Business Accounting and Finance

Second edition

Tony Davies
and
Tony Boczko

London Boston Burr Ridge, IL Dubuque, IA Madison, WI New York San Francisco
St. Louis Bangkok Bogotá Caracas Kuala Lumpur Lisbon Madrid Mexico City
Milan Montreal New Delhi Santiago Seoul Singapore Sydney Taipei Toronto

Business Accounting and Finance, Second edition
Tony Davies and Tony Boczko
ISBN-10: 0-07-710809-4
ISBN-13: 978-0-07-710809-0

Education

Published by McGraw-Hill Education
Shoppenhangers Road
Maidenhead
Berkshire
SL6 2QL
Telephone: 44 (0) 1628 502 500
Fax: 44 (0) 1628 770 224
Website: www.mcgraw-hill.co.uk

British Library Cataloguing in Publication Data
A catalogue record for this book is available from the British Library

Library of Congress Cataloguing in Publication Data
The Library of Congress data for this book has been applied for from the Library of Congress

Acquisitions Editor: Mark Kavanagh
Development Editor: Rachel Crookes
Senior Marketing Manager: Marca Wosoba
Senior Production Editor: Eleanor Hayes

Text Design by Jonathan Coleclough
Cover design by Fielding Design Ltd
Typeset by Mathematical Composition Setters Ltd, Salisbury, Wiltshire
Printed and bound in Great Britain by CPI Bath Press

Dedication

I dedicate this book with love to
my wife Fran
and my daughters Joanna and Polly

Brief Table of Contents

Detailed Table of Contents

Features

Case Studies

Press Extracts

Figures

Preface

Introduction

There were two key aims in writing the first edition of *Business Accounting and Finance* (BAF). One aim was to provide undergraduates, postgraduates and others with an accounting and finance book in a practical business context that was clear and easy to understand. In BAF we have maintained a rigorous approach and full coverage of all the theoretical and technical aspects of accounting and finance, together with their practical application. At the same time, we have tried to remove the fear and intimidation that sometimes accompany these subjects, by making them more user-friendly and a little more fun to study.

The other aim was to provide a comprehensive and flexible teaching and learning resource, with a wide range of study and assessment material supported by an 'easy to use' accessible website. There are links between each of the chapters, which follow a structure that has been designed to facilitate effective teaching and learning of accounting and finance in a progressive way. Alternatively, each chapter may be used on a standalone basis; chapters may also be excluded if they relate to subjects that are not essential for a specific module. Basic bookkeeping is a topic that may or may not be a requirement of some modules and so it has been placed in an appendix towards the end of the text. Therefore, the text is intended to be suitable for modules of either one or two semesters' duration.

Feedback from lecturers and students, particularly those for whom English may not be their first language, positively confirmed that these aims were largely met. The second edition of BAF has built on that success with its user-friendly approach to the principles and techniques of accounting and finance, its increased linkage with the real business world, and coverage of contemporary issues and topics of growing importance.

Accounting and finance are of critical importance in the support of all business activities. The formal study of accounting and finance is exciting because it introduces a toolkit that enables a better understanding of the performance of businesses, and the decisions and problems they face. These issues are discussed daily by managers and in the media. The second edition of this textbook provides you with the toolkit and shows you how to apply it in practice, utilising a comprehensive range of learning features, illustrative examples and assessment material to support and reinforce your study.

This textbook is aimed primarily at students who are not majoring in accounting or finance, but who are undertaking an introductory-level module as part of their degree or diploma course in business management, economics or any other subject. BAF is a tightly-written, clear and engaging text which distils the core principles of accounting and finance for those students who may not have the luxury of devoting all their time to its study.

Second edition

The structure of the first edition of BAF has been maintained but enhanced in the second edition. The content of the second edition has been expanded and completely updated and now includes six full-length case studies, 35 new chapter-end exercises, and a completely new chapter with eight chapter-end exercises, which are provided with Excel spreadsheet model solutions.

Each topic in BAF has been carefully researched to closely follow the typical current requirements of introductory undergraduate and MBA modules. The text assumes no prior knowledge of the subject, starting at square one and taking you step-by-step through the concepts and application of techniques, with clear explanations and numerous worked examples.

The second edition has been increased to 16 chapters, structured into three parts. Each part of the book and the component chapters are outlined in the introductory section to each part of the text, and cover the main areas of accounting and finance:

- **Financial accounting** is broadly concerned with the recording and analysis of historical financial data, the presentation of financial information, and compliance with current legislation, and accounting rules and standards.
- **Management accounting** uses financial and non-financial information and also provides information for the costing of products for the valuation of stocks, the pricing of products and services, and the planning, control, and decision-making functions. It is mainly involved in the support of the management of an organisation in dealing with current problems and in the evaluation of the future outcomes of various different scenarios and decisions.
- **Business finance** (or financial management) includes the appraisal of decisions relating to investments in capital projects, the ways in which a business and the investment in any new projects may be financed, and the efficient and effective management of the assets of the organisation.

Each of the three parts of the second edition provides some wider coverage of existing topics and many new sections that include, for example:

Part I

- the international approach to the development of a common set of accounting rules to be used by businesses in groups of countries, for example the European Union
- the up-to-date position regarding corporate governance, and the responsibilities of directors, primarily in the UK
- the reporting of corporate social responsibility (CSR) by companies

Part II

- a look at how a company may find its break-even point when it produces many different products
- measurement of the performance of the individual divisions within a business
- lean accounting, which provides the support and motivation for lean thinking – businesses are becoming leaner as they endeavour to create greater value from even less resources

Part III

- increased coverage of sources of business funding, including hybrid finance, leasing, and UK Government and European funding
- a new chapter, which looks at the significant impact of information technology on accounting and finance.

The additional new chapter about IT and accounting emphasises how the continuing development of IT has resulted in changes in the role of the accounting and finance function, and a broadening of the range of other business disciplines in which it is now involved. It explains how IT has impacted on every area within a business: design; engineering; manufacturing; human resources management; purchasing; distribution; sales; marketing; and how these operational areas have increasingly become totally integrated with the accounting and finance function. The spreadsheet has now become an indispensable tool in every aspect of business life. Accounting and finance Excel spread-sheet applications are fully illustrated in worked examples and chapter-end assessment material.

Just as the principles and practice of, for example, genetics or information technology are continually questioned, refined, and improved, so accounting and finance continue to develop, sometimes in exciting ways. This is illustrated in BAF by the introduction of topics not typically covered in some of the more traditional introductory accounting texts, for example corporate governance, and lean accounting. It also includes a number of contemporary issues and areas of increasing importance such as *kaizen*, target costing, quality costing, balanced scorecard, throughput accounting, and activity based costing.

This text has been written primarily for non-specialist students, and so each chapter aims to help students understand the broader context and relevance of accounting and finance in the business environment, and how accounting and financial statements and non-financial information can be used to improve the quality of management decision-making. Every chapter in the second edition provides completely new examples and commentary on company activity, including at least one press extract. Companies featured include: Microsoft; NTL; Easyjet; Samsung; Marks & Spencer; Corus; Matalan; Shearings; Tyco International; Royal Doulton; Network Rail. In addition, two of the chapters feature extracts and analysis of the Report and Accounts 2004 of Johnson Matthey plc.

Using this book

To support your study and reinforce the topics covered, we have included an enhanced, and comprehensive, range of learning features and assessment material in each chapter, including:

- learning objectives
- introduction
- highlighted key terms
- fully-worked examples
- Excel spreadsheet worked examples
- integrated progress checks
- key points summary
- questions
- discussion points
- exercises
- Excel spreadsheet exercises.

Within each chapter we have also included numerous diagrams and charts that illustrate and reinforce important concepts and ideas. The double-page *Guided Tour* that follows on pages xxv–xxvi summarises the purpose of these learning features and the chapter-end assessment material. To gain maximum benefit from this text and to help you succeed in your study and exams, you are encouraged to familiarise yourself with these elements now, before you start the first chapter.

Accounting is essentially a 'hands-on' subject; just reading about it is not enough. Believe us, from our own experience we know that repeated practice of examples and exercises is the only way to become proficient in its techniques. You may think that reading through this book or your lecture notes, highlighting the odd sentence and gliding through the worked examples, progress checks and chapter-end questions and exercises, will instill the knowledge and expertise required to pass your exams. This would be a big mistake. Active learning needs to be interactive: if you have not followed a topic or an example, go back and work through it again; try to think of other examples to which particular topics may be applied. The only way to check you have a comprehensive understanding of things is to attempt all the integrated progress checks and worked examples, and the chapter-end assessment material, and then to compare with the text and answers provided. Full solutions are given for each worked example, and solutions to 45% of the chapter-end exercises (those with their numbers in colour) are provided in Appendix 4. The book's supporting website (www.mcgraw-hill.co.uk/textbooks/davies) provides an extensive range of learning and teaching resources (see below). Additional self-assessment material is available in the student centre of the website.

Case studies

Each of the three main parts of the book includes two case studies that may be tackled either individually or as a team. The case studies are a little more weighty than the chapter-end exercises; in addition, they integrate many of the topics included in the chapters in each part of the text to which they relate, although not exclusively. Each case study therefore gives you an opportunity to apply the knowledge and techniques gained from each part of the book, and to develop these together with the analytical skills and judgement required to deal with real-life business problems. Additional cases are provided on the accompanying website.

We hope that this textbook continues to put the sparkle into your study of accounting and finance to enhance your interest, and increase your understanding and skills. Above all, relax, learn and enjoy!

Online learning centre (OLC)

The website accompanying this text

www.mcgraw-hill.co.uk/textbooks/davies

includes an extensive range of chapter-based student and lecturer resources, and comprises three main sections. See page xxvii for details.

Remember to check the website frequently throughout your studies, as these resources will be regularly updated.

Acknowledgements

Thank you to the following lecturers who were involved in either the initial market research and/or in providing useful review comments and technical checks of the draft chapters during the development phase of this project:

- Graham Ball
- Mike Barker
- Tariq Bashir
- Bruce Bowhill
- Mary Canny
- Giovanni Cozzi
- Cedric McCallum
- Ian Crawford
- Robert Devlin
- Barbara Dexter
- Graham Diggle
- Steve Dungworth
- Steward Hughes
- Carolyn Isaaks
- Chris Knight
- Danny Leiwy

- John Lyons
- Jenny Maynard
- Rona O'Brien
- Gary Owen
- Richard Pike
- Graeme Reid
- Mark Richer
- Clare Roberts
- Zeljko Seviç
- Jon Simon
- Chris Simpson
- John Syer
- Brian Telford
- Tony Wall
- Pauline Willis

Thank you to CIMA (the Chartered Institute of Management Accountants) for their permission to include extracts from their Management Accounting Official Terminology 2000 edition.

Thank you to *Financial Management*, *Accountancy Age*, *The Daily Telegraph*, *The Times*, and *The Guardian* for their permission to use extracts from their publications, and to *HSBC Bank Group Archives* for their permission to use photographic images.

Thank you to Johnson Matthey plc for permission to use extracts of their Report and Accounts 2004 as an excellent example of the information provided to shareholders by a major UK plc.

Thank you to systems analyst, Norrette Moore, for her invaluable review comments with regard to the chapter about IT and accounting.

Thank you to Mark Kavanagh for his support and encouragement in the writing of this book.

Guided Tour

Learning objectives

Listed at the start of each chapter, these bullet points identify the core learning outcomes you should have acquired after completing each chapter.

Key terms

These are colour highlighted the first time they are introduced, alerting you to the core concepts and techniques in each chapter. A full explanation is contained in the glossary of key terms section at the end of the book.

Introduction

This section gives you a brief overview of the coverage and purpose of each chapter, and how it links to the previous chapter.

Worked examples

The numerous worked examples in each chapter provide an application of the learning points and techniques included within each topic. By following and working through the step-by-step solutions, you have an opportunity to check your knowledge at frequent intervals.

Progress checks

Each topic within each chapter includes one or more of these short questions that enable you to check and apply your understanding of the preceding key topics before you progress to the next one in the chapter.

Press extracts

These topical extracts used in every chapter feature real company examples from the press, including commentary that highlights the practical application of accounting and finance in the business environment.

Summary of key points

Following the final section in each chapter there is a comprehensive summary of the chapter topics. These allow you to check that you understand all the main points covered before moving on to the next chapter.

Questions

These are short narrative-type questions that encourage you to review and check your understanding of all the key topics. There are typically 8 to 11 of these questions at the end of each chapter.

Discussion points

This section typically includes 2 to 4 thought-provoking ideas and questions that encourage you to critically apply your understanding and/or further develop some of the topics introduced in each chapter, either individually or in team discussion.

Exercises

These comprehensive examination-style questions are graded by their level of difficulty, as well as by the time typically required to complete them. Designed to assess your knowledge and application of the principles and techniques covered in a chapter, there are typically 7 to 9 exercises at the end of each chapter. Full solutions to the colour-highlighted exercise numbers are provided in Appendix 4 to allow you to self-assess your progress.

Glossary of key terms

At the end of the book a glossary of key terms in alphabetical order provides full definitions of all main terms that have been introduced throughout each chapter, as identified by the symbol ◀━━. The numbers of the pages on which key term definitions appear are colour-highlighted in the index.

Online Learning Centre (OLC)

After completing each chapter, log on to the supporting Online Learning Centre website. Take advantage of the study tools offered to reinforce the material you have read in the text, and to develop your knowledge of business accounting and finance in a fun and effective way.

Resources for students include:

- Additional chapter-based exercises
- Excel spreadsheet solutions to worked examples
- Additional part-based case studies
- Self-testing multiple-choice questions organised by chapter with automatic grading
- Revision notes organised by chapter
- Glossary of key terms
- The press room
- Useful weblinks
- International and UK accounting standards

Additionally available for lecturers:

- Solutions to all chapter-based exercises
- Excel spreadsheet solutions to chapter-based exercises
- Debriefings to all case studies
- Large multiple-choice questions test bank
- PowerPoint lecture slides
- Textbook figures
- PageOut

Visit **www.mcgraw-hill.co.uk/textbooks/davies** today

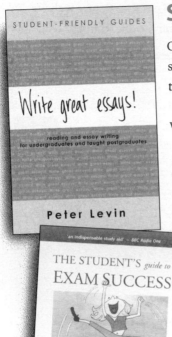

Study Skills

Open University Press publishes guides to study, research and exam skills, to help undergraduate and postgraduate students through their university studies.

Visit **www.openup.co.uk/ss/** to see the full selection.

Computing Skills

If you'd like to brush up on your computing skills, we have a range of titles covering MS Office applications such as Word, Excel, PowerPoint, Access and more.

Get a £2 discount off these titles by entering the promotional code app when ordering online at **www.mcgraw-hill.co.uk/app**

1

Underlying principles: the building blocks

Contents

Learning objectives

Completion of this chapter will enable you to:

- outline the uses and purpose of accounting and the practice of accountancy
- explain the development of the conceptual frameworks of accounting
- outline the contents of the UK Statement of Principles (SOP)
- explain the main UK accounting concepts and accounting and financial reporting standards
- appreciate the meaning of true and fair view
- consider the increasing importance of international accounting standards
- explain what is meant by financial accounting, management accounting, and financial management
- illustrate the different types of business entity: sole traders, partnerships, private limited companies, public limited companies
- explain the nature and purpose of financial statements
- identify the wide range of users of financial information
- consider the issues of accountability and financial reporting.

Introduction

This chapter explains why accounting and finance are such key elements of business life. Both for aspiring accountants, and those of you who may not continue to study accounting and finance beyond the introductory level, the fundamental principles of accounting and the ways in which accounting is regulated to protect owners of businesses, and the public in general, are important topics. A broad appreciation will be useful not only in dealing with the subsequent text, but also in the context of the day-to-day management of a business.

This chapter will look at why accounting is needed and how it is used and by whom. Accounting and finance are wide subjects, which often mean many things to many people. They are broadly concerned with the organisation and management of financial resources. Accounting and accountancy are two terms which are sometimes used to mean the same thing, although they more correctly relate separately to the subject and the profession.

Accounting and accountancy are generally concerned with measuring and communicating the financial information provided from accounting systems, and the reporting of financial results to shareholders, lenders, creditors, employees and Government. The owners or shareholders of the wide range of business entities that use accounting, may be assumed to have the primary objective of maximisation of the wealth of their business. Directors of the business manage the resources of the business to meet shareholders' objectives.

Accounting operates through basic principles and rules. This chapter will examine the development of conceptual frameworks of accounting, which in the UK are seen in the Statement of Principles (SOP). We will discuss the rules of accounting, which are embodied in what are termed accounting concepts and accounting standards.

Over the past few years there has been an increasing focus on trying to bring together the rules, or standards, of accounting that apply in each separate country, into one set of accounting standards. For example, with effect from January 2005 all the large companies within the European Union are required to comply with one such set of accounting standards relating to the way in which they report financial information. We will discuss how this may affect the topics we shall be covering in this book.

We will consider the processes used in accounting and look at an overview of the financial statements used in financial reporting, and the way in which financial reporting is used to keep shareholders informed. The timely and accurate disclosure of truthful information is a fundamental requirement in the preparation of appropriate statements of the financial performance and the financial position of a business. Directors and managers are responsible for running businesses and their accountability to shareholders is maintained through their regular reporting on the activities of the business.

A large number of accounting concepts and terms are used throughout this book, the definitions of which may be found in the glossary of key terms at the end of the book.

What is accounting, and its uses and purposes?

The original, basic purposes of accounting were to classify and record monetary transactions (see Appendix 1) and present the financial results of the activities of an entity, in other words the scorecard that shows how the business is doing. The accounting profession has evolved and accounting techniques have been developed for use in a much broader business context. To look at the current nature of accounting and the broad purposes of accounting systems we need to consider the three questions these days generally answered by accounting information:

- how are we doing, and are we doing well or badly? **a scorecard (like scoring a game of cricket, for example)**
- which problems should be looked at? **attention-directing**
- which is the best alternative for doing a job? **problem solving.**

Although accountants and the accounting profession have retained their fundamental roles they have grown into various branches of the profession, which have developed their own specialisms and responsibilities.

Accounting is a part of the information system within an organisation (see Appendix 1, which explains double-entry bookkeeping, and how data is identified, recorded and presented as information in the ways required by the users of financial information). Accounting also exists as a service function, which ensures that the financial information that is presented meets the needs of the users of financial information. To achieve this, accountants must not only ensure that information is accurate, reliable and timely but also that it is relevant for the purpose for which it is being provided, consistent for comparability, and easily understood (see Fig. 1.1).

In order to be useful to the users of financial information, the accounting data from which it is prepared, together with its analysis and presentation, must be:

- accurate – free from error of content or principle
- reliable – representing the information that users believe it represents
- timely – available in time to support decision-making

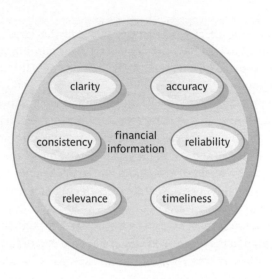

Figure 1.1 Features of useful financial information

- relevant – applicable to the purpose required, for example a decision regarding a future event or to support an explanation of what has already happened
- consistent – the same methods and standards of measurement of data and presentation of information to allow like-for-like comparison
- clear – capable of being understood by those for whom the information has been prepared.

In the next few sections we will see just how important these features are, and the ways they are included in the development of various conceptual frameworks of accounting, and the accounting policies selected by companies.

The conceptual frameworks of accounting

How can the credibility and usefulness of accounting and financial information be ensured? Accounting operates within a framework. This framework is constantly changing and evolving as new problems are encountered, as new practices and techniques are developed, and the objectives of users of financial information are modified and revised.

The search for a definitive conceptual framework, a theoretical accounting model, which may deal with any new accounting problem that may arise, has resulted in many conceptual frameworks having been developed in a number of countries worldwide. The basic assumption for these conceptual frameworks is that financial statements must be useful. The general structure of conceptual frameworks deals with the following six questions:

1. What is the purpose of financial statement reporting?
2. Who are the main users of accounting and financial information?
3. What type of financial statements will meet the needs of these users?
4. What type of information should be included in financial statements to satisfy these needs?
5. How should items included in financial statements be defined?
6. How should items included in financial statements be recorded and measured?

In 1989 the International Accounting Standards Board (IASB) issued a conceptual framework that largely reflected the conceptual frameworks of the USA, Canada, Australia, and the UK. This was based on the ideas and proposals made by the accounting profession since the 1970s in both the USA and UK. In 1999 the Accounting Standards Board (ASB) in the UK published its own conceptual framework called the Statement of Principles (SOP) for Financial Reporting.

> **Progress check 1.1** **What is meant by a conceptual framework of accounting?**

The Statement of Principles (SOP)

The 1975 Corporate Report was the first UK attempt at a conceptual framework. This, together with the 1973 Trueblood Report published in the USA, provided the basis for the conceptual framework issued by the IASB in 1989, referred to in the previous section. It was followed by the publication of the SOP by the ASB in 1999. The SOP is a basic structure for determining objectives, in which there is a thread from the theory to the practical application of accounting standards to transactions that are reported in published accounts. The SOP is not an accounting standard and its use is not mandatory, but it is a statement of guidelines; it is, by virtue of the subject, constantly in need of revision.

The SOP identifies the main users of financial information as:

- investors
- lenders
- employees
- suppliers and creditors
- customers and debtors
- Government
- the general public.

The SOP focuses on the interests of investors and assumes that each of the other users of financial information is interested in or concerned about the same issues as investors.

The SOP consists of eight chapters that deal with the following topics:

1. The objectives of financial statements, which are fundamentally to provide information that is useful for the users of that information.
2. Identification of the entities that are required to provide financial statement reporting by virtue of the demand for the information included in those statements.
3. The qualitative characteristics required to make financial information useful to users:
   - materiality (inclusion of information that is not material may distort the usefulness of other information)
   - relevance
   - reliability
   - comparability (enabling the identification and evaluation of differences and similarities)
   - comprehensibility.
4. The main elements included in the financial statements – the 'building blocks' of accounting such as assets and liabilities.
5. When transactions should be recognised in financial statements.
6. How assets and liabilities should be measured.
7. How financial statements should be presented for clear and effective communication.
8. The accounting by an entity in its financial statements for interests in other entities.

The UK SOP can be seen to be a very general outline of principles relating to the reporting of financial information. The SOP includes some of the basic concepts that provide the foundations for the preparation of financial statements. These accounting concepts will be considered in more detail in the next section.

> **Progress check 1.2** What are the aims of the UK Statement of Principles and how does it try to achieve these aims?

UK accounting concepts

The accounting framework revolves around the practice of accountancy and the accounting profession, which is bounded by rules, or concepts (see Fig. 1.2, in which the five most important concepts are shown shaded) of what data should be included within an accounting system and how that data should be recorded.

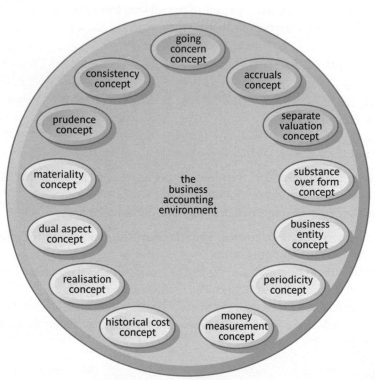

Figure 1.2 Accounting concepts

Accounting concepts are the principles underpinning the preparation of accounting information relating to the ethical rules, boundary rules, and recording and measurement rules of accounting. Ethical rules, or principles, are to do with limiting the amount of judgement (or indeed creativity) that may be used in the reporting of financial information. Boundary rules are to do with which types of data, and the amounts of each, that should be held by organisations, and which elements of financial information should be reported. Recording and measurement rules of accounting relate to how the different types of data should be recorded and measured by the organisation.

Fundamental accounting concepts are the broad basic assumptions, which underlie the periodic financial accounts of business enterprises. The five most important concepts, which are included in the Companies Act 1985/89, are as follows.

The prudence concept

Prudence means being careful or cautious. The prudence concept is an ethical concept, which is based on the principle that revenue and profits are not anticipated, but are included in the profit and loss account only when realised in the form of either cash or other assets, the ultimate cash realisation of which can be assessed with reasonable certainty. Provision must be made for all known liabilities and expenses, whether the amount of these is known with certainty or is a best estimate in the light of information available, and for losses arising from specific commitments, rather than just guesses. Therefore, companies should record all losses as soon as they are known, but should record profits only when they have actually been achieved in cash or other assets.

The consistency concept

The consistency concept is an ethical rule that is based on the principle that there is uniformity of accounting treatment of like items within each accounting period and from one period to the next. However, as we will see in Chapter 3, judgement may be exercised as to the application of accounting rules to the preparation of financial statements. For example, a company may choose from a variety of methods to calculate the depreciation of its machinery and equipment, or how to value its stocks of a product. Until recently, once a particular approach had been adopted by a company for one accounting period then this approach should normally have been adopted in all future accounting periods, unless there were compelling reasons to change. The ASB now prefers the approaches adopted by companies to be revised by them, and the ASB encourages their change, if those changes result in showing a truer and fairer picture. If companies do change their approaches then they have to indicate this in their annual reports and accounts.

The going concern concept

The going concern concept is a boundary rule that assumes that the entity will continue in operational existence for the foreseeable future. This is important because it allows the original, historical costs of assets to continue to be used in the balance sheet on the basis of their being able to generate future income. If the entity was expected to cease functioning then such assets would be worth only what they would be expected to realise if they were sold off separately (their break-up values) and therefore usually considerably less.

The National Botanic Garden of Wales faced a threat to its future existence because it had suffered a slump in visitor numbers since it opened as a 2000 Millennium project. This resulted in the attraction having difficulties in generating sufficient cash to meet its operational requirements and to pay the contractors who were developing the gardens.

In March 2004 the National Botanic Garden of Wales was offered a £2.3m package to keep it open. However, the independent trustees of the attraction were warned that the garden had to bring in more money from visitors and private sponsors to secure its future as a going concern.

A going concern or an expensive failure?

Trustees for the National Botanic Garden of Wales are to meet today to decide whether it should be put into liquidation after the Welsh Assembly's refusal to provide £3 million to keep it open.

The attraction, in Llanarthne, Carmarthenshire, is funded by the Millennium Commission. It was opened by the Prince of Wales three years ago and was Britain's first national botanic garden for 200 years.

Visitor numbers are down, however, and it may close within days. In a statement, the Prince, a patron, said he hoped 'a situation can be found to allow the garden to remain open'. The trustees said last night that only a 'last-minute miracle' could save it.

A spokesman said liquidation, in which assets would be sold to recoup money for creditors, was the most likely outcome of today's meeting.

The garden was a showpiece Millennium project, using National Lottery funds. The commission is expected to call back the £21 million given to the garden if it is liquidated.

Brian Charles, deputy chairman of the trustees, said closure would be a tragedy. 'It's an outstanding attraction for Wales. We will open the doors today, but it will be up to the administrators whether they open again.'

Carwyn Jones, the Welsh Assembly rural affairs minister, said the garden was in the wrong place and should have been opened in Cardiff.

A report by an independent panel sponsored by the Wales Tourist Board said it had no commercial future.

National botanic garden on brink of liquidation, by Richard Savill

© *Daily Telegraph*, 15 December 2003

The accruals concept

➡ The accruals concept (or the matching concept) is a recording and measurement rule that is based on the principle that revenues and costs are recognised as they are earned or incurred, are matched with one another, and are dealt with in the profit and loss account of the period to which they relate, irrespective of the period of receipt or payment. It would be misleading to report profit as the difference between cash received and cash paid during a period because some trading and commercial activities of the period would be excluded, since many transactions are based on credit.

Most of us are users of electricity. We may use it over a period of 3 months for heating, lighting, and running our many home appliances, before receiving an invoice from the electricity supplier for the electricity we have used. The fact that we have not received an invoice until much later doesn't mean we have not incurred a cost for each month. The costs have been accrued over each of those months, and we will pay for them at a later date.

The separate valuation concept

➡ The separate valuation concept is a recording and measurement rule that relates to the determination of the aggregate amount of any item. In order to determine the aggregate amount of an asset or a liability, each individual asset or liability that comprises the aggregate must be determined separately. This is important because material items may reflect different economic circumstances. There must be a review of each material item to comply with the appropriate accounting standards:

- FRS 11 (Impairment of Fixed Assets and Goodwill)

- FRS 12 (Provisions, Contingent Liabilities and Contingent Assets)
- FRS 15 (Tangible Fixed Assets).

(See the later section, which discusses UK accounting and financial reporting standards called Financial Reporting Standards (FRSs), and Statements of Standard Accounting Practice (SSAPs).)

Note the example of the Millennium Dome 2000 project, which was developed in Greenwich, London, throughout 1999 and 2000 and cost around £800m. At the end of the year 2000 a valuation of the individual elements of the attraction resulted in a total of around £100m.

The further eight fundamental accounting concepts are as follows.

The substance over form concept

Where a conflict exists, the substance over form concept, which is an ethical rule, requires the structuring of reports to give precedence to the representation of financial or economic reality over strict adherence to the requirements of the legal reporting structure. This concept is dealt with in another accounting standard FRS 5, Reporting the Substance of Transactions. An example of this is where a company leases an asset, for example a machine, and discloses it in its balance sheet even though not holding legal title to the asset, whilst also disclosing separately in its balance sheet the amount that the company still owes on the machine. The reason for showing the asset in the balance sheet is because it is being used to generate income for the business, in the same way as a purchased machine. The substance of this accounting transaction (treating a leased asset as though it had been purchased) takes precedence over the form of the transaction (the lease itself).

The business entity concept

The business entity concept is a boundary rule that ensures that financial accounting information relates only to the activities of the business entity and not to the other activities of its owners. An owner of a business may be interested in sailing and may buy a boat and pay a subscription as a member of the local yacht club. These activities are completely outside the activities of the business and such transactions must be kept completely separate from the accounts of the business.

The periodicity concept

The periodicity concept (or time interval concept) is a boundary rule. It is the requirement to produce financial statements at set time intervals. This requirement is embodied, in the case of UK companies, in the Companies Act 1985/1989 (all future references to the Companies Act will relate to the Companies Act 1985/1989 unless otherwise stated). Both annual and interim financial statements are required to be produced by public limited companies (plcs) each year.

Internal reporting of financial information to management may take place within a company on a monthly, weekly, daily, or even an hourly basis. But owners of a company, who may have no involvement in the running of the business or its internal reporting, require the external reporting of their company's accounts on a 6-monthly and yearly basis. The owners of the company may then rely on the regularity with which the reporting of financial information takes place, which enables them to monitor company performance, and compare figures year on year.

The money measurement concept

The money measurement concept is a recording and measurement rule that enables information relating to transactions to be fairly compared by providing a commonly-accepted unit of converting quantifiable amounts into recognisable measures. Most quantifiable data is capable of being converted, using a common denominator of money, into monetary terms. However, accounting deals only with those items capable of being translated into monetary terms, which imposes a limit on the scope of accounting reporting to such items. You may note, for example, that in a University's balance sheet there is no value included for its human resources, that is its lecturers, its managers, and secretarial and support staff.

The historical cost concept

The **historical cost concept** is a recording and measurement rule that relates to the practice of valuing assets at their original acquisition cost. For example, you may have bought a mountain bike two years ago for which you were invoiced and paid £150, and may now be wondering what it is currently worth. One of your friends may consider it to be worth £175 because they feel that the price of new mountain bikes has increased over the past two years. Another friend may consider it to be worth only £100 because you have used it for two years and its condition has deteriorated. Neither of your friends may be incorrect, but their views are subjective and they are different. The only measure of what your bike is worth on which your friends may agree is the price shown on your original invoice, its historical cost.

Although the historical cost basis of valuation may not be as realistic as using, for instance, a current valuation, it does provide a consistent basis for comparison and almost eliminates the need for any subjectivity.

The realisation concept

The **realisation concept** is a recording and measurement rule and is the principle that increases in value should only be recognised on realisation of assets by arms-length sale to an independent purchaser. This means, for example, that sales revenue from the sale of a product or service is recognised in accounting statements only when it is realised. This does not mean when the cash has been paid over by the customer; it means when the sale takes place, that is when the product or service has been delivered, and ownership is transferred to the customer. Very often, salespersons incorrectly regard a 'sale' as the placing of an order by a customer because they are usually very optimistic and sometimes forget that orders can get cancelled. Accountants, being prudent individuals, correctly record a sale by issuing an invoice when services or goods have been delivered (and installed).

The dual aspect concept

The **dual aspect concept** is the recording and measurement rule that provides the basis for double-entry bookkeeping. It reflects the practical reality that every transaction always includes both the giving and receiving of value. For example, a company may pay out cash in return for a delivery into its warehouse of a consignment of products, which it subsequently aims to sell. The company's reduction in its cash balance is reflected in the increase in its stock of products.

The materiality concept

Information is material if its omission or misstatement could influence the economic decisions of users taken on the basis of the financial statements. Materiality depends on the size of the item or error judged, its significance, in the particular circumstances of its omission or misstatement. Thus, materiality provides a threshold or cut-off point rather than being a primary qualitative characteristic that information must have if it is to be useful. The materiality concept is the overriding recording and measurement rule, which allows a certain amount of judgement in the application of all the other accounting concepts. The level of materiality, or significance, will depend on the size of the organisation and the type of revenue or cost, or asset or liability being considered. For example, the cost of business stationery is usually charged as an expense regardless of whether or not all the items have been used; it would be pointless to try and attribute a value to such relatively low-cost unused items.

True and fair view

The term true and fair view was introduced in the Companies Act 1947, requiring that companies' reporting of their accounts should show a true and fair view. It was not defined in that Act and has not been defined since. Some writers have suggested that conceptually it is a dynamic concept but over the years it could be argued that it has failed, and various business scandals and collapses have occurred without users being alerted. The concept of true and fair was adopted by the European Community Council in its fourth directive, implemented by the UK in the Companies Act 1981, and subsequently in the implementation of the seventh directive in the Companies Act 1989 (section 226 or 227). Conceptually the directives require additional information where individual provisions are insufficient.

In practice true and fair view relates to the extent to which the various principles, concepts, and standards of accounting have been applied. It may therefore be somewhat subjective and subject to change as new accounting rules are developed, old standards replaced and new standards introduced. It may be interesting to research the issue of derivatives and decide whether the true and fair view concept was invoked by those companies that used or marketed these financial instruments, and specifically consider the various collapses or public statements regarding losses incurred over the past few years. Before derivatives, the issue which escaped disclosure in financial reporting under true and fair view was leasing.

UK accounting and financial reporting standards

A number of guidelines, or standards (some of which we have already discussed), have been developed by the accounting profession to ensure truth, fairness, and consistency in the preparation and presentation of financial information.

A number of bodies have been established to draft accounting policy, set accounting standards, and to monitor compliance with standards and the provisions of the Companies Act. The Financial Reporting Council (FRC), whose chairman is appointed by the Department of Trade and Industry (DTI) and the Bank of England, develops accounting standards policy and gives guidance on issues of public concern. The ASB, which is composed of members of the accountancy profession, and on which the Government has an observer status, has responsibility for development, issue, and withdrawal of accounting standards.

The accounting standards are called Financial Reporting Standards (FRSs). Up to 1990 the accounting standards were known as Statements of Standard Accounting Practice (SSAPs), and were issued by the Accounting Standards Committee (ASC), the forerunner of the ASB. Although some SSAPs have now been withdrawn there are, in addition to the new FRSs, a large number of SSAPs that are still in force. A list of all FRSs and SSAPs that are currently in force may be found in Appendix 3 at the end of this book. The website accompanying this book contains the up-to-date position with regard to changes in accounting standards.

The ASB is supported by the Urgent Issues Task Force (UITF). Its main role is to assist the ASB in areas where an accounting standard or Companies Act provision exists, but where unsatisfactory or conflicting interpretations have developed or seem likely to develop. The UITF also deals with issues that need to be resolved more quickly than through the issuing of an accounting standard. A recent example of this was the Y2K problem, which involved ensuring that computerised accounting transactions were not corrupted when we moved from the year 1999 to the year 2000.

The Financial Reporting Review Panel (FRRP) reviews comments and complaints from users of financial information. It enquires into the annual accounts of companies where it appears that the requirements of the Companies Act, including the requirement that annual accounts shall show a true and fair view, might have been breached. The Stock Exchange rules covering financial disclosure of publicly quoted companies require such companies to comply with accounting standards and reasons for non-compliance must be disclosed.

Pressure groups, organisations and individuals may also have influence on the provisions of the Companies Act and FRSs (and SSAPs). These may include some Government departments (for example, Inland Revenue, HM Customs & Excise, Office of Fair Trading) in addition to the DTI and employer organisations such as the Confederation of British Industry (CBI), and professional bodies like the Law Society, Institute of Directors, and Chartered Management Institute.

There are therefore many diverse influences on the form and content of company accounts. In addition to legislation, standards are continually being refined, updated and replaced and further enhanced by various codes of best practice. As a response to this the UK Generally Accepted Accounting Practices (UK GAAP), first published in 1989, includes all practices that are considered to be permissible or legitimate, either through support by statute, accounting standard or official pronouncement, or through consistency with the needs of users and of meeting the fundamental requirement to present a true and fair view, or even simply through authoritative support in the accounting literature. UK GAAP is therefore a dynamic concept, which changes in response to changing circumstances.

→ Within the scope of current legislation, best practice and accounting standards, each company needs to develop its own specific accounting policies. Accounting policies are the specific accounting bases selected and consistently followed by an entity as being, in the opinion of the management, appropriate to its circumstances and best suited to present fairly its results and financial position. Examples are the various alternative methods of valuing stocks of materials, or charging the cost of a machine over its useful life, that is, its depreciation.

The accounting standard that deals with how a company chooses, applies and reports on its accounting policies is called FRS 18, Accounting Policies, and was issued in 2000 to replace SSAP 2, Disclosure of Accounting Policies. FRS 18 clarified when profits should be recognised (the realisation concept), and the requirement of 'neutrality' in financial statements in neither overstating gains nor understating losses (the prudence concept). This standard also emphasised the increased importance of the going concern concept and the accruals concept. The aims of FRS 18 are:

- to ensure that companies choose accounting policies that are most suitable for their individual circumstances, and incorporate the key characteristics stated in Chapter 3 of the SOP
- to ensure that accounting policies are reviewed and replaced as necessary on a regular basis
- to ensure that companies report accounting policies, and any changes to them, in their annual reports and accounts so that users of that information are kept informed.

Whereas FRS 18 deals with the disclosure by companies of their accounting policies, FRS 3, Reporting Financial Transactions, deals with the reporting by companies of their financial performance. Financial performance relates primarily to the profit and loss account, whereas financial position relates primarily to the balance sheet. FRS 3 aims to ensure that users of financial information get a good insight into the company's performance during the period to which the accounts relate. This is in order that decisions made about the company may be made on an informed basis. FRS 3 requires the following items to be included in company accounts to provide the required level of reporting on financial performance (which will all be discussed in greater detail in Chapter 3, which is about the profit and loss account, and Chapter 6, which looks at published reports and accounts):

■ analysis of turnover, cost of sales, operating expenses, and profit before interest
■ exceptional items
■ extraordinary items
■ statement of recognised gains and losses (a separate financial statement along with the balance sheet, profit and loss account, and cash flow statement).

Progress check 1.3 What is meant by accounting concepts and accounting standards, and why are they needed? Give some examples.

International accounting standards

The International Accounting Standards Committee (IASC) set up in 1973, which is supported by each of the major professional accounting bodies, fosters the harmonisation of accounting standards internationally. To this end each UK FRS (Financial Reporting Standard) includes a section explaining its relationship to any relevant international accounting standard.

There are wide variations in the accounting practices that have been developed in different countries. These reflect the purposes for which financial information is required by the different users of that information, in each of those countries. There is a different focus on the type of information and the relative importance of each of the users of financial information in each country. This is because each country may differ in terms of:

■ who finances the businesses – individual equity shareholders, institutional equity shareholders, debenture holders, banks, etc.
■ tax systems either aligned with or separate from accounting rules
■ the level of government control and regulation
■ the degree of transparency of information.

The increase in international trade and globalisation has led to a need for convergence, or harmonisation, of accounting rules and practices. The IASC was created in order to develop international accounting standards, but these have been slow in appearing because of the difficulties in bringing together differences in accounting procedures. Until 2000 these standards were called International Accounting Standards (IASs). The successor to the IASC, the IASB (International Accounting Standards Board) was set up in April 2001 to make financial statements more comparable on a worldwide basis. The IASB publishes its standards in a series of pronouncements called International Financial Reporting Standards (IFRSs). It has also adopted the body of standards issued by the IASC, which continue to designated IASs.

The chairman of the IASB, Sir David Tweedie, has said that 'the aim of the globalisation of accounting standards is to simplify accounting practices and to make it easier for investors to compare the financial statements of companies worldwide'. He also said that 'this will break down barriers to investment and trade and ultimately reduce the cost of capital and stimulate growth' (*Business Week*, 7 June 2004). On 1 January 2005 there was convergence in the mandatory application of the IFRSs by listed companies within each of the European Union member states. The impact of this should be negligible with regard to the topics covered in the book, since UK accounting standards have already moved close to international standards. The reason for this is that the UK SOP was drawn up using the 1989 IASB conceptual framework for guidance. A list of current IFRSs and IASs is shown in Appendix 3 at the end of this book.

At the time of writing this book, major disagreements continued about convergence from 1 January 2005. For example, there was disagreement by European banks and insurers concerning the IASB rules requiring listed companies to record the gains and losses of various derivatives at fair market value in their published reports and accounts. The French banks, in particular, feared that the IASB may be imposing Anglo-Saxon views of accounting on the rest of the world! (See 'When bankers kept saying NON', *Business Week*, 1 March 2004).

> **Progress check 1.4** **What is the significance of the International Financial Reporting Standards (IFRSs) that have been issued by the IASB?**

Worked Example 1.1

Young Gordon Brown decided that he would like to start to train to become an accountant. Some time after he had graduated (and after an extended backpacking trip across a few continents) he registered with the Chartered Institute of Management Accountants (CIMA). At the same time Gordon started employment as part of the graduate intake in the finance department of a large engineering group. The auditors came in soon after Gordon started his job and he was intrigued and a little confused at their conversations with some of the senior accountants. They talked about accounting concepts and this standard and that standard, SSAPs and FRSs, all of which meant very little to Gordon. Gordon asked his boss, the Chief Accountant Angela Jones, if she could give him a brief outline of the framework of accounting one evening after work over a drink.

Angela's outline might have been something like this:

- Accounting is supported by a number of rules, or concepts, that have evolved over many hundreds of years, and by accounting standards to enable consistency in reporting through the preparation of financial statements.
- Accounting concepts relate to the framework within which accounting operates, ethical considerations and the rules relating to measurement of data.
- A number of concepts relate to the boundaries of the framework: business entity; going concern; periodicity.
- A number of concepts relate to accounting principles or ethics: consistency; prudence; substance over form.
- A number of concepts relate to how data should be measured and recorded: accruals; separate valuation; money measurement; historical cost; realisation; materiality; dual aspect.

- Accounting standards are formulated by a body comprised of members of the accounting institutes (Accounting Standards Board   ASB) and are guidelines which businesses are recommended to follow in the preparation of their financial statements.
- The original standards were the Statements of Standard Accounting Practice (SSAPs) which have been and continue to be superseded by the Financial Reporting Standards (FRSs).
- The aim of the SSAPs/FRSs is to cover all the issues and problems that are likely to be encountered in the preparation of financial statements and they are the authority to ensure that 'financial statements of a reporting entity give a true and fair view of its state of affairs at the balance sheet date and of its profit or loss for the financial period ending on that date' (as quoted from the ASB foreword to *Accounting Standards*).
- SSAPs were promulgated by the Accounting Standards Committee (ASC).
- FRSs are promulgated by the ASB.

Financial accounting, management accounting and financial management

The provision of a great deal of information, as we shall see as we progress through this book, is mandatory; it is needed to comply with, for example, the requirements of Acts of Parliament, the Inland Revenue, and HM Customs & Excise. However, there is a cost of providing information that has all the features that have been described, which therefore renders it potentially useful information. The benefits from producing information, in addition to mandatory information, should therefore be considered and compared with the cost of producing that information to decide on which information is 'really' required.

Accountants may be employed by accounting firms, which provide a range of accounting-related services to individuals, companies, public services and other organisations. Alternatively, accountants may be employed within companies, public services, and other organisations. Accounting firms may specialise in audit, corporate taxation, personal taxation, VAT, or consultancy (see the right hand column of Fig. 1.3). Accountants within companies, public service organisations etc., may be employed in the main functions of financial accounting, management accounting, and treasury

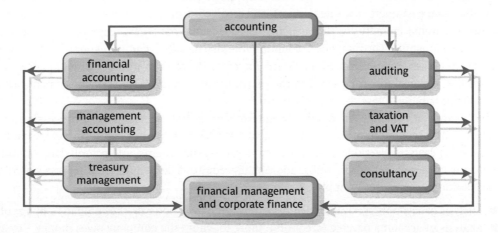

Figure 1.3 Branches of accounting

⟹ management (see the left hand column of Fig. 1.3), and also in general management. Accounting
⟹ skills may also be required in the areas of financial management, and corporate finance. Within companies this may include responsibility for investments, and the management of cash and foreign currency risk. External to companies this may include advice relating to mergers and acquisitions, and
⟹ Stock Exchange flotations.

Financial accounting

Financial accounting is primarily concerned with the first question answered by accounting information, the scorecard function. Taking a car-driving analogy, financial accounting makes greater use of
the rear-view mirror than the windscreen; financial accounting is primarily concerned with historical
information.

Financial accounting is the function responsible in general for the reporting of financial information to the owners of a business, and specifically for preparation of the periodic external reporting of
financial information, statutorily required, for shareholders. It also provides similar information as
required for Government and other interested third parties, such as potential investors, employees,
lenders, suppliers, customers, and financial analysts. Financial accounting is concerned with the
⟹ three key financial statements: the balance sheet; profit and loss account; cash flow statement. It
assists in ensuring that financial statements are included in published reports and accounts in a way
that provides ease of analysis and interpretation of company performance.

The role of financial accounting is therefore concerned with maintaining the scorecard for the
entity. Financial accounting is concerned with the classification and recording of the monetary transactions of an entity in accordance with established concepts, principles, accounting standards and
legal requirements and their presentation, by means of profit and loss accounts, balance sheets and
⟹ cash flow statements, during and at the end of an accounting period.

Within most companies, the financial accounting role usually involves much more than the preparation of the three main financial statements. A great deal of analysis is required to support such
statements and to prepare information both for internal management and in preparation for the
⟹ annual audit by the company's external auditors. This includes sales analyses, bank reconciliations,
and analyses of various types of expenditure.

A typical finance department has the following additional functions within the financial
⟹ accounting role: control of accounts payable to suppliers (the purchase ledger); control of accounts
receivable from customers (the sales ledger), and credit control; control of cash (and possible wider
treasury functions) including cash payments, cash receipts, managers' expenses, petty cash, and
banking relationships. The financial accounting role also usually includes responsibility for payroll,
whether processed internally or by an external agency. However, a number of companies elect to
transfer the responsibility for payroll to the personnel, or human resources department, bringing
⟹ with it the possibility of loss of internal control.

The breadth of functions involved in financial accounting can require the processing of high
volumes of data relating to purchase invoices, supplier payments, sales invoices, receipts from customers, other cash transactions, petty cash, employee expense claims, and payroll data. Control and
monitoring of these functions therefore additionally requires a large number of reports generated by
the accounting systems, for example:

- analysis of accounts receivable (debtors): those who owe money to the company – by age of debt
- analysis of accounts payable (creditors): those to whom the company owes money – by age of
  invoice

- sales analyses
- cheque and automated payments
- records of fixed assets
- invoice lists.

Management accounting

Past performance is never a totally reliable basis for predicting the future. However, the vast amount of data required for the preparation of financial statements, and maintenance of the further subsidiary accounting functions, provides a fertile database for use in another branch of accounting, namely management accounting.

Management accounting is primarily concerned with the provision of information to managers within the organisation for product costing, planning and control, and decision-making, and is to a lesser extent involved in providing information for external reporting.

The functions of management accounting are wide and varied. As we shall discover in Part II, whereas financial accounting is primarily concerned with past performance, management accounting makes use of historical data, but focuses almost entirely on the present and the future. Management accounting is involved with the scorecard role of accounting, but in addition is particularly concerned with the other two areas of accounting, namely problem solving and attention directing. These include cost analysis, decision-making, sales pricing, forecasting and budgeting, all of which will be discussed later in this book.

Financial management

Financial management has its roots in accounting, although it may also be regarded as a branch of applied economics. It is broadly defined as the management of all the processes associated with the efficient acquisition and deployment of both short- and long-term financial resources. Financial management assists an organisation's operations management to reach its financial objectives. This may include, for example, responsibility for corporate finance and treasury management, which is concerned with cash management, and the management of interest rate and foreign currency exchange rate risk.

The management of an organisation generally involves the three overlapping and inter-linking roles of strategic management, risk management, and operations management. Financial management supports these roles to enable management to achieve the financial objectives of the shareholders. Financial management assists in the reporting of financial results to the users of financial information, for example shareholders, lenders, and employees.

The responsibility of the finance department for financial management includes the setting up and running of reporting and control systems, raising and managing funds, the management of relationships with financial institutions, and the use of information and analysis to advise management regarding planning, policy and capital investment. The overriding requirement of financial management is to ensure that the financial objectives of the company are in line with the interests of the shareholders; the underlying fundamental objective of a company is to maximise shareholder wealth.

Financial management, therefore, includes both accounting and treasury management. Treasury management includes the management and control of corporate funds, in line with company policy. This includes the management of banking relationships, borrowings, and investment. Treasury management may also include the use of the various financial instruments, which may be used to hedge the risk to the business of changes in interest rates and foreign currency exchange rates, and advising on how company strategy may be developed to benefit from changes in the economic environment and the market in which the business operates. This book will identify the relevant areas within these subjects, which will be covered as deeply as considered necessary to provide a good introduction to financial management.

As management accounting continues to develop its emphasis on decision-making and strategic management, and broaden the range of activities that it supports, the distinction between management accounting and financial management is slowly disappearing.

Worked Example 1.2

A friend of yours is thinking about pursuing a career in accounting and would like some views on the major differences between financial accounting, management accounting and financial management.

The following notes provide a summary that identifies the key differences.

Financial accounting: The financial accounting function deals with the recording of past and current transactions, usually with the aid of computerised accounting systems. Of the various reports prepared, the majority are for external users, and include the profit and loss account, balance sheet, and the cash flow statement. In a plc, such reports must be prepared at least every 6 months, and must comply with current legal and reporting requirements.

Management accounting: The management accounting function works alongside the financial accounting function, using a number of the day-to-day financial accounting reports from the accounting system. Management accounting is concerned largely with looking at current issues and problems and the future in terms of decision-making and forecasting, for example the consideration of 'what if' scenarios during the course of preparation of forecasts and budgets. Management accounting outputs are mainly for internal users, with much confidential reporting, for example to the directors of the company.

Financial management: Financial management may include responsibilities for corporate finance and the treasury function. This includes the management and control of corporate funds, within parameters specified by the board of directors. The role often includes the management of company borrowings, investment of surplus funds, the management of both interest rate and exchange rate risk, and giving advice on economic and market changes and the exploitation of opportunities. The financial management function is not necessarily staffed by accountants. Plcs report on the treasury activities of the company in their periodic reporting and financial review.

The article on page 19 which appeared in the *Daily Telegraph* illustrates some of the important applications of accounting and financial management. These include:

- the planning activities, particularly with regard to restructuring of the business
- negotiations with bankers
- evaluation of investments in new steelworks
- union negotiations
- costs of compliance with environmental requirements.

In February 2004 St Modwen Properties announced it had purchased some of the Corus surplus property, the former Llanwern steelworks site in Wales. They also revealed plans to invest more than

Accounting and financial management in action

Corus, the troubled steel producer, is quietly marketing around 7,000 acres of surplus property in a bid to raise funds and streamline its business as it prepares for a radical restructuring of its UK operations.

Corus, formed though a merger of British Steel and Hoogovens of the Netherlands in 1999, requires around £250m to pay for redundancies and investments in its plan to turn around its ailing UK business.

Corus is unable to put a value on its surplus property because of the expensive cleaning up which some sites may require. Corus is legally liable to carry out the remediation work which can sometimes cost more than the value of the site.

Since the merger, Corus has cut around 10,000 jobs in the UK and is planning to cut a further 1,100 as it closes more unprofitable plants. The number of redundancies could rise by another 2,000 if its Teesside steel plant cannot be brought into profit.

However, the company intends to invest in modernising two or three steelworks in the UK in order to boost its output.

Earlier this month Corus announced that it had secured a new £800m debt facility, but the £250m needed for the UK restructuring is likely to come from either a rights issue or from fresh loans.

It is also planning to dispose of most of its US business after years of poor performance.

Philippe Varin, the new Corus chief executive who was appointed three months ago from the French aluminium producer Pechiney, has said the money is required 'the sooner the better'.

Despite selling several smaller portfolios earlier this year – including one to Threadneedle, the fund manager, for £48m in July – realising the value of its property portfolio is likely to be a slow process.

The company won planning permission in April to redevelop the 1,125 acre site of the former Ravenscraig steelworks in Scotland more than 11 years after the last steel was poured there.

Corus puts land up for sale to raise funds for rescue package, by Edward Simkins and Mary Fagan

© *Daily Telegraph*, 24 August 2003

£200m in the site over the next 10 years. The project would create 7,000 jobs and lead to a total end value of £750m and they hoped to be on site towards the end of 2005. The acquisition of the Llanwern site was the fifth major land deal St Modwen completed with Corus, which retained a further 1,500 acres at Llanwern, including the operational steelworks.

> **Progress check 1.5** **What are the main differences between financial accounting, management accounting, and financial management?**

Accounting and accountancy

Accounting is sometimes referred to as a process of identifying, measuring and communicating economic information to permit informed judgements and decisions by users of the information, and also to provide information, which is potentially useful for making economic and social decisions. The term 'accounting' may be defined as:

- the classification and recording of monetary transactions
- the presentation and interpretation of the results of those transactions in order to assess performance over a period and the financial position at a given date

- the monetary projection of future activities arising from alternative planned courses of action.

Accounting processes are concerned with how data is measured and recorded and how the accounting function ensures the effective operation of accounting and financial systems. Accounting processes follow a system of recording and classification of data, followed by summarisation of financial information for subsequent interpretation and presentation. An accounting system is a series of tasks and records of an entity by which the transactions are processed as a means of maintaining financial records. Such systems identify, assemble, analyse, calculate, classify, record, summarise and report transactions.

Most companies prepare an accounting manual that provides the details and responsibilities for each of the accounting systems. The accounting manual is a collection of accounting instructions governing the responsibilities of persons, and the procedures, forms and records relating to preparation and use of accounting data.

There may be separate accounting manuals for the constituent parts of the accounting system, for example:

- financial accounting manual – general ledger and coding
- management accounting manual – budget and cost accounting
- financial management/treasury manual – bank reconciliations and foreign currency exposure management.

Accountancy is defined as the practice of accounting. A **qualified accountant** is a member of the accountancy profession, and in the UK is a member of one of the six professional accountancy bodies (see Fig. 1.4). An accountant becomes qualified within each of these institutes through passing a large number of extremely technically-demanding examinations and completion of a mandatory period of three years' practical training. The examination syllabus of each of the professional bodies tends to be very similar; each body provides additional emphasis on specific areas of accounting.

Chartered Management Accountants (qualified members of CIMA) receive their practical training

Figure 1.4 The professional accounting bodies

in industrial and commercial environments, and in the public sector, for example the NHS. They are involved in practical accounting work and development of broader experience of strategic and operational management of the business. Certified Accountants (qualified members of ACCA) and Chartered Accountants (qualified members of ICAEW, ICAS, or ICAI) usually receive training while working in a practising accountant's office, which offers services to businesses and the general public, but may also receive training while employed in industrial and commercial organisations. Training focuses initially on auditing, and may then develop to include taxation and general business advice. Many accountants who receive training while specialising in central and local government usually, but not exclusively, are qualified members of CIPFA.

There are also a number of other accounting bodies like the Association of Accounting Technicians (AAT), Association of International Accountants, and Association of Authorised Public Accountants. The AAT, for example, provides bookkeeping and accounting training through examination and experience to a high level of competence, but short of that required to become a qualified accountant. Treasury management is served by the Association of Corporate Treasurers (ACT). This qualification has tended to be a second qualification for accountants specialising in corporate funding, cash and working capital management, interest rate and foreign currency exchange rate risk management. In the same way, the Institute of Taxation serves accountants who are tax specialists.

> **Progress check 1.6** **What services does accounting offer and why do businesses need these services?**

Worked Example 1.3

Of which professional bodies are accountants likely to be members if they are employed as auditors, or if they are employed in the industrial and commercial sectors, or if they are employed in local government?

The following list of each of the types of professional accounting bodies links them with the sort of accounting they may become involved in.

Chartered Institute of Management Accountants (CIMA): management accounting and financial accounting roles with a focus on management accounting in the industrial and commercial sectors, and strategic and operational management

Institutes of Chartered Accountants (ICAEW, ICAS, ICAI): employment within a firm of accountants, carrying out auditing, investigations, taxation and general business advice – possible opportunities to move into an accounting role in industry

Chartered Institute of Public Finance and Accountancy (CIPFA): accounting role within central government or local government

Association of Chartered Certified Accountants (ACCA): employment either within a firm of accountants, carrying out auditing etc., or management accounting and financial accounting roles within commerce/industry

Association of Corporate Treasurers (ACT): commercial accounting roles with almost total emphasis on treasury issues: corporate finance; funding; cash management; working capital management; financial risk management

Types of business entity: sole traders; partnerships; limited companies; public limited companies

Business entities are involved either in manufacturing (for example, food and automotive components) or in providing services (for example, retailing, hospitals or television broadcasting). Such entities include profit-making and not-for-profit organisations, and charities. The main types of entity, and the environments in which they operate, represented in Fig. 1.5 and the four main types of profit-making organisations are explained in the sections that follow.

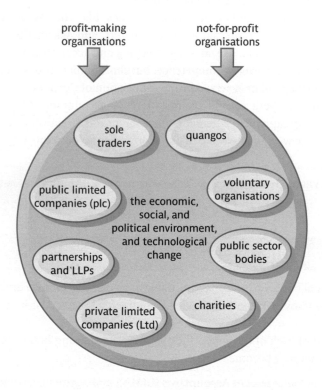

Figure 1.5 Types of business entity

The variety of business entities can be seen to range from quangos (quasi-autonomous non-government organisations) to partnerships to limited companies. Most of the topics covered in this book apply to any type of business organisation that has the primary aim of maximising the wealth of its owners: limited liability companies, both private (Ltd) companies and public (plc) limited companies, sole traders, and partnerships.

> **Progress check 1.7 What are the different types of business entity? Can you think of some examples of each?**

Sole traders

A sole trader entity is applicable for most types of small business. It is owned and financed by one individual, who receives all the profit made by the business, even though more than one person may work in the business.

The individual sole trader has complete flexibility regarding:

- the type of (legal) activities in which the business may be engaged
- when to start up or cease the business
- the way in which business is conducted.

The individual sole trader also has responsibility for:

- financing the business
- risk-taking
- decision-making
- employing staff
- any debts or loans that the business may have (the responsibility of which is unlimited, and cases of financial difficulty may result in personal property being used to repay debts).

A sole trader business is simple and cheap to set up. There are no legal or administrative set-up costs as the business does not have to be registered since it is not a legal entity separate from its owner. As we shall see, this is unlike the legal position of owners, or shareholders, of limited companies who are recognised as separate legal entities from the businesses they own.

Accounting records are needed to be kept by sole traders for the day-to-day management of the business and to provide an account of profit made during each tax year. Unlike limited companies, sole traders are not required to file a formal report and accounts each year with the Registrar of Companies. However, sole traders must prepare accounts on an annual basis to provide the appropriate financial information for inclusion in their annual tax return for submission to the Inland Revenue.

Sole traders normally remain quite small businesses, which may be seen as a disadvantage. The breadth of business skills is likely to be lacking since there are no co-owners with which to share the management and development of the business.

Partnerships

Partnerships are similar to sole traders except that the ownership of the business is in the hands of two or more persons. The main differences are in respect of how much each of the partners puts into the business, who is responsible for what, and how the profits are to be shared. These factors are normally set out in formal partnership agreements, and if the partnership agreement is not specific then the provisions of the Partnership Act 1890 apply. There is usually a written partnership agreement (but this is not absolutely necessary) and so there are initial legal costs of setting up the business.

A partnership is called a firm and is usually a small business, although there are some very large partnerships, for example firms of accountants like PriceWaterhouseCoopers. Partnerships are formed by two or more persons and, apart from certain professions like accountants, architects and solicitors, the number of persons in a partnership is limited to 20.

A partnership:

- can carry out any legal activities agreed by all the partners
- is not a legal entity separate from its partners.

The partners in a firm:

- can all be involved in running the business
- all share the profits made by the firm

- are all jointly and severally liable for the debts of the firm
- all have unlimited liability for the debts of the firm (and cases of financial difficulty may result in personal property being used to repay debts)
- are each liable for the actions of the other partners.

Accounting records are needed to be kept by partnerships for the day-to-day management of the business and to provide an account of profit made during each tax year. Unlike limited companies, partnership firms are not required to file a formal report and accounts each year with the Registrar of Companies, but they must submit annual accounts for tax purposes to the Inland Revenue.

A new type of legal entity was established in 2001, the limited liability partnership (LLP). This is a variation on the traditional partnership, and has a separate legal identity from the partners, which therefore protects them from personal bankruptcy.

One of the main benefits of a partnership is that derived from its broader base of business skills than that of a sole trader. A partnership is also able to share risk-taking, decision-making, and the general management of the firm.

Limited companies

A limited company is a legal entity separate from the owners of the business, which may enter into contracts, own property, and take or receive legal action. The owners limit their obligations to the amount of finance they have put into the company by way of the share of the company they have paid for. Normally, the maximum that may be claimed from shareholders is no more than they have paid for their shares, regardless of what happens to the company. Equally, there is no certainty that shareholders may recover their original investment if they wish to dispose of their shares or if the business is wound up, for whatever reason.

A company with unlimited liability does not give the owners, or members, of the company the protection of limited liability. If the business were to fail, the members would be liable, without limitation, for all the debts of the business.

The legal requirements relating to the registration and operation of limited companies is contained within the Companies Act 1985 as amended by the Companies Act 1989. Limited companies are required to be registered with the Registrar of Companies as either a private limited company (designated Ltd) or a public limited company (designated plc).

Private limited companies (Ltd)

Private limited companies are designated as Ltd. There are legal formalities involved in setting up a Ltd company which result in costs for the company. These formalities include the drafting of the company's Memorandum and Articles of Association (M and A) that describe what the company is and what it is allowed to do, registering the company and its director(s) with the Registrar of Companies, and registering the name of the company.

The shareholders provide the financing of the business in the form of share capital, of which there is no minimum requirement, and are therefore the owners of the business. The shareholders must appoint at least one director of the company, who may also be the company secretary, who carries out the day-to-day management of the business. A Ltd company may only carry out the activities included in its M and A.

Limited companies must regularly produce annual accounts for their shareholders and file a copy with the Registrar of Companies, and therefore the general public may have access to this information. A Ltd company's accounts must be audited by a suitably qualified accountant, unless it is exempt from this requirement, currently (with effect from 30 March 2004) by having annual sales of less than £5.6m and a balance sheet total of less than £2.8m. The exemption is not compulsory and having no audit may be a disadvantage: banks, financial institutions, customers and suppliers may rely on information from Companies House to assess creditworthiness and they are usually reassured by an independent audit. Limited companies must also provide copies of their annual accounts for the Inland Revenue and also generally provide a separate computation of their profit on which corporation tax is payable. The accounting profit of a Ltd company is adjusted for:

- various expenses that may not be allowable in computing taxable profit
- tax allowances that may be deducted in computing taxable profit.

Limited companies tend to be family businesses and smaller businesses with the ownership split among a few shareholders, although there have been many examples of very large private limited companies. The shares of Ltd companies may be bought and sold but they may not be offered for sale to the general public. Since ownership is usually with family and friends there is rarely a ready market for the shares and so their sale usually requires a valuation of the business.

Public limited companies (plc)

Public limited companies are designated as plc. A plc usually starts its life as a Ltd company and then becomes a plc by applying for a listing of its shares on the Stock Exchange or the Alternative Investment Market, and making a public offer for sale of shares in the company. Plcs must have a minimum issued share capital of (currently) £50,000. The offer for sale, dealt with by a financial institution and the company's legal representatives, is very costly. The formalities also include the re-drafting of the company's M and A, reflecting its status as a plc, registering the company and its director(s) with the Registrar of Companies, and registering the name of the plc.

The shareholders must appoint at least two directors of the company, who carry out the day-to-day management of the business, and a suitably qualified company secretary to ensure the plc's compliance with company law. A plc may only carry out the activities included in its M and A.

Plcs must regularly produce annual accounts, which they copy to their shareholders. They must also file a copy with the Registrar of Companies, and therefore the general public may have access to this information. The larger plcs usually provide printed glossy annual reports and accounts which they distribute to their shareholders and other interested parties. A plc's accounts must be audited by a suitably qualified accountant, unless it is exempt from this requirement by (currently) having annual sales of less than £5.6m and a balance sheet total of less than £2.8m. The same drawback applies to having no audit as applies with a Ltd company. Plcs must also provide copies of their annual accounts for the Inland Revenue and also generally provide a separate computation of their profit on which corporation tax is payable. The accounting profit of a plc is adjusted for:

- various expenses that may not be allowable in computing taxable profit
- tax allowances that may be deducted in computing taxable profit.

The shareholders provide the financing of the plc in the form of share capital and are therefore the owners of the business. The ownership of a plc can therefore be seen to be spread amongst many shareholders (individuals and institutions like insurance companies and pension funds), and the shares may be freely traded and bought and sold by the general public.

Worked Example 1.4

Ike Andoowit is in the process of planning the setting up of a new residential training centre.

Ike has discussed with a number of his friends the question of registering the business as a limited company, or being a sole trader. Most of Ike's friends have highlighted the advantages of limiting his liability to the original share capital that he would need to put into the company to finance the business. Ike feels a bit uneasy about the whole question and decides to obtain the advice of a professional accountant to find out:

(i)   the main disadvantages of setting up a limited company as opposed to a sole trader
(ii)   if Ike's friends are correct about the advantage of limiting one's liability
(iii)   what other advantages there are to registering the business as a limited company.

The accountant may answer Ike's questions as follows:

Setting up as a sole trader is a lot simpler and easier than setting up a limited company. A limited company is bound by the provisions of the Companies Act 1985 as amended by the Companies Act 1989, and for example, is required to have an independent annual audit. A limited company is required to be much more open about its affairs.

The financial structure of a limited company is more complicated than that of a sole trader. There are also additional costs involved in the setting up, and in the administrative functions of a limited company.

Running a business as a limited company requires registration of the business with the Registrar of Companies.

As Ike's friends have pointed out, the financial obligations of a shareholder in a limited company are generally restricted to the amount he/she has paid for his/her shares. In addition, the number of shareholders is potentially unlimited, which widens the scope for raising additional capital.

It should also be noted that:

- a limited company is restricted in its choice of business name
- if its annual sales exceed £1m, a limited company is required to hold an annual general meeting (AGM)
- any additional finance provided for a company by a bank is likely to require a personal guarantee from one or more shareholders.

> **Progress check 1.8** There are some differences between those businesses that have been established as sole traders and those established as partnerships, and likewise there are differences between private limited companies and public limited companies. What are these differences, and what are the similarities?

An introduction to financial statement reporting

Limited companies produce financial statements for each accounting period to provide adequate information about how the company has been doing. There are three main financial statements –

balance sheet, profit and loss account (or income statement), and cash flow statement. Companies are also obliged to provide similar financial statements at each year end to provide information for their shareholders, the Inland Revenue, and the Registrar of Companies. This information is frequently used by City analysts, investing institutions and the public in general.

After each year end companies prepare their annual report and accounts for their shareholders. Copies of the annual report and accounts are filed with the Registrar of Companies and copies are available to other interested parties such as financial institutions, major suppliers and other investors. In addition to the profit and loss account and cash flow statement for the year and the balance sheet as at the year end date, the annual report and accounts includes notes to the accounts, and much more financial and non-financial information such as company policies, financial indicators, corporate governance compliance, directors' remuneration, employee numbers, business analysis, and segmental analysis. The annual report also includes an operating and financial review of the business, a report of the auditors of the company, and the chairman's statement.

The auditors' report states compliance or otherwise with accounting standards and that the accounts are free from material misstatement, and that they give a true and fair view prepared on the assumption that the company is a going concern. The chairman's statement offers an opportunity for the chairman of the company to report in unquantified and unaudited terms on the performance of the company during the past financial period and on likely future developments. However, the auditors would object if there was anything in the chairman's statement that was inconsistent with the audited accounts.

Progress check 1.9 **What are the three main financial statements reported by a business? How are business transactions ultimately reflected in financial statements?**

Worked Example 1.5

Gordon Brown soon settled into his graduate trainee role in the finance department of the large engineering group, and pursued his CIMA studies with enthusiasm. Although Gordon was more interested in business planning and getting involved with new development projects, his job and his studies required him to become totally familiar with, and to be able to prepare, the financial statements of a company. Gordon was explaining the subject of financial statements and what they involved to a friend of his, Jack, another graduate trainee in human resources. Where? – you have guessed it – over an after-work drink.

Gordon explained the subject of financial statements to Jack, bearing in mind that he is very much a non-financial person.

Limited companies are required to produce three main financial statements for each accounting period with information about company performance for:

- shareholders
- the Inland Revenue
- banks
- City analysts
- investing institutions
- the public in general.

The three key financial statements are the:

(a)   balance sheet

(b)   profit and loss account (or income statement)

(c)   cash flow statement.

(a)   **Balance sheet:** a financial snapshot at a moment in time, or the financial position of the company comparable with pressing the 'pause' button on a DVD. The DVD in 'play' mode shows what is happening as time goes on second by second, but when you press 'pause' the DVD stops on a picture; the picture does not tell you what has happened over the period of time up to the pause (or what is going to happen after the pause). The balance sheet is the consequence of everything that has happened up to the balance sheet date. It does not explain how the company got to that position.

(b)   **Profit and loss account:** this is the DVD in 'play' mode. It is used to calculate whether or not the company has made a gain or deficit on its operations during the period, its financial performance, through producing and selling its goods or services. Net earnings or net profit is calculated from revenues derived throughout the period between two 'pauses', minus costs incurred in deriving those revenues.

(c)   **Cash flow statement:** this is the DVD again in 'play' mode, but net earnings is not the same as cash flow, since revenues and costs are not necessarily accounted for when cash transfers occur. Sales are accounted for when goods or services are delivered and accepted by the customer but cash may not be received until some time later. The profit and loss account does not reflect non-trading events like an issue of shares or a loan that will increase cash but are not revenues or costs. The cash flow statement summarises cash inflows and cash outflows and calculates the net change in the cash position for the company throughout the period between two 'pauses'.

Users of accounting and financial information

Financial information is important to a wide range of groups both internal and external to the organisation. Such information is required, for example, by individuals outside the organisation to make decisions about whether or not to invest in one company or another, or by potential suppliers who wish to assess the reliability and financial strength of the organisation. It is also required by managers within the organisation as an aid to decision-making. The main users of financial information are shown in Fig. 1.6.

> **Progress check 1.10** How many users of financial information can you think of and in what ways do you think they may use this information?

Figure 1.6 Users of financial and accounting information

Worked Example 1.6

Kevin Green, a trainee accountant, has recently joined the finance department of a newly formed public limited company. Kevin has been asked to work with the company's auditors who have been commissioned to prepare some alternative formats for the company's annual report.

As part of his preparation for this, Kevin's manager has asked him to prepare a draft report about who is likely to use the information contained in the annual report, and how they might use such information.

Kevin's preparatory notes for his report included the following:

- **Competitors** as part of their industry competitive analysis studies to look at market share, and financial strength
- **Customers** to determine the ability to provide a regular, reliable supply of goods and services, and to assess customer dependence
- **Employees** to assess the potential for providing continued employment and assess levels of remuneration
- **General public** to assess general employment opportunities, social, political and environmental issues, and to consider potential for investment
- **Government** VAT and corporate taxation, Government statistics, grants and financial assistance, monopolies and mergers
- **Investment analysts** investment potential for individuals and institutions with regard to past and future performance, strength of management, risk versus reward
- **Lenders** the capacity and the ability of the company to service debt and repay capital
- **Managers/directors** to a certain extent an aid to decision-making, but such relevant information should already have been available internally
- **Shareholders/investors** a tool of accountability to maintain a check on how effectively the

directors/managers are running the business, to assess the financial strength and future developments

■ **Suppliers** to assess the long-term viability and whether the company is able to meet its obligations and pay suppliers on an ongoing basis.

Accountability and financial reporting

When we talk about companies we are generally referring to limited companies, as distinct from sole traders and partnerships (or firms – although this term is frequently wrongly used to refer to companies). As we have discussed, limited liability companies have an identity separate from their owners, the shareholders, and the liability of shareholders is limited to the amount of money they have invested in the company, that is their shares in the company. Ownership of a business is separated from its stewardship, or management, by the shareholders' assignment to a board of directors the responsibility for running the company. The directors of the company are accountable to the shareholders, and both parties must play their part in making that accountability effective.

The directors of a limited company may comprise one or more professionally qualified accountants (usually including a finance director). The directors of the company necessarily delegate to middle managers and junior managers the responsibility for the day-to-day management of the business. It is certainly likely that this body of managers, who report to the board of directors, will include a further one or more qualified accountants responsible for managing the finance function.

Accountability is maintained by reporting on the financial performance and the financial position of the business to shareholders on both a yearly and an interim basis. The reporting made in the form of the financial statements includes the balance sheet, profit and loss account, and cash flow statement, which will be considered in detail in Part I of this book.

You may question why all the accounting regulation that we have discussed in the earlier sections of this chapter is necessary at all. Well, there are a number of arguments in favour of such regulation:

■ It is very important that the credibility of financial statement reporting is maintained so that actual and potential investors are protected as far as possible against inappropriate accounting practices.

■ Generally, being able to distinguish between the good and not so good companies also provides some stability in the financial markets.

■ The auditors of companies must have some rules on which to base their true and fair view of financial position and financial performance, which they give to the shareholders and other users of the financial statements.

External auditors are appointed by, and report independently to, the shareholders. They are professionally qualified accountants who are required to provide objective verification to shareholders and other users that the financial statements have been prepared properly and in accordance with legislative and regulatory requirements; that they present the information truthfully and fairly; and that they conform to the best accounting practice in their treatment of the various measurements and valuations.

The audit is defined by the Auditing Practices Board (APB) as 'an independent examination of, and expression of an opinion on, the financial statements of the enterprise'. There is a requirement for all companies registered in the UK to have an annual audit, except for those companies that (currently) have an annual turnover of less than £5.6m and a balance sheet total of less than £2.8m.

The financial reporting of the company includes preparation of the financial statements, notes and reports, which are audited and given an opinion on by the external auditors. A regulatory framework exists to see fair play, the responsibility for which is held jointly by the Government and the private sector, including the accountancy profession and the Stock Exchange.

The Government exercises influence through bodies such as the Department of Trade and Industry (DTI) and through Parliament by the enactment of legislation, for example the Companies Act. Such legal regulation began with the Joint Stock Companies Act 1844.

Subsequent statutes exerted greater influence on company reporting: the Companies Acts 1948, 1967, and 1981. The provisions included in these Acts were consolidated into the Companies Act 1985, which was then amended in 1989. The Companies Act 1985, as amended in 1989, contains the overall current legal framework.

It may be argued that the increasing amount of accounting regulation itself stifles responses to changes in economic and business environments, and discourages the development of improved financial reporting. We have already seen that the development of various conceptual frameworks indicates that there is wide disagreement about what constitutes accounting best practice. The resistance to acceptance of international accounting standards may be for political reasons, the rules perhaps reflecting the requirements of specific interest groups or countries.

It is also true that despite increasing accounting regulation there have been an increasing number of well-publicised financial scandals in the USA in particular, where the accounting systems are very much 'rule-based', as well as in the UK, Italy, and Japan. However, these scandals have usually been the result of fraudulent activity. This leads to another question as to why the auditors of such companies did not detect or prevent such fraud. The answer is that, despite the widespread perception of the general public to the contrary, auditors are not appointed to detect or prevent fraud. Rather, they are appointed by the shareholders to give their opinion as to whether the financial statements show a true and fair view and comply with statutory, regulatory, and accounting and financial reporting standards requirements.

> **Progress check 1.11 In what ways may the reliability of financial reporting be ensured?**

Worked Example 1.7

You are thinking of changing jobs (within marketing) and moving from a local, well-established retailer that has been in business for over 20 years. You have been asked to attend an interview at a new plc that started up around two years ago. The plc is a retailer via the Internet. Your family has suggested that you investigate the company thoroughly before your interview, paying particular attention to its financial resources. There is a chance the plc may not be a going concern if its business plan does not succeed.

You will certainly want to include the following questions at your interview.

(a) Are any published accounts available for review?
(b) What is the share capital of the company (for example, is it £10,000 or £1,000,000)?

(c) Is the company profitable?

(d) Does the company have loan commitments?

(e) Is the company working within its bank overdraft facilities?

(f) Are any press analyses of the company available?

(g) What is the current customer base?

The answers may suggest whether the company can continue trading for the foreseeable future.

Summary of key points

- The three main purposes of accounting are: to provide records of transactions and a scorecard of results; to direct attention to problems; to evaluate the best ways of solving problems.
- Accountancy is the practice of accounting.
- Conceptual frameworks of accounting have been developed in many countries and the UK conceptual framework is embodied in the Statement of Principles (SOP).
- The framework of accounting is bounded by concepts (or rules) and standards, covering what data should be included within an accounting system and how that data should be recorded.
- International accounting standards have been developed, which should be adopted by listed companies within the European Union with effect from 1 January 2005.
- The main branches of accounting within commercial and industrial organisations are financial accounting, management accounting, treasury management, financial management and corporate finance.
- The main services, in addition to accounting, that are provided by accountants to commercial and industrial organisations are auditing, corporate taxation, personal taxation, VAT advice, and consultancy.
- The large variety of types of business entity includes profit and not-for-profit organisations, both privately and Government owned, involved in providing products and services.
- The four main types of profit-making businesses in the UK are sole traders, partnerships, limited companies (Ltd), and public limited companies (plc).
- Accounting processes follow a system of recording and classifying data, followed by a summarisation of financial information for subsequent interpretation and presentation.
- The three main financial statements that appear within a business's annual report and accounts, together with the chairman's statement, directors' report, and auditors' report, are the balance sheet, profit and loss account, and cash flow statement.
- There is a wide range of users of financial information external and internal to an organisation. External users include: potential investors; suppliers; financial analysts. Internal users include: managers; shareholders; employees.
- Accountability is maintained by the reporting to shareholders on a yearly and half-yearly basis of sales and other activities and profits or losses arising from those activities, and the audit function.

Questions

Q1.1 (i) How many different types of business entity can you think of?

(ii) In what respect do they differ fundamentally?

Q1.2 (i) Why are accountants required to produce financial information?

(ii) Who do they produce it for and what do they do with it?

Q1.3 Describe the broad regulatory, professional, and operational framework of accounting.

Q1.4 What are conceptual frameworks of accounting?

Q1.5 (i) What are accounting concepts?

(ii) What purpose do they serve?

Q1.6 What is the UK Statement of Principles (SOP)?

Q1.7 (i) What is accountancy?

(ii) What is an accountant?

(iii) What do accountants do?

Q1.8 What do accountants mean by SSAPs and FRSs, and what are they for?

Q1.9 What are IASs and IFRSs and why are they important?

Q1.10 (i) What is financial management?

(ii) How does financial management relate to accounting and perhaps other disciplines?

Q1.11 How do financial statements ensure accountability for the reporting of timely and accurate information to shareholders is maintained?

Discussion points

D1.1 The managing director of a large public limited company stated: 'I've built up my business over the past 15 years from a one man band to a large plc. As we grew we seemed to spend more and more money on accountants, financial managers, and auditors. During the next few months we are restructuring to go back to being a private limited company. This will be much simpler and we can save a fortune on accounting and auditing costs.' Discuss.

(Hint: You may wish to research Richard Branson and, for example, Virgin Air, on the Internet to provide some background for this discussion.)

D1.2 The managing director of a growing private limited company stated: 'All these accounting concepts and standards seem like a lot of red tape to me, and we've got financial accountants and management accountants as well as auditors. Surely all I need to know at the end of the day is how much have we made.' Discuss.

D1.3 Is accounting objective? Discuss with reference to at least six different accounting concepts.

Exercises

Exercises E1.1 to E1.10 require an essay-type approach. You should refer to the relevant sections in Chapter 1 to check your solutions.

Level I

E1.1 *Time allowed – 15 minutes*
Discuss the implications of preparation of the profit and loss account if there were no accounting concepts.

E1.2 *Time allowed – 30 minutes*
At a recent meeting of the local branch of the Women's Institute they had a discussion about what sort of organisation they were. The discussion broadened into a general debate about all types of organisation, and someone brought up the term 'business entity'. Although there were many opinions, there was little sound knowledge about what business entities are. Jane Cross said that her husband was an accountant and she was sure he would not mind spending an hour one evening to enlighten them on the subject. Chris Cross fished out his textbooks to refresh his knowledge of the subject and came up with a schedule of all the different business entities he could think of together with the detail of their defining features and key points of difference and similarity.

Prepare the sort of schedule that Chris might have drafted for his talk and identify the category that the Women's Institute might fall into.

E1.3 *Time allowed – 30 minutes*
Mary Andrews was an accountant but is now semi-retired. She has been asked by her local comprehensive school careers officer to give a talk entitled: 'What is an accountant and what is accounting, its use and its purpose?'.

Prepare a list of bullet points that covers everything necessary for Mary to give a comprehensive and easy-to-understand presentation to a group of sixth-formers at the school.

Level II

E1.4 *Time allowed – 30 minutes*
Accounting standards in general are reasonably clear and unambiguous.

Are there any major areas where accountants may disagree in balance sheet accounting?

E1.5 *Time allowed – 30 minutes*
Financial statements are produced each year by businesses, using prescribed formats.

Should major plcs be allowed to reflect their individuality in their own financial statements?

E1.6 *Time allowed – 45 minutes*
Professionals in the UK, for example, doctors, solicitors, accountants etc., normally work within partnerships. Many tradesmen, such as plumbers, car mechanics, carpenters, and so on, operate as sole traders. Software engineers seem to work for corporations and limited companies.

Consider the size of operation, range of products, financing, the marketplace, and the geographical area served, to discuss why companies like Microsoft and Yahoo should operate as plcs.

E1.7 *Time allowed – 60 minutes*
Bill Walsh has just been appointed Finance Director of a medium-sized engineering company, Nutsan Ltd, which has a high level of exports and is very sensitive to economic changes throughout the UK and the rest of the world. One of the tasks on Bill's action list is a review of the accounting and finance function.

What are the senior financial roles that Bill would expect to be in place and what are the important functions for which they should be responsible?

E1.8 *Time allowed – 60 minutes*

The Millennium Dome was opened to the general public in the UK for the year 2000 and was planned to close at the end of 2000 for the site to be used for some other purpose. There were problems financing the construction and the general day-to-day operations. There were many crises reported in the press during 2000. A proposed takeover of the site fell through in September 2000, with various reasons given by the potential acquirer.

You are required to research into the Dome using the BBC, *Financial Times* and the other serious newspapers, and the Internet, and summarise the financial aspects of the project that you gather. You should focus on the attitudes expressed by the general public, select committees of MPs, Government ministers, the Opposition, the Dome's management, and consider examples of bias, non-timeliness, and lack of transparency.

E1.9 *Time allowed – 60 minutes*

Conceptual frameworks of accounting have been developed over many years and in many countries.

Explain how these culminated in the publication of the UK Statement of Principles (SOP) in 1999, and discuss the implications of each of the eight chapters.

E1.10 *Time allowed – 60 minutes*

The International Accounting Standards Board (IASB) decreed the adoption of the International Financial Reporting Standards (IFRSs) by all listed companies within the European Union mandatory with effect from 1 January 2005.

Discuss the practical and political issues surrounding this decision.

Part I

Financial accounting

Part contents

Part I is about financial accounting. The first three chapters deal with the three key financial statements: balance sheet; profit and loss account; cash flow statement; and in particular those relating to limited companies. In most respects these also apply to other profit-making and not-for-profit organisations in both the private and public sectors.

Chapter 2 begins with an introduction to the preparation of simple financial statements and then goes on to consider the balance sheet in detail.

Chapter 3 looks in detail at the profit and loss account. It looks at how to recognise that a profit (or loss) has been made and how it is linked with the balance sheet and cash flow.

Chapter 4 deals with the cash flow statement, which shows from where an organisation has received cash during an accounting period and how cash was used.

Chapter 5 is headed *Business performance analysis*. The three financial statements provide information about business performance. Much more may be gleaned about the performance of the business through further analysis of the financial statements, using financial ratios and other techniques, for example trend analysis, industrial and inter-firm analysis.

Chapter 6 looks at the analysis and interpretation of the published accounts of a business. It uses the report and accounts for the year ended 31 March 2004 of Johnson Matthey plc to illustrate the type of financial and non-financial information provided by a major UK public company.

In Chapter 7 we broaden the scope of our study of accounting and finance to provide an introduction to corporate governance, a topic that is becoming increasingly important, as the responsibilities of directors continue to increase. The burden lies with management to run businesses in strict compliance with statutory, regulatory and accounting requirements, so it is crucial that directors are aware of the rules and codes of practice in place to regulate the behaviour of directors of limited companies.

2

Financial statements of limited companies – balance sheet

Contents

Learning objectives

Completion of this chapter will enable you to:

- explain the differences in accounting treatment of capital expenditure and revenue expenditure
- identify the financial information shown in the financial statements of a company: balance sheet; profit and loss account; cash flow statement
- construct simple financial statements
- outline the structure of the balance sheet of a limited company
- classify the broad balance sheet categories of shareholders' equity, liabilities, assets
- outline the alternative balance sheet formats
- prepare a balance sheet
- evaluate some of the alternative methods of asset valuation
- appreciate the limitations of the conventional balance sheet.

Introduction

We talked about business entities in general in Chapter 1. The financial accounting and reporting of limited companies are similar to those of sole traders and partnerships, except that they are more detailed and require a greater disclosure of information. This is to comply with current legislation and the requirements for reporting of financial information to the owners of the business (the shareholders).

Each type of business is required to prepare periodic financial statements in one form or another for internal control purposes, the shareholders and, for example, the Inland Revenue. The current chapter and Chapters 3 and 4 provide a comprehensive coverage of financial statements, which are the basis for the subsequent chapters about business performance analysis and published reports and accounts.

We will be looking in a little more detail at the profit and loss account in Chapter 3 and the balance sheet later in this chapter. Each of these financial statements includes expenditure of one form or another. This chapter begins by broadly looking at types of expenditure and explaining what is meant by revenue expenditure and capital expenditure. Most items may be clearly identified in terms of revenue or capital expenditure, but there are also a number of uncertain areas in these classifications with regard to the rules used in accounting and in the way that expenditure may be analysed for taxation purposes.

Before dealing specifically with the balance sheets of limited companies we will discuss the subject of financial statements that was introduced in Chapter 1. We will see how these are constructed and interrelated, by working through a comprehensive example that illustrates how transactions are reflected in the profit and loss account, balance sheet and cash flow statement of a business.

This chapter deals with how balance sheets are structured and how the accounts within the balance sheet are categorised. Each of the items within each of the balance sheet categories will be described in detail and form the basis to enable the preparation of a balance sheet of a limited company in the appropriate format.

The chapter closes by illustrating the subjective nature of the balance sheet and considers one of the areas in which this is apparent through looking at examples of the alternative methods for valuation of assets that are available to companies.

Capital expenditure and revenue expenditure

Expenditure made by an entity falls generally within two types:

- revenue expenditure
- capital expenditure.

Revenue expenditure relates to expenditure incurred in the manufacture of products, the provision of services or in the general conduct of the company, which is normally charged to the profit and loss account in the accounting period in which it is incurred or when the products and services are sold. This expenditure includes repairs and depreciation of fixed assets as distinct from the provision of these assets. Revenue expenditure relates to expenditure on those items where the full benefit is received within the normal accounting period. The accruals (matching) concept says that sales must be recognised in the period in which they are earned, and the costs incurred in achieving those sales must also be recognised in the same period. Therefore the costs of revenue expenditure appear under the appropriate headings within the profit and loss account of the period in which the benefits are consumed and the costs are therefore incurred.

In some circumstances expenditure, which would normally be treated as revenue expenditure, is not written off in one period. This is called deferred revenue expenditure and relates to, for example, extensive expenditure on an advertising campaign over a period of months.

Capital expenditure (not to be confused with share capital or capital account, which are something completely different) relates to the cost of acquiring, producing or enhancing fixed assets. Capital expenditure is extremely important because it is usually much higher in value and follows the appropriate authorisation of expenditure on items of plant or equipment, or on a specific project. Such expenditure is usually expected to generate future earnings for the entity, protect existing revenue or profit levels, or provide compliance with, for example, health and safety or fire regulation requirements. Capital expenditure does not necessarily relate directly to sales derived in the period that the expenditure was made. It relates to expenditure on those items where the benefit from them is received over a number of future accounting periods. Therefore, capital expenditure items are held and carried forward to subsequent accounting periods until such time as their costs must be matched with sales or other benefits derived from their use. Accordingly, such items should appear in the balance sheet under the heading fixed assets. The values of these items are reduced during each subsequent accounting period as the appropriate portions of their cost are charged to the profit and loss account to match the sales or other benefits deriving from their use. Receipts from the disposal of fixed assets also appear under the fixed assets heading in the balance sheet. They are not treated as sales in the profit and loss account.

Control over capital expenditure is maintained through procedures for authorisation and subsequent monitoring of capital expenditure. Capital expenditure proposals are formal requests for authority to incur capital expenditure. Organisations usually require capital expenditure proposals to be supported by detailed qualitative and quantitative justifications for the expenditure, in accordance with the company's capital investment criteria. Levels of authority for expenditure must be clearly

reporting structure of actual expenditure must also be aligned with the appropriate
els.

n to the actual plant or equipment cost some revenue-type expenditure such as delivery
tion costs may also, where appropriate, be treated as capital expenditure. Such expenditure is described as being capitalised. In many circumstances revenue items must be capitalised as they are considered part of the acquisition cost, and in other circumstances revenue items may optionally be capitalised as part of the acquisition cost. In many circumstances it is not always possible to provide a clear ruling.

The general rule is that if the expenditure is as a result of: (a) a first-time acquisition, delivery, and commissioning of a fixed asset; or relates to (b) improving the asset from when it was first acquired, then it is capital expenditure. If the expenditure is neither of these two types then it is normally revenue expenditure. The following examples of expenditure illustrate some of the circumstances that may prompt the question 'is it revenue or capital expenditure?'.

Repairs are usually treated as revenue expenditure, but if, for example, some second-hand plant is purchased and some immediate repair costs are incurred necessary to make it efficient for the company's purpose, then such repairs become capital expenditure and are therefore added to the plant cost as part of the acquisition cost. Salaries and wages are revenue items. However, salaries and wages paid to employees to erect and fit some new machinery that has been acquired must be considered as an addition to the cost of the machinery.

Legal expenses are usually treated as revenue expenditure. But the legal expenses of conveyancing when purchasing a factory must be treated as part of the cost of the factory. Finance charges incurred during, say, the building of a factory or installation of plant and machinery may be capitalised so long as such a policy is applied consistently.

Apportionment of expenditure

Some items of expenditure require an apportionment of costs. This means that part of the cost is charged as capital expenditure and the balance is written off immediately as revenue expenditure. This is frequently the case within the uncertain area of improvements, alterations, and extensions to plant and buildings. Capitalisation of the whole may not be prudent, since the value of the plant or building may not be enhanced to anything near the amount of money that may have been spent. The prudent policy may be not to permanently capitalise any expenditure that is not represented by assets, although legally this may be acceptable.

You may question why the distinction between capital and revenue expenditure is so important. We have already touched on the prudence concept and the consistency concept. The matching concept requires a company to match income, sales or turnover, and costs as closely as possible to the time period to which they relate. If the expected life of a fixed asset acquired to generate income is, say, 5 years then the costs of that asset should be spread over 5 years to match the realisation of the income it generates. It is therefore important to ensure that all the costs associated with the acquisition, installation and commissioning of the asset are included as part of its capitalised cost.

The amount of corporation tax that a company must pay on the profits it has generated is not computed simply as a percentage of profit. Depending on the tax rules currently in force, many revenue items may be disallowable expenses so far as taxable profit is concerned. In a similar way the treatment of capital expenditure in terms of allowances against taxation also has an impact on the amount of tax payable by the company.

Worked Example 2.1

The following table illustrates how various items of expenditure are normally classified as either capital expenditure or revenue expenditure.

Revenue expenditure	**Capital expenditure**
Wages and salaries	Computer software
Interest payable	Goodwill
Travel expenses	Enhancement of a moulding machine
Repairs to the factory building	Patents
Professional fees	Office desk

Financial statements of limited companies

In Chapter 1 we introduced the topic of the financial statements that businesses need to prepare for each accounting period to provide adequate information about the financial performance and the financial position of the business.

We will now look in more detail at the three key financial statements (see Fig. 2.1): balance sheet, profit and loss account (or income statement), and cash flow statement.

Balance sheet

The balance sheet summarises the financial position of the business; it is a financial snapshot at a moment in time. It may be compared to looking at a DVD. In 'play' mode the DVD is showing what is happening as time goes on second by second. If you press 'pause' the DVD stops on a picture. The picture does not tell you what has happened over the period of time up to the pause (or what is going to happen after the pause). The balance sheet is the financial position of the company at the 'pause' position. It is the consequence of everything that has happened up to that time. It does not explain how the company got to that position, it just shows the results of financial impacts of events and decisions up to the balance sheet date. The year end may be 31 December, but other dates may be chosen. A company's year end date is (normally) the same date each year.

The balance sheet comprises a number of categories, within the three main elements (see Fig. 2.2), which are labelled assets, liabilities or shareholders' equity (usually referred to as just ←

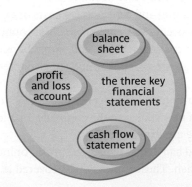

Figure 2.1 The three key financial statements

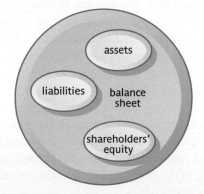

Figure 2.2 The main elements of the balance sheet

➡ equity). The assets are debit balances and the liabilities and shareholders' equity are credit balances. (Note: the concepts of debit and credit, and double-entry bookkeeping are fully covered in Appendix 1.) The balance sheet is always in balance so that

$$\text{total assets (TA)} = \text{equity (E)} + \text{total liabilities (TL)}$$

➡ The balance sheet is a summary of the general ledger in which the total assets equal the shareholders' equity plus total liabilities.

If the balance sheet is the financial snapshot at a moment in time – the 'pause' on the DVD – the two other financial statements are the equivalent of what is going on throughout the accounting period – the 'play' mode on the DVD.

Profit and loss account

The profit and loss account and income statement are two terms that really mean the same thing. Profit (or loss) may be considered in two ways, which both give the same result.

The profit and loss account shows the change in wealth of the business over a period. The wealth of the business is the amount it is worth to the owners, the shareholders. The accumulation of the total change in wealth since the business began, up to a particular point in time, is reflected within the equity section of the balance sheet under the heading 'retained profits'. The profit and loss account measures the change in the balance sheet from one 'pause' to another. An increase in equity is a profit and a decrease in equity is a loss.

The profit and loss account may also be considered in its measurement of the trading performance of the business (see Fig. 2.3). The profit and loss account calculates whether or not the company has made a profit or loss on its operations during the period, through producing and selling its goods or
➡ services. The result, the net earnings or net profit (or loss), is derived from deducting expenses incurred from revenues derived throughout the period between two 'pauses'. The profit and loss account is dealt with in detail in Chapter 3.

The total of the expenses (debits) and revenues (credits) accounts within the general ledger comprise the profit and loss account. The total of these may be a net debit or a net credit. A net debit represents a loss and a net credit represents a profit. The net profit or loss is reflected in the balance sheet of the business under the heading 'retained profits', which is part of 'shareholders' equity'. All the other accounts within the general ledger, other than expenses and revenues, may be summarised into various other non-profit and loss account categories and these represent all the other balances that complete the overall balance sheet of the business.

There are three main points to consider regarding the profit and loss account and how it differs
➡ from the cash flow statement. First, revenues (or sales or income) and expenses (or costs or expenditure) are not necessarily accounted for when cash transfers occur. Sales are normally accounted for when goods or services are delivered and accepted by the customer. Cash will rarely be received immediately from the customer, except in businesses like high-street retailers and supermarkets; it is normally received weeks or months later.

Second, the profit and loss account does not take into account all the events that impact on the
➡ financial position of the company. For example, an issue of new shares in the company, or a loan to the company, will increase cash but they are neither revenue nor expenses.

Third, non-cash flow items, for example depreciation and bad debts, reduce the profit, or increase the loss, of the company but do not represent outflows of cash. These topics will be covered in detail in the next chapter.

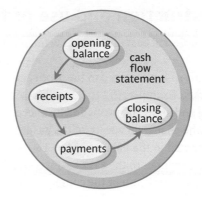

Figure 2.3 The main elements of the profit and loss account

Figure 2.4 The main elements of the cash flow statement

Therefore it can be seen that net profit is not the same as cash flow. A company may get into financial difficulties if it suffers a severe **cash** shortage even though it may have positive net earnings (profit).

Cash flow statement

Between them, the balance sheet and profit and loss account show a company's financial position at the beginning and at the end of an accounting period and how the profit or loss has been achieved during that period.

The balance sheet and profit and loss account do not show or directly analyse some of the key changes that have taken place in the company's financial position, for example:

■ How much capital expenditure (for example, equipment, machinery and buildings) has the company made, and how did it fund the expenditure?

■ What was the extent of new borrowing and how much **debt** was repaid?

■ How much did the company need to fund new **working capital** (which includes, for example, an increase in **debtors** and **stock** requirements as a result of more business activity)?

■ How much of the company's funding was met by funds generated from its trading activities, and how much by new external funding (for example, from banks and other lenders, or new shareholders)?

The profit and loss account and the cash flow statement (see Fig. 2.4) are the two 'DVDs' which are running in parallel between the two 'pauses' – the balance sheets at the start and the finish of an accounting period. However, the cash flow statement goes further in answering the questions like those shown above. The aim of the cash flow statement is to summarise the cash inflows and outflows and calculate the net change in the cash position for the company throughout the period between two 'pauses'.

> **Progress check 2.1** Explain the fundamental differences between the types of information presented in each of the three key financial statements.

Construction and use of financial statements

An example will best illustrate how financial statements may be constructed. We will use the example of Mr Bean's business, Ayco (see also Example A1.1, Appendix 1), to track how some simple transactions are reflected in the profit and loss account, cash flow statement, and balance sheet.

Worked Examples 2.2 to 2.5 will look at the four one-week periods during Ayco's first month of trading and show the profit and loss account reflecting the trading transactions of the business. The result, the change in wealth of the business, is shown as the resources held at the end of each period and reflected in the balance sheet. The example will show the cash flow statement as movements in cash and changes to the cash balance, which is reflected in the balance sheet that gives a summary of the financial position of the company at the end of each period.

Worked Example 2.2

Mr Bean decides to set up a wholesale business, Ayco, on 1 January 2005. He has his own cash resources for the purpose of setting up the business and has estimated that an initial £50,000 would be required for this purpose. During the first four-week period in business, January 2005, **Ayco** will enter into the following transactions:

		£
Week 1	Receipt of cheque from Mr Bean	50,000
Week 1	Purchase for cash the freehold of a shop	30,000
Week 1	Purchase for cash the shop fittings	5,000
Week 2	Cash paid for printing and stationery used	200
Week 3	Purchases of stock, from Beeco Ltd, of Aymen toys, payable two months later (12,000 toys at £1 each)	12,000
Week 3	Sales of Aymen toys to Ceeco Ltd for cash (1,000 toys at £2 each)	2,000
Week 4	Sales of Aymen toys to Deeco Ltd, receivable one month later (8,000 toys at £2 each)	16,000

		Week 1 £	Total £
Profit and loss account	Sales	0	0
	Cost of sales	0	0
	Gross profit	0	0
	Expenses	0	0
	Profit/(loss)	0	0
	Cumulative profit/(loss)	0	0
Cash flow statement	Opening balance	0	0
	Cash received ex Mr Bean	50,000	50,000
	Cash received from customers	0	0
	Cash paid for shop freehold	(30,000)	(30,000)

	Cash paid for shop fittings	(5,000)	(5,000)
	Cash paid for stationery	0	0
	Closing balance	15,000	15,000
Balance sheet	Cash closing balance	15,000	15,000
	Freehold shop	30,000	30,000
	Shop fittings	5,000	5,000
	Stocks	0	0
	Debtors	0	0
	Creditors	0	0
	Total wealth	50,000	50,000
	Represented by:		
	Mr Bean's original capital	50,000	50,000
	Profit/(loss) to date	0	0
	Total capital	50,000	50,000

The statement above shows that no trading took place during the first week of January. Mr Bean paid £50,000 of his personal funds into the bank account of Ayco, representing his capital invested in Ayco. The company immediately used £35,000 of this to purchase the freehold of a shop together with shop fittings.

We can summarise the financial position at the end of the first week as follows:
- There was neither a profit nor a loss.
- Cash has been increased by Mr Bean's capital invested, less payments for the shop and fittings, to give a closing cash (bank) balance of £15,000.
- The wealth of the business at the end of the first week was Mr Bean's original capital of £50,000. Wealth had not been increased or decreased as there was no profit or loss.

The wealth was represented by the shop, its fittings, and the closing bank balance. Totals for the month to date are of course the same as for week 1.

Let's look at the subsequent three weeks' accounting periods, one week at a time, beginning with week 2.

Worked Example 2.3

		Week 1	Week 2	Total
		£	£	£
Profit and loss account	Sales	0	0	0
	Cost of sales	0	0	0
	Gross profit	0	0	0
	Expenses	0	(200)	(200)

	Profit/(loss)	0	(200)	(200)
	Cumulative profit/(loss)	0	(200)	(200)
Cash flow statement	Opening balance	0	15,000	0
	Cash received ex Mr Bean	50,000	0	50,000
	Cash received from customers	0	0	0
	Cash paid for shop freehold	(30,000)	0	(30,000)
	Cash paid for shop fittings	(5,000)	0	(5,000)
	Cash paid for stationery	0	(200)	(200)
	Closing balance	15,000	14,800	14,800
Balance sheet	Cash closing balance	15,000	14,800	14,800
	Freehold shop	30,000	30,000	30,000
	Shop fittings	5,000	5,000	5,000
	Stocks	0	0	0
	Debtors	0	0	0
	Creditors	0	0	0
	Total wealth	50,000	49,800	49,800
	Represented by:			
	Mr Bean's original capital	50,000	50,000	50,000
	Profit/(loss) to date	0	(200)	(200)
	Total capital	50,000	49,800	49,800

We can summarise the financial position at the end of the second week as follows:

- There was still no trading but printing and stationery had been used, and there was a charge for their expense to the profit and loss account, therefore there was a loss for the week. The cumulative two weeks is obtained by adding across each line in the profit and loss account, which is also the sum of the totals, to give a cumulative two-week loss of £200.
- Cash was reduced in week 2 by the cash paid for printing and stationery expenses to give a closing balance of £14,800. It can be seen that the two-week cumulative cash position is calculated by starting with the week 1 opening balance and then adding across all the payment and receipt elements. The sum of the total column will give the same closing balance as that shown for week 2.
- The wealth of the business at the end of the second week was Mr Bean's original capital reduced by the cumulative loss of £200 to give £49,800. The wealth was represented by the shop, its fittings, and the closing bank balance.

Note that the cumulative balance sheet at the end of week 2 is exactly the same as that shown in the week 2 column and not the totals of each of the elements added across in weeks 1 and 2. This is always true for however many weeks or any other period we may be looking at, which is what we would expect since the balance sheet does show the financial position at a point in time, in this example the position at the end of week 2.

Progress check 2.2 How can a business have made a loss during an accounting period if it hasn't been involved in any trading during the period?

Worked Example 2.4

Let's now look at accounting period week 3.

		Week 1 £	Week 2 £	Week 3 £	Total £
Profit and loss account	Sales	0	0	2,000	2,000
	Cost of sales	0	0	(1,000)	(1,000)
	Gross profit	0	0	1,000	1,000
	Expenses	0	(200)	0	(200)
	Profit/(loss)	0	(200)	1,000	800
	Cumulative profit/(loss)	0	(200)	800	800
Cash flow statement	Opening balance	0	15,000	14,800	0
	Cash received ex Mr Bean	50,000	0	0	50,000
	Cash received from customers	0	0	2,000	2,000
	Cash paid for shop freehold	(30,000)	0	0	(30,000)
	Cash paid for shop fittings	(5,000)	0	0	(5,000)
	Cash paid for stationery	0	(200)	0	(200)
	Closing balance	15,000	14,800	16,800	16,800
Balance sheet	Cash closing balance	15,000	14,800	16,800	16,800
	Freehold shop	30,000	30,000	30,000	30,000
	Shop fittings	5,000	5,000	5,000	5,000
	Stocks	0	0	11,000	11,000
	Debtors	0	0	0	0
	Creditors	0	0	(12,000)	(12,000)
	Total wealth	50,000	49,800	50,800	50,800
	Represented by:				
	Mr Bean's original capital	50,000	50,000	50,000	50,000
	Profit/(loss) to date	0	(200)	800	800
	Total capital	50,000	49,800	50,800	50,800

We can summarise the financial position at the end of the third week as follows:

- There was some trading, which gave a profit for the week of £1,000. The cumulative three weeks is obtained by adding across each line in the profit and loss account, which is also the sum of the totals, to give a cumulative three-week profit of £800.

- Cash was increased in week 3 by the cash received from customers, and with no cash payments the closing balance was £16,800. It can be seen that the three-week cumulative cash position is calculated by starting with the week 1 opening balance and then adding across all the payment and receipt elements. The sum of the total column will give the same closing balance as that shown for week 3.
- The wealth of the business at the end of the third week was Mr Bean's original capital increased by the cumulative profit of £800 to give £50,800. The wealth was represented by the shop, its fittings, the closing bank balance, plus stocks less creditors (two new categories introduced in this example). The first category is stocks. Stocks had been purchased in the month, but had been reduced by the amount used in trading. The second new category is the result of the purchase of stock for £12,000, which had not yet been paid out in cash but nevertheless was a claim against the company. This claim is an amount due to be paid to suppliers, or creditors of the business, and therefore a reduction in the wealth of the company.

The amount of stocks used in trading to provide the sales of £2,000 is called cost of sales, which in this example is £1,000. Note again that the cumulative balance sheet at the end of week 3 is exactly the same as that shown in the week 3 column and not the totals added across each of the elements in weeks 1, 2 and 3.

Worked Example 2.5

Let's now look at the final accounting period, week 4.

		Week 1 £	Week 2 £	Week 3 £	Week 4 £	Total £
Profit and loss account	Sales	0	0	2,000	16,000	18,000
	Cost of sales	0	0	(1,000)	(8,000)	(9,000)
	Gross profit	0	0	1,000	8,000	9,000
	Expenses	0	(200)	0	0	(200)
	Profit/(loss)	0	(200)	1,000	8,000	8,800
	Cumulative profit/ (loss)	0	(200)	800	8,800	8,800
Cash flow statement	Opening balance	0	15,000	14,800	16,800	0
	Cash received ex Mr Bean	50,000	0	0	0	50,000
	Cash received from customers	0	0	2,000	0	2,000
	Cash paid for shop freehold	(30,000)	0	0	0	(30,000)
	Cash paid for shop fittings	(5,000)	0	0	0	(5,000)

	Cash paid for stationery	0	(200)	0	0	(200)
	Closing balance	15,000	14,800	16,800	16,800	16,800
Balance sheet	Cash closing balance	15,000	14,800	16,800	16,800	16,800
	Freehold shop	30,000	30,000	30,000	30,000	30,000
	Shop fittings	5,000	5,000	5,000	5,000	5,000
	Stocks	0	0	11,000	3,000	3,000
	Debtors	0	0	0	16,000	16,000
	Creditors	0	0	(12,000)	(12,000)	(12,000)
	Total wealth	50,000	49,800	50,800	58,800	58,800
	Represented by:					
	Mr Bean's original capital	50,000	50,000	50,000	50,000	50,000
	Profit/(loss) to date	0	(200)	800	8,800	8,800
	Total capital	50,000	49,800	50,800	58,800	58,800

We can summarise the final financial position at the end of the fourth week as follows:

- There was further trading, which gave a profit for the week of £8,000. The cumulative four weeks is obtained by adding across each line in the profit and loss account, which is also the sum of the totals, to give a cumulative four-week profit of £8,800.
- No cash was received or paid during week 4, and so the closing balance remained at £16,800. It can be seen that the four-week cumulative cash position is calculated by starting with the week 1 opening balance and then adding across all the payment and receipt elements. The sum of the total column will give the same closing balance as that shown for week 4.
- The wealth of the business at the end of the fourth week was Mr Bean's original capital increased by the cumulative profit of £8,800 to give £58,800. The wealth was represented by the shop, its fittings, closing bank balance, stock, less creditors, and now another additional element: debtors. Sales of £16,000 had been made in the month, none of which had been paid in cash. The amount remaining due from customers, the debtors of the company, at the end of the week was £16,000 which represented an element of the wealth of Ayco. The stock used for those sales had reduced the stock from the end of the previous week £11,000 to £3,000 at the end of week 4.

Note again that the cumulative balance sheet at the end of week 4 is exactly the same as that shown in the week 4 column and not the totals of each of the elements added across in weeks 1, 2, 3 and 4.

> **Progress check 2.3 Why is there usually a difference between profit and cash in an accounting period?**

Examples 2.2 to 2.5 introduced a number of terms relating to financial statements. Whilst they gave an introduction to the principles and put things in context they were by no means exhaustive. In this chapter and the next two, we will consider each of the financial statements in more detail, beginning with the balance sheet.

What does the balance sheet tell us?

In theory the balance sheet of a private limited company or a public limited company should be able to tell us all about the company's financial structure and liquidity – the extent to which its assets and liabilities are held in cash or in a near cash form (for example, bank accounts and deposits). It should also tell us about the assets held by the company, the proportion of current assets and the extent to which they may be used to meet current obligations. In later chapters we will look at many of the important ratios used to evaluate the strength of a company's balance sheet. We will also see how the balance sheet tells us about the financial structure of companies and the sources of such financing.

An element of caution should be noted in analysing balance sheet information. The balance sheet is an historical document. It may have looked entirely different six months or a year ago, or even one week ago. There is not always consistency between the information included in one company's balance sheet with that of another company. Two companies even within the same industry are usually very difficult to compare. Added to that, very often different analysts use the same ratios in different ways.

We will look at some of the variety of methods used to value the various items contained in the balance sheet. However, in addition to the wide choice of valuation methods, the information in a typical published balance sheet does not tell us anything about the quality of the assets, their real value in money terms or their value to the business.

'Off balance sheet financing' and 'window dressing' are two terms that often crop up in discussions about the accuracy of balance sheet information. The former relates to the funding of operations in such a way that the relevant assets and liabilities are not disclosed in the balance sheet of the company concerned. The latter is a creative accounting practice in which changes in short-term funding have the effect of disguising or improving the reported liquidity (cash and near cash) position of the reporting organisation.

Structure of the balance sheet

Assets are acquired by a business to generate future benefits, for example from trading or whatever activities the business has been set up to provide. To acquire assets the business must first raise the necessary funds. In doing so the claims or obligations are created in the form of shareholders' equity or liabilities.

Shareholders' equity and both long-term and current liabilities represent claims, or obligations, on the company to provide cash or other benefits to a third party. Equity, or capital, represents a claim by the owners, or shareholders, of the business against the business.

Liabilities represent claims by persons other than the owners of the business, against the business. These claims arise from transactions relating to the provision of goods or services, or lending money to the business.

An example of a balance sheet format adopted by a limited company, Flatco plc, is shown in Fig. 2.5. It is shown in what is termed an horizontal format in order to illustrate the grouping of the assets categories, the total of which equal the total of the liabilities and equity categories. UK companies invariably adopt the vertical format (see Fig. 2.7), rather than the horizontal format balance sheet, which we shall discuss in a later section of this chapter.

```
                              Flatco plc
                    Balance sheet as at 31 December 2005


Figures in £000
                  Assets                      Liabilities
                                              Capital and reserves
                  Fixed assets                (shareholders' equity)
operational       Intangible      416         Capital             1,200      financial
operational       Tangible      1,884         Premiums              200      financial
operational       Financial       248         Profit and loss account 1,594 financial
                                2,548                              2,994
                                              Long-term liabilities
                                              (over one year)
                                              Financial debt        173      financial
                                              Creditors             154      operational
                                              Provisions            222      operational
                                                                     549

                  Current assets              Current liabilities
operational       Stocks          311         (less than one year)
operational       Debtors         573         Financial debt         50      financial
operational       Prepayments     589         Creditors             553      operational
financial         Cash            327         Accruals              202      operational
                                1,800                                805
                                4,348                              4,348
```

Figure 2.5 A typical horizontal balance sheet format showing the balancing of assets with liabilities

The detail of each of the categories within the balance sheet will be explained in the sections that follow. As we have shown in Fig. 2.5, each balance sheet category, both assets and liabilities, may be described as either financial or operational. Capital and reserves and financial debt are financial resources, whereas fixed assets, stocks, debtors, prepayments, long-term liabilities and short-term liabilities are operational, relating to the manufacturing, commercial and administrative activities of the company. Cash, which is also financial, represents the temporary difference between the financial resources and its uses.

We will now look at each of the balance sheet categories in detail, beginning with shareholders' equity and liabilities.

Capital and reserves or shareholders' equity

Shareholders' equity is usually simply called 'equity'. It represents the total investment of the shareholders in the company, the total wealth. Equity comprises capital, premiums, and retained earnings. The cost of shareholders' equity is generally regarded as the dividends paid to shareholders, the level of which is usually dependent on how well the company has performed during the year.

Capital

The nominal value of a share is the value of each share, decided at the outset by the promoters of the company. The nominal value is the same for each of the shares and may be, for example, 25p, 50p, or

➡ £1 (the usual maximum). The initial share capital is the number of shares in the company multiplied by the nominal value of the shares (for example, 2 million shares at 50p per share is £1,000,000, or at £1 per share is £2,000,000). Each share is a title of ownership on the assets of the company. This is an important issue in respect of control and growth of the company.

Worked Example 2.6

Arthur King is setting up a small limited company, Round Table Ltd, for which he needs initial capital of £10,000. Arthur creates 100 shares each having a nominal value of £100. Arthur decides to start off as king of his empire and keep 90% of the shares for himself and so buys 90 shares at £100 each and pays £9,000 out of his personal account into the bank account of the new company, Round Table Ltd. The remaining 10 shares are purchased by ten of Arthur's friends, each for £100. Arthur owns 90% of the company, and each friend owns 1% of the company, has 1% of the voting rights at shareholders' meetings and will receive 1% of dividends paid by the company.

Round Table Ltd does well and after some time Arthur considers that he needs additional capital of a further £10,000 to fund its growth. Arthur may issue 100 new shares at £100 each.

We may discuss the implications for Arthur if he is unable to afford any additional shares himself and the new shares are sold to new investors. The total number of shares will become 200 of which he will own 90, that is 45%.

Because Arthur will have less than 50% of the shares we may say that he therefore loses control of the company. There are two main considerations regarding the issue of shares and control.

The first point is that the founder of a growing business must face a difficult dilemma: growing, but losing control, or keeping control but losing growth opportunities. An alternative may be to go to the bank and fund growth with a loan. However, along with this goes a vulnerability to failure at the first cash crisis the company may face.

The second point is that the issue of new shares at the same price as the existing original shares may be considered unfair. When Round Table Ltd was created it was worth only the money that the original shareholders invested in it. The company's credibility has now been built up through successful operations and an understanding of the market. Surely this must have a value so that the new share issue should be made at a higher price? The difference in price between the original nominal value and the price new investors will have to pay is the share premium.

Premiums

➡ The share premium may be best illustrated with an example.

Worked Example 2.7

Using the company in Worked Example 2.6, let's assume that for potential investors the value of one share is now £400. This means that 25 shares of £400 would be needed to raise additional capital of £10,000.

We will look at how these new shares should appear in the company's balance sheet.

(i) These new shares cannot appear in the balance sheet with a nominal value of £400 because it would then mean that legally the shareholders would have voting and dividend rights four times those of the £100 nominal shares.

(ii) The capital in the balance sheet will need to be increased by 25 × £100, the nominal value of the shares, that is £2,500.

(iii) A new category, share premiums, is required on the balance sheet.

(iv) Share premiums will have a value of 25 × (£400 − £100), that is £7,500.

Retained earnings

Retained earnings is the final element within the equity of the company. The profit or net earnings generated from the operations of the company belongs to the shareholders of the company. It is the shareholders who decide how much of those earnings are distributed to shareholders as dividends, the balance being held and reinvested in the business. The retained earnings of the company are increased by the annual net profit less any dividends payable; they are part of the shareholders' wealth and therefore appear within the equity of the company. Similarly, any losses will reduce the retained earnings of the company.

Liabilities

Current, or short-term, liabilities

Short-term liabilities are items that are expected to become payable within one year from the balance sheet date. These comprise trade creditors (or accounts payable) within one year, financial debts, accruals, tax, and dividends.

Short-term financial debt

Short-term financial debts are the elements of overdrafts, loans and leases that are payable within one year of the balance sheet date.

Trade creditors or accounts payable

Whereas there is a cost associated with equity and financial debt in the form of dividends and interest payable, creditors are sometimes considered 'free' of such cost. This, however, is not really true. Creditors payable within one year comprise taxes, national insurance, VAT, etc. as well as accounts payable to suppliers of materials, goods and services provided to the company. Accounts payable, for example, are not free debt.

Worked Example 2.8

A supplier may offer to a company payment terms of three months from delivery date.

We will look at the effect of the company proposing to the supplier payment terms of two months from delivery date, for which the supplier may for example offer 1% or 2% early settlement discount.

A discount of 1% for settlement one month early is equivalent to over 12% per annum. Consequently, it becomes apparent that the supplier's selling price must have included some allowance for financial charges; accounts payable to suppliers are therefore not a free debt.

Accruals

Accruals are allowances made for costs and expenses incurred and payable within one year of the balance sheet date but for which no invoices have yet been processed through the accounts. This is in line with the matching (or accruals) concept we discussed in Chapter 1. Expense recognition is an important concept. Expenses should be recognised immediately they are known about. Accruals are treated in a similar way to payables but the invoices for these charges have not yet been processed by the entity. They are charges or expenses, which are brought into the period because, although goods (or services) have been provided, they have not yet been included in the supplier's accounts. Some examples are telephone and electricity charges which are incurred but for which invoices may not normally be received until the end of each quarter. On the other hand, revenues or profits should not be recognised until they are earned.

Worked Example 2.9

We know that in the Ayco example the business had used and had been invoiced for and paid for £200 worth of stationery. If we assume, for example, that more than £200 worth of stationery had been used in the month of January, say £1,000, we can consider:

(i)   What would be the impact on Ayco if £500 worth of the additional stationery had been used, and an invoice had been received but not processed through the ledgers?

(ii)   What would be the impact on Ayco if £300 worth of the additional stationery had been used, and an invoice had not yet been received but was still in the mail?

Both amounts would have to be charged to printing and stationery expenses for a total of £800. The balancing entries that would have to be made would be to credit a total of £800 to accruals. Ayco knew they had used stationery for which there was a cost even though an invoice may not have been processed.

The net impact of the above on Ayco would have been a reduction in profit, a debit of £800 and an increase in liabilities, a credit of £800 to accruals.

Long-term liabilities

Long-term liabilities are items that are expected to become payable after one year from the balance sheet date. These comprise long-term trade creditors (or accounts payable), financial debt, and provisions.

Long-term financial debt

Long-term financial debts are the elements of loans and leases that are payable after one year of the balance sheet date. To help the company finance its operations it may take on further debt – financial debt for a limited period of time. The company has to pay interest on financial debt, over the period of the loan, regardless of how well or not the company performs, that is, regardless of whether it has made a profit or a loss.

Financial debt, provided by various financial institutions such as banks, may take the form of overdrafts, loans, *debentures* and leases. Interest rates vary according to the risk of the investment. The level of interest payable, and thus the choice of which type of debt the company may wish to take on, will be determined by how risky the potential lender regards this particular company.

A banker or investor may wish to invest in Government securities, which are risk free, and receive the low rate of return offered by such investments. For a company, which is not risk free, the investor will expect a higher rate of interest as an incentive or compensation for the risk being taken. The higher the risk of a security, the higher the expected rate of return (see Fig. 2.6).

The difference between the interest rate paid on Government securities and the interest rate that a company pays on loans is called the risk premium. Shareholders' equity is even riskier than shorter-term corporate debt (for example, a loan made to the company). Therefore, the company should not only make a profit but the level of profit should be such that the shareholders get a return in line with their level of risk. This should be the return on Government securities plus a risk premium which is even higher than the risk premium payable on the corporate debt.

Long-term trade creditors or accounts payable

Creditors payable after one year mainly comprise accounts payable to suppliers of goods and services provided to the company that may typically, for example, relate to capital projects taking place over an extended period.

Provisions

Provisions are amounts charged against profit to provide for an expected liability or loss even though

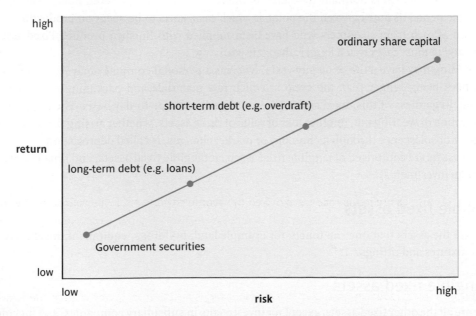

Figure 2.6 An illustration of the relationship between risk and return

the amount or date of the liability or loss is uncertain. This is in line with the prudence concept we discussed in Chapter 1.

> **Progress check 2.4** **Which of the following do you think may be classified as liabilities or shareholders' equity within a balance sheet, and under which headings should they appear?**
>
> - bank overdraft
> - computer   ■ accruals
> - five-year bank loan
>
> - amounts owed to suppliers
> - ordinary shares
> - amounts owed by customers

Assets

We have seen that assets are acquired by a business to generate future benefits, for example from trading or whatever activities the business has been set up to provide. In addition to providing benefits from transactions, accounting assets have a number of other characteristics. Assets must be capable of being measured in monetary units; the business must have exclusive control over such assets.

The assets side of the balance sheet is more homogeneous than the equity and liabilities side of the balance sheet. The liabilities side of the balance sheet generally describes where the financing comes from, whereas the assets side generally represents how the money has been used.

Fixed assets

Fixed assets include land and buildings, equipment, machinery, furniture, fittings, computers, software, and motor vehicles, which the company has purchased to enable it to meet its strategic objectives. They have a very important common feature, namely that they are not renewed within the operating cycle, which is normally measured in months, weeks, days, or even hours. The operating cycle is the period of time between the point at which cash starts to be spent on production, and the collection of cash from customers who have been supplied with finished product. Fixed assets last longer, and in most cases much longer, than one year.

A building may have a life of twenty years, whereas a personal computer may have a life of three years, both being longer than the cycle in which raw materials and packaging are renewed, for example. Regardless of this, fixed assets are 'consumed' on a day-to-day basis. The measure of this consumption or wearing out, or other loss of value of these assets, whether arising from use, passage of time or obsolescence through technology or market changes, is called depreciation.

Fixed assets are comprised of tangible fixed assets, intangible fixed assets, and financial assets (or long-term investments).

Tangible fixed assets

These are the assets that one can touch, for example land, buildings, equipment, machinery, computers, fixtures and fittings.

Intangible fixed assets

These are all the other fixed assets, except for investments in subsidiary companies, and include software, patents, trademarks, and goodwill.

Financial assets

Financial assets include investments in subsidiaries, and other specific items such as loans to subsidiary companies.

Current assets

In addition to the investment in its whole fixed environment (buildings, equipment, machinery, computers, and furniture) the company has to invest additional funds in its operating cycle, which involves the management of its current assets and current liabilities. We will look in detail at the operating cycle in Chapter 15 when we look at the management of working capital.

Stocks

Stocks comprise raw materials, partly completed finished goods, work in progress and finished goods. They may also include sundry other consumable items purchased for use over a period of time such as stationery, replacement parts, and cleaning materials, if these are of any significant value, so that the inclusion of their total cost on acquisition would provide a distortion in the profit and loss account.

Debtors or accounts receivable

Debtors represent money owed to the company by customers.

Cash

Cash includes bank balances and actual cash held.

Prepayments

A prepayment is expenditure on goods (or services) for future benefit, which is to be charged to future operations. Such amounts are similar to debtors and are included in current assets in the balance sheet.

Prepayments include prepaid expenses for services not yet used, for example rent, insurance, subscriptions, or electricity charges in advance, and also accrued income. Accrued income relates to sales of goods or services that have occurred and have been accounted for within the trading period but have not yet been invoiced to the customer. This is in accord with the matching (or accruals) concept discussed in Chapter 1.

Worked Example 2.10

In the Ayco example we may assume, for example, that Ayco had received an invoice in January for £2,000 for advertising to be paid in March, but the advertising was not taking place until February.

An invoice may have been received and processed through the ledgers, which has an additional impact on Ayco.

Payables would be increased by (or credited with) £2,000 and advertising expenses charged with (or debited with) £2,000 in the month of January. However, because the advertising had not yet taken place the charge of £2,000 would be considered as being in advance, or to use its technical term, a prepayment. The payables entry remains as a credit of £2,000, but an additional entry is required to credit advertising expenses with £2,000 and debit prepayments with £2,000.

The net impact of the above on Ayco would have been no change to profit.

Progress check 2.5

(i)   Which of the following items do you think may be classified as assets within a balance sheet?
(ii) Which ones are fixed assets and which ones are current assets?
(iii) In which categories should the assets appear?

- long-term debt
- goodwill
- an invoice not yet received for photocopy expenses already incurred
- share premium
- products for sale to customers
- computer printer
- materials held to be used in production
- water charges paid in advance

Flatco plc
Balance sheet as at 31 December 2005

Figures in £000

Fixed assets		
Intangible		416
Tangible		1,884
Financial		248
		2,548
Current assets		
Stocks	311	
Debtors	573	
Prepayments	589	
Cash	327	
		1,800
Current liabilities (less than one year)		
Financial debt	50	
Creditors	553	
Accruals	202	
	805	
Net current assets (working capital)		995
Total assets less current liabilities		3,543
less		
Long-term liabilities (over one year)		
Financial debt	173	
Creditors	154	327
less		
Provisions		222
Net assets		2,994
Capital and reserves		
Capital		1,200
Premiums		200
Profit and loss account		1,594
		2,994

Figure 2.7 A vertical format balance sheet

Balance sheet formats

The summary balance sheet that we saw in Fig. 2.5 is known as the horizontal format. Although now rarely used in practice within businesses, it was a conventional format in which assets are shown in one column and liabilities (and equity) in the other column. Such a presentation clearly illustrated how total assets equalled the total of liabilities (and equity).

The horizontal balance sheet format can be represented by the equation

$$\text{total assets (TA)} = \text{equity (E)} + \text{total liabilities (TL)}$$
$$\text{TA} = \text{E} + \text{TL}$$

or

$$\text{fixed assets (FA)} + \text{current assets (CA)}$$
$$= \text{equity (E)} + \text{long-term liabilities (LTL)} + \text{current liabilities (CL)}$$
$$\text{FA} + \text{CA} = \text{E} + \text{LTL} + \text{CL}$$

An alternative, more commonly used format is the vertical format. The vertical format simply rearranges the above equation to become

$$\text{FA} + (\text{CA} - \text{CL}) - \text{LTL} = \text{E}$$

Each element in the equation is represented vertically with total assets less total liabilities equal to, or represented by, the equity of the company.

Using the data from Fig. 2.5 the balance sheet for Flatco plc is shown in a vertical format in Fig. 2.7. The vertical format balance sheet has some advantages over the horizontal format. It shows a balance sheet total, that is the equity, or total capital, of the business; it is the total wealth that is represented by the net assets of the business. A balance sheet is probably easier to read down the page rather than across, and the vertical format does clearly highlight each of the main sections of the balance sheet.

The Companies Act requires comparative figures for the previous year for each line in the balance sheet (not shown in the Flatco plc balance sheet example). These are normally shown in a column to the right of the current year's figures.

In Appendix 1, the concept of the trial balance, and its links with the profit and loss account and balance sheet are examined in detail. Worked Example 2.11 uses the trial balance of Perfecto Ltd to identify the various categories of assets, and liabilities and equity (the debits and the credits).

Worked Example 2.11

The balances extracted from the trial balance of Perfecto Ltd at 30 September 2005 are presented in an alphabetical list:

	£000
Accruals	100
Bank and cash balances	157
Creditors due within one year	277
Creditors due after one year	77
Debtors	284
Intangible fixed assets	203

Long-term loans	85
Prepaid expenses and accrued income	295
Profit and loss account year to 30 September 2005 (profit)	130
Provisions	103
Retained earnings at 30 September 2004	525
Share capital	600
Share premium	105
Stocks of finished goods	95
Stocks of materials	37
Tangible fixed assets	902
Work in progress	29

It should be noted that a provision is similar to an accrual. If the total of the debit balances is equal to the total of the credit balances it may be assumed that the information is complete.

First, we need to identify which are assets (debit balances) and which are liabilities and equity (credit balances). Second, we can check that the trial balance is actually in balance, and if there is any missing information. Third, we can prepare a balance sheet for Perfecto Ltd as at 30 September 2005 using a vertical format.

	Assets (debits) £000	Liabilities and equity (credits) £000
Accruals		100
Bank and cash balances	157	
Creditors due within one year		277
Creditors due after one year		77
Debtors	284	
Intangible fixed assets	203	
Long-term loans		85
Prepaid expenses and accrued income	295	
Profit and loss account year to 30 September 2005 (profit)		130
Provisions		103
Retained earnings at 30 September 2004		525
Share capital		600
Share premium		105
Stocks of finished goods	95	
Stocks of materials	37	
Tangible fixed assets	902	
Work in progress	29	
Total	2,002	2,002

The total of the assets is £2,002,000, which is equal to the total of the liabilities plus equity. The trial balance is therefore in balance and there doesn't appear to be any information missing. However, errors of omission, for example, or transposed figures, may not be spotted from the information given. There could be equal and opposite debit and credit balances that have been excluded from the list in error.

Given that the data is correct, an accurate balance sheet for Perfecto Ltd as at 30 September 2005 may be prepared.

Perfecto Ltd
Balance sheet as at 30 September 2005

	£000	£000	£000
Fixed assets			
Intangible			203
Tangible			902
			1,105
Current assets			
Stocks [95 + 37 + 29]	161		
Debtors	284		
Prepayments	295		
Cash	157		
		897	
Current liabilities (less than one year)			
Creditors	277		
Accruals	100		
		377	
Net current assets (working capital)			520
Total assets less current liabilities			1,625
less			
Long-term liabilities (over one year)			
Financial debt	85		
Creditors	77		
			162
less			
Provisions			103
Net assets			1,360
Capital and reserves			
Capital			600
Premiums			105
Profit and loss account [130 + 525]			655
			1,360

> **Progress check 2.6** **What does the horizontal format balance sheet tell us? Why is the vertical format balance sheet preferred by most UK companies?**

Many of the larger businesses in the UK consist of a number of companies rather than just one company. The control of such companies, or groups of companies, rests with a parent company, which is called the holding company. The other companies within the group are called subsidiaries. The holding company holds the required number of shares in each of the subsidiaries to give it the required control.

Businesses operate in a group structure for a variety of reasons. It may be because they cover different countries, different products, or different market sectors; it may be to provide independence, or separate accountability, or may very often be a result of successive takeovers or mergers of businesses.

The Companies Act 1985/1989 requires group accounts to be prepared for the holding company in addition to the accounts that are required to be prepared for each of the individual companies within the group. These 'consolidated accounts' exclude all transactions between companies within the group, for example inter-company sales and purchases, to avoid double counting of transactions. In most other respects, the group consolidated accounts reflect an amalgamation of each of the components of the balance sheets of all the companies within the group.

Valuation of assets

The question of valuation of assets at a specific balance sheet date arises in respect of choosing the most accurate methods relating to fixed assets, stocks and debtors (and similarly creditors), which support the fundamental requirement to give a true and fair view.

Companies must be very careful to ensure that their assets are valued in a way that realistically reflects their ability to generate future cash flows. This applies to both current assets such as stocks, and fixed assets such as land and buildings. The balance sheets of companies rarely reflect either the current market values of fixed assets, or their future earnings potential, since they are based on historical costs. During 2004, Marks and Spencer plc was facing a takeover bid from entrepreneur Philip Green (see the extract below). The directors of Marks and Spencer plc prepared to fight off the takeover bid on the basis that the offer price was a long way short of the value of its assets. Marks and Spencer was revaluing its portfolio of freehold property, which the directors felt was worth £2bn more than stated in its balance sheet.

Marks and Spencer's revaluation of its property portfolio was a measure to protect it against takeover. Directors of companies must take care in such valuation increases that reflect the impact of property price inflation, which may not be sustained, and ignore the future earning potential of the assets. Marks and Spencer was also carrying out a review of its underperforming businesses, headed by Lifestore, the home furnishings shop, so that the company could decide on what changes needed to be made.

Differences between the methods chosen to value various assets (and liabilities) at the end of accounting periods may have a significant impact on the results reported in the profit and loss account for those periods. Examples of this may be seen in:

- fixed assets and depreciation
- stocks valuations and cost of sales
- valuations of accounts payable and accounts receivable denominated in foreign currencies
- provisions for doubtful debts.

The real value of a company's assets

Retail entrepreneur Philip Green is this week expected to table a fresh bid for Marks & Spencer, as the high street giant considers ditching its flagship £15m homeware store.

Mr Green, who owns Top Shop and BHS, is preparing to raise his offer for M&S, following the board's near-instant rejection of his previous bid earlier this month.

Insiders expect the new offer – tabled through bid vehicle Revival – to be worth up to £8.8 billion. It would value the company's shares at between 380p and 390p, and would offer current M&S shareholders the opportunity to hold equity in the new company, so as to reap any returns made by Mr Green.

The previous bid of 290p–310p in cash plus a 25 pc stake in Revival was rejected within hours by the M&S board, under its newly appointed chief executive Stuart Rose. A number of M&S insiders, as well as city analysts, do not expect an offer below 400p to be accepted, although Mr Green has indicated that this is more than he regards the company is worth.

M&S is preparing to fight off a new bid by revaluing its portfolio of freehold property, which some reckon is worth up to £4 billion – £2 billion more than its valuation in the group's accounts. Mr Rose has brought in close adviser Charles Wilson to help mastermind the retail group's recovery.

Paul Myners has been drafted in as a temporary replacement for chairman Luc Vandevelde. It emerged yesterday that Mr Vandevelde's private equity fund, Change Capital Partners, is one of the bidders for £200m retailer Pets at Home.

Yesterday, Mr Rose was working at the company's Baker Street headquarters on a review of M&S's underperforming businesses. Top of the list is Lifestore, the home furnishings shop launched by ousted clothing chief Vittorio Radice. M&S has admitted that the pioneer Gateshead store is not meeting performance targets, but a spokesman warned yesterday that its fate may take some time to be decided.

'Stuart and Charles have only been at the company for 10 days,' he said. 'It will take a certain amount of time for them to decide what needs changing and what doesn't. Lifestore is clearly not performing well at the moment so it is the subject of a review. Our revaluing of the property portfolio is already under way, and we should have the results in a matter of weeks.'

The spokesman played down suggestions that the value of the properties would be released and passed on to shareholders. 'We need to be able to point to the inherent value of the company if there is another bid,' he said. 'For the moment, though, our main tactic here is to wait and see what Philip Green does next.'

Mr Green is expected to return from his home in Monaco this afternoon to put the finishing touches to the new bid. Yesterday he said: 'All I'm going to say at the moment is that we are considering our position. Other than that I can't make any comment.'

The M&S spokesman said Mr Rose was unavailable to talk to the press.

Green to bid £8.8bn as M&S considers selling flagship Lifestore, by Edmund Conway

© *Daily Telegraph*, 14 June 2004

The valuation of assets and liabilities will all be covered in detail in Chapter 3 when we look at the profit and loss account. The rules applicable to the valuation of balance sheet items are laid down in the Companies Act 1985, as amended by the Companies Act 1989. These rules allow companies to prepare their financial statements under the historical cost convention (the gross value of the asset being the purchase price or production cost), or alternative conventions of historical cost modified to include certain assets at a revalued amount or current cost.

Under alternative conventions, the gross value of the asset is either the market value at the most recent valuation date or its current cost: tangible fixed assets should be valued at market value or at current cost; investments (fixed assets) are valued at market value or at any value considered appropriate by the directors; investments (current assets) are valued at current cost; stocks are valued at current cost. If a reduction in value of any fixed assets is expected to be permanent then provision for this must be made. The same applies to investments even if the reduction is not expected to be permanent.

Fixed assets with finite lives are subject to depreciation charges. Current assets must be written down to the amount for which they could be disposed of (their **net realisable value**), if that value is lower than cost or an alternative valuation. It should be noted that provisions for reductions in value no longer considered necessary must be written back to the profit and loss account.

There is an element of choice between alternative valuation methods that may be adopted by businesses. Because of this, difficulties may arise in trying to provide consistent comparisons of the performance of companies even within the same industrial sectors. If changes in accounting policies have been introduced, further inconsistencies arise in trying to provide a realistic comparison of just one company's performance between one accounting period and another.

The Companies Act 1985/1989, accounting concepts, and the accounting standards (SSAPs and FRSs) lay down certain rules for the valuation of balance sheet items. We will look at some of the most important valuation rules in respect of fixed assets and current assets.

Fixed assets

Capital expenditure on fixed assets is defined in the Companies Act 1985 as those assets intended for use on a continuing basis in the company's activities. As we have already discussed, fixed assets comprise tangible assets, **intangible assets**, and investments (financial assets). Within tangible fixed assets there are various categories of asset: land and buildings (freehold, long leasehold and short leasehold); plant and machinery; fixtures, fittings, tools and equipment; assets in the course of construction.

Capital expenditure relates to acquisition of fixed assets and includes all the costs of putting an asset into service with the company so that the company will benefit from the services of the asset for more than one trading period.

Interest charges incurred in the financing of the production of an asset may be added to and included in the total cost of the asset. Such charges are said to have been capitalised, and if they are included in the total fixed asset cost this must be disclosed in a note to the financial statements.

Which other acquisition costs should be added to the asset price to give the total acquisition cost? The total amount recorded in the accounts of a company, the capitalised cost, for each category of fixed asset, should include various acquisition costs in addition to the purchase price of the asset, as follows:

- land
  - agent's commissions
  - legal fees
  - survey fees
  - draining, clearing, landscaping, demolition costs
- buildings
  - repair, alteration and improvement costs
- other assets
  - freight costs
  - customs duty
  - installation charges
- building construction
  - subcontract work
  - materials costs
  - labour costs
  - direct construction overheads
  - excavation costs
  - construction offices
  - professional fees
- own-built plant and machinery
  - materials costs
  - labour costs
  - production overheads.

Overheads that may be capitalised relate to costs of wages, salaries and expenses not directly incurred in the construction of buildings or machinery, but which nevertheless are necessary costs incurred to enable construction to take place. Examples may be a proportion or the full costs of management and supervision of projects, and a share of electricity or similar charges incurred on such projects.

Worked Example 2.12

We have been asked to decide which of the following items should be disclosed in the balance sheet and which should be disclosed in the profit and loss account.

		£
1.	Extension to the factory	500,000
2.	New plant	100,000
3.	Architect's fee for supervising the building of the extension	10,000
4.	Haulier's invoice for delivering the plant	5,000
5.	Invoice from decorators for painting the reception area	2,000
6.	Insurance premium for twelve months on new cars	15,000
7.	Invoice from garage for ten new cars	200,000

The disclosure should be as follows:

		£
1.	Balance sheet – fixed assets	500,000
2.	Balance sheet – fixed assets	100,000
3.	Balance sheet – fixed assets	10,000
4.	Balance sheet – fixed assets	5,000
5.	Profit and loss account – repairs	2,000
6.	Profit and loss account – insurance	15,000
7.	Balance sheet – fixed assets	200,000

A valuation problem arises with regard to fixed assets because such assets have been 'consumed' over time and will currently be worth less than at the time of acquisition. The total cost of using a fixed asset over its life is generally defined as the original investment less a portion of its cost recovered (its residual value) at the end of the asset's useful life. Depreciation is allocated to charge a fair proportion of the total cost (or valuation) of the asset to each accounting period expected to benefit from its use. The net fixed asset figure reported in each period's balance sheet will reflect the reduction to the historical cost, or revalued amount, of the asset using the depreciation calculated for each period.

Intangible assets include: deferred development costs; concessions; patents; licences; trademarks; goodwill; brand names. Investments (financial assets) primarily include shares and loans in non-consolidated group companies.

Progress check 2.7 **Does it really matter if the year-end balance sheet of a company shows fixed assets at cost, less depreciation, but ignores any change in their value? This should be discussed from the points of view of an investor and a lender as two major users of financial statements.**

Brand names

Some organisations have included brand names for products like chocolate bars and beers in their balance sheets as intangible assets, therefore inflating the totals of their balance sheets. Examples of companies that have capitalised brand names have been:

- Ranks Hovis McDougall (1991) capitalised non-purchased brand names
- Guinness (1993) capitalised purchased brand names.

Brands purchased by a company may be capitalised, whereas non-purchased brands may not normally be capitalised. The ASB have viewed the inclusion of non-purchased brands as undesirable because of the difficulty in ascertaining historical costs and the inappropriateness of trying to capitalise the earnings or cash flows that have been generated by the brand names. Capitalisation of purchased brand names is permitted under FRS 10. Purchased brands have proved to be as desirable as traditional tangible fixed assets, and so should be disclosed in the balance sheet.

Goodwill

FRS 10 defines goodwill as the difference between the value of the business as a whole and the aggregate of the fair values of its separable net assets. It can only appear on the balance sheet if a business has been acquired for a value in either cash or shares, so a company may not capitalise internally generated goodwill. FRS 10 requires purchased goodwill to be capitalised, along with all other purchased fixed assets. It may be amortised (depreciated) through the profit and loss account over its useful economic life, or left in the balance sheet at its purchased cost indefinitely, and justified annually.

Research and development costs

Development costs do not include research costs. A development cost is defined in SSAP 13 as the cost of scientific or technical knowledge in order to produce new or substantially improved materials, devices, products or services; to install new processes or systems prior to the commencement of commercial production or commercial applications; or to improve substantially those already produced or installed. Development expenditure on new products or services is normally undertaken with an expectation of future commercial benefits, either from increased profits or reduced costs, and so to the extent that such costs are recoverable they may be matched against the future revenues.

Pure research costs are defined in SSAP 13 as the costs of experimental or theoretical work undertaken primarily to acquire new scientific or technical knowledge and understanding, not primarily directed towards any specific practical aim or application. Applied research costs are the costs of original or critical investigation undertaken in order to gain new scientific or technical knowledge and directed towards a specific practical aim or objective. In general, no one particular period rather than any other will be expected to benefit and so these costs should be charged to the profit and loss account as they are incurred.

Stocks

Problems arise in the area of valuation of stocks for three main reasons. First, homogeneous items within various stock categories are purchased continuously and consumed continuously in the manufacturing processes. The purchase prices of these homogeneous items may vary considerably. How do we know the specific prices of each item as we take them from stock and use them?

The general rule is that stocks must be valued at the lower of purchase cost (or production cost) and their net realisable value. The Companies Act 1985/1989 allows a number of alternative methods to be used to determine the cost of stock, the most common being FIFO (first in first out, where the oldest items of stock or their costs are assumed to be the first to be used), LIFO (last in first out, where the most recently acquired items of stock or their costs are assumed to be the first to be used), average cost, and market value. LIFO is not permitted in the UK by the accounting standard for Stocks and Long-term Contracts, SSAP 9, and is not acceptable for taxation purposes.

Second, materials may be purchased from a variety of geographical locations. Additional costs such as duty, freight, and insurance may be incurred. How should these be accounted for? The costs of stocks should comprise the expenditure that has been incurred in the normal course of business in bringing the product or service to its present location and condition.

Third, as materials, packaging and other consumable items are used during the production processes to manufacture work in progress, partly finished product and fully finished product, how should costs be correctly apportioned to give a true cost? Which costs should be included and which should be excluded?

Stocks are disclosed as a main heading in the balance sheet and comprise raw materials and consumables, work in progress, finished goods, and long-term contracts. SSAP 9 requires that companies must disclose accounting policies adopted in respect of stocks and work in progress.

Debtors

Debtors, or accounts receivable, are normally paid to the company according to contractual terms of trading agreed at the outset with each customer. However, economic and trading circumstances may have changed. Can the company be sure that it will receive payment in full against all outstanding receivables? If not, what is a more realistic valuation of such debtors?

Accounts receivable may need to be reduced by an assessment of debts that will definitely not be paid (bad debts), or debts that are unlikely ever to be paid (doubtful debts). Bad and doubtful debts and their impact on the profit and loss account will be examined in detail in Chapter 3 which looks at the profit and loss account.

When goods or services are supplied to a customer they are invoiced at the agreed price and on the trading terms that have been contracted. The trading terms may be, for example, 30 days. In this case the sales value will have been taken into the current period profit and loss account but the debt, or the account receivable, will remain unpaid in the sales ledger account until it is settled after 30 days.

Foreign currency transactions

A general factor that may impact on the valuation of all asset types (and liabilities) is foreign currency exchange rate risk. For example, a customer in the USA may insist on being invoiced by the company in US$, say 10,000 US$. At the time of delivery of the goods or services the value of the US$ sale in £ at the exchange rate on the day will be, say, £6,250 (£ = 1.60 US$). The sales invoice may be issued a few days later and the exchange rate may have changed, for example £6,173 (£ = 1.62 US$). The customer may have agreed payment for two months later and the exchange rate may have moved again, say £5,714 (£ = 1.75 US$). What value should have been attributed to the account receivable at the balance sheet date?

The value attributed to a sales invoice is its £ value on the day if invoiced in £ sterling. If a sales invoice is rendered in foreign currency SSAP 20 requires it to be valued at the exchange rate at the date of the transaction, or at an average rate for the period if exchange rates do not fluctuate significantly.

If the transaction is to be settled at a contracted exchange rate then the exchange rate specified in the contract should be used. Such a trading transaction is then said to be covered by a matching forward contract.

> **Progress check 2.8** UK International Ltd invoiced a customer in the USA for goods to the value of 100,000 US$ on 31 December 2005. The US$ cheque sent to UK International by the customer was received on 31 January 2006 and was converted into £ sterling by the bank at 1.45 US$ to £1. Discuss the two transactions, the invoice and its settlement, and their impact on UK International's profit and loss account and its balance sheet as at 31 December 2005.

A foreign exchange forward contract is a contract, for example between a company and a bank, to exchange two currencies at an agreed exchange rate. Note also the foreign exchange forward option contract which extends this idea to allow the bank or the company to call for settlement of the contract, at two days' notice, between any two dates that have been agreed between the bank and the company at the time of agreeing the contract.

At the end of each accounting period, all debtors denominated in foreign currency should be translated, or revalued, using the rates of exchange ruling at the period-end date, or, where appropriate, the rates of exchange fixed under the terms of the relevant transactions. Where there are related or matching forward contracts in respect of trading transactions, the rates of exchange specified in those contracts may be used. A similar treatment should be applied to all monetary assets and liabilities denominated in a foreign currency, that is, cash and bank balances, loans, and amounts payable and receivable.

An exchange gain or loss will result during an accounting period if a business transaction is settled at an exchange rate which differs from that used when the transaction was initially recorded, or, where appropriate, that used at the last balance sheet date. An exchange gain or loss will also arise on unsettled transactions if the rate of exchange used at the balance sheet date differs from that used previously. Such gains and losses are recognised during each accounting period and included in the profit or loss from ordinary activities.

Summary of key points

- Items of expenditure may be generally classified as either capital expenditure or revenue expenditure, although some items may need to be apportioned between the two classifications.
- Limited companies are required to prepare periodically three main financial statements: balance sheet; profit and loss account; cash flow statement.
- Financial statements are required for the shareholders and the Registrar of Companies, and are also used by, for example, analysts, potential investors, customers, suppliers.
- Categories within the balance sheet are classified into shareholders' equity, liabilities, and assets.
- The structure of the balance sheet lends itself to two main formats: horizontal format and vertical format, the latter being the most popular and having many advantages.
- Valuation of the various items within the balance sheet is covered by the Companies Act 1985 as amended by the Companies Act 1989, and accounting concepts and standards, but nevertheless gives rise to problems and differences in approach.
- Within the rules alternative methods may be used to value the different categories of assets (and liabilities) within the balance sheet.

> ■ There are limitations to the conventional balance sheet arising not only from the fact that it is an historical document, but also from inconsistencies in its preparation between companies and industries, the employment of various asset valuation methods, off-balance sheet financing, and window dressing.

Questions

Q2.1   (i)   What are the three main financial statements?

(ii)   What is their purpose?

Q2.2   Consider two ways of looking at the profit of a business: an increase in the wealth of the company; and the net result of the company's trading operations (sales less expenses). What do these terms mean, and is the result different using the two approaches?

Q2.3   Explain the vertical format structure of the balance sheet for a typical limited company.

Q2.4   Explain what assets, liabilities and shareholders' equity are, and give some examples of each.

Q2.5   Illustrate the difference between current liabilities and long-term liabilities with some examples of each.

Q2.6   (i)   What accounting convention is generally used in the valuation of fixed assets?

(ii)   What additional costs may sometimes be included and to which assets may these be applied?

Q2.7   Why are current assets and fixed assets shown under different balance sheet classifications?

Q2.8   Describe what are meant by intangible assets and give some examples of their valuation.

Q2.9   What factors influence the accurate valuation of a company's debtors?

Q2.10   Why should a potential investor exercise caution when analysing the balance sheets of potential companies in which to invest?

Discussion points

D2.1   'Surely the purchase of fixed assets is expenditure just like spending on stationery or photocopy expenses so why should it appear as an entry in the balance sheet?' Discuss.

D2.2   'It has often been said that the value of every item in a balance sheet is a matter of opinion and the cash balance is the one and only number that can truly be relied upon.' Discuss.

Exercises

Solutions are provided in Appendix 4 to all exercise numbers highlighted in colour.

Level I

E2.1   *Time allowed – 30 minutes*

Mr IM Green – Manager Ian admired the sign on the door to his new office, following his appointment as manager of the human resources department. The previous manager left fairly suddenly to join another company but had left Ian with some papers about costs of his department, which showed a total of £460,000 together with a list of items of expenditure. This seemed rather a high figure to Ian for a department of five people. Ian's boss muttered something to him about capital expenditure and revenue expenditure, but this was an area about which Ian had never been very clear. The list left with Ian by his predecessor was as follows:

	£
Legal fees	42,000
5 personal computers	15,000
Specialist software	100,000
3 laser printers	10,000
Salaries	158,000
National Insurance costs	16,000
Pension costs	14,000
Building repairs	25,000
Equipment repairs	8,000
Health and safety costs	20,000
Staff recruitment fees	10,000
Training costs	20,000
Subsistence and entertaining	10,000
Office furniture	12,000
	460,000

Assume that you are the finance manager whom Ian has asked for advice and provide him with a list that separates the items into capital and revenue expenditure.

E2.2 *Time allowed – 30 minutes*
The balances in the accounts of Vertico Ltd at 31 July 2005 are as follows:

	£000
Accrued expenses	95
Bank overdraft	20
Debtors	275
Plant and equipment	309
Finished product	152
Computer system	104
Petty cash	5
Share capital	675
Trade creditors	293
Final payment on computer system due 1 September 2006	52
Loan for a factory building	239
Buildings	560
Raw materials	195

(i) **An important number has been omitted. What is that?**
(ii) **Using the data provided and the missing data prepare a balance sheet for Vertico Ltd as at 31 July 2005 in a vertical format.**

E2.3 *Time allowed – 45 minutes*

You are required to prepare a balance sheet for Trainer plc as at 31 December 2005 using the trial balance at 31 December 2005 and the additional information shown below.

Trial balance at 31 December 2005	Debit £000	Credit £000
Bank	73	
Ordinary share capital		320
Land and buildings at cost	320	
Plant and machinery at cost	200	
Cumulative depreciation provision (charge for year 2005 was £20,000)		80
Stocks	100	
Sales		1,000
Cost of sales	600	
Operating expenses	120	
Depreciation	20	
Bad debts written off	2	
Debtors	100	
Accruals		5
Trade creditors		130
	1,535	1,535

Additional information: The company will be paying £20,000 for corporation tax on the 2005 profits during 2006.

E2.4 *Time allowed – 45 minutes*

The following information relates to Major plc at 31 December 2005, and the comparative numbers at 31 December 2004.

	2004 £000	2005 £000
Accruals	800	1,000
Bank overdraft		16,200
Cash at bank	600	
Plant and machinery at cost	17,600	23,900
Debentures (interest at 15% per annum)	600	750
Plant and machinery depreciation	9,500	10,750
Proposed dividends	3,000	6,000
Ordinary share capital	5,000	5,000
Preference share capital	1,000	1,000
Prepayments	300	400
Profit and loss account	3,000	10,100
Stocks	5,000	15,000
Taxation	3,200	5,200
Trade creditors	6,000	10,000
Trade debtors	8,600	26,700

Prepare a balance sheet in the format adopted by most of the leading UK plcs showing the previous year comparative figures.

E2.5 *Time allowed – 60 minutes*

From the trial balance of Gremlins plc at 31 March 2005 identify the assets and expenses (debit balances) and income, liabilities and equity (credit balances), confirm that the trial balance is in balance, then prepare a balance sheet for Gremlins plc as at 31 March 2005 using a vertical format.

	£000
Depreciation on office equipment and furnishings (administrative expenses)	156
Bank overdraft	609
Accountancy and audit fees	30
Electricity paid in advance	45
Computer system (net book value)	441
Advertising and promotion	135
Share premium account	240
Interest received	15
Plant and equipment (net book value)	927
Amount for final payment on factory machine due March 2007	252
Trade debtors	1,110
Goodwill	204
12-year lease on factory	330
Rents received	63
Prepaid expenses	885
Interest paid	120
Office electricity	66
Retained earnings at 31 March 2004	513
Stocks of materials at 31 March 2005	585
Telephone	87
Distribution costs	162
Other office utilities	72
Cost of goods sold	1,659
Administrative salaries	216
Sales salaries	267
Furniture and fixtures (net book value)	729
Sales	3,267
Office rent	165
Finished product at 31 March 2005	84
Debenture	750
Trade creditors	1,257
Cash	51
Share capital	1,560

Level II

E2.6 *Time allowed – 60 minutes*

Prepare a balance sheet in vertical format as at 31 December 2004 for Gorban Ltd based on the following trial balance, and the further information shown below.

	£	£
Share capital		200,000
Profit and loss account		108,968
Building at cost	130,000	
Machinery at cost	105,000	
Provision for depreciation as at 31 December 2004		30,165
Provision for doubtful debts at 31 December 2004		1,725
Creditors (accounts payable)		35,112
Debtors (accounts receivable)	42,500	
Bank	67,050	
Loan		20,000
Stocks as at 31 December 2004	51,420	
	395,970	395,970

You are given the following additional information, which is not reflected in the above trial balance.

(a) The authorised and issued share capital is divided into 200,000 shares at £1 each.
(b) Wages unpaid at 31 December 2004 amounted to £1,173.
(c) Stocks at 31 December 2004 were found to have been undervalued by £48,000.
(d) The provision for doubtful debts is to be increased by £1,870.
(e) Additional machinery was purchased on 31 December 2004 for cash at a cost of £29,368.
(f) The company issued £50,000 £1 ordinary shares at par on 31 December 2004.
(g) A customer owing £10,342 went into liquidation on 9 January 2005, a bad debt which had not previously been provided for.
(h) The loan was repaid on 31 December 2004.

E2.7 *Time allowed – 60 minutes*
You are required to prepare a balance sheet as at 31 December 2005 from the following summary of Pip Ltd's financial position at 31 December 2005.
Brands worth £10,000 (director's opinion)
Reputation in the local area £10,000 (director's opinion)
Stocks at cost £50,000 and resale value £85,000, with obsolete stocks £5,000 within the £50,000
Bank overdraft facilities £20,000 agreed by the bank manager
Cash in the office £1,000
Cash in the bank number one current account £10,000
Overdraft in the bank number two current account £10,000, per the bank statement
Land and buildings at cost £100,000
Plant and equipment at cost £150,000
Plant and equipment cumulative depreciation £50,000
Plant and equipment market value £110,000
Trade creditors £81,000
Invoices outstanding by all customers £50,000, including an invoice of £5,000 owed by a customer in liquidation (Pip Ltd have been advised by the receiver that 1p in the £1 will be paid to creditors)
Past unspent profits re-invested in the business £110,000
Ordinary shares issued £100,000 (authorised ordinary shares £200,000)

3

Financial statements of limited companies – profit and loss account

Contents

Learning objectives

Completion of this chapter will enable you to:

- describe what is meant by profit (or loss)
- outline the structure of the profit and loss account (income statement) of a limited company
- classify the categories of income and expenditure that comprise the profit and loss account
- appreciate the alternative profit and loss account formats
- prepare a profit and loss account
- explain the links between the profit and loss account and the balance sheet, particularly with regard to the valuation of fixed assets and depreciation, stock and cost of sales, and debtors and the doubtful debt provision
- explain the links between the profit and loss account and cash flow
- appreciate the subjective aspects of profit measurement.

Introduction

In Chapter 2 we looked at how to prepare simple financial statements from transactions carried out by a business during an accounting period. We then looked in a little more detail at the first of these financial statements, namely the balance sheet. This chapter will be concerned with the second of the financial statements, the profit and loss account (or income statement). Although profit and loss accounts are prepared by all forms of business entity, this chapter, in a similar way to Chapter 2, deals primarily with the profit and loss accounts of limited companies, both private and public.

This chapter deals with how profit and loss accounts are structured and how the accounts within the profit and loss account are categorised. Each of the items within each of the profit and loss account categories will be described in detail and form the basis to enable the preparation of a profit and loss account of a limited company in the appropriate format.

We will look at the relationship between the profit and loss account and the balance sheet and provide an introduction to the relationship between profit (or loss) and cash flow. Like the balance sheet, the profit and loss account is subjective largely because of the impact on costs of the variety of approaches that may be taken to the valuation of assets and liabilities.

What does the profit and loss account tell us?

The profit and loss account of a private limited company or a public limited company should be able to tell us all about the results of the company's activities over specified accounting periods. The profit and loss account shows us what revenues have been generated and what costs incurred in generating those revenues, and therefore the increase or decrease in wealth of the business during the period.

The same note of caution we mentioned in Chapter 2 that should be exercised in the analysis of balance sheet information, applies to profit and loss account information. The profit and loss account is an historical statement and so it does not tell us anything about the ability of the business to sustain or improve upon its performance over subsequent periods.

There is not always consistency between the information included in one company's profit and loss account and that of another company. As with the balance sheet, the profit and loss accounts of two companies even within the same industry may be very difficult to compare. This will be illustrated in the wide variety of methods of depreciation calculations and stock valuation methods examined in this chapter. In addition, the bases of financial ratios (to be examined in detail in Chapter 5) used by analysts in looking at a company's profit and loss account may often be different.

It is often said of profit and loss statements, as well as of balance sheets, that the value of every item included in them is a matter of opinion. This is due not only to the alternative stock valuation and depreciation methods, but also because of the subjective assessment of whether the settlement of a customer account is doubtful or not, and the sometimes imprecise evaluation of accruals and provisions.

What is profit?

We saw from the worked examples in Chapter 2 that profit (or loss) may be considered from two perspectives. We may consider these perspectives to illustrate the links between the profit and loss account and the balance sheet.

The first perspective, which is not suggested as a method for calculating profit in practice, compares the balance sheet of an entity at the start of an accounting period with the balance sheet at the end of the accounting period. We may see from these that the values of each of the components of the balance sheet may have changed. For example, levels of stocks, debtors, creditors, cash, fixed assets, and accruals may have changed during an accounting period. We have seen that the net value of the assets and liabilities in the balance sheet represents the capital, or equity, or the wealth of the business at a point in time. The change in wealth over an accounting period between the beginning and end of the accounting period is the profit or loss for the period reflected in the retained earnings category in the balance sheet.

Profit (or loss) considered in this way can be represented in the equation:

total assets (TA) – total liabilities (TL) = equity (E) + profit (P)

Worked Example 3.1

Using the opening balance sheet 1 March 2005 below and the further transactions (a) and (b), we are able to:

   (i)   show how the balance sheet will change after these transactions/events have taken place
   (ii) identify the profit which the shareholders should consider is potentially distributable as a dividend.

Opening balance sheet 1 March 2005	£
Fixed assets	100,000
Current assets	100,000

less

Current liabilities	(100,000)
	100,000
Shareholders' funds	100,000

During March

    (a)   The fixed assets were re-valued from £100,000 to £120,000

    (b)   All the stock of £20,000 was sold for £40,000 cash (that is, not on credit)

(i)

Closing balance sheet 31 March 2005	**£**
Fixed assets [100,000 + 20,000]	120,000
Current assets [100,000 − 20,000 + 40,000]	120,000
Current liabilities [no change]	(100,000)
	140,000
Shareholders' funds [100,000 + 20,000 + 20,000]	140,000

(ii)

The revised balance sheet reflects two profits:

- The revaluation surplus of £20,000 is a paper profit; as no cash has been involved it is not prudent to pay a dividend from this profit (and legally it is not permitted).
- The other £20,000 profit is from trading and is a cash profit; it is quite prudent to pay a dividend from this profit.

The balance sheets show the categories of assets, liabilities and capital, but it can be seen that there must be an analysis of the movements between the balance sheets to appreciate their fundamental nature.

    The second perspective, as we discussed in Chapter 2, considers the profit and loss account by summarising all the trading and non-trading transactions that have occurred during an accounting period (see Fig. 3.1). This is the method used in practice to calculate the profit or loss for an accounting period. This summary, or profit and loss account, gives the same result as that derived by simply looking at the change in wealth between the beginning and end of the accounting period. It is the same because all the transactions relating to items contained in the profit and loss account are also all reflected in some way within one or more balance sheet categories. For example, sales are reflected in debtors, expenses are reflected in creditors, cost of goods that have been sold came out of stocks.

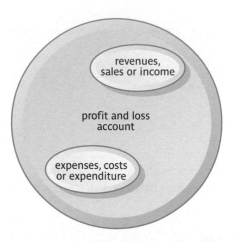

Figure 3.1 The main elements of the profit and loss account

Profit (or loss) considered in this way can be represented in the equation:

$$\textbf{profit (P)} = \textbf{total revenue (TR)} - \textbf{total costs (TC)}$$

Worked Example 3.2

A trading company, Squirrel Ltd, has an accounting period that covers the 12 months to 31 December 2005. During that period the company entered into the following transactions:

Sales of £1,300,000, included a sales invoice for January 2006, amounting to £100,000. Expenses of £1,000,000, included a payment of £60,000 for rent relating to the 6 months to 31 March 2006.

The expenses excluded some heating costs relating to the last 2 weeks of December 2005, for which the estimated cost was around £5,000. The quarterly invoice covering that period was not expected until late March 2006.

The above information may be used to look at why the annual net profit should be revenues less expenses, and why there should be accounting concepts applied to the treatment of those expenses.

The profit and loss account for a year tries to match revenues and expenses for that year (complying with the matching concept – see Chapter 1). The term 'net profit' means the difference between revenues and expenses. Gross profit is derived from sales less the costs of those sales, and net profit is derived from deducting expenses from gross profit. Net profit is not the difference between cash receipts and cash payments. Cash inflows and outflows suffer from timing differences.

The reported sales for the year must relate only to the 12 months to 31 December. Sales for Squirrel Ltd for the year 2005 are £1,200,000 (£1,300,000 less £100,000). Using the matching concept, the expenses must also be for 12 months. So, the estimated heating costs of £5,000 for the last 2 weeks of December 2005 must be added, and the rent relating to January to March 2006 of £30,000 (£60,000/2) must be deducted from the total expenses of £1,000,000. Without these adjustments, the expenses would not represent 12 months' expenses.

Net profit for the 12 months to 31 December 2005 for Squirrel Ltd is therefore:

Sales   £1,200,000   [£1,300,000 less £100,000]

less Expenses   £975,000   [£1,000,000 plus £5,000 less £60,000 plus £30,000]

which equals   £225,000

There must be an application of concepts and standard practices in arriving at net profit, otherwise users of financial information would not have reasonable confidence in the amounts being shown in the accounts reported by companies, large or small.

In this chapter we will look at the profit and loss account from the second perspective. We will look at how a profit and loss account is constructed and prepared by deducting total costs from total revenues, as the second of the three key financial statements that are required to be prepared by a limited company.

> **Progress check 3.1** Explain the perspectives from which we may consider the profit (or loss) of a business.

Structure of the profit and loss account

As we have seen previously, the profit and loss account measures whether or not the company has made a profit or loss on its operations during the period, through producing or buying and selling its goods or services. It measures whether total sales or revenues are higher than the total costs (profit), or whether total costs are higher than total sales or revenues (loss).

The total revenue of a business is generated from the provision of goods or services and may be, for example, in the form of:

- sales (goods)
- interest received (on loans)
- rents (from property)
- subscriptions (to TV channels)
- fees (professions)
- royalties (books, CDs).

The total costs of a business include the expenditure incurred as a result of the generation of revenue. The total costs of a business include, for example:

- costs of goods purchased for resale
- costs of manufacturing goods for sale
- transport and distribution costs
- advertising
- promotion
- insurance
- costs of the 'consumption' of fixed assets over their useful lives (depreciation)

- wages and salaries
- interest paid
- stationery costs
- photocopy costs
- communications costs
- electricity
- water and effluent costs
- travel expenses
- entertaining expenses
- postage.

Each of the above examples of costs (by no means an exhaustive list) incurred in the generation of revenue by a business appears itself as a separate heading, or is grouped within one or other of the other main headings within the profit and loss account. Figure 3.2 shows each of the levels of profit that are derived after allowing for the various categories of revenues and expenses.

We will look at how a basic profit and loss account is constructed to arrive at the profit on ordinary activities after taxation (or net profit) for the company. Net profit is also sometimes called net earnings, from which may be deducted dividends payable to ordinary shareholders. The net result is then the retained profit for the financial year.

Figure 3.3 shows an example of the profit and loss account format adopted by a public limited company, Flatco plc.

Each of the categories of revenue and cost within the profit and loss account (see Fig. 3.4) can be examined in a little more detail.

Turnover

The main source of income for a company is its turnover, primarily comprised of sales of its products and services to third-party customers. Revenues and costs are not necessarily accounted for when

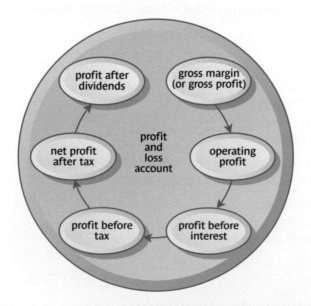

Figure 3.2 Levels of profit within the profit and loss account

Flatco plc
Profit and loss account for the year ended 31 December 2005

	£000
Turnover	3,500
Cost of sales	(2,500)
Gross profit	1,000
Distribution costs	(300)
Administrative expenses	(250)
	450
Other operating income	100
Operating profit	550
Income from other investments	100
Profit before interest and tax	650
Net interest	(60)
Profit before tax	590
Tax on profit on ordinary activities	(50)
Net profit (or profit on ordinary activities after tax)	540
Dividends	(70)
Net result (or retained profit for the financial year)	470

Figure 3.3 A profit and loss account format

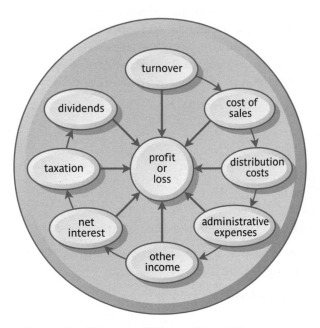

Figure 3.4 Elements of the profit and loss account

cash transfers occur. Sales are normally accounted for when goods or services are delivered and invoiced, and accepted by the customer, even if payment is not received until some time later, even in a subsequent trading period.

It should be noted that a cost or expense is the financial result of the 'consumption' that occurred during the accounting period that relates directly or indirectly to the production or sales of the goods or services, and is accounted for as it is incurred rather than on a cash payment basis. Costs may be cash-related, invoiced costs such as raw materials or non-cash items like depreciation charges.

Cost of sales (COS)

The sum of direct costs of goods sold plus any manufacturing expenses relating to the sales (or turnover) is termed cost of sales, or production cost of sales, or cost of goods sold. These costs include:

- costs of raw materials stocks
- costs of inward-bound freight paid by the company
- packaging costs
- direct production salaries and wages
- production expenses, including depreciation of trading-related fixed assets.

Gross margin (or gross profit)

The difference between turnover, or sales, and COS is gross profit or gross margin. It needs to be positive and large enough to at least cover all other expenses.

Other operating expenses: distribution costs and administrative expenses

Although not directly related to the production process, but contributing to the activity of the company, there are further costs that are termed 'other operating expenses'. These include distribution costs and selling costs, administration costs, and research and development costs (unless they relate to specific projects and the costs may be deferred to future periods).

Distribution costs include the costs of selling and delivering goods and services. Such costs may include:

- advertising
- market research
- promotion
- costs of the sales department
- outbound freight costs
- delivery fleet costs
- costs of the warehouse and goods outward department.

Administrative expenses effectively include all costs not included in cost of sales, distribution costs, and financial costs. They may include:

- costs of service departments such as
  - finance
  - human resources
  - research and development
  - engineering
- telephone costs
- computer costs
- amortised goodwill.

Distribution costs and administrative expenses include all expenses related to the 'normal' operations of the company, except those directly related to manufacturing like the costs of the purchasing department, logistics department, and quality department. They also exclude the share of overhead costs, for example, heating and lighting, business rates, water and effluent costs, relating to manufacturing activities. Administrative expenses exclude financial expenses and revenues, because these are really a function of the financial structure of the company (the extent of its funding by owners' share capital and by lenders' debt, or loans), and any other non-operational expenses and revenues.

Other operating income

Other operating income includes all other revenues that have not been included in other parts of the profit and loss account. It does not include sales of goods or services, reported turnover, or any sort of interest receivable, reported within the net interest category.

Operating profit (OP)

Operating profit (see Fig. 3.2 and Fig. 3.3), or

$$OP = turnover - COS - other\ operating\ expenses + other\ operating\ income$$

The operating profit is the net of all operating revenues and costs, regardless of the financial structure of the company and whatever exceptional events occurred during the period that resulted in exceptional costs. Operating profit is not required to be disclosed according to the Companies Act 1985/1989, but its disclosure is one of the specific recommendations within the standard on Reporting Financial Performance, FRS 3. It is therefore an extremely important profit/loss subtotal because it allows inter-firm comparisons of companies operating in the same markets but having different financial policies.

Income from other fixed asset investments

Income from other fixed asset investments specifically excludes interest receivable, but includes dividends receivable from subsidiary or fellow subsidiary companies and from non-related companies.

Profit before interest and tax (PBIT)

Profit before interest and tax, or

$$PBIT = OP + income\ from\ other\ fixed\ asset\ investments$$

PBIT is a measure of the profitability of the operations of a company regardless of the amount of interest payable and receivable on overdrafts and loans, and regardless of the amount of corporation tax it may have to pay.

Net interest

Net interest is the difference between financial revenues and charges, interest receivable and payable, and includes other financial costs like bank charges, and costs of transferring funds. The overall level of cost (or revenue) will be dependent on the type of company and level of interest rates and debt/equity mix within the funding of the company.

Profit before tax (PBT)

➡ Profit before tax, or

$$PBT = PBIT +/- \text{ net interest}$$

Tax on profit on ordinary activities

➡ Corporation tax is payable on profits of limited companies. The companies, as entities, are responsible for the tax, rather than individuals as with sole traders and partnerships. Tax is shown in the profit and loss accounts, balance sheets and cash flow statements of limited companies.

The corporation tax shown on the face of the profit and loss account will have been based on a computation carried out prior to the exact amount payable, having been agreed with the Inland Revenue. There may therefore be some differences from year to year between the tax payable numbers reported and tax actually paid.

Profit after tax (PAT)

PAT, or net profit, is the profit on ordinary activities after tax. The final charge that a company has to suffer, provided it has made sufficient profits, is therefore corporate taxation.

$$PAT = PBT - \text{ corporation tax}$$

> **Progress check 3.2** **What exactly do we mean by cost of sales? What types of expense does cost of sales include and what types of expense does it exclude?**

The net profit has resulted from the following processes. The assets, owned by the shareholders, have generated the operating profit. Operating profit has been used to pay interest to bankers and other lenders, and corporation tax to the Inland Revenue. What is left belongs to the owners of the assets, the shareholders. The net profit is the increase in wealth of the company.

The directors propose how much will be distributed to shareholders in dividends, and how much will be held as retained earnings as part of the equity of the company and reinvested in the operations of the company. The shareholders vote on whether to accept or reject the directors' proposal. The net profit is used to provide the shareholders' returns, the dividends they receive from their total investment in the equity of the company. So, not only does the net profit have to be positive, but it has to be high enough to reward the risk the shareholders took in investing in the company. In some circumstances a dividend may be paid out of retained earnings, even though the company may have made a loss during the period. This is obviously only acceptable in the short term and cannot be continued for successive accounting periods.

Dividends

The Companies Acts do not have a specific requirement for dividends to be shown in the profit and loss account, but both the Acts and FRS 3 imply that dividends are usually deducted from the profit or loss for the financial year in arriving at the profit or loss retained for the year. The dividend line in the profit and loss account includes any interim payment that may have been made and any final dividend proposed by the directors to be paid to shareholders later in the year.

Retained profit for the financial year

The retained profit for the year is what is left on the profit and loss account after deducting dividends ⟵ for the year. The balance on the profit and loss account forms part of the capital (or equity, or share-holders' funds) of the company. The company's annual report is required to include a statement that discloses the reconciliation of the movement in shareholders' funds that has taken place between the beginning and the end of the financial year (see Fig. 3.5).

Flatco plc Reconciliation of movement in shareholders' funds for the year ended 31 December 2005		
	£000	£000
Shareholders' funds at start of year		2,524
Profit for the financial year	510	
Dividends	(70)	470
Shareholders' funds at end of year		2,994

Figure 3.5 Reconciliation of movement in shareholders' funds

Progress check 3.3 **The profit or loss that a business has earned or suffered during an accounting period may be ascertained by deducting the total costs from the total revenues for the period. Identify in which category of the profit and loss account the following items may appear.**

- interest received
- share premiums
- interest paid
- depreciation on factory machinery for the year
- CD royalties received
- outward freight costs
- sales of redundant stocks
- travel and subsistence

- accountancy fees
- electricity standing charge
- rents received
- telephone charges
- advertising and promotion
- raw materials purchases
- stocks of work in progress
- sales of finished product

Profit and loss account formats

The Companies Act 1985, as amended in 1989, outlines the permitted formats for published financial statements. There are four alternative formats for the profit and loss account.

In formats 1 and 3, expenses are classified by function, for example cost of sales, distribution costs, administrative expenses. Both formats require identical information and have much in common with the internal management accounts prepared monthly by most UK companies.

In formats 2 and 4, expenses are classified by type, for example raw materials and consumables, staff costs, and depreciation. Formats 3 and 4 are rarely used. Format 1 is seen more frequently than format 2, and is the format adopted by most of the larger UK plcs. The profit and loss account in the example adopted by Flatco plc (Fig. 3.3) has been based on format 1.

FRS 3, Reporting Financial Performance, contains supplementary provisions relating to the format of the profit and loss account, in addition to the four alternative formats allowed in the Companies Act. One of the main provisions of FRS 3 relates to the separate identification within the profit and loss account of turnover and operating profit relating to continuing operations and discontinued operations.

The other important provisions of FRS 3 relate to the treatment of:

1. Extraordinary items

2. Exceptional items

3. Earnings per share

4. Reconciliation of the movement in shareholders' funds.

1. Extraordinary items

Extraordinary items, defined as material (significant) income or costs which are derived or incurred from events or transactions outside the ordinary activities of the company which were not expected to occur frequently or regularly, were previously required to be disclosed in a separate line on the profit

Flatco plc
Profit and loss account for the year ended 31 December 2005

		£000
Turnover		
Continuing operations		3,500
Discontinued operations		–
		3,500
Cost of sales		(2,500)
Gross profit		1,000
Distribution costs	(300)	
Administrative expenses	(155)	
Other operating costs		
Exceptional items: redundancy costs	(95)	(550)
Other operating income		100
Operating profit		
Continuing operations	550	
Discontinued operations	–	550
Income from other investments		100
Profit before interest and tax		650
Net interest		(60)
Profit before tax		590
Tax on profit on ordinary activities		(50)
Profit on ordinary activities after tax		540
Dividends		(70)
Retained profit for the financial year		470

Figure 3.6 Format 1 profit and loss account in compliance with the Companies Act 1985/89 and FRS 3

and loss account. A company's ordinary activities have now been defined so broadly that extraordinary items have now effectively disappeared from the face of the profit and loss account.

The costs resulting from the complete destruction of a factory may be sufficiently extraordinary to warrant the appearance of extraordinary items as a separate item on the profit and loss account.

2. Exceptional items

Exceptional items are items of abnormal size and incidence, which are derived from the ordinary activities of the business. FRS 3 requires exceptional items to be included under the statutory format headings to which they relate and disclosed on the face of the profit and loss account if necessary to give a true and fair view.

3. Earnings per share

FRS 3 also refers to earnings per share, which would normally be disclosed after the retained profit for the year (not shown in the Flatco plc example).

4. Reconciliation of the movement in shareholders' funds

The movement in shareholders' funds for Flatco plc, disclosed in accordance with the requirements of FRS 3, is shown in Fig. 3.5. The actual report would of course include the previous year 2004 comparative figures.

Figure 3.6 shows the profit and loss account for Flatco plc restated in line with format 1 and illustrating the provisions of FRS 3. The Companies Act requires comparative figures for the previous year for each line in the profit and loss account (not shown in the example), usually shown in a column to the right of the current year's figures.

Worked Example 3.3

The relevant profit and loss account balances, representing the costs and revenues for the year to date as extracted from the trial balance of Perfecto Ltd at 30 September 2005, are presented below in an alphabetical list:

	£000
Advertising and promotion	54
Corporation tax	70
Costs of administration departments	146
Costs of production departments	277
Costs of purchasing and logistics department	77
Depreciation on factory machinery	284
Depreciation on office equipment	35
Direct labour cost of sales	203
Freight out costs	230
Interest paid	20
Interest received	10

Materials cost of sales	611
Rent and utilities (2/3 factory, 1/3 office)	48
Sales	2,279
Warehousing and goods outward costs	84

We will prepare a profit and loss account for Perfecto Ltd for the year to 30 September 2005, using format 1, and which complies as far as possible with the provisions included in FRS 3.

Perfecto Ltd
Profit and loss account for the year ended 30 September 2005

Figures in £000

Turnover		2,279
Cost of sales [277 + 77 + 284 + 203 + 611 + 32 (2/3 of 48)]		(1,484)
Gross profit		795
Distribution costs [54 + 230 + 84]	(368)	
Administrative expenses [146 + 35 + 16 (1/3 of 48)]	(197)	
		(565)
Operating profit		230
Net interest [20 – 10]		(10)
Profit before tax		220
Tax on profit on ordinary activities		(70)
Profit on ordinary activities after tax		150

The Companies Act 1985/1989 requires group accounts to be prepared for the holding company in addition to the accounts that are required to be prepared for each of the individual companies within the group. Consolidated accounts exclude all transactions between companies within the group, for example inter-company sales and purchases. In most other respects the group consolidated accounts reflect an amalgamation of each of the components of the profit and loss accounts of all the companies within the group.

> **Progress check 3.4** There are four profit and loss account formats that comply with the requirements of the Companies Act 1985/1989. How do formats 1 and 3 differ from formats 2 and 4? Which format appears to be favoured by the majority of UK companies?

Profit and loss and the balance sheet

The balance sheet and the profit and loss account, whilst they are both historical statements, are not alternatives or competing options. They show different financial information, as we have discussed. The balance sheet shows the financial position at the start and at the end of an accounting period, and the profit and loss account shows what has happened during the period, the financial performance.

The profit and loss account and the balance sheet are linked in two ways:

- the cumulative balance on the profit and loss account is reflected within the equity, or the shareholders' funds, category of the balance sheet representing the increase in the wealth of the business
- some of the items contained in the profit and loss account are also all reflected in some way within one or more balance sheet categories.

In Chapter 2 we saw how the balance on the profit and loss account was reflected in retained earnings, within the equity of the company. We will now look at some of the types of adjusting entries used to prepare the profit and loss account, which are also reflected in the balance sheet. Two of these types of adjusting entries, accruals and prepayments, are described in Appendix 1.

In this chapter we will look at some further categories of adjusting entries:

- depreciation, the depreciation provision, and fixed assets
- the cost of sales, and the valuation of stocks
- bad and doubtful debts, and trade debtors.

Worked Example 3.4

Ronly Bonly Jones Ltd, or RBJ, buys and sells giftware. It made a profit of £10,000 during the month of January 2005.

We will use the balance sheet as at 1 January 2005 as the starting point and then look at how each of the elements in the profit and loss account for January is reflected in the balance sheet to derive the balance sheet as at 31 January 2005.

The profit and loss account for January 2005 and the balance sheet as at 1 January 2005 are as follows:

Profit and loss account for January 2005		£000
Sales		650
Cost of goods sold		
Opening stocks	45	
Purchases	424	
	469	
less Closing stocks	79	(390)
Gross profit		260
Depreciation		(5)
Expenses		(245)
Profit for January [650 − 390 − 5 − 245]		10

Additional information

RBJ acquired fixed assets in January for £20,000 cash, and raised additional share capital of £10,000.

Creditors were paid £422,000 in the month and £632,000 was received from customers. The bank account at the end of January 2005 was overdrawn by £39,000.

Balance sheet as at 1 January 2005   **£000**

Fixed assets at cost	130
Depreciation provision	(20)
Stocks	45
Debtors	64
Cash and bank	6
	225
Creditors	(87)
Share capital	(50)
Profit and loss account	(88)
	(225)

Let's derive the 31 January 2005 balance sheet from the information that has been provided.

Figures in £000	Fixed assets	Depn	Stocks	Debtors	Cash	Creditors	Equity	Profit/loss account
1 January 2005	130	(20)	45	64	6	(87)	(50)	(88)
Sales				650				(650)
Cash from customers				(632)	632			0
Purchases			424			(424)		0
Cash to creditors					(422)	422		0
Stock sold			(390)					390
Depreciation		(5)						5
Expenses					(245)			245
Fixed asset additions	20				(20)			0
Issue of shares					10		(10)	0
31 January 2005	150	(25)	79	82	(39)	(89)	(60)	(98)

Ronly Bonly Jones Ltd

Balance sheet at 1 January 2005 and at 31 January 2005 is as follows:

	1 January 2005 £000	31 January 2005 £000
Fixed assets at cost	130	150
Depreciation provision	(20)	(25)
Stocks	45	79
Debtors	64	82
Cash and bank	6	–
	225	286

Creditors	(87)	(89)
Bank overdraft	–	(39)
Share capital	(50)	(60)
Profit and loss account	(88)	(98)
	(225)	(286)

Worked Example 3.4 shows the changes in the balance sheet that have taken place over the month of January. The 31 January balance sheet has been derived from considering each element in the profit and loss account for January and its impact on the balance sheet, and movements between accounts within the balance sheet:

- sales to customers on credit are the starting point for the profit and loss account, which also increase debtors
- cash received from customers increases cash and reduces debtors
- purchases of goods on credit for resale increase stock and increase creditors
- cash paid to creditors reduces cash and reduces creditors
- stock sold reduces stock and is a cost to the profit and loss account
- depreciation of fixed assets increases the depreciation provision and is a cost to the profit and loss account
- payments of expenses reduce cash and are a cost to the profit and loss account
- payments for additions to fixed assets increase fixed assets and reduce cash
- issues of ordinary shares increase equity capital and increase cash.

In Worked Example 3.4, depreciation is a relatively small number. Normally, profit and loss account movements may have significant impacts on the balance sheet in the areas of both stocks and depreciation:

- during the years 1999 and 2000 several major retailers had to announce that their profits would be lower due to their stocks having to be heavily discounted (for example, Marks and Spencer plc)

- depreciation of an automotive assembly line may need to be changed due to a revision in its estimated useful economic life following a reassessment of the life cycle of a vehicle.

> **Progress check 3.5** Describe the ways in which a company's profit and loss account and its balance sheet are linked.

We have already discussed the links between the various categories in the profit and loss account and those within the balance sheet. Consequently, the ways in which specific balance sheet items are valued have a significant impact on the profit reported for an entity for a particular period. The requirement for the valuation, or revaluation of, for example, assets like machinery, raw materials, and finished product may be a result of their consumption or being used up; it may be because of their deterioration or obsolescence, or significant changes in their market value. For whatever reason, such changes in the valuation of assets must be reflected in the profit and loss account in the period in which they occur. We will focus here on the valuation of the three key areas of:

- fixed assets, reflected in the profit and loss account within *depreciation*
- stocks, reflected in the profit and loss account within *cost of sales*
- debtors, reflected in the profit and loss account within *bad and doubtful debts*.

Depreciation

Generally, the total cost of using a fixed asset over its life may be defined as the original investment less an estimate of the portion of its cost that may be recovered (its residual value) at the end of the asset's useful life. FRS 15 defines depreciation as a measure of the wearing out, consumption or other reduction in the useful economic life of a fixed asset, whether arising from use, passage of time or obsolescence through technological or market changes. In accordance with the accruals (matching) concept a fair proportion of the total cost (or valuation) of a fixed asset, its depreciation, should be charged to the profit and loss account during each period that sales or other benefits are received from the use of that asset. At the same time as the depreciation charge is made to the profit and loss account, the value of the fixed asset is reduced by the same amount from a corresponding entry to credit the cumulative **depreciation provision** account. The cumulative balance at any point in time on the depreciation provision account for a fixed asset is deducted from its historical cost to provide its net value shown in the balance sheet at that time.

Worked Example 3.5

Many companies operate and succeed in one market for many years. One of many business 'facts of life' is that recurring profits can come to an abrupt end when a successful business model develops a basic flaw. Changes in technology can cause a change in trading or force a complete review of the equipment that has been highly profitable in the past. Photo-Me International, the photo-booth operator, announced a £24.1m non-cash write-down of its old analogue photo-booths in January 2001.

There a number of reasons why this type of equipment review might affect the annual profits:

(i) The profit and loss account for a year aims to match incomes and expenses for that year, complying with the matching concept (see Chapter 1).

(ii) One of the expenses relates to the use of plant and equipment, which normally represents wear and tear, and is called depreciation.

(iii) The choice of method of depreciating an asset will result in differing amounts of depreciation for the year and so the annual profit and loss account can be quite different because of this subjective decision (which involves opinions that may vary from manager to manager).

(iv) The Accounting Standards Board (ASB) introduced FRS 11, Impairment of Fixed Assets and Goodwill, to force companies to formally review the fixed assets for any changes in circumstances (impairment is not recurring, whereas depreciation or wear and tear is recurring).

(v) In the Photo-Me circumstances outlined above, the company would have had to acknowledge a change in technology from analogue to digital. The result is that the balance

> sheet net book values of its fixed assets would no longer be tenable because of their sharp decline. The remaining net book value of the amount that was paid for their original acquisition can no longer be regarded as a fixed asset for current and future balance sheet purposes, and therefore must be written off against the current profits.

The useful life of an asset is the period of its service relevant to the business entity. With regard to the useful life of the asset, there are a number of problems in dealing with depreciation of fixed assets:

- determining the useful life of the asset
- determining the correct way to spread the total cost of the asset over the useful life
- physical limitations regarding the useful life
  - intensity of use of the asset
  - the actions of the elements
  - adequacy of maintenance
  - the simple passage of time (e.g. legal rights or patents)
- economic limitations in respect of useful life
  - technological developments
  - business growth.

There are three main depreciation methods:

- straight line
- reducing balance
- sum of the digits.

We will consider each of these in detail in Worked Example 3.6. However, the straight line and the reducing balance methods are the ones that are most frequently used by businesses.

Straight line depreciation is calculated by deducting the residual value from the acquisition cost and dividing the result by the life of the asset.

The reducing balance method is used to derive the rate required (d) to reduce the cost of the asset, period by period, to the residual value by the end of its life. This may be expressed as:

$$d = 1 - \sqrt[\text{life}]{\text{residual value/original cost}}$$

The sum of the digits method considers the life of the asset, say for example 5 years, and allocates the total cost of the asset over that period as follows:

For a 5-year life the sum of digits is $5 + 4 + 3 + 2 + 1 = 15$

So each year's depreciation is calculated:

1st year $5/15 \times$ (acquisition cost − residual value)
2nd year $4/15 \times$ (acquisition cost − residual value)
3rd year $3/15 \times$ (acquisition cost − residual value)
4th year $2/15 \times$ (acquisition cost − residual value)
5th year $1/15 \times$ (acquisition cost − residual value)

Worked Example 3.6

Castle Ltd purchases an item of equipment for £16,000 and estimates its residual value, at the end of its useful economic life of 5 years, at £1,000. At the start of year 1 the net book value (NBV) is the acquisition cost of the asset £16,000.

Net book values may be derived by using any of the three methods:

– straight line
– reducing balance
– sum of the digits

Straight line divides acquisition cost less residual value by 5 (the number of years' economic life).

Reducing balance calculates

$$d = 1 - \sqrt[5]{1,000/16,000} = 42.5659\%$$

Sum of the digits is (5 + 4 + 3 + 2 + 1) = 15

Figures in £000

Year	Straight line			Reducing balance			Sum of the digits		
	Start NBV	Depn	End NBV	Start NBV	Depn	End NBV	Start NBV	Depn	End NBV
1	16,000	3,000	13,000	16,000	6,810	9,190	16,000	5,000	11,000
2	13,000	3,000	10,000	9,190	3,912	5,278	11,000	4,000	7,000
3	10,000	3,000	7,000	5,278	2,247	3,031	7,000	3,000	4,000
4	7,000	3,000	4,000	3,031	1,290	1,741	4,000	2,000	2,000
5	4,000	3,000	1,000	1,741	741	1,000	2,000	1,000	1,000

The resultant cost of £1,000 in the balance sheet under the fixed assets category at the end of year 5 is the same using each of the methods. This cost is likely to be offset exactly by the proceeds of £1,000 expected to be received on disposal of the asset.

In addition to the methods already discussed, it should be noted that there are many alternative methods that may be used to account for depreciation. We will not look at the detailed calculations of any further methods, but you may consider Worked Example 3.7, which serves only to illustrate the wide variations in yearly depreciation (and therefore net book values) that may be derived from a selection of alternative methods, compared with the straight line method.

We have already seen from Worked Example 3.6 that there may be large variations in the amounts of depreciation charged to the profit and loss account in each year, dependent on which method is adopted by a company. Worked Example 3.7 further illustrates the wide variation in first year depreciation, from £2,840 to £4,400 on an asset costing £20,000, using six alternative methods of calculation. The particular depreciation method used by a company, therefore, may result in widely differing levels of profit reported each year. This sometimes makes it difficult to compare the profit of a company from one year to the next on a like-for-like basis. Likewise, it may sometimes be difficult to compare the yearly performance of two or more businesses, which may be similar in every respect other than the difference in the methods they have used to depreciate their fixed assets.

Worked Example 3.7

Consider a company van, which cost £20,000 to purchase new. Its residual value is considered to be zero at the end of its useful life of 5 years. The rate of inflation is 10% and the cost of capital is 15%.

The depreciation for the first year and the net book value (NBV) at the end of year 1 may be evaluated using six alternative methods, including straight line depreciation.

		Depreciation in year 1	NBV at end of year 1
1. Straight line depreciation over 5 years, i.e. 20% per annum using an historical cost of £20,000	£20,000 at 20%	£4,000	£16,000
2. Constant purchasing power, which means allowing for an inflationary price increase (in this case 10%), and using straight line depreciation at 20% per annum	£20,000 × 1.10 at 20%	£4,400	£17,600
3. Replacement value for an identical one-year-old van based on used van market value of say £17,000. Depreciation would be £20,000 – £17,000 = £3,000		£3,000	£17,000
4. Replacement cost of a new van less one year's depreciation based on an estimated replacement cost of say	£21,600 at 20%	£4,320	£17,280
5. Net realisable value – net proceeds from a trade auction say £16,000. Depreciation would be £20,000 – £16,000 = £4,000		£4,000	£16,000
6. Economic value using estimated net cash flow from using the van for each year 1: £6,000; 2: £6,000; 3: £6,000; 4: £6,000 present values of future cash flows, using a cost of capital of 15% per annum (see the discounted cash flow technique in Chapter 13) $£6,000/1.15 + £6,000/1.15^2 + £6,000/1.15^3 + £6,000/1.15^4$ Depreciation will be £20,000 − £17,160		£2,840	£17,160

Whichever method of depreciation is used, it must be consistent from one accounting period to another. The depreciation method adopted must be disclosed within the company's accounting policies that accompany the financial statements and include the depreciation rates applied to each of the categories of fixed asset.

> **Progress check 3.6** **What are the various methods that may be used to depreciate an asset? Describe two of the most commonly used methods.**

The amount of depreciation calculated for an accounting period is charged as a cost in the profit and loss account, the depreciation charge. A corresponding amount is also reflected in an account in the balance sheet, the cumulative depreciation provision account, the effect of which is to reduce the original cost of the fixed assets at the end of each accounting period.

The difference between depreciation cost and other costs such as wages is that it is not a cash expense, that is, it will generate no cash inflow or outflow. The only cash outflow relating to depreciation took place when the asset was originally purchased. The depreciation is really only the 'memory' of that earlier cash outflow.

> **Progress check 3.7** **Why are assets depreciated and what factors influence the decision as to how they may be depreciated?**

Cost of sales

As we saw in Chapter 2, stocks of raw materials, work in progress, finished product, and consumable stores, pose problems in their valuation for three main reasons:

- raw materials may be purchased from a variety of geographical locations, and additional costs such as duty, freight, and insurance may be incurred – the costs of stocks should comprise the expenditure that has been incurred in the normal course of business in bringing the product or service to its present location and condition
- packaging and other consumable items, in addition to raw materials, are used during the production processes to manufacture work in progress, partly finished product and fully finished product, and such costs must be correctly apportioned to give a true cost – stocks are disclosed as a main heading in the balance sheet and comprise raw materials and consumables, work in progress, finished goods, and long-term contracts
- homogeneous items within various stock categories are purchased continuously and consumed continuously in the manufacturing processes and the purchase prices of these homogeneous items may vary considerably – stocks must be valued at the lower of purchase cost (or production cost) and their net realisable value.

There are many alternative methods that may be used to determine the cost of stock. The four methods that are most commonly used by businesses are:

- first in first out (FIFO)
- last in first out (LIFO)
- average cost
- market value.

The choice of method adopted by individual companies depends largely on their particular requirements and will be influenced by a number of factors:

- ease of use
- volumes of stocks
- costs of stocks
- management information requirements.

The FIFO method of stock valuation is by far the most popular. FIFO (first in first out, where the oldest items of stock, or their costs, are assumed to be the first to be used) assumes that costs are matched with the physical flow of stock.

LIFO (last in first out, where the most recently acquired items of stock, or their costs, are assumed to be the first to be used) matches current costs with current revenues. LIFO is not permitted in the UK by the accounting standard for SSAP 9, Stocks and Long-term Contracts, and is not acceptable for taxation purposes.

The average cost method smoothes income and stock values and assumes that individual units cannot be tracked through the system. The use of market values begs the questions as to which market value is most appropriate and should replacement or realisable values be used.

> Progress check 3.8 **What factors must be considered regarding the valuation of stocks?**

The following worked example looks at the four main methods of valuation of stocks to enable us to provide a comparison in numerical terms and represent this graphically.

Worked Example 3.8

A retailing company at 1 January 2005 has 400 units in stock of a product that cost £3 each, and therefore a total cost of £1,200. The company's purchases over January and February are:

	Units	Price £	Value £	
January	600	4.00	2,400	
	800	5.00	4,000	Total £6,400
February	200	6.00	1,200	
	1,000	4.00	4,000	Total £5,200

and its sales over the same periods are

	Units	Price £	Value £
January	1,400	12.00	16,800
February	1,400	12.00	16,800

The market value of a unit of each product is

	Price £
January	6.00
February	3.00

FIFO – first in first out, matching costs with physical stock flows

	Units	£		Units	£
January opening stock	400	1,200	Sales	1,400	16,800
Purchases	1,400	6,400			
	1,800	7,600			
January closing stock	400	2,000			
Cost of goods sold	1,400	5,600			
Gross profit		11,200			
		16,800			16,800
February opening stock	400	2,000	Sales	1,400	16,800
Purchases	1,200	5,200			
	16,00	7,200			
February closing stock	200	800			
Cost of goods sold	1,400	6,400			
Gross profit		10,400			
		16,800			16,800

Note that purchases are always valued at their actual cost regardless of which stock valuation method is used.

There were 400 units in stock at the beginning of January that cost £3 each and then 600 units were purchased at £4 each and then 800 purchased at £5 each. On a FIFO basis it is assumed that the 1,400 units sold in January first used the 400 opening stock and then the 600 units first purchased and then 400 of the 800 units next purchased. The cost of these units was $(400 \times £3) + (600 \times £4) + (400 \times £5) = £5,600$. The 400 units of stock remaining at the end of January (which becomes the opening stock at the beginning of February) are the 400 units left from the purchase of 800 units at £5 each and so are valued at £2,000. Using the same basis, the cost of the 1,400 units sold in February was $(400 \times £5) + (200 \times £6) + (800 \times £4) = £6,400$. The 200 units of stock remaining at the end of February are the 200 units left from the purchase of 1,000 units at £4 each and so are valued at £800.

The result is a gross profit of £11,200 for January and £10,400 for February.

LIFO – last in first out, matching current costs with current revenues

	Units	£		Units	£
January opening stock	400	1,200	Sales	1,400	16,800
Purchases	1,400	6,400			
	1,800	7,600			
January closing stock	400	1,200			
Cost of goods sold	1,400	6,400			
Gross profit		10,400			
		16,800			16,800

	Units	£		Units	£
February opening stock	400	1,200	Sales	1,400	16,800
Purchases	1,200	5,200			
	1,600	6,400			
February closing stock	200	600			
Cost of goods sold	1,400	5,800			
Gross profit		11,000			
		16,800			16,800

There were 400 units in stock at the beginning of January that cost £3 each and then 600 units were purchased at £4 each and then 800 purchased at £5 each. On a LIFO basis it is assumed that the 1,400 units sold in January used the 800 last purchased at £5 each and then the 600 units purchased at £4 each. The cost of these units was $(800 \times £5) + (600 \times £4) = £6,400$. The 400 units of stock remaining at the end of January (which becomes the opening stock at the beginning of February) are the 400 units left from opening stock at £3 each and so are valued at £1,200. Using the same basis, the cost of the 1,400 units sold in February was $(1,000 \times £4) + (200 \times £6) + (200 \times £3) = £5,800$. The 200 units of stock remaining at the end of February are the 200 units left from the opening stock of 400 units at £3 each and so are valued at £600.

The result is a gross profit of £10,400 for January and £11,000 for February.

Average cost – smoothing of revenues and stock values, assuming that individual units purchased cannot be followed through to actual sales so total purchases combined to calculate an average cost per unit

	Units	£		Units	£
January opening stock	400	1,200	Sales	1,400	16,800
Purchases	1,400	6,400			
	1,800	7,600			
January closing stock	400	1,689			
Cost of goods sold	1,400	5,911			
Gross profit		10,889			
		16,800			16,800

$$\text{Average cost per unit for January} = \frac{(1,200 + 6,400)}{(400 + 1,400)} = \frac{7,600}{1,800} = £4.222$$

$$\text{January closing stock} = 400 \times \frac{7,600}{1,800} = £1,689$$

	Units	£		Units	£
February opening stock	400	1,689	Sales	1,400	16,800
Purchases	1,200	5,200			
	1,600	6,889			
February closing stock	200	861			
Cost of goods sold	1,400	6,028			
Gross profit		10,772			
		16,800			16,800

$$\text{Average cost per unit for February} = \frac{(1,689 + 5,200)}{(400 + 1,200)} = \frac{6,889}{1,600} = £4.305$$

$$\text{February closing stock} = 200 \times \frac{6,889}{1,600} = £861$$

The result is a gross profit of £10,889 for January and £10,772 for February

The lower of FIFO or market value

	Units	£		Units	£
January opening stock	400	1,200	Sales	1,400	16,800
Purchases	1,400	6,400			
	1,800	7,600			
January closing stock	400	2,000			
Cost of goods sold	1,400	5,600			
Gross profit		11,200			
		16,800			16,800

	Units	£		Units	£
February opening stock	400	2,000	Sales	1,400	16,800
Purchases	1,200	5,200			
	1,600	7,200			
February closing stock	200	600			
Cost of goods sold	1,400	6,600			
Gross profit		10,200			
		16,800			16,800

January closing stock using FIFO is £2,000. Using market value, January closing stock is 400 units at £6 per unit – £2,400. Using the lower value, stock at the end of January is £2,000. February closing stock using FIFO is £800. Using market value, February closing stock is 200 units at £3 per unit – £600. Using the lower value, stock at the end of February is £600.

The result is a gross profit of £11,200 for January and £10,200 for February.

Summary of stock valuation methods

	FIFO	LIFO	Average cost	Lower of cost or market value
	£	£	£	£
Profit				
January	11,200	10,400	10,889	11,200
February	10,400	11,000	10,772	10,200
Stock valuation				
January	2,000	1,200	1,689	2,000
February	800	600	861	600

Graphical representations of the summary of stock valuation methods used in Worked Example 3.8 are shown in Fig. 3.7 and Fig. 3.8.

It can be seen from the summary of results in Worked Example 3.8 that wide variations in profit may be reported from period to period. However, over the long run the total result will eventually be the same, as all stocks become used up. It is important to stress that a method may not be chosen to give, for example, a required result for one period. There must be consistency in the use of stock valuation method from one period to the next.

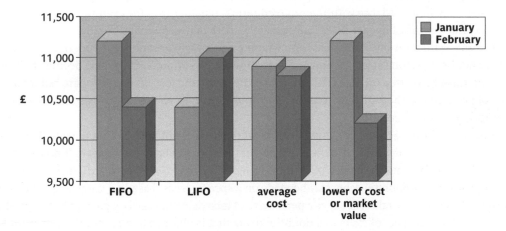

Figure 3.7 Profit comparison from use of various stock valuation methods

Progress check 3.9 Why does stock valuation cause such problems and why is it so very important?

Figure 3.8 Stock value comparison from use of various stock valuation methods

Bad and doubtful debts

The term 'provision' often means very much the same thing as accrued expenses. The difference is that a provision is normally an amount charged against profit to provide for an expected liability or loss even though the amount or date of the liability or loss is uncertain. However, the word 'provision' is sometimes used in a different context, most commonly the depreciation provision relating to a fixed asset. It is also used in dealing with debtors at the end of an accounting period.

When goods or services are sold to a customer on credit, an invoice is issued to record the transaction and to obtain settlement. The sale is reflected in the profit and loss account within the turnover of the business for the relevant period. The 'other side' of the entry is debited to the sales ledger, appearing as an account receivable from the customer in line with the agreed payment terms. Most customers pay in accordance with their agreed terms, whether it is for example within 10 days, 1 month, or 2 months of invoice date. Unfortunately, there may sometimes be slow payers; there may be customers, for a variety of reasons, from whom payment will never be received. In the event of an invoice not being settled at all, as soon as this is known with certainty, the debt is deemed to be a **bad debt** and must be written off. The effect of this on the profit and loss account is not to reduce sales. It is a cost charged to the bad debt account. The double-entry is to the debtor account to cancel the appropriate account receivable.

At the end of each accounting period debtors who have still not paid, falling outside their normal credit terms, must be reviewed as to the likelihood of their not paying in full or at all. If non-payment is certain then the debt must be written off. If there is uncertainty as to whether or not a debt will be settled then a provision for **doubtful debts** may be made on a specific basis, based on knowledge of particular customers, or on a general basis, say as a percentage of total debtors, based on past trading experience.

An amount in respect of estimated doubtful debts that is charged to an account in the profit and loss account, the bad and doubtful debt account, is also reflected as a credit to an account in the balance sheet, the **doubtful debt provision**. The effect of the provision for doubtful debts is to reduce the value of the debtors in the balance sheet but without permanently eliminating any accounts receivable. Debtors that are deemed to be bad debts are actually written off (charged as a cost to the profit and loss account) and the debts are permanently eliminated from accounts receivable.

> **Progress check 3.10** What are bad debts and doubtful debts and how are they reflected in the profit and loss account and balance sheet of a business?

Worked Example 3.9

Trade debtors on the books of Sportswear Wholesalers Ltd at 31 January 2005 were £429,378: current month £230,684, month 2 £93,812, 3 to 6 months £64,567, over 6 months £40,315. On 18 January 2005 one of Sportswear's customers, Road Runner Ltd, had gone into liquidation owing Sportswear £15,342, which had been invoiced over 6 months previously. Sportswear's policy was to provide for doubtful debts on the basis of 3 to 6 months' debts 5%, and over 6 months' debts 10%.

Let's consider what entries would appear in Sportwear's cumulative profit and loss account to January 2005 and its balance sheet at 31 January 2005 in respect of bad and doubtful debts. We may assume that no other debts have been written off during the year to date.

Road Runner Ltd has gone into liquidation owing Sportswear £15,342, of which it is assumed there is no chance of any recovery, therefore it must be written off as a bad debt in the profit and loss account in January 2005.

The effect of the bad debt write off is to reduce trade debtors by £15,342, and the debts over 6 months old will reduce down to £24,973 [£40,315 − £15,342].

The doubtful debt provision at 31 January in line with Sportswear's policy is

5% × £64,567   = £3,228
10% × £24,973 = £2,497
Total   = £5,725 (assuming no opening doubtful debt provision at 1 January 2005)

Profit and loss account for the year to 31 January 2005:

Bad and doubtful debts

Road Runner Ltd write off 31/01/05	£15,342
Doubtful debt provision at 31/01/05	£5,725
Balance at 31 January 2005	£21,067

Balance sheet as at 31 January 2005:

Trade debtors:

Balance per accounts receivable at 31/01/05	£429,378
Road Runner Ltd write off 31/01/05	£15,342
Balance at 31 January 2005	£414,036

Doubtful debt provision:

Doubtful debt provision at 31/01/05	£5,725
Balance at 31 January 2005	£5,725

Trade debtors in Sportswear's balance sheet as at 31 January 2005 would be £408,311 [£414,036 − £5,725]

Such bad and doubtful debt entries would not be individually apparent from inspection of Sportswear Wholesalers Ltd's financial statements. Bad and doubtful debt charges are normally included under the profit and loss account heading *Distribution Costs*, and the corresponding balance sheet entries are reflected within the total *Trade Debtors* heading.

Profit and loss and cash flow

During the last decade of the twentieth century there was a great deal of activity in the birth and growth of so-called dot.com companies. Their aim was to exploit the use of the Internet to provide opportunities to sell products and services in wider markets and on an increasingly global basis. The apparent success of the majority of these businesses was initially based on growth of potential in both market share and profitability reflected in the numbers of subscribers attracted to their websites. Actual and potential profitability do not necessarily inevitably result in a healthy cash position. Such companies invariably required large amounts of cash for them to continue operating for extended periods prior to achieving profitability and to generate their own cash flows. Many dot.com businesses from that era failed to survive and flourish, but there were also many successes, for example, Amazon.com, Sportingbet.com, and Lastminute.com.

In Chapter 2 we discussed how profit and cash flow do not mean the same thing. In fact, the profit earned and the net cash generated during an accounting period are usually very different, and often significantly different. How often do we see cases reported of businesses in serious financial difficulties because of severe cash shortages, even though they may appear to be trading profitably?

However, it is invariably the reported profits, or more usually estimated profits, that are closely monitored by investors and financial analysts. It is these numbers on which analysts base their business forecasts, and which influence investor confidence in a business, and therefore its share price.

June 2004 saw a severe profits warning from the budget airline Easyjet (see the *Accountancy Age* extract below). Easyjet's chief executive actually gave a full year profit forecast for 2004 that indicated that it was likely to be 50% worse than analysts had expected. This had a huge impact on the share price, which fell by 19%.

Nevertheless, cash flow is very important. There is a relationship between cash and profit, and it is possible to identify and quantify the factors within this relationship. The profit or loss made by a business during an accounting period differs from the net cash inflows and outflows during the period because of:

- cash expected to be paid or received relating to transactions during a period may in fact not be paid or received until the following or subsequent periods

Profits warning – the writing on the wall

Chris Walton, the finance director of troubled budget airline EasyJet, has come under pressure from shareholders to step down over the manner in which the company communicated its recent profit warnings.

The Independent reported that institutional shareholders have raised the issue with the airline's non-executive directors although Sir Colin Chandler, chairman of EasyJet, has backed his FD, saying the company was not contemplating any board changes 'at the moment'.

Last week EasyJet warned that rising fuel prices and fare cuts could hurt fiscal 2004 earnings sending the share price tumbling by 19% – the company's share price has almost halved in value since the beginning of May.

EasyJet founder and its biggest shareholder Stelios Haji-Ioannou, who has a 41% stake in the airline, has also been critical of the manner in which the warnings have been handled saying there was 'room for improvement'.

Easyjet FD under threat

© *Accountancy Age*, 14 June 2004

- cash may have been paid or received in advance of goods or services being received or provided and invoices being received or issued
- cash may have been paid or received relating to non-manufacturing, non-trading, or non-profit items – for example, cash received for shares in the business, and cash paid out on capital expenditure
- profit will have been calculated to include the impact of non-cash items such as depreciation.

When we look at the cash flow statement in the next chapter we shall see that one of the schedules that is required to be prepared in support of the cash flow statement is in fact a reconciliation of operating profit to net cash flow.

Prior to that, we can consider the following example, which is not in strict compliance with the cash flow reconciliation schedule requirement, but will serve to illustrate how profit and cash flow are linked and how the links may be identified.

Worked Example 3.10 shows that despite making a profit of £10,000 during an accounting period the company in fact had a shortfall of cash of £45,000 for the same period. After adjusting profit for the non-cash item of depreciation and adding the increase in share capital it effectively had an increase in funds during the month of £25,000. It then had to finance the purchase of fixed assets of £20,000 and finance an increase in its working capital requirement of £50,000 (stocks £34,000 plus debtors £18,000 less creditors £2,000). This resulted in its cash deficit for the month of £45,000. The company therefore went from having a positive cash balance of £6,000 at the start of the month to an overdraft of £39,000 at the end of the month.

Worked Example 3.10

In Worked Example 3.4 we saw that Ronly Bonly Jones Ltd made a profit of £10,000 during the month of January 2005. A summary of its balance sheet at 1 January 2005, and the 31 January 2005 balance sheet that we derived, are as follows:

	1 January 2005 £000	31 January 2005 £000
Fixed assets at cost	130	150
Depreciation provision	(20)	(25)
Stocks	45	79
Debtors	64	82
Cash and bank	6	–
	225	286
Creditors	(87)	(89)
Bank overdraft	–	(39)
Share capital	(50)	(60)
Profit and loss account	(88)	(98)
	(225)	(286)

We can provide a reconciliation of Ronly Bonly Jones Ltd's profit for the month of January with the cash flow for the same period.

| | January 2005 |
	£000
Profit for the month	10
Add back non-cash item	
Depreciation for month	5
	15
Cash gained from	
Increase in creditors	2
Additional share capital	10
	27
Cash reduced by	
Purchase of fixed assets	(20)
Increase in stocks	(34)
Increase in debtors	(18)
	(72)
Cash outflow for month	(45)
Cash and bank 1 January 2005	6
Cash outflow for month	(45)
Cash and bank 31 January 2005	(39)

Both the company and its bankers would obviously need to monitor RBJ Ltd's performance very closely over future months! A company will normally continuously review its cash, overdraft, accounts payable, and accounts receivable position. The bank manager will regularly review a company's balances and require advance notice of potential breaches of its overdraft limits.

> **Progress check 3.11** In what ways does the profit earned by a business during an accounting period differ from the cash generated during the same period? In what ways are profit and cash affected by the settlement (or not) of their accounts by the customers of the business?

Summary of key points

- Profit and loss account and income statement are two terms usually used to mean the same thing.
- The profit (or loss) of an entity may be considered from two perspectives: by considering the change in wealth between the start and end of an accounting period; by deducting total costs from total revenues (sales) generated during the accounting period.

- Categories within the profit and loss account are classified into turnover, cost of sales, other operating costs, other operating income, net interest, taxation, and dividends.
- There are four alternative profit and loss account formats permitted by the Companies Act 1985/1989, and in line with the provisions of FRS 3; format 1 is the most widely used by the majority of limited companies.
- The profit and loss account is closely linked with the balance sheet in two ways: they both reflect the change in wealth of the business; most transactions are reflected once in the profit and loss account and once in the balance sheet.
- Valuation of the various items within the balance sheet in accordance with the Companies Act 1985/1989, accounting concepts and standards, has a significant impact on the level of profit (or loss) earned by a business during an accounting period.
- The profit (or loss) earned during an accounting period is not the same as the cash flow generated during the period, but the links between the two measures may be quantified and reconciled.
- There are limitations to the profit and loss account, which like the balance sheet is an historical document, primarily due to the impact on costs of the employment of alternative methods of valuation of assets and liabilities.

Questions

Q3.1   How would you define the profit (or loss) earned by a business during an accounting period?

Q3.2   Outline a profit and loss account showing each of the main category headings.

Q3.3   (i)   What are the requirements that determine the format of the profit and loss account of a limited company?

(ii)   Which accounting standard contains provisions relating to the format of the profit and loss account?

(iii)   What are the main requirements relevant to the formats?

Q3.4   The profit and loss account and the balance sheet report on different aspects of a company's financial status. What are these different aspects and how are they related?

Q3.5   (i)   Why are the methods used for the valuation of the various types of assets so important?

(ii)   Describe the three main categories of asset that are most relevant.

Q3.6   What is depreciation and what are the problems encountered in dealing with the depreciation of fixed assets?

Q3.7   Describe the three most commonly used methods of accounting for depreciation.

Q3.8   Describe the four most commonly used methods of valuing stocks.

Q3.9   How does the valuation of trade debtors impact on the profit and loss account of a business?

Q3.10   Profit does not equal cash, but how can the one be reconciled with the other for a specific accounting period?

Discussion points

D3.1 'My profit for the year is the total of my pile of sales invoices less the cash I have paid out during the year.' Discuss.

D3.2 'The reason why companies make a provision for depreciation on their fixed assets is to save up enough money to buy new ones when the old assets reach the end of their lives.' Discuss.

D3.3 Why is judgement so important in considering the most appropriate method to use for valuing stocks? What are the factors that should be borne in mind and what are the pros and cons of the alternative methods? (Hint: Research Marks and Spencer plc and Laura Ashley plc to collect background material for this discussion.)

Exercises

Solutions are provided in Appendix 4 to all exercise numbers highlighted in colour.

Level I

E3.1 *Time allowed – 30 minutes*

Mr Kumar's chemist shop derives income from both retail sales and from prescription charges made to the NHS and to customers. For the last 2 years to 31 December 2003 and 31 December 2004 his results were as follows:

	2003 £	2004 £
Sales and prescription charges to customers	196,500	210,400
Prescription charges to the NHS	48,200	66,200
Purchases of stocks	170,100	180,600
Opening stock at the start of the year	21,720	30,490
Closing stock at the end of the year	30,490	25,300
Wages	25,800	27,300
Mr Kumar drawings*	20,500	19,700
Rent and rates	9,400	13,200
Insurance	1,380	1,620
Motor vehicle expenses	2,200	2,410
Other overheads	14,900	15,300

* Note that Mr Kumar's drawings are the amounts of money that he has periodically taken out of the business for his own use and should be shown as a deduction from the profits earned by the business rather than an expense in the profit and loss account.

Rent for the year 2003 includes £2,400 paid in advance for the half year to 31 March 2004, and for 2004 includes £3,600 paid in advance for the half year to 31 March 2005. Other overheads for 2003 do not include the electricity invoice for £430 for the final quarter (included in 2004 other overheads). There is a similar electricity invoice for £510 for 2004. Depreciation may be ignored.

   (i)   Prepare a profit and loss account for the two years to 31 December.

   (ii)   Why do you think that there is a difference in the gross profit to sales % between the two years?

   (iii) Using Mr Kumar's business as an example, explain the accruals accounting concept and examine whether it has been complied with.

E3.2 *Time allowed – 30 minutes*

Discuss the concepts that may apply and practical problems that may be encountered when accounting for:

   (i)   the acquisition of desktop personal computers, and

   (ii)   popular brands of products supplied by retailers

with specific comments regarding their depreciation charged to the profit and loss account and their net book values shown in the balance sheet.

E3.3 *Time allowed – 30 minutes*

A friend of yours owns a shop selling CDs and posters for the 12–14-year-old market. From the following information advise him on the potential problems that may be encountered in the valuation of such items for balance sheet purposes:

   (i)   greatest hits compilation CDs have sold consistently over the months and cost £5,000 with a retail value of £7,000

   (ii)   sales of specific group CDs, which ceased recording in the previous year, have now dropped off to zero and cost £500 with a total retail value of £700

   (iii) specific group CDs, which are still constantly recording and selling in the shop every week, cost £1,000 with a total retail value of £1,400

   (iv) specific artist posters are currently not selling at all (although CDs are), and cost £50 with a retail value of £100.

E3.4 *Time allowed – 30 minutes*

The Partex company began trading in 2002, and all sales are made to customers on credit. The company is in a sector that suffers from a high level of bad debts, and a provision for doubtful debts of 4% of outstanding debtors is made at each year end.

Information relating to 2002, 2003 and 2004 was as follows:

	Year to 31 December		
	2002	**2003**	**2004**
Outstanding debtors at 31 December*	£88,000	£110,000	£94,000
Bad debts to be written off during year	£4,000	£5,000	£4,000

* before bad debts have been written off

You are required to state the amount that will appear:

   (i)   in the balance sheet for debtors, and

   (ii)   in the profit and loss account for bad debts.

E3.5 *Time allowed – 45 minutes*

Tartantrips Ltd, a company in Scotland, operates several ferries and has a policy of holding several in reserve, due to the weather patterns and conditions of various contracts with local authorities. A ferry costs £5 million and has an estimated useful life of 10 years, at which time its realisable value is expected to be £1 million.

Calculate and discuss three methods of depreciation available to the company:

(i)   sum of the digits
(ii) straight line
(iii) reducing balance.

E3.6 *Time allowed – 60 minutes*

From the following profit and loss information that has been provided by Lazydays Ltd, for the year ended 31 March 2005 (and the corresponding figures for the year to 31 March 2004), construct a profit and loss account, using the format adopted by the majority of UK plcs, including comparative figures.

	2005 £	2004 £
Administrative expenses	22,000	20,000
Depreciation	5,000	5,000
Closing stock	17,000	15,000
Distribution costs	33,000	30,000
Dividends paid	32,000	30,000
Dividends received from non-related companies	5,000	5,000
Interest paid	10,000	10,000
Interest received	3,000	3,000
Opening stock	15,000	10,000
Purchases	99,000	90,000
Redundancy costs	5,000	
Sales	230,000	200,000
Taxation	25,000	24,000

(a)   Depreciation is to be included in the administrative expenses
(b)   Redundancy costs are to be regarded as an exceptional item

Level II

E3.7 *Time allowed – 60 minutes*

Llareggyb Ltd started business on 1 January 2005 and its year ended 31 December 2005. Llareggyb entered into the following transactions during the year.

Received funds for share capital of £25,000

Paid suppliers of materials £44,000

Purchased 11,000 units of materials at £8 per unit, one of which was required in one unit of finished goods

Heating and lighting costs paid for cash £16,000

Further heating and lighting costs £2,400 were incurred within the year, but still unpaid at 31 December 2005

Mr D Thomas loaned the company £80,000 on 1 January 2005 at 8% per annum

Loan interest was paid to Mr Thomas for January to June 2005

8,000 finished goods units were sold to customers at £40 each

Customers paid £280,000 to Llareggyb for sales of finished goods

Rent on the premises £60,000 was paid for 18 months from 1 January 2005, and business rates for the
same period of £9,000 were also paid

Salaries and wages were paid for January to November amounting to £132,000 but the December
payroll cost of £15,000 was not paid

A lorry was purchased for £45,000 on 1 January 2005 and was expected to last for 5 years after which
it could be sold for £8,000

The company uses the straight line method of depreciation

Prepare a profit and loss account for Llareggyb Ltd for the year ended 31 December 2005.

E3.8 *Time allowed – 60 minutes*

**From the trial balance of Retepmal Ltd at 31 March 2004 prepare a profit and loss account for the
year to 31 March 2004 and a balance sheet as at 31 March 2004 using the vertical formats used by
most UK companies.**

	£
Premises (net book value)	95,000
Trade debtors	75,000
Purchases of stocks	150,000
Retained earnings at 31 March 2003	130,000
Stocks at 31 March 2003	15,000
Furniture and fixtures	30,000
Sales	266,000
Distribution costs and administrative expenses	90,000
Trade creditors	54,000
Motor vehicles (net book value)	40,000
Cash and bank	35,000
Share capital	80,000

Additional information:

(a) Stocks at 31 March 2004 were £25,000.

(b) Dividend proposed for 2004 was £7,000.

(c) An accrual for expenses of £3,000 was required at 31 March 2004.

(d) A prepayment of expenses of £5,000 was required at 31 March 2004.

(e) Corporation tax estimated to be payable on 2003/2004 profits was £19,000.

(f) Annual depreciation charges on premises and motor vehicles for the year to 31 March
2004 are included in administrative expenses and distribution costs respectively, and in the
cumulative depreciation provisions used to calculate the net book values of £95,000 and
£40,000, shown in the trial balance at 31 March 2004.

The furniture and fixtures balance of £30,000 relates to purchases of assets during the year to 31
March 2004. The depreciation charge to administrative expenses and the corresponding depreciation
provision are not included in the trial balance at 31 March 2004. They are required to be calculated for
a full year to 31 March 2004, based on a useful economic life of eight years and an estimated residual
value of £6,000.

4

Financial statements of limited companies – cash flow statement

Contents

Learning objectives

Completion of this chapter will enable you to:

- describe what is meant by cash flow
- outline the structure of the cash flow statement of a limited company, and its supporting schedules
- classify the categories of cash inflows and cash outflows that comprise the cash flow statement
- illustrate how both the direct and indirect cash flow approaches are used to derive net cash flows from operating activities
- prepare a cash flow statement
- explain the links between the cash flow statement and the balance sheet
- explain the links between the cash flow statement and the profit and loss account
- consider the merits of cash flow versus profit as a measure of financial performance.

Introduction

Chapters 2 and 3 have been concerned with the first two of the three key financial statements required to be prepared periodically by limited companies: the balance sheet and the profit and loss account. This chapter will be concerned with the third of the financial statements, the cash flow statement. The cash flow statement, in one form or another, is prepared and used as an important management tool by all businesses. However, as in the previous two chapters, this chapter deals primarily with the cash flow statements of limited companies, both private and public.

Chapter 4 looks at how cash flow statements are structured and how each of the different types of cash inflows and cash outflows is categorised. This forms the basis to enable the preparation of a cash flow statement of a limited company, and its supporting schedules, in the appropriate format.

We will look at the relationship between the cash flow statement and the balance sheet and the profit and loss account. In Chapters 2 and 3 we have seen the subjective aspects of both the balance sheet and the profit and loss account. Cash flow is not subjective in any way but is a matter of fact.

What does the cash flow statement tell us?

Cash is a crucial requirement for any business to develop and survive, whether involved in the public services, manufacturing, retailing, or in a major national project like the Millennium Dome 2000 project (see the press extract below).

The Millennium Dome project demonstrated the need for realistic and timely cash planning both prior to and during its life, through the preparation of regular, clearly understood cash reports. Such cash planning and reporting may have avoided the problems faced by the managers throughout and subsequent to the life of the project.

The definition of cash includes not only cash in hand but also deposits and overdrafts, including those denominated in foreign currencies, repayable on demand with any bank or other financial institutions. Deposits repayable on demand include any kind of account where additional funds may be deposited at any time or funds withdrawn at any time without prior notice. All charges and credits on these accounts such as bank interest, bank fees, deposits or withdrawals, other than movements wholly within them, represent cash inflows and outflows of the reporting entity.

Virtually all transactions are conducted ultimately by cash or near cash (for example, bank accounts and credit cards). Sales of goods or services, or any other business assets, whether they are settled immediately or settled at some future date, are settled by cash or cash equivalents. Cash is an asset like any other asset, such as fixed asset machinery, or current asset debtors. Cash has the same properties as other assets, but also many more.

Cash is:

- a unit of measurement – we evaluate transactions and report financial information in £ sterling or whatever other foreign currency denominated
- a medium of exchange – rather than using the exchange or barter of other assets, cash is used as the accepted medium, having itself a recognisable value
- a store of value – cash may be used for current requirements or held for future use.

The inability of a business to pay its creditors, and other claims on the business, is invariably the reason for that business to fail. Cash, therefore, is a key asset and different from all other assets, which is why the performance of cash as a measure of business performance is so important.

In Chapters 2 and 3 we have discussed how the balance sheet and the profit and loss account do not show or directly deal with some of the key changes that have taken place in the company's

Cash planning is crucial for success

Plans to stage a New Year's Eve extravaganza for 20,000 people at the Millennium Dome last night were scrapped because organisers feared the event would be disrupted by a tube strike. Then the planned strike was called off.

Winter Wonderland, a theme park which ran at the Greenwich site throughout December, attracted up to 250,000 visitors. But the highlight was to have been last night's grand finale, with live bands and indoor fireworks.

But the organisers cancelled the event on December 19 because of the threat of strike action on the London Underground by members of the Rail, Maritime and Transport Union. Five days later, the strike was called off.

A spokesman for the organisers said yesterday: 'We were not confident that people would be able to get to the Dome. We decided to act. Subsequently, the strikes have not occurred but we had to make a decision at that time.'

The Dome's troubled history began on New Year's Eve four years ago with the government's attempts to mark the Millennium.

Last year the Guardian revealed the £800m structure is costing taxpayers £250,000 a month to maintain. By the time the government hands over responsibility for the Dome taxpayers will have paid £10.5m on maintenance alone.

The Dome is being taken over by the Meridian consortium, which includes US entertainment giant AEG.

Curse of Dome hits celebration, by Hugh Muir

© *The Guardian*, 1 January 2004

financial position. We will see in this chapter how the cash flow statement addresses this shortfall of information provided by the other two key financial statements, by answering questions like:

- How much capital expenditure (for example, machines and buildings) has the company made, and how did it fund the expenditure?
- What was the extent of new borrowing and how much debt was repaid?
- How much did the company need to fund new working capital requirements (for example, increases in debtors and stock requirements as a result of more business activity)?
- How much of the company's funding was met by funds generated from its trading activities, and how much was met by new external funding (for example, from banks and other lenders, or new shareholders)?

We introduced the DVD analogy in Chapters 2 and 3 with regard to the balance sheet and the profit and loss account. In the same way as profit (or loss), cash represents the dynamic DVD of changes in the cash position of the business throughout the period between the two 'pauses' – the balance sheets at the start and the finish of an accounting period. The cash flow statement summarises the cash inflows and outflows and calculates the net change in the cash position throughout the period. In this way it provides answers to the questions shown above. Analysis and summary of the cash inflows and outflows of the period answers those questions by illustrating:

- changes in the level of cash between the start and end of the period
- how much cash has been generated, and from where
- for what purpose cash has been used.

Structure of the cash flow statement

The basic purpose of a cash flow statement, as we saw in Chapter 2, is to report the cash receipts and cash payments that take place within an accounting period (see Fig. 4.1), and to show how the cash balance has changed from the start of the period to the balance at the end of the period. This can be seen to be objective and clearly avoids the problems of allocation associated with the preparation of a conventional profit and loss account.

However, a more useful presentation would describe:

- how the company generated or lost cash

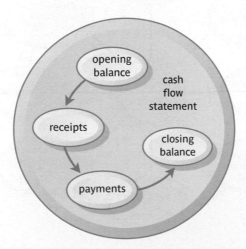

Figure 4.1 The main elements of the cash flow statement

- how the company financed its growth and investments
- the extent to which the company was funded by debt and equity.

The cash flow statement is covered in FRS 1, Cash Flow Statements, and its objective is to ensure that **reporting entities** fall within its scope:

- for companies to report their cash generation and cash absorption for a period by highlighting the significant components of cash flow in a way that facilitates comparison of the cash flow performances of different businesses
- for companies to provide information that assists in the assessment of their liquidity, solvency and financial adaptability.

SSAP 10, Statements of Source and Application of Funds, was the original accounting standard that required companies to provide a statement of source and application of funds. This statement was difficult to understand and did not provide a clear explanation of the cash flows of the company. SSAP 10 was replaced in September 1991 by the ASB with FRS 1, requiring companies to publish a cash flow statement. FRS 1 was subsequently revised in 1996. FRS 1 requires that the company's cash flow statement should list its cash flows for the period, and be classified under standard headings. These headings are represented in Fig. 4.2.

> **Progress check 4.1 Explain what is meant by a cash flow statement.**

The headings under which cash inflows and outflows for the period are itemised follow a particular order. We will look at explanations of each of the headings and how they are put together to provide an analysis of the cash movements of the business over an accounting period.

> **Progress check 4.2 What are the aims and purposes of the cash flow statement?**

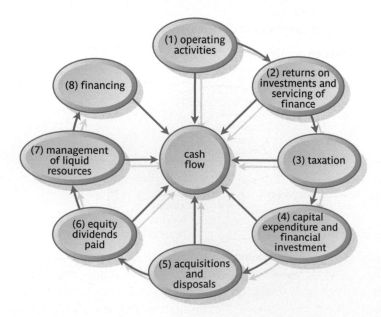

Figure 4.2 Cash inflows and cash outflows reflected in the cash flow statement

1. Operating activities (using either the direct or indirect method)

Net cash flows from operating activities include the cash effects of transactions and other events relating to the operating or trading activities of the business. They are the movements in cash and cash equivalents of the operations that are included in the profit and loss account to derive operating profit. Net cash flows from operating activities include the cash effects only and not all the revenues and costs that together represent the profit and loss account.

Reference to the direct and **indirect method** relates to the choice of two options that are available for a business to derive the net cash flows from operating activities. The **direct method** involves individual identification of each of the cash items during the period that have been included in the profit and loss account. They are:

- cash received from customers in respect of sales
- cash paid to suppliers in respect of purchases
- cash paid to employees
- cash paid for all other expenses.

The indirect method involves use of the net operating profit for the period adjusted for non-cash items and movements in working capital to arrive at net cash flows from operating activities. We will look at examples of both these techniques in a later section of this chapter.

2. Returns on investments and servicing of finance

Returns on investments and servicing of finance are receipts of cash that result from owning an investment, and payments of cash to providers of finance. This includes interest received on long-term and short-term loans, interest paid on overdrafts and long-term and short-term loans, and dividends paid to other than equity shareholders (preference shareholders and minority interests). Returns on investments and servicing of finance excludes all other returns included elsewhere in the cash flow statements under operating activities, investing or **financing** activities.

3. Taxation

The taxation heading should include all items in respect of tax on revenue and capital profits. These include all payments relating to corporation tax, and receipts from rebate claims, overpayments, etc. Payments and receipts in respect of Value Added Tax (VAT) are not included within the taxation heading. VAT payments and receipts are netted against the cash flows to which they relate, for example operating activities and fixed assets investments.

4. Capital expenditure and financial investment

Capital expenditure and financial investment includes payments and receipts for the acquisition and disposal of fixed assets. It does not include any income derived from these investments, since these are shown under the heading returns on investments and servicing of finance.

5. Acquisitions and disposals

Cash payments and receipts for acquisitions and disposals relate to the acquisition and sale of investments in subsidiary undertakings, or investment and sales of investments in other undertakings. As with capital expenditure investments, this category does not include any income derived from these investments, which is included under the heading returns on investments and servicing of finance.

6. Equity dividends paid

This heading includes all dividends actually paid in cash during the accounting period to equity (ordinary share) shareholders. It does not include proposed dividends or dividends declared, which will not be paid until a subsequent accounting period.

7. Management of liquid resources

→ The management of liquid resources is concerned with cash payments and cash receipts from the acquisition and disposal of investments held as a result of short-term cash surpluses. Such investments may include investments in equity shares or short-term Government loans.

8. Financing

Financing cash flow generally includes the receipts and payments of cash relating to the long-term financing of the business. It relates to the financing itself rather than the servicing of such finance through dividends and interest. Financing cash flows include receipts from:

- share issues
- debentures
- loans
- notes
- bonds
- other long-term borrowings.

The last two headings may be shown in a single section, provided that a subtotal is given for each heading. Individual categories of inflows and outflows under the standard headings should be disclosed separately either in the cash flow statement or in a note to it unless they are allowed to be shown net. In some circumstances cash inflows and outflows may be shown net if they relate to the management of liquid resources or financing. The requirement to show cash inflows and outflows separately does not apply to cash flows relating to operating activities.

> **Progress check 4.3** **Explain what cash inflows and outflows are reflected within each of the headings in the cash flow statement.**

Worked Example 4.1

The following is a list of some of the different types of cash inflows and cash outflows of a typical plc. We will identify within which of the cash flow statement headings they would normally be reported.

- sale of a subsidiary
- dividends paid to ordinary shareholders
- VAT
- interest paid
- purchase of a copyright (intangible fixed asset)

- interest received
- issue of debentures
- corporation tax
- short-term Government loans (for example, Treasury Stock)

- purchase of a building
- income from investments
- receipts from trade debtors
- payments to trade creditors (due within one year)
- purchase of factory machinery

Net cash flow from operating activities
  Receipts from trade debtors
  Payments to trade creditors (due within one year)
Returns on investments and servicing of finance
  Interest received
  Interest paid
  Income from investments
Taxation
  Corporation tax
  VAT? No, because VAT is netted against the cash flow to which it relates
Capital expenditure and financial investment
  Purchase of a copyright
  Purchase of a building
  Purchase of factory machinery
Acquisitions and disposals
  Sale of a subsidiary
Equity dividends paid
  Dividends paid to ordinary shareholders
Management of liquid resources
  Short-term Government loans
Financing
  Issue of debentures

> **Progress check 4.4** **What questions does the cash flow statement set out to answer and how does it achieve this?**

Direct and indirect cash flow

As touched on earlier, the heading relating to net operating cash flow can be presented by using either the direct method or indirect method. We shall consider both methods in a little more detail, although the indirect method is by far the easiest to use in practice and is the method used by most companies.

Direct method

The direct method involves an analysis of all the cash transactions for the appropriate period to identify all receipts and payments relating to the operating activities for the period. The analysis therefore shows the relevant constituent cash flows, operating cash receipts and cash payments including in particular cash receipts from customers, cash payments to suppliers, and cash payments to and on behalf of employees.

An example of the adoption of the direct method by Flatco plc is illustrated in Fig. 4.3. The standard FRS 1 makes it mandatory to provide a reconciliation between operating profit and net cash flow from operating activities, even where the direct method is adopted. Because of this, the amount of time, and other resources required to analyse the relevant cash information, the direct method has not been popular with many companies, although it does provide some very useful information.

Flatco plc Cash flow statement for the year ended 31 December 2005 Cash flow from operating activities	
	£000
Operating activities	
Net cash received from customers	3,472
Cash payments to suppliers	(1,694)
Cash paid to and on behalf of employees	(631)
Other cash payments	(211)
Net cash inflow from operating activities	936

Figure 4.3 Cash flow from operating activities – direct method

Indirect method

The indirect method is by far the one most frequently adopted by UK companies. The basis of this approach is that operating revenues and costs are generally associated with cash receipts and cash payments and so profits earned from operating activities during an accounting period will approximate the net cash flows generated during the period. The actual operating cash flow may be determined from adjustment to the operating profit reported in the profit and loss account for non-cash items and changes in working capital during the period:

- stocks
- debtors
- creditors.

Worked Example 4.2

Indirect Ltd earned operating profits of £247,000 during 2004/2005, and its retained profit for the year was also £247,000. Indirect Ltd had acquired fixed assets totalling £290,000 during the year and had made no disposals of fixed assets. Indirect's balance sheets as at 1 July 2004 and 30 June 2005 were as follows:

	1 July 2004	30 June 2005
	£000	£000
Fixed assets	385	525
Stocks	157	277
Debtors	224	287
	766	1,089

Creditors due within 1 year	(305)	(312)
Bank overdraft	(153)	(222)
Equity	(308)	(555)
	(766)	(1,089)

The indirect method may be used to calculate the net cash flow from operating activities:

Calculation of depreciation	**£000**
Fixed assets at the start of the year were	385
Additions during the year were	290
Disposals during the year were	zero
	675
Fixed assets at the end of the year were	525
Therefore, depreciation for the year was	150

Indirect Ltd
Cash flow statement for the year ended 30 June 2005
Reconciliation of operating profit to net cash inflow from operating activities

	£000
Operating profit	247
Depreciation charges	150
Increase in stocks [277 – 157]	(120)
Increase in debtors [287 – 224]	(63)
Increase in creditors due within 1 year [312 – 305]	7
Net cash inflow from operating activities	221

The above worked example shows how the net cash inflow from operating activities of £221,000 was calculated by starting with the operating profit for the year of £247,000 and adjusting for changes in depreciation and working capital over the year.

The only other cash activity during the year appears to be the acquisition of fixed assets totalling £290,000. If we deduct that from the net cash inflow from operating activities of £221,000 we get a net cash outflow of £69,000. This agrees with the movement in the cash and bank balances, which have worsened from an overdraft of £153,000 at the beginning of the year to an overdraft of £222,000 at the end of the year.

> **Progress check 4.5** Describe the direct and the indirect cash flow methods that may be used to derive net operating cash flow, their differences and their purpose.

Cash flow statement formats

There is no statutory requirement for companies to prepare a cash flow statement. FRS 1 requires all reporting entities that prepare financial statements, intended to give a true and fair view of their financial position and profit and loss, to include a cash flow statement as a primary statement within their financial statements, except for small companies which are specifically exempted.

There is one standard format for the cash flow statement prescribed by FRS 1, which includes the headings we have discussed above. The cash flow statement actually comprises a number of statements:

- reconciliation of operating profit to net operating cash flows (Fig. 4.4)
- cash flow statement of cash inflows and outflows (Fig. 4.5)
- reconciliation of net cash flow to movement in net debt (Fig. 4.6)
- note on gross cash flows (Fig. 4.7)
- note on analysis of changes in net debt (Fig. 4.8).

Figures 4.4 to 4.8 illustrate the format of the cash flow statements and have been prepared from the balance sheet and profit and loss account for Flatco plc included in Chapter 2 and Chapter 3.

The comparative figures for the previous year (not shown in the Flatco plc illustrations, Figs 4.3 to 4.8) are usually reported in columns to the right of the current year's figures. Each of the statements shown in Figs 4.4 to 4.8 is important for the following reasons:

- the reconciliation of operating profit to net cash flow from operating activities (Fig. 4.4) shows how the net cash flow from operating activities is derived from adjusting operating profit for non-cash items and movements in working capital
- the cash flow statement (Fig. 4.5) reports the net cash flow for an accounting period, derived from the net cash flow from operating activities and adjusted for all non-operating categories of cash inflows and outflows
- the reconciliation of net cash flow to movement in net debt (Fig. 4.6) shows how the net cash flow for an accounting period is the difference between the net debt at the beginning of the period and the net debt at the end of the period
- note 1 – gross cash flows (Fig. 4.7) provides more detail with regard to the non-operating cash inflows and outflows used in the cash flow statement (Fig. 4.5)
- note 2 – analysis of changes in net debt (Fig. 4.8) analyses the net debt movement shown in Fig. 4.6 in greater detail to show each of the categories that comprise net debt.

Flatco plc
Cash flow statement for the year ended 31 December 2005
Reconciliation of operating profit to net cash flow from operating activities

	£000
Operating profit	550
Depreciation charges	345
Increase in stocks	(43)
Increase in debtors	(28)
Increase in creditors	112
Net cash inflow from operating activities	936

Figure 4.4 Reconciliation of operating profit to net cash flow from operating activities

Cash flow statement	
	£000
Net cash inflow from operating activities	936
Returns on investments and servicing of finance (note 1)	40
Taxation	(44)
Capital expenditure (note 1)	(299)
	633
Equity dividends paid	(67)
	566
Management of liquid resources (note 1)	–
Financing (note 1)	373
Increase in cash	939

Figure 4.5 Cash flow statement

Reconciliation of net cash flow to movement in net debt/funds (note 2)	
	£000
Increase in cash for the period	939
Cash inflow from increase in long-term debt	(173)
Change in net debt	766
Net debt at 1 January 2005	(662)
Net funds at 31 December 2005	104

Figure 4.6 Reconciliation of net cash flow to movement in net debt/funds

Note 1 to the cash flow statement – gross cash flows		
	£000	£000
Returns on investments and servicing of finance		
Income from investments	100	
Interest received	11	
Interest paid	(71)	
		40
Capital expenditure		
Payments to acquire tangible fixed assets	(286)	
Payments to acquire intangible fixed assets	(34)	
Receipts from sales of tangible fixed assets	21	
		(299)
Management of liquid resources		
Purchase of Government bills (short-term investments)	(200)	
Sale of Government bills (short-term investments)	200	
		–
Financing		
Issue of ordinary share capital	200	
Debenture loan	173	
		373

Figure 4.7 Note 1 – gross cash flows

Note 2 to the cash flow statement – analysis of change in net debt/funds			
	At 1 January 2005 £000	Cash flows £000	At 31 December 2005 £000
Cash in hand and at bank	17	310	327
Overdraft	(679)	629	(50)
Debenture	–	(173)	(173)
Total (debt)/funds	662	766	104

Figure 4.8 Note 2 – analysis of change in net debt/funds

Worked Example 4.3

The reconciliation of operating profit to net cash flow from operating activities shown below is an extract from the published accounts of Tomkins plc, which is a diversified multinational UK plc with interests in the UK, USA and other parts of the world. Tomkins has been acquisitive in the past, but sold off activities it wished not to develop in the future.

We can use this table to comment on the working capital movements for the year 2000.

Figures in £m	2000	1999
Operating profit	519.1	495.3
Depreciation	197.9	175.0
Profit/(loss) on sale of fixed assets	(1.0)	(6.1)
(Increase)/decrease in stocks	(64.4)	4.7
(Increase)/decrease in debtors	(73.2)	7.2
Increase/(decrease) in creditors	(0.9)	(89.7)
Other	0.5	1.3
Net cash inflow from operating activities	578.0	587.7

Operating profits may initially be considered to be on a plateau, but as the group is not solely involved in one industrial sector, further analysis is difficult.

The stocks movement of £64.4m is quite significant and the company may be expected to explain what activity or decision brought this about.

The debtors movement of £73.2m is also worthy of separate comment to assist users of the cash flow statement to make their economic judgement.

The creditors movement of £0.9m is most unexpected as many companies would use creditors in part to finance increases in stocks and debtors.

Net cash inflows for the two years are so similar that the company may have set internal targets to ensure sufficient cash flows were achieved, allowing for acquisitions, disposals and trading.

Worked Example 4.4

The extract from a leading UK supermarket retailer's cash flow statement shown below is its net debt note for the year to February 2000.

Figures in £m	Opening balance 1 Mar 1999	Cash flow	Closing balance 28 Feb 2000
Cash at bank	127	(39)	88
Overdrafts	(31)	(4)	(35)
	96	(43)	53
Liquid resources	201	57	258
Short-term loans	(799)	(13)	(812)
Long-term loans	(1,218)	(341)	(1,559)
Net debt	(1,720)	(340)	(2,060)

We will discuss each of the elements in the net debt note and comment briefly on the cash flow movements over the year.

(a) Both cash and overdraft balances have contributed to the increase in net debt. This apparent policy of reducing cash balances and increasing overdrafts may be questioned. The actual policy can be established by looking at the trends over several years and any comments made by the company in its published report and accounts.

(b) The liquid resources were in fact increased, possibly to take advantage of the increase in interest rates being paid in the UK. The company was actually publicly criticised in late 2000 by the UK Government for holding on to suppliers' funds for too long.

(c) The company is obviously using short-term funds to finance the business. The users of financial information usually require information on the timing of repayments of loans (in this case the bulk of the £812 million short-term debt is owed to banks), which plcs are required by the Companies Act to disclose in their published reports and accounts.

(d) All major UK plcs provide an overview of their treasury activities in their published reports and accounts, which links current policies with the components of net debt (for example, banking facilities).

(e) The financial press sometimes comment on net debt movement. This may vary from year to year and from analyst to analyst. A typical comment might be 'the £340 million increase has pushed net borrowings of the company to over £2 billion for the first time'.

The Companies Act 1985/1989 requires group accounts to be prepared for the holding company in addition to the accounts that are required to be prepared for each of the individual companies within the group. These 'consolidated accounts' exclude all transactions between companies within the group, for example inter-company sales and purchases. Undertakings preparing consolidated financial statements should prepare a consolidated cash flow statement and related notes; they are not then required to prepare an entity cash flow statement.

Progress check 4.6 What are the schedules that are used to support the main cash flow statement and what is their purpose?

Worked Example 4.5

We may use the following data, extracted from the financial records of Zap Electronics plc, to prepare a cash flow statement in compliance with the provisions of FRS 1, together with the appropriate notes and reconciliations. The data relate to the financial statements prepared for the year ended 31 July 2005.

	£000
Dividends paid on ordinary shares	49
Purchase of Government bills (short-term investments)	200
Issue of ordinary share capital	100
Reduction in stocks	25
Corporation tax paid	120
Interest paid	34
Operating profit	830
Bank and cash balance 31 July 2005	527
Purchase of machinery	459
Sale of Government bills	100
Interest received	18
Purchase of a copyright (intangible fixed asset)	78
Depreciation charge for the year	407
Purchase of a building	430
Sale of a patent (intangible fixed asset)	195
Increase in trade debtors	35
Reduction in trade creditors (due within 1 year)	85
Bank and cash balance 1 August 2004	342

Zap Electronics plc
Cash flow statement for the year ended 31 July 2005
Reconciliation of operating profit to net cash flow from operating activities

	£000
Operating profit	830
Depreciation charge	407
Reduction in stocks	25
Increase in debtors	(35)
Reduction in creditors	(85)
Net cash inflow from operating activities	1,142

Cash flow statement

	£000
Net cash inflow from operating activities	1,142
Returns on investments and servicing of finance (note 1)	(16)
Taxation	(120)
Capital expenditure (note 1)	(772)
	234
Equity dividends paid	(49)
	185
Management of liquid resources (note 1)	(100)
Financing (note 1)	100
Increase in cash	185

Reconciliation of net cash flow to movement in net debt/net funds (note 2)

	£000
Increase in cash for the period	185
Change in net debt	185
Net funds at 1 August 2004	342
Net funds at 31 July 2005	527

Note 1 to the cash flow statement – gross cash flows

	£000	£000
Returns on investments and servicing of finance		
Interest received	18	
Interest paid	(34)	
		(16)
Capital expenditure		
Payments to acquire intangible fixed assets	(78)	
Payments to acquire tangible fixed assets [430 + 459]	(889)	
Receipts from sales of intangible fixed assets	195	
		(772)
Management of liquid resources		
Purchase of Government bills	(200)	
Sale of Government bills	100	
		(100)
Financing		
Issue of ordinary share capital		100

Note 2 to the cash flow statement – analysis of change in net debt/funds

	At 1 August 2004	Cash flows	At 31 July 2005
	£000	£000	£000
Bank and cash	342	185	527
Overdraft	–	–	–
	342	185	527

Worked Example 4.6

Perfecto Ltd
Profit and loss account for the year ended 30 September 2005

	£000	£000
Turnover		2,279
Cost of sales		(1,484)
Gross profit		795
Distribution costs	(368)	
Administrative expenses	(197)	
		(565)
Operating profit		230
Net interest		(10)
Profit before tax		220
Tax on profit on ordinary activities		(70)
Profit on ordinary activities after tax		150
Dividends [20 + 20]		(40)
Retained profit for the financial year		110

Perfecto Ltd
Balance sheet as at 30 September 2005

	2005	2004
	£000	£000
Fixed assets		
Intangible	203	193
Tangible	902	1,071
	1,105	1,264
Current assets		
Stocks	161	142
Debtors	284	193
Prepayments	295	278
Cash	157	–
	897	613

Current liabilities (less than one year)

Bank overdraft	–	20
Creditors	187	231
Corporation tax	70	55
Proposed dividend	20	20
Accruals	100	81
	377	407
Net current assets	520	206
Total assets less current liabilities	1,625	1,470
less		
Long-term liabilities (over one year)		
Creditors	77	184
Financial debt	85	126
Provisions	103	185
	265	495
Net assets	1,360	975
Capital and reserves		
Capital	600	450
Premiums	105	–
Profit and loss account	655	525
	1,360	975

During the year Perfecto Ltd acquired new plant and machinery for £150,000, bought a patent for £10,000, and made no disposals of either tangible or intangible fixed assets.

Perfecto Ltd paid an interim dividend of £20,000 during the year and declared a final dividend of £20,000. Interest paid was £20,000 and interest received was £10,000. The company paid corporation tax of £55,000 during the year.

We have all the data required to prepare a cash flow statement for the year ended 30 September 2005 complying with FRS 1, including all supporting reconciliations and notes.

	£000
Fixed assets at the start of the year were	1,264
Additions during the year were	160 [150 + 10]
Disposals during the year were	zero
	1,424
Fixed assets at the end of the year were	1,105
Therefore, depreciation for the year was	319

	30 Sep 2004	30 Sep 2005	Difference
	£000	£000	£000
Stocks	142	161	19 increase
Debtors and prepayments	471 [193 + 278]	579 [284 + 295]	108 increase
Creditors, accruals, and provisions	681 [231 + 81 + 184 + 185]	467 [187 + 100 + 77 + 103]	214 decrease

Perfecto Ltd
Cash flow statement for the year ended 30 September 2005
Reconciliation of operating profit to net cash flow from operating activities

	£000
Operating profit	230
Depreciation charges	319
Increase in stocks	(19)
Increase in debtors	(108)
Reduction in creditors	(214)
Net cash inflow from operating activities	208

Cash flow statement

	£000
Net cash inflow from operating activities	208
Returns on investments and servicing of finance (note 1)	(10)
Taxation	(55)
Capital expenditure (note 1)	(160)
	(17)
Equity dividends paid	(20)
	(37)
Management of liquid resources (note 1)	–
Financing (note 1)	214
Increase in cash	177

Reconciliation of net cash flow to movement in net debt/funds (note 2)

	£000
Increase in cash for the period	177
Cash outflow from decrease in long-term debt	41
Change in net debt	218
Net debt at 30 September 2004	(146)
Net funds at 30 September 2005	72

Note 1 to the cash flow statement – gross cash flows

	£000	£000
Returns on investments and servicing of finance		
Interest received	10	
Interest paid	(20)	
		(10)
Capital expenditure		
Payments to acquire tangible fixed assets	(150)	
Payments to acquire intangible fixed assets	(10)	
		(160)
Financing		
Issue of ordinary share capital [600 + 105 – 450]	255	
Repayment of loans [126 – 85]	(41)	
		214

Note 2 to the cash flow statement – analysis of change in net debt/funds

	At 30 September 2004 £000	Cash flows £000	At 30 September 2005 £000
Cash	–	157	157
Bank overdraft	(20)	20	–
Long-term debt	(126)	41	(85)
Total (debt)/funds	(146)	218	72

Cash flow links to the balance sheet and profit and loss account

The diagram shown in Fig. 4.9 is a representation of some simple links between cash flow and the profit and loss account, and the relationship with the balance sheet. It shows how, for example:

- a purchase of fixed assets for cash of £50 has
  - increased fixed assets in the balance sheet from the opening balance of £100 to the closing balance of £150
  - decreased the opening cash balance by £50
- a profit of £100, that has been realised in cash, has
  - increased by £100 the opening cash balance of £100 which, less the outflow of £50 for fixed assets, gives a closing balance of £150
  - increased the profit and loss account from the opening balance of £100 to the closing balance of £200.

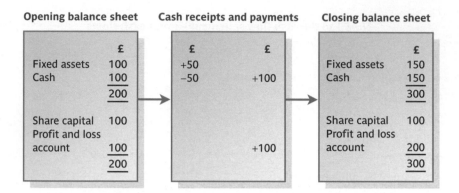

Figure 4.9 Some simple links between cash flow and the profit and loss account, and the balance sheet

The effect of the above transactions is

- cash has increased by £50
- fixed assets have been increased by £50
- profit has increased by £100
- the balance sheet is still in balance with increased total assets and total liabilities.

We may see from the more detailed information given as part of cash flow statement reporting how cash flow may be appreciated in the context of the information given by the balance sheet and the profit and loss account. The accounting standard FRS 1, Cash Flow Statements requires companies to provide two reconciliations included as part of the cash flow statement reporting, between:

- operating profit and the net cash flow from operating activities

and between:

- the net cash flow during the period and the movement in net debt.

These reconciliations do not form part of the cash flow statement but each is provided in a supporting schedule and in a separate note. The links between cash flow and the profit and loss account may therefore be observed by way of the operating profit adjusted for non-cash items and the changes in working capital, to arrive at net cash flow from operating activities.

Opening and closing balances of cash do not appear on the face of the cash flow statement and so do not provide a direct link with the corresponding numbers reported in the balance sheet. It is for this reason that the increase or decrease in cash that appears in the cash flow statement must be reconciled with the opening and closing balance sheet numbers – the movement in net debt.

Usually this reconciliation is a simple matter of adding the increase or decrease in cash during the accounting period to the opening balance of cash and cash equivalents to agree the closing balance of cash. However, there are some situations when, in addition to the cash flows of the entity, the movement in net debt has to identify specific items, which must be reconciled to the opening and closing balance sheet amounts:

- the acquisition or disposal of subsidiaries (excluding cash balances)
- other non-cash charges
- the recognition of changes in market value and exchange rate movements.

> **Progress check 4.7** **How is the cash flow statement of a business related to its other financial statements, the profit and loss account and the balance sheet?**

Worked Example 4.7

Detailed below are the cash flow statement and direct cash flow analysis for Ronly Bonly Jones Ltd for the month of January 2005, and its balance sheet as at 1 January 2005. Rather than deriving a cash flow statement from a profit and loss account and a balance sheet this example aims to derive the following information from a cash flow statement:

(i) reconciliation of the cash flow for the month with the profit for the month
(ii) derivation of the profit and loss account for the month
(iii) derivation of the changes in the balance sheet during the month from the 1 January balance sheet
(iv) preparation of the balance sheet as at 31 January 2005.

Figures in £000

Reconciliation of operating profit to net cash flow from operating activities

Operating profit	10
Depreciation charges	5
Increase in stocks	(34)
Increase in debtors	(18)
Increase in creditors	2
Net cash outflow from operating activities	(35)

Cash flow statement

Net cash outflow from operating activities	(35)
Capital expenditure – tangible fixed asset additions	(20)
	(55)
Financing – increase in equity share capital	10
Decrease in cash	(45)

Direct method

Operating activities	
Net cash received from customers	632
Cash payments to suppliers	(422)
Cash paid to and on behalf of employees	(190)
Other cash payments	(55)
Net cash outflow from operating activities	(35)

Balance sheet as at 1 January 2005

	£000
Fixed assets at cost	130
Depreciation provision	(20)
Stocks	45
Debtors	64
Cash and bank	6
	225
Creditors	(87)
Share capital	(50)
Profit and loss account	(88)
	(225)

We may reconcile the cash flow for the month with the profit for the month as follows:

	January 2005	
	£000	
Increase in debtors during the month	18	
Cash received from customers	632	
Sales for the month	650	
Increase in stocks during the month	(34)	
Purchases of materials from suppliers	424	[increase in creditors 2 +
		cash payments to suppliers 422]
Cost of goods sold in the month	390	
Depreciation charge in the month	5	
Cash paid to and on behalf of employees	190	
Other cash payments	55	
Expenses for the month	245	

Therefore the profit and loss account for January 2005 is

	£000
Sales	650
Cost of goods sold	(390)
Depreciation	(5)
Expenses	(245)
Profit for January	10

Let's derive the 31 January 2005 balance sheet from the information that has been provided:

Figures in £000	Fixed assets	Depn	Stocks	Debtors	Cash	Creditors	Equity	Profit/loss account
1 January 2005	130	(20)	45	64	6	(87)	(50)	(88)
Sales				650				(650)
Cash from customers				(632)	632			0
Purchases			424			(424)		0
Cash to creditors					(422)	422		0
Stock sold			(390)					390
Depreciation		(5)						5
Expenses					(245)			245
Fixed asset additions	20				(20)			0
Issue of shares					10		(10)	0
31 January 2005	150	(25)	79	82	(39)	(89)	(60)	(98)

Therefore the balance sheets at 1 January 2005 and at 31 January 2005 are as follows:

	1 January 2005 £000	31 January 2005 £000
Fixed assets at cost	130	150
Depreciation provision	(20)	(25)
Stocks	45	79
Debtors	64	82
Cash and bank	6	(39)
	225	247
Creditors	(87)	(89)
Share capital	(50)	(60)
Profit and loss account	(88)	(98)
	(225)	(247)

In Worked Example 4.7, we have

- used the cash flow statement to derive the profit and loss account for the month

and we have then used the

- 1 January 2005 balance sheet
- profit and loss account for the month of January 2005
- non-profit and loss items also shown in the January cash flow statement

to derive the balance sheet for 31 January 2005.

In this way, we can see how the balance sheet, profit and loss account and cash flow statement of a business are inextricably linked.

Worked Example 4.8

We can use the cash flow reconciliation statement to provide an explanation of the net cash outflow of £45,000, shown in Worked Example 4.7, to shareholders in Ronly Bonly Jones Ltd.

During January 2005 there was a profit before depreciation of £15,000 (£10,000 + £5,000). This, together with the increase in share capital of £10,000, provided a total cash inflow for the month of £25,000. However, there was a net outflow of cash on increased working capital of £50,000 (£34,000 + £18,000 – £2,000) and capital expenditure of £20,000. This all resulted in a net cash outflow of £45,000 (£25,000 – £50,000 – £20,000).

The net cash outflow may be in line with what the company had planned or forecast for January 2005. Alternatively, the outflow may not have been expected. Changes in trading circumstances and/or management decisions may have been the reason for the difference between the actual and expected cash flow for January 2005.

The shareholders of Ronly Bonly Jones Ltd need to be reassured that the current cash position is temporary, and under control, and within the overdraft facility agreed with the company's bankers. The shareholders must also be reassured that the company is not in financial difficulty or that if problems are being experienced then the appropriate remedial actions are in place.

Summary of key points

- Cash flow includes not only cash in hand but also deposits and overdrafts, repayable on demand with any bank or other financial institutions.
- The cash flow statement lists the inflows and outflows of cash for a period classified under the standard headings of: operating activities; returns on investments and servicing of finance; taxation; capital expenditure and financial investment; acquisitions and disposals; equity dividends paid; management of liquid resources; financing.
- The preparation of a cash flow statement is not a legal requirement. However, FRS 1 requires all reporting entities which prepare financial statements intended to give a true and fair view of their financial position and profit and loss to include a cash flow statement as a primary statement within their financial statements, unless specifically exempted.
- There is only one standard format for the cash flow statement prescribed by FRS 1, comprising a main statement of cash inflows and outflows, supported by schedules and notes reconciling net operating cash flow to operating profit and reconciling net cash flow to changes in net debt.
- Net cash flow from operating activities may be derived using the direct method or the indirect method, with both methods giving the same result.
- The cash flow statement is directly related to both the profit and loss account and the balance sheet and the links between them may be quantified and reconciled.
- The preparation of the cash flow statement is a highly objective exercise, in which all the headings and amounts are cash based and therefore easily measured.
- The cash flow generated during an accounting period is a matter of fact and does not rely on judgement or the use of alternative conventions or valuation methods.

Questions

Q4.1   (i)   How would you define cash generated by a business during an accounting period?

(ii)   Which accounting standard deals with cash flow?

Q4.2   Give an example of the main cash flow statement showing each of the main categories.

Q4.3   Give an example of the reconciliations and notes that are prepared in support of the main cash flow statement.

Q4.4   Describe the ways in which both the direct method and the indirect method may be used to derive the net operating cash flow during an accounting period of a business.

Q4.5   (i)   Which reconciliation statement is used to link the cash flow statement to the profit and loss account?

(ii)   How does it do that?

Q4.6   (i)   Which reconciliation statement is used to link the cash flow statement to the balance sheet?

(ii)   What are the links?

Q4.7   Why is cash so important, compared to the other assets used within a business?

Q4.8   (i)   What questions does the cash flow statement aim to answer?

(ii)   How far does it go towards answering them?

Discussion points

D4.1 Why is the information disclosed in the profit and loss account and the balance sheet not considered sufficient for users of financial information? What was so important about cash flow that it was considered necessary for the Accounting Standards Board to issue FRS 1 (Cash Flow Statements) in 1991, which was subsequently revised in 1996?

D4.2 'Forget your profit and loss accounts and balance sheets, at the end of the day it's the business's healthy bank balance that is the measure of its increase in wealth.' Discuss.

Exercises

Solutions are provided in Appendix 4 to all exercise numbers highlighted in colour.

Level I

E4.1 *Time allowed – 60 minutes*

Candice-Marie James and Flossie Graham obtained a one-year lease on a small shop which cost them £15,000 for the year 2005, and agreed to pay rent of £4,000 per year payable one year in advance. Candyfloss started trading on 1 January 2005 as a florist, and Candice and Flossie bought a second-hand, white delivery van for which they paid £14,500. The business was financed by Candice and Flossie each providing £9,000 from their savings and an interest free loan from Candice's uncle of £3,000. Candice and Flossie thought they were doing OK over their first six months but they weren't sure how to measure this. They decided to try and see how they were doing financially and looked at the transactions for the first six months:

	£
Cash sales of flowers	76,000
Rent paid	4,000
Wages paid	5,000
Payments for other operating expenses	7,000
Purchases of stocks of flowers for resale	59,500
Legal expenses paid for the lease acquisition	1,000

In addition, at 30 June 2005 they owed a further £4,000 for the purchase of flowers and £1,000 for other operating expenses. Customers had purchased flowers on credit and the sum still owed amounted to £8,000. One customer was apparently in financial difficulties and it was likely that the £1,500 owed would not be paid. Stocks of flowers at 30 June 2005 valued at cost were £9,500. They estimated that the van would last four years, at which time they expected to sell it for £2,500, and that depreciation would be spread evenly over that period.

(i)   Prepare a cash flow statement for Candyfloss for the first 6 months of the year 2005 using the direct method.

(ii)   Prepare a conventional profit and loss account statement for Candyfloss, on an accruals basis.

(iii) Why is the profit different from the cash flow?

(iv)   Which statement gives the best indication of the first 6 months' performance of Candyfloss?

E4.2 *Time allowed – 60 minutes*

Using the information from Exercise E4.1 prepare a cash flow statement for Candyfloss for the first six months of the year 2005, using the indirect method.

E4.3 *Time allowed – 60 minutes*

Jaffrey Packaging plc have used the following information in the preparation of their financial statements for the year ended 31 March 2005.

	£000
Dividends paid	25
Issue of a debenture	200
Reduction in stocks	32
Corporation tax paid	73
Interest paid	28
Operating profit for the year	450
Bank and cash balance 31 March 2005	376
Purchase of factory equipment	302
Dividends payable at 31 March 2005	25
Interest received	5
Depreciation charge for the year	195
Purchase of a new large computer system	204
Sale of a patent (intangible fixed asset)	29
Increase in trade debtors	43
Reduction in short-term creditors	62
Bank and cash balance 1 April 2004	202

You are required to prepare a cash flow statement in compliance with the provisions of FRS 1, together with the appropriate supporting schedules and reconciliations.

E4.4 *Time allowed – 60 minutes*

From the profit and loss account for the year ended 31 December 2004 and balance sheets as at 31 December 2003 and 31 December 2004, prepare a complete cash flow statement for Medco Ltd for the year to 31 December 2004.

During the year 2004 the company:

(i)   acquired new fixed assets that cost £12,500

(ii)   issued new share capital for £5,000

(iii) sold fixed assets for £2,000 that had originally cost £3,000 and had a net book value of £2,500

(iv) depreciated its fixed assets by £2,000.

Figures in £

	2004
Profit and loss account	
Operating profit	2,500
Interest	(100)
Profit before tax	2,400
Tax	(500)
Profit on ordinary activities after tax	1,900
Interim dividend	(300)
Final dividend	(600)
Retained profit	1,000

Balance sheet as at 31 December	2004	2003
Fixed assets	28,000	20,000
Current assets		
Stocks	6,000	5,000
Debtors	4,000	3,000
Investments	5,100	3,000
Cash and bank	2,150	5,000
Creditors due in less than one year		
Overdraft	(6,000)	(2,000)
Trade creditors	(4,000)	(6,000)
Taxation	(500)	(400)
Dividend (proposed)	(600)	(450)
Creditors due in over one year		
Loan	(2,000)	(1,000)
Net assets	32,150	26,150
Capital and reserves		
Ordinary shares	14,000	10,000
Share premium	6,000	5,000
Profit and loss account	12,150	11,150
	32,150	26,150

Level II

E4.5 *Time allowed – 90 minutes*

Llareggyb Ltd started business on 1 January 2005 and its year ended 31 December 2005. Llareggyb made the following transactions during the year.

Received funds for share capital of £25,000

Paid suppliers of materials £44,000

Purchased 11,000 units of materials at £8 per unit, one of which was required in one unit of finished goods

Heating and lighting costs paid for cash £16,000

Further heating and lighting costs £2,400 were incurred within the year, but unpaid at 31 December 2005

Mr D Thomas loaned the company £80,000 on 1 January 2005 at 8% per annum

Loan interest was paid to Mr Thomas for January to June 2005

8,000 finished goods units were sold to customers at £40 each

Customers paid £280,000 to Llareggyb for sales of finished goods

Rent on the premises £60,000 was paid for 18 months from 1 January 2005, and business rates of £9,000 for the same period were also paid

Salaries and wages were paid for January to November amounting to £132,000 but the December payroll cost of £15,000 had not been paid

A lorry was purchased for £45,000 on 1 January 2005 and was expected to last for 5 years after which it could be sold for £8,000. The company uses the straight line method of depreciation.

You are required to:

(i)   **prepare a balance sheet for Llareggyb Ltd as at 31 December 2005**
(ii)   **prepare a cash flow statement for Llareggyb Ltd for the year ended 31 December 2005.**

(Note: you may use the profit or loss figure calculated in Exercise E3.7 to complete this exercise.)

E4.6 *Time allowed – 90 minutes*

The balance sheets for Victoria plc as at 30 June 2003 and 30 June 2004 are shown below:

Victoria plc
Balance sheet as at 30 June

Figures in £000	2003	2004
Fixed assets		
Cost	6,900	9,000
Depreciation provision	(900)	(1,100)
	6,000	7,900
Current assets		
Stocks	2,600	4,000
Trade debtors	2,000	2,680
Cash and bank	200	–
	4,800	6,680

Creditors due within one year

Overdraft	–	600
Trade creditors	2,000	1,800
Tax payable	300	320
Dividend payable	360	480
	2,660	3,200
Net current assets	2,140	3,480
Total assets less current liabilities	8,140	11,380
less		
Creditors due in over one year		
10% Debentures	(1,000)	(1,000)
Net assets	7,140	10,380
Capital and reserves		
Ordinary share capital	4,000	5,500
Share premium	–	1,240
Profit and loss account	3,140	3,640
	7,140	10,380

The following information is also relevant:

1. During the years 2003 and 2004 Victoria plc disposed of no fixed assets.
2. Interim dividends were not paid during the years ended 30 June 2003 and 2004.
3. Debenture interest was paid on 10 February in each year.

You are required to:

(i)   calculate:
  (a)   **profit before tax for the year ended 30 June 2004**
  (b)   **operating profit for the year ended 30 June 2004**
(ii) **prepare a cash flow statement for Victoria plc for the year to 30 June 2004 that includes all supporting schedules and an analysis of change in net debt.**

E4.7 *Time allowed – 90 minutes*
Sparklers plc have completed the preparation of their profit and loss account for the year ended 31 October 2004 and their balance sheet as at 31 October 2004. During the year Sparklers sold for £2m some fixed assets that had originally cost £11m. The cumulative depreciation on those assets at 31 October 2003 was £7.6m.

You have been asked to prepare a full cash flow statement for the same period in compliance with the provisions contained in FRS 1. The directors are concerned about the large bank overdraft at 31 October 2004 which they believe is due mainly to the increase in trade debtors as a result of apparently poor credit control. What is your assessment of the reasons for the increased overdraft?

Sparklers plc
Profit and loss account for the year ended 31 October 2004

	2004 £m	2003 £m
Operating profit	41.28	18.80
Interest paid	(0.56)	–
Interest received	0.08	0.20
Profit before tax	40.80	19.00
Tax on profit on ordinary activities	(10.40)	(6.40)
Profit after tax	30.40	12.60
Dividends		
Preference paid	(0.20)	(0.20)
Ordinary: interim paid	(4.00)	(2.00)
final proposed	(12.00)	(6.00)
Retained profit for the financial year	14.20	4.40

Sparklers plc
Balance sheet as at 31 October 2004

	2004 £m	2003 £m
Fixed assets		
Tangible at cost	47.80	35.20
Depreciation	(21.50)	(19.00)
	26.30	16.20
Current assets		
Stocks	30.00	10.00
Debtors	53.40	17.20
Prepayments	0.80	0.60
Cash and bank	–	1.20
	84.20	29.00
Current liabilities (less than one year)		
Overdraft	32.40	–
Creditors	20.00	12.00
Accruals	2.00	1.60
Dividends	12.00	6.00
Taxation	10.40	6.40
	76.80	26.00
Net current assets	7.40	3.00
Total assets less current liabilities	33.70	19.20
less		
Long-term liabilities (over one year)		
Debenture	1.50	1.20
Net assets	32.20	18.00

Capital and reserves

£1 ordinary shares	10.00	10.00
£1 preferences shares 10%	2.00	2.00
Profit and loss account	20.20	6.00
	32.20	18.00

E4.8 *Time allowed – 90 minutes*

Dimarian plc's profit and loss account for the year ended 31 December 2004, and its balance sheets as at 31 December 2004 and 2003, are shown below. Dimarian plc issued no new ordinary shares during the year.

During 2004 Dimarian plc spent £100,000 on fixed assets additions. There were no fixed assets disposals during 2004.

Dimarian plc
Profit and loss account for the year ended 31 December 2004

Figures in £000

Turnover	850
Cost of sales	(500)
Gross profit	350
Distribution and administrative costs	(120)
	230
Other operating income	20
Operating profit	250
Interest receivable	10
	260
Interest payable	(30)
Profit before tax	230
Tax on profit on ordinary activities	(50)
Profit on ordinary activities after tax	180
Retained profit 1 January 2004	230
	410
Proposed dividends	(80)
Retained profit 31 December 2004	330

Dimarian plc
Balance sheet as at 31 December 2004

Figures in £000	**2004**	**2003**
Fixed assets		
Intangible	40	50
Tangible	750	800
	790	850

Current assets

Stocks	50	60
Debtors	170	160
Prepayments	20	40
Cash and bank	20	10
	260	270

Current liabilities (less than one year)

Overdraft	20	10
Creditors	40	60
Accruals	30	20
Dividends	80	70
Taxation	50	30
	220	190
Net current assets	40	80

Total assets less current liabilities	830	930

less

Long-term liabilities (over one year)

Debenture	100	300
Net assets	730	630

Capital and reserves

Share capital	260	260
Share premium	50	50
Revaluation reserve	90	90
Profit and loss account	330	230
	730	630

Required:

(i)   Prepare an operating cash flow reconciliation statement for the year to 31 December 2004.

(ii) Prepare a cash flow statement for the year ended 31 December 2004, in the format used by UK plcs.

(iii) Include an analysis of change in net debt/funds from 31 December 2003 to 31 December 2004.

5

Business performance analysis

Contents

Learning objectives

Completion of this chapter will enable you to:

- carry out a performance review of a business, including the use of SWOT analysis
- critically evaluate the limitations of the performance review process
- differentiate between divisional manager performance measurement and economic performance measurement
- analyse business performance through the use of ratio analysis of profitability; efficiency; liquidity; investment; financial structure
- use both profit and cash flow in the measurement of business performance
- critically compare the use of cash flow versus profit as the best measure in the evaluation of financial performance
- use earnings before interest, tax, depreciation and amortisation (EBITDA) as a close approximation of a cash flow performance measure.

Introduction

Chapters 2, 3, and 4 introduced us to the financial statements of limited companies. This chapter is concerned with how the performance of a business may be reviewed through analysis and evaluation of the balance sheet, the profit and loss account, and the cash flow statement. Business performance may be considered from outside or within the business for a variety of reasons. The performance review process provides an understanding of the business which, together with an analysis of all the relevant information, enables interpretation and evaluation of its financial performance during successive accounting periods and its financial position at the end of those accounting periods.

The chapter begins with an outline of the steps involved in the performance review process and also considers the limitations of such a process. The main body of this chapter is concerned with ratio analysis. Financial ratio analysis looks at the detailed use of profitability, efficiency, liquidity, investment, and financial structure ratios in the evaluation of financial performance.

The chapter closes with a discussion about which is the best measure of performance – cash or profit. The use of earnings per share and cash flow in performance measurement are discussed along with the measurement of earnings before interest, tax, depreciation and amortisation (EBITDA) as an approximation of cash flow. The debate continues as to whether cash flow or profit represents the best basis for financial performance measurement.

In Chapter 6 we shall build on the knowledge gained from the current chapter when we examine the published report and accounts of a major UK plc, Johnson Matthey.

The performance review process

A performance review using financial statements may be undertaken for a number of reasons, for example:

- to assist in investment decisions

- to identify possible takeover targets
- to evaluate the financial strength of potential or existing customers or suppliers.

The main aim of a performance review is to provide an understanding of the business, and, together with an analysis of all the relevant information, provide an interpretation of the results. A performance review is generally undertaken using a standard format and methodology. The most effective performance review is provided from a balanced view of each of the activities of the organisation, which necessarily involves the close cooperation of each role: marketing; research and development; design; engineering; manufacturing; sales; logistics; finance; human resources management.

The performance review process begins with a SWOT analysis and works through a number of steps to the conclusions, as outlined in Fig. 5.1. A SWOT analysis includes an internal analysis of the company, and an analysis of the company's position with regard to its external environment.

1. SWOT analysis

SWOT is shorthand for strengths, weaknesses, opportunities and threats. The first look at a company's performance usually involves listing the key features of the company by looking internally at its particular strengths and weaknesses, and externally at risks or threats to the company and opportunities that it may be able to exploit. The SWOT analysis may give some indication of, for example, the strength of the company's management team, how well it is doing on product quality, and areas as yet untapped within its marketplace.

To keep the analysis focused, a cruciform chart may be used for SWOT analysis. An example is outlined in Fig. 5.2, relating to a fictitious company in the 1990s which manufactured components for supply to automotive manufacturers.

Figure 5.1 The stages of performance review

STRENGTHS	WEAKNESSES
Market share	Slow product development
Part of a large diversified group	Products designed not easy to manufacture
OPPORTUNITIES	THREATS
European joint ventures	Japanese transplant manufacturers
Market share of Japanese manufacturers	European economic recession

Figure 5.2 An example of a SWOT analysis

2. Consideration of major features

The increasing amount of information now provided in published financial statements enables the analyst to look in detail at the various industrial and geographical sectors of the business, the trends within these and the business in general. Further background information may be extracted from the accounting policies, the auditors' report, chairman's report and details of any significant events that have been highlighted.

3. Profitability

A number of financial indicators and ratios may be considered to assess the profitability of the company, which include:

- ROCE (return on capital employed), or ROI (return on investment)
- return on sales (ROS)
- gross margin to sales
- asset turnover
- earnings per share (eps)
- dividend cover
- price earnings ratio (P/E).

4. Efficiency

The efficiency of the company may be considered in terms of:

- its operating cycle – its debtor days, creditor days, and stock days
- its operating gearing
- vertical analysis of its profit and loss account (which we will look at in Chapter 6).

In a vertical analysis of the profit and loss account (which may also be applied to the balance sheet) each item is expressed as a percentage of the total sales. The vertical analysis provides evidence of structural changes in the accounts such as increased profitability through more efficient production.

5. Growth

Growth of the organisation may relate to sales growth and gross margin growth. Horizontal analysis (which we will look at in Chapter 6), or common size analysis, of the profit and loss account allows a line-by-line analysis of the accounts compared with those of the previous year. It may provide over a number of years a trend of changes showing either growth or decline in these elements of the accounts by calculation of annual percentage growth rates in profits, sales, stock or any other item.

6. Liquidity

Liquidity is concerned with the short-term solvency of the company. It is assessed by looking at a number of key ratios:

- current ratio
- acid test
- defensive interval
- cash ROCE
- cash interest cover.

7. Finance

How the company is financed is concerned with the long-term solvency of the company. It is assessed by looking at a number of other key ratios:

- gearing – the proportion of capital employed financed by lenders rather than shareholders, expressed in a number of ways, for example the debt/equity ratio (long-term loans and preference shares/ordinary shareholders' funds)
- dividend cover (eps/dividend per share)
- interest cover (PBIT/interest payable)
- various forms of off balance sheet financing.

Off balance sheet financing is defined as the funding or refinancing of a company's operations in such a way that, under legal requirements and existing accounting conventions, some or all of the finance may not be disclosed in its balance sheet. The Accounting Standards Board (ASB) has tried (and indeed continues to try) to introduce regulations forcing the inclusion of this type of financing.

8. Management of financial risk

The global market is here. Companies increasingly trade multinationally with greater levels of sophistication in products, operations, and finance. Risk assessment and the management of risk are therefore now assuming increasing importance. The main areas of risk are the areas of investment, foreign currency exchange rates and interest rates, and levels of trade credit.

9. Investment

Investment ratios examine whether or not the company is undertaking sufficient investment to ensure its future profitability. These ratios include, for example:

- capital expenditure/sales
- capital expenditure/depreciation
- capital expenditure/gross fixed assets.

10. Conclusions

The conclusion of the performance review will include consideration of the company's SWOT analysis and the main performance features. It will consider growth and profitability and whether or not this is maintainable, as well as levels of finance and investment, and whether there is sufficient cash flow, and the future plans of the business.

All performance reviews must use some sort of benchmark. Comparisons may be made against past periods and against budget; they may also be made against other companies and using general data relating to the industry within which the company operates. Later in this chapter we will look in more detail at the use of profitability, efficiency, liquidity, and investment ratios, and ratios relating to financial structure.

> **Progress check 5.1 Describe each of the stages in a business performance review process.**

Limitations of the performance review process

There are many obvious limitations to the above approach. In comparing performance against other companies (and sometimes within the company in comparing past periods), or looking at industrial data, it should be borne in mind that:

- there may be a lack of uniformity in accounting definitions and techniques
- the balance sheet is only a snapshot in time, and only represents a single estimate of the company's position
- there may actually be no standards for comparison
- changes in the environment and changes in money values, together with short-term fluctuations, may have a significant impact
- the past should really not be relied on as a good predictor of the future.

The volatility and unpredictability of the computer games market is well understood by John Menzies who enjoyed considerable success with their sales of Pokemon games. The press extract on p. 153 indicates that John Menzies did not assume that they would continue indefinitely to be profitable in that market.

As the extract illustrates, John Menzies decided (as a likely result of a strategic review of their business) that it may not continue its distribution agreement with Nintendo, the maker of games consoles and the Pokemon games, and may also dispose of its toyshop chain the Early Learning Centre.

Diversified companies present a different set of problems. Such companies by their very nature are comprised of companies engaged in various industrial sectors, each having different market conditions, financial structures and expectations of performance. The notes to the accounts, which appear in each company's annual report and accounts, invariably present a less than comprehensive picture of the company's position.

As time goes by, and accounting standards and legislation get tighter and tighter, the number of

> **Progress check 5.2 What are the main limitations encountered in carrying out the performance review of a business?**

loopholes which allow any sort of window dressing of a company's results are reduced. Inevitably, however, there will always remain the possibility of the company's position being presented in ways that may not always represent the 'truth'. We will now look at the type of information that may be used and the important financial ratios and their meaning and relevance.

The past is not a good predictor of the future

Pikachu, the cuddly Pokémon character, helped to propel John Menzies, the distribution, retail and aviation services group, to pre-tax profits of £15.7 million before exceptionals, compared with just £4.1 million last time.

But David Mackay, John Menzies' chief executive, believes the Pokémon craze is dying out and the company will not extend the exclusive distribution agreement with Nintendo, maker of games consoles and Pokémon games.

Mr Mackay said: 'Pokémon was a unique and wonderful phenomenon but it is on the decline.' He added that the games market was volatile, unpredictable and about to suffer intense competition.

John Menzies is in the throes of being transformed into an aviation services business and, unsurprisingly, a raft of exceptionals clouded its interim account.

A £2.5 million gain on one disposal was more than offset by a £26.4 million loss on another, resulting in a pre-tax loss after exceptionals of £8.2 million.

A fall in operating losses at the Early Learning Centre, the toyshop chain, means that its disposal is likely.

Mr Mackay said: 'We are on track to be in profit this year but there will be no fire sale.'

John Menzies bought Ogden Ground Services, a major airport services group, for £76 million last November and will seek a reclassification from distribution to support services once ELC has been sold.

Robin Althaus, an analyst at Seymour Pierce, said: 'Menzies cannot be faulted so far in its re-invention but it is still an emerging picture.'

The interim dividend rises to 5.5p a share from 5p. The shares rose $5\frac{1}{2}$p to $426\frac{1}{2}$p yesterday.

Pokémon helps to lift Menzies, by Mark Court

© *The Times*, London, 24 January 2001

Economic performance measurement

Most large organisations are divided into separate divisions in which their individual managers have autonomy and total responsibility for investment and profit. Within each division there is usually a functional structure comprising many departments. Divisionalisation is more appropriate for companies with diversified activities. The performance of the managers of each division may be measured in a number of ways, for example return on investment (ROI) and residual income (RI).

The relationships between divisions should be regulated so that no division, by seeking to increase its own profit, can reduce the profitability of the company as a whole. Therefore, there are strong arguments for producing two broad types of performance measure. One type of measure is used to evaluate managerial performance and the other type of measure is used to evaluate economic performance.

Divisional performance measurement is discussed in Chapter 11. In the current chapter we are primarily concerned with the performance of the organisation as a whole. We will look at ratios that measure economic performance, which focus not only on profit and profitability, but on a range of other areas of performance that include, for example, cash and working capital.

Ratio analysis

The reasons for a performance review may be wide and varied. Generally, it is required to shed light on the extent to which the objectives of the company are being achieved. These objectives may be:

- to earn a satisfactory return on capital employed (ROCE)
- to maintain and enhance the financial position of the business with reference to the management of working capital, fixed assets and bank borrowings
- to achieve cost targets and other business targets such as improvements in labour productivity.

Ratio analysis is an important area of performance review. It is far more useful than merely considering absolute numbers, which on their own may have little meaning. Ratios may be used:

- for a subjective assessment of the company or its constituent parts
- for a more objective way to aid decision-making
- to provide cross-sectional analysis and inter-firm comparison
- to establish models for loan and credit ratings
- to provide equity valuation models to value businesses
- to analyse and identify underpriced shares and takeover targets
- to predict company failure.

There are various models that may be used to predict company failure such as those developed by John Argenti (*Corporate Collapse – the Causes and Symptoms*, 1976), and Edward Altman (*Corporate Financial Distress – A Complete Guide to Predicting, Avoiding and Dealing with Bankruptcy*, 1983). Altman's model is sometimes used for prediction of corporate failure by calculating what is called a *Z score* for each company. For a public industrial company if the *Z score* is greater than 2.99 then it is unlikely to fail, and if the score is less than 1.81 then it is likely to fail. Statistical analyses of financial ratios may further assist in this area of prediction of corporate failure, using for example time series and line of business analyses.

As we saw in our examination of the performance review process, the key ratios include the following categories:

- profitability
- efficiency
- liquidity
- investment
- financial structure.

The financial structure, or gearing, of the business will also be considered in further detail in Chapter 14 when we look at sources of finance and the cost of capital. In the current chapter we will use the financial statements of Flatco plc, an engineering company, shown in Figs. 5.3 to 5.9, to illustrate the calculation of the key financial ratios. The profit and loss account and cash flow statement are for the year ended 31 December 2005 and the balance sheet as at 31 December 2005. Comparative figures are shown for 2004.

Profitability ratios

It is generally accepted that the primary objective for the managers of a business is to maximise the wealth of the owners of the business. To this end there are a number of other objectives, subsidiary to the main objective. These include:

- survival
- stability
- growth
- maximisation of market share
- maximisation of sales

Flatco plc Balance sheet as at 31 December 2005		
Figures in £000	2005	2004
Fixed assets		
Intangible	416	425
Tangible	1,884	1,921
Financial	248	248
	2,548	2,594
Current assets		
Stocks	311	268
Debtors	573	517
Prepayments	589	617
Cash	327	17
	1,800	1,419
Current liabilities (less than one year)		
Financial debt	50	679
Creditors	553	461
Taxation	50	44
Dividends	70	67
Accruals	82	49
	805	1,300
Net current assets	995	119
Total assets		
less current liabilities	3,543	2,713
less		
Long-term liabilities		
Financial debt	173	–
Creditors	154	167
	327	167
less		
Provisions	222	222
Net assets	2,994	2,324
Capital and reserves		
Capital	1,200	1,000
Premiums	200	200
Profit and loss account	1,594	1,124
	2,994	2,324

Figure 5.3 Flatco plc balance sheet as at 31 December 2005

- maximisation of profit
- maximisation of return on capital.

Each group of financial ratios is concerned to some extent with survival, stability, growth and maximisation of shareholder wealth. We will first consider ratios in the broad area of profitability (see Fig. 5.10), which give an indication of how successful the business has been in its achievement of the wealth maximisation objective.

$$\text{gross margin } \% = \frac{\text{gross margin}}{\text{sales}} = \frac{\text{sales} - \text{cost of sales (COS)}}{\text{sales}}$$

Flatco plc
Profit and loss account for the year ended 31 December 2005

Figures in £000		2005		2004
Turnover				
Continuing operations		3,500		3,250
Discontinued operations		–		–
		3,500		3,250
Cost of sales		(2,500)		(2,400)
Gross profit		1,000		850
Distribution costs	(300)		(330)	
Administrative expenses	(155)		(160)	
Other operating costs				
Exceptional items: redundancy costs	(95)		–	
		(550)		(490)
Other operating income		100		90
Operating profit				
Continuing operations	550		450	
Discontinued operations	–		–	
		550		450
Income from other fixed asset investments		100		80
Profit before interest and tax		650		530
Net interest		(60)		(100)
Profit before tax		590		430
Tax on profit on ordinary activities		(50)		(44)
Profit on ordinary activities after tax		540		386
Dividends		(70)		(67)
Retained profit for the financial year		470		319

Additional information
Authorised and issued share capital 31 December 2005, 1,200,000 £1 ordinary shares
(1,000,000 in 2004).
Total assets less current liabilities 31 December 2003, £2,406,000.
Trade debtors 31 December 2003, £440,000.
Market value of ordinary shares in Flatco plc 31 December 2005, £2.75 (£3.00, 2004).
Tangible fixed assets depreciation provision 31 December 2005, £1,102,000 (£779,000, 2004).

Figure 5.4 Flatco profit and loss account for the year ended 31 December 2005

Flatco plc
Cash flow statement for the year ended 31 December 2005
Reconciliation of operating profit to net cash flow from operating activities

Figures in £000	2005	2004
Operating profit	550	450
Depreciation charges	345	293
Increase in stocks	(43)	(32)
Increase in debtors and prepayments [– 573 + 517 – 589 + 617]	(28)	(25)
Increase in creditors and accruals [553 – 461 + 82 – 49 + 154 – 167]	112	97
Net cash inflow from operating activities	936	783

Figure 5.5 Reconciliation of operating profit to net cash flow from operating activities

Cash flow statement

Figures in £000	2005	2004
Net cash inflow from operating activities	936	783
Returns on investments and servicing of finance (note 1)	40	(20)
Taxation	(44)	(40)
Capital expenditure (note 1)	(299)	(170)
	633	553
Equity dividends paid	(67)	(56)
	566	497
Management of liquid resources (note 1)	–	–
Financing (note 1)	373	290
Increase in cash	939	787

Figure 5.6 Cash flow statement

Reconciliation of net cash flow to movement in net debt (note 2)

Figures in £000	2005	2004
Increase in cash for the period	939	787
Cash inflow from increase in long-term debt	(173)	–
Change in net debt	766	787
Net debt at 1 January [17 – 679 – 0]	(662)	(1,449)
Net funds/net debt at 31 December [327 – 50 – 173]	104	(662)

Figure 5.7 Reconciliation of net cash flow to movement in net debt

Note 1 to the cash flow statement – gross cash flows

Figures in £000	2005	2004
Returns on investments and servicing of finance		
Income from investments	100	80
Interest received	11	–
Interest paid	(71)	(100)
	40	(20)
Capital expenditure		
Payments to acquire tangible fixed assets	(286)	(170)
Payments to acquire intangible fixed assets	(34)	–
Receipts from sales of tangible fixed assets	21	–
	(299)	(170)
Management of liquid resources		
Purchase of treasury bills	(200)	–
Sale of treasury bills	200	–
	–	–
Financing		
Issue of ordinary share capital	200	300
Debenture loan	173	–
Expenses paid in connection with share issues	–	(10)
	373	290

Figure 5.8 Note 1 – gross cash flows

Note 2 to the cash flow statement – analysis of change in net debt/funds			
Figures in £000	**At 1 January 2005**	**Cash flows**	**At 31 December 2005**
Cash in hand and at bank	17	310	327
Overdraft	(679)	629	(50)
Debenture	–	(173)	(173)
Total (debt)/funds	(662)	766	104
	At 1 January 2004	**Cash flows**	**At 31 December 2004**
Cash in hand and at bank	–	17	17
Overdraft	(1,449)	770	(679)
Total (debt)/funds	(1,449)	787	(662)

Figure 5.9 Note 2 – analysis of change in net debt/funds

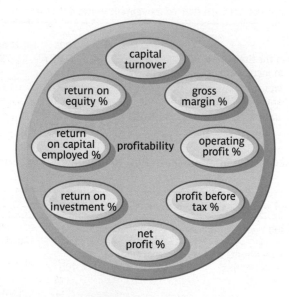

Figure 5.10 Profitability ratios

This is used to gain an insight into the relationship between production/purchasing costs and sales revenues. The gross margin needs to be high enough to cover all other costs incurred by the company, and leave an amount for profit. If the gross margin percentage is too low then sales prices may be too low, or the purchase costs of materials or production costs may be too high.

$$\text{operating profit \%} = \frac{\text{operating profit}}{\text{sales}} = \frac{\text{sales} - \text{COS} - \text{other operating expenses}}{\text{sales}}$$

The operating profit (or profit before interest and tax (PBIT) excluding other operating income) ratio is a key ratio that shows the profitability of the business before incurring financing costs. If the numerator is not multiplied by 100 to give a percentage, it shows the profit generated by each £1 of turnover.

$$\text{profit before tax (PBT) } \% = \frac{\text{profit before tax}}{\text{sales}} = \frac{\text{operating profit } +/- \text{ net interest}}{\text{sales}}$$

This is the profit ratio that uses profit after financing costs, that is, having allowed for interest payable and interest receivable. It should be remembered that profit before tax (PBT) is a profit measure that goes further than dealing with the trading performance of the business, in allowing for financing costs. It provides an indication of pre-tax profit-earning capability from the sales for the period.

$$\text{net profit } \% = \frac{\text{net profit}}{\text{sales}} = \frac{\text{profit before tax (PBT)} - \text{corporation tax}}{\text{sales}}$$

This is the final profit ratio after allowing for financing costs and corporation tax. Net profit or return on sales (ROS) is the profit available for distribution to shareholders in the form of dividends and/or future investment in the business.

$$\begin{array}{l}\text{return on investment (ROI)}\\ \text{or return on capital employed (ROCE) } \%\end{array} = \frac{\text{operating profit}}{\text{total assets} - \text{current liabilities}\\ \text{(usually averaged)}}$$

This is a form of return on capital employed (using pre-tax profit) which compares income with the operational assets used to generate that income. Profit is calculated before financing costs and tax. This is because the introduction of interest charges introduces the effect of financing decisions into an appraisal of operating performance, and tax levels are decided by external agencies (governments).

The average cost of the company's finance (equity, debentures, loans), weighted according to the proportion each element bears to the total pool of capital, is called WACC, the weighted average cost of capital. The difference between a company's ROI and its WACC is an important measure of the extent to which the organisation is endeavouring to optimise its use of financial resources. In their 1999 annual report, Tomkins plc reported on the improvement in their ROI versus WACC gap and stated that 'to be successful a company must consistently deliver a return on investment (ROI) above its weighted cost of capital (WACC) and must actively manage both variables'. A company manages its ROI through monitoring its operating profit as a percentage of its capital employed. A company manages its WACC by planning the proportions of its financing through either equity (ordinary shares) or debt (loans), with regard to the relative costs of each, dividends and interest.

In looking at acquisitions the importance of WACC is emphasised in the Tomkins plc 1999 annual report : 'Tomkins' strategy is to focus on strategic business activities and within this only to make acquisitions which add to shareholder value by enhancing earnings in the first year and deliver an ROI above the WACC hurdle rate (internal cost of capital) within three years.' This refers to the importance of WACC as a factor used in the evaluation of investment in projects undertaken (or not) by a business (see Chapters 13 and 14).

$$\text{return on equity (ROE)} = \frac{\text{profit after tax}}{\text{equity}}$$

Another form of return on capital employed, ROE measures the return to the owners on the book value of their investment in a company. The return is measured as the residual profit after all expenses and charges have been made, and the equity is comprised of share capital and reserves.

$$\text{capital turnover} = \frac{\text{sales}}{\text{average capital employed in year}}$$

The capital turnover expresses the number of times that capital is turned over in the year, or alternatively the sales generated by each £1 of capital employed. This ratio will be affected by capital additions that may have taken place throughout a period but have not impacted materially on the performance for that period. Further analysis may be required to determine the underlying performance.

The profitability performance measures discussed above consider the general performance of organisations as a whole. It is important for managers also to be aware of particular areas of revenue or expenditure that may have a significant importance with regard to their own company and that have a critical impact on the net profit of the business. Companies may, for example:

- suffer large warranty claim costs
- have to pay high royalty fees
- receive high volumes of customer debit notes (invoices) for a variety of product or service problems deemed to be the fault of the supplier.

All managers should fully appreciate such key items of cost specific to their own company and be innovative and proactive in identifying ways that these costs may be reduced and minimised.

Managers should also be aware of the general range of costs for which they may have no direct responsibility, but nevertheless may be able to reduce significantly by:

- improved communication
- involvement
- generation of ideas for waste reduction, increased effectiveness and cost reduction.

Such costs may include:

- the cost of the operating cycle
- costs of warehouse space
- project costs
- costs of holding stock
- depreciation (as a result of capital expenditure)
- warranty costs
- repairs and maintenance
- stationery costs
- telephone and fax costs
- photocopy costs.

The relative importance of these costs through their impact on profitability will of course vary from company to company.

Worked Example 5.1

We will calculate the profitability ratios for Flatco plc for 2005 and the comparative ratios for 2004, and comment on the profitability of Flatco plc.

Gross margin, GM

$$\text{gross margin \% 2005} = \frac{\text{gross margin}}{\text{sales}} = \frac{£1,000 \times 100\%}{£3,500} = 28.6\%$$

$$\text{gross margin \% 2004} = \frac{£850 \times 100\%}{£3,250} = 26.2\%$$

Profit before interest and tax, PBIT

$$\text{PBIT \% 2005} = \frac{\text{PBIT}}{\text{sales}} = \frac{£650 \times 100\%}{£3,500} = 18.6\%$$

$$\text{PBIT \% 2004} = \frac{£530 \times 100\%}{£3,250} = 16.3\%$$

Net profit, PAT (return on sales, ROS)

$$\text{PAT \% 2005} = \frac{\text{net profit}}{\text{sales}} = \frac{£540 \times 100\%}{£3,500} = 15.4\%$$

$$\text{PAT \% 2004} = \frac{£386 \times 100\%}{£3,250} = 11.9\%$$

Return on capital employed, ROCE (return on investment, ROI)

$$\text{ROCE \% 2005} = \frac{\text{operating profit}}{\substack{\text{total assets} - \text{current liabilities} \\ \text{(average capital employed)}}} = \frac{£550 \times 100\%}{(£3,543 + £2,713)/2}$$

$$= \frac{£550 \times 100\%}{£3,128} = 17.6\%$$

$$\text{ROCE \% 2004} = \frac{£450 \times 100\%}{(£2,713 + £2,406)/2} = \frac{£450 \times 100\%}{£2,559.5} = 17.6\%$$

Return on equity, ROE

$$\text{ROE \% 2005} = \frac{\text{PAT}}{\text{equity}} = \frac{£540 \times 100\%}{£2,994} = 18.0\%$$

$$\text{ROE \% 2004} = \frac{£386 \times 100\%}{£2,324} = 16.6\%$$

Capital turnover

$$\text{capital turnover 2005} = \frac{\text{sales}}{\text{average capital employed in year}} = \frac{£3,500 \times 100\%}{£3,128} = 1.1 \text{ times}$$

$$\text{capital turnover } 2004 = \frac{£3,250 \times 100\%}{£2,559.5} = 1.3 \text{ times}$$

Report on the profitability of Flatco plc

Sales for the year 2005 increased by 7.7% over the previous year, partly through increased volumes and partly through higher selling prices.

Gross margin improved from 26.2% to 28.6% of sales, as a result of increased selling prices but also lower costs of production.

PBIT improved from 16.3% to 18.6% of sales (and operating profit improved from 13.8% to 15.7%). If the one-off costs of redundancy of £95,000 had not been incurred in the year 2005 operating profit would have been £645,000 (£550,000 + £95,000) and the operating profit ratio would have been 18.4% of sales, an increase of 4.6% over 2004. The underlying improvement in operating profit performance (excluding the one-off redundancy costs) was achieved from the improvement in gross margin and from the benefits of lower distribution costs and administrative expenses.

ROCE was static at 17.6% because the increase in capital employed as a result of additional share capital of £200,000 and long-term loans of £173,000 was matched by a similar increase in operating profit.

Return on equity increased from 16.6% to 18%, despite the increase in ordinary share capital. This was because of improved profit after tax (up 3.5% to 15.4%) arising from increased income from fixed asset investments and lower costs of finance. Corporation tax was only marginally higher than the previous year despite higher pre-tax profits.

Capital turnover for 2005 dropped to 1.1 times from 1.3 times in 2004. The new capital introduced into the company in the year 2005 to finance major new projects is expected to result in significant increases in sales levels over the next few years, which will see improvements in capital turnover over and above 2004 levels.

> **Progress check 5.3** **How may financial ratio analysis be used as part of the process of review of business performance?**

Efficiency ratios

The regular monitoring of efficiency ratios by companies is crucial because they relate directly to how effectively business transactions are being converted into cash. For example, if companies are not regularly paid in accordance with their terms of trading:

- their profit margins may be eroded by the financing costs of funding overdue accounts
- cash flow shortfalls may put pressure on their ability to meet their day-to-day obligations to pay employees, replenish stocks, etc.

Despite the introduction of legislation to combat slow payment of suppliers, the general situation in the UK is poor in comparison with other European countries (see the following extract from *Accountancy Age*).

Companies that fail to pay suppliers on time

UK businesses could be losing up to £20bn every year in unpaid invoices, according to a report out today.

Intrum Justitia's UK Payment Index estimates that almost half (47%) of UK invoices are overdue – on average 18 days late – and 1.9% of total revenues are never paid at all.

The credit management service provider said the results of the survey clearly illustrated that payment delays put British businesses at risk. The increasing debt-to-income ratios significantly reduced profitability for companies – particularly SMEs who are vulnerable to variations in cash flow and often rely on a limited number of customers, it said.

Compared with Europe, the UK ranked poorly for payment delays, according to the company. The average 18 day UK payment delay is two days longer than in Ireland or the EU.

The research also reveals that UK creditors believe that one of the principal reasons for late payment is a deliberate decision on the part of debtors to use them as a 'source of free finance'. Another key reason cited was 'debtors' financial problems'.

'The consequence of payment delays on the public purse is also worrying – the UK government could be losing up to £10bn each year in lost VAT and corporation tax – the equivalent of the entire UK transport budget,' the report found.

Late payment costs UK companies £20bn, by Damian Wild

© *Accountancy Age*, 26 June 2004

The range of efficiency ratios is illustrated in Fig. 5.11.

Efficiency generally relates to the maximisation of output from resources devoted to an activity or the output required from a minimum input of resources. Efficiency ratios measure the efficiency with which such resources have been used.

$$\text{debtor days} = \frac{\text{trade debtors} \times 365}{\text{sales}}$$

Debtor days indicate the average time taken, in calendar days, to receive payment from credit

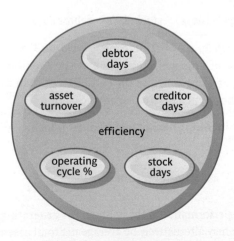

Figure 5.11 Efficiency ratios

customers. Adjustment is needed if the ratio is materially distorted by VAT (or other taxes). This is because sales invoices to customers, and therefore trade debtors (accounts receivable), include the net sales value plus VAT. However, sales are reported net of VAT. To provide a more accurate ratio, VAT may be eliminated from the trade debtors' figures as appropriate. (Note: for example, export and zero-rated sales invoices, which may be included in debtors, do not include VAT and so an adjustment to total trade debtors by the standard percentage rate for VAT may not be accurate.)

$$\text{creditor days} = \frac{\text{trade creditors} \times 365}{\text{cost of sales}} \quad \text{(or purchases)}$$

Creditor days indicate the average time taken, in calendar days, to pay for supplies received on credit. For the same reason, as in the calculation of debtor days, adjustment is needed if the ratio is materially distorted by VAT or other taxes.

$$\text{stock days} = \frac{\text{stock value}}{\text{average daily cost of sales in period}}$$

Stock days (or stock turnover) are the number of days that stocks could last at the forecast or most recent usage rate. This may be applied to total stocks, finished goods, raw materials, or work in progress. The weekly internal efficiency of stock utilisation is indicated by the following ratios:

$$\frac{\text{finished goods}}{\text{average weekly despatches}} \qquad \frac{\text{raw materials}}{\text{average weekly raw material usage}} \qquad \frac{\text{work in progress}}{\text{average weekly production}}$$

These ratios are usually calculated using values but may also be calculated using quantities where appropriate.

$$\text{stock weeks} = \frac{\text{total stock value}}{\text{average weekly cost of sales}} \text{ (total COS for the year divided by 52)}$$

Financial analysts usually only have access to published accounts and so they often use the stock weeks ratio using the total closing stocks value in relation to the cost of sales for the year.

$$\text{operating cycle (days)} = \text{stock days} + \text{debtor days} - \text{creditor days}$$

We discussed the operating cycle, or working capital cycle, in Chapter 2 when we looked at the balance sheet. It is the period of time which elapses between the point at which cash begins to be expended on the production of a product, and the collection of cash from the customer. The operating cycle may alternatively be calculated as a percentage using:

$$\text{operating cycle \%} = \frac{\text{working capital requirement (stocks + debtors - creditors)}}{\text{sales}}$$

$$\text{asset turnover (times)} = \frac{\text{sales}}{\text{total assets}}$$

Asset turnover measures the performance of the company in generating sales from the assets under its control. The denominator may alternatively be average net total assets.

Worked Example 5.2

We will calculate the efficiency ratios for Flatco plc for 2005 and the comparative ratios for 2004, and comment on the working capital performance of Flatco plc.

Debtor days

$$\text{debtor days } 2005 = \frac{\text{trade debtors} \times 365}{\text{sales}} = \frac{£573 \times 365}{£3,500} = 60 \text{ days}$$

$$\text{debtor days } 2004 = \frac{£517 \times 365}{£3,250} = 58 \text{ days}$$

Creditor days

$$\text{creditor days } 2005 = \frac{\text{trade creditors} \times 365}{\text{cost of sales}} = \frac{£553 \times 365}{£2,500} = 81 \text{ days}$$

$$\text{creditor days } 2004 = \frac{£461 \times 365}{£2,400} = 70 \text{ days}$$

Stock days (stock turnover)

$$\text{stock days } 2005 = \frac{\text{stock value}}{\text{average daily cost of sales in period}} = \frac{£311}{£2,500/365}$$

$$= 45 \text{ days (6.5 weeks)}$$

$$\text{stock days } 2004 = \frac{£268}{£2,400/365} = 41 \text{ days (5.9 weeks)}$$

Operating cycle days

$$\text{operating cycle } 2005 = \text{stock days} + \text{debtor days} - \text{creditor days}$$

$$= 45 + 60 - 81 = 24 \text{ days}$$

$$\text{operating cycle } 2004 = 41 + 58 - 70 = 29 \text{ days}$$

Operating cycle %

$$\text{operating cycle \% } 2005 = \frac{\text{working capital requirement}}{\text{sales}}$$

$$= \frac{(£311 + £573 - £553) \times 100\%}{£3,500} = 9.5\%$$

$$\text{operating cycle \% } 2004 = \frac{(£268 + £517 - £461) \times 100\%}{£3,250} = 10.0\%$$

Asset turnover

$$\text{asset turnover } 2005 = \frac{\text{sales}}{\text{total assets}} = \frac{£3,500}{£4,348} = 0.80 \text{ times} \quad [2,548 + 1,800]$$

$$\text{asset turnover } 2004 = \frac{£3,250}{£4,013} = 0.81 \text{ times} \qquad [2,594 + 1,419]$$

Report on the working capital performance of Flatco plc

The major cash improvement programme introduced late in the year 2005 began with the implementation of new cash collection procedures and a reinforced credit control department. This was not introduced early enough to see an improvement in the figures for the year 2005. Average customer settlement days actually worsened from 58 to 60 days.

The purchasing department negotiated terms of 90 days with a number of key large suppliers. This had the effect of improving the average creditors settlement period from 70 to 81 days.

A change in product mix during the latter part of the year 2005 resulted in a worsening of the average stock turnover period from 41 to 45 days. This is expected to be a temporary situation. An improved just in time (JIT) system and the use of vendor managed inventory (VMI) with two main suppliers in the year 2006 are expected to generate significant improvements in stock turnover.

Despite the poor stock turnover, the operating cycle improved from 29 days to 24 days (operating cycle % from 10.0% to 9.5%). Operating cycle days are expected to be zero or better by the end of year 2006.

Asset turnover dropped from 0.81 in 2004 to 0.80 times in the year 2005. The new capital introduced into the company in 2005 to finance major new projects is expected to result in significant increases in sales levels over the next few years which will see improvements in asset turnover over and above 2004 levels.

> **Progress check 5.4 What do the profitability and efficiency ratios tell us about the performance of a business?**

Liquidity ratios

The degree to which assets are held in a cash or near-cash form is determined by the level of obligations that need to be met by the business. Liquidity ratios (see Fig. 5.12) reflect the health or otherwise of the cash position of the business and its ability to meet its short-term obligations.

$$\text{current ratio (times)} = \frac{\text{current assets}}{\text{current liabilities}}$$

The current ratio is an overall measure of the liquidity of the business. It should be appreciated that this ratio will be different for different types of business. For example, an automotive manufacturer may have a higher ratio because of its relatively high level of stock (mainly work in progress) compared with a supermarket retailer which holds a very high percentage of fast-moving stocks.

$$\text{acid test (times)} = \frac{\text{current assets} - \text{stocks}}{\text{current liabilities}}$$

The acid test (or quick ratio) indicates the ability of the company to pay its creditors in the short term. This ratio may be particularly meaningful for supermarket retailers because of the speed with which their stocks are converted into cash.

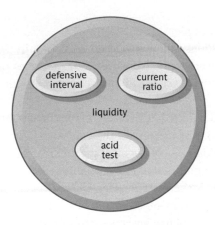

Figure 5.12 Liquidity ratios

$$\text{defensive interval (days)} = \frac{\text{quick assets}}{\text{average daily cash from operations}} \quad \text{(current assets - stocks)}$$

The defensive interval shows how many days a company could survive at its present level of operating activity if no inflow of cash were received from sales or other sources.

Worked Example 5.3

We will calculate the liquidity ratios for Flatco plc for 2005 and the comparative ratios for 2004, and comment on the liquidity of Flatco plc.

Current ratio

$$\text{current ratio } 2005 = \frac{\text{current assets}}{\text{current liabilities}} = \frac{£1,800}{£805} = 2.2 \text{ times}$$

$$\text{current ratio } 2004 = \frac{£1,419}{£1,300} = 1.1 \text{ times}$$

Acid test (quick ratio)

$$\text{quick ratio } 2005 = \frac{\text{current assets} - \text{stocks}}{\text{current liabilities}} = \frac{£1,800 - £311}{£805} = 1.8 \text{ times}$$

$$\text{quick ratio } 2004 = \frac{£1,419 - £268}{£1,300} = 0.9 \text{ times}$$

Defensive interval

$$\text{defensive interval } 2005 = \frac{\text{quick assets}}{\text{average daily cash from operations}}$$

$$\frac{}{(\text{opening debtors} + \text{sales} - \text{closing debtors})/365}$$

$$= \frac{£1,800 - £311}{(£517 + £3,500 - £573)/365} = 158 \text{ days}$$

$$\text{defensive interval } 2004 = \frac{£1,419 - £268}{(£440 + £3,250 - £517)/365} = 132 \text{ days}$$

Report on the liquidity of Flatco plc

Net cash flow from operations improved from £783,000 in 2004 to £936,000 in 2005. Investments in fixed assets were more than covered by increases in long-term finance in both years. Therefore, the operational cash flow improvement was reflected in the net cash flow of £939,000 (£787,000 2004).

The improved cash flow is reflected in increases in the current ratio (1.1 to 2.2 times) and the quick ratio (0.9 to 1.8 times). The increase in the defensive interval from 132 to 158 days has strengthened the position of the company against the threat of a possible downturn in activity.

Although there has been a significant improvement in cash flow, the increase in investment in working capital is a cause for concern. Actions have already been taken since the year end to try and maximise the returns on investment: reduction in stock levels (noted above); further reductions in trade debtors and prepayments; investment of surplus cash in longer term investments.

> **Progress check 5.5 What are liquidity ratios and why are they so important?**

Investment ratios

Investment ratios (see Fig. 5.13) generally indicate the extent to which the business is undertaking capital expenditure to ensure its survival, and stability and its ability to sustain current revenues and generate future increased revenues.

$$\text{earnings per share} = \frac{\text{profit after tax} - \text{preference share dividends}}{\text{number of ordinary shares in issue}}$$

Earnings per share, or eps, measures the return per share of earnings available to shareholders. The eps of companies may be found in the financial pages sections of the daily press.

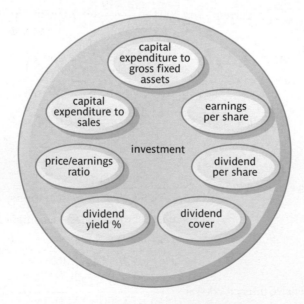

Figure 5.13 Investment ratios

$$\text{dividend per share} = \frac{\text{total dividends paid to ordinary shareholders}}{\text{number of ordinary shares in issue}}$$

Dividend per share is the total amount declared as dividends per each ordinary share in issue. It is the dividend per share actually paid in respect of the financial year. The amount must be adjusted if additional equity shares are issued during the financial year.

$$\text{dividend cover} = \frac{\text{earnings per share}}{\text{dividend per share}}$$

This shows the number of times the profits attributable to equity shareholders cover the dividends payable for the period.

$$\text{dividend yield \%} = \frac{\text{dividend per share}}{\text{share price}}$$

The dividend yield shows the dividend return on the market value of the shares, expressed as a percentage.

$$\text{price/earnings ratio} = \frac{\text{current share price}}{\text{eps}}$$

The price/earnings or P/E ratio shows the number of years it would take to recoup an equity investment from its share of the attributable equity profit. The P/E ratio values the shares of the company as a multiple of current or prospective earnings, and therefore gives a market view of the quality of the underlying earnings.

$$\text{capital expenditure to sales \%} = \frac{\text{capital expenditure for year}}{\text{sales}}$$

This ratio gives an indication of the level of capital expenditure incurred to sustain a particular level of sales.

$$\text{capital expenditure to gross fixed assets \%} = \frac{\text{capital expenditure for year}}{\text{gross value of tangible fixed assets}}$$

This is a very good ratio for giving an indication of the replacement rate of new for old fixed assets.

Worked Example 5.4

We will calculate the investment ratios for Flatco plc for 2005 and the comparative ratios for 2004, and comment on the investment performance of Flatco plc.

Earnings per share, eps

$$\text{eps 2005} = \frac{\text{profit after tax} - \text{preference share dividends}}{\text{number of ordinary shares in issue}} = \frac{£540,000 \times 100}{1,200,000} = 45\text{p}$$

$$\text{eps 2004} = \frac{£386,000 \times 100}{1,000,000} = 38.6\text{p}$$

Dividend per share

$$\text{dividend per share } 2005 = \frac{\text{total dividends paid to ordinary shareholders}}{\text{number of ordinary shares in issue}}$$

$$= \frac{£70,000}{1,200,000} = 5.8\text{p per share}$$

$$\text{dividend per share } 2004 = \frac{£67,000}{1,000,000} = 6.7\text{p per share}$$

Dividend cover

$$\text{dividend cover } 2005 = \frac{\text{earnings per share}}{\text{dividend per share}}$$

$$= \frac{45\text{p}}{5.8\text{p}} = 7.8\text{ times}$$

$$\text{dividend cover } 2004 = \frac{38.6\text{p}}{6.7\text{p}} = 5.8\text{ times}$$

Dividend yield %

$$\text{dividend yield } 2005 = \frac{\text{dividend per share}}{\text{share price}}$$

$$= \frac{5.8\text{p} \times 100\%}{£2.75} = 2.11\%$$

$$\text{dividend yield } 2004 = \frac{6.7\text{p} \times 100\%}{£3.00} = 2.23\%$$

Price/earnings ratio, P/E

$$\text{P/E ratio } 2005 = \frac{\text{current share price}}{\text{eps}} = \frac{£2.75}{45\text{p}} = 6.1\text{ times}$$

$$\text{P/E ratio } 2004 = \frac{£3.00}{38.6\text{p}} = 7.8\text{ times}$$

Capital expenditure to sales %

$$\text{capital expenditure to sales } 2005 = \frac{\text{capital expenditure for year}}{\text{sales}} = \frac{£286 \times 100\%}{£3,500} = 8.2\%$$

$$\text{capital expenditure to sales } 2004 = \frac{£170 \times 100\%}{£3,250} = 5.2\%$$

Capital expenditure to gross fixed assets %

$$\text{capital expenditure to gross fixed assets } 2005 =$$

$$\frac{\text{capital expenditure for year}}{\text{gross value of tangible fixed assets}} = \frac{£286 \times 100\%}{(£1,884 + £1,102)} = 9.6\%$$

$$\text{net book value + cumulative depreciation provision}$$

$$\text{capital expenditure to gross fixed assets } 2004 = \frac{£170 \times 100\%}{(£1,921 + £779)} = 6.3\%$$

Report on the investment performance of Flatco plc

The improved profit performance was reflected in improved earnings per share from 38.6p to 45p. However, the price/earnings ratio dropped from 7.8 to 6.1 times.

The board of directors reduced the dividend for the year to 5.8p per share from 6.7p per share in 2004, establishing a dividend cover of 7.8 times. The dividend yield reduced from 2.23% at 31 December 2004 to 2.11% at 31 December 2005. The increase in the capital expenditure to sales ratio from 5.2% to 8.2% indicates the company's ability to both sustain and improve upon current sales levels.

The increase in the capital expenditure to gross fixed assets ratio from 6.3% to 9.6% demonstrates the policy of Flatco for ongoing replacement of old assets for new in order to keep ahead of the technology in which the business is engaged.

> **Progress check 5.6** **What are investment ratios and what is their purpose?**

Financial ratios

Financial ratios (see Fig. 5.14) are generally concerned with the relationship between debt and equity capital, the financial structure of an organisation. This relationship is called gearing. Gearing is discussed in detail in Chapter 14. The ratios that follow are the two most commonly used. Both ratios relate to financial gearing, which is the relationship between a company's borrowings, which includes both prior charge capital and long-term debt, and its shareholders' funds (share capital plus reserves).

$$\text{gearing} = \frac{\text{long-term debt}}{\text{equity} + \text{long-term debt}}$$

and

$$\text{debt/equity ratio or leverage} = \frac{\text{long-term debt}}{\text{equity}}$$

These ratios are both equally acceptable in describing the relative proportions of debt and equity used to finance a business. Gearing calculations can be made in other ways, and in addition to those based on capital values may also be based on earnings/interest relationships, for example:

$$\text{dividend cover (times)} = \frac{\text{earnings per share (eps)}}{\text{dividend per share}}$$

This ratio indicates the number of times the profits attributable to the equity shareholders covers the actual dividends paid and payable for the period. Financial analysts usually adjust their calculations for any exceptional or extraordinary items of which they may be aware.

$$\text{interest cover (times)} = \frac{\text{profit before interest and tax}}{\text{interest payable}}$$

This ratio calculates the number of times the interest payable is covered by profits available for such payments. It is particularly important for lenders to determine the vulnerability of interest payments to a drop in profit.

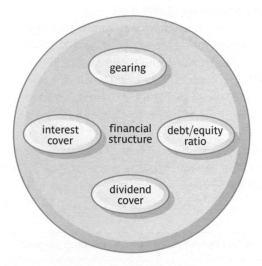

Figure 5.14 Financial ratios

Worked Example 5.5

We will calculate the financial ratios for Flatco plc for 2005 and the comparative ratios for 2004, and comment on the financial structure of Flatco plc.

Gearing

$$\text{gearing } 2005 = \frac{\text{long-term debt}}{\text{equity} + \text{long-term debt}} = \frac{£173 \times 100\%}{(£2{,}994 + £173)} = 5.5\%$$

$$\text{gearing } 2004 = \frac{£0 \times 100\%}{(£2{,}324 + £0)} = 0\%$$

Debt/equity ratio

$$\text{debt/equity ratio } 2005 = \frac{\text{long-term debt}}{\text{equity}} = \frac{£173 \times 100\%}{£2{,}994} = 5.8\%$$

$$\text{debt/equity ratio } 2004 = \frac{£0 \times 100\%}{£2{,}324} = 0\%$$

Dividend cover

$$\text{dividend cover } 2005 = \frac{\text{earnings per share (eps)}}{\text{dividend per share}} = \frac{45p}{5.8p} = 7.8 \text{ times}$$

$$\text{dividend cover } 2004 = \frac{38.6p}{6.7p} = 5.8 \text{ times}$$

Interest cover

$$\text{interest cover } 2005 = \frac{\text{profit before interest and tax}}{\text{interest payable}} = \frac{£650}{£71} = 9.2 \text{ times}$$

$$\text{interest cover } 2004 = \frac{£530}{£100} = 5.3 \text{ times}$$

Report on the financial structure of Flatco plc

In 2004 Flatco plc was financed totally by equity, reflected in its zero gearing and debt/equity ratios for that year. Flatco plc was still very low geared in 2005, with gearing of 5.5% and debt/equity of 5.8%. This is because its debt of £173,000 at 31 December 2005 is very small compared with its equity of £2,994,000 at the same date.

Earnings per share increased by 16.6% in 2005 compared with 2004. However, the board of directors reduced the dividend, at 5.8p per share for 2005, by 13.4% from 6.7p per share in 2004. This resulted in an increase in dividend cover from 5.8 times in 2004 to 7.8 times in 2005.

Interest payable was reduced by £29,000 in 2005 from the previous year, but PBIT was increased by £120,000 year on year. The result was that interest cover was nearly doubled from 5.3 times in 2004 to 9.2 times in 2005.

Progress check 5.7 **What are financial ratios and how may they be used to comment on the financial structure of an organisation?**

In this chapter we have looked at most of the key ratios for review of company performance and their meaning and relevance. However, the limitations we have already identified generally relating to performance review must always be borne in mind. In addition, it should be noted that the calculations used in business ratio analysis are based on past performance. These may not, therefore, reflect the current position of an organisation. Performance ratio analyses can also sometimes be misleading if their interpretation does not also consider other factors that may not always be easily quantifiable, and may include non-financial information, for example customer satisfaction, and delivery performance (see the section about non-financial performance indicators in Chapter 9). There may be inconsistencies in some of the measures used in ratio analysis. For example, sales numbers are reported net of VAT, but debtors and creditors numbers normally include VAT. Extreme care should therefore be taken with the conclusions used in any performance review to avoid reaching conclusions that may perhaps be erroneous.

If all the financial literature were thoroughly researched the number of different ratios that would be discovered would run into hundreds. It is most helpful to use a limited set of ratios and to fully understand their meaning. The ratios will certainly help with an understanding of the company but do not in themselves represent the complete picture.

Calculation of the ratios for one company for one year is also very limited. It is more relevant to compare companies operating in the same market and to analyse how a company has changed over the years. However, difficulties inevitably arise because it is sometimes impossible to find another company that is strictly comparable with the company being analysed. In addition, the company itself may have changed so much over recent years as to render meaningless any conclusions drawn from changes in ratios.

The best performance measure – cash or profit?

The importance of cash flow versus profit (or earnings per share) as a measure of company performance has increased over the past few years. The advantages and disadvantages in the use of each are shown in Figs. 5.15 and 5.16.

advantages	disadvantages
it cannot be hidden – like air in a balloon, one can see if it is going in or out	there are a number of different methods of analysing cash flow
generation of long-term cash flow is the real value of a company	cash flow analysis is not straightforward – it can sometimes be extremely complex
use of the discounted cash flow (DCF) method shows the added value to a company	it is sometimes difficult to obtain cash flow information
	it is difficult to compare the cash flows of different companies

Figure 5.15 The advantages and disadvantages of using cash flow as a measure of company performance

Worked Example 5.6

We will calculate the cash ROCE % for Flatco plc for 2005 and the comparative ratio for 2004, and compare with the equivalent profit ratio for Flatco plc.

Cash ROCE %

$$\text{cash ROCE \% 2005} = \frac{\text{net cash flow from operations}}{\text{average capital employed}} = \frac{£936 \times 100\%}{(£3{,}543 + £2{,}713)/2}$$

$$= \frac{£936 \times 100\%}{£3{,}128} = 29.9\%$$

$$\text{cash ROCE \% 2004} = \frac{£783 \times 100\%}{(£2{,}713 + £2{,}406)/2} = \frac{£783 \times 100\%}{£2{,}559.5} = 30.6\%$$

Report on the cash and profit ROCE of Flatco plc

Whilst the profit ROCE % was static at 17.6% for 2004 and 2005, the cash ROCE % reduced from

30.6% to 29.9%. Operating cash flow for 2005 increased by only 19.5% over 2004, despite the fact that operating profit for 2005 increased by 22.2% over 2004.

Operating profit before depreciation (EBITDA) was £895,000 [£550,000 + £345,000] for 2005, which was an increase of 20.5% over 2004 [£450,000 + £293,000 = £743,000]. If pre-depreciation operating profit had been used to calculate ROCE, it would have been 28.6% for 2005 compared with 29.0% for 2004, a reduction of 0.4% and more in line with the picture shown by the cash ROCE.

The chairman of Flatco plc expects that ROCE will be improved in 2006 as a result of:

- increased profitability resulting from higher sales levels generated from the investments in new projects
- reduction in levels of working capital, with more efficient use of company resources.

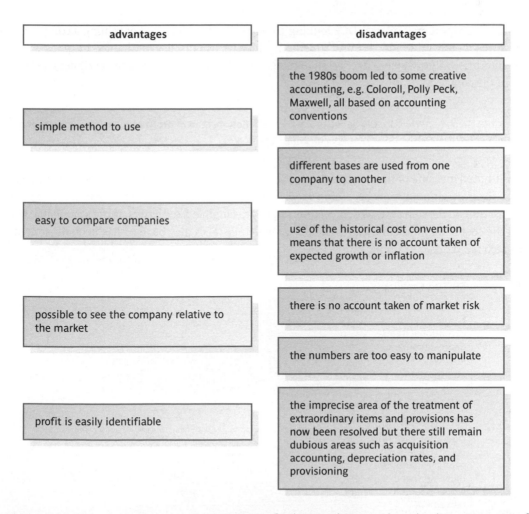

Figure 5.16 The advantages and disadvantages of using earnings per share (eps) as a measure of company performance

Cash flow has assumed increasing importance and has gained popularity as a measure of performance because the profit and loss account has become somewhat discredited due to the unacceptable degree of subjectivity involved in its preparation. Some of the financial ratios that we have already looked at may be considered in cash terms, for example:

$$\text{cash ROCE \%} = \frac{\text{net cash flow from operations}}{\text{average capital employed}}$$

and

$$\text{cash interest cover} = \frac{\text{net cash inflow from operations} + \text{interest received}}{\text{interest paid}}$$

which, in cash terms, calculates the number of times the interest payable is covered by cash available for such payments.

The increasing importance of cash flow as a measure of performance has led to new methods of measurement:

- the Rappaport method uses DCF looking 10 years ahead as a method of valuing a company
- the economic value added (EVA™) method, which we will discuss in Chapter 14 (p. 539)
- enterprise value, which is a very similar method to EVA, which excludes the peripheral activities of the company.

> **Progress check 5.8** **What are the benefits of using cash flow instead of profit to measure financial performance? What are the disadvantages of using cash flow?**

A profit-based measure of financial performance EBITDA, or earnings before interest, tax, depreciation, and amortisation, is now becoming widely used as an approximation to operational cash flow. Amortisation, in the same way as depreciation applies to tangible fixed assets, is the systematic write-off of the cost of an intangible asset. The way in which EBITDA may be used has been illustrated in the Flatco plc Worked Example 5.6.

Figure 5.17 Tomkins plc EBITDA and operating cash flow for 1998 to 2002

Tomkins plc, in their 1999 annual report, commented on their use of EBITDA as a performance measure. 'Sophisticated investors increasingly employ a range of measures when assessing the financial health and value of a company, diversifying into cash-based yardsticks from a simplistic earnings per share test. EBITDA is becoming widely accepted as a reliable guide to operational cash flow.'

Graphs showing Tompkins plc's EBITDA and operating cash flows derived from EDITDA for the years 1998 to 2002, which were included in the group's annual report for the year 2002, are shown in Fig. 5.17.

We have seen that the method of performance measurement is not a clear-cut cash or profit choice. It is generally useful to use both. However, many analysts and the financial press in general continue to depend heavily on profit performance measures with a strong emphasis on earnings per share (eps) and the price/earnings ratio (P/E).

Summary of key points

- The main aims of a business performance review are to provide an understanding of the business and provide an interpretation of results.
- Care must be taken in reviewing business performance, primarily because of lack of consistency in definitions, and changes in economic conditions.
- An important area of business performance review is the use of ratio analysis looking at profitability, efficiency, liquidity, investment, and also growth and financial structure.
- Cash flow and cash ratios are becoming increasingly as important as profit and profitability ratios in the measurement of business performance.
- There is no best way of evaluating financial performance and there are advantages and disadvantages in using earnings per share or cash flow as the basis of measurement.
- Earnings before interest, tax, depreciation and amortisation – EBITDA – is now commonly used as a close approximation of a cash flow performance measure.

Questions

Q5.1 (i) Who is likely to carry out a business performance review?

(ii) Describe what may be required from such reviews giving some examples from different industries and differing perspectives.

Q5.2 (i) Outline how the business performance review process may be used to evaluate the position of a dot.com company like Amazon UK.

(ii) What are the limitations to the approach that you have outlined?

Q5.3 How is ratio analysis, in terms of profitability ratios, efficiency ratios, liquidity ratios, and investment ratios, used to support the business review process?

Q5.4 Why should we be so careful when we try to compare the profit and loss account of a limited company with a similar business in the same industry?
(Hint: Research Tesco and Sainsbury on the Times CD-ROM for 1999 and 2000 for USA earnings and Far East earnings.)

Q5.5 (i) Why does profit continue to be the preferred basis for evaluation of the financial performance of a business?

(ii) In what ways can cash flow provide a better basis for performance evaluation, and how may cash flow be approximated?

Discussion points

D5.1 In what ways may the performance review process be used to anticipate and react to change?

D5.2 'Lies, damned lies, and statistics.' In which of these categories do you think ratio analysis sits, if at all?

Exercises

Solutions are provided in Appendix 4 to all exercise numbers highlighted in colour.

Level I

E5.1 *Time allowed – 30 minutes*
The information below relates to Priory Products plc's actual results for 2004 and 2005 and their budget for the year 2006.

Figures in £000

	2004	2005	2006
Cash at bank	100	0	0
Overdraft	0	50	200
Loans	200	200	600
Ordinary shares	100	200	400
Profit and loss account	200	300	400

You are required to calculate the following financial ratios for Priory Products for 2004, 2005, and 2006:

(i)   **debt/equity ratio (net debt to equity)**
(ii) **gearing (long-term loans to equity and long-term loans).**

E5.2 *Time allowed – 60 minutes*

From the financial statements of Freshco plc, a Lancashire-based grocery and general supplies chain supplying hotels and caterers, for the year ended 30 June 2005, prepare a report on performance using appropriate profitability ratios for comparison with the previous year.

Freshco plc
Balance sheet as at 30 June 2005

	2005	2004
	£m	£m
Fixed assets	146	149
Current assets		
Stocks	124	100
Debtors	70	80
Cash and bank	14	11
	208	191
Current liabilities (less than one year)		
Creditors	76	74
Dividends	20	13
Taxation	25	20
	121	107
Net current assets	87	84
Total assets less current liabilities	233	233
less		
Long-term liabilities (over one year)		
Debenture	20	67
Net assets	213	166
Capital and reserves		
Capital	111	100
General reserve	14	9
Profit and loss account	88	57
	213	166

Freshco plc
Profit and loss account for the year ended 30 June 2005

	2005 £m	2004 £m
Turnover	894	747
Cost of sales	(690)	(581)
Gross profit	204	166
Distribution and administrative costs	(101)	(79)
Operating profit	103	87
Other costs	(20)	(5)
Profit before interest and tax	83	82
Net interest	(2)	(8)
Profit before tax	81	74
Tax on profit on ordinary activities	(25)	(20)
Profit on ordinary activities after tax	56	54
Retained profit brought forward	57	16
	113	70
Dividends	(20)	(13)
	93	57
Transfer to general reserve	(5)	–
Retained profit for the financial year	88	57

Additional information:

(i)   Authorised and issued share capital 30 June 2005, £222m £0.50 ordinary shares (£200m, 2004).

(ii) Total assets less current liabilities 30 June 2003, £219m. Trade debtors 30 June 2003, £60m.

(iii) Market value of ordinary shares in Freshco plc 30 June 2005, £3.93 (£2.85, 2004).

(iv) Fixed assets depreciation provision 30 June 2005, £57m (£44m, 2004).

(v)   Depreciation charge for the year to 30 June 2005, £13m (£10m, 2004).

Freshco plc
Cash flow statement for the year ended 30 June 2005

Reconciliation of operating profit to net cash flow from operating activities

	2005 £m	2004 £m
Operating profit	103	87
Depreciation charges	13	10
Increase in stocks	(24)	(4)
Increase in debtors	(10)	(20)
Increase in creditors	2	4
Net cash inflow from operating activities	84	77

Cash flow statement

	2005 £m	2004 £m
Net cash inflow from operating activities	84	77
Returns on investments and servicing of finance	(2)	(8)
Taxation	(20)	(15)
Capital expenditure	(10)	(40)
	52	14
Equity dividends paid	(13)	(11)
	39	3
Management of liquid resources	–	–
Financing	(36)	7
Increase in cash	3	10

E5.3 *Time allowed – 60 minutes*
Using the financial statements of Freshco plc from Exercise E5.2, for the year ended 30 June 2005, prepare a report on performance using appropriate efficiency ratios for comparison with the previous year.

E5.4 *Time allowed – 60 minutes*
Using the financial statements of Freshco plc from Exercise E5.2, for the year ended 30 June 2005, prepare a report on performance using appropriate liquidity ratios for comparison with the previous year.

E5.5 *Time allowed – 60 minutes*
Using the financial statements of Freshco plc from Exercise E5.2, for the year ended 30 June 2005, prepare a report on performance using appropriate investment ratios for comparison with the previous year.

E5.6 *Time allowed – 60 minutes*
Using the financial statements of Freshco plc from Exercise E5.2, for the year ended 30 June 2005, prepare a report on performance using appropriate financial ratios for comparison with the previous year.

Level II

E5.7 *Time allowed – 60 minutes*

The summarised profit and loss account for the years ended 31 March 2003 and 2004 and balance sheets as at 31 March 2003 and 31 March 2004 for Boxer plc are shown below:

Boxer plc
Profit and loss account for the year ended 31 March

Figures in £000

	2003	2004
Turnover	5,200	5,600
Cost of sales	(3,200)	(3,400)
Gross profit	2,000	2,200
Expenses	(1,480)	(1,560)
Profit before tax	520	640

Boxer plc
Balance sheet as at 31 March

Figures in £000

	2003	2004
Fixed assets	4,520	5,840
Current assets		
Stocks	1,080	1,360
Trade debtors	640	880
Prepayments	40	80
Cash and bank	240	–
	2,000	2,320
Creditors due within one year		
Overdraft	–	160
Trade creditors	360	520
Tax payable	240	120
Dividend payable	280	384
	880	1,184
Net current assets	1,120	1,136
Total assets less current liabilities	5,640	6,976
less		
Creditors due in over one year		
Debentures	(1,200)	(1,200)
Net assets	4,440	5,776
Capital and reserves		
Ordinary share capital	4,000	5,200
Profit and loss account	440	576
	4,440	5,776

Required:

(i) Calculate the following ratios for the years 2003 and 2004:
 - (a) gross profit percentage
 - (b) profit before tax percentage
 - (c) return on capital employed
 - (d) debtor collection days
 - (e) creditor payment days
 - (f) stock turnover
 - (g) current ratio
 - (h) acid test ratio.

(ii) Comment on Boxer plc's financial performance over the two years and explain the importance of effective management of working capital.

E5.8 *Time allowed – 90 minutes*

The chief executive of Laurel plc, Al Chub, wants to know the strength of the financial position of Laurel's main competitor, Hardy plc. From Hardy's financial statements for the past three years he has asked you to write a report that evaluates the financial performance of Hardy plc and to include:

(i) a ratio analysis that looks at profitability, working capital, and liquidity

(ii) an identification of the top five areas which should be investigated further

(iii) details of information that has not been provided, but if it were available would improve your analysis of Hardy's performance.

Hardy plc
Balance sheet as at 31 March 2005

Figures in £m

	2003	2004	2005
Fixed assets	106	123	132
Current assets			
Stocks	118	152	147
Debtors	53	70	80
Cash and bank	26	29	26
	197	251	253
Current liabilities (less than 1 year)			
Trade creditors	26	38	38
Other creditors	40	52	55
	66	90	93
Net current assets	131	161	160
Total assets less current liabilities	237	284	292
less			
Long-term liabilities (over 1 year)			
Debenture	37	69	69
Net assets	200	215	223

Capital and reserves

Capital	50	50	50
Profit and loss account	150	165	173
	200	215	223

Hardy plc
Profit and loss account for the year ended 31 March 2005

Figures in £m

	2003	2004	2005
Turnover	420	491	456
Cost of sales	(277)	(323)	(295)
Gross profit	143	168	161
Distribution and administrative costs	(93)	(107)	(109)
Operating profit	50	61	52
Other costs	–	–	–
Profit before interest and tax	50	61	52
Net interest	(3)	(7)	(9)
Profit before tax	47	54	43
Tax on profit on ordinary activities	(22)	(26)	(23)
Profit on ordinary activities after tax	25	28	20
Dividends	(12)	(12)	(12)
Retained profit for the financial year	13	16	8

E5.9 *Time allowed – 120 minutes*
Locate the website for HSBC Bank plc on the Internet. Use their most recent annual report and accounts to prepare a report that evaluates their financial performance, financial position, and future prospects. Your report should include calculations of the appropriate ratios for comparison with the previous year.

E5.10 *Time allowed – 120 minutes*
Locate the websites for Tesco plc and Morrisons plc on the Internet. Use their most recent annual report and accounts to prepare a report that evaluates and compares their financial performance, and financial position. Your report should include calculations of the appropriate ratios for comparing the two groups, and an explanation of their differences and similarities.

Case Study I

BUZZARD LTD

Buzzard Ltd is a first-tier supplier to major passenger car and commercial vehicle manufacturers. As a first-tier supplier Buzzard provides systems that fit directly into motor vehicles, which they have manufactured from materials and components acquired from second, third, fourth-tier, etc., suppliers. During the 1990s, through investment in R&D and technology, Buzzard became regarded as one of the world's leaders in design, manufacture and supply of innovative automotive systems.

In the mid-1990s Buzzard started business in one of the UK's many development areas. It was established through acquisition of the business of Firefly from the Stonehead Group. Firefly was a traditional, mass-production automotive component manufacturer, located on a brownfield site in Gentbridge, once a fairly prosperous mining area. Firefly had pursued short-term profit rather than longer-term development strategies, and had a poor image with both its customers and suppliers. This represented a challenge but also an opportunity for Buzzard to establish a world-class manufacturing facility.

A major part of Buzzard's strategic plan was the commitment to investing £30m to relocate from Gentbridge to a new, fully equipped 15,000 square metre purpose-built factory on a 20-acre greenfield site in Bramblecote, which was finally completed during the year 2004. At the same time, it introduced the changes required to transform its culture and implement the operating strategies required to achieve the highest level of industrial performance. By 2004 Buzzard Ltd had become an established supplier of high quality and was close to achieving its aim of being a world-class supplier of innovative automotive systems.

In December 2004 a seven-year bank loan was agreed with interest payable half-yearly at a fixed rate of 8% per annum. The loan was secured with a floating charge over the assets of Buzzard Ltd.

The financial statements of Buzzard Ltd, its accounting policies and extracts from its notes to the accounts, for the year ended 31 December 2004, are shown below, prior to the payment of any proposed dividend. It should be noted that Note 3 to the accounts – Profit on ordinary activities before taxation – reports on some of the key items included in the profit and loss account for the year and is not a complete analysis of the profit and loss account.

Required

(i)   Prepare a SWOT analysis for Buzzard Ltd based on the limited information available.

(ii) What do you consider to be the main risks faced by Buzzard Ltd, both internally and external to the business, based on your SWOT analysis and your own research about the automotive industry in the UK?

(iii) Prepare a report for shareholders that describes Buzzard's performance, supported by the appropriate profitability, efficiency, liquidity, and investment ratios required to present as complete a picture as possible from the information that has been provided.

(iv) The company has demonstrated its achievement of high levels of quality and customer satisfaction but would you, as a shareholder, be satisfied with the financial performance of Buzzard Ltd?

Profit and loss account
for the year ended 31 December 2004

	Notes	2004 £000	2003 £000
Turnover	1	115,554	95,766
Cost of sales		(100,444)	(80,632)
Gross profit		15,110	15,134
Distribution costs		(724)	(324)
Administrative expenses		(12,348)	(10,894)
Operating profit		2,038	3,916
Net interest	2	(868)	(972)
Profit on ordinary activities before taxation	3	1,170	2,944
Taxation		–	–
Profit for the financial year		1,170	2,944

The company has no recognised gains and losses other than those included above, and therefore no separate statement of total recognised gains and losses has been presented.

Balance sheet
as at 31 December 2004

	Notes	2004 £000	2003 £000
Fixed assets			
Tangible assets	8	42,200	29,522
Current assets			
Stocks	9	5,702	4,144
Debtors	10	18,202	16,634
Cash at bank and in hand		4	12
		23,908	20,790
Creditors: amounts falling due within one year	11	(23,274)	(14,380)
Net current assets		634	6,410
Total assets less current liabilities		42,834	35,932
Creditors: amounts falling due after more than one year			
Borrowings and finance leases	12	(6,000)	–
Provisions for liabilities and charges	13	(1,356)	(1,508)
Accruals and deferred income	14	(1,264)	(1,380)
Net assets		34,214	33,044

Capital and reserves

Share capital	15	22,714	22,714
Profit and loss account		11,500	10,330
Shareholders' funds	16	34,214	33,044

Cash flow statement
for the year ended 31 December 2004

	2004	2003
	£000	**£000**
Net cash inflow from operating activities	12,962	3,622
Returns on investments and servicing of finance		
Interest received	268	76
Interest paid	(1,174)	(1,044)
Net cash outflow from returns on investments		
and servicing of finance	(906)	(968)
Capital expenditure		
Purchase of tangible fixed assets	(20,490)	(14,006)
Sale of tangible fixed assets	12	30
Government grants received	1,060	1,900
Net cash outflow from investing activities	(19,418)	(12,076)
Net cash inflow/(outflow) before financing	(7,362)	(9,422)
[Hint: 12,962 – 906 – 19,418]		
Financing		
Issue of ordinary share capital	–	8,000
Increase in borrowings	6,000	–
Net cash (outflow)/inflow from financing	6,000	8,000
Decrease in cash in the period	(1,362)	(1,422)

	2004	2003
	£000	**£000**
Note – reconciliation of net cash flows to the		
movement in net funds		
Decrease in cash in the period	(1,362)	(1,422)
Cash inflow from movement in borrowings	(6,000)	–
Opening net debt	(1,974)	(552)
Closing net debt	(9,336)	(1,974)

	2003 £000	Cash flow £000	2004 £000
Note – analysis of changes in net debt during the year			
Cash at bank and in hand	12	(8)	4
Overdraft	(1,986)	(1,354)	(3,340)
Borrowings due after one year	–	(6,000)	(6,000)
Net debt	(1,974)	(7,362)	(9,336)

Accounting policies

The financial statements have been prepared in accordance with applicable accounting standards. A summary of the more important accounting policies which have been applied consistently is set out below.

Basis of accounting   The accounts are prepared under the historical cost convention.

Research and development   Expenditure on research and development is written off as it is incurred.

Tangible fixed assets   Tangible fixed assets are stated at their purchase price together with any incidental costs of acquisition.

Depreciation is calculated so as to write off the cost of tangible fixed assets on a straight line basis over the expected useful economic lives of the assets concerned. The principal annual rates used for this purpose are:

Freehold buildings	20 years
Plant and machinery (including capitalised tooling)	4–8 years
Office equipment and fixtures and fittings	5–8 years
Motor vehicles	4 years

Freehold land is not depreciated.

Government grants   Grants received on qualifying expenditure or projects are credited to deferred income and amortised in the profit and loss account over the estimated useful lives of the qualifying assets or over the project life as appropriate.

Stocks and work in progress   Stocks and work in progress are stated at the lower of cost and net realisable value. In general, cost is determined on a first in first out basis; in the case of manufactured products cost includes all direct expenditure and production overheads based on the normal level of activity. Net realisable value is the price at which stocks can be sold in the normal course of business after allowing for the costs of realisation and, where appropriate, the cost of conversion from their existing state to a finished condition. Provision is made where necessary for obsolescent, slow-moving and defective stocks.

Foreign currencies   Assets, liabilities, revenues and costs denominated in foreign currencies are recorded at the rate of exchange ruling at the date of the transaction; monetary assets and liabilities at the balance sheet date are translated at the year-end rate of exchange or where there are related forward foreign exchange contracts, at contract rates. All exchange differences thus arising are reported as part of the results for the period.

Turnover   Turnover represents the invoiced value of goods supplied, excluding value added tax.

Warranties for products   Provision is made for the estimated liability arising on all known warranty claims. Provision is also made, using past experience, for potential warranty claims on all sales up to the balance sheet date.

Notes to the accounts

1 Segmental analysis

	Turnover		Profit on ordinary activities before taxation	
	2004 £000	2003 £000	2004 £000	2003 £000
Class of business				
Automotive components	115,554	95,766	1,170	2,944
Geographical segment				
United Kingdom	109,566	92,020		
Rest of Europe	5,290	3,746		
Japan	698	–		
	115,554	95,766		

2 Net interest

	2004 £000	2003 £000
Interest payable on bank loans and overdrafts	(1,182)	(1,048)
Interest receivable	314	76
	(868)	(972)

3 Profit on ordinary activities before taxation

	2004 £000	2003 £000
Profit on ordinary activities before taxation is stated **after crediting:**		
Amortisation of Government grant	1,176	796
(Loss)/profit on disposal of fixed assets	(18)	10
And after charging		
Depreciation charge for the year:		
Tangible owned fixed assets	7,782	4,742
Research and development expenditure	7,694	6,418
Auditors' remuneration for:		
Audit	58	58
Other services	40	52
Hire of plant and machinery – operating leases	376	346
Hire of other assets – operating leases	260	314
Foreign exchange losses	40	20

4 Directors and employees

The average weekly number of persons (including executive directors) employed during the year was:

	2004 number	2003 number
Production	298	303
Engineering, quality control and development	49	52
Sales and administration	56	45
	403	400

	2004 £000	2003 £000
Staff costs (for the above persons):		
Wages and salaries	6,632	5,837
Social security costs	562	483
Other pension costs	286	218
	7,480	6,538

8 Tangible fixed assets

	Freehold land and buildings	Motor vehicles	Plant, machinery and tooling	Office equipment, fixtures and fittings	Total
	£000	£000	£000	£000	£000
Cost					
At 1 January 2004	15,450	114	20,648	4,600	40,812
Additions	20	28	19,808	634	20,490
Disposals	–	–	(80)	(10)	(90)
At 31 December 2004	15,470	142	40,376	5,224	61,212
Depreciation					
At 1 January 2004	834	54	7,932	2,470	11,290
Charge for year	734	22	6,226	800	7,782
Eliminated in respect of disposals	–	–	(58)	(2)	(60)
At 31 December 2004	1,568	76	14,100	3,268	19,012
Net book value at 31 December 2004	13,902	66	26,276	1,956	42,200
Net book value at 31 December 2003	14,616	60	12,716	2,130	29,522

9 Stocks

	2004 £000	2003 £000
Raw materials and consumables	4,572	3,274
Work in progress	528	360
Finished goods and goods for resale	602	510
	5,702	4,144

10 Debtors

	2004 £000	2003 £000
Amounts falling due within one year		
Trade debtors	13,364	8,302
Other debtors	4,276	7,678
Prepayments and accrued income	562	654
	18,202	16,634

11 Creditors: amounts falling due within one year

	2004 £000	2003 £000
Overdraft	3,340	1,986
Trade creditors	13,806	8,646
Other taxation and social security payable	2,334	1,412
Other creditors	122	350
Accruals and deferred income	3,672	1,986
	23,274	14,380

12 Borrowings

	2004 £000	2003 £000
Bank and other loans repayable otherwise than by instalments		
Over five years	6,000	–

13 Provisions for liabilities and charges

	Pensions £000	Warranties for products £000	Total £000
At 1 January 2004	732	776	1,508
Expended in the year	(572)	(494)	(1,066)
Charge to profit and loss account	562	352	914
At 31 December 2004	722	634	1,356

14 Accruals and deferred income

	2004 £000	2003 £000
Government grants		
At 1 January 2004	1,380	2,176
Amount receivable	1,060	–
Amortisation in year	(1,176)	(796)
At 31 December 2004	1,264	1,380

15 Share capital

	2004 £000	2003 £000
Authorised		
28,000,000 (2003: 28,000,000) ordinary shares of £1 each	28,000	28,000
Issued and fully paid		
22,714,000 (2003: 22,714,000) ordinary shares of £1 each	22,714	22,714

16 Reconciliation of movement in shareholders' funds

	2004 £000	2003 £000
Opening shareholders' funds	33,044	22,100
Issue of ordinary share capital	–	8,000
Profit for the financial year	1,170	2,944
Closing shareholders' funds	34,214	33,044

17 Capital commitments

	2004 £000	2003 £000
Capital expenditure that has been contracted for but has not been provided for in the financial statements	1,506	162
Capital expenditure that has been authorised by the directors but has not yet been contracted for	6,768	5,404

18 Financial commitments

At 31 December 2004 the company had annual commitments under non-cancellable operating leases as follows:

	Land and Buildings 2004 £000	Other 2004 £000	Land and buildings 2003 £000	Other 2003 £000
Expiring within 1 year	–	96	112	210
Expiring within 2 to 5 years	–	254	–	360
Expiring after 5 years	–	120	–	90
	–	470	112	660

6

Published reports and accounts

Contents

Learning objectives

Completion of this chapter will enable you to:

- explain why annual reports and accounts of limited companies are filed and published
- recognise the key elements of the contents of the annual report and accounts of a typical public limited company
- evaluate the information disclosed within the annual report and accounts
- carry out a horizontal analysis of the profit and loss account and the balance sheet
- carry out a vertical analysis of the profit and loss account and the balance sheet
- interpret the information provided by segmental reporting
- critically evaluate the quality of corporate social responsibility (CSR) performance reporting within annual reports
- appreciate the impact of inflation on the financial performance of companies
- prepare and describe an alternative perception of the profit and loss account illustrated by the value added statement.

Introduction

This chapter builds on the business performance analysis techniques we introduced in Chapter 5. It is concerned with the type of information, both financial and non-financial, that is included in company annual reports and accounts. We will use the annual report and accounts of Johnson Matthey plc for the year 2004 to illustrate the financial statements of a large UK plc. We will not consider the whole of the Johnson Matthey plc annual report, a copy of which may be obtained from their head office in Trafalgar Square, London, UK. Further information about the company and copies of its report and accounts 2004 may be obtained from the Johnson Matthey website which is linked to the website accompanying this book at www.mcgraw-hill.co.uk/text-books/davies.

We will look at extracts from Johnson Matthey plc's report and accounts 2004, including the:

- chairman's statement
- chief executive's statement
- financial review
- accounting policies
- financial highlights
- financial statements
- segmental reporting
- corporate social responsibility (CSR) reporting
- directors' report.

The information disclosed in Johnson Matthey plc's report and accounts 2004 provides us with a broad picture of what sort of company Johnson Matthey is. The report and accounts include not only Johnson Matthey's historical financial performance, but also an indication of Johnson Matthey's prospects for the future. Included within the financial review is an example of how such a group manages risk.

In Chapter 5 we considered ratio analysis in our review of business performance. In this chapter we will look at some further tools of analysis. The first is horizontal analysis, or common size analysis, which provides a line-by-line comparison of the accounts of a company (profit and loss account and balance sheet) with those of the previous year. The second approach is the vertical analysis, where each item in the profit and loss account and balance sheet is expressed as a percentage of the total.

The reports and accounts of companies are now including more and more non-financial information, for example employee accident rates. Companies are also increasing generally their reporting on their corporate social responsibility performance. This includes areas such as health and safety, the environment, equal opportunities, employee development, and ethical issues. Johnson Matthey's report and accounts 2004 includes a comprehensive report on its corporate social responsibility performance, which is reproduced within this chapter.

The chapter closes with a look at the nature and purpose of the value added statement and its preparation. The value added statement is a variation on the profit and loss account and is concerned with measuring the value added by a business rather than the profit earned by the business.

An area of increasing importance now reported on in the annual reports and accounts of UK plcs is corporate governance. Corporate governance, including the role of auditors, will be covered in detail in Chapter 7.

Why are annual accounts filed and published?

After each year end, companies prepare their annual report and accounts, which include the financial statements and the auditors' report, for their shareholders. Copies of the annual report and accounts must be filed with the Registrar of Companies, and presented for approval by the shareholders at the company's annual general meeting (AGM). Further copies are usually made available to other interested parties such as financial institutions, major suppliers and other investors. The annual report and accounts of a plc usually takes the form of a glossy booklet which includes photographs of the directors, products and activities and other promotional material, and many non-financial performance measures, as well as the statutory legal and financial information. Large companies also issue half-yearly, or interim reports, which include the standard financial information, but the whole report is on a much smaller scale than the annual report.

The following press extract includes comments on the interim financial report published by Johnson Matthey plc for the first half of their financial year to 30 September 2003.

Johnson Matthey plc's pre-tax profits fell by 5% for the first six months of its financial year to 31 March 2004. Despite this, financial analysts lifted their share price forecasts because the results were better than they had expected, and because of the underlying strength of the company.

The publication of the annual report and accounts is of course always the time when such forecasts may be seen to have been justified or not. As it turned out, the figures were slightly below market expectations, and so the share price actually fell by 13% on announcement of the full year results to 31 March 2004. Johnson Matthey plc's report and accounts 2004 saw the profits of its pharmaceuticals division, which uses platinum products to create cancer drugs, increase by 16% over the previous year. Profits for the Johnson Matthey group as a whole rose 2.6% to £178m, while turnover increased

Interim financial reporting

Johnson Matthey, the precious metals and chemicals firm, said yesterday it is selling its ceramics business to concentrate on making catalytic converters.

The company said it expected a number of offers for its tiles and tableware businesses, which generate two-thirds of the profits at its colours and coatings arms.

Meanwhile, the company reported that total turnover had fallen 4pc to £2.17 billion in the first half.

Profits fell 5pc to £88.9m. It also raised its interim dividend 5pc to 8.2p.

The shares fell 3.3pc to £10.20 as investors digested that Johnson's renegotiated contract with producer Anglo Platinum would earn the company £1.5m less each year into the next decade.

It said the main reason for the loss was a 10pc drop in revenue from precious metals sales because of low palladium and rhodium prices. The weak US dollar also drove profits down by £2.8m.

Chief executive Chris Clark said: 'The new contract with Anglo Platinum is at a lesser rate than in previous years, but we expect the company's platinum output to increase considerably in coming years, which will more than outweigh the negative effects.'

The group said its catalytic converters arm, which nets just over half its earnings, was aided by buoyant car sales in Asia, offsetting disappointment in the West.

Pharmaceuticals, based on its platinum-based cancer drug, grew 8pc.

Johnson to sell ceramics side, by Edmund Conway

© *The Daily Telegraph*, 28 November 2003

by 3.9% to £4.5bn. The weakness of the US$, in which Johnson Matthey makes most of its sales, had a big impact on its 2004 results, and took £6.7m off the group's pre-tax profits.

Financial statements, whether to internal or external parties, are defined as summaries of accounts to provide information for interested parties. The key reports and statements within the published annual report and accounts are illustrated in Fig. 6.1.

In 1993 the Accounting Standards Board (ASB) issued a statement of good practice that supported the earlier suggestion made in the report of the Cadbury Committee (1992) that companies should include in their annual reports an operating and financial review (OFR) of the business. The reason for this suggestion was that businesses had become increasingly diversified and complex, and it had become increasingly difficult to understand information contained in financial reporting. Complex financial and organisational structures made it difficult to analyse and interpret financial information. It was felt that the OFR was needed to provide a greater insight into the affairs of the company, in addition to the information traditionally already provided by the chairman's statement and the directors' report.

The OFR was intended to cover the business as a whole for the year under review, and to include issues relevant to the assessment of future prospects. The OFR should include:

- brief reports that are easy to understand
- reports on each of the individual aspects of the business
- explanations of non-recurring aspects of the business
- discussion of matters that underpin the financial results for the period
- consideration of factors that might impact on the future performance of the business.

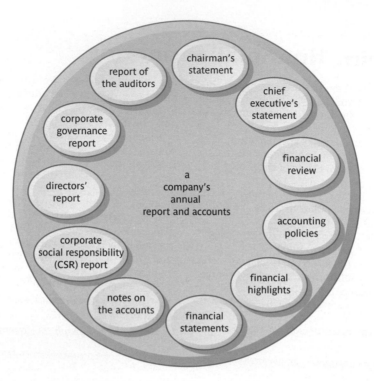

Figure 6.1 The key reports and statements within a company's annual report and accounts

The OFR includes two separate reports:

- an operating review, which includes:
  - new product development information
  - details of shareholders' returns
  - sensitivities of the financial results to specific accounting policies
  - risks and uncertainties
  - future investment
- a financial review, which includes:
  - current cash position
  - sources of funding
  - treasury policy
  - capital structure
  - confirmation that the business is a going concern
  - factors outside the balance sheet impacting on the value of the business
  - taxation.

We will look at each of the reports and statements included in Fig. 6.1 in this chapter, using the annual report and accounts 2004 of Johnson Matthey plc as an illustration, except for the last two reports, the corporate governance report and the report of the auditors, which will be discussed in Chapter 7. It should be noted that Johnson Matthey's operating review is included within the chief executive's statement. With regard to the notes on the accounts, in this chapter we will consider only note 1 that relates to **segmental reporting**.

Progress check 6.1 **Why are annual accounts filed and published?**

Chairman's statement

In addition to the profit and loss account and cash flow statement for the year and the balance sheet as at the year-end date, the annual report and accounts includes much more financial and non-financial information such as:

- company policies
- financial indicators
- directors' remuneration
- employee numbers
- business analysis.

The annual report and accounts includes the chairman's statement. This offers an opportunity for the chairman of the company to report in unquantified and unaudited terms on the performance of the company during the past financial period and on likely future developments. Let's take a look at the Johnson Matthey chairman's statement from its chairman, Michael Miles, OBE (see pp. 200–201).

The Johnson Matthey chairman's statement can be seen to include his general comments about the performance of the company over the past year, its current position, and its outlook for the future. A couple of paragraphs describe the strategy of the group. As with most chairmen's statements, Johnson Matthey's statement includes comments about the board of directors, investments in research and development and in people, and the achievements of the management team and other employees over the preceding year. The Johnson Matthey statement devotes a large section to the importance of the company's employees, their training and development. It also includes reference to the importance of the company's full commitment to its reporting on its corporate social responsibility performance, including environmental issues (which we shall deal with later in this chapter). Michael Miles' report concludes with a return to the company's goal of delivering superior shareholder value, and the importance of its employees and investment in research and development and manufacturing technology in achieving that goal.

Progress check 6.2 **What is the purpose of a chairman's statement?**

Chief executive's statement

Chief executives' statements generally include detail on the performance of the business particularly relating to products, markets, technology and the various geographical areas of activity. These statements include brief comments on the financial highlights of the preceding year and the recommended dividend payable to shareholders. The chief executive's statement includes a review of operations, which outlines the main factors underlying the business and identifies any changes or expected future changes which may impact on the business. It normally concludes with an outlook on the future prospects of the business.

Chairman's Statement

"The company's most important investment will always be the one it makes in its people. We place an absolute priority on the continuing development of our management talent and the skills of all our employees."

Michael Miles OBE
Chairman

I am pleased to report to shareholders that despite some quite strong headwinds, generated by the weak US dollar and the challenging conditions in some of our markets, Johnson Matthey made good progress in 2003/04.

The board's commitment to investment in research & development and manufacturing technology has enabled the company to remain at the forefront of the high technology industries that it serves and to continue its record of growth.

In 2003/04 we took a number of important steps in the strategic development of the group. The former Synetix businesses, which were acquired from ICI last year, have been successfully integrated into Johnson Matthey's Process Catalysts and Technologies business. These businesses have not only made a good contribution to the year but provide important opportunities for the group's future growth, especially in catalysts for the emerging gas to liquids market, an area where we have begun a significant programme of investment. The year also witnessed a further example of our strategy of making bolt-on acquisitions in core areas of activity with the acquisition of AMC in the United States which further enhances Catalysts Division's product portfolio.

The board is also committed to investment in growth markets around the world. Asia continues to be a major focus. In Shanghai, we are increasing capacity at our autocatalyst manufacturing facility to serve the rapidly growing Chinese vehicle market. In Japan, we achieved significant sales of retrofit heavy duty diesel catalysts. In India, we constructed a new platinum group metal catalyst manufacturing facility to serve the fast growing pharmaceutical and speciality chemical markets in that region.

The company's most important investment will always be the one it makes in its people. We place an absolute priority on the continuing development of our management talent and the skills of all our employees to enable them to perform to the highest standards to meet the challenges of the future. On behalf of the board I would like to thank all of our employees around the world for their hard work and dedication during the year.

I would like to welcome two new executive directors who joined the board in August 2003; Pelham Hawker, Executive Director, Environmental Catalysts and Technologies and Larry Pentz, Executive Director, Process Catalysts and Technologies. Both have made important contributions to recent developments in Johnson Matthey's Catalysts Division. Pelham has overseen a period of strong growth and technological change in our autocatalyst business and Larry has undertaken a leading role in the successful integration of the former Synetix businesses since their acquisition from ICI.

Johnson Matthey is very fortunate to have a strong group of independent directors who bring to the board many years of invaluable experience of international business from across a wide range of industrial sectors. I would also like to thank them for their valuable contribution during the year.

In July 2003 we announced that Chris Clark, our Chief Executive, will retire following this year's Annual General Meeting in July after 42 years with Johnson Matthey, the last six as Chief Executive. Chris has had a long and distinguished career with Johnson Matthey since joining the company in 1962. He has great experience of all of the group's operations and has run all of its major businesses. Chris has made an outstanding contribution to Johnson Matthey. As Chief Executive he has overseen the evolution of the group into a world leading speciality chemicals company. Through his strong leadership, Chris has steered the company through a successful period of strategic change and growth. As I said at the time of his appointment as Chief Executive in June 1998, I can think of no person better suited to have undertaken this task. On behalf of the whole board, and indeed all of us at Johnson Matthey, I would like to thank Chris for the key role that he has played in the development and success of the group and wish him all the best for a well deserved, long and very happy retirement.

As we also announced last July, Chris Clark will be succeeded as Chief Executive by Neil Carson, Executive Director, Catalysts and Precious Metals. Neil has 23 years of experience of working at Johnson Matthey and will be an excellent successor to Chris. The board is particularly pleased to have been able to appoint its new Chief Executive from within the company.

Your board is fully committed to reporting on Johnson Matthey's corporate social responsibility performance. Once again, this year's annual report features a review of the company's policies and performance in this important area. This is to be found on pages 24 to 28. Our comprehensive web based corporate social responsibility report was published last year for the first time. This report has been very well received and has generated a good deal of valuable feedback from shareholders. The 2004 edition of our corporate social responsibility report can be accessed on Johnson Matthey's corporate website at www.matthey.com.

I am very pleased that Johnson Matthey continues to make good progress towards our goal of delivering superior shareholder value. I remain confident that with our talented staff and our commitment to investment in research & development and world leading manufacturing technology, your company is well positioned to deliver continued growth in the years ahead.

Michael Miles

Michael Miles OBE
Chairman

Chief Executive's Statement

"Johnson Matthey made good progress in 2003/04. Operating profit before exceptional items and goodwill amortisation was 9% up on prior year despite the fall in the value of the US dollar."

Chris Clark
Chief Executive

Johnson Matthey made good progress in 2003/04. Operating profit before exceptional items and goodwill amortisation was 9% up on prior year despite the fall in the value of the US dollar. Both Catalysts and Pharmaceutical Materials divisions achieved 15% profit growth. We continue to see excellent prospects for both these divisions and we have increased our investment in research and development to take full advantage of anticipated market growth over the next few years.

Our Catalysts Division has leading positions in market segments which will expand rapidly in the next few years. These include catalysts for heavy duty diesel (HDD) emission control, where legislation is due to take full effect in 2007 in the USA and 2008 in Europe, and catalysts for the gas to liquids process which uses a series of different catalytic steps to convert stranded natural gas to sulphur free diesel fuel.

We are increasing our investment in R&D to support these opportunities, and are also selectively looking at possible acquisitions to expand our range of catalyst products. We are pleased to have concluded the acquisition of AMC in March 2004, which strengthens our position in the pharmaceutical and speciality chemicals catalyst markets.

As well as growing revenues we are also focusing on improving efficiency. In these results we have taken a £12.7 million exceptional provision to improve efficiency across the Catalysts Division. One element of this relates to restructuring our platinum group metal (pgm) refining business, which has been adversely affected by the downturn in the palladium market. In addition, we will be phasing out our older autocatalyst manufacturing process technology now that precision coating technology has been fully installed in all our worldwide autocatalyst manufacturing plants. We expect this rationalisation programme to reduce costs in the division by £8 million in 2005/06.

Diesel emission control continues to be a focus for environmentalists and regulators worldwide and remains a key priority for us. The market for diesel cars is mainly in Europe where we have increased our market share. Whilst oxidation catalysts remain the key current product, there is growing interest in the use of soot filter technology for particulate emission control and we have been nominated for several important customer programmes.

Worldwide, Johnson Matthey's award winning Continuously Regenerating Trap (CRT®) technology is the most widely used method of controlling particulate emissions from heavy duty diesel vehicles already on the road. New regulations in both Europe and the USA will drive the need for engine makers to fit catalyst technologies to new HDD vehicles starting in 2005. In the last few years we have increased the resource needed to support these customers and the benefits of this strategy are now coming through in contracts for future business.

The acquisition of Synetix from ICI in 2002 has led to a major expansion of Process Catalysts and Technologies (PCT). The former Synetix businesses are now fully integrated and we are building on the opportunities presented by merging Johnson Matthey's leading precious metals catalysis technology with Synetix's leading base metals catalyst technology. One example of this is the opening in May 2004 of a new precious metals catalyst manufacturing facility at Taloja in India. The acquisition of ICI India's catalyst business provided Johnson Matthey with a strong presence in base metal catalysts in the region, to which we have now been able to add precious metals catalyst manufacturing.

The acquisition of AMC for $43 million in March 2004 was another important step in strengthening our position in the worldwide catalyst market. AMC is based in Tennessee, USA and is the global market leader in Sponge Nickel™ catalysts. These nickel catalysts are extensively used in hydrogenation and reductive alkylation reactions throughout the pharmaceutical industry as well as in a wide range of other chemical processes. They are often the first catalyst to be evaluated when designing a new process and the acquisition widens our catalyst product offering to this important market.

The Fuel Cells business continues to make encouraging progress both in the scale up of membrane electrode assembly (MEA) manufacturing at its facility in Swindon, UK and in collaborative programmes with key customers and suppliers. Johnson Matthey Fuel Cells has been awarded £3.2 million in funding by the Department of Trade and Industry as part of the Government's commitment to the development of renewable energy and to the building of a

world class fuel cell industry in the United Kingdom. This grant has been given for a major three year programme to develop the next generation of MEAs for automotive applications and will see the Fuel Cells business working in collaboration with a number of key suppliers as well as leading global automobile manufacturers.

We announced in November 2003 that we had renewed our long term contracts with Anglo Platinum which extends the relationship well into the next decade. The revised terms of these renewed contracts came into effect on 1st January 2004 and resulted in a reduction in Precious Metals Division's income in the final quarter of roughly £1.5 million. As demand for platinum grows this shortfall will be more than offset by increased volumes, and the renewed contracts with Anglo Platinum firmly underpin the longer term growth of the division.

The fundamentals for platinum remain very robust. Demand will continue to be driven by its use in autocatalysts, particularly as diesels continue to take a growing share of the light duty vehicle market in Europe and as heavy duty diesel legislation begins to take effect around the world. While jewellery demand has been impacted by the high price of platinum, it remains remarkably resilient and we are seeing signs of improved demand from the manufacturers. The platinum producers are increasing their output to meet this growing demand and move the market closer to equilibrium.

Palladium demand is also expected to increase, benefiting from growth in consumption by the auto manufacturers. However, supplies are expected to rise substantially as South African producers expand their output and the palladium market is expected to continue to remain in surplus.

As we also announced in November, the Board has reviewed the group's strategy for the Structural Ceramics and Speciality Coatings businesses which form the majority of Colours & Coatings Division. A process is now underway to consider offers for those two businesses. We expect to make a further announcement in the next few months.

Pharmaceutical Materials Division enjoyed another very successful year. At West Deptford in the USA we have expanded the product range with two new platinum anticancer products performing well in 2003/04. The patent for carboplatin which we manufacture for Bristol-Myers

Chief Executive's Statement (continued)

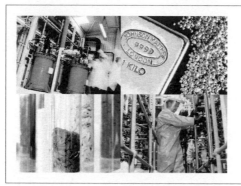

Squibb will expire this year and we anticipate the contribution from this product will fall. However, we expect to see an increased contribution from other products, including semi-synthetic opiates where we will benefit from the new morphine and codeine extraction facility at West Deptford. Our Edinburgh based business, Macfarlan Smith, has achieved excellent growth over the last three years and we are continuing to invest in new capacity there to meet anticipated future growth. We have completed a new facility to produce a range of specialist products (mainly highly potent analgesics) which we expect to make a useful contribution this year. At Pharm-Eco we have commissioned the new small scale manufacturing suites at Devens in Massachusetts, USA which are being used to manufacture products for clinical trials.

Financial Highlights
Sales for the financial year ending 31st March 2004 rose by 4% to £4.5 billion. Excluding the value of precious metals sales increased by 6% to £1.2 billion.

Operating profit before exceptional items and goodwill amortisation rose by 9% to £206.0 million despite adverse exchange translation. Profit before tax, exceptional items and goodwill amortisation increased by 3% to £195.7 million.

Earnings per share before exceptional items and goodwill amortisation rose by 4% to 64.0 pence and we are recommending that the dividend for the year is increased by the same percentage to a total of 26.4 pence.

Operations
Catalysts Division's sales rose by 5% to £1,143 million despite the fall in the average palladium price and the weaker US dollar. Sales excluding the value of precious metals rose by 10% to £720 million. The division's operating profit increased by 15% to £109.2 million benefiting from a full year's contribution from the former Synetix businesses.

Environmental Catalysts and Technologies (ECT), which encompasses Johnson Matthey's worldwide autocatalyst, heavy duty diesel and stationary source emission control businesses, achieved strong profit growth in Asia and good growth in Europe, but profits declined in the US. Our autocatalyst business in Asia benefited from strong growth in the Chinese market where sales of light duty vehicles (cars and vans) rose

by 37% in 2003. Car sales in Europe were flat but demand for diesel cars continues to grow and now represents 46% of all cars sold. Johnson Matthey has leading technology in diesel emission control and we increased our share of this growing market. In North America our domestic customers' share of the NAFTA market declined and inventories were trimmed by lowering production, reducing demand for autocatalysts.

Sales of heavy duty diesel products were ahead of prior year in all three regions with particularly strong sales in Japan in the first half of the year supported by an incentive programme from the Tokyo Metropolitan Government. Sales of HDD catalysts to original equipment manufacturers continued to grow in the USA and we increased our investment in joint development programmes with the major manufacturers worldwide, gaining several programmes that will enter commercial production from 2005/06.

Process Catalysts and Technologies, which sells catalysts to the chemicals, pharmaceutical, oil and gas and other markets, was well ahead benefiting from the contribution from the former Synetix businesses. The integration of those businesses into Johnson Matthey has progressed very well and results are in line with our expectations at the time of the acquisition. Sales and profits from process catalysts were well up on prior year, despite weakness in some parts of the market. Platinum group metal refining was adversely affected by the weak palladium and rhodium prices and profits were down. Research Chemicals, our catalogue business, continued to achieve good growth.

Our Fuel Cells business made encouraging progress. Revenues showed significant growth on prior year, reducing the net expense for the year to £11.5 million (down 12%). Much of the growth this year has come from sales to the automotive sector as more prototype fuel cell powered vehicles have been developed for durability testing.

Precious Metals Division's sales grew by 3% to £2,956 million with a recovery in the second half of the year reflecting strong demand and higher prices for platinum. Operating profit for the year fell by 8% to £44.2 million, as a result of subdued trading conditions for palladium and rhodium for most of the year, and the impact of the renewed contracts with Anglo Platinum in the final quarter.

"In the next few years we should start to see significant benefits from Johnson Matthey's investment in new product areas."

Demand for platinum remained strong and the average price of the metal for Johnson Matthey's financial year 2003/04 was $744 per ounce, an increase of 27% over 2002/03. Purchases for use in autocatalysts increased robustly in response to further growth in diesel car sales in Europe. In addition, North American car companies stepped up their purchases of platinum having largely depleted inventories of the metal the year before. However, platinum demand from the Chinese jewellery market dropped after almost a decade of rapid growth, as the rise in the platinum price reduced profit margins throughout the industry.

In contrast with platinum, the average price of palladium was $200 per ounce, 34% below the average in 2002/03, and trading conditions remained subdued for most of the year. Physical demand for palladium began to recover from the fall in the previous year, with purchases by the auto and electronics industries increasing significantly. The surplus between supply and demand, however, widened considerably as Russian sales of palladium recovered and South African production was expanded.

The division's platinum fabrication businesses achieved further growth with good demand for both medical components and industrial products. Operating profit for the gold refining businesses was down on last year with the stronger gold price having little immediate impact on mine output.

Colours & Coatings Division's sales were very similar to last year at £254 million. Operating profit rose by 6% to £26.7 million with an improvement in margins.

The glass coatings business achieved good growth in sales and profits benefiting from new product introductions and market share gains. The Structural Ceramics sector, which sells largely to the tile industry, experienced weaker demand for most of the year and profits were down, but demand picked up in the final quarter and the outlook is now much stronger. Profits for Speciality Coatings were well up on prior year, benefiting from the rationalisation programme undertaken in 2002/03.

Pharmaceutical Materials Division's sales rose by 9% to £140 million despite the impact of the weaker US dollar. The division's operating profit increased by 15% to £42.3 million.

The division's US business at West Deptford, NJ achieved strong growth in the year, benefiting from an expanded range of platinum based anticancer compounds. One new product has recently been launched and another is in phase three clinical trials. The new opiate extraction facility was completed in the year and is now operational. Macfarlan Smith also achieved excellent growth in profits benefiting from increasing sales of high margin specialist opiates. Additional capacity is being installed to meet future growth. Pharm-Eco experienced the industry-wide drop in demand for contract research in the first quarter of the year but was able to respond by gaining new business and its performance in the second half of the year was much stronger.

Outlook In 2004/05 we expect to see further growth in Catalysts and Pharmaceutical Materials. However, exchange translation may be adverse if the US dollar remains at its current level.

In the next few years we should start to see significant benefits from Johnson Matthey's investment in new product areas, including heavy duty diesel catalysts which represents a major opportunity once legislation comes into force in 2007 and 2008. In Pharmaceutical Materials we have a strong worldwide position in the manufacture of controlled drugs and complex molecules, such as prostaglandins, where the generic market should see significant growth. Excellent progress is also being made in other long term growth markets, such as gas to liquids catalysts and fuel cells, where revenues are expected to grow in the years ahead.

Overall, supported by a strong balance sheet, the group is very well positioned to deliver good long term growth.

Chris Clark
Chief Executive

Financial Review

"*Johnson Matthey's balance sheet remains strong with shareholders' funds rising by £74.9 million to £862.2 million and gearing of 45%.*"

John Sheldrick
Group Finance Director

Review of Results Total sales for the financial year ending 31st March 2004 rose by 4% to £4.5 billion. Sales excluding the value of precious metals rose by 6% to £1.2 billion.

Operating profit before exceptional items and goodwill amortisation increased by 9% to £206.0 million, despite the effects of adverse exchange translation. The group has adopted FRS 17, the new accounting standard for pensions, and last year's results have been restated accordingly. Divisional results are discussed in the Chief Executive's Statement on pages 4 to 7, and in the individual divisional reports on pages 16 to 23.

Interest also rose, partly reflecting higher average borrowings following the acquisition of Synetix, but also as a consequence of the change to FRS 17 and the reduction in pension fund surplus at 31st March 2003. Profit before tax, exceptional items and goodwill amortisation rose by 3% to £195.7 million.

Earnings per share before exceptional items and goodwill amortisation increased by 4% to 64.0 pence.

Exceptional items gave rise to a net credit of £2.1 million before tax, compared with a £2.7 million charge last year. Goodwill amortisation increased by £6.1 million to £19.8 million reflecting the full year's ownership of Synetix which was acquired in November 2002. After exceptional items and goodwill amortisation, profit before tax rose by 3% to £178.0 million. Earnings per share on the same basis increased by 1% to 56.0 pence.

The board is recommending to shareholders a final dividend of 18.2 pence, making a total dividend for the year of 26.4 pence, an increase of 4%. The proposed dividend would be covered 2.4 times by earnings before exceptional items and goodwill amortisation.

Sales and Margins Johnson Matthey's turnover is heavily impacted by the high value of precious metals sold by the group particularly in the Precious Metals Division (PMD). The total value of sales each year varies according to the mix of metals sold and level of trading activity. The value of the precious metals included in sales is generally separately invoiced and payment made within a few days. Consequently, although return on sales (operating profit / total external sales) for the precious metals businesses is low, return on investment is high.

To provide a more useful measure of return on sales, the adjacent table shows sales by division excluding the value of precious metals. Total sales excluding precious metals were £1,224 million which was 6% up on last year and return on these sales averaged 16.8% which was 0.5% up on 2002/03 (restated for FRS 17). The group's target for each of its divisions is to achieve a return on sales excluding precious metals in excess of 10%. All four divisions were ahead of that target in 2003/04.

Catalysts achieved 10% growth in sales excluding precious metals benefiting from a full year's ownership of former Synetix businesses. A significant proportion of the division's operations are located in the USA, and both sales and profits were adversely affected by exchange translation as a result of the decline in value of the US dollar. Margins improved, benefiting from sales of new, technologically advanced products.

PMD's sales excluding precious metals were down 9% reflecting subdued trading conditions for palladium and rhodium for most of the year and the impact of the renewed contracts with Anglo Platinum in the final quarter.

Colours & Coatings' sales were very similar to last year but margins improved as a result of good growth in our glass coatings business, which has higher margins than other parts of the division.

Pharmaceutical Materials achieved 8% growth in sales excluding precious metals, despite adverse exchange translation, with good growth in sales of platinum anticancer compounds and opiates. Margins improved at our Edinburgh based business, Macfarlan Smith, as a result of increased sales of high margin specialist opiates.

Exchange Rates

March 2002 — March 2003 — March 2004

—— $/£   ⊏⊐ Euro/£

	Sales excluding precious metals		Return on sales excluding precious metals	
	2004	2003	2004	2003 restated
	£ million	£ million	%	%
Catalysts	720	652	15.2	14.6
Precious Metals	121	132	36.7	36.4
Colours & Coatings	252	253	10.6	10.0
Pharmaceutical Materials	131	122	32.2	30.1
	1,224	1,159	16.8	16.3

Return on Investment We set a target of 20% for the pre-tax return on assets (ROA) for all our businesses. For the group as a whole ROA was 16.2% (see pages 70 and 71) compared with 16.8% in 2002/03. The decline in the overall return reflects the impact of the acquisition of Synetix which is expected to take a few years to meet the group's target.

On a post tax basis the return on invested capital was 11.4% which was above the estimated weighted average cost of capital (WACC) for the group of 8%. The margin above the cost of capital for the year was 3.4%, which was below last year's restated figure of 3.8% but still satisfactory.

Exceptional Items and Goodwill Amortisation Exceptional items included in operating profit gave rise to a net credit of £2.1 million.

The group benefited by £14.8 million from the settlement of litigation with Research Corporation and Research Corporation Technologies, Inc. relating to royalties earned under a licence agreement with Bristol-Myers Squibb Company in respect of carboplatin.

This exceptional credit was partly offset by a charge of £12.7 million for the rationalisation of Catalysts Division. The rationalisation costs relate to the reorganisation of PCT's pgm refining business and the phasing out of ECT's older autocatalyst process technology now that precision coating technology has been fully installed across the group. This rationalisation is expected to improve the division's profits by £8 million in 2005/06.

Goodwill amortisation increased by £6.1 million to £19.8 million, reflecting the full year's ownership of the former Synetix businesses, which were acquired in November 2002.

Interest The group's net interest charge rose by £3.1 million to £16.3 million as a result of the increase in average net borrowings following the acquisition of Synetix. The average interest rate was lower than last year benefiting from lower US dollar interest rates and reduced rates on gold leases.

The group has adopted FRS 17, the new accounting standard for pensions. Under FRS 17 the net return on retirement benefits assets and liabilities fell by £7.9 million to £6.0 million. The drop reflected the fall in the value of the pension fund surplus in 2002/03 as measured on 31st March 2003, when the world equity markets were particularly depressed. Equity markets recovered somewhat in 2003/04 and the group's UK pension fund surplus has increased. The net return on retirement benefits assets and liabilities is likely to be roughly £3 million higher in 2004/05.

Exchange Rates Over a third of the group's profits were made in North America, mainly in the USA. The average rate for the US dollar weakened significantly, from $1.55/£ in 2002/03 to $1.69/£ in 2003/04, which reduced reported group profit before tax by £6.7 million.

The group has significant operations in several euro-zone countries and in South Africa whose currencies have strengthened against sterling. The group benefited by £2.4 million from the translation of profits made in euros, of which £1.7 million related to Colours & Coatings, but the euro's strength also had a negative impact on demand for that division's products. The overall impact of the appreciation of the South African rand was negative. The products the group manufactures in South Africa are generally for export with pricing mainly related to euros and US dollars, whereas costs are in rands, and margins were adversely affected by currency movements.

Financial Review (continued)

Taxation The group's tax charge increased by £4.2 million to £57.9 million. The increase largely reflected higher profits. The group's average tax rate on profit before tax, exceptional items and goodwill amortisation rose slightly from 29.7% to 29.8%.

Cash Flow Johnson Matthey's net cash flow from operations increased by 13% to £259.7 million. Capital expenditure was £13.4 million lower than prior year at £113.1 million and represented 1.8 times depreciation. We are planning to spend at a lower rate in 2004/05 although still maintaining investment to support future growth opportunities. Free cash flow for the group (after dividends, but before acquisitions and share purchases) was strong at £29.9 million.

The group spent £18.4 million on acquisitions (mainly AMC) and made a net purchase of shares (for the employee share ownership trusts) which cost £8.5 million, leaving a net cash inflow of £3.0 million.

After taking into account favourable exchange translation of £6.1 million on the group's foreign currency borrowings (mainly US dollars), and £1.1 million of loan notes issued to acquire subsidiaries, net borrowings fell by £8.0 million to £394.5 million. Johnson Matthey's balance sheet remains strong with shareholders' funds rising by £74.9 million to £862.2 million and gearing (net borrowings / shareholders' funds and minority interests) of 45%. The comparative figures for last year have been restated for FRS 17 and UITF 38, under which shares held in employee share ownership trusts are accounted for in the same way as treasury shares. Restated for these new accounting standards, last year's gearing was 50%.

Pensions For the financial year 2003/04 the group has adopted FRS 17, and the figures for 2002/03 have been restated accordingly. The value of the assets in the group's pension funds increased significantly in 2003/04, partly reflecting the recovery in equity prices from their depressed levels at 31st March 2003. The surplus on the group's UK schemes increased by £42.6 million to £43.3 million at 31st March 2004 after taking into account the results of the triennial actuarial revaluation (see page 51).

Worldwide, including provisions for the group's post-retirement healthcare schemes and pension related deferred tax assets and liabilities, the group had a net surplus of £3.5 million on retirement benefits net assets compared with a net deficit of £25.4 million at 31st March 2003.

Financing The group financed the acquisition of Synetix on 1st November 2002 out of additional borrowings. Initially this was done using bank facilities. Most of this additional debt was refinanced on 26th March 2003 with the proceeds of a long term private placement bond issue. The issue included a range of maturities, from 7 to 12 years, and comprised £40 million in sterling bonds and $230 million in US dollar bonds. Some $65 million of the dollar bonds were swapped into sterling to raise a total of £81.1 million of fixed rate sterling with an average maturity of just under 10 years at an average interest cost (including fees) of 5.15%. The remaining $165 million of bonds issued had a 12 year maturity and a fixed rate interest cost in dollars (including fees) of 4.98%. This part of the issue was swapped into floating rate dollars to provide attractively priced variable rate debt.

At 31st March 2004 the maturity profile of the group's debt was as follows:

Borrowings and Finance Leases	31st March 2004 £ million	%	31st March 2003 £ million	%
Over ten years	111.3	22	126.6	25
Five to ten years	66.6	13	67.5	14
Two to five years	210.9	42	151.1	30
One to two years	65.7	13	111.2	22
Within one year	46.5	10	46.5	9
Gross borrowings	501.0	100	502.9	100
Less: cash and deposits	106.5		100.4	
Net borrowings	394.5		402.5	

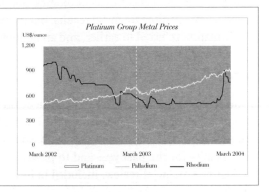

Platinum Group Metal Prices

Financial Risk Management The group uses financial instruments, in particular forward currency contracts and currency swaps, to manage the financial risks associated with the group's underlying business activities and the financing of those activities. The group does not undertake any trading activity in financial instruments. Our Treasury department is run as a service centre rather than a profit centre.

Interest Rate Risk At 31st March 2004 the group had net borrowings of £394.5 million. Some 35% of this debt is at fixed rates with an average interest rate of 5.6%. The remaining 65% of the group's net borrowings are funded on a floating rate basis. A 1% change in all interest rates would have a 1.4% impact on group profit before tax. This is within the range the board regards as acceptable.

Liquidity Policy The group's policy on funding capacity is to ensure that we always have sufficient long term funding and committed bank facilities in place to meet foreseeable peak borrowing requirements. The group has committed bank facilities of £280 million. Borrowings drawn under these facilities at 31st March 2004 amounted to £219.8 million. The group also has a number of uncommitted facilities and overdraft lines.

Foreign Currency Risk Johnson Matthey's operations are global in nature with the majority of the group's operating profits earned outside the UK. The group has operations in 34 countries with the largest single investment being in the USA. In order to protect the group's sterling balance sheet and reduce cash flow risk, the group finances most of its US investment by US dollar borrowings. Although most of this funding is obtained by directly borrowing US dollars, some is achieved by using currency swaps to reduce costs and credit exposure. The group also uses local currency borrowings to fund its operations in other countries (see page 59).

The group uses forward exchange contracts to hedge foreign exchange exposures arising on forecast receipts and payments in foreign currencies. Currency options are occasionally used to hedge foreign exchange exposures, usually when the forecast receipt or payment amounts are uncertain. Details of the contracts outstanding on 31st March 2004 are shown on page 61.

Precious Metal Prices Fluctuations in precious metal prices can have a significant impact on Johnson Matthey's financial results. Our policy for all our manufacturing businesses is to limit this exposure by hedging against future price changes where such hedging can be done at acceptable cost. The group does not take material exposures on metal trading.

All the group's stocks of gold and silver are fully hedged by leasing or forward sales. Currently the majority of the group's platinum stocks are unhedged because of the lack of liquidity in the platinum market.

John Sheldrick
Group Finance Director

The Johnson Matthey chief executive's statement for 2004, presented by Chris Clark (see pp. 202–5, provides details about developments in the various divisions of the company including acquisitions. The report provides a great deal of information of particular interest to current and potential new shareholders relating to future growth opportunities, planned major investments, the development of new and existing technologies, and new product development. This report includes some detail of the headline financial results, but its main focus is the operating review containing the sort of information referred to earlier, and an outlook for the business over the next few years.

Financial review

The financial review goes into further financial detail than the chief executive's statement and is normally prepared by the finance director. In the case of Johnson Matthey, the financial review has been prepared by its group finance director, John Sheldrick. The purpose of the financial review is to review the results for the past year and to provide an overview of financial policy. Let's look at the Johnson Matthey financial review, included in its annual report and accounts for the year 2004 (see pp. 206–9).

The Johnson Matthey financial review begins with a review of the results for the year to 31 March 2004, with an initial focus on sales, profit before tax, earnings per share and dividends. The review goes on to look in a little more detail at:

- sales and margins
- exceptional items and goodwill amortisation
- exchange rates
- cash flow
- financing

- return on investment
- interest rates
- taxation
- pensions
- financial risk management.

We can see that the review includes many of the financial performance measures we have discussed in Chapter 5. Examples are return on sales and return on investment, which are analysed by each area of business activity.

Johnson Matthey has commented with regard to the impacts of both the strength of the euro, and the weakness of the US$. The group benefited by £2.4m from the translation of profits of euro-zone companies made in euros, but the strength of the euro also had a negative impact on demand for products in the Colours & Coatings division. The group's pre-tax profit suffered from an 8% deterioration of the US$, with a large part of the group's operating income being derived from North America. The group's net cash flow was at around the same level as the previous year; operating cash flow increased, but there was reduced capital expenditure.

The first part of the financial review concludes with a comment on the refinancing of the group's acquisition of Synetix in 2002. The initial financing of the acquisition, using its existing bank facilities, was refinanced at the end of March 2003 with the proceeds of a long-term private placement bond issue amounting to £40m plus 230m US$.

The final part of the review is devoted to the group's policy on financial risk management. Risk management is a key strategic area for the type of business in which Johnson Matthey is involved. Policy is explained relating to interest rate, liquidity, and foreign currency risk and the financial instruments that are used by Johnson Matthey to manage financial risks.

Risk relating to precious metals prices is also outlined in terms of policy and the way in which that area of risk is managed. The group finance director indicated in an outline of its policy the extent to which the group is risk averse. The group hedges against future changes in precious metal prices, using leasing or forward sales, except for platinum because of the lack of liquidity in that market.

Johnson Matthey has not reported on its share price performance in its report and accounts for the year 2004. This information, available from Johnson Matthey plc, is illustrated in Fig. 6.2 for each 31 March from 1995 to 2004.

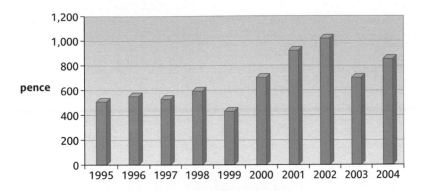

Figure 6.2 Johnson Matthey plc year-end 31 March share price 1995 to 2004

Accounting policies

The statement of accounting policies informs readers of the policies the company has pursued in preparation of the report and accounts, and of any deviation from the generally accepted fundamental accounting concepts and conventions. Johnson Matthey devotes a large part of its statement of accounting policies to the management of risk, (see pp. 213–14).

> **Progress check 6.3** **What information do the chief executive's statement and the financial review provide and how do these reports differ?**

Financial highlights

The section headed financial highlights serves to focus on the headline numbers of sales, profit before tax, earnings per share, and dividends. Johnson Matthey's financial highlights are illustrated in both summary and graphical form on p. 215.

Worked Example 6.1

We can use the Johnson Matthey plc ten-year record, which you will find on pp. 244–5 in the **Exercises** section at the end of this chapter, to present earnings per share and dividends per share for 1995 to 2004:

(i) in tabular form, and
(ii) in one bar chart for comparison.

	Earnings per share (pence)	Dividends per share (pence)
1995	30.9	13.50
1996	32.5	14.50
1997	34.2	15.50
1998	46.7	17.80
1999	47.8	19.00
2000	50.5	20.30
2001	57.3	23.30
2002	49.0	24.60
2003	55.4	25.50
2004	56.0	26.40

Figure 6.3 Johnson Matthey plc eps and dividend per share at each 31 March 1995 to 2004

Profit and loss account, balance sheet, and cash flow statement

The three financial statements that are shown on pp. 216–18 illustrate Johnson Matthey plc's consolidated profit and loss account, and consolidated cash flow statement for the year to 31 March 2004, and its consolidated and parent company balance sheets as at 31 March 2004.

The profit and loss account is consolidated to include the results of all the companies within the group, which together with the parent company, Johnson Matthey plc, total 34. Profit is stated both before exceptional items and after exceptional items, and the consolidated profit and loss account also shows previous year comparative figures.

The balance sheet is presented in consolidated form, also showing previous year comparative figures, and includes a separate balance sheet for the parent company only.

The cash flow statement is consolidated to include the cash flows of all the companies within the group, and includes the parent company, Johnson Matthey plc.

We will look at the financial performance of Johnson Matthey in Worked Examples 6.2 and 6.3 using the two approaches to ratio analysis that were mentioned in the introduction to this chapter:

■ horizontal analysis, or common size analysis, which provides a line-by-line comparison of the profit and loss account (and balance sheet) with those of the previous year

Accounting Policies

for the year ended 31st March 2004

Accounting convention: The accounts are prepared in accordance with applicable accounting standards under the historical cost convention.

Basis of consolidation: The consolidated accounts comprise the accounts of the parent company and all its subsidiary undertakings and include the group's interest in associates.

The results of companies acquired or disposed of in the year are dealt with from or up to the effective date of acquisition or disposal respectively. The net assets of companies acquired are incorporated in the consolidated accounts at their fair values to the group at the date of acquisition.

The parent company has not presented its own profit and loss account as permitted by section 230 of the Companies Act 1985.

Turnover: Comprises all invoiced sales of goods and services exclusive of sales taxes.

Financial instruments: The group uses financial instruments, in particular forward currency contracts and currency swaps, to manage the financial risks associated with the group's underlying business activities and the financing of those activities. The group does not undertake any trading activity in financial instruments.

A discussion of how the group manages its financial risks is included in the Financial Review on page 11. Financial instruments are accounted for as follows:

> Forward exchange contracts are used to hedge foreign exchange exposures arising on forecast receipts and payments in foreign currencies. These forward contracts are revalued to the rates of exchange at the balance sheet date and any aggregate unrealised gains and losses arising on revaluation are included in other debtors / other creditors. At maturity, or when the contract ceases to be a hedge, gains and losses are taken to the profit and loss account.

> Currency options are occasionally used to hedge foreign exchange exposures, usually when the forecast receipt or payment amounts are uncertain. Option premia are recognised at their historic cost in the group balance sheet as prepayments or accruals and released to the profit and loss account, net of any realised gains, on a straight line basis over the remaining term of the option when the outcome becomes certain.

> Interest rate swaps are occasionally used to hedge the group's exposure to movements in interest rates. The interest payable or receivable on such swaps is accrued in the same way as interest arising on deposits or borrowings. Interest rate swaps are not revalued to fair value prior to maturity.

> Currency swaps are used to reduce costs and credit exposure where the group would otherwise have cash deposits and borrowings in different currencies. The difference between spot and forward rate for these contracts is recognised as part of the net interest payable over the period of the contract. These swaps are revalued to the rates of exchange at the balance sheet date and any aggregate unrealised gains or losses arising on revaluation are included in other debtors / other creditors. Realised gains and losses on these currency swaps are taken to reserves in the same way as for the foreign investments and borrowings to which the swaps relate.

The aggregate fair values at the balance sheet date of the hedging instruments described above are disclosed as a note on the accounts.

The group has taken advantage of the exemption available for short term debtors and creditors.

Foreign currencies: Profit and loss accounts in foreign currencies and cash flows included in the cash flow statement are translated into sterling at average exchange rates for the year. Foreign currency assets and liabilities are translated into sterling at the rates of exchange at the balance sheet date. Gains or losses arising on the translation of the net assets of overseas subsidiaries and associated undertakings are taken to reserves, less exchange differences arising on related foreign currency borrowings. Other exchange differences are taken to the profit and loss account.

Research and development expenditure: Charged against profits in the year incurred.

Goodwill: Goodwill arising on acquisitions made after 1st April 1998 is capitalised and amortised on a straight line basis over the estimated useful economic life, which is 20 years or less if it is considered appropriate. Goodwill previously eliminated against reserves has not been reinstated, but will be charged to the profit and loss account on subsequent disposal of the businesses to which it relates.

Depreciation: Freehold land and certain office buildings are not depreciated. The depreciation charge and accumulated depreciation of these properties would be immaterial and they are reviewed for impairment annually. Other fixed assets are depreciated on a straight line basis at annual rates which vary according to the class of asset, but are typically: leasehold property 3.33% (or at higher rates based on the life of the lease); freehold buildings 3.33%; and plant and equipment 10% to 33%.

Leases: The cost of assets held under finance leases is included under tangible fixed assets and the capital element of future lease payments is included in borrowings. Depreciation is provided in accordance with the group's accounting policy for the class of asset concerned. Lease payments are treated as consisting of capital and interest elements and the interest is charged to the profit and loss account using the annuity method. Rentals under operating leases are expensed as incurred.

Accounting Policies

for the year ended 31st March 2004

Grants in respect of capital expenditure: Grants received in respect of capital expenditure are included in creditors and released to the profit and loss account in equal instalments over the expected useful lives of the related assets.

Precious metal stocks: Stocks of gold, silver and platinum group metals are valued according to the source from which the metal is obtained. Metal which has been purchased and committed to future sales to customers or hedged in metal markets is valued at the price at which it is contractually committed or hedged, adjusted for unexpired contango or backwardation. Leased metal is valued at market prices at the balance sheet date. Other precious metal stocks owned by the group, which are unhedged, are valued at the lower of cost and net realisable value.

Other stocks: These are valued at the lower of cost, including attributable overheads, and net realisable value.

Deferred taxation: Provided on all timing differences that have originated but not reversed by the balance sheet date and which could give rise to an obligation to pay more or less tax in the future.

Pensions and other retirement benefits: The group operates a number of contributory and non-contributory schemes, mainly of the defined benefit type, which require contributions to be made to separately administered funds.

The cost of the defined contribution schemes is charged to the profit and loss account as incurred.

For defined benefit schemes, the group recognises the net assets or liabilities of the schemes in the balance sheet, net of any related deferred tax liability or asset. The changes in scheme assets and liabilities, based on actuarial advice, are recognised as follows:

> The current service cost, based on the most recent actuarial valuation, is deducted in arriving at operating profit.

> The interest cost, based on the present value of scheme liabilities and the discount rate at the beginning of the year and amended for changes in scheme liabilities during the year, is included as interest.

> The expected return on scheme assets, based on the fair value of scheme assets and expected rates of return at the beginning of the year and amended for changes in scheme assets during the year, is included as interest.

> Actuarial gains and losses, representing differences between the expected return and actual return on scheme assets, differences between the actuarial assumptions underlying the scheme liabilities and actual experience during the year, and changes in actuarial assumptions, are recognised in the statement of total recognised gains and losses.

> Past service costs are spread evenly over the period in which the increases in benefit vest and are deducted in arriving at operating profit. If an increase in benefits vests immediately, the cost is recognised immediately.

> Gains or losses arising from settlements or curtailments not covered by actuarial assumptions are included in operating profit.

Employee share ownership trusts (ESOTs) and long term incentive plan (LTIP): The cost of shares held by the ESOTs are deducted in arriving at shareholders' funds until they vest unconditionally in employees. The cost to the group of the LTIP is recognised on a straight line basis over the period to which the performance criteria relate, adjusted for changes in the probability of performance criteria being met or conditional awards lapsing. The creditor arising from the charge is deducted in arriving at shareholders' funds.

Changes in accounting policies: Under the provisions of Financial Reporting Standard (FRS) 17 – 'Retirement Benefits', which the group adopted on 1st April 2003, the group has restated its accounts to reflect the revised recognition of its retirement benefits schemes and the resultant changes to deferred tax and amounts recognised in the profit and loss account and statement of total recognised gains and losses. Consequently, the group has restated its comparatives for the year ended 31st March 2003. The effect is to decrease the profit after taxation by £1.8 million in the year ended 31st March 2003. The group's net assets at 31st March 2003 have decreased by £95.7 million. No calculation has been performed of the effect on the results for the year ended 31st March 2004 because it was not considered practicable.

Under the provisions of Urgent Issues Task Force (UITF) Abstract 38 – 'Accounting for ESOP Trusts', which the group adopted on 1st April 2003, the group has restated its accounts to recognise amounts related to the group's ESOTs and LTIP as a component of shareholders' funds. The effect is to decrease short term investments by £13.8 million and to decrease other creditors falling due within one year by £1.2 million, resulting in net assets decreasing by £12.6 million at 31st March 2003. There is no effect on the profit and loss account.

	2004	2003 restated[1]	% change
Turnover	£4,493m	£4,324m	+4
Sales excluding precious metals	£1,224m	£1,159m	+6
Operating profit	£188.3m	£167.9m	+12
Profit before tax	£178.0m	£173.5m	+3
Earnings per share	56.0p	55.4p	+1
Before Exceptional Items and Goodwill Amortisation:			
Operating profit	£206.0m	£189.2m	+9
Profit before tax	£195.7m	£189.9m	+3
Earnings per share	64.0p	61.8p	+4
Dividend per share	26.4p	25.5p	+4

[1] Restated for FRS 17

Financial
Highlights
2004

Divisional Operating Profit

Earnings Per Share Before Exceptional Items and Goodwill Amortisation

Dividend Per Share

Consolidated Profit and Loss Account

for the year ended 31st March 2004

	Notes	2004 Before exceptional items and goodwill amortisation £ million	2004 Exceptional items and goodwill amortisation £ million	2004 Total £ million	2003 Before exceptional items and goodwill amortisation restated £ million	2003 Total restated £ million
Turnover	1	4,492.9	–	4,492.9	4,323.9	4,323.9
Operating profit	1					
Before goodwill amortisation		205.3	–	205.3	188.7	188.7
Goodwill amortisation		–	(19.7)	(19.7)	–	(13.7)
Before exceptional items		205.3	(19.7)	185.6	188.7	175.0
Exceptional items	2	–	2.1	2.1	–	(7.4)
Group operating profit	5	205.3	(17.6)	187.7	188.7	167.6
Share of profit in associates		0.7	–	0.7	0.5	0.5
Goodwill amortisation on associates		–	(0.1)	(0.1)	–	–
Share of exceptional items in associates	2	–	–	–	–	(0.2)
Total operating profit		206.0	(17.7)	188.3	189.2	167.9
Profit on sale of continuing operations						
Sale of an interest in Johnson Matthey Fuel Cells Limited		–	–	–	–	10.9
Exchange of Australian gold operations for share of AGR Matthey		–	–	–	–	(6.0)
Profit on ordinary activities before interest		206.0	(17.7)	188.3	189.2	172.8
Net interest	3	(16.3)	–	(16.3)	(13.2)	(13.2)
Net return on retirement benefits assets and liabilities	4	6.0	–	6.0	13.9	13.9
Profit on ordinary activities before taxation	6	195.7	(17.7)	178.0	189.9	173.5
Taxation	8	(58.3)	0.4	(57.9)	(56.4)	(53.7)
Profit after taxation		137.4	(17.3)	120.1	133.5	119.8
Minority interests	26	1.7	–	1.7	0.4	0.4
Profit attributable to shareholders		139.1	(17.3)	121.8	133.9	120.2
Dividends	9	(57.4)	–	(57.4)	(55.5)	(55.5)
Retained profit for the year	27	81.7	(17.3)	64.4	78.4	64.7

		pence		pence	restated pence	restated pence
Earnings per ordinary share						
Basic	10	64.0		56.0	61.8	55.4
Diluted	10	63.7		55.8	61.4	55.1
Dividend per ordinary share	9	26.4		26.4	25.5	25.5

The notes on pages 46 to 69 form an integral part of the accounts.

Consolidated and Parent Company Balance Sheets

as at 31st March 2004

	Notes	Group 2004 £ million	Group 2003 restated £ million	Parent company 2004 £ million	Parent company 2003 restated £ million
Fixed assets					
Goodwill	12	**377.1**	373.4	**106.6**	110.0
Tangible fixed assets	13	**608.1**	601.1	**200.2**	196.1
Investments	14	**5.5**	6.4	**462.0**	463.4
		990.7	980.9	**768.8**	769.5
Current assets					
Stocks	16	**417.3**	438.4	**268.8**	232.8
Debtors: due within one year	17	**387.4**	365.7	**556.9**	599.3
Debtors: due after more than one year	17	**–**	–	**320.9**	344.5
Short term investments	18	**1.6**	1.5	**–**	–
Cash at bank and in hand	19	**106.5**	100.4	**2.7**	33.4
		912.8	906.0	**1,149.3**	1,210.0
Creditors: amounts falling due within one year					
Borrowings and finance leases	19	**(46.5)**	(46.5)	**(16.4)**	(27.5)
Precious metal leases	21	**(127.4)**	(128.0)	**(142.5)**	(107.9)
Other creditors	22	**(358.9)**	(382.6)	**(750.3)**	(757.4)
Net current assets		**380.0**	348.9	**240.1**	317.2
Total assets less current liabilities		**1,370.7**	1,329.8	**1,008.9**	1,086.7
Creditors: amounts falling due after more than one year					
Borrowings and finance leases	19	**(454.5)**	(456.4)	**(448.4)**	(450.3)
Other creditors	22	**(0.7)**	(0.6)	**(103.4)**	(153.0)
Provisions for liabilities and charges	23	**(47.4)**	(49.3)	**(18.9)**	(13.8)
Net assets excluding retirement benefits assets and liabilities		**868.1**	823.5	**438.2**	469.6
Retirement benefits net assets	11	**31.5**	1.5	**–**	–
Retirement benefits net liabilities	11	**(28.0)**	(26.9)	**(9.3)**	(7.0)
Net assets including retirement benefits assets and liabilities		**871.6**	798.1	**428.9**	462.6
Capital and reserves					
Called up share capital	25	**220.6**	219.5	**220.6**	219.5
Share premium account	27	**137.1**	131.8	**137.1**	131.8
Capital redemption reserve	27	**4.9**	4.9	**4.9**	4.9
Shares held in employee share ownership trusts	27	**(28.8)**	(14.8)	**(28.4)**	(14.4)
Associates' reserves	27	**(0.5)**	0.1	**–**	–
Profit and loss account	27	**528.9**	445.8	**94.7**	120.8
Shareholders' funds		**862.2**	787.3	**428.9**	462.6
Minority interests	26	**9.4**	10.8	**–**	–
		871.6	798.1	**428.9**	462.6

The accounts were approved by the Board of Directors on 1st June 2004 and signed on its behalf by:

C R N Clark

J N Sheldrick

Directors

The notes on pages 46 to 69 form an integral part of the accounts.

Consolidated Cash Flow Statement

for the year ended 31st March 2004

	Notes	2004 £ million	2003 restated £ million
Reconciliation of operating profit to net cash inflow from operating activities			
Operating profit		187.7	167.6
Depreciation, amortisation and net loss on disposal of fixed assets and investments		83.5	68.6
Net retirement benefit charge less contributions		1.0	(6.7)
Decrease / (increase) in owned stocks		17.3	(7.7)
(Increase) / decrease in debtors		(41.7)	13.9
Increase / (decrease) in creditors and provisions		11.9	(5.8)
Net cash inflow from operating activities		259.7	229.9

Cash Flow Statement

	Notes	2004 £ million	2003 restated £ million
Net cash inflow from operating activities		259.7	229.9
Dividends received from associates		0.5	0.1
Returns on investments and servicing of finance	28	(16.4)	(13.4)
Taxation		(43.1)	(42.4)
Capital expenditure and financial investment	28	(114.4)	(124.7)
Acquisitions and disposals			
Acquisitions	28	(18.4)	(271.2)
Disposals	28	–	22.4
Net cash outflow for acquisitions and disposals		(18.4)	(248.8)
Equity dividends paid		(56.4)	(54.0)
Net cash flow before use of liquid resources and financing		11.5	(253.3)
Management of liquid resources	28	1.1	1.0
Financing			
Issue and purchase of share capital	28	(8.5)	2.8
Increase in borrowings and finance leases	28	6.3	259.7
Net cash (outflow) / inflow from financing		(2.2)	262.5
Increase in cash in the period		10.4	10.2

	Notes	2004 £ million	2003 restated £ million
Reconciliation of net cash flow to movement in net debt			
Increase in cash in the period		10.4	10.2
Cash inflow from movement in borrowings and finance leases	29	(6.3)	(259.7)
Cash inflow from term deposits included in liquid resources		(1.1)	(1.0)
Change in net debt resulting from cash flows		3.0	(250.5)
Borrowings acquired with subsidiaries		–	(0.4)
Loan notes (issued) / cancelled to acquire subsidiaries	29	(1.1)	(6.8)
Translation difference	29	6.1	14.2
Movement in net debt in year		8.0	(243.5)
Net debt at beginning of year	29	(402.5)	(159.0)
Net debt at end of year	29	(394.5)	(402.5)

The notes on pages 46 to 69 form an integral part of the accounts.

■ vertical analysis, where each item in the profit and loss account (and balance sheet) is expressed as a percentage of the total sales (total assets).

Horizontal analysis

We introduced the technique of horizontal analysis in Chapter 5. The following example illustrates the technique applied to a summary of the Johnson Matthey plc profit and loss account for the years to 31 March 2004 and 31 March 2003.

Worked Example 6.2

We can prepare a horizontal analysis using a summary of the profit and loss account results for Johnson Matthey plc for 2003 and 2004, using 2003 as the base year.

(You may note that a part of the profit and loss account refers to profit on sale of continuing operations. Continuing operations, as distinct from discontinued operations, are defined in the glossary at the end of this book.)

Johnson Matthey plc
Summary consolidated profit and loss account for the year ended 31 March 2004

Figures in £m

	2004		2003	
Turnover		4,492.9		4,323.9
Operating profit				
Before goodwill amortisation	205.3		188.7	
Goodwill amortisation	(19.7)		(13.7)	
Before exceptional items	185.6		175.0	
Exceptional items	2.1		(7.4)	
Group operating profit	187.7		167.6	
Share of profit in associates	0.7		0.5	
Goodwill amortisation on associates	(0.1)		(0.0)	
Share of exceptional items in associates	(0.0)		(0.2)	
Total operating profit		188.3		167.9
Profit on sale of continuing operations				
Sale of interest in Fuel Cells Ltd		–		10.9
Exchange of Australian gold operations for share of AGR Matthey		–		(6.0)
Profit on ordinary activities before interest		188.3		172.8
Net interest		(16.3)		(13.2)
Net return on retirement benefits assets and liabilities		6.0		13.9
Profit on ordinary activities before taxation		178.0		173.5
Taxation		(57.9)		(53.7)

Profit after tax	120.1	119.8
Minority interests	1.7	0.4
Profit attributable to shareholders	121.8	120.2
Dividends	(57.4)	(55.5)
Retained profit for the year	64.4	64.7

Johnson Matthey plc
Consolidated profit and loss account for the year ended 31 March 2004

Horizontal analysis	2003	2004
Turnover	100.0	103.9
Operating profit		
Before goodwill amortisation	100.0	108.8
Goodwill amortisation	100.0	143.8
Before exceptional items	100.0	106.1
Exceptional items	100.0	(28.4)
Group operating profit	100.0	112.0
Share of profit in associates	100.0	140.0
Goodwill amortisation on associates	100.0	–
Share of exceptional items in associates	100.0	–
Total operating profit	100.0	112.2
Profit on sale of continuing operations		
Sale of interest in Fuel Cells Ltd	100.0	–
Exchange of Australian gold operations for share of AGR Matthey	100.0	–
Profit on ordinary activities before interest	100.0	109.0
Net interest	100.0	123.5
Net return on retirement benefits assets and liabilities	100.0	43.2
Profit on ordinary activities before taxation	100.0	102.6
Taxation	100.0	107.8
Profit after tax	100.0	100.3
Minority interests	100.0	–
Profit attributable to shareholders	100.0	101.3
Dividends	100.0	103.4
Retained profit for the year	100.0	99.5

Worked Example 6.2 has considered only two years, and has used 2003 as the base year 100. This means, for example·

if   turnover for 2003 of £4,323.9m = 100

then   turnover for 2004 of £4,492.9m = $\dfrac{£4,492.9m \times 100}{£4,323.9m} = 103.9$

Subsequent years may be compared with 2003 as base 100, using the same sort of calculation.

This technique is particularly useful to make a line-by-line comparison of a company's accounts for each accounting period over say five or ten years, using the first year as the base year. When we look at a set of accounts we may by observation automatically carry out this process of assessing percentage changes in performance over time. However, presentation of the information in tabular form, for a number of years, gives a very clear picture of trends in performance in each area of activity and may provide the basis for further analysis.

We can see from the above horizontal analysis how the net profit for the year has been derived compared with that for 2003. Despite an increase of 3.9% in sales, operating profit before tax was increased by only 2.6%. Higher average corporation tax levels incurred by the company meant that Johnson Matthey was able to increase the level of profit attributable to shareholders by only 1.3% compared with the previous year.

> **Progress check 6.4** **What can a horizontal analysis of the information contained in the financial statements of a company add to that provided from ratio analysis?**

Vertical analysis

Worked Example 6.3 uses total turnover as the basis for calculation. The following analysis confirms the conclusions drawn from the horizontal analysis.

Worked Example 6.3

We can prepare a vertical analysis using a summary of the consolidated profit and loss account results for Johnson Matthey plc for 2003 and 2004.

Johnson Matthey plc
Consolidated profit and loss account for the year ended 31 March 2004

Vertical analysis	2004	2003
Turnover	100.0	100.0
Operating profit		
Before goodwill amortisation	4.6	4.3
Goodwill amortisation	(0.4)	(0.3)
Before exceptional items	4.2	4.0
Exceptional items	(0.0)	(0.1)

Group operating profit	4.2	3.9
Share of profit in associates	0.0	0.0
Goodwill amortisation on associates	(0.0)	0.0
Share of exceptional items in associates	0.0	0.0
Total operating profit	4.2	3.9
Profit on sale of continuing operations		
Sale of interest in Fuel Cells Ltd	0.0	0.2
Exchange of Australian gold operations for share of AGR Matthey	(0.0)	(0.1)
Profit on ordinary activities before interest	4.2	4.0
Net interest	(0.3)	(0.3)
Net return on retirement benefits assets and liabilities	0.1	0.3
Profit on ordinary activities before taxation	4.0	4.0
Taxation	(1.3)	(1.2)
Profit after tax	2.7	2.8
Minority interests	0.0	0.0
Profit attributable to shareholders	2.7	2.8
Dividends	(1.3)	(1.3)
Retained profit for the year	1.4	1.5

Profit on ordinary activities before interest was increased from 4.0% in 2003 to 4.2% in 2004. Net interest charges and other financial items were higher than the previous year, and so profit before tax was the same for both years at 4% of sales. An increase in the percentage burden of taxation reduced the profit attributable to shareholders from 2.8% in 2003 to 2.7% in 2004. Dividends were 1.3% of sales for both years, giving a retained profit for the year of 1.4% (2003 1.5%).

> **Progress check 6.5 What can a vertical analysis of the information contained in the financial statements of a company add to the information provided from a horizontal analysis and a ratio analysis?**

Notes on the accounts

The section headed 'Notes on the Accounts' in the annual report and accounts contains information that must be reported additional to, and in support of, the financial statements. This may be used to comment on financial performance. Generally, the information disclosed in notes to the accounts includes:

- segmental information – analysis by business and geographical area relating to turnover, operating profit and net assets
- exceptional items
- operating profit
- net interest
- net return on retirement benefits assets and liabilities
- profit before taxation
- fees paid to auditors
- taxation
- earnings per share
- dividends
- employees/directors information – employee numbers, costs, and retirement benefits
- fixed assets
- stocks
- debtors
- investments
- borrowings
- derivatives and financial instruments
- creditors
- finance leases
- provisions for liabilities and charges
- deferred taxation
- share capital
- minority interests
- reserves
- cash flows
- analysis of net debt
- commitments and contingent liabilities ⬅
- acquisitions and disposals
- post balance sheet events. ⬅

Segmental reporting

The first note in the Notes on the Accounts in Johnson Matthey's report and accounts for 2004 is headed segmental information. Accounting standard SSAP 25, Segmental Reporting, requires large companies to disclose segmental information by each class of business, and by geographical region, unless the directors feel that by doing so they may seriously damage the competitive position of the company. This analysis is required in order that users of financial information may carry out more meaningful financial analysis.

Most large companies are usually comprised of diverse businesses supplying different products and services, rather than being engaged in a single type of business. Each type of business activity may have:

- a different structure
- different levels of profitability
- different levels of growth potential
- different levels of risk exposure.

The financial statements of such diversified companies are consolidated to include all business activities, which is a potential problem for the users of financial information. For analysis and interpretation of financial performance, aggregate figures are not particularly useful for the following reasons:

- difficulties in evaluation of performance of a business which has interests that are diverse from the aggregated financial information
- difficulties of comparison of trends over time and comparison between companies because the various activities undertaken by the company are likely to differ in size and range in comparison with other businesses
- differences in conditions between different geographical markets, in terms of levels of risk, profitability and growth

- differences in conditions between different geographical markets, in terms of political and social factors, environmental factors, currencies and inflation rates.

Segmental reporting analysis enables:

- the further analysis of segmental performance to determine more accurately the likely growth prospects for the business as a whole
- evaluation of the impact on the company of changes in conditions relating to particular activities
- improvements in internal management performance, because it may be monitored through disclosure of segmental information to shareholders
- evaluation of the acquisition and disposal performance of the company.

Worked Example 6.4

The information in the table below relates to global sales by Guinness plc for the years 2000 and 1999.

Figures in £m

	2000	1999
Global Sales	4,730	4,681
Asia/Pacific – B	349	324
Asia/Pacific – S	454	426
North America – B	166	151
North America – S	491	551
Rest of Europe – B	1,025	954
Rest of Europe – S	723	741
Rest of the World – B	203	198
Rest of the World – S	402	384
UK – B	519	495
UK – S	398	457

S = spirits B = beer

(i) Using the information provided we may prepare a simple table that compares the sales for 1999 with the sales for the year 2000.

(ii) We can also consider how a simple sales analysis can provide an investor with information that is more useful than just global sales for the year.

(i)

Global sales	2000 £m Spirits	2000 versus 1999 %	2000 £m Beers	2000 versus 1999 %	2000 £m Total	2000 versus 1999 %	1999 £m Spirits	1999 £m Beers	1999 £m Total
UK	398	−12.9	519	+4.8	917	−3.7	457	495	952
Rest of Europe	723	−2.4	1,025	+7.4	1,748	+3.1	741	954	1,695
North America	491	−10.9	166	+9.9	657	−6.4	551	151	702
Asia/Pacific	454	+6.6	349	+7.7	803	+7.1	426	324	750
Rest of the World	402	+4.7	203	+2.5	605	+3.9	384	198	582
Total global sales					4,730	+1.0			4,681

(ii)

Numbers that are blandly presented in a global format do not usually reveal trends. Analysis of information by area, for example, may reveal trends and may illustrate the impact of new policies or the changes in specific economic environments. The analysis of the Guinness sales for two years shows:

- in which geographical area sales have increased or decreased
- for which products sales have increased or decreased.

Analysis of the results over several years is usually needed to provide meaningful trend information as a basis for investigation into the reasons for increases and decreases.

Class of business is a part of the overall business, which can be identified as providing a separate product or service, or group of related products or services. A geographical segment may comprise an individual country or a group of countries in which the business operates.

If a company operates in two or more classes of business activity or two or more geographical segments, there should normally be separate disclosure of information for each segment, which should include:

- sales to external customers and sales to other segments within the business, according to origin, and also by destinations of the goods and services if they are substantially different from the geographical region from which they were supplied
- operating profit before accounting for finance charges, taxation, minority interests and extra-ordinary items
- net assets.

Let's take a look at Johnson Matthey's segmental reporting, (see pp. 226–7). This may be used to provide even more useful information through horizontal and vertical analysis of the numbers. Such an analysis over a 5 or 10-year period would be particularly useful to identify trends in performance,

Notes on the Accounts

for the year ended 31st March 2004

1 *Segmental information*

	Turnover		Operating profit		Net operating assets	
	2004	2003	2004	2003 restated	2004	2003 restated
	£ million	£ million	£ million	£ million	£ million	£ million
Activity analysis						
Catalysts	**1,142.7**	1,083.4	**109.2**	95.3	**819.7**	747.2
Precious Metals	**2,956.4**	2,857.1	**44.2**	48.0	**19.0**	48.4
Colours & Coatings	**254.1**	255.7	**26.7**	25.3	**204.7**	210.3
Pharmaceutical Materials	**139.7**	127.7	**42.3**	36.7	**281.4**	281.3
Corporate	**–**	–	**(16.4)**	(16.1)	**(62.2)**	(61.2)
	4,492.9	4,323.9	**206.0**	189.2	**1,262.6**	1,226.0
Goodwill amortisation (note 12)			**(19.7)**	(13.7)		
Goodwill amortisation on associates			**(0.1)**	–		
Exceptional items included in operating profit (note 2)			**2.1**	(7.6)		
			188.3	167.9	**1,262.6**	1,226.0
Profit on sale of continuing operations			**–**	4.9		
Net interest			**(16.3)**	(13.2)		
Net return on retirement benefits assets and liabilities			**6.0**	13.9		
Profit on ordinary activities before taxation			**178.0**	173.5		
Net borrowings and finance leases					**(394.5)**	(402.5)
Net assets excluding retirement benefits assets and liabilities					**868.1**	823.5
Retirement benefits net assets / (liabilities)					**3.5**	(25.4)
Net assets including retirement benefits assets and liabilities					**871.6**	798.1

	Turnover		Operating profit		Net operating assets	
	2004	2003	2004	2003 restated	2004	2003 restated
	£ million	£ million	£ million	£ million	£ million	£ million
Geographical analysis by origin						
Europe	**3,235.1**	2,964.7	**81.0**	59.3	**916.6**	871.9
North America	**965.7**	1,082.2	**72.3**	87.3	**229.4**	234.4
Asia	**838.1**	844.7	**19.3**	12.4	**55.4**	74.6
Rest of the World	**277.6**	234.2	**33.4**	30.2	**61.2**	45.1
	5,316.5	5,125.8	**206.0**	189.2	**1,262.6**	1,226.0
Less inter-segment sales	**(823.6)**	(801.9)				
Total turnover	**4,492.9**	4,323.9				
Goodwill amortisation (note 12)			**(19.7)**	(13.7)		
Goodwill amortisation on associates			**(0.1)**	–		
Exceptional items included in operating profit (note 2)			**2.1**	(7.6)		
			188.3	167.9	**1,262.6**	1,226.0
Profit on sale of continuing operations			**–**	4.9		
Net interest			**(16.3)**	(13.2)		
Net return on retirement benefits assets and liabilities			**6.0**	13.9		
Profit on ordinary activities before taxation			**178.0**	173.5		
Net borrowings and finance leases					**(394.5)**	(402.5)
Net assets excluding retirement benefits assets and liabilities					**868.1**	823.5
Retirement benefits net assets / (liabilities)					**3.5**	(25.4)
Net assets including retirement benefits assets and liabilities					**871.6**	798.1

Notes on the Accounts

for the year ended 31st March 2004

1   Segmental information *(continued)*

	2004 £ million	2003 £ million
External turnover by geographical destination		
Europe	**2,011.4**	1,800.2
North America	**1,144.8**	1,228.7
Asia	**1,020.0**	1,023.0
Rest of the World	**316.7**	272.0
Total turnover	**4,492.9**	4,323.9

Turnover by destination relating to the United Kingdom amounted to £1,255.4 million (2003 £1,050.3 million).

2   Exceptional items

An exceptional credit of £2.1 million (2003 charge of £7.6 million) has been included in operating profit. This comprises:

	2004 £ million	2003 £ million
Litigation settlement (Pharmaceutical Materials)	**14.8**	–
Cost of integrating Synetix	**–**	(6.5)
Other Catalysts' rationalisation costs	**(12.7)**	(4.8)
Profit on sale of unhedged palladium	**–**	5.1
Cost of rationalising Australian operations following the set up of AGR Matthey	**–**	(1.2)
Exceptional items in group operating profit	**2.1**	(7.4)
Share of exceptional items in associates – AGR Matthey	**–**	(0.2)
Exceptional items in total operating profit	**2.1**	(7.6)

These charges arise in Europe (£10.5 million, 2003 £4.8 million), North America (credit £13.7 million, 2003 charge £1.4 million), Asia (£0.2 million, 2003 £ nil) and Rest of the World (£0.9 million, 2003 £1.4 million).

3   Net interest

	2004 £ million	2003 £ million
Interest payable on bank loans and overdrafts	**(9.0)**	(8.5)
Interest payable on other loans	**(17.2)**	(13.6)
	(26.2)	(22.1)
Interest receivable from associates	**–**	0.2
Other interest receivable	**10.2**	9.0
Net interest – group	**(16.0)**	(12.9)
Share of interest payable by associates – payable to group	**–**	(0.2)
Share of interest payable by associates – other	**(0.3)**	(0.1)
Net interest	**(16.3)**	(13.2)

4   Net return on retirement benefits assets and liabilities

	2004 £ million	2003 restated £ million
Expected return on scheme assets	**37.5**	46.4
Interest on scheme liabilities	**(31.5)**	(32.5)
Net return on retirement benefits assets and liabilities	**6.0**	13.9

and changes that may have taken place in the activities of the business and the areas of the world in which the company has operated.

There are many problems relating to the principle of disclosure of segmental information, some of which we have already identified:

- directors may be reluctant to disclose information that may damage the competitive position of the company – foreign competitors may not have to disclose similar data
- segmental information may not be useful since the total company results are what should be relevant to shareholders
- some users of information may not be sufficiently financially expert to avoid being confused by the segmental information
- conglomerates may choose not to disclose segmental information, whereas a single activity company by definition is unable to hide anything.

There are, in addition, some accounting problems concerned with the preparation of segmental reports:

- identification of business class and geographical segments is not defined in SSAP 25, but is left to the judgement of the directors of the company
- lack of definition of segments results in difficulty in comparison of companies
- difficulties in analysis and apportionment of costs that are common between activities and geographical regions
- difficulties in the treatment of costs of transfers of goods and services between segments.

> Progress check 6.6 **Describe what is meant by segmental reporting and to whom it is useful.**

Worked Example 6.5

If we refer to note 1 in the Johnson Matthey plc Notes on the Accounts in their annual report and accounts 2004 we can identify activity – turnover for 2004 and 2003. This will enable us to present the data in both pie chart and bar chart format, and more clearly explain JM's sales results for 2004 and 2003.

Figure 6.4 Johnson Matthey plc
turnover 2004

Figure 6.5 Johnson Matthey plc
turnover 2003

The pie charts give a broad indication of turnover by type of business, and show that for both years precious metals provide just below two thirds of the turnover, catalysts provide around one quarter of the turnover. Colours and coatings, and pharmaceutical materials are small sectors that provide the balance. The bar chart is probably more useful in showing more clearly that turnover from the two largest sectors has increased in 2004 over 2003 but the two small sectors have remained at around the same volume.

Figure 6.6 Johnson Matthey plc turnover 2004 and 2003

Corporate social responsibility (CSR) reporting

An inspection of Johnson Matthey's report and accounts 2004 will reveal that environmental issues and the health and safety of its employees, customers, and the community, rank highly amongst the company's priorities. This is demonstrated in the coverage given to such issues in the chairman's statement and in the separate five-page section devoted to these issues (see pp. 231–5).

Throughout the past 10 years or so companies have started to show greater interest in their position with regard to environmental and social issues. General corporate awareness has increased as to how the adoption of particular policies may have adverse social and environmental effects. Environmental issues naturally focus on our inability to sustain our use of non-renewable resources, the disappearance of the ozone layer and forestation, pollution and waste treatment. Social issues may include problems associated with race, gender, disability, sexual orientation, and age, and the way that companies manage bullying, the incidence of accidents, employee welfare, training and development.

The increase in awareness of environmental and social issues has followed the concern that the focus of traditional reporting has been weighted too heavily towards the requirements of shareholders, with too little regard for the other stakeholders. This has led to an over-emphasis on the financial performance, particularly the profitability, of the business. The accountancy profession and other interested parties have given thought to the widening of the annual report and accounts to meet the requirements of all stakeholders, and not just the shareholders of the business.

In March 2000, the UK Government appointed a Minister for Corporate Social Responsibility. The Government's first report on CSR was published in March 2001, which has been followed by subsequent reports, all of which can be accessed from its website devoted to CSR, www.CSR.gov.uk. The

Government sees CSR as the business contribution to sustainable development goals. They regard CSR as essentially about how business takes account of its economic, social and environmental impacts in the way it operates – maximising the benefits and minimising the downsides. CSR is about companies moving beyond a base of legal compliance to integrating socially responsible behaviour into their core values, in recognition of the sound business benefits in doing so. In principle, CSR applies to SMEs as well as to large companies.

There is currently no consensus of 'best practice' in the area of social and environmental reporting. Nor is there a compulsory requirement for companies to include such statements in their annual reports and accounts. The Government's approach is to encourage the adoption and reporting of CSR through best practice guidance, including development of its Corporate Responsibility Index and, where appropriate, intelligent regulation and fiscal incentives. Most large companies have reacted positively to the need for such reporting, although the quality, style and content, and the motives for inclusion, may vary. Motives may range from a genuine wish to contribute to the goal of sustainable development to simple reassurance, or attempts to mould and change opinion, and political lobbying.

Companies that include CSR reporting in their annual reports and accounts are now endeavouring to go beyond a simple outline of their environmental and social policies. Many companies include reports expanding on these policies in qualitative terms, which explain the performance of the business in its compliance with national and international standards. Some companies have taken the next step to provide detailed quantitative reports of targets, and performance and the financial impact of social and environmental issues.

CSR performance reporting is still in its infancy. The current UK Government is actively supporting the creation of a shift in the UK enterprise culture. It has emphasised how companies engaged in CSR are reporting benefits to their reputation and their bottom line. It seems likely that as the focus on standardisation of targets, indicators and audit of social and environmental performance increases, then the pressure for wider reporting will increase, and be supported by a CSR performance reporting standard.

> **Progress check 6.7** **What is CSR performance reporting and why is it becoming increasingly important to companies and the UK Government?**

Directors' report

The directors' report includes financial and non-financial information, and it is a statutory requirement for a copy of this report, along with the accounts of the business, to be sent to shareholders. The directors' report includes a great deal of detail, for example:

- details of the principal activities of the business
- information about directors and their share ownership
- details about auditors
- company employment policy
- proposed dividends payable to shareholders
- major fixed assets acquisitions and disposals, and changes in valuation
- changes to share capital
- charitable and political donations made by the company.

Corporate Social Responsibility

"The application of Johnson Matthey's leading technology and its commitment to operational excellence make significant contributions to sustainable development."

> *3 Day Accident Rate per 1,000 Employees*

99/00	00/01	01/02	02/03	03/04
19.60	12.76	12.03	11.99	9.22

Johnson Matthey operates according to well established ethical, social and environmental policies. Over the last year the board has led a number of initiatives to improve our operational performance in these areas. Details of these initiatives can be found in the Johnson Matthey corporate social responsibility (CSR) review and are presented here in summary. The full report can be found at www.matthey.com.

The corporate social responsibility disclosure follows the guidelines issued by the Association of British Insurers and the format recommended by the Global Reporting Initiative has been used to guide the development of the corporate social responsibility review. As outlined in the Corporate Governance section (page 31) the board has embedded corporate social responsibility into its risk management process. Corporate social responsibility is championed at the highest level at Johnson Matthey and the board has reviewed and endorsed the full report.

Johnson Matthey has a culture of constant improvement in all aspects of performance. In this area improvement is driven through corporate policies, a comprehensive management system and the commitment of our staff. There are three key policy areas which provide the framework for the management of corporate social responsibility: the Environment, Health and Safety policies; the Employment policies; and the Business Integrity and Ethics policy.

Johnson Matthey Products

Many of our products have a particularly positive social and environmental benefit. They range from anticancer compounds to our autocatalyst technologies, which improve air quality around the world. In addition, our fuel cell technologies aim to make a significant contribution to the generation of clean energy and security of supply.

Product safety is critical to Johnson Matthey and sophisticated systems are in place to ensure that a high level of protection is afforded to our customers.

Whilst Johnson Matthey's main contribution to sustainable development will be through the excellence of our products we also seek to achieve similar levels of excellence in the management of the business and in the quality of our manufacturing operations. Our expertise in processing valuable precious metal materials provides us with a core competence in the conservation, re-use and recycling of natural resources, principles which are now applied throughout our business.

Environment, Health and Safety

Johnson Matthey is firmly committed to managing its activities throughout the group so as to provide the highest level of protection to the environment and to safeguard the health and safety of its employees, customers and the community.

The company's Environment, Health and Safety (EHS) policies provide the guiding principles that ensure high standards are achieved at all sites around the world and afford a means of promoting continuous improvement based on careful risk assessment and comprehensive EHS management systems. These policies, summarised in the company's policy statement (page 26) are reviewed at regular intervals. This work has given greater emphasis to formal management systems, which bring a systematic improvement in performance. Corporate policies provide a framework for all Johnson Matthey businesses to formulate site specific policies to meet local requirements.

EHS compliance audits are an integral part of Johnson Matthey's corporate EHS management system. 69 facilities from our operations worldwide are included in the audit programme. 30 audits have been carried out in 2003 (2002 – 32). Formal exit interviews with local site management are a feature of the audits and audit reports are reviewed by the Chief Executive's Committee with routine follow up on any outstanding issues. During the year further site visits were made to oversee health surveillance programmes by the Group Occupational Physician.

Over the past year Johnson Matthey has undertaken a number of initiatives to improve environmental and health and safety performance. This has included considerable investment in manufacturing processes to reduce safety risks, improvements to planning of site health and safety actions and the installation of new emission control technology.

*Total Acid Gas Emissions**
Tonnes SO$_2$ equivalent

*Total Global Warming Potential**
Million tonnes CO$_2$ equivalent

*Total Water Supply**
Thousands m^3

* On an equivalent basis, over the last year, key environmental emissions have reduced. For the first time the data now includes emissions due to the Synetix and other smaller acquisitions. This growth in the business has given rise to increases in emissions for the year which are highlighted on the graphs in the lighter shade. Plans are in place to return emissions to a downward trend. The environmental data is for the calendar year.

ISO 14001   Over the past year significant strides have been made in the implementation of ISO 14001. This progress has been led by the Environmental Catalysts and Technologies business where a programme to certify the entire business has been initiated. At present 16 sites are certified to the standard with a further two sites in the final stages of assessment. 45% of our staff work at sites with ISO 14001 accreditation, representing some 3,554 people.

Training   Training is vital to ensuring continuous improvements in health and safety at all our sites. Over the past year staff of all grades have received training. There is a wide range of courses available to staff including courses on managing safely and site safety practices. Our major sites employ health and safety training specialists. Expert external trainers supplement in house capabilities where necessary.

Target Setting   One of the key aims of Johnson Matthey's EHS policies is to demonstrate continuous improvement in EHS performance. The group performance against targets is shown below. The targets are set in line with the UK Health and Safety Executive Revitalising Health and Safety initiative with a baseline year of 2000 for our worldwide operations.

1   Reduction of working days lost by 15% by 2004 and by 30% by 2010.
    Target – 35,639 working days lost per 100,000 employees
    Actual – 30,630 working days lost per 100,000 employees

2   Reduction in the incidence rate of major injuries by 5% by 2004 and 10% by 2010.
    Target – 1,862 > 3 day accidents per 100,000 employees
    Actual – 922 > 3 day accidents per 100,000 employees

    Given current performance we will be revising our future targets in the next year.
    A group wide review of environmental performance is undertaken annually.

Targets are also set locally by business units to drive improvement in environmental, health and safety. Typical targets include:
>   Reduction in waste or emissions to air or water.
>   Reduction in energy or commodity use.
>   Training of a certain number of employees on EHS issues.
>   Undertaking a certain number of inspection programmes.
>   Reviewing a target number of risk assessments and implementing new controls.

Supply Chains   Johnson Matthey supports the principles set out within the United Nations Universal Declaration of Human Rights and International Labour Organisation Core Conventions. Management of supply chains and contractor activities is a core component of the group EHS management system. Whilst we are confident of the human rights performance of our own operations we recognise that business practices in the supply chain are not always transparent and represent a risk that must be managed.

Community Activities   The CSR review includes details of the community activities carried out by Johnson Matthey. In the UK the charity of the year programme has so far raised £30,000 for Diabetes UK. The company also supports many other charities locally and nationally through donations, employee time or loans of company facilities. As noted in the Directors' Report, total charitable giving in 2003/04 was £313,000.

Verification   The board and audit committee review CSR issues as part of the company's risk management processes. A review of site based environment, health and safety reporting systems forms part of the group environmental, health and safety audit programme. The board believes that the measures taken to review the CSR information provide a suitable level of confidence without external audit. Johnson Matthey utilises external specialists where specific CSR issues are identified.

Corporate Social Responsibility (continued)

Environment, Health and Safety Policy Statement

Johnson Matthey is firmly committed to managing its activities throughout the group so as to provide the highest level of protection to the environment and to safeguard the health and safety of its employees, customers and the community.

The company's Environment, Health and Safety policies have been widely disseminated and provide the guiding principles necessary to ensure that high standards are achieved at all sites around the world. They also afford a means of promoting continuous improvement based on careful risk assessment and comprehensive EHS management systems, against which all sites are audited.

This policy and its associated procedures are designed to achieve the following corporate objectives:

> That all locations meet legal and group environment, health and safety requirements.

> That the design, manufacture and supply of products is undertaken so as to satisfy the highest standards of health, safety, environmental protection and resource efficiency.

> That management systems are effective in maintaining standards and fulfilling the challenge of securing continuous improvement in environmental, health and safety performance.

In order to achieve these objectives we will:

> Provide leadership and commitment as an expression of the importance that the board and the senior management team places on EHS issues.

> Ensure accountability by holding corporate management and senior executives within each operating division and business unit responsible for EHS performance.

> Provide the financial and human resources to allow EHS issues to be given an appropriate level of priority.

> Provide good communication internally and externally and encourage employee involvement and cooperation at all levels in the organisation in meeting EHS objectives.

> Ensure competence on EHS matters through education, training and awareness at all levels in the organisation, including creating an understanding of individual responsibilities for health and safety and the environment.

> Undertake assessments to identify the risks to health, safety and the environment from company operations and ensure that appropriate control measures are implemented.

> Ensure that new investments are designed and operated to the latest standards so as to eliminate or minimise risks to health, safety and the environment.

> Investigate incidents to identify the root cause and take action to prevent recurrence.

> Promote programmes to achieve energy and resource efficiency.

> Set key corporate objectives and performance targets that can be measured and assessed, reporting results in a meaningful and transparent way both internally and externally.

> Undertake regular EHS inspections and internal audits of operations, and review performance to ensure continuous improvement in EHS management.

The group EHS management system will be reviewed regularly to ensure that it reflects international best practice and our growing understanding of the practical application of sustainable development.

Employment Policies and Business Integrity and Ethics Policy Statement

Employment Policies

Equal Opportunities It is the policy of the group to recruit, train and manage employees who meet the requirements of the job, regardless of gender, ethnic origin, age or religion. Employees who become disabled and disabled people are offered employment consistent with their capabilities.

Training and Development of People Johnson Matthey recognises the importance of recruiting the very highest calibre of employees, training them to achieve challenging standards in the performance of their jobs, and developing them to their maximum potential.

Our policy requires careful review of organisation structure, succession and the development of high potential people to meet our business goals. The Management Development and Remuneration Committee of the board takes a special interest in ensuring compliance with the Training and Development of People Policy.

Training and Development of People Policy

> Ensure highest standards in the recruitment of staff.
> Assess training needs in the light of job requirements.
> Ensure relevance of training and link with business goals.
> Employ and evaluate effective and efficient training methods.
> Promote from within, from high potential pools of talent.
> Understand employees' aspirations.
> Provide development opportunities to meet employees' potential and aspirations.

Employee Relations and Communication Johnson Matthey recognises the importance of effective employee communications. Information and comment is exchanged with employees through the company's in house magazine, regular news bulletins, presentations to staff and team briefings.

Business Integrity and Ethics Policy Statement
A reputation for integrity has been a cornerstone of Johnson Matthey's business since it was founded by Percival Norton Johnson in 1817. It gives customers the confidence that the company's products meet the standards claimed for them and that they may safely

entrust their own precious metals to Johnson Matthey for processing and safe keeping. Employees at all levels are required to protect Johnson Matthey's reputation for integrity.

The company strives to maintain the highest standards of ethical conduct and corporate responsibility worldwide through the application of the following principles:

> Compliance with national and international laws and regulations is required as a minimum standard.
> Reputable business practices must be applied worldwide.
> Conflicts of interest must be declared and appropriate arrangements made to ensure those with a material interest are not involved in the decision making process.
> Improper payments of any kind are prohibited, similarly no gift whose value is material and which may be interpreted as a form of inducement should be accepted or offered by Johnson Matthey employees.
> Reporting of business performance should be undertaken in such a way that senior management is fully and properly informed concerning the business' true performance, risks and opportunities in a timely manner.
> Ethical issues must be dealt with in an efficient and transparent manner.
> A positive contribution to society as a whole, and specifically the communities in which we operate, must be ensured.
> We must seek to influence our suppliers to operate to similar high standards as ourselves.

We support the principles set out within the United Nations Universal Declaration of Human Rights and International Labour Organisation Core Conventions.

All employees have a duty to follow the principles set out in this policy statement. It is the responsibility of directors and senior management to ensure that all employees who directly or indirectly report to them are fully aware of Johnson Matthey's policies and values in the conduct of the company's businesses. It is also the responsibility of directors and senior management to lead by example and to demonstrate the highest standards of integrity in carrying out their duties on behalf of the company. These issues are further safeguarded through corporate governance processes and monitoring by the board and sub-committees to the board.

Corporate Social Responsibility (continued)

Celebrating **30 years**
of Johnson Matthey autocatalysts

When the first car to be fitted with a catalytic converter rolled off a production line in the USA in 1974, it was a huge landmark for both the platinum group metals markets and the global auto industry. In 2004 Johnson Matthey celebrates 30 years in the development of autocatalysts.

1950s...
Automotive exhaust emissions are proved to be a major source of photochemical smog in Los Angeles.

1960s...
The first federal emission standards to control pollution from automobiles are set in the US in 1965. These targets are met without catalysts.

1970s...
> In 1970, US Congress substantially lowers vehicle emissions limits and lead is phased out in gasoline in the USA from 1972 onwards.

> Johnson Matthey files a patent in 1971 covering the use of a rhodium promoted platinum catalyst to control NOx and gaseous organic compounds.

> In 1972, Johnson Matthey proves to the Environmental Protection Agency that the US emissions regulations can be met using rhodium-platinum catalysts.

> The first cars fitted with oxidation catalysts reach showrooms in the USA in 1975; unleaded gasoline is widely available.

> Japanese vehicle emissions standards to control HC, CO and NOx come into effect in 1976.

> US Clean Air Act amendments made in 1977 agree to tighten emissions standards further from 1981 onwards.

> Increased substrate surface area helps to improve pollution conversion efficiency of catalysts.

1980s...
> More sophisticated 'three-way' catalytic converters are introduced in 1981 to meet strict NOx limits.

> Performance of three-way catalytic converters significantly enhanced by use of improved oxygen storage materials (based on cerium dioxide) in catalyst washcoats.

> Vehicle emissions regulations introduced in Australia, incentives introduced in Germany.

1990s...
> In 1990, Johnson Matthey files a patent covering the use of NO_2 to reduce the combustion temperature of diesel particulate matter in a filter, a system subsequently commercialised as the Continuously Regenerating Trap (CRT®).

> New legislation introduced in Japan in 1991 sets much more stringent vehicle NOx emissions limits.

> European Union emissions regulations that necessitate the use of catalytic converters (Euro 1) come into effect from 1993.

> In 1996, European Union emissions regulations tighten as Euro 2 standards are applied. Californian Low Emission Vehicle (LEV) standards come into force, emphasising the cold-start control of pollutants; palladium based catalysts found to be particularly suited to controlling HC emissions on engine start-up.

> Further improvements made in substrate surface area of catalysts.

> National Low Emissions Vehicle (NLEV) emissions standards take effect in the USA from 1999, requiring very substantial reductions in NOx.

2000 Onwards
> EU emissions standards for all road vehicles become more stringent with introduction of Euro 3 regulations in 2000.

> A substantial retrofit programme is created by the Tokyo Metropolitan Government in a move to improve particulate pollution from diesel trucks and buses in the city.

> Diesel car sales in Europe surpass six million vehicles for the first time.

> Phase in of US Tier II emissions standards begins in 2004. These mandate further large reductions in NOx and particulate matter emissions. Tier II compliant vehicles are up to 99% cleaner than vehicles sold in the 1960s.

> Regulations will be introduced in the EU and USA between 2005 and 2010 which will create a significant new original equipment market for exhaust aftertreatment products.

Directors' Report

The directors submit to shareholders their one hundred and thirteenth annual report, together with the audited accounts of the group for the year ended 31st March 2004. Pages 1 to 38 are an integral part of the report.

Principal Activities

The group's principal activities are summarised on page 15.

Dividends

The interim dividend of 8.2 pence per share, up 0.4 pence, was paid in February 2004. A final dividend, which will be paid as an ordinary dividend, of 18.2 pence per share, up 0.5 pence, is being proposed to shareholders as Resolution 3 at the Annual General Meeting (AGM), making a total for the year of 26.4 pence, an increase of 4% over last year. Dividends for the year total £57.4 million.

A low cost Dividend Reinvestment Plan is in place for the benefit of shareholders. This allows them to purchase additional shares in Johnson Matthey with their dividend payment. Further information and a mandate can be obtained from the Company Secretary at the company's registered office.

Share Capital

Allotments of ordinary shares of £1 each of the company were made during the year as set out in note 25 on page 63.

The board will again seek shareholders' approval to renew the annual authority for the company to make purchases of its own ordinary shares through the market. No shares were purchased under this authority during the year ended 31st March 2004.

Employee Share Schemes

4,636 current and former employees, representing approximately 63% of employees worldwide as at 31st March 2004, are shareholders in Johnson Matthey through the group's employee share schemes, which held 3,507,288 shares (1.59% of ordinary share capital) at 31st March 2004. A total of 834 current and former executives hold options over 6,183,642 shares through the company's executive share option schemes.

Directors

Details of the directors of the company are shown on pages 12 and 13. Dr P N Hawker and Mr L C Pentz, both appointed to the board on 1st August 2003, offer themselves for election at the forthcoming AGM. In accordance with the company's Articles of Association, Mr M B Dearden, Mr C D Mackay, Mr J N Sheldrick and Mr I C Strachan retire by rotation and, being eligible, offer themselves for re-election at the AGM.

Directors' Material Interests in Contracts

Other than service contracts, no director had any interest in any material contract with any group company at any time during the year.

Substantial Shareholdings

The company has been advised of the following interest in its ordinary share capital as at 28th May 2004:

Schroder Investment Management Ltd	7.66%	Legal & General Assurance Society Ltd	4.38%
Merrill Lynch Investment Managers	7.61%	Deutsche Asset Management	3.74%
Scottish Widows Investment Partnership Ltd	4.96%	AXA Investment Managers UK Ltd	3.05%

Auditors

In accordance with section 384 of the Companies Act 1985, a resolution is to be proposed at the forthcoming AGM for the reappointment of KPMG Audit Plc as auditors of the company.

Policy on Payment of Commercial Debts

The group's policy in relation to the payment of all suppliers (set out in its Group Control Manual, which is distributed to all group operations) is that payment should be made within the credit terms agreed with the supplier. At 31st March 2004, the company's aggregate level of 'creditor days' amounted to 5 days. Creditor days are calculated by dividing the aggregate of the amounts which were owed to trade creditors at the end of the year by the aggregate of the amounts the company was invoiced by suppliers during the year and multiplying by 365 to express the ratio as a number of days.

Donations

During the year the group donated £313,000 (2003 £323,000) to charitable organisations, of which £279,000 (2003 £299,000) was in the UK. There were no political donations made in the year (2003 £ nil).

Going Concern

The directors have a reasonable expectation that the group has sufficient resources to continue in operational existence for the foreseeable future and have, therefore, adopted the going concern basis in preparing the accounts.

This report was approved by the directors on 1st June 2004 and is signed on their behalf by:

Simon Farrant
Company Secretary

The Johnson Matthey plc directors' report (see pp. 236), includes a section on each of the headings we have outlined above. In addition, it includes a section on directors' (lack of) material interests in contracts, and the group policy on payment of commercial debts. The inclusion of the company's 'creditor days' performance is important. There has been general pressure for companies to rely less on funding from extended credit from suppliers, over and above agreed terms.

Following the publication of the Cadbury Committee report in 1992, the directors' report now includes a section on corporate governance (see Chapter 7), and includes details about the company's system of internal control, and its various committees, for example the remuneration committee. Johnson Matthey has reported on the many committees it has in place, and their functions:

- chief executive's committee: strategy, planning and executive management
- audit committee: financial reporting, corporate control, internal and external audit
- nomination committee: appointment of executive and non-executive directors
- management development and remuneration committee: senior management remuneration.

> **Progress check 6.8 What purpose does the directors' report serve and what information does it usually include?**

Inflation and reporting

Inflation is a general increase in the price level over time. We will consider the impact of inflation on the financial statements prepared under the traditional, historical cost convention. In this book we will not cover in detail the alternative approaches to reporting the effect of inflation, other than to highlight the level of awareness of the problem. The accountancy profession has, over the years, considered many proposals of methods to try and deal with inflation-related problems requiring financial reports to reflect the effects of inflation. The proposals relating to the treatment of inflation in financial reporting have revolved around two schools of thought:

- the purchasing power approach, using a price index like the Retail Price Index, to adjust the historical costs of transactions
- the current cost accounting approach, which requires fixed assets and stocks to be included in the accounts at their current value rather than their historical cost.

We have previously discussed the reasons for using money as the unit of measurement, which include its properties as a medium of exchange and a store of value. Its use implies some stability in its value, which in the real world is patently not the case. One £ held today does not have the same value as one £ held in a year's time; it will purchase less in a year's time despite the relatively low levels of inflation prevailing in the UK over recent years – but note how in the mid-1970s the inflation level reached nearly 25% per annum!

The basic problem of inflation in financial reporting is that it tends to overstate profit calculated using traditional historical costs. In periods of inflation the impact on profit is seen in four key areas:

- borrowing and extended credit received are worth less in real terms when settled compared to when the borrowing took place or the credit was received, which is a gain for the business
- financial investments made and extended credit allowed are worth less in real terms when settled compared to when the investments took place or the credit was granted, which is a loss for the business
- depreciation of fixed assets is understated, being based on fixed assets' historical costs and so

when assets eventually have to be replaced the replacement cost will be higher, for which the company may have provided insufficient cash resources
- closing stocks will be more likely to have higher values, on a like-for-like basis, compared with opening stocks and so profit may be overstated, but the pressure on cash resources will be felt when stocks have been sold and then need to be replaced at higher prices.

It is important for the non-accounting specialist to be aware that the published financial statements of UK limited companies have not been adjusted to allow for the effects of inflation. Over extended periods there is therefore significant distortion in the accounting information that has been presented based on historical costs. However, the non-specialist may be assured that the accountancy profession continues to grapple with the problem of inflation in financial reporting.

> **Progress check 6.9 Why should users of financial information be aware of the effects of inflation on financial reporting?**

Value added statements

Value added is a measure of the wealth created by a company through its activities. It is the difference between the value of its sales and the cost of the materials and services that it has bought in.

The value added statement is effectively a rearrangement of the profit and loss account. It shows how value added is distributed among the relevant parties:

- employees
- lenders
- shareholders
- Government

and the amount to provide maintenance and expansion of the business.

The value added statement has often been compared with a cake or a pie (see Fig. 6.7 and Fig. 6.8), with interested parties asking 'are we getting our fair share of the cake?' This question is often the basis of trade union employee wage negotiations with companies.

The Accounting Standards Committee in 1975 published *The Corporate Report*, which described the value added statement as 'the simplest and most immediate way of putting profit into a proper perspective *vis à vis* the whole enterprise as a collective effort of capital, management and employees'. The value added statement has certain advantages as a business performance measure:

- is simple to calculate
- enables comparison between companies with different activities
- improves relationships between shareholders, managers and employees
- cannot be manipulated to the same extent as accounting profit
- enables further analysis for example vertical analysis against turnover
- lends itself to integration with employee incentive schemes.

The value added statement for Johnson Matthey plc shown in Worked Example 6.6 illustrates how value added has been derived and how it has been applied in absolute terms for the years 2003 and 2004. A vertical analysis of the numbers would perhaps provide a better basis for comparison, which is illustrated in Worked Example 6.7.

Worked Example 6.6

We can prepare a value added statement for Johnson Matthey plc using the consolidated profit and loss accounts, and consolidated cash flow statements for 2004 and 2003. Employee costs for 2004 were £262.3m (2003, £253.6m).

Johnson Matthey plc
Consolidated value added statement for the year ended 31 March 2004

Figures in £m	2004	2003
Turnover (from the consolidated profit and loss account)	4,492.9	4,323.9
Bought in materials and services (balancing number)	3,951.1	3,814.6
Value added	541.8	509.3
Applied as follows:		
To pay employees	262.3	253.6
To pay providers of capital (from the consolidated profit and loss account)		
Net interest on loans	16.3	13.2
Dividends to shareholders	57.4	55.5
To pay Government		
Corporation tax	57.9	53.7
To provide maintenance and expansion		
Depreciation (from the consolidated cash flow statement)	83.5	68.6
Retained profits (from the consolidated profit and loss account)	64.4	64.7
	541.8	509.3

The vertical analysis of the value added statement for Johnson Matthey plc shows us that around one half of the value generated by the business is distributed to employees in the form of salaries, wages and benefits (49.8% for 2003 down to 48.4% for 2004). This is far greater than the proportion distributed to the providers of capital (lenders and shareholders), which is at 13.6% for 2004 (13.5% for 2003), although the proportion paid to lenders was higher in 2004 than 2003. Corporation tax has increased from 10.5% in 2003 to 10.7% in 2004.

The remainder of value added is retained for maintenance and expansion of assets. This has increased from 26.2% in 2003 to 27.3% in 2004, indicating an increase in the financing of growth of the business through internally generated sources. Whilst retained profits have decreased from 12.7% to 11.9%, depreciation has increased from 13.5% in 2003 to 15.4% in 2004.

Worked Example 6.7

We can use the value added statement from Worked Example 6.6 to:

(i) prepare a vertical analysis of the data
(ii) present the results in a pie chart format (see Figs 6.7 and 6.8).

Johnson Matthey plc
Consolidated vertical analysis value added statement for the year ended 31 March 2004

	2004	2003
Value added	100.0	100.0
Applied as follows:		
To pay employees	48.4	49.8
To pay providers of capital		
Net interest on loans	3.0	2.6
Dividends to shareholders	10.6	10.9
To pay Government		
Corporation tax	10.7	10.5
To provide maintenance and expansion		
Depreciation	15.4	13.5
Retained profits	11.9	12.7

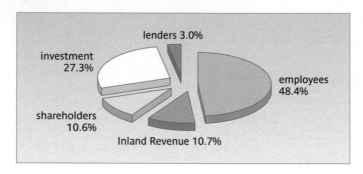

Figure 6.7 Johnson Matthey plc % distribution of value added for the year 2004

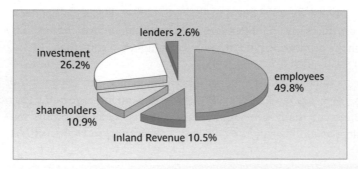

Figure 6.8 Johnson Matthey plc % distribution of value added for the year 2003

The value added statement provides a great deal of clarification on company performance, but, of course, also has disadvantages:

- some difficulty encountered in measurement and reporting
- classification of items – for example taxation, which normally excludes employee tax and National Insurance, and business rates
- unstandardised format with varying treatment of items in the value added statement
- current lack of popularity among companies, despite the inclusion of a value added statement by a large percentage of large companies up to the early 1980s in their annual reports and accounts.

The value added statement seems unlikely to replace the conventional profit and loss account, or cash flow statement as a decision-making tool or as a measure of business performance. However, it may continue to be useful for internal communication of company financial performance to employees, and in support of employee incentive schemes.

> **Progress check 6.10** **What is a value added statement and what does it tell us?**

Summary of key points

- Limited companies prepare their annual reports and accounts to keep shareholders informed about financial performance and the financial position of the business.
- The annual report and accounts of a public limited company now requires disclosure of a great deal of both financial and non-financial information in addition to the financial statements.
- The annual report and accounts allows evaluation of a public limited company in a wider context than was possible from the sort of financial information traditionally required by the shareholders.
- Horizontal analysis of the profit and loss account (which may also be applied to the balance sheet) for two or more years starts with a base year 100 and shows each item, line-by-line, indexed against the base year, and is particularly useful in looking at performance trends over a number of years.
- Vertical analysis of the profit and loss account (which may also be applied to the balance sheet) shows every item as a percentage of turnover (balance sheet-total assets), and is also particularly useful in looking at performance trends over a number of years.
- Segmental reporting provides a further dimension to the financial statements through analysis of turnover, operating profit and net assets, by business class and geographical segments.
- The quality and depth of corporate social responsibility (CSR) performance reporting, in both qualitative and quantitative terms, is becoming increasingly important as annual reports and accounts are required to meet the needs of all stakeholders, not just the shareholders.
- Although the financial statements of limited companies are not adjusted for the effects of inflation, the impact of inflation is a factor that must be considered in evaluation of business performance.
- The value added statement, which is an alternative presentation of the traditional profit and loss statement, measures wealth as the value added by the business rather than the profit earned by the business.

Questions

Q6.1 (i) Why, and for whom, do the annual reports and accounts of limited companies have to be prepared?

(ii) Where do they have to be filed?

(iii) Who are the main users of the information contained in the annual report and accounts?

(iv) How do they use the information?

Q6.2 (i) Why do you think that the chairman, chief executive, and finance director of a plc each need to provide a statement or report for inclusion in the annual report and accounts?

(ii) What purpose do these reports serve and in what ways do they differ?

Q6.3 (i) Describe the key elements of Johnson Matthey's financial review that are included in their report and accounts for 2004, and what these indicate about the performance of the business.

(ii) Why do you think that a third of this report is devoted to financial risk management?

(iii) What does risk management mean?

(iv) What are the financial risks faced by Johnson Matthey?

Q6.4 Describe the technique of horizontal analysis and how it may be used to evaluate, explain and compare company performance.

Q6.5 Describe the technique of vertical analysis and how it may be used to evaluate, explain and compare company performance.

Q6.6 (i) What were the inadequacies in financial statement reporting that SSAP 25, Segmental Reporting, sought to address and how did it do this?

(ii) What are the practical problems that companies face associated with their compliance with SSAP 25?

Q6.7 (i) Why do you think that corporate social responsibility (CSR) reporting has become increasingly important in terms of corporate awareness, and with regard to the awareness of the non-business community?

(ii) Examine the annual reports and accounts of a number of large UK plcs to critically evaluate and compare their CSR reporting with that provided by Johnson Matthey in its 2004 report and accounts.

Q6.8 (i) How does inflation distort accounting information that has been prepared under the historical cost convention?

(ii) In what ways has the accountancy profession considered some alternative approaches to try and deal with the problem of inflation?

Q6.9 (i) Explain what is meant by a value added statement.

(ii) In what ways may a value added statement be used to measure financial performance?

(iii) What are the disadvantages in using value added statements?

(iv) Why do you think the levels of popularity they enjoyed in the 1980s have not been maintained?

Q6.10   What information included in the annual report and accounts of UK public listed companies (plcs) may influence prospective investors and in what ways? How impartial do you think this information is?

Discussion points

D6.1 'The annual reports and accounts prepared by the majority of UK plcs serve to ensure that shareholders, and other stakeholders, are kept very well informed about the affairs of their businesses.' Discuss.

D6.2 'In the global competitive world in which we live, company directors should be able to exercise their full discretion as to the amount of information they disclose in their annual reports and accounts. If they are not allowed this discretion in disclosure, their companies may be driven out of business by their competitors, particularly foreign competitors who may not have the restriction of such extensive reporting requirements.' Discuss.

D6.3 'The main reason that companies increasingly include corporate social responsibility (CSR) reports in their annual reports and accounts is to change the views of users and regulators about the activities in which their businesses are engaged, in order to pre-empt and avoid any negative or harmful reactions.' Discuss this statement by drawing on examples of the type of businesses to which this might apply.
(Hint: You may wish to research Railtrack, and British Gas, as well as Johnson Matthey plc, to provide material for this discussion.)

Exercises

Solutions are provided in Appendix 4 to all exercise numbers highlighted in colour.

Level I

E6.1 *Time allowed – 60 minutes*
Refer to note 1 in Johnson Matthey plc's Notes on the Accounts in their Annual Report & Accounts 2004 and identify the geographical analysis by origin for 2004 and 2003 for:

(a)   turnover

(b)   operating profit.

    (i)   Present each of the data from (a) and (b) in both pie chart and bar chart format.

    (ii)   What do the charts you have prepared tell you about Johnson Matthey's sales and operating profit for 2004 and 2003?

E6.2 *Time allowed – 60 minutes*

    (i)   Use the 10-year record of Johnson Matthey (see pp. 244–5) to prepare a horizontal analysis of the profit and loss account for the 5 years 2000 to 2004, using 2000 as the base year.

    (ii)   What does this analysis tell us about Johnson Matthey's financial performance over that period?

Ten Year Record

	1995 £ million	1996 £ million	1997 £ million	1998 £ million	1999 £ million
Turnover					
Parent and subsidiaries	2,177.8	2,528.9	2,423.2	3,138.8	3,385.4
Share of joint ventures	97.1	156.7	156.9	128.8	–
Total	2,274.9	2,685.6	2,580.1	3,267.6	3,385.4
Operating profit before exceptional items and goodwill amortisation	100.4	111.0	116.3	139.2	147.1
Goodwill amortisation	–	–	–	–	–
Exceptional items	–	–	–	(4.5)	(1.9)
Total operating profit	100.4	111.0	116.3	134.7	145.2
Other exceptional items	(0.7)	–	–	4.4	8.8
Profit before interest	99.7	111.0	116.3	139.1	154.0
Net interest	(4.3)	(8.8)	(8.0)	(9.0)	(15.9)
Net return on retirement benefits assets and liabilities	–	–	–	–	–
Profit before taxation	95.4	102.2	108.3	130.1	138.1
Taxation	(34.3)	(34.3)	(33.0)	(28.5)	(35.1)
Profit after taxation	61.1	67.9	75.3	101.6	103.0
Minority interests	(1.0)	(1.7)	(1.2)	(0.3)	0.7
Profit attributable to shareholders	60.1	66.2	74.1	101.3	103.7
Dividends	(25.9)	(31.4)	(33.6)	(38.7)	(41.3)
Profit retained	34.2	34.8	40.5	62.6	62.4
Earnings per ordinary share (graph 2)	30.9p	32.5p	34.2p	46.7p	47.8p
Earnings per ordinary share before exceptional items and goodwill amortisation (graph 1)	31.2p	32.5p	34.2p	42.8p	42.8p
Dividend per ordinary share (graph 3)	13.5p	14.5p	15.5p	17.8p	19.0p
Summary Balance Sheet					
Assets employed:					
Goodwill	–	–	–	–	4.2
Tangible fixed assets	256.1	321.7	337.7	461.5	480.2
Fixed assets investments / joint ventures / associates	70.9	100.4	84.2	4.2	1.8
Stocks	153.2	196.6	184.7	244.8	243.7
Debtors and short term investments	190.9	231.7	252.5	379.8	434.0
Other creditors and provisions	(223.4)	(304.0)	(291.1)	(409.8)	(418.8)
Retirement benefits net assets / (liabilities)	–	–	–	–	–
	447.7	546.4	568.0	680.5	745.1
Financed by:					
Net borrowings and finance leases / (cash)	102.4	134.2	143.7	225.1	221.6
Retained earnings	151.6	99.8	107.8	130.9	200.9
Share capital, share premium, capital redemption and shares held in ESOTs	195.7	313.1	316.3	318.4	316.8
Minority interests	(2.0)	(0.7)	0.2	6.1	5.8
Capital employed	447.7	546.4	568.0	680.5	745.1
Cumulative goodwill taken directly to reserves	57.5	150.3	156.3	171.4	171.4
Return on assets	21.3%	18.5%	16.4%	17.7%	16.6%

(Operating profit before exceptional items and goodwill amortisation /
average capital employed and cumulative goodwill taken directly to reserves)

Figures for 2003 have been restated for the adoption of FRS 17 – 'Retirement Benefits'. Prior year figures have not been restated for FRS 17 because comparatives are not available. Apart from this, 2003 and prior years have been restated to reflect all changes in accounting policies.

Ten Year Record

2000 £ million	2001 £ million	2002 £ million	2003 £ million	2004 £ million
3,866.0	5,903.7	4,830.1	4,323.9	**4,492.9**
–	–	–	–	**–**
3,866.0	5,903.7	4,830.1	4,323.9	**4,492.9**
146.2	175.0	193.3	189.2	**206.0**
(0.2)	(0.3)	(6.8)	(13.7)	**(19.8)**
(9.8)	(0.6)	(18.1)	(7.6)	**2.1**
136.2	174.1	168.4	167.9	**188.3**
23.4	1.1	(5.6)	4.9	**–**
159.6	175.2	162.8	172.8	**188.3**
(2.4)	5.3	(6.1)	(13.2)	**(16.3)**
–	–	–	13.9	**6.0**
157.2	180.5	156.7	173.5	**178.0**
(47.3)	(54.2)	(50.2)	(53.7)	**(57.9)**
109.9	126.3	106.5	119.8	**120.1**
(0.2)	(0.6)	0.3	0.4	**1.7**
109.7	125.7	106.8	120.2	**121.8**
(44.3)	(51.3)	(53.2)	(55.5)	**(57.4)**
65.4	74.4	53.6	64.7	**64.4**
50.5p	57.3p	49.0p	55.4p	**56.0p**
46.6p	57.2p	60.4p	61.8p	**64.0p**
20.3p	23.3p	24.6p	25.5p	**26.4p**
5.1	8.6	182.6	373.4	**377.1**
311.3	386.8	495.1	601.1	**608.1**
1.0	1.0	2.7	6.4	**5.5**
253.2	278.8	414.3	438.4	**417.3**
434.7	522.9	456.0	367.2	**389.0**
(452.5)	(534.7)	(584.4)	(560.5)	**(534.4)**
–	–	–	(25.4)	**3.5**
552.8	663.4	966.3	1,200.6	**1,266.1**
(165.8)	(139.9)	159.0	402.5	**394.5**
389.2	465.9	466.4	445.9	**528.4**
324.9	332.8	337.0	341.4	**333.8**
4.5	4.6	3.9	10.8	**9.4**
552.8	663.4	966.3	1,200.6	**1,266.1**
46.0	46.0	46.0	40.6	**40.6**
19.3%	26.8%	22.5%	16.8%	**16.2%**

1. Earnings Per Share Before Exceptional Items and Goodwill Amortisation

2. Earnings Per Share

3. Dividend Per Share

E6.3 *Time allowed – 60 minutes*

(i)   Use the 10-year record of Johnson Matthey (see pp. 244–5) to prepare a horizontal analysis of the balance sheet for the 5 years years 2000 to 2004, using 2000 as the base year.

(ii)   What does this analysis tell us about Johnson Matthey's financial position over that period?

Level II

E6.4 *Time allowed – 60 minutes*

(i)   Use the 10-year record of Johnson Matthey (see pp. 244–5) to prepare a vertical analysis of the profit and loss account for the 5 years years 2000 to 2004.

(ii)   What does this analysis tell us about Johnson Matthey's financial performance over that period?

E6.5 *Time allowed – 60 minutes*

Note 1 to the report and accounts of Johnson Matthey provides segmental analysis for the years 2004 and 2003.

Prepare a horizontal analysis from this information, with 2003 as the base year, and use it to explain the appropriate elements of financial performance and the changes in the financial position of the business.

E6.6 *Time allowed – 60 minutes*

Refer to the financial statements included in Johnson Matthey's report and accounts 2004 to calculate the appropriate ratios for comparison with the previous year, and include them in a report on the profitability of the group (see Chapter 5).

E6.7 *Time allowed – 60 minutes*

Refer to the financial statements included in Johnson Matthey's report and accounts 2004 to calculate the appropriate ratios for comparison with the previous year, and to give your assessment of the company's sources and uses of cash, and include them in a report on the group's cash position (see Chapter 5).

E6.8 *Time allowed – 60 minutes*

Refer to the financial statements included in Johnson Matthey's report and accounts 2004 to calculate the appropriate ratios for comparison with the previous year, and include them in a report on the working capital of the group (see Chapter 5).

E6.9 *Time allowed – 60 minutes*

Refer to the financial statements included in Johnson Matthey's report and accounts 2004 to calculate the appropriate ratios for comparison with the previous year, and include them in a report on the investment performance of the group (see Chapter 5).

E6.10 *Time allowed – 60 minutes*

Refer to the financial statements included in Johnson Matthey's report and accounts 2004 to calculate the appropriate ratios for comparison with the previous year, and include them in a report on the financial structure of the group (see Chapter 5).

E6.11 *Time allowed – 90 minutes*

The notes and five-year profit and loss account extracts from the financial statements of Guinness plc are shown below.

You are required to use these to carry out an appropriate analysis and provide a report on the likely explanations of differences in performance over the five years.

Notes:

- The group sells alcohol-based products to consumers and operates in nearly every major country throughout the world.
- Local and global competition is intense in many markets.
- Brands have been sold during the five years.
- New products are invariably variants on the group's basic products of beers, wines and spirits.
- The group share price had been relatively static due to the maturity of the market and the pattern of profits.
- Other investment income shown in the five-year analysis related to an investment in a French luxury goods group.
- Soon after year 6 the group merged with another international food and drinks business, which also had an extensive portfolio of own and purchased brands.
- After the merger several brands were sold to competitors.
- After the merger many of the directors left the group's management team.
- Exchange rates over the five-year period in several of the group's markets were quite volatile.
- The group had £1.4 billion of brands in its balance sheet.

Guinness plc five-year profit and loss account

Figures in £m

	Year 5	Year 4	Year 3	Year 2	Year 1
Turnover	4,730	4,681	4,690	4,663	4,363
Gross profit	961	943	956	938	1,023
Other investment income	113	47	89	(48)	(24)
Profit before interest and tax (operating profit)	1,074	990	1,045	890	999
Net interest	(99)	(114)	(130)	(188)	(204)
Profit before tax	975	876	915	702	795
Tax on profit on ordinary activities	(259)	(251)	(243)	(247)	(242)
Profit on ordinary activities after tax	716	625	672	455	553
Minority interests	(31)	(30)	(31)	(22)	(29)
Profit for financial year	685	595	641	433	524
Dividends	(295)	(302)	(279)	(258)	(237)
Retained profit	390	293	362	175	287
Earnings per share	35.1p	29.4p	31.8p	22.9p	28.1p
Interest cover	10.8	8.7	8.0	4.7	4.9
Dividend cover	2.2	2.0	2.3	1.8	2.3

E6.12 *Time allowed – 90 minutes*

The BOC Group is a company in the chemical industry, in the same industrial sector as Johnson Matthey. Locate the website for BOC Group plc on the Internet. Carry out a review of their most recent annual report and accounts and prepare a report that compares it with Johnson Matthey's report and accounts for the same year. Your report should include comments that relate to specific items that have been covered in Chapter 6, and also the differences and the similarities between the two companies.

7

Corporate governance

Contents

Learning objectives

Completion of this chapter will enable you to:

- describe how the framework for establishing good corporate governance and accountability has been established in a Combined Code of Practice, developed from the work of the Cadbury, Greenbury, Hampel, and Turnbull Committees
- explain the statutory requirement for the audit of limited companies, the election by shareholders of suitably qualified, independent auditors, and the role of the auditors
- outline directors' specific responsibility to shareholders, and responsibilities to society in general, for the management and conduct of companies
- recognise the fiduciary duties that directors have to the company, and their duty of care to all stakeholders and to the community at large, particularly with regard to the Companies Act 1985/1989, Health and Safety at Work Act 1974, and Financial Services Act 1986
- explain the implications for companies and their directors that may arise from the UK Government's promised legislation on the issue of corporate manslaughter
- appreciate the importance of directors' duties regarding insolvency, the Insolvency Act 1986, and the Enterprise Act 2002
- consider the implications for directors of wrongful trading, and recognise the difference between this and the offence of fraudulent trading, and the possibility of criminal penalties
- outline the implication for directors of the Company Directors Disqualification Act 1986, and the Enterprise Act 2002
- explain the actions that directors of companies should take to ensure compliance with their obligations and responsibilities, and to protect themselves against possible non-compliance.

Introduction

In Chapter 6 we saw that a large part of Johnson Matthey plc's report and accounts 2004 was devoted to the subject of corporate governance, the systems by which companies are directed and controlled. This chapter turns to the statutory and non-statutory rules that surround the accounting for limited companies.

In earlier chapters we discussed the way in which the limited company exists in perpetuity as a legal entity, separate from the lives of those individuals who both own and manage it. The limited company has many rights, responsibilities, and liabilities in the same way as individual people. As a separate legal entity the company is responsible for its own liabilities. These are not the obligations of the shareholders who have paid for their shares, being the limit of their obligations to the company.

The directors of a limited company are appointed by, and are responsible to, the shareholders for the management of the company, maintained through their regular reporting on the activities of the business. The responsibilities of directors, however, are wider than to just the shareholders. They are also responsible for acting correctly towards their employees, suppliers, customers, and the public at large.

The annual audit of the accounts is a statutory requirement for all limited companies, excluding smaller limited companies. As with directors, the auditors of a limited company are also appointed by, and are responsible to, the shareholders. Their primary responsibility is to make an objective report to shareholders and others as to whether, in their opinion, the financial statements show a true and fair view, and compliance with statutory, regulatory and accounting standard requirements. Therefore, the management and regulation of a company as a separate legal entity lies with the directors and the auditors. The directors are within, and part of, the company, and the auditors are external to, and not part of, the company.

This chapter will look at roles and responsibilities of directors and auditors. It will also consider the obligations of directors, particularly with regard to the corporate governance Combined Code of Practice, and the many Acts that are now in place to regulate the behaviour of directors of limited companies. The chapter closes with a look at some of the steps that directors may take to protect themselves against possible non-compliance.

Corporate governance code of practice

Concerns about financial reporting and accountability, and the impact on the business community (see Fig. 7.1), grew during the 1980s following increasing numbers of company failures and financial scandals.

During the 1980s and 1990s there was huge concern within the business community following the financial scandals surrounding BCCI, Polly Peck and Robert Maxwell's companies. The concerns increased as we saw even larger scandals involving companies such as Enron and WorldCom, and particularly the involvement of the consulting arms of firms like Arthur Andersen. These concerns were seen in a lack of confidence in financial reporting, and in shareholders and others being unable

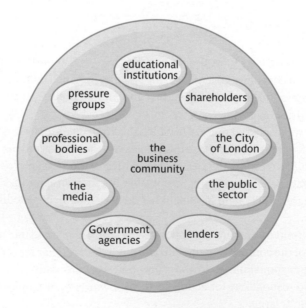

Figure 7.1 The business community

to rely on auditors to provide the necessary safeguards for their reliance on company annual reports. The main factors underlying the lack of confidence in financial reporting were:

- loose accounting standards, which allowed considerable latitude (an example has been the treatment of extraordinary items and exceptional items in financial reporting)
- lack of a clear framework to ensure directors were able to continuously review business controls
- competitive pressure within companies and on auditors, making it difficult for auditors to maintain independence from demanding boards
- lack of apparent accountability regarding directors' remuneration and compensation for loss of office.

The Cadbury Committee, chaired by Sir Adrian Cadbury, was set up in May 1991 by the Financial Reporting Council, the London Stock Exchange, and the accounting profession, to address these concerns and make recommendations on good practice.

The Cadbury Committee defined corporate governance (see Fig. 7.2) as 'the system by which companies are directed and controlled. Boards of directors are responsible for the governance of their companies. The shareholders' role in governance is to appoint the directors and the auditors and to satisfy themselves that an appropriate governance structure is in place. The responsibilities of the board include setting the company's strategic aims, providing the leadership to put them into effect, supervising the management of the business and reporting to shareholders on their stewardship. The board's actions are subject to laws, regulations and the shareholders in general meeting.'

The financial aspects within the framework described by Cadbury are the ways in which the company's board sets financial policy and oversees its implementation, the use of financial controls, and how the board reports on activities and progress of the company to shareholders.

The framework for establishing good corporate governance and accountability set up by the

Figure 7.2 The context of corporate governance

Cadbury Committee was formulated as the Committee's Code of Best Practice, published in December 1992. This provided a benchmark against which to assess compliance. The Cadbury Code was updated in 1998 by the Hampel Committee, to include their own Committee's work, and the Greenbury Committee report on directors' remuneration (published July 1995). In September 1999 the Turnbull Committee report on *Internal Control: Guidance for Directors on the Combined Code* was published by the ICAEW.

In May 2000 the original Cadbury Code and subsequent reports were all consolidated by the Committee on Corporate Governance and published in the Combined Code of Practice.

The underlying principles of the Code are:

- openness
- integrity
- accountability.

Openness

Openness from companies is constrained within the limits of their competitive position but is the basis for the confidence that needs to exist between business and all those who have a stake in its success. Openness in disclosure of information adds to the effectiveness of the market economy. It forces boards to take action and allows shareholders and others to be able to look more closely and thoroughly into companies.

Integrity

Integrity means straightforward dealing and completeness. Financial reporting should be honest and present a balanced view of the state of the company's affairs. The integrity of the company's reports will depend on the integrity of the people responsible for preparing and presenting them.

The annual reports and financial statements of the majority of UK plcs now include a section headed *Corporate Governance*. These sections of the annual reports are required to aim to comply with provisions set out in a Combined Code of Practice (principles of good governance and code of best practice), embracing the principles of the Cadbury, Greenbury and Hampel Committees, appended to the Listing Rules of the London Stock Exchange.

The corporate governance section of a company's annual report and accounts should contain details under the following headings:

- directors' biographies
- board responsibilities
- board composition and functions
- board committees
  - audit committee
  - nomination committee
  - remuneration committee
  - IT committee
  - capital expenditure committee
  - non-executive directors' committee

- directors' remuneration
- relations with shareholders

- internal financial control
- incentive compensation
- directors' pensions
- corporate strategy.

This may not be a complete list but it gives a broad indication of the areas of compliance under the Combined Code of Practice. This compliance can be seen as set out in the annual reports and accounts of UK plcs.

Accountability

Accountability of boards of directors to their shareholders requires the commitment from both to make the accountability effective. Boards of directors must play their part by ensuring the quality of information that is provided to shareholders. Shareholders must exercise their responsibilities as owners of the business. The major investing institutions (for example, pension funds and insurance companies) are in regular contact with the directors of UK plcs to discuss past, current, and future performance.

Subsequent to 1998, further reviews of various aspects of corporate governance were set up:

- *Review of the role and effectiveness of non-executive directors*, by Derek Higgs and published January 2003
- *Audit Committees Combined Code guidance*, by a group led by Sir Robert Smith and published January 2003.

The above reviews were undertaken during a period in which investor confidence had been badly shaken both by lapses in corporate governance and by the high-profile failure of some corporate strategies, the latter two being very much in response to these events. The reviews were reflected in a revision to the 1998 Combined Code of Practice, which was published by the Financial Reporting Council (FRC) in July 2003 – the Revised Code on Corporate Governance.

Companies listed on the Stock Exchange are requested to comply with the Code, but other companies may also benefit from compliance. It is not compulsory for any company, but rather a target of best practice to aim for. The revised Code continued to include the 'comply or explain' approach that was introduced by Cadbury. This means that companies listed on the Stock Exchange are required to include in their annual report and accounts a statement to confirm that they have complied with the Code's provisions throughout the accounting period, or to provide an explanation if that is not the case.

> **Progress check 7.1 What is corporate governance and how is it implemented?**

Let's take a look at the Johnson Matthey section on corporate governance, included in pages 30 to 38 of their report and accounts 2004, and reproduced on pages 254–62 of this book. This section includes the corporate governance report itself, and the audit committee report, remuneration committee report, remuneration of the directors, and the responsibility of directors report. The company states that 'The group was in compliance with the provisions of the Code throughout the year'.

A number of the headings required as part of corporate governance reporting are not included within Johnson Matthey plc's main corporate governance report, but are shown elsewhere in the report and accounts. For example, the composition and functions of the board, and directors'

Corporate Governance

Statement of Compliance with the Combined Code

The company has applied all of the principles set out in section 1 of the Combined Code on Corporate Governance (the Code) relating to the structure and composition of the board, the remuneration of the directors, relations with shareholders and procedures for financial reporting, internal control and audit. This statement describes how the principles of the Code have been applied. The group was in compliance with the provisions of the Code throughout the year.

Directors and the Board

The board is responsible to the company's shareholders for the group's system of corporate governance, its strategic objectives and the stewardship of the company's resources and is ultimately responsible for social, environmental and ethical matters. The board met eight times in the year and delegated specific responsibilities to board committees, as described below. The board reviews the key activities of the business and receives papers and presentations to enable it to do so effectively. The Company Secretary is responsible to the board, and is available to individual directors, in respect of board procedures.

The board comprises the Chairman, the Chief Executive, five other executive directors and five independent non-executive directors. Following the retirement of Mr C R N Clark at the company's Annual General Meeting (AGM) to be held on 20th July 2004, half of the board, excluding the Chairman, will comprise independent non-executive directors. The Chairman's other commitments are disclosed on page 12. The roles of Chairman and Chief Executive are separate. The Chairman leads the board, ensuring that each director, particularly the independent non-executive directors, is able to make an effective contribution. He monitors, with assistance from the Company Secretary, the information distributed to the board to ensure that it is sufficient, accurate, timely and clear. The Chief Executive maintains day-to-day management responsibility for the company's operations, implementing group strategies and policies agreed by the board.

Mr C D Mackay was appointed Senior Independent Director upon the retirement of Mr H R Jenkins on 16th July 2003. The role of non-executive directors is to enhance the independence and objectivity of the board's deliberations and decisions. All non-executive directors are independent of management and free from any business or other relationship which could materially interfere with the exercise of their independent judgment. The executive directors have specific responsibilities, which are detailed on pages 12 and 13, and have direct responsibility for all operations and activities.

All directors submit themselves for re-election at least once every three years. The board composition allows for changes to be made with minimum disruption. The board annually reviews the senior managers and their succession and development plans.

Committees of the Board

The **Chief Executive's Committee** is responsible for the recommendation to the board of strategic and operating plans and on decisions reserved to the board where appropriate. It is also responsible for the executive management of the group's business. The Committee is chaired by the Chief Executive and meets at least monthly. It comprises the executive directors and four senior executives of the company.

The **Audit Committee** is a sub-committee of the board whose purpose is to assist the board in the effective discharge of its responsibilities for financial reporting and corporate control. The Committee meets quarterly and, since the retirement of Mr H R Jenkins on 16th July 2003, is chaired by Mr A M Thomson. It comprises all the independent non-executive directors with the Chairman, the Chief Executive, the Group Finance Director and the external and internal auditors attending by invitation. A report from the Committee on its activities is given on page 32.

The **Nomination Committee** is a sub-committee of the board responsible for advising the board and making recommendations on the appointment of new directors. The Committee is chaired by Mr H M P Miles and comprises the Chairman and all the independent non-executive directors.

The **Management Development and Remuneration Committee** (MDRC) is a sub-committee of the board, which determines on behalf of the board the remuneration of the executive directors. The Committee is chaired by Mr C D Mackay and comprises all the independent non-executive directors. The Committee meets at least four times per year. The Chairman attends by invitation. The Chief Executive also attends by invitation except when his own performance and remuneration are discussed.

Attendance at board and board committee meetings in 2003/04 was as follows:

Director	Full Board		MDRC		Nomination Committee		Audit Committee	
	Eligible to attend	Attended	Eligible to attend	Attended	Eligible to attend	Attended	Eligible to attend	Attended
H M P Miles	8	8	5[1]	6[3]	1	1	2[1]	4[3]
C R N Clark	8	8	–	6[3]	–	1[3]	–	4[3]
N A P Carson	8	8	–	3[3]	–	–	–	–
M B Dearden	8	8	7	7	1	1	4	3
P N Hawker	5	4	–	–	–	–	–	–
H R Jenkins[2]	3	3	3	3	1	1	1	1
C D Mackay	8	8	7	7	1	1	4	3
D W Morgan	8	8	–	–	–	–	–	–
L C Pentz	5	5	–	–	–	–	–	–
J N Sheldrick	8	8	–	–	–	–	–	4[3]
I C Strachan	8	7	7	6	1	1	4	4
A M Thomson	8	7	7	7	1	1	4	4
R J W Walvis	8	8	7	7	1	1	4	3

[1] Mr Miles ceased to be a member of the Audit Committee and the MDRC on 25th November 2003.
[2] Retired July 2003.
[3] Includes meetings attended by invitation for all or part of meeting.

Corporate Governance

Directors' Remuneration

The Remuneration Report on pages 33 to 38 includes details of remuneration policies and of the remuneration of the directors.

Relations with Shareholders

The board considers effective communication with shareholders, whether institutional investors, private or employee shareholders, to be extremely important.

The company reports formally to shareholders twice a year, when its half year and full year results are announced and an interim report and a full report are issued to shareholders. These reports are posted on Johnson Matthey's website (www.matthey.com). At the same time, executive directors give presentations on the results to institutional investors, analysts and the media in London and other international centres. Copies of major presentations are also posted on the company's website.

The company's Annual General Meeting takes place in London and formal notification is sent to shareholders with the annual report at least 20 working days in advance of the meeting. The directors are available, formally during the AGM and informally afterwards, for questions. Details of the 2004 AGM are set out in the notice of the meeting enclosed with this annual report.

There is a programme of regular dialogue with major institutional shareholders and fund managers. The Chairman and the Senior Independent Director are always available to shareholders on all matters relating to governance.

Accountability, Audit and Control

The statement of directors' responsibilities in relation to the accounts is set out on page 38.

In its reporting to shareholders, the board aims to present a balanced and understandable assessment of the group's financial position and prospects.

The group's organisational structure is focused on its four divisions. These entities are all separately managed, but report to the board through a board director. The executive management team receives monthly summaries of financial results from each division through a standardised reporting process.

The group has in place a comprehensive annual budgeting process including forecasts for the next two years. Variances from budget are closely monitored.

The board has overall responsibility for the group's system of internal controls and for reviewing its effectiveness. The internal control systems are designed to meet the group's needs and address the risks to which it is exposed. Such a system can provide reasonable but not absolute assurance against material misstatement or loss.

There is a continuous process for identifying, evaluating and managing the significant risks faced by the company which has been in place during the year under review and up to the date of approval of the annual report and accounts. The board regularly reviews this process.

The assessment of group and strategic risks is reviewed by the board and updated on an annual basis. At the business level the processes to identify and manage the key risks are an integral part of the control environment. Key risks and internal controls are the subject of regular reporting to the Chief Executive's Committee.

The Group Control Manual, which is distributed to all group operations, clearly sets out the composition, responsibilities and authority limits of the various board and executive committees and also specifies what may be decided without central approval. It is supplemented by other specialist policy and procedures manuals issued by the group, divisions and individual business units or departments. The high intrinsic value of many of the metals with which the group is associated necessitates stringent physical controls over precious metals held at the group's sites.

The internal audit function is responsible for monitoring the group's systems of internal financial controls and the control of the integrity of the financial information reported to the board. The Audit Committee approves the plans for internal audit reviews and receives the reports produced by the internal audit function on a regular basis. Actions are agreed with management in response to the internal audit reports produced.

In addition, significant business units provide assurance on the maintenance of financial and non-financial controls and compliance with group policies. These assessments are summarised by the internal audit function and a report is made annually to the Audit Committee.

The directors confirm that the system of internal control for the year ended 31st March 2004 and the period up to 31st May 2004 has been established in accordance with the Turnbull Guidance included with the Code and that they have reviewed the effectiveness of the system of internal control.

Corporate Social Responsibility

Measures to ensure responsible business conduct and the identification and assessment of risks associated with social, ethical and environmental matters are managed in conjunction with all other business risks and reviewed at regular meetings of the board and Chief Executive's Committee.

A summary report on the group's policies and targets for corporate social responsibility is set out on pages 24 to 28. A full version of the report is available on the company's website.

The identification, assessment and management of environment, health and safety (EHS) risks are standing items at the Chief Executive's Committee. Performance is monitored using monthly statistics and detailed site audit reports. An annual review of EHS performance is undertaken by the board.

Risks from employment and people issues are identified and assessed by the Chief Executive's Committee and reported through to the board.

Employment contracts, handbooks and policies specify acceptable business practices and the group's position on ethical issues. The Group Control Manual and security manuals provide further operational guidelines to reinforce these.

The Audit Committee reviews risks associated with corporate social responsibility on an annual basis and monitors performance through the annual control self-assessment process conducted by the internal audit function.

Audit Committee Report

Role of the Audit Committee

The Audit Committee is a sub-committee of the board whose responsibilities include:

> Reviewing the interim and full year accounts and results announcements of the company and any other formal announcements relating to the company's financial performance and recommending them to the board for approval;

> Reviewing the group's systems for internal financial control and risk management;

> Monitoring and reviewing the effectiveness of the company's internal audit function and considering regular reports from Internal Audit on internal financial controls and risk management;

> Considering the appointment of the external auditors; overseeing the process for their selection; and making recommendations to the board in relation to their appointment (to be put to shareholders for approval at a general meeting);

> Monitoring and reviewing the effectiveness and independence of the external auditors, agreeing the nature and scope of their audit, their remuneration, and considering their reports on the company's accounts and systems of internal financial control and risk management.

The full terms of reference of the Audit Committee are provided on our website at www.matthey.com.

Composition of the Audit Committee

The Audit Committee comprises all the independent non-executive directors. Biographical details of the independent directors are set out on pages 12 and 13. Their remuneration is set out on page 34. The Chairman of the Audit Committee is Mr A M Thomson who took over from Mr H R Jenkins following his retirement from the board at the Annual General Meeting on 16th July 2003. The group Chairman, Mr H M P Miles, stepped down as a member of the Audit Committee on 25th November 2003 and now attends by invitation. The Chief Executive, Group Finance Director, Head of Internal Audit and external auditors (KPMG Audit Plc) attend Audit Committee meetings by invitation. The Committee also meets separately with the Head of Internal Audit and with the external auditors without management being present. The Company Secretary, Mr S Farrant, is secretary to the Audit Committee.

Main Activities of the Audit Committee

The Audit Committee met four times during the financial year ended 31st March 2004. At its meeting on 29th May 2003 the Committee reviewed the company's preliminary announcement of the results for the financial year ended 31st March 2003, and the draft report and accounts for that year. The Committee received reports from the internal auditors on control matters and the external auditors on the conduct of their audit, their review of the accounts, including accounting policies and areas of judgment, and their comments on risk management and control matters. The Committee also reviewed the group's corporate social responsibility (CSR) review which is available on our website at www.matthey.com.

The Audit Committee met on 31st July 2003 to receive a presentation by the external auditors setting out their audit approach and procedures, including matters relating to scope, auditor independence and audit fees. Following this presentation, and further discussion and review, the Committee recommended to the board that KPMG Audit Plc should be re-appointed as the company's external auditors.

At its meeting on 25th November 2003 the Audit Committee reviewed the company's interim results, the half year report and the external auditors' review.

At its meeting on 25th February 2004 the Audit Committee reviewed management's and internal audit's reports on the effectiveness of the company's systems for internal financial control and risk management. In addition the Committee reviewed and approved revised policies on whistleblowing and ethics.

Independence of External Auditors

Both the board and the external auditors have for many years had safeguards to avoid the possibility that the auditors' objectivity and independence could be compromised. Our policy in respect of services provided by the external auditors is as follows:

> Audit related services – the external auditors are invited to provide services which, in their position as auditors, they must or are best placed to undertake. It includes formalities relating to borrowings, shareholders' and other circulars, various other regulatory reports and work in respect of acquisitions and disposals.

> Tax consulting – in cases where they are best suited, we use the external auditors. All other significant tax consulting work is put out to tender.

> General consulting – in recognition of public concern over the effect of consulting services on auditors' independence, our policy is that the external auditors are not invited to tender for general consulting work.

Internal Audit

During the year the Audit Committee reviewed the performance of the internal audit function, the findings of the audits completed during the year, the department's resource requirements and also approved the internal audit plan for the year ending 31st March 2005.

A M Thomson
Chairman of the Audit Committee

CORPORATE GOVERNANCE CODE OF PRACTICE 257

. . . .

Remuneration Report

Remuneration Report to Shareholders

Management Development and Remuneration Committee and its Terms of Reference

The Management Development and Remuneration Committee of the board comprises all the non-executive directors of the company, other than the group Chairman, as set out on pages 12 and 13. Mr Jenkins retired from the Committee on 16th July 2003 and Mr Miles stepped down from the Committee on 25th November 2003.

The Committee's terms of reference are to determine on behalf of the board competitive remuneration for the executive directors, which recognises their individual contributions to the company's overall performance. The Committee believes strongly that remuneration policy should be completely aligned with shareholder interests. In addition the Committee assists the board in ensuring that the senior management of the group are recruited, developed and remunerated in an appropriate fashion.

The remuneration of the non-executive directors is determined by the board, within the limits prescribed by the company's Articles of Association.

Executive Remuneration Policy

The Committee recognises that, in order to maximise shareholder value, it is necessary to have a competitive pay and benefits structure. The Committee also recognises that there is a highly competitive market for successful executives and that the provision of appropriate rewards for superior performance is vital to the continued growth of the business. To assist with this the Committee appoints and receives advice from independent remuneration consultants on the pay and incentive arrangements prevailing in comparably sized industrial companies in each country in which Johnson Matthey has operations. During the year such advice was received from The Hay Group, which also provided advice on job evaluation, and the Monks Partnership. Watson Wyatt provided actuarial services. The Committee also receives recommendations from the Chief Executive on the remuneration of those reporting to him as well as advice from the Director of Human Resources. Total potential rewards are earned through the achievement of demanding performance targets based on measures that represent the best interests of shareholders.

The remuneration policy was reviewed by the Committee in 2002 and consists of basic salary, annual bonus, a long term incentive plan, share options and other benefits as detailed below. Salaries are based on median market rates with incentives providing the opportunity for upper quartile total remuneration, but only for achieving outstanding performance. Following a further comprehensive review by the Committee in 2003/04, which included advice from independent consultants, changes are proposed to the annual bonus, long term incentive plan and share options. These require shareholder approval and are the subject of a separate circular.

Executive directors' remuneration consists of the following:

Basic Salary – which is in line with the median market salary for each director's responsibilities as determined by independent surveys. Basic salary is normally reviewed on 1st August each year and the Committee takes into account individual performance and promotion during the year. Where an internal promotion takes place, the median salary relative to the market would usually be reached over a period of a few years, which can give rise to higher than normal salary increases while this is being achieved.

Annual Bonus – which is paid as a percentage of basic salary under the terms of the company's Executive Compensation Plan (which also applies to the group's 150 or so most senior executives). The executive directors' bonus award is based on consolidated profit before tax, exceptional items and goodwill amortisation (PBT) compared with the annual budget. The board of directors rigorously reviews the annual budget to ensure that the budgeted PBT is sufficiently stretching. An annual bonus payment of 30% of basic salary (prevailing at 31st March) is paid if the group meets the annual budget. This bonus may rise to 50% of basic salary if the group achieves PBT of 107.5% of budget. There is a provision that a maximum 105% of basic salary may be paid to the Chief Executive and 85% to other executive directors if 125% of budgeted PBT is achieved. PBT must reach 95% of budget for a minimum bonus to be payable. The Committee has discretion to vary the awards made. The bonus awarded to executive directors in 2003/04 was 42.5% of salary at 31st March 2004.

Long Term Incentive Plan (LTIP) – which was introduced in August 1998, is designed to achieve above average performance and growth. Shares are allocated to directors and key executives subject to performance conditions. For shares allocated in the years 1998, 1999 and 2000 the number of shares released to the individual was dependent upon growth in Johnson Matthey's relative total shareholder return (TSR) compared with the FTSE 250 over a three year performance period. 100% of the allocated shares will be released to the individual if the company's relative TSR is in the 75th percentile or above. Between 35% and 100% of the allocated shares will be released pro rata between the 50th and the 75th percentiles. No shares will be released at or below 50th percentile performance. Earnings per share (EPS) is used as a second performance measure and requires an increase in EPS to be at least equal to the increase in UK RPI plus 2% p.a. over the performance period before any release is made.

In 2001 shareholder approval was obtained for certain changes to the LTIP. The LTIP will continue to provide for the release of half of the allocated shares based on the company's relative TSR and EPS measures, as described above. The other half of the allocation will be released subject to the achievement of absolute TSR growth over a three year period. Under this test no shares will be released should the absolute TSR growth be less than 30%. 100% of the allocated shares will be released should the absolute TSR growth be 45% or more. Pro rata allocations will be made for absolute TSR growth between 30% and 45%.

On 12th June 2002 Johnson Matthey moved into the FTSE 100, and as a consequence of this the Committee decided that a comparator group of those companies ranked 51 – 150 in the FTSE index would be more appropriate than the FTSE 250 previously used. Hence the August 2002 and 2003 allocations will be tested against this revised comparator group for that half of the allocation subject to the relative TSR test.

Remuneration Report

Executive Remuneration Policy (continued)

Share Options – option grants were not made to executive directors in the years 1998, 1999 and 2000. Previously, options were granted to executive directors under the 1985 scheme (under which the final grant was made in November 1994) and the 1995 schemes with the latter having a performance target of EPS growth of UK RPI plus 2% over a three year period. Options under all the schemes were granted in annual tranches, up to the maximum permitted of four times earnings.

Following the review by independent remuneration consultants, the Committee obtained shareholder approval in 2001 for the introduction of a new employee share option scheme, known as the Johnson Matthey 2001 Share Option Scheme. The executive directors and approximately 800 employees are awarded an annual grant of share options under the terms of this scheme. For executive directors the Committee will award options each year up to a maximum value equal to basic annual salary. The options will only be exercisable upon the achievement of appropriate performance targets. The performance target is EPS growth of UK RPI plus 4% p.a. over any three year period. The Committee has discretion to alter the performance targets for future options, but not so as to make the targets less challenging, and would only do so after consultation with institutional investors.

Pensions – all the executive directors are members of the Johnson Matthey Employees Pension Scheme in the UK, with the exception of Mr Pentz who is a member of the Johnson Matthey Inc. Salaried Employees Pension Plan in the US. Under the UK scheme, members are entitled to a pension based on their service and final pensionable salary subject to Inland Revenue limits. The scheme also provides life assurance cover of four times annual salary. The normal pension age for directors is 60. None of the non-executive directors are members of the schemes. Details of the individual arrangements for executive directors are given on page 37.

Other Benefits – available to the executive directors are private medical insurance, a company car and membership of the group's employee share incentive plans which are open to all employees in the countries in which the group operates such schemes.

Service Contracts – Mr Clark was appointed to the board on 1st March 1990, Mr Sheldrick on 1st September 1990, Messrs Carson and Morgan on 1st August 1999 and Dr Hawker and Mr Pentz on 1st August 2003. All are employed on contracts subject to one year's notice at any time. On early termination of their contracts the directors would normally be entitled to 12 months' salary and benefits.

Non-executive directors' remuneration consists of fees, which are set following advice taken from independent consultants. They are reviewed at three year intervals.

Remuneration

Directors' Emoluments 2003/04

	Fees £'000	Salary £'000	Annual bonus £'000	Benefits £'000	Total excluding pension £'000	Total prior year excluding pension[10] £'000
Executive						
C R N Clark[8]	–	603	264	30	897	819
N A P Carson[9]	–	283	128	23	434	366
P N Hawker[1]	–	127	54	10	191	–
D W Morgan	–	233	102	25	360	320
L C Pentz[1] [2]	–	146	52	53	251	–
J N Sheldrick	–	317	138	12	467	426
Total	–	1,709	738	153	2,600	1,931
Non-Executive[3]						
H M P Miles (Chairman)	180			20	200	198
M B Dearden	33			–	33	33
H R Jenkins[4]	12			–	12	37
C D Mackay	37[5]			–	37	33
I C Strachan	33			–	33	33
A M Thomson	36[6]			–	36	17[7]
R J W Walvis	33			–	33	17[7]
Total	364			20	384	368

Notes:

[1]   Appointed August 2003.

[2]   Mr Pentz's emoluments are based on US basic salary adjusted for the cost of living differential in the UK including UK taxation. He will be provided, for two years only, with an expatriation package commensurate with the company's policy on international assignments, including accommodation costs, education expenses and relocation expenses. One-off costs associated with Mr Pentz's move to the UK were £24,316. These costs are not included in the above table.

[3]   Non-executive fees were last reviewed on 1st April 2001 for all non-executives and on 1st October 2001 for the Chairman.

[4]   Retired July 2003. Includes £4,000 per annum for chairmanship of the Audit Committee.

[5]   Includes £4,000 per annum for chairmanship of the Management Development and Remuneration Committee.

[6]   Includes £4,000 per annum for chairmanship of the Audit Committee. Appointed July 2003.

[7]   Appointed September 2002.

[8]   Mr Clark is a non-executive director of Rexam PLC and FKI plc. His annual fees are £90,000 from Rexam PLC and £35,000 from FKI plc. These amounts are excluded from the table above and retained by him.

[9]   Mr Carson is a non-executive director of Avon Rubber plc. His annual fee is £25,000. This amount is excluded from the table above and retained by him.

[10]   Excludes emoluments of £281,000 for directors who retired in the year ended 31st March 2003.

Remuneration Report

Directors' Interests

The interests of the directors as at 31st March 2004 in the shares of the company according to the register required to be kept by section 325(1) of the Companies Act 1985, were:

1   Ordinary Shares

	31st March 2004	31st March 2003
C R N Clark	17,840	65,770
N A P Carson	44,959	36,773
M B Dearden	2,000	2,000
P N Hawker	7,034	6,703[1]
C D Mackay	12,500	12,500
H M P Miles	562	562
D W Morgan	35,396	34,913
L C Pentz	9,442	8,686[1]
J N Sheldrick	52,355	91,860
I C Strachan	1,000	1,000
A M Thomson	2,056	2,000
R J W Walvis	1,000	1,000

[1]   at date of appointment

The directors are also deemed to be interested in the shares held by two employee share ownership trusts (see note 27 on page 64).

2   Share Options

As at 31st March 2004, individual holdings under the company's executive share option schemes were as set out below. Options are not granted to the non-executive directors.

	Date of grant	Ordinary shares under option	Exercise price (pence)	Date from which exercisable	Expiry date	Total number of ordinary shares under option
C R N Clark	18.7.01	48,938	1083.00	18.7.04	18.7.11	
	17.7.02	65,895	865.00	17.7.05	17.7.12	114,833
						(2003: 156,212)
N A P Carson	14.7.98	15,964	524.00	14.7.01	14.7.08	
	22.7.99	18,035	585.50	22.7.02	22.7.09	
	18.7.01	19,391	1083.00	18.7.04	18.7.11	
	17.7.02	28,901	865.00	17.7.05	17.7.12	
	17.7.03	33,407	898.00	17.7.06	17.7.13	115,698
						(2003: 82,291)
P N Hawker	19.7.00	6,130	942.00	19.7.03	19.7.10	
	18.7.01	10,253	1083.00	18.7.04	18.7.11	
	17.7.02	15,606	865.00	17.7.05	17.7.12	
	17.7.03	21,158	898.00	17.7.06	17.7.13	53,147
						(2003: 53,147[1])
D W Morgan	14.7.98	15,835	524.00	14.7.01	14.7.08	
	22.7.99	17,472	585.50	22.7.02	22.7.09	
	18.7.01	18,098	1083.00	18.7.04	18.7.11	
	17.7.02	25,433	865.00	17.7.05	17.7.12	
	17.7.03	26,726	898.00	17.7.06	17.7.13	103,564
						(2003: 108,071)
L C Pentz	14.7.98	12,981	524.00	14.7.01	14.7.08	
	22.7.99	12,158	585.50	22.7.02	22.7.09	
	19.7.00	8,224	942.00	19.7.03	19.7.10	
	18.7.01	12,952	1083.00	18.7.04	18.7.11	
	17.7.02	17,730	865.00	17.7.05	17.7.12	
	17.7.03	22,185	898.00	17.7.06	17.7.13	86,230
						(2003: 86,230[1])
J N Sheldrick	27.11.97	35,488	553.00	27.11.00	27.11.07	
	18.7.01	25,854	1083.00	18.7.04	18.7.11	
	17.7.02	34,682	865.00	17.7.05	17.7.12	
	17.7.03	36,191	898.00	17.7.06	17.7.13	132,215
						(2003: 96,024)

[1]   at date of appointment

Remuneration Report

Directors' Interests (continued)

2   Share Options (continued)

Notes:

a   Between 1st April 2003 and 31st March 2004 the following options were exercised:

	Date of grant	Date of exercise	Options exercised	Exercise price (pence)	Market price on exercise (pence)
C R N Clark	17.7.96	1.8.03	41,379	574.50	908.00
P N Hawker	22.7.99	18.7.03	9,299	585.50	907.00
D W Morgan	17.7.96	1.8.03	12,233	574.50	903.97
	6.1.97	1.8.03	19,000	553.00	903.97
L C Pentz	17.7.97	24.7.03	10,879	556.00	895.00

b   Gains made on exercise of options by directors during the year totalled £311,763 (2003: £1,318,863).

c   The closing market price of the company's shares at 31st March 2004 was 879.5 pence and the range during 2003/04 was 763.5 pence to 1055 pence.

3   LTIP Allocations

Number of allocated shares:

	As at 31st March 2003	Allocations during the year	Shares released during the year	Allocations lapsed during the year	As at 31st March 2004
C R N Clark	188,617	–	33,889	21,667	133,061
N A P Carson	65,819	33,936	12,991	8,305	78,459
P N Hawker	25,219[1]	21,493	2,471	1,580	42,661
D W Morgan	60,399	27,149	12,285	7,854	67,409
L C Pentz	30,693[1]	22,537	3,315	2,120	47,795
J N Sheldrick	85,804	36,764	18,103	11,574	92,891

[1]   and at date of appointment

On 1st August 2003 the 2000 LTIP allocation was released to participants. The company's TSR performance relative to the FTSE 250 was in the 60th percentile during the periods under measurement and EPS performance targets as described on page 33 were also achieved. The outcome was that EPS increased by 34.3% over the performance period compared to the minimum target of 12.0%. 61% of the shares were therefore released in accordance with the rules as approved by shareholders. This resulted in the following gains:

	Number of shares released	Share price when released (pence)	Gain £
C R N Clark	33,889	900.3	305,103
N A P Carson	12,991	900.3	116,958
P N Hawker	2,471	900.3	22,246
D W Morgan	12,285	900.3	110,602
L C Pentz	3,315	900.3	29,845
J N Sheldrick	18,103	900.3	162,981

Directors' interests at 28th May 2004 were unchanged from those listed above with the following exceptions:

The Trustees of the Johnson Matthey Share Incentive Plan have purchased on behalf of Messrs Clark, Carson, Hawker, Morgan and Sheldrick a further 84 ordinary shares each.

The Trustees of the Johnson Matthey Salaried Employees Savings Investment Plan (US) have purchased a further 236 ordinary shares on behalf of Mr Pentz.

Remuneration Report

Pensions

Pensions and life assurance benefits for UK executive directors are provided through the company's final salary occupational pension scheme for UK employees – the Johnson Matthey Employees Pension Scheme (JMEPS) – which is constituted under a separate Trust Deed. JMEPS is an exempt approved scheme under Chapter I of Part XIV of the Income & Corporation Taxes Act 1988 and its members are contracted out of the State Earnings Related Pension Scheme and the State Second Pension. With the agreement of the scheme actuary, the company paid contributions to JMEPS of 10% of basic salaries during the year.

In previous years' accounts, disclosure of directors' pension benefits has been made under the requirement of the Financial Services Authority Listing Rules. These rules are still in place, but it is now also necessary to make disclosures in accordance with the Directors' Remuneration Report Regulations 2002. The information below sets out the disclosures under the two sets of requirements.

a.   Financial Services Authority Listing Rules

	Age at 31st March 2004	Years of service at 31st March 2004	Director's contributions to JMEPS during the year[1] £'000	Increase in accrued pension during the year (net of inflation)[2] £'000 pa	Total accrued pension at 31st March 2004[3] £'000 pa	Total accrued pension at 31st March 2003 £'000 pa	Transfer value of increase (less director's contributions)[4] £'000	FURBS contribution in the year[5] £'000	FURBS related tax payments[5] £'000
C R N Clark	62	41	–	26	433	396	460	–	–
N A P Carson	46	23	11	24	129	103	184	–	–
P N Hawker[6]	50	17	5	18	80	61	180	–	–
D W Morgan	46	15	4	2	32	29	14	55	37
J N Sheldrick	54	13	4	2	38	34	27	76	51
L C Pentz[6] [7]	48	19	–	(2)	35	37	(8)	–	–

b.   Directors' Remuneration Report Regulations 2002

	Years of service at 31st March 2004	Director's contributions to JMEPS during the year[1] £'000	Increase in accrued pension during the year £'000 pa	Total accrued pension at 31st March 2004[3] £'000 pa	Transfer value of accrued pension at 31st March 2004[4] £'000	Transfer value of accrued pension at 31st March 2003[4] £'000	Increase in transfer value (less director's contributions) £'000	FURBS contribution for the year[5] £'000	FURBS related tax payment[5] £'000
C R N Clark	41	–	37	433	7,625	6,968	657	–	–
N A P Carson	23	11	26	129	1,065	654	400	–	–
P N Hawker[6]	17	5	19	80	810	545	260	–	–
D W Morgan	15	4	3	32	252	176	72	55	37
J N Sheldrick	13	4	4	38	475	356	115	76	51
L C Pentz[6] [7]	19	–	(2)	35	118	112	6	–	–

Notes:

[1]   Members' contributions are at the general scheme rate of 4% of pensionable pay, i.e. basic salary excluding bonuses. In accordance with the JMEPS' rules, Mr Clark ceased contributing to the scheme on attaining his normal retirement date at age 60.

[2]   The increase in accrued pension during the year excludes any increase for inflation from 31st March 2003.

[3]   The entitlement shown under "Total accrued pension at 31st March 2004" is the pension which would be paid annually on retirement, based on pensionable service to 31st March 2004. The pension would, however, be subject to an actuarial reduction of 0.3% per month for each month that retirement precedes age 60.

[4]   The transfer values have been calculated on the basis of actuarial advice in accordance with Actuarial Guidance Note 11, less directors' contributions. No allowance has been made in the transfer values for any discretionary benefits that have been or may be awarded under JMEPS. The transfer values in the Directors' Remuneration Report Regulations 2002 have been calculated at the start and the end of the year and, therefore, take into account market movements.

[5]   The JMEPS' benefits and contributions for Messrs Morgan and Sheldrick are restricted by reference to the 'earnings cap' imposed by the Finance Act No. 2, 1989. Contributions have therefore been paid to Funded Unapproved Retirement Benefit Schemes (FURBS) established by the company, independently of JMEPS, with effect from 1st April 2000. The purpose of each FURBS is to provide retirement and death benefits in relation to basic salary in excess of the earnings cap. Because FURBS are not exempt approved under Chapter I of Part XIV of the Income & Corporation Taxes Act 1988, payments have been made to meet the tax liabilities in respect of these contributions.

[6]   Dr Hawker and Mr Pentz were appointed to the board with effect from 1st August 2003. Pensions shown are the amounts accrued since appointment. The contributions are those that have been paid since appointment.

[7]   Mr Pentz is a US citizen and is not a member of the UK pension scheme. Instead, he is a member of the US salaried pension plan, which is a non-contributory defined benefit arrangement. The entitlements shown in the tables are those arising out of his membership of this arrangement converted into sterling by reference to the exchange rates on 31st July 2003 and 31st March 2004. The reduction in accrued pension is the result of exchange rate differences. Mr Pentz is also a member of a savings plan (401k), to which the company contributed $8,000 between 1st August 2003 and 31st March 2004. This is not included in the tables above but is included in his benefits in the table on page 34.

Remuneration Report

Johnson Matthey Total Shareholder Return, FTSE 100 and FTSE 250 rebased to 100

(31st March 1999 to 31st March 2004)

Johnson Matthey ———— FTSE 100 ———— FTSE 250

C D Mackay
Chairman of the Management Development and Remuneration Committee

Responsibility of Directors

for the preparation of the accounts

Company law requires the directors to prepare accounts for each financial year which give a true and fair view of the state of affairs of the company and group and of the profit or loss for that period. In preparing those accounts, the directors are required to:

> select suitable accounting policies and apply them consistently;

> make judgments and estimates that are reasonable and prudent;

> state whether applicable accounting standards have been followed, subject to any material departures disclosed and explained in the accounts;

> prepare the accounts on the going concern basis unless it is inappropriate to presume that the group will continue in business.

The directors are responsible for keeping proper accounting records which disclose with reasonable accuracy at any time the financial position of the company and enable them to ensure that the accounts comply with the Companies Act 1985. They have general responsibility for taking such steps as are reasonably open to them to safeguard the assets of the group and to prevent and detect fraud and other irregularities.

Worked Example 7.1

A number of basic problems may be encountered by shareholders with small shareholdings as they enter a new relationship with the company they effectively part own.

Most major plcs are owned by shareholders with both large and small shareholdings, the analysis of which can be found in their annual reports and accounts.

Usually within a very short time of acquiring their shares, most new small shareholders realise they have neither influence nor power.

As plcs have become multi-activity and multinational, so the directors have become more distanced from the shareholders. (Compare this with, for example, locally based building societies.)

During the move towards growth and expanded activities by companies, considerable disquiet regarding accountability developed in the business community and the Committee on the Financial Aspects of Corporate Governance (Cadbury Committee) was appointed, which produced its report in December 1992.

There has been unease regarding remuneration, bonus schemes, option schemes and contracts. The various committees on corporate governance, subsequent to Cadbury, have reviewed each of these areas.

biographies are shown on pages 12 to 14 of the report and accounts 2004, and are not reproduced in this book.

Non-executive directors are represented on all the main committees, except the chief executive's committee. The company does not appear to have an information technology (IT) committee or a capital expenditure committee, and so IT and capital expenditure are presumably the responsibility of the chief executive's committee.

The importance of CSR is again emphasised. As well as in the chairman's report, and in its own separate section of the report and accounts, CSR is also referred to in the corporate governance section.

Together with the section covering corporate governance, the reports of Johnson Matthey plc's audit committee and remuneration committee are included for reference.

The audit and the role of auditors

As we have noted earlier, an annual audit of the accounts is a statutory requirement for all limited companies, except for those currently having an annual turnover of less than £5.6 million and a balance sheet total of less than £2.8 million (refer to the Department of Trade and Industry website www.dti.com for changes to these limits). The shareholders of a limited company are responsible for appointing suitably qualified, independent persons, either individually or as a firm, to act as auditors. The external auditors are not part of the company but are responsible to the shareholders, with a main duty of objectively reporting to shareholders and others as to whether, in their opinion, the financial statements show a true and fair view, and comply with statutory, regulatory and accounting standard requirements. Such an opinion is referred to as an unqualified opinion.

The report of the auditors is usually very short and additionally includes:

- reference to the directors' responsibility for preparation of the annual report and accounts
- reference to the responsibility as auditors being established by

– UK statute
→ – the **Auditing Practices Board (APB)**
– the Listing Rules of the Financial Services Authority
– the accountancy profession's ethical guidance.

The auditors are required to explain the basis of the audit, and report if in their opinion:

- the directors' report is not consistent with the accounts
- the company has not kept proper accounting records
- they have not received all the information and explanations required for the audit
- information specified by law, or the Listing Rules regarding directors' remuneration and transactions with the company, is not disclosed
- company policies are appropriate and consistently applied and adequately disclosed
- all information and explanations considered necessary provide sufficient evidence to give reasonable assurance that the accounts are free from material misstatement
- the overall presentation of information in the accounts is adequate.

There may very occasionally be circumstances when the financial statements may be affected by an inherent, and fundamental uncertainty. In such cases the auditors are obliged to draw attention to the fundamental uncertainty. If the fundamental uncertainty is adequately accounted for and disclosed in the financial statements then the opinion of the auditors may remain unqualified. If there is inadequate disclosure about the fundamental uncertainty then the auditors must give what is termed a
→ qualified opinion. A qualified **audit report** is something that may destroy company credibility and create uncertainty, and is obviously something to be avoided.

In addition to their reporting on the financial statements of the company, the auditors' reports now include a statement of the company's corporate governance compliance with the seven provisions of the Combined Code of Practice. This review is in accordance with guidelines issued by the Auditing Practices Board. The auditors are not required to:

- consider whether the statements by the directors on internal control cover all risks and controls
- form an opinion on the effectiveness of the company's corporate governance procedures or its risk management and internal control procedures
- form an opinion on the ability of the company to continue in operational existence.

The audit and the perceived role of auditors has been the subject of much criticism over the years. The responsibility of the auditors does not include guarantees that:

- the financial statements are correct
- the company will not fail
- there has been no fraud.

This gap, 'the expectations gap', between public expectation and what the audit actually provides is understandable in the light of the numerous examples of company failures and financial scandals in the 1980s and 1990s. These have led to a lack of confidence of the business community in financial reporting, and in shareholders being unable to rely on safeguards they assumed would be provided by their auditors.

The problem is that 'correctness' of financial statements is an unachievable result. We have seen from our consideration of both the balance sheet and profit and loss account the inconsistency in asset valuation and the level of subjective judgement required in their preparation. Directors are required to prepare, and auditors give an opinion on, accounts that give a true and fair view rather than accounts that are deemed 'correct'.

Companies increasingly face a greater diversity and level of risk:

- financial risk
- commercial risk
- operational risk

and the increasing possibility of corporate failure is very real. Although the financial statements of companies are based on the going concern concept, the directors and auditors cannot realistically give any assurance that those businesses will not fail.

An area of risk that is of increasing concern to companies is fraud. This is perhaps due to:

- increasing pace of change
- widespread use of computer systems
- ease and speed of communications and transfer of funds
- use of the Internet
- increase in staff mobility
- increasing dependence on specific knowledge (for example, Nick Leeson and Barings, and dot.com companies' IT experts).

Fraud is perhaps something on which auditors may arguably be expected to give an opinion. This is not something that is currently required from an external audit. It is something for which an **internal audit** department may be responsible. In the same way, external auditors could be requested to report on the adequacy or otherwise of systems of internal control.

Most major corporate fraud is now associated with communications and information technology systems. The use of internal (or external) audit for the:

- detection of fraud
- minimisation of fraud
- elimination of fraud

therefore tends to be specialised and is something for which the costs and benefits must be carefully evaluated.

> Progress check 7.2 **What is the audit and to whom are the auditors responsible, and for what?**

The report of the independent auditors to the shareholders of Johnson Matthey plc, included in the report and accounts 2004, is illustrated on page 266. It can be seen to have complied with the standard audit reporting requirements outlined above. It may be interesting to compare the auditors report for, say, 1994 with the same report for the year 2004, in which so many more areas are covered, to confirm the importance of corporate governance.

Worked Example 7.2

The audit is the objective review (or sometimes the detailed examination) of business systems and transactions. A business may employ internal and external auditors. The latter are considered the more independent, although both are paid by the business. External auditors are appointed by, and report to, the shareholders, whereas the internal auditors report to the company's audit committee.

Report of the Independent Auditors

to the members of Johnson Matthey Public Limited Company

We have audited the accounts on pages 40 to 69. We have also audited the tabulated information and related footnotes set out in the directors' remuneration report on pages 33 to 38 disclosing the directors' emoluments and compensation, share options, long term incentive plan, pensions and other matters specified by Part 3 of Schedule 7A to the Companies Act 1985.

This report is made solely to the company's members, as a body, in accordance with section 235 of the Companies Act 1985. Our audit work has been undertaken so that we might state to the company's members those matters we are required to state to them in an auditor's report and for no other purpose. To the fullest extent permitted by law, we do not accept or assume responsibility to anyone other than the company and the company's members as a body, for our audit work, for this report, or for the opinions we have formed.

Respective Responsibilities of Directors and Auditors

The directors are responsible for preparing the annual report and the directors' remuneration report. As described on page 38 this includes responsibility for preparing the accounts in accordance with applicable United Kingdom law and accounting standards. Our responsibilities, as independent auditors, are established in the United Kingdom by statute, the Auditing Practices Board, the Listing Rules of the Financial Services Authority, and by our profession's ethical guidance.

We report to you our opinion as to whether the accounts give a true and fair view and whether the accounts and the part of the directors' remuneration report to be audited have been properly prepared in accordance with the Companies Act 1985. We also report to you if, in our opinion, the directors' report is not consistent with the accounts, if the company has not kept proper accounting records, if we have not received all the information and explanations we require for our audit, or if information specified by law or the Listing Rules regarding directors' remuneration and transactions with the group is not disclosed.

We review whether the statement on pages 30 and 31 reflects the company's compliance with the seven provisions of the Combined Code specified for our review by the Listing Rules, and we report if it does not. We are not required to consider whether the board's statements on internal control cover all risks and controls, or form an opinion on the effectiveness of the group's corporate governance procedures or its risk and control procedures.

We read the other information contained in the annual report, including the corporate governance statement and the unaudited part of the directors' remuneration report, and consider whether it is consistent with the audited accounts. We consider the implications for our report if we become aware of any apparent misstatements or material inconsistencies with the accounts.

Basis of Audit Opinion

We conducted our audit in accordance with Auditing Standards issued by the Auditing Practices Board. An audit includes examination, on a test basis, of evidence relevant to the amounts and disclosures in the accounts and the part of the directors' remuneration report to be audited. It also includes an assessment of the significant estimates and judgments made by the directors in the preparation of the accounts, and of whether the accounting policies are appropriate to the group's circumstances, consistently applied and adequately disclosed.

We planned and performed our audit so as to obtain all the information and explanations which we considered necessary in order to provide us with sufficient evidence to give reasonable assurance that the accounts and the part of the directors' remuneration report to be audited are free from material misstatement, whether caused by fraud or other irregularity or error. In forming our opinion we also evaluated the overall adequacy of the presentation of information in the accounts and the part of the directors' remuneration report to be audited.

Opinion

In our opinion:

> the accounts give a true and fair view of the state of affairs of the company and the group as at 31st March 2004 and of the profit of the group for the year then ended; and

> the accounts and the part of the directors' remuneration report to be audited have been properly prepared in accordance with the Companies Act 1985.

KPMG Audit Plc
Chartered Accountants
Registered Auditor
London
2nd June 2004

(i)   Why should the external auditors of a plc report direct to the shareholders and not to the chairman of the company?

(ii)   Why should the internal auditors of a plc report to the audit committee and not to the finance director?

(iii) In what ways may the independence of a company's audit committee be demonstrated?

The answers to these questions are:

(i)   The external auditors are appointed by and are responsible to the shareholders. The annual general meeting (AGM) is the formal meeting of directors, shareholders and auditors. Conceivably, the chairman could shelve the report, with shareholders unaware of the contents. The law is quite strict on auditors' access to the shareholders.

(ii)   The finance director is responsible for the system of recording transactions. The finance director could prevent vital information from the internal auditors being distributed to others in the organisation.

(iii) The audit committee may request the non-executive directors to review specific areas, for example, the output from the internal auditors. The audit committee meets many times during the year and it offers a degree of objectivity. The careers of its members do not depend on the continuance of their directorship.

The directors of a company may not be accountants and they very rarely have any hands-on involvement with the actual putting-together of a set of accounts for the company. However, directors of companies must make it their business to be fully conversant with the content of the accounts of their companies. Directors are responsible for ensuring that proper accounting records are maintained, and for ensuring reasonably accurate reporting of the financial position of their company, and ensuring their compliance with the Companies Act 1985/1989. Johnson Matthey plc's report and accounts 2004 includes a section headed 'Responsibility of Directors (for the preparation of the accounts)' that follows the remuneration committee report on page 38, which details the responsibilities of its directors in the preparation of its accounts.

We will now consider the role of directors and their responsibilities in more detail, and with regard to the corporate governance Combined Code of Practice. We will also look at some of the circumstances in which directors of limited companies are particularly vulnerable, and how these may lead to disqualification of directors.

The fact that a corporate governance Code of Practice exists or even that the appropriate corporate governance committees have been established is not necessarily a guarantee of effective corporate governance. There have been many examples of companies that have had corporate governance committees in place relating to directors and their remuneration, relations with shareholders, accountability and audit. Nevertheless, these companies have given cause for great concern from shareholders following much-publicised revelations about financial scandals and apparent loosely-adhered-to corporate governance practices.

Such examples have been by no means confined to the UK, as the press extract on pp. 268–69 illustrates. Dennis Kozlowski was the head of the conglomerate Tyco International from 1992 to 2002, which enjoyed phenomenal growth from the acquisition of hundreds of companies involved in

Another huge fraud case in the USA?

Dennis Kozlowski fancied himself as Jack Welch and Warren Buffett genetically melded into the body of a beefy, regular guy from New Jersey.

As head of the conglomerate Tyco International from 1992 to 2002, he oversaw the dizzying takeover of hundreds of big and small companies at a cost of $60bn (£34bn), in businesses as diverse as surgical equipment, disposable nappies and security systems. What's more, Koz pitched himself as a legendary tight-fist, and became a Wall Street darling.

For a company with more than 200,000 employees scattered across 2,342 subsidiaries and generating $36bn in annual revenues, Tyco's head office in a bland two-storey wooden building in Exeter, New Hampshire, housed just 20 full-time employees.

'We don't believe in perks,' Kozlowski once told a visiting journalist. 'Not even executive parking spots.'

It turns out Koz may have been fudging it a smidge. In the indictment against Kozlowski and his chief financial officer, Mark Swartz, by the New York District Attorney Robert Morgenthau, Tyco's headquarters while under their command is charmingly referred to as TEXCE. That is short for 'Top Executive Criminal Enterprise'.

The DA's case against them argues that the perception of 'frugality' and the tiny number of people with their hands in the till helped make Tyco a 'personal piggy bank' for the duo. For the past six months Koz, 57, and Swartz, 43, have been on trial for allegedly pilfering a staggering $600m (£341m).

Prosecutors say they snagged $170m through unauthorised bonuses and abuses of a company loan programme and netted another $430m by pumping Tyco shares by misleading the stock market about Tyco's results and then dumping their holdings.

Compared with the 'Marthathon', the lengthy and complex Tyco proceedings haven't received heaps of attention. (There is one odd similarity, however: both Koz and Stewart – her maiden name is Koystra – hailed from working-class Polish families in New Jersey.)

But Koz may be ready for his close-up now that the trial is wrapped up: the jury could deliver its verdict as soon as this week.

In fact, Stewart's obstruction of justice doesn't even register compared with the epic scale of the charges against Kozlowski. It is the first real attempt by a criminal court to hold accountable corporate executives for the alleged fraudulent pumping of their stocks during the bull market.

Indeed, as 'nothing exceeds like excess' scandals go, Koz's ordeal offered something for everyone. Toys? Check. Koz has plenty, including three Harley-Davidson motorcycles, a classic sailing yacht and a private plane to whisk him between his grand homes in New York, New Hampshire, Nantucket and Florida.

Furnishings and antiques – including the now legendary $6,000 wastebasket and $15,000 umbrella stand – were charged to the company account.

Ladies? Check. The trial featured testimony from former Koz paramours and the disclosure of his divorce agreement with former wife Angie, who was entitled to $30m in cash plus two New York apartments and homes in Connecticut, New Hampshire and Florida – not to mention a new Mercedes every three years. These obligations were depicted by prosecutors as the potential motivation for a successful executive making millions a year to carry on looting his company for much more.

Parties? Check. There was of course the infamous 40th birthday party held for his wife Karen in Sardinia in 2001, half of its $2m cost – including a vodka-peeing ice sculpture and Jimmy Buffett performance – on the Tyco tab.

Interesting pals? Check. Probably the most fascinating tale to emerge during the testimony was Koz's closeness to Phua Young, an analyst hired to cover Tyco for Merrill Lynch after Koz complained to Merrill's CEO about his company's coverage in 1999.

In addition to being unfailingly bullish on Tyco stock – Young once described himself as being 'indirectly paid by Tyco' – the analyst also fell in love during those heady times with a woman he met in Singapore. Young then did what any person in that situation would do: he asked Tyco for assistance in hiring a private detective to investigate her, which Kozlowski agreed to do at a cost of some $20,000.

Fortunately, the woman checked out, and she and the analyst were married. Unfortunately, Young was fired by Merrill in

2002 for improper conduct and has been charged by securities regulators with publishing misleading research on Tyco.

'Greed is greed, and sometimes when you have a lot you want more,' Ann Donnelly, the assistant district attorney, said of Kozlowski and Swartz. 'They have an extravagant lifestyle and there is nothing wrong with that. But you have to pay for it. Don't these guys have credit cards? Don't they have chequebooks? Why does Tyco have to buy a house for every place they travel to?'

For their closing arguments last week, Donnelly and her colleagues displayed a large chart outlining for the jury the 32 counts against Koz and Swartz, just as they did when the case opened. The charges include grand larceny, conspiracy, falsifying business records and violating state business laws.

The grand larceny charge alone is punishable by up to 25 years in prison. (Earlier this month the judge did throw out a charge of 'enterprise corruption', a statute normally applied to mob figures.)

It all seems very sensational, but the reality is that the proceedings have been convoluted and tiring. Kozlowski's lawyer, Stephen Kaufman, argued to the jury that his client might be culpable in a civil court for misusing shareholder funds but he is no criminal.

And he played a bit of a post-Martha card when he urged the jury not to view his client's case as a chance to 'win one for the little guy'. He pointed out that 'we're not WorldCom, we're not Adelphia, we're not Enron'.

Indeed, those three companies, whose former CEOs are being prosecuted for fraud, are all now bankrupt. Tyco stock isn't the high flier it was in Koz's day, but it's still plugging along.

In his two hours of instruction to the jury, Judge Michael Obus told them that their purpose is a 'narrow one' and that they should not 'evaluate any other cases you might have heard about' or be 'judges of corporate governance'.

Indeed, the only question is whether Kozlowski, the man who 'doesn't believe in perks', was legally entitled to an obscenely super-sized helping of them.

Time for Kozlowski to pick up the tab?, by Richard Sykes

© *Daily Telegraph*, 21 March 2004

widely diverse industries. Kozlowski once told a reporter: 'We don't believe in perks, not even executive parking spots.' In the USA, during an extremely long and complicated case against Kozlowski for fraud, it appears that he in fact received an inordinate portion of perks himself, either legally or illegally.

The case against Mr Kozlowski and the former chief financial officer of Tyco, Mark Swartz, collapsed in a mistrial in April 2004 when a juror began receiving threats. However, a retrial was expected.

Directors' responsibilities

The responsibilities of directors, in terms of the Combined Code of Practice, can be seen to be important and far-reaching. It has been said that being a director is easy, but being a responsible director is not. It is important for all directors to develop an understanding and awareness of their ever-increasing legal obligations and responsibilities to avoid the potential personal liabilities, and even disqualification, which are imposed if those obligations are ignored.

It can be seen that the aims of most of the codes of practice and legislation have been to promote better standards of management in companies. This has also meant penalising irresponsible directors, the effect of which has been to create an increasingly heavy burden on directors regardless of the size or nature of the business they manage. The Government is actively banning offending directors.

Directors' duties are mainly embodied in the:

- Companies Act 1985/1989
- Insolvency Act 1986 (as amended by the Enterprise Act 2002)
- Company Directors Disqualification Act 1986 (as amended by the Enterprise Act 2002)
- Enterprise Act 2002
- Health and Safety at Work Act 1974
- Financial Services Act 1986

and there is

- potential for legal action on corporate manslaughter.

In addition, it should be noted that further statutory provisions giving rise to vicarious liability of directors for corporate offences are included in Acts of Parliament, which currently number well over 200! Directors can be:

- forced to pay a company's losses
- fined
- prevented from running businesses
- imprisoned.

The Directors' Remuneration Report Regulations 2002 (Statutory Instrument 2002 No. 1986) are now in force and require the directors of a company to prepare a remuneration report that is clear, transparent and understandable to shareholders. Many smaller companies without continuous legal advice are unaware about how much the rules have tightened. It is usually not until there is wide publicity surrounding high-profile business problems that boards of directors are alerted to the demands and penalties to which they may be subjected if things go wrong.

It was not only the 1980s and early 1990s that saw corporate scandals and irregularities (for example, Polly Peck, and the Maxwell companies). At the end of 1999, accounting irregularities caused trading in engineering company TransTec shares to be suspended, with Arthur Andersen called in as administrative receiver. The case was fuelled by the revelation by former TransTec chief accountant Max Ayris that nearly £500,000 of a total of £1.3m in grants from the Department of Trade and Industry was obtained fraudulently. TransTec, founded by former Government minister Geoffrey Robinson, collapsed in December 1999, after the accounting irregularities were discovered, with debts of more than £70m. Following the collapse of the company the role of the auditors to the company, PricewaterhouseCoopers, was also to be examined by the Joint Disciplinary Scheme, the accountancy professions' senior watchdog.

Also during 1999, the trade finance group Versailles discovered that there had been some double counting of transactions, which prompted the Department of Trade and Industry to take a close interest in its affairs. Actual and apparent corporate misdemeanours continued, on an even larger scale, through the late 1990s and on into the twenty-first century (note the Barings debacle, Enron, WorldCom, and Tyco).

Non-executive directors are legally expected to know as much as executive directors about what is going on in the company. Ignorance is not a defence. Directors must be aware of what is going on and have knowledge of the law relating to their duties and responsibilities. Fundamentally, directors must:

- use their common sense
- be careful in what they do

- look after shareholders
- look after creditors
- look after employees.

> **Progress check 7.3** **What are the main responsibilities of directors with regard to the accounting and financial reporting of their companies?**

Duty of care

It is the duty of a director to exercise his/her powers in the best interests of the company, which includes not acting for his/her personal benefit, nor for an improper use. In the year 2000, Greg Hutchings, the chairman of a major plc, Tomkins, was criticised for alleged excessive perks, unauthorised donations, and inclusion of members of his family and household staff on the company payroll, without proper disclosure. Investors' concern over corporate governance practices at the group had been triggered by a fall in the share price of over 50% in two years. The resignation of the chairman followed an initial investigation. The new chairman very quickly launched a full inquiry into executive perks within the group, overseen by him personally.

Duty of care means doing the job with the skill and care that somebody with the necessary knowledge and experience would exercise if they were acting on their own behalf. Delegation of directors' power must be 'properly and sensibly done'. If a director of a company does not choose the right people or supervise them properly, all the directors may be liable for the misdeeds and mistakes of the people they have appointed.

When a company fails and is found to be insolvent, the receiver appointed will leave no stone unturned to identify whether any money may be recovered in order to pay off creditors. This will include checking for any oversights by directors for items they should have spotted 'if they had exercised their proper level of skill'.

Fiduciary duty

Directors must act in the best interests of the company. Courts will support directors who act honestly and in good faith. Acting in the best interests of the company includes not making personal profit at the company's expense, not letting personal interest interfere with the proper running of the business, or doing business which favours directors or their close associates. In the late 1990s and early 2000s there were several business failures within the dot.com sector, where directors did act in the best interests of the company although their business plans may not have been commercially successful (for example, www.breathe.com).

Corporate manslaughter

There is an offence of corporate manslaughter, which a company may be guilty of if a failure by its management is the cause of a person's death, and their failure is because their conduct is well below what can be reasonably expected. Before 1999 there were only five prosecutions in the UK for corporate manslaughter, resulting in two convictions. The risk for companies and their directors is remote but very real, and should therefore be managed in terms of awareness, training, preventative measures, and liability insurance.

In earlier years companies were outside the criminal law. As one judge put it, 'a company had a soul to damn and no body to kick', meaning that because a company did not have an actual existence it could not be guilty of a crime because it could not have a guilty will. In 1965 a case established the validity of the indictment of a company for manslaughter. Since then over 19,000 people have been killed as a result of corporate activity, but no company stood trial for manslaughter, apart from P&O European Ferries (Dover) Ltd after the capsize and sinking of the *Herald of Free Enterprise* off Zeebrugge in 1987. The directors of P&O Ferries did stand trial, but were acquitted because the trial collapsed halfway through. Currently, to succeed in a case of corporate manslaughter against a company there is a need to prove gross negligence and to prove that at least one sufficiently senior official was guilty of that same gross negligence.

Although each year hundreds of people are killed at work or in commercially related activity, if companies have been prosecuted at all they have been charged under the Health and Safety at Work Act (1974) and other regulatory legislation. Many of the companies implicated in work fatalities and public transport disasters operate with diffuse management systems and much delegated power. Such systems that appear to have no 'controlling mind' make it difficult to meet the requirement of the law because of the difficulty in identifying the individual(s) who may possess the mental element for the crime.

A case that was successfully prosecuted involved a small company, OLL Ltd, which organised a canoe expedition at Lyme Bay in 1993, in which four teenage schoolchildren died. In 1994 the jury in the case found OLL Ltd guilty of manslaughter – an historic decision. Peter Kite, the managing director of the activity centre responsible for the canoeing disaster, was jailed for three years for manslaughter, and OLL Ltd was fined £60,000. OLL Ltd was the first company in the UK ever to be found guilty of manslaughter, in a decision that swept away 400 years of legal history.

The Lyme Bay case was atypical of corporate homicide incidents. The company was small, so it was

Corporate manslaughter and the 'controlling mind'

Six senior managers from Network Rail and Balfour Beatty were charged with manslaughter today in connection with the Hatfield train disaster. The two companies – Railtrack's successor and its maintenance firm – have also been charged with manslaughter and failure to discharge a duty under the Health and Safety at Work Act, the Crown Prosecution Service announced. Another six men received summonses for an offence under health and safety legislation, including Gerald Corbett, the former chief executive of Railtrack who is now the chairman of Woolworths.

British Transport Police confirmed that six men – four from Railtrack and two from Balfour – had been charged with gross negligence manslaughter and a health and safety offence. The maximum sentence for individuals is life in prison, while the companies face unlimited fines if found guilty. The prosecutions were revealed in *The Times* earlier this week. All are due to appear before Central Hertfordshire Magistrates' Court in St Albans on Monday morning.

Four people died in the October 17 2000 crash when a GNER express train derailed half a mile south of Hatfield station in Hertfordshire. Thirty police officers are understood to have been working on the case and to have interviewed about 100 people. The London to Leeds train derailed because of a broken rail, which both Railtrack and Balfour Beatty allegedly knew about.

The accident led to a network-wide inspection of tracks and speed restrictions on trains while work took place. Train punctuality has still not returned to pre-Hatfield levels and is not expected to for some years.

Solicitors representing the injured and families of the victims welcomed news of prosecutions, as did rail safety groups. Carol Bell, co-chairman of the Safe Trains Action Group, said: 'It is going to be really important for the families because it gives them a chance to put some kind of closure on it. If they decide to go to court it will be difficult but they will be glad that someone is taking responsibility for it'. Mrs Bell is a survivor of the 1997 Southall rail crash. But Balfour Beatty criticised the decision and defended its safety record.

In a statement, the company said: 'The charge of manslaughter against our maintenance business will be firmly defended as we see no plausible basis for it in law or on the evidence. The individuals charged will have the company's fullest support in their defence of the charges against them'. Network Rail also pledged to defend itself and its employees against the charges. 'As the company stated last week, we believe that our employees conduct their duties to the best of their abilities with the sole intention of delivering a safe, reliable and efficient railway network. It is now a matter for the courts and it would be inappropriate to comment further,' a statement said.

Andrew Faiers, a Crown Prosecutor, said that the decision to press charges was based on 'substantial evidence'. More than 1,500 witnesses gave evidence during the two-and-a-half year long probe. The police seized more than one million pages of documentary evidence.

The families of those who died at Hatfield have campaigned for a corporate manslaughter prosecution, as have relatives of victims of other rail accidents. It is difficult to obtain a conviction on such a charge, however. Great Western Trains was acquitted of the charge on a point of law when it was prosecuted for the 1997 Southall rail crash, but it was fined £1.5 million under health and safety legislation. Labour promised to update corporate manslaughter law in its 1997 manifesto and the Home Secretary has said that he intends to introduce a draft law in October to make it easier to prosecute companies, but that would not target individual directors. Under present corporate manslaughter law, a company can be convicted only if a person is identified as its 'controlling mind' and is found responsible for someone's death. If he or she is found not guilty, the company is cleared as well.

If a junior member of staff is responsible for safety, he or she is not regarded as a controlling mind and again the company escapes prosecution. In the Southall case, the CPS did not charge any individual with manslaughter, so the case against the company failed. Only small companies, where it is easy to establish the lines of responsibility, have been convicted of corporate manslaughter.

In 1994 Peter Kite, managing director of an activity centre responsible for a canoeing disaster that killed four children, was jailed for three years after his company became the first in the country to be convicted of manslaughter. It was fined £60,000. P&O European Ferries was prosecuted after the 1987 Zeebrugge disaster, but the case collapsed half-way through the trial.

Rail chiefs on Hatfield manslaughter charges, by PA News and Angela Jameson

© *The Times*, 9 July 2003

relatively easy to discover the 'controlling mind'; the risks to which pupils were exposed were serious and obvious and, critically, they were not technical or esoteric in any way. Moreover, very unusually, the directors could not claim ignorance of the risks because of a damning letter they had received from former instructors telling them to improve safety at the centre.

Great Western Trains was fined £1.5m over the Southall (1997) rail crash in which seven people were killed, following a Health and Safety Executive (HSE) prosecution. But no individual within the company was charged with manslaughter.

The Paddington (1999) rail crash case, again brought by the HSE, resulted in 31 people killed and over 400 injured. The company, Thames Trains, was fined £2m in April 2004, but even though the HSE said its enquiries had revealed 'serious failing in management', there was no prosecution for corporate manslaughter.

A few years ago the legal profession considered that the promised review of the Law Commission's recommendation for an Involuntary Homicide Act 'could result in company directors being made personally responsible for safety and therefore potentially liable in cases of avoidable accidents'. The current Government has promised to legislate on the issue of corporate manslaughter. In its consultation document in 2000 it considered a proposed offence of corporate killing, allowing easier prosecution of any employing organisation for a death that results from a serious management failure. In May 2003 the Government said that it would issue a draft Bill on corporate manslaughter, and that it would target the companies themselves and not the criminal liability of individual directors, and would not set up a system of standards in parallel to existing health and safety standards. In November 2004 the Government included the issue of corporate manslaughter in the Queen's Speech, and placed it on their legislative agenda for 2005.

Other responsibilities

Directors do not owe a direct duty to shareholders, but to the company itself. Directors have no contractual or fiduciary duty to outsiders and are generally not liable unless they have acted in breach of their authority. Directors must have regard to the interests of employees but this is enforceable against directors only by the company and not by the employees.

> Progress check 7.4 **What is meant by a duty of care and fiduciary duty with regard to company directors?**

Insolvency

Insolvency, or when a company becomes insolvent, is when the company is unable to pay creditors' debts in full after realisation of all the assets of the business. The penalties imposed on directors of companies continuing to trade while insolvent may be disqualification and personal liability. Many directors have lost their houses (as well as their businesses) as a result of being successfully pursued by the receivers appointed to their insolvent companies.

The Insolvency Act 1986 (as amended by the Enterprise Act 2002) provides guidance on matters to be considered by liquidators and receivers in the reports, which they are required to prepare on the conduct of directors. These matters include:

- breaches of fiduciary and other duties to the company
- misapplication or retention of monies or other property of the company
- causing the company to enter into transactions which defrauded the creditors
- failure to keep proper accounting and statutory records
- failure to make annual returns to the Registrar of Companies and prepare and file annual accounts.

If a company is insolvent, the courts assess the directors' responsibility for:

- the cause of the company becoming insolvent
- the company's failure to supply goods or services which had been paid for
- the company entering into fraudulent transactions or giving preference to particular creditors

- failure of the company to adhere to the rules regarding creditors' meetings in a creditors' voluntary winding-up
- failure to provide a statement of affairs or to deliver up any proper books or information regarding the company.

> **Progress check 7.5** **How does insolvency impact on directors and what are their responsibilities in this regard?**

Wrongful trading

A major innovation of the Insolvency Act 1986 was to create the statutory tort (civil wrong) of wrongful trading. It occurs where a director knows or ought to have known before the commencement of winding up that there was no reasonable prospect of the company avoiding insolvency and he/she does not take every step to minimise loss to creditors. If the court is satisfied of this it may:

- order the director to contribute to the assets of the business, and
- disqualify him/her from further involvement in corporate management for a specified period.

A director will not be liable for wrongful trading if he/she can show that from the relevant time he/she 'took every step with a view to minimising the potential loss to the company's creditors as (assuming him/her to have known that there was no reasonable prospect that the company would avoid going into insolvent liquidation) he/she ought to have taken'. A company goes into insolvent liquidation, for this purpose, if it does so at a time when its assets are insufficient for the payment of its debts and other liabilities and the expenses of winding-up.

Both subjective tests and objective tests are made with regard to directors. A director who is responsible, for example, for manufacturing, quality, purchasing, or human resources, is likely to have less skill and knowledge regarding the financial affairs of the company than the finance director, unless otherwise fully briefed. Directors with financial or legal experience will certainly be expected to bear a greater responsibility than other directors because of their specialist knowledge.

Fraudulent trading

Fraudulent trading is an offence committed by persons who are knowingly party to the continuance of a company trading in circumstances where creditors are defrauded, or for other fraudulent purposes. Generally, this means that the company incurs more debts at a time when it is known that those debts will not be met. Persons responsible for acting in this way are personally liable without limitation for the debts of the company. The offence also carries criminal penalties.

The offence of fraudulent trading may apply at any time, not just in or after a winding-up. If a company is wound up and fraudulent trading has taken place, an additional civil liability arises in respect of any person who was knowingly a party to it.

> **Progress check 7.6** **Are there any differences between wrongful trading and fraudulent trading? If so, what are they?**

Disqualification of directors

Worked Example 7.3

A director of a Hampshire building and double-glazing contractor was disqualified for six years after his company collapsed owing creditors £364,000. Ronald Norris, director of the Aldershot-based Berg Group, which was wound up on 6 January 1999, was found guilty of trading while insolvent since 3 December 1997. Norris from West Sussex, stood before Reading County Court on 8 January 1999. The other grounds for his disqualification were the transfer of a pension fund, of which Norris was a beneficiary on a property owned by Berg, failing to ensure that VAT was collected as due, and failing to ensure that monies due to Berg from connected companies were collected.

There are some fundamental reasons why it is necessary for society to ban certain individuals from becoming directors of limited companies.

The limited liability company is a very efficient means of conducting business, but if used by unscrupulous persons then innocent people can lose money, through no fault of their own.

The limited liability company can offer a financial shield to protect employees and investors if things go wrong and the company ceases trading, unable to pays its creditors.

UK law is now quite strict and will attack an obviously unscrupulous person taking advantage of the limited liability company and leaving various creditors out of pocket.

In recent times the UK Government has been banning an increasing number of persons from becoming directors, as well as publishing their names in the public domain (for example, on the Internet). Almost certainly the recently introduced regime is showing its teeth and punishing guilty directors in a most practical manner.

Disqualification means that a person cannot be, for a specified period of time, a director or manager of any company without the permission of the courts. Disqualification is governed under the Company Directors (Disqualification) Act 1986, and may result from breaches under:

- the Companies Act 1985/1989
  - from cases of fraud or other breaches of duty by a director
- the Insolvency Act 1986 (as amended by the Enterprise Act 2002)
  - if the courts consider that the conduct of a director makes him/her unfit to be concerned in the future management of a company.

Whilst there are serious implications for directors of companies under the Company Directors (Disqualification) Act 1986, it should be noted that the Act is not restricted to company directors. Over one half of the liabilities fall on 'any persons' as well as company directors. 'Any persons' in this context potentially includes any employee within the organisation.

The following offences, and their penalties, under the Act relate to any persons:

- being convicted of an indictable offence – disqualification from company directorships for up to five years, and possibly for up to 15 years
- fraud in a winding up – disqualification from company directorships for up to 15 years
- participation in fraudulent or wrongful trading – disqualification from company directorships for up to 15 years

- acting as a director while an undischarged bankrupt, and failure to make payments under a county court administration order – imprisonment for up to two years, or a fine, or both
- personal liability for a company's debts where the person acts while disqualified – civil personal liability.

The following offences, and their penalties, under the Act relate to directors (but in some instances include other managers or officers of the company):

- persistent breaches of company legislation – disqualification from company directorships for up to five years
- convictions for not less than three default orders in respect of a failure to comply with any provisions of companies' legislation requiring a return, account or other document to be filed, delivered, sent, etc., to the Registrar of Companies (whether or not it is a failure of the company or the director) – disqualification from company directorships for up to five years
- finding of unfitness to run a company in the event of the company's insolvency – disqualification from company directorships for a period of between two years and 15 years
- if after investigation of a company the conduct of a director makes him unfit to manage a company – disqualification from company directorships for up to 15 years
- attribution of offences by the company to others if such persons consent, connive or are negligent – imprisonment for up to two years, or a fine, or both, or possibly imprisonment for not more than six months, or a fine.

In some circumstances directors may be disqualified automatically. Automatic disqualification occurs in the case of an individual who revokes a county court administration order, and in the case of an undischarged bankrupt unless leave of the court is obtained. In all other situations the right to act as a director may be withdrawn only by an order of the court, unless a company through its Articles of Association provides for specific circumstances in which a director's appointment may be terminated. The City of London has seen a major toughening of the regime where persons have found themselves unemployable (for example, the fallout from the Baring Bank debacle in the mid-1990s).

> Progress check 7.7 **In what circumstances may a director be disqualified?**

Summary of directors' obligations and responsibilities

In summary, the following may serve as a useful checklist of directors' obligations and responsibilities:

- both executive and non-executive directors must act with care, look after the finances and act within their powers, and look after employees
- directors are responsible for keeping proper books of account and presenting shareholders with accounts, and failure to do so can result in disqualification
- directors should understand the accounts and be able to interpret them
- the board of directors is responsible for filing accounts with the Registrar of Companies and must also notify changes to the board of directors and changes to the registered address
- shareholders must appoint auditors
- the directors are responsible for calling and holding annual general meetings, and ensuring minutes of all meetings are appropriately recorded

- directors are responsible for ensuring that the company complies with its memorandum and articles of association
- if a company continues to trade while technically insolvent and goes into receivership a director may be forced to contribute personally to repaying creditors
- a director trading fraudulently is liable to be called on for money
- any director who knew or ought to have known that insolvency was unavoidable without minimising loss to the creditors becomes liable
- directors can be disqualified for paying themselves too much
- inadequate attention paid to the financial affairs of the company can result in disqualification
- directors are required to prepare a remuneration report.

We have seen the onerous burden of responsibility placed on directors of limited companies in terms of compliance with guidelines and legislation. The obligations of directors continue to grow with the increase in Government regulation and legislation. Sixteen new directives were introduced during the two years to 2001, relating to such issues as employee working conditions, health and safety and, for example, administration of a minimum wage policy.

How can directors make sure that they comply and cover themselves in the event of things going wrong?

Actions to ensure compliance

Directors of companies need to be aware of the dividing line between the commission of a criminal offence and the commission of technical offences of the Companies Act. Directors should take the necessary actions to ensure compliance with their obligations and responsibilities, and to protect themselves against possible non-compliance:

- directors may delegate their responsibilities within or outside the company and in such circumstances they must ensure that the work is being done by competent, able and honest people
- directors of small companies in particular should get professional help to ensure compliance with statutory responsibilities
- directors must ensure that they are kept fully informed about the affairs of the company by having regular meetings and recording minutes and material decisions
- directors should ensure they have service contracts that cover the company's duties, rights, obligations, and directors' benefits
- directors must ensure that detailed, timely management accounts are prepared, and, if necessary, professional help sought to provide, for example, monthly reporting systems and assistance with interpretation of information produced and actions required.

It is essential that directors carefully watch for warning signs of any decline in the company's position, for example:

- falling sales/market share
- overdependence on one product/customer/supplier
- overtrading (see Chapter 15)
- pressure on bank borrowings
- increases in trade creditors
- requirements for cash paid in advance

- increasing stock levels
- poor financial controls.

The protection that directors may obtain is extremely limited. All directors should certainly take out individual professional liability insurance. But above all it is probably more important that all directors clearly understand their obligations and responsibilities, closely watch company performance, and take immediate, appropriate action as necessary, to ensure compliance and minimise their exposure to the type of personal risks we have discussed above.

> **Progress check 7.8** **What actions should directors take to ensure they meet their obligations, and to protect themselves should things go wrong?**

Summary of key points

- The framework for establishing good corporate governance and accountability has been established in a revised Combined Code of Practice, developed from the work of the Cadbury, Greenbury, Hampel, and Turnbull Committees.
- There is a statutory requirement for the audit of the accounts of limited companies, except for smaller limited companies.
- The election of suitably qualified, independent auditors is the responsibility of the shareholders, to whom they are responsible.
- Directors of limited companies have a specific responsibility to shareholders, and general responsibilities to all stakeholders and the community, for the management and conduct of companies. (Note the continued activities of pressure groups such as Greenpeace and Friends of the Earth.)
- Directors of limited companies have a fiduciary duty to act in the best interests of the company, and a duty of care to all stakeholders and to the community at large, particularly with regard to the Companies Act 1985/1989, Health and Safety at Work Act 1974, Financial Services Act 1986, Insolvency Act 1986, and Enterprise Act 2002.
- The risk for companies and their directors from the UK Government's promised legislation on the issue of corporate manslaughter may be remote but very real, and should therefore be managed in terms of awareness, training, preventative measures, and liability insurance.
- The implications for directors for wrongful trading may be to contribute to the assets of the business, and disqualification from further involvement in corporate management for a specified period.
- The implications for directors for fraudulent trading may be to contribute to the assets of the business without limit, disqualification, and possible criminal and civil penalties.
- The implications of the Company Directors (Disqualification) Act 1986 (as amended by the Enterprise Act 2002) apply not only to company directors, and over 50% of the provisions relate to any persons.
- Directors of limited companies, in addition to taking out individual professional liability insurance, must ensure that they clearly understand their obligations and responsibilities.

Questions

Q7.1 (i)   How was the corporate governance Combined Code of Practice developed?

(ii) Why was it considered necessary?

Q7.2 Refer to the Johnson Matthey section on corporate governance in their annual report and accounts 2004, pp. 254–5 to illustrate the areas of compliance under the Combined Code of Practice.

Q7.3 (i)   Which areas of the business do auditors' opinions cover?

(ii) What happens if there is any fundamental uncertainty as to compliance?

Q7.4 Explain the implications of the 'expectation gap' with regard to external auditors.

Q7.5 Explain the obligations of directors of limited companies in terms of their duty of care, their fiduciary duty, and the forthcoming introduction of an Involuntary Homicide Act.

Q7.6 If the severity of the penalty is determined by the seriousness of the offence, describe the half dozen or so most serious offences under the Company Directors (Disqualification) Act 1986 (as amended by the Enterprise Act 2002), which relate to directors of limited companies.

Q7.7 Outline the general responsibilities of a director of a limited company with regard to the company, its shareholders, and other stakeholders.

Q7.8 What are the key actions that a director of a limited company may take to ensure compliance with his/her obligations and responsibilities?

Discussion points

D7.1 Discuss, and illustrate with some examples, how far you think the corporate governance Combined Code of Practice goes to preventing the kind of corporate excesses we have seen in the recent past.

D7.2 'I pay my auditors a fortune in audit fees. I look upon this almost as another insurance premium to make sure that I'm protected against every kind of financial risk.' Discuss.

D7.3 'Everyone who embarks on a career in industry or commerce aspires to becoming a director of their organisation, because then all their troubles are over! Directors just make a few decisions, swan around in their company cars, and pick up a fat cheque at the end of each month for doing virtually nothing.' Discuss.

D7.4 In an age of increasingly sophisticated computer systems is the traditional role of the auditor coming to an end?

Exercises

Solutions are provided in Appendix 4 to all exercise numbers highlighted in colour.

Level I

E7.1 *Time allowed – 30 minutes*

Discuss why users of financial statements should have information on awards to directors of share options, allowing them to subscribe to shares at fixed prices in the future.

E7.2 *Time allowed – 30 minutes*

Outline the basic reasons why there should be openness regarding directors' benefits and 'perks'.

E7.3 *Time allowed – 30 minutes*

Can you think of any reasons why directors of UK plcs found that their contracts were no longer to be open-ended under the new regime of corporate governance?

E7.4 *Time allowed – 60 minutes*

William Mason is the managing director of Classical Gas plc, a recently formed manufacturing company in the chemical industry, and he has asked you as finance director to prepare a report that covers the topics, together with a brief explanation, to be included in a section on corporate governance in their forthcoming annual report and accounts.

Level II

E7.5 *Time allowed – 60 minutes*

After the birth of her twins Vimla Shah decided to take a couple of years away from her career as a company lawyer. During one of her coffee mornings with Joan Turnbull, Joan confided in her that although she was delighted at her husband Ronnie's promotion to commercial director of his company, which was a large UK plc in the food industry, she had heard many horror stories about problems that company directors had encountered, seemingly through no fault of their own. She was worried about the implications of these obligations and responsibilities (whatever they were) that Ronnie had taken on. Vimla said she would write some notes about what being a director of a plc meant, and provide some guidelines as to the type of things that Ronnie should be aware of, and to include some ways in which Ronnie might protect himself, that may all offer some reassurance to Joan.

    Prepare a draft of what you think Vimla's notes for Joan may have included.

E7.6 *Time allowed – 60 minutes*

Li Nan has recently been appointed managing director of Pingers plc, which is a company that supplies table tennis equipment to clubs and individuals throughout the UK and Europe. Lin Nan is surprised at the high figure that appeared in last year's accounts under audit fees.

    Li Nan is not completely familiar with UK business practices and has requested you to prepare a detailed report on what the audit fees cover, and to include the general responsibilities of directors in respect of the external audit.

E7.7 *Time allowed – 60 minutes*

Use the following information, extracted from Tomkins plc report and accounts for 2000, as a basis for discussing the users of financial information's need for information on directors' remuneration.

	Basic salary	Benefits in kind	Bonuses
G Hutchings, executive director	£975,000	£45,000	£443,000
G Gates (USA), non-executive director	nil, but has a 250,000 US$ consultancy agreement		
R Holland, non-executive director	£23,000	Nil	nil

E7.8 *Time allowed – 60 minutes*

Explain what is meant by insolvency and outline the responsibilities of receivers appointed to insolvent companies.

Case Study II

DESIGN PIERRE LTD

Design Pierre Ltd is a designer and manufacturer of gift and presentation packaging, aimed particularly at the mass market, via jewellery shops and large retail chains, and mail order companies. The company was founded many years ago by Pierre Girault, who was the managing director and was involved in the sales and marketing side of the business.

Towards the end of 2001 when Pierre was due to retire, Marie Girault, Pierre's daughter, joined the company as managing director, along with Erik Olsen as marketing director. Marie had worked as a senior manager with Saturn Gifts plc, a large UK designer and manufacturer of giftware, of which Erik had been a director. Marie and Erik capitalised on their experience with Saturn to present some very innovative ideas for developing a new product range for Design Pierre. However, Marie and Erik's ideas for expanding the business required additional investment, the majority of which was spent during the financial year just ended on 31 March 2004.

The share capital of Design Pierre Ltd, 800,000 £1 ordinary shares, had all been owned by Pierre himself. On retirement he decided to transfer 390,000 of his shares to his daughter Marie, and to sell 390,000 shares to Erik Olsen (to help fund his pension). Pierre gifted his remaining 20,000 shares to Nigel Finch, who was the production director and had given the company many years of loyal service. Although Marie had received her share in the company from her father, Erik had used a large part of his personal savings and had taken out an additional mortgage on his house to help finance his investment in the business. This was, of course, paid to Pierre Girault and did not provide any additional capital for the business.

In order to raise additional share capital, Marie and Erik asked Pierre's advice about friends, family and business contacts who may be approached. Pierre suggested approaching a venture capital company, Fishtale Ltd, which was run by a friend of his, Paul Fish. Fishtale already had a wide portfolio of investments in dot.com and service businesses, and Paul was interested in investing in this type of growing manufacturing business. He had known Pierre and the Girault family for many years, and was confident that Marie and Erik would make a success of the new ideas that they presented for the business. Additional capital was therefore provided from the issue of 800,000 new £1 shares at par to Fishtale Ltd, to become the largest shareholder of Design Pierre Ltd. Design Pierre Ltd also had a bank loan, which it increased during 2003/04, and bank overdraft facility.

The directors of the newly structured Design Pierre Ltd and its shareholders were as follows:

Marie Girault	Managing director	390,000 shares
Erik Olsen	Marketing director	390,000 shares
Nigel Finch	Production director	20,000 shares
Paul Fish	Non-executive director	
Fishtale Ltd		800,000 shares

As a non-executive director of Design Pierre Ltd, Paul Fish attended the annual general meetings, and review meetings that were held every 6 months. He did not have any involvement with the day-to-day management of the business.

The new range at Design Pierre did quite well and the company also began to export in a small way to the USA and Canada. Marie and Erik were pleased by the way in which the sales of the business had grown, and in the growth of their customer base. They had just received a large order from Norbox, a Swedish company, which was regarded as an important inroad into the Scandinavian market. If Norbox became a regular customer, the sales of the company were likely to increase rapidly over the next few years and would establish Design Pierre as a major player in the market.

In the first week of May 2004, the day that Design Pierre received the order from Norbox, Marie also received a letter from the bank manager. The bank manager requested that Design Pierre Ltd immediately and considerably reduce their overdraft, which he felt was running at a level which exposed the bank and the company to a higher level of risk than he was prepared to accept. Marie Girault was very angry and felt very frustrated. Marie, Erik, and Nigel agreed that since they had just had such a good year's trading and the current year looked even better, the reduction in the overdraft facility was going to seriously jeopardise their ability to meet the commitments they had to supply their customers.

When they joined the company, Marie and Erik decided that Design Pierre, which had always been production led, would become a design and marketing led business. Therefore, a great deal of the strategic planning was concerned with integrating the product design and development with the sales and marketing operations of the business. Over the past three years Marie and Erik had invested in employing and training a young design team to help continue to develop the Design Pierre brand. The marketing team led by Erik had ensured that the enthusiasm of their key customers was converted into new firm orders, and that new orders were received from customers like Norbox. The order book grew until it had now reached the highest level ever for the company.

In addition to his role as production director, Nigel had always tended to look after the books and any financial matters. Nigel was not an accountant and he had not had any formal financial training. But, as he said, he had a small and experienced accounts team who dealt with the day-to-day transactions; if ever there had been a problem, they would ask Design Pierre's auditors for some advice.

As soon as she received the letter from the bank, Marie called the bank manager to try and persuade him to continue to support the overdraft facility at the current level, but with no success. Marie also convened an urgent meeting of the directors, including Paul Fish, to talk about the letter and the draft accounts of the business for the year ended 31 March 2004. The letter from the bank was distributed to all the directors before the meeting.

Erik Olsen was very worried about his investment in the company. He admitted that his accounting knowledge was fairly limited. He thought that the company was doing very well, and said that the draft accounts for the year to 31 March 2004 seemed to confirm their success. Profit before tax was more than double the profit for 2003. He could not understand why the cash flow was so bad. He appreciated that they had spent a great deal of money on the additional plant and equipment, but they had already had a bank loan to help with that. He thought that the cash situation should really be even better than the profit because the expenses included £1.5m for depreciation, which does not involve any cash at all.

Marie Girault still appeared very angry at the lack of support being given by the bank. She outlined the impact that the overdraft reduction would have on their ability to meet their commitments over the next year. She said that the bank's demand to cut their overdraft by 50% over the next 3 months put them in an impossible position with regard to being able to meet customer orders. Design Pierre Ltd could not find an alternative source of such a large amount of money in such a short time.

Erik, Marie, and Nigel had, before the meeting, hoped that Paul Fish would be prepared to help out by purchasing further additional new shares in the company or by making a loan to the company. However, it was soon made clear by Paul that further investment was not a possible option. Fishtale Ltd had made a couple of new investments over the past few months and so did not have the money to invest further in Design Pierre. As a venture capitalist, Fishtale had actually been discussing the possible exit from Design Pierre by selling and trying to realise a profit on the shares. Finding a prospective buyer for their shares, or floating Design Pierre on the alternative investment market (AIM), did not currently appear to be a realistic option.

Paul Fish had been so much involved in running his own business, Fishtale Ltd, that he had neglected to monitor the financial position of Design Pierre Ltd as often and as closely as he should have done. At the directors' meeting he realised that he should have been much more attentive and there was now a possibility that Design Pierre would not provide the returns his company expected, unless things could be drastically improved.

The accounts of Design Pierre Ltd for the past two years are shown below.

Profit and loss account for the year ended 31 March

	2003 £000	2004 £000
Turnover	7,000	11,500
Cost of sales	3,700	5,800
Gross profit	3,300	5,700
Operating expenses	2,200	3,100
Operating profit	1,100	2,600
Interest payable	200	500
Profit before taxation	900	2,100
Taxation	200	400
Profit after taxation	700	1,700
Dividend	200	300
Retained profit for the year	500	1,400
Retained profit brought forward	1,100	1,600
Retained profit carried forward	1,600	3,000

Balance sheet as at 31 March

	2003		2004	
	£000	£000	£000	£000
Fixed assets		4,300		7,200
Current assets				
Stocks	1,200		2,900	
Trade debtors	800		1,900	
Other debtors	100		200	
Cash at bank and in hand	100		–	
	2,200		5,000	
Creditors: Amounts falling due within one year				
Trade creditors	600		1,300	
Other creditors	100		200	
Taxation	200		400	
Dividends	200		300	
Bank overdraft	–		2,100	
	1,100		4,300	
Net current assets		1,100		700
		5,400		7,900
Creditors: Amounts falling due after more than one year				
Loan		2,200		3,300
		3,200		4,600
Capital and reserves				
Ordinary shares (£1)		1,600		1,600
Retained profit		1,600		3,000
		3,200		4,600

The directors of Design Pierre Ltd were unable to agree on a way of dealing with the financial problem faced by the company. Marie thought it best that she continue to try and negotiate with the bank manager, and believed that she could change the bank managers mind if she:

- presented him with the accounts for 31 March 2004, which showed such good results, and
- made him fully aware of the implications of the reduction in the overdraft facility on the future of Design Pierre.

However, Erik and Nigel said that they were aware that Design Pierre Ltd had exceeded its agreed overdraft limit a few times over the past two years and so they were not confident that Marie could persuade the bank to change its mind. They suggested that they should try and find another investor prepared to provide additional funds for the business, to keep the business going. They really believed that the year-end accounts showed how successful Design Pierre had been over the past 2 years and that their track record was sufficient to attract a potential new investor in the business. Paul did not agree. He felt that this would not be a practical solution. More importantly, Fishtale did not want to have another large shareholder in the company because it would dilute its shareholding, and also reduce its influence over the future direction of the business. However, Paul agreed that immediate and radical action needed to be taken by the company.

After hours of argument and discussion, it became apparent that the problem would not be resolved at the meeting. Therefore, it was agreed by all present that expertise from outside the company should be sought to help the company find an acceptable and viable solution to the problem. The directors decided to approach Lucis Consulting, which specialises in helping businesses with financial problems, and to ask them to produce a plan of action for their consideration.

Required

As a member of the Lucis team, prepare a report for the board of directors of Design Pierre Ltd which analyses the problems faced by the company and which sets out a detailed plan of action for dealing with its financing problem.

Your report should be supported by the appropriate analyses, and a full cash flow statement for the year ended 31 March 2004.

Part II

Management accounting

Part II is about management accounting. In contrast with financial accounting, which deals with historical information, management accounting is more concerned with looking at current issues and the future in terms of providing information to assist managers in decision-making, forecasting, planning and achievement of plans.

Chapter 8 provides an introduction to management accounting and the framework in which it operates. It looks at the nature and behaviour of costs and how they change in response to changes in levels of activity.

Chapter 9 takes a broad approach to the management of costs, and the relationships between costs, activity volumes, and profit. This chapter introduces the topic of break-even analysis, and various approaches to the treatment of costs, and goes on to consider some of the more recently developed techniques of cost management, such as activity based costing (ABC), and includes non-financial performance measurement and the balanced scorecard.

Chapter 10 considers how some of the techniques of management accounting may be used in the decision-making process. Decision-making is looked at in the context of both costs and sales pricing.

Chapter 11 deals with the way in which businesses, as part of their strategic management process, translate their long-term objectives and plans into forecasts, short-term plans and budgets.

Chapter 12 deals with budgetary control. This is concerned with the periods after the budgeting process has been completed, in which actual performance may be compared with the budget. This chapter looks at how actual performance comparisons with budget may be made and analysed to explain deviations from budget, and to identify appropriate remedial actions.

8

Cost behaviour

Contents

Learning objectives

Completion of this chapter will enable you to:

- outline the additional accounting concepts that relate to management accounting
- explain what is meant by the term cost, its nature and limitations
- identify the bases for allocation and apportionment of costs
- determine the costs of products, services or activities using the techniques of absorption costing and marginal costing
- critically compare the techniques of absorption costing and marginal costing.

Introduction

The chapters included in Part I of this book were concerned with financial accounting, with particular emphasis on the three key financial statements: balance sheet; profit and loss account; cash flow statement. This has necessarily focused on the historical aspect of accounting. To use a car-driving analogy, we have made far more use of the rear view mirror than the view through the windscreen. We have concentrated on the accumulation of data and the reporting of past events, rather than the consideration of current and future activities.

We have previously identified accounting as having the three roles of maintaining the score-card, problem solving, and attention directing. The scorecard role, although primarily a financial accounting role, remains part of the responsibility of management accounting. However, its more important roles are those of problem solving and attention directing. These roles focus on current and future activities, with regard to the techniques involved in decision-making, planning and control that will be covered in this and subsequent chapters.

This chapter introduces management accounting by looking at some further concepts to those that were covered in Chapter 1. Management accounting is concerned with costs. We will look at what cost is, how costs behave and how costs are ascertained. This will include some of the approaches used to determine the costs of products and services. Management accountants may be involved in the preparation of financial information that frequently requires senior management attention, resulting in decisions that are not always popular, for example down-sizing of businesses. They may also be involved in many more positive ways in the development of businesses, as illustrated in the extract below from *Financial Management*, the journal of the Chartered Institute of Management Accountants.

We can see from the Figleaves example below that the management accounting function is extremely important in adding value to the business through its involvement in:

- investment decision-making
- scorecard design
- development of budgetary control systems
- capacity planning.

The importance of management accounting

Internet lingerie retailer Figleaves.com is expanding its management accounting function in recognition of the key contribution it made to the firm's first break-even result.

In December 2002 the company reported break-even at EBITDA on net sales of £1 million. This compares with Amazon.com's break-even on turnover of £550 million in September 2002.

'We are in rarefied territory for dotcoms,' said Figleaves.com's finance director, Howard Bryant ACMA. 'The management accounting team is crucial to that success, continually adding value to the business. The unique role of management accountants, experts in everything from investment to general manage-ment, makes them ideal for a smaller firm such as Figleaves.'

Over the past year the management accounting team has been involved in projects including the introduction of a scorecard design covering key metrics and interrelationships for discussion at company meetings; the development of budget and forecast control mechanisms; and the integration of rolling sales forecasts with inventory capacity planning.

Uplifting growth for on-line underwear company, by Cathy Hayward

© *Financial Management*, March 2003

The management accounting function may also be involved in many more important areas of business activity, for example:

- planning and preparation of business plans
- directing attention to specific areas and providing proposed solutions to actual and anticipated problems
- formulation of cost-cutting proposals and the evaluation of their impact on current and future operations
- preparation of forecasts
- negotiation with bankers for funding
- analysis and interpretation of internal and external factors in support of strategic decision-making.

Management accounting concepts

Management accounting is an integral part of management, requiring the identification, generation, presentation, interpretation and use of information relevant to the activities outlined in Fig. 8.1:

- formulating business strategy involves setting the long-term objectives of the business
- planning and controlling activities deal with short-term objectives and investigations into the differences that may arise from actual outcomes against the plan and the recommendation and implementation of remedial actions
- decision-making includes identification of those items of information relevant to a particular decision and those items that may be ignored
- efficient resource usage may be determined from the process of setting short-term budget plans and in their implementation
- performance improvement and value enhancement includes cost reduction and profit

Figure 8.1 The areas of business activity supported by management accounting

improvement exercises and the implementation of improvement initiatives such as quality costing, continuous improvement, and **benchmarking**

■ safeguarding tangible and intangible assets – the management of fixed assets and working capital (which we shall look at in more detail in Chapter 15) are key accounting responsibilities in ensuring that there is no undue diminution in the value of assets such as buildings, machinery, stocks and debtors, as a result, for example, of poor management, and weak physical controls, and to ensure that every endeavour is made to maximise returns from the use of those assets

■ corporate governance and internal control were considered in Chapter 7 and are concerned with the ways in which companies are controlled, the behaviour and accountability of directors and their levels of remuneration, and disclosure of information.

Therefore, it can be seen that management accounting, although providing information for external reporting, is primarily concerned with the provision of information to people within the organisation for:

■ product costing
■ forecasting, planning and control
■ decision-making.

> **Progress check 8.1** **Outline what is meant by management accounting and give examples of areas of business activity in which it may be involved.**

In addition to the fundamental accounting concepts that were discussed in Chapter 1, there are further fundamental management accounting concepts (see Fig. 8.2). These do not represent any form of external regulation but are fundamental principles for the preparation of internal management accounting information. A brief outline of these principles is as follows.

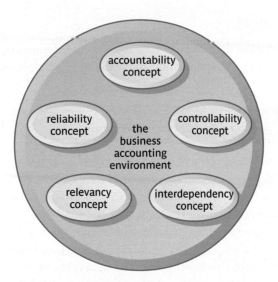

Figure 8.2 Management accounting concepts

The accountability concept

Management accounting presents information measuring the achievement of the objectives of an organisation and appraising the conduct of its internal affairs in that process. In order that further action can be taken, based on this information, the accountability concept makes it necessary at all times to identify the responsibilities and key results of individuals within the organisation.

The controllability concept

The controllability concept requires that management accounting identifies the elements or activities which management can or cannot influence, and seeks to assess risk and sensitivity factors. This facilitates the proper monitoring, analysis, comparison and interpretation of information which can be used constructively in the control, evaluation and corrective functions of management.

The interdependency concept

The interdependency concept requires that management accounting, in recognition of the increasing complexity of business, must access both internal and external information sources from interactive functions such as marketing, production, personnel, procurement and finance. This assists in ensuring that the information is adequately balanced.

The relevancy concept

The relevancy concept ensures that flexibility in management accounting is maintained in assembling and interpreting information. This facilitates the exploration and presentation, in a clear, understandable and timely manner, of as many alternatives as are necessary for impartial and confident decisions to be taken. This process is essentially forward-looking and dynamic. Therefore, the information must satisfy the criteria of being applicable and appropriate.

The reliability concept

→ The reliability concept requires that management accounting information must be of such quality that confidence can be placed on it. Its reliability to the user is dependent on its source, integrity and comprehensiveness.

Worked Example 8.1

During 1999 the UK Government promoted the building of the Dome in Greenwich, London, to celebrate the Millennium. It was opened on time for 31 December 1999. The projected number of visitors during the year was 12 million. That target was not reached. We can consider the Dome and its visitor targets with regard to the controllability concept.

The visitor numbers proved to be a major problem from the outset. Various attempts were made to increase the number of visitors, for example free tickets to schools. The visitor numbers were frequently reported in the national press. The management was changed to try and get somewhere near the targets. All measures taken and effort expended throughout the year unfortunately failed. The Internet is a rich source of information about the Dome, for example www.telegraph.co.uk, which you may use for further research.

> **Progress check 8.2** **Explain in what ways the additional concepts have been developed to support the profession of management accounting.**

The nature of costs

→ Costs and revenues are terms that are inextricably linked to accounting. Revenues relate to inflows of assets such as cash and accounts receivable from debtors, or reductions in liabilities, resulting from trading operations. Costs generally relate to what was paid for a product or a service. It may be a past cost:

- a particular use of resources forgone to achieve a specific objective
- a resource used to provide a product or a service
- a resource used to retain a product or a service.

A cost may be a future cost in which case the alternative uses of resources other than to meet a specific objective may be more important, or relevant, to the decision whether or not to pursue that objective.

Cost is not a word that is usually used without a qualification as to its nature and limitations. On the face of it cost may obviously be described as what was paid for something. Cost may, of course, be used as a noun or a verb. As a noun it is an amount of expenditure (actual or notional) incurred on, or attributable to, a specified thing or activity; it relates to a resource sacrificed or forgone, expressed in a monetary value. As a verb, we may say that to cost something is to ascertain the cost of a specified thing or activity.

A number of terms relating to cost are regularly used within management accounting. A comprehensive glossary of key terms appears at the end of the book. These terms will be explained as we go on to discuss each of the various topics and techniques.

Cost accumulation relates to the collection of cost data. Cost data may be concerned with past costs or future costs. Past costs, or historical costs, are the costs that we have dealt with in Chapters 2, 3 and 4, in the preparation of financial statements.

Costs are dependent on, and generally change with, the level of activity. The greater the volume or complexity of the activity, then normally the greater is the cost. We can see from Fig. 8.3 that there are three main elements of cost:

- fixed cost
- variable cost
- semi-variable cost.

Fixed cost is a cost which is incurred for an accounting period, and which, within certain manufacturing output or sales turnover limits, tends to be unaffected by fluctuations in the level of activity (output or turnover). An example of a fixed cost is rent of premises that will allow activities up to a particular volume, but which is fixed regardless of volume, for example a car production plant. In the

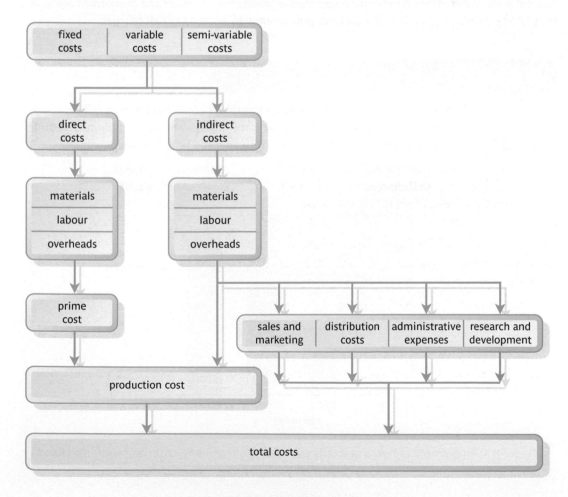

Figure 8.3 The elements of total costs

longer term, when volumes may have increased, the fixed cost of rent may also increase from the need to provide a larger factory. Discussion on fixed overheads invariably focuses on when the fixed costs should no longer be 'fixed'. Since most businesses these days need to be dynamic and constantly changing, changes to fixed costs inevitably follow changes in their levels of activity.

A variable cost varies in direct proportion to the level, or volume, of activity, and again strictly speaking, within certain output or turnover limits. The variable costs incurred in production of a car: materials; labour costs; electricity costs; and so on, are the same for each car produced and so the total of these costs varies as volume varies. The relationship holds until, for example, the cost prices of materials or labour change.

> **Progress check 8.4** **Discuss whether or not knowledge of labour costs can assist management in setting prices for products or services.**

A semi-variable cost is a cost containing both fixed and variable components and which is thus partly affected by a change in the level of activity, but not in direct proportion. Examples of semi-variable costs are maintenance costs comprising regular weekly maintenance and breakdown costs, and telephone expenses that include line and equipment rental in addition to call charges.

Worked Example 8.2

Quarterly telephone charges that may be incurred by a business at various levels of call usage are shown in the table below, and in the chart in Fig. 8.4. If the business makes no calls at all during the quarter it will incur costs of £200, which cover line rentals and rental of equipment.

Calls (units)	1,000	2,000	3,000
Call charges	£700	£1,400	£2,100

Figure 8.4 An example of how a quarterly semi-variable telephone cost comprises both fixed and variable elements

The total costs of an entity comprise three categories:

- staff costs, the costs of employment which include
    - gross pay
    - paid holidays
    - employer's contributions to National Insurance
    - pension schemes
    - sickness benefit schemes
    - other benefits, for example protective clothing and canteen subsidies
- materials, which include
    - raw materials purchased for incorporation into products for sale
    - consumable items
    - packaging
- expenses, relating to all costs other than materials and labour costs.

Each of the above three categories may be further analysed into:

- direct costs
- indirect costs.

> **Progress check 8.5** **Are managers really interested in whether a cost is fixed or variable when assessing cost behaviour within an organisation?**

Direct costs are those costs that can be traced and identified with, and specifically measured with respect to, a relevant cost object. A cost object is the thing we wish to determine the cost of. Direct costs include direct labour, direct materials, and direct overheads. The total cost of direct materials, direct labour and direct expenses, or overheads, is called prime cost.

Indirect costs, or overheads, are costs untraceable to particular units (compared with direct costs). Indirect costs include expenditure on labour, materials or services, which cannot be identified with a saleable cost unit. The term 'burden' used by American companies is synonymous with indirect costs or overheads.

Indirect costs may relate to:

- the provision of a product
- the provision of a service
- other 'sales and administrative' activities.

Total indirect costs may therefore be generally categorised as:

- production costs
- sales and marketing costs
- distribution costs
- administrative costs
- research and development costs.

Indirect costs relating to production activities have to be allocated, that is, assigned as allocated overheads to any of the following:

- a single cost unit
  a unit of product or service in relation to which costs are ascertained

- a cost centre
  a production or service location, function, activity or item of equipment for which costs are accumulated
- a cost account
  a record of the expenditure of a cost centre or cost unit
- a time period.

Worked Example 8.3

Are managers really interested in whether a cost is fixed or variable when assessing cost behaviour within their departments?

A manager should know how a cost will behave when setting a departmental budget. As time goes by and the manager routinely reports actual compared to budget, several differences will be caused by the behaviour of the cost. For example, certain wage costs may be greater per hour for hours worked after 6.00 pm each day.

Progress check 8.6 **Explain costs in terms of the hierarchy of costs that comprise the total costs of a business.**

Cost allocation and cost apportionment

The indirect costs of service departments may be allocated both to other service departments and to production departments. An idea of the range of departments existing in most large businesses can be gained by simply looking at the newspaper job advertisements of major companies, where each department may represent an 'allocation of costs' problem.

Allocation of overheads is the charging to a cost centre of those overheads that result solely from the existence of that cost centre. Cost assignment defines the process of tracing and allocating costs to the cost object. Overheads are allocated where possible, but allocation can only be done if the exact amount incurred is known without having to carry out any sort of sharing. For example, a department in a factory may have a specific machine or a type of skilled labour that is only used in that department. The depreciation cost of the specific machine and the cost of the skilled labour would be allocated to that department. If the amount is not known and it is not possible to allocate costs then the total amount must be apportioned.

Worked Example 8.4

A degree of subjectivity is involved in the allocation of expenses to a department, or cost centre, which can frequently cause problems. However, the allocation of wage costs to the Millennium Dome project should have been fairly straightforward.

The Dome was very unusual since it was a large capital project with a very short life, starting on 31 December 1999 and finishing 31 December 2000. The ticket office would also have a very short life – it would have had no tickets to sell after 31 December 2000! The costs of staff working in the ticket office would also be easy to identify.

Apportionment is the charging to a cost centre of a fair share of an overhead on the basis of the benefit received by the cost centre in respect of the facilities provided by the overhead. For example, a factory may consist of two or more departments that occupy different amounts of floor space. The total factory rent cost may then be apportioned between the departments on the basis of floor space occupied.

Therefore, if an overhead cannot be allocated then it must be apportioned, involving use of a basis of apportionment, a physical or financial unit, so that the overhead will be equitably shared between the cost centres. Bases of apportionment, for example, that may be used are:

- area – for rent, heating and lighting, building depreciation
- number of employees – for personnel and welfare costs, safety costs
- weights or sizes – for materials handling costs, warehousing costs.

The basis chosen will use the factor most closely related to the benefit received by the cost centres.

Worked Example 8.5

The Millennium Dome had many areas that were financed by outside companies, which had signed contracts for the year. The contracts would have included clauses regarding recovery of certain costs from them, by the Millennium Company. It is likely that different bases of apportionment would need to have been chosen for the costs of cleaning and security.

The cleaning costs would have been fairly straightforward to apportion, probably on a surface area basis (square metres).

The security costs may have been more problematical, for example using a basis of value of contents, area of concession and so on.

Once overheads have been allocated and apportioned, perhaps via some service cost centres, ultimately to production cost centres, they can be charged to cost units. For example, in a factory with three departments the total rent may have been apportioned to the manufacturing department, the assembly department, and the goods inwards department. The total overhead costs of the goods inwards department may then be apportioned between the manufacturing department and the assembly department. The total costs of the manufacturing department and the assembly department may then be charged to the units being produced in those departments, for example television sets, or cars. The same process may be used in the service sector, for example theatre seats, and hospital beds. A cost unit is a unit of product or service in relation to which costs are ascertained. A **unit cost** is the average cost of a product or service unit based on total costs and the number of units.

Worked Example 8.6

The unit cost ascertainment process illustrated in Fig. 8.5 involves taking each cost centre and sharing its overheads among all the cost units passing through that centre.

This example considers one cost centre, the manufacturing department, which is involved with the production of three different products, A, B, and C. The process is similar to apportionment but in this case cost units (which in this case are products) are charged instead of cost centres. This process of charging costs to cost units is absorption and is defined as the charging of overheads to cost units.

		Manufacturing department				
	Number of units	Production time	Rate per hour	Total charge on the basis of hours		Charge per unit
Overhead costs	3,000 product A	1,000 hours	£5	£5,000	[£5,000/3,000]	£1.67
for January	2,000 product B	4,000 hours	£5	£20,000	[£20,000/2,000]	£10.00
£50,000	5,000 product C	5,000 hours	£5	£25,000	[£25,000/5,000]	£5.00
	10,000 units	10,000 hours		£50,000		

Figure 8.5 An example of unit cost ascertainment

The cost of converting material into finished products, that is, direct labour, direct expense and production overhead, is called the conversion cost. An example of this may be seen in the manufacture of a car bumper, which may have started out as granules of plastic and 'cans of paint'. After the completion of carefully controlled processes that may use some labour and incur overhead costs, the granules and paint are converted into a highly useful product.

> Progress check 8.7 **What is cost allocation and cost apportionment? Give some examples of bases of cost apportionment.**

Within the various areas of management accounting there is greater interest in future costs. The future costs that result from management decisions are concerned with relevant costs and opportunity costs, which are described briefly below but which will be illustrated in greater detail when we consider the techniques of decision-making in Chapter 10.

Relevant costs (and revenues) are the costs (and revenues) appropriate to a specific management decision. They are represented by future cash flows whose magnitude will vary depending upon the outcome of the management decision made. If stock is sold to a retailer, the relevant cost, used in the determination of the profitability of the transaction, would be the cost of replacing the stock, not its original purchase price, which is a sunk cost. Sunk costs, or irrecoverable costs, are costs that have been irreversibly incurred or committed prior to a decision point and which cannot therefore be considered relevant to subsequent decisions.

An opportunity cost is the value of the benefit sacrificed when one course of action is chosen in preference to an alternative. The opportunity cost is represented by the forgone potential benefit from the best of the alternative courses of action that have been rejected.

Worked Example 8.7

A student may have a Saturday job that pays £7 per hour. If the student gave up one hour on a Saturday to clean the car instead of paying someone £5 to clean it for them, the opportunity cost would be:

One hour of the student's lost wages	£7
less: **Cost of car cleaning**	£5
Opportunity cost	£2

Absorption costing

In this section we are looking at profit considered at the level of total revenue less total cost. If a CD retailer, for example, uses absorption costing it includes a proportion of the costs of its premises, such as rent and utilities costs, in the total unit cost of selling each CD. The allocation and apportionment process that has been outlined in the past few paragraphs is termed absorption costing, or full costing. This process looks at costing in terms of the total costs of running a facility like a hospital, restaurant, retail shop, or factory, being part of the output from that facility. This is one method of costing that, in addition to direct costs, assigns all, or a proportion of, production overhead costs to cost units by means of one or a number of overhead absorption rates. There are two steps involved in this process:

- computation of an overhead absorption rate
- application of the overhead absorption rate to cost units.

The basis of absorption is chosen in a similar way to choosing an apportionment base. The overhead rate is calculated using:

$$\text{overhead absorption rate} = \frac{\text{total cost centre overheads}}{\text{total units of base used}}$$

Worked Example 8.8

Albatross Ltd budgeted to produce 44,000 dining chairs in the month of January, but actually produced 48,800 dining chairs (units). Its sales were 40,800 units at a price of £100 per unit.

Budgeted costs for January:

Direct material	£36 per unit
Direct labour	£8 per unit
Variable production costs	£6 per unit
Fixed costs	
Production costs	£792,000
Administrative expenses	£208,000
Selling costs	£112,000

Sales commission is paid at 10% of sales revenue. There was no opening stock and budgeted costs were the same as actual costs.

We can prepare the profit and loss account for January using absorption costing techniques, on the basis of the number of budgeted units of production.

$$\text{Overhead absorption rate} = \frac{\text{budgeted fixed production cost}}{\text{budgeted units of production}}$$
$$= \frac{£792,000}{44,000} = £18 \text{ per unit}$$

Over-absorption of fixed production overheads
= (actual production − budgeted production) × fixed production overhead rate per unit
= (48,800 − 44,000) × £18 per unit = £86,400

Production costs per unit

	£	
Direct material	36	
Direct labour	8	
Variable production overhead	6	
Variable production cost	50	
Fixed production overhead	18	see above
Full production cost per unit	68	

Profit and loss account

	£	£
Sales (40,800 × £100)		4,080,000
Full production costs (48,800 × £68)	3,318,400	
plus Opening stock	–	
less Closing stock (8,000 units × £68)	(544,000)	
Cost of sales		2,774,400
Gross profit		1,305,600
less Other expenses		
Sales commission (£4,080,000 × 10%)	408,000	
Administrative expenses	208,000	
Selling costs	112,000	
		728,000
		577,600
plus		
Over-absorbed fixed production overheads		86,400 see above
Net profit for January, before tax		664,000

Under/over-absorbed overheads represent the difference between overheads incurred and overheads absorbed. Over-absorbed overheads are credited to the profit and loss account, increasing the profit, as in the above example (refer to Appendix 1 to refresh your knowledge of debits and credits). Under-absorbed overheads are debited to the profit and loss account, reducing the profit. In this example, the over-absorption of overheads was caused by the actual production level deviating from the budgeted level of production. Deviations, or variances, can occur due to differences between actual and budgeted volumes and/or differences between actual and budgeted expenditure.

There are many bases that may be used for calculation of the overhead absorption rate, for example:

■ units of output
■ direct labour hours
■ machine hours.

Desktop IT systems can assist in these calculations and provide many solutions to the problem of the 'overhead absorption rate', allowing consideration of a number of 'what-if' scenarios before making a final decision.

It can be seen that absorption costing is a costing technique whereby each unit of output is charged with both fixed and variable production costs. The fixed production costs are treated as part of the actual production costs. Stocks, in accordance with SSAP 9, are therefore valued on a full production cost basis and 'held' within the balance sheet until the stocks have been sold, rather than charged to the profit and loss account in the period in which the costs of the stocks are incurred. When the stocks are sold in a subsequent accounting period these costs are matched with the sales revenue of that period and charged to the profit and loss account. The objective of absorption costing is to obtain an overall average economic cost of carrying out whatever activity is being costed.

In order for costings to be carried out from the first day of operations, overhead rates are invariably calculated on the basis of expected future or budgeted overheads and the number of units of manufacturing capacity. Actual overheads and levels of production are unlikely to exactly equal budgeted amounts and so the use of budgeted overhead absorption rates will inevitably lead to an overhead over- or under-absorption (as we have seen in Worked Example 8.8), which is transferred (usually) monthly to the profit and loss account, for internal management accounting reporting.

> **Progress check 8.8** What is absorption costing and how is it used? Give some examples of bases that may be used for the calculation of overhead absorption rates applied to cost units.

Worked Example 8.9

The total costs for one specific manufacturing process have been incurred at various levels of output as shown in the table below. We can assume that the fixed costs and the variable cost per unit remain constant over this range of output, that is to say there is a linear relationship between total costs and output.

Output units	Total cost £
28,750	256,190
30,000	261,815
31,250	267,440
32,500	273,065
33,750	278,690
35,000	284,315

From the table above we can use a high–low analysis to determine:

(i)   the variable costs per unit for the process
(ii) the fixed cost of the process

(i)

	Total cost	Units output
	£	
High	35,000	284,315
Low	28,750	256,190
Difference	6,250	28,125

Variable cost per unit:

$$\frac{£28,125}{6,250} = £4.50$$

(ii) Using the answer from (i) we can calculate the total variable costs at any level of output, for example at 30,000 units we have:

Variable costs = 30,000 units × £4.50 = £135,000

We can now use this to determine fixed costs:

Total costs at an output level of 30,000 units	= £261,815
Less: variable cost element	= £135,000
Therefore fixed overhead	= £126,815

Alternatively, you may like to try and achieve the same result for Worked Example 8.9 using a graphical approach. If you plot the data in the table you should find that at the point where the graph crosses the y-axis (total costs) output is zero. At that point total costs are £126,815, which is the fixed cost – the cost incurred even when no output takes place. The slope of the graph represents the variable cost per unit, which may be calculated as £4.50 per unit.

We shall now consider another costing technique, marginal costing, which is also known as variable costing or period costing. We will return later to Worked Example 8.8, using the marginal costing technique and contrast it with the absorption costing technique.

Marginal costing

We have considered above a costing method that looks at profit considered at the level of total revenue, or total sales, less total cost. We will now look at another way of considering profit, called contribution, and its corresponding costing system called marginal costing (see Fig. 8.6).

contribution = total revenue – variable costs

Marginal costing, variable costing, or period costing, is a costing technique whereby each unit of output is charged only with variable production costs. The costs which are generated solely by a given cost unit are the variable costs associated with that unit, including the variable cost elements of any associated semi-variable costs. Marginal cost ascertainment includes all unit direct costs plus the variable overhead cost per unit incurred by the cost unit. The marginal cost of a unit may be defined as the additional cost of producing one such unit. The marginal cost of a number of units is the sum

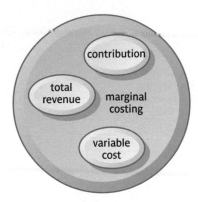

Figure 8.6 The elements of marginal costing

of all the unit marginal costs. Whereas absorption costing deals with total costs and profits, marginal costing deals with variable costs and contribution. Contribution is defined as the sales value less the variable cost of sales. Contribution may be expressed as:

- total contribution
- contribution per unit
- contribution as a percentage of sales.

If a business provides a series of products that all provide some contribution, the business may avoid being severely damaged by the downturn in demand of just one of the products. Fixed production costs are not considered to be the real costs of production, but costs which provide the facilities, for an accounting period, that enable production to take place. They are therefore treated as costs of the period and charged to the period in which they are incurred against the aggregate contribution. Stocks are valued on a variable production cost basis that excludes fixed production costs.

Marginal cost ascertainment assumes that the cost of any given activity is only the cost that that activity generates; it is the difference between carrying out and not carrying out that activity. Each cost unit and each cost centre is charged with only those costs that are generated as a consequence of that cost unit and that cost centre being a part of the company's activities.

We will now return to Worked Example 8.8 and consider the results using marginal costing techniques, and contrast them with those achieved using absorption costing in Worked Example 8.10.

Worked Example 8.10

Using the information for Albatross Ltd from Worked Example 8.8, we may prepare a profit and loss account for January using marginal costing.

The variable (marginal) production costs per unit from Worked Example 8.8 are:

	£
Direct material	36
Direct labour	8
Variable production overhead	6
Variable production cost	50

Profit and loss account

	£	£
Sales (40,800 × £100)		4,080,000
Variable production costs (48,800 × £50)	2,440,000	
plus Opening stock	–	
less Closing stock (8,000 units × £50)	(400,000)	
Cost of sales		2,040,000
Gross contribution		2,040,000
less Sales commission (£4,080,000 × 10%)		408,000
Net contribution		1,632,000
less Fixed costs		
Production costs	792,000	
Administrative expenses	208,000	
Selling costs	112,000	
		1,112,000
Net profit for January, before tax		520,000

It can be seen that profit calculated using the marginal costing technique is £144,000 less than that using the absorption costing technique, because under absorption costing stock is valued at full production costs, the fixed production costs being carried forward in the stock to the next period instead of being charged to the current period as under marginal costing.

Note: The activity is the same regardless of the costing technique that has been used. It is only the method of reporting that has caused a difference in the profit.

Stock valuation difference

Closing stock units × (absorption cost per unit – marginal cost per unit) = profit difference

8,000 units × (£68 – £50) = £144,000

Some specific features of the marginal costing technique are:

- its recognition of cost behaviour, providing better support for sales pricing and decision-making, which we shall explore further in Chapter 10
- it allows better control reports to be prepared because contribution is based on, and varies with, the sales level, which we shall examine when we look at cost and overhead relationships in Chapter 9
- fixed costs may be addressed within the period that gives rise to them.

However, marginal costing is not suitable for stock valuation in line with accounting standard SSAP 9, because there is no fixed cost element included. SSAP 9 requires closing stocks to consist of direct materials, direct labour and appropriate overheads. A great many companies, large and small, adopt marginal costing for monthly management reporting and stocks valuation for each of their accounting periods throughout their financial year. Such companies overcome the problems of non-compliance with SSAP 9 by making an adjustment to their stocks valuation and their profit and loss accounts to include an allowance for fixed overhead costs, in the final accounting period at their year end.

Absorption costing versus marginal costing

A more comprehensive list of the advantages and disadvantages of both techniques is summarised in Figs 8.7 and 8.8.

> **Progress check 8.9** **Should managers participate in the accounting exercise of allocation of fixed costs?**
>
> **(Hint: You may wish to consider the cyclical nature of the building industry as an example that illustrates the difficulty of allocating fixed costs.)**

In the long run, over several accounting periods, the total recorded profit of an entity is the same regardless of whether absorption costing or marginal costing techniques are used. The difference is one of timing. The actual amounts of the costs do not differ, only the period in which they are charged against profits. Thus, differences in profit occur from one period to the next depending on which method is adopted.

Figure 8.9 illustrates and contrasts the formats of the trading and profit and loss account using absorption costing and marginal costing.

Marginal costing is a powerful technique since it focuses attention on those costs which are affected by, or associated with, an activity. We will return to marginal costing in Chapter 9, with regard to cost/volume/profit (CVP) relationships and break-even analysis. It is also particularly useful in the areas of decision-making and relevant costs, and sales pricing which we shall be looking at in Chapter 10.

Management accounting continues to change and develop as it meets the needs presented by:

- changing economic climates
- globalisation
- information technology
- increasing competition.

Marginal costing developed from absorption costing in recognition of the differences in behaviour between fixed costs and variable costs. In most industries, as labour costs continue to become a smaller and smaller percentage of total costs, traditional costing methods, which usually absorb costs on the basis of direct labour hours, have been seen to be increasingly inappropriate.

In Chapter 9, we will look at some management accounting techniques that have been developed more recently in response to some of the criticisms of traditional costing methods:

- activity based costing (ABC)
- throughput accounting (TA)
- life cycle costing
- target costing
- benchmarking
- *kaizen*.

> **Progress check 8.10** **What is marginal costing and in what ways is it different from absorption costing?**

advantages	disadvantages
it is simple to use, and based on a formula that uses an estimated or planned fixed overhead rate included in the calculation of unit costs of the products and services	fixed costs are not necessarily avoidable and they have to be paid regardless of whether sales and production volumes are high, low or zero
it is easy to apply using cost or a percentage mark-up to achieve a reasonable profit	fixed costs are not variable in the short run
apportionment and allocation of fixed costs to cost centres makes managers aware of costs and services provided and ensures that they remember that all costs need to be covered for the company to be profitable	there are different alternative bases of overhead allocation which therefore result in different interpretations
cost price or full cost pricing ensures that all costs are covered	the capacity levels chosen for overhead absorption rates are based on historical information and are therefore open to debate
it conforms with the accrual concept by matching costs with revenue for a particular accounting period, as in the full costing of stocks	activity must be equal to or greater than the budgeted level of activity or else fixed costs will be under-absorbed
stock valuation complies with SSAP 9, as an element of fixed production costs is absorbed into stocks	if sales are depressed then profits can be artificially increased by increasing production thus increasing stocks
it avoids the separation of costs into fixed and variable elements, which are not easily and accurately identified	
analysis of over- and under-absorbed overheads highlights any inefficient utilisation of production resources	

Figure 8.7 Advantages and disadvantages of absorption costing

advantages	disadvantages
it is market based not cost based; exclusion of fixed production costs on a marginal basis enables the company to be more competitive	pricing at the margin may lead to underpricing with too little contribution and non-recovery of fixed costs, particularly in periods of economic downturn
it covers all incremental costs associated with the product, production and sales	stock valuation does not comply with SSAP 9, as no element of fixed production costs is absorbed into stocks
it enables the analysis of different market price/volume levels to allow selection of optimal contributions and it enables strategic analysis of competitors and customers	
it enables the company to determine break-even points and plan profit, and to use the opportunity cost approach	
it avoids the arbitrary apportionment of fixed costs and avoids the problem of determining a suitable basis for the overhead abortion rate, e.g. units, labour hours, machine hours etc.	
most fixed production overheads are periodic, or time-based, and incurred regardless of levels of production, and so should be charged to the period in which they are incurred, e.g. factory rent, salaries and depreciation	
fixed production costs may not be controllable at departmental level and so should not be included in production costs at the cost centre level – control should be matched with responsibility	
profits cannot be manipulated by increasing stocks in times of low sales because stocks exclude fixed costs and profits therefore vary directly with sales	
it facilitates control through easier pooling of separate fixed costs and variable costs totals, and preparation of flexible budgets to provide comparisons for actual levels of activity	
stock valued on a variable cost basis supports the view that the additional cost of stock is limited to its variable costs	
marginal costing is prudent because fixed costs are charged to the period in which they are incurred, not carried forward in stock which may prove to be unsaleable and result in earlier profits having been overstated	

Figure 8.8 Advantages and disadvantages of marginal costing

Absorption costing		Marginal costing	
	Net turnover		Net turnover
less:		less variable costs:	
Direct materials		Direct materials	
Direct labour		Direct labour	
Production overhead		Variable production overhead	
		Variable selling and distribution overhead	
	Production cost of sales		Production cost of sales
	Gross profit		**Contribution**
less:		less fixed costs:	
		Production costs	
Selling costs		Selling costs	
Distribution costs		Distribution costs	
Administrative expenses		Administrative expenses	
Research and development costs		Research and development costs	
	Non-production costs		Total fixed costs
	Net profit before tax		**Net profit before tax**

Figure 8.9 Trading and profit and loss account absorption and marginal costing formats

Worked Example 8.11

Management accounting provides information to various departments within a business. Fast-moving businesses need this information very quickly. Hotel groups have invested in central booking systems and these systems are used to reveal times of the year when reservations are down because of national and local trends. Let us consider how the marketing department and the management accounting function might work together to generate extra bookings.

The marketing department may assess the periods and times in which each hotel has gaps in its reservations. The management accountant may assess the direct costs associated with each reservation, for example the costs of cleaning and food. The two departments may then suggest a special offer for a fixed period of time (for example, Travelodge special offers in the press during January and February 2001). The special offer may allow for local conditions by varying the price within a range, for example £20 to £30 per night.

Summary of key points

- There are a number of additional accounting concepts that relate to management accounting.

- Cost (as a noun) is an amount of expenditure attributable to a specified thing or activity, but also relates to a resource sacrificed or forgone, expressed in a monetary value.
- Cost (as a verb) may be used to say that to cost something is to ascertain the cost of a specified thing or activity, but cost is not a word that is usually used without a qualification as to its nature and limitations.
- Direct costs are directly identified with cost objects.
- Indirect costs have to be allocated or apportioned to cost units, cost centres, or cost accounts using appropriate bases for allocation and apportionment.
- Unit costs of products, services or activities may be determined using the traditional costing techniques of absorption costing and marginal costing.
- There are many arguments for and against the use of the techniques of both absorption costing and marginal costing, revolving mainly around the basis chosen for allocation and apportionment of overheads.

Questions

Q8.1 (i) What are the main roles of the management accountant?

 (ii) How does management accounting support the effective management of a business?

Q8.2 (i) What are the differences between fixed costs, variable costs and semi-variable costs?

 (ii) Give some examples of each.

Q8.3 (i) Why do production overheads need to be allocated and apportioned, and to what?

 (ii) Describe the processes of allocation and apportionment.

Q8.4 (i) Which costing system complies with the provisions outlined in SSAP 9?

 (ii) Describe the process used in this technique.

Q8.5 What is marginal costing and how does it differ from absorption costing?

Q8.6 What are the main benefits to be gained from using a system of marginal costing?

Discussion points

D8.1 Surely an accountant is an accountant! Why does the function of management accounting need to be separated from financial accounting and why is it seen as such an integral part of the management of the business? Discuss.

D8.2 Do the benefits from using marginal costing outweigh the benefits from using absorption costing sufficiently to replace absorption costing in SSAP 9 as the basis for stock valuation and the preparation of financial statements? Discuss.

Exercises

Solutions are provided in Appendix 4 to all exercise numbers highlighted in colour.

Level I

E8.1 *Time allowed – 45 minutes*

Bluebell Woods Ltd produces a product for which the following standard cost details have been provided based on production and sales of 4,300 units in a four-week period:

Direct material cost	£0.85 per kg
Direct material usage	2 kg per unit
Direct labour rate	£4.20 per hour
Direct labour time per unit	42 minutes
Selling price	£5.84 per unit
Variable production costs	£0.12 per unit
Fixed production costs	£3,526 per four-week period

Prepare a standard profit statement for a four-week period using:

(i)   **absorption costing**

(ii) **marginal costing.**

E8.2 *Time allowed – 45 minutes*

A manufacturing company, Duane Pipes Ltd, uses predetermined rates for absorbing manufacturing overheads based on the budgeted level of activity. A total rate of £35 per direct labour hour has been calculated for the Assembly Department for March 2004, for which the following overhead expenditure at various activity levels has been estimated:

Total manufacturing overheads £	Number of direct labour hours
465,500	12,000
483,875	13,500
502,250	15,000

You are required to calculate the following:

(i)   **the variable overhead absorption rate per direct labour hour**

(ii)   **the estimated total fixed overheads**

(iii) **the budgeted level of activity for March 2004 in direct labour hours**

(iv)   **the amount of under/over-recovery of overheads, and state which, if the actual direct labour hours were 13,850 and actual overheads were £509,250**

and

(v)   **outline the reasons for and against using departmental absorption rates as opposed to a single blanket factory-wide rate.**

Level II

E8.3 *Time allowed – 75 minutes*

Square Gift Ltd is located in Wales, where the national sales manager is also based, and has a sales force of 15 salesmen covering the whole of the UK. The sales force, including the national sales manager, all have the same make and model of company car. A new car costs £16,000, and all cars are traded in for a guaranteed £6,000 when they are two years old.

The salesman with the lowest annual mileage, of 18,000 miles, operates in the South East of England.
The salesman with the highest annual mileage, of 40,000 miles, operates throughout Scotland.
The annual average mileage of the complete sales team works out at 30,000 miles per car.

The average salesman's annual vehicle running cost is:

	£
Petrol and oil	3,000
Road tax	155
Insurance	450
Repairs	700
Miscellaneous	300
Total	4,605

Annual vehicle repair costs include £250 for regular maintenance.
Tyre life is around 30,000 miles and replacement sets cost £350.
No additional repair costs are incurred during the first year of vehicle life because a special warranty agreement exists with the supplying garage to cover these, but on average £200 is paid for repairs in the second year – repair costs are averaged over the two years with regular maintenance and repairs being variable with mileage rather than time.
Miscellaneous vehicle costs include subscriptions to motoring organisations, vehicle cleaning costs, parking, and garaging allowances.

Analyse the total vehicle costs into fixed costs and variable costs separately to give total annual costs for:

(i)   the lowest mileage per annum salesman

(ii)   the highest mileage per annum salesman.

You may ignore cost of capital, and possible impacts of tax and inflation.
(Hints: Assume that insurance costs are the same for each area.
          Assume that miscellaneous operating costs are fixed.
          Repairs are based on amount of mileage.)

E8.4 *Time allowed – 75 minutes*

Rocky Ltd manufactures a single product, the budget for which was as follows for each of the months July and August 2005:

		Total £		Per unit £
Sales (6,000 units)		60,000		10.00
Production cost of sales:				
Variable overhead	45,000		7.50	
Fixed overhead	3,000	48,000	0.50	8.00
		12,000		2.00
Selling and distribution costs (fixed)		4,200		0.70
Administrative expenses (fixed)		3,000		0.50
Profit		4,800		0.80

Actual units produced, sold and in stock in July and August were:

	July	August
Opening stock	–	900
Production	5,300	4,400
Sales	4,400	5,000
Closing stock	900	300

Prepare profit and loss accounts for each of the months July and August, assuming that fixed production overhead is absorbed into the cost of the product at the normal level shown in the monthly budget.

(Hint: This is the absorption costing approach.)

E8.5 *Time allowed – 75 minutes*

Using the data for Rocky Ltd from Exercise E8.4, prepare profit and loss accounts for each of the months July and August, assuming that fixed production overhead is not absorbed into the cost of the product, but is treated as a cost of the period and charged against sales.

(Hint: This is the marginal costing approach.)

E8.6 *Time allowed – 75 minutes*

Using your answers to Exercises E8.4 and E8.5, explain why the profits for July and August are different using the two costing methods, and support your explanation with an appropriate reconciliation of the results.

9

Cost management

Contents

Learning objectives

Completion of this chapter will enable you to:

- explain cost/volume/profit (CVP) relationships and break-even analysis
- identify the limitations of CVP analysis
- outline the more recently developed techniques of activity based costing (ABC), and throughput accounting (TA)
- identify the conditions appropriate to the use of life cycle costing
- apply the principles of target costing
- consider benchmarking as a technique to identify best practice and enable the introduction of appropriate performance improvement targets
- outline *kaizen* as a technique for continuous improvement of all aspects of business performance
- explain the types of information and measurements used in lean accounting systems
- use cost of quality (COQ) to identify areas for improvement and cost reduction within each of the processes throughout the business
- appreciate the importance of both financial and non-financial indicators in the evaluation of business performance
- consider the use of both financial and non-financial measures incorporated into performance measurement systems such as the balanced scorecard.

Introduction

In Chapter 8 we introduced costs, contribution and profit. This chapter develops the importance of contribution as a measure of profitability and begins with an examination of the relationship between costs, volumes of activity, and profit, or CVP analysis. We will look at a particular application of CVP analysis in break-even analysis, and consider some of the advantages and limitations of its use.

This chapter looks at some of the more recently developed management accounting techniques, some of which have been developed in response to the criticisms of traditional costing methods, for example: activity based costing; throughput accounting; life cycle costing; target costing; benchmarking; *kaizen*; quality costing; non-financial performance indicators; and the balanced scorecard.

The broadening of the range of activities supported by management accounting has resulted in a gradual disappearance of the boundaries between itself and financial management. Management accounting continues to develop with an emphasis on decision-making and strategic management, and financial management. Financial management is usually defined as the management of the processes that deal with the efficient acquisition and deployment of short- and long-term financial resources. It was interesting to note in September 2000 that CIMA renamed its monthly journal from *Management Accounting* to *Financial Management*.

This chapter provides an introduction to the development of lean accounting systems, and closes with an examination of the important area of non-financial indicators in the evaluation of business performance. The contribution of financial and non-financial measures is examined in their incorporation into performance measurement systems such as the balanced scorecard, developed by David Norton and Robert Kaplan in the early 1990s.

Cost/volume/profit (CVP) relationships and break-even analysis

It is sometimes said that accountants think in straight lines whereas economists think in curves. We can see this in the way that economists view costs and revenues. Generally, economists are looking at the longer term when they consider a company's total costs and total revenues.

We can see from Fig. 9.1 that the total revenue curve starts where the volume is zero and therefore the total revenue is zero (nothing is sold and so there is no sales value). The economist says that as the selling price (which the economist calls marginal revenue) is increased then total revenue will continue to increase, but by proportionately less and less. This continues up to a point where the decrease in selling price starts to have less and less impact on volume and so total revenue starts to decline. The result of this is a total revenue curve that increases but which becomes gradually less steep until it eventually flattens out and then falls away.

The total cost curve starts some way up the £ axis because fixed costs are incurred even when sales are zero. Total costs are comprised of fixed costs and variable costs (or marginal costs). As volumes increase then total costs increase. The economist assumes that fixed costs continue to be unchanged, and when volumes increase unit costs decrease because the fixed cost is spread amongst a greater number of products. Therefore, the total costs increase but proportionately less and less. In addition, the economist says that the total costs further benefit from decreases in variable costs as volume increases. This happens as a result of economies of scale:

- as labour becomes more experienced then less is required for a given level of output
- materials cost prices reduce as purchasing power increases from greater volumes.

Economies of scale continue until further economies are not possible, and we begin to see diminishing returns. This happens when variable costs start to increase, which may be due to the overloading of processes at high volumes, leading to possible malfunctions, breakdowns, and bottlenecks.

Figure 9.1 Economist's cost and revenue curves

Initially the total cost curve does not rise steeply because of the fixed costs effect and the positive impact of economies of scale on variable costs. As the business reaches its most efficient volume level further economies of scale are not possible and the total cost curve quickly becomes very steep as a result of the adverse impact of diminishing returns on variable costs.

It can be seen from Fig. 9.1 that profit is maximised at a specific point shown where the gap between the two curves is greatest. Also, because of the shapes of the economist's longer-term total cost and total revenue curves, it can be seen that they cross at two points. At these points total costs are equal to total revenues and so for the economist there are two break-even points. This contrasts with the accountant's view of costs, volumes, and break-even, which is explained below. This chapter will focus on the accountant's view of CVP analysis and break-even.

The break-even point is an important measure for NTL, the largest British cable company (see the press extract below):

- the company had needed to be able to determine the point at which it would break even
- one of the company's initial targets is likely to have been to be able to reach break-even within a given number of years from start-up.

When does a company break even?

NTL, Britain's largest cable company, today said losses in the first three months of the year fell by 63% as over 61,000 new customers joined its NTL Home internet, phone and TV service.

The cable giant said the performance of NTL Home, combined with increased profitability in its other divisions, meant it had reached break-even in terms of operating income for the first time in its history.

Operating income in the first quarter rose to £2.2m compared with a £54.1m loss in the same period last year, as turnover rose 7% to £585m.

The cable group, which is expected to merge with Telewest once a lengthy financial restructuring process is completed, said net losses for the quarter fell by over 62% to £65.4m compared with the £174.7m it lost in the first three months of 2003.

Simon Duffy, the chief executive of NTL, said the company's complex financial restructuring, coupled with last year's share issue, had reduced the company's annual interest charges by 37% to £235m.

'The first quarter results demonstrate a strong start to the year with increased profitability across all divisions compared to the first quarter of 2003. The progress made in the first quarter positions NTL well for continued revenue growth and sustainable margin expansion over the balance of the year,' said Mr Duffy.

NTL added 61,500 subscribers to NTL Home, a quarterly record according to the company. It has 2.9 million subscribers who each spent just under £42 in the first three months of 2004 on either TV, telephone, internet or a mix of all three.

The cable company, which recently announced free speed upgrades for its broadband customers, said it had added 81,000 new high speed internet customers since December, taking the total to 1.03 million.

The number of people taking its TV services also rose, reversing consecutive quarters of decline. It added 16,600 TV subscribers in the first three months, boosting overall numbers to 2.05 million.

It also revealed for the first time that churn – the rate by which customers sign off services – stands at 13.2% annually, or 1.1% per month.

Customer drive boosts NTL hopes, by Dominic Timms

© *The Guardian*, 5 May 2004

NTL reported in May 2004 that it had reached a milestone in its development in breaking even at its operating income (profit) level for the first time in the company's history.

For the accountant the total cost and total revenue functions are not represented as curves, but as straight lines. There are a number of assumptions made by the accountant that support this, as follows:

- fixed costs may remain unchanged over a specific range of volumes but they increase in steps over higher ranges of volumes, because when volumes are significantly increased additional fixed costs are incurred on items like new plant and machinery, factories, etc. – the accountant considers a short-term relevant range of volumes over which fixed costs remain unchanged
- over the short term the selling price may be considered to be constant
- over the short term the unit variable cost may be considered to be constant.

The result of these assumptions is that, unlike the economist, the accountant views income from sales (total revenue) and total cost as straight lines over the relevant short-term period. This means that profit continues to increase as volume increases. Profit is maximised at the volume where maximum capacity is reached. Also, there is only one point where the total revenue and total cost lines cross and so for the accountant there is only one break-even point.

Cost/volume/profit (CVP) analysis studies the effects on future profit of changes in fixed costs, variable costs, volume, sales mix and selling price. Break-even (B/E) analysis is one application of CVP, which can be useful for profit planning, sales mix decisions, production capacity decisions and pricing decisions.

There are three fundamental cost/revenue relationships which form the basis of CVP analysis:

total costs = variable costs + fixed costs

contribution = total revenue − variable costs

profit (or operating income) = total revenue − total costs

The break-even point is the level of activity at which there is neither profit nor loss. It can be ascertained by using a break-even chart or by calculation. The break-even chart indicates approximate profit or loss at different levels of sales volume within a limited range. Break-even charts may be used to represent different cost structures and also to show contribution break-even positions and profit-volume relationships (see Figs. 9.2, 9.3, 9.4, and 9.5). Computerised spreadsheets can be used to convert profit/volume relationship 'what-ifs' into either charts or tables that may be used for presentation or decision-making purposes. They provide the means of exploring any area within fixed costs, variable costs, semi-variable costs, and sales, in terms of values and volumes.

The slopes of the total cost lines in Fig. 9.2 and Fig. 9.3 represent the unit variable costs. The break-even chart shown in Fig. 9.2 shows a relatively low level of fixed costs with variable costs rising quite steeply as the level of activity increases. Where the total sales (or income) line intersects the total cost line is the point at which total sales or total revenue equals total costs. This activity of 40 units is the break-even point.

The break-even chart shown in Fig. 9.3 shows the impact of a higher level of fixed costs with a higher break-even point at around 60 units, even though variable costs are lower than the cost structure shown in Fig. 9.2. If variable costs had stayed the same, the break-even point would be even higher at over 80 units of activity.

The margin of safety shown in each of these charts will be explained when we look a little further at some break-even relationships.

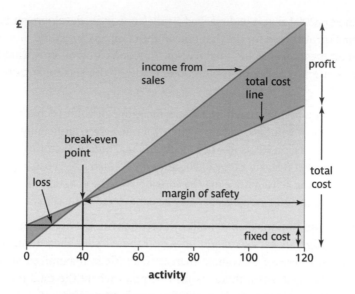

Figure 9.2 Break-even chart – low fixed costs, high variable costs

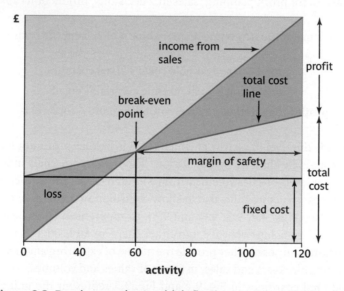

Figure 9.3 Break-even chart – high fixed costs, low variable costs

Progress check 9.1 **Explain how a break-even analysis could be used within the planning of a 'one-off' event that involves:**

- **the sales of tickets**
- **provision of hotel accommodation**
- **live music.**

Figure 9.4 shows a contribution break-even chart, which is just a variation of the previous charts. In this chart, variable costs are shown starting from the zero x/y axes in the same way as sales. The effect of adding fixed costs to variable costs (or marginal costs) is shown in the total costs line. Where the sales line intersects the total costs line there is zero profit. This is the break-even point.

Figure 9.5 shows a profit volume chart. The horizontal line represents fixed costs and the diagonal line represents the total contribution at each level of activity. The break-even point, where total sales equals total costs, is also where total contribution equals fixed costs.

We will look at why the break-even point is where total contribution equals fixed costs and also consider some further break-even relationships.

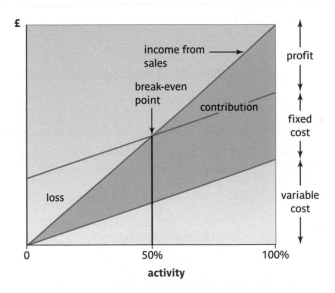

Figure 9.4 Contribution break-even chart

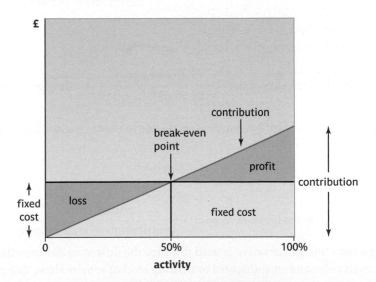

Figure 9.5 Profit volume (PV) chart

Consider:

Total revenue = R
Variable costs = V
Fixed costs = F
Profit = P
Contribution = C

Profit equals total revenue less total costs (variable costs and fixed costs)

$$P = R - V - F$$

Contribution equals total revenue less variable costs

$$C = R - V$$

Therefore, substituting C for R – V, profit equals contribution less fixed costs

$$P = C - F$$

At the break-even point total revenue equals totals costs, and profit is zero, therefore

$$0 = C - F$$

Or at the break-even point

$$C = F$$
$$\textbf{contribution} = \textbf{fixed costs} \tag{BE1}$$

It follows that the:
Number of units at the break-even point × contribution per unit = fixed costs, or

$$\textbf{number of units at break-even point} = \frac{\textbf{fixed costs}}{\textbf{contribution per unit}} \tag{BE2}$$

Therefore the break-even point in £ sales value is:
Number of units at the break-even point × selling price per unit, or

$$\textbf{£ sales value at break-even point} = \frac{\textbf{fixed costs}}{\textbf{contribution per unit}} \times \textbf{selling price per unit}$$

But the selling price per unit divided by contribution per unit is the same as total sales revenue divided by total contribution, which is:

The reciprocal of the contribution to sales ratio percentage
So, an alternative expression is:

$$\textbf{£ sales value at break-even point} = \frac{\textbf{fixed costs}}{\textbf{contribution to sales ratio \%}} \tag{BE3}$$

**The term 'margin of safety' is used to define the difference between the
break-even point and an anticipated or existing level of activity above that point.** (BE4)

In other words, the margin of safety measures the extent to which anticipated or existing activity can fall before a profitable operation turns into a loss-making one (see Figs. 9.2 and 9.3).

> **Progress check 9.2** **Discuss how departmental stores might use the concept of contribution and break-even analysis when analysing their financial performance.**

The following example uses the relationships we have discussed to illustrate the calculation of a break-even point.

Worked Example 9.1

	£
Sales (1,000 units)	10,000
Variable costs (direct materials and direct labour)	6,000
Contribution	4,000
Fixed costs	2,000
Profit	2,000

From the above table of sales and cost data we can find the break-even point in number of units and the sales value at that point.

Number of units sold	1,000
Therefore, contribution/unit	$\dfrac{£4,000}{1,000} = £4$ per unit
And, contribution to sales ratio %	$= \dfrac{£4,000}{£10,000} \times 100\% = 40\%$
Using BE2 number of units at break-even point	$= \dfrac{\text{fixed costs}}{\text{contribution per unit}}$
	$= £2,000/£4$
	$= 500$ units
Using BE3 £ sales value at break-even point	$= \dfrac{\text{fixed costs}}{\text{contribution to sales ratio \%}}$
	$= £2,000/40\%$
	$= £5,000$

The CVP technique may also be used to derive a target cost estimate, by subtracting a desired margin or target profit from a competitive market price. This cost may be less than the planned initial product cost, but will be a cost that is expected to be achieved by the time the product reaches the mature production stage. Sales volumes or sales values may be calculated that are required to achieve a range of profit targets.

Worked Example 9.2

Bill Jones, who had worked for many years as an engineer in the automotive industry, had recently been made redundant. Bill, together with a number of colleagues, now had the opportunity to set up a business to make and sell a specialised part for motor vehicle air-conditioning units. Bill had already decided on a name for the company. It would be called Wilcon Ltd. Bill had some good contacts in the industry and two automotive components manufacturers had promised him contracts that he estimated would provide sales of 15,000 units per month, for the foreseeable future.

The business plan was based on the following data:

Selling price per unit	£17.50
Variable costs per unit	£13.00
Fixed costs for month	£54,000 including salaries for 5 managers @ £1,500 each

Bill and his colleagues are very interested in determining the break-even volume and sales value for Wilcon Ltd.

Contribution/unit

	£
Selling price	17.50
Variable cost	13.00
Contribution/unit	4.50

Break-even volume

If the number of units sold is n Total contribution = $n \times £4.50$

At the break-even point fixed costs equal total contribution (see BE1)

$$£54,000 = £4.50 \times n$$

Therefore, $n = £54,000/£4.50 = 12,000$ units

Sales value at break-even point   = number of units at break-even point × selling price per unit

          = $12,000 \times £17.50 = £210,000$

Bill and his colleagues are also interested in looking at the break-even points at different levels of sales, costs and profit expectation, which are considered in Worked Examples 9.3 to 9.7.

Worked Examples 9.3 to 9.7 have used the technique of sensitivity analysis. We have considered the sensitivity of the break-even point against expected volumes of activity. We have also considered the impact on the break-even point of changes to fixed costs and variable costs, and how costs and price levels need to change to achieve a planned level of profit. Sales price sensitivity may be considered in terms of volume through analysis of fixed labour and overhead costs, and variable material, labour and overhead costs.

Worked Example 9.3

The data from Worked Example 9.2 can be used to find the margin of safety (volume and value) for Wilcon Ltd if the predicted sales volume is 12,500 units per month.

Margin of safety (volume and value) if the predicted sales volume is 12,500 units per month

The predicted or forecast volume is 12,500 units, with a sales value of $12,500 \times £17.50$

$$= £218,750$$

The margin of safety is predicted volume – break-even volume (see BE4)

$$= 12,500 - 12,000 = 500 \text{ units}$$

Margin of safety sales value

$$= £218,750 - £210,000$$

$$= £8,750$$

Worked Example 9.4

The data from Worked Example 9.2 can be used to find the reduction in break-even volume if one less manager were employed by Wilcon Ltd.

Reduction in break-even volume if one less manager were employed

Fixed costs become $£54,000 - £1,500$

$$= £52,500$$

If the number of units sold is n

$$£52,500 = £4.50 \times n$$

Therefore, $n = £52,500/£4.50 = 11,667 \text{ units}$

Therefore reduction in volume from break-even is $12,000 - 11,667$, or 333 units

Worked Example 9.5

The data from Worked Example 9.2 can be used to find the volume of units to be sold by Wilcon Ltd to make £9,000 profit per month.

Volume of units to be sold to make £9,000 profit

Profit = contribution – fixed costs
If n equals the number of units, for a profit of £9,000

$$£9,000 = (n \times £4.50) - £52,500 \,[54,000 - 1,500]$$

Or, $n = £61,500/£4.50 = 13,667 \text{ units}$

Worked Example 9.6

The data from Worked Example 9.2 can be used to find the revised break-even volume if fixed costs are reduced by 10% and variable costs are increased by 10% by Wilcon Ltd.

Revised break-even volume if fixed costs are reduced by 10% and variable costs are increased by 10%

If fixed costs are $\quad\quad\quad\quad\quad\quad 90\% \times £54,000 = £48,600$
And variable costs are $\quad\quad\quad\quad 110\% \times £13 = £14.30$
Then unit contribution becomes $£17.50 - £14.30 = £3.20$
$$£48,600 = £3.20 \times n$$
Therefore, $\quad\quad\quad\quad\quad\quad\quad\quad n = £48,600/£3.20 = 15,188 \text{ units}$

Worked Example 9.7

The data from Worked Example 9.2 can be used to find the revised selling price that must be charged by Wilcon Ltd to show a profit of £6,000 on 10,000 sales units.

Revised selling price that must be charged to show a profit of £6,000 on 10,000 sales units

Profit = contribution – fixed costs
If total contribution is TC
$$£6,000 = TC - £54,000$$
$$TC = £60,000$$
Therefore
Contribution/unit = £60,000/10,000 = £6 per unit
Variable cost is £13 per unit
Therefore revised selling price is
$$£13 + £6 = £19 \text{ per unit}$$

CVP analysis may therefore be used in:

- profit planning
- project planning
- establishing points of indifference between projects
- make or buy decision-making
- shut down or continuation decisions
- product mix decisions
- sales pricing.

We shall consider many of these applications of CVP analysis in Chapter 10 when we look at decision-making.

> **Progress check 9.3** What is a break-even point? Why is it important for a business to know its break-even point, and what types of sensitivity can it be used to analyse?

Limitations of CVP analysis

We have seen that break-even analysis is just one of the applications of CVP analysis that may be viewed differently by the economist and the accountant. The many assumptions made by the accountant, on which CVP analysis relies, include:

- that output is the only factor affecting costs – there may be others including inflation, efficiency, economic and political factors
- the simplistic approach to cost relationships: that total costs are divided into fixed and variable costs – in reality costs cannot be split easily, even into variable and fixed costs
- the likelihood that fixed costs do not remain constant beyond certain ranges
- the behaviour of both costs and revenue is linear – linearity is rare with regard to costs and revenue
- there is no uncertainty – there is much uncertainty involved in the prediction of costs and sales
- there is a single product – businesses usually provide more than one product and sales mix is not constant but continually changes due to changes in demand
- that stock levels do not change
- the time value of money is ignored (see Chapter 13)
- that these assumptions hold over the relevant range (the activity levels within which assumptions about cost behaviour in break-even analysis remain valid: it is used to mitigate the impact of some of the limitations of CVP analysis mentioned above).

In real-life situations the above assumptions clearly do not hold because, as has been noted previously, cost relationships are not simple and straightforward. Factors affecting the costs and volumes of products and services do change frequently. Such factors do not usually change only one at a time but more usually change all at once. The above limitations to CVP analysis are very real and should be borne in mind when using the technique, for example, to consider alternative pricing options that use both the marginal and full absorption costing approach. Nevertheless, the principles of CVP analysis continue to hold true, and some of the above limitations may be overcome.

Multiple product break-even analysis

The break-even analyses that we have considered thus far have assumed that only one product or service is being provided. In practice however this is rarely the case. Businesses usually offer a range of products or services.

In the same way as we have calculated for a single product, the weighted average contribution may be used to calculate the selling prices required to achieve targeted profit levels, and revised break-even volumes and sales values resulting from changes to variable costs and fixed costs.

Worked Example 9.8

Curtis E. Carr & Co provides a range of three limousines for hire. The proprietor, Edna Cloud, has prepared the following details of estimated activity for 2005.

Limousine	Elvis	JR Ewing	Madonna
Estimated number of hours of hire	600	900	500
Hire price per hour	£25	£20	£24
Variable costs per hour of hire	£5	£3	£4

Fixed costs for the year   £5,595

Edna would like to know what is the break-even position for the firm in total hours of hire and sales value.

We can summarise the estimated sales, contribution and profit from the information given by Edna, as follows:

Limousine	Elvis	JR Ewing	Madonna	Total
Contribution per hour of hire	£20 (£25 – £5)	£17 (£20 – £3)	£20 (£24 – £4)	
Estimated number of hours of hire	600	900	500	2,000
Total sales	£15,000	£18,000	£12,000	£45,000
Total contribution	£12,000	£15,300	£10,000	£37,300
Fixed costs for 2005				£5,595
Estimated profit for 2005				£31,705

To calculate the break-even position we need to weight the level of activity of each of the products, the hours of hire of each of the limousines:

	Hours	% of total hours
Elvis	600	30
JR Ewing	900	45
Madonna	500	25
	2,000	100

The weighting percentages of each product may then be used to calculate a weighted average contribution per hour:

	Contribution per hour	Weighting %	Weighted contribution
Elvis	£20	30	£6.00
JR Ewing	£17	45	£7.65
Madonna	£20	25	£5.00
Weighted average contribution per hour			£18.65

The multiple product break-even point is derived from:

$$\frac{\text{total fixed costs}}{\text{weighted average contribution}} = \frac{£5,595}{£18.65} = 300 \text{ hours}$$

The break-even level of activity (300 hours) may then be used to calculate the proportion of total hours for each product and the contribution for each product and the business.

		Break-even hours	Contribution per hour	Total contribution
Elvis	30% × 300 hours	90	£20	£1,800
JR Ewing	45% × 300 hours	135	£17	£2,295
Madonna	25% × 300 hours	75	£20	£1,500
		300		£5,595

The total contribution can be seen to equal total fixed costs at the break-even point.

Break-even sales may be calculated by first calculating the:

$$\text{weighted average contribution to sales ratio \%} = \frac{\text{total contribution}}{\text{total sales}} = \frac{£37,300}{£45,000}$$

$$= 0.8289$$

$$\text{£ sales value at the break-even point} = \frac{\text{total fixed costs}}{\text{contribution to sales ratio \%}}$$

$$= \frac{£5,595}{0.8289} = £6,750$$

for the total 300 hours of hire.

A greater degree of sophistication may be achieved from more dynamic and complex models, and using computerised simulation models. Uncertainty will always remain, but the impact of the results of the occurrence of uncertain events, within given constraints, may be evaluated using sensitivity analysis. Spreadsheets like Excel can provide very sensitive 'what-if' solutions, and the linking features in modelling systems can speedily provide a range of alternative values.

Progress check 9.4 Discuss the usefulness of a sensitivity analysis of the factors used in calculation of the break-even point of a national chain fast food outlet that uses television advertising campaigns.

In addition to break-even analysis, cost/volume/profit (CVP) analysis techniques may be used in a number of decision-making scenarios, some of which we will look at in Chapter 10. Very often, for example, in a decision-making scenario there are two or more limiting factors, in which case a linear programming model would need to be used to determine optimum solutions. Linear programming is not covered in this book.

Progress check 9.5 What is CVP analysis and on what assumptions is it based?

Activity based costing (ABC)

The activities of businesses across the entire chain of value-adding organisational processes have a considerable impact on costs and therefore profit. A recently developed management accounting approach to evaluating the extent of this impact and to dealing with the root causes of costs is activity based costing (ABC).

Activity based costing provides an alternative approach to the costing of products in response to some of the criticisms that have been aimed at the more traditional approaches. Before we examine the concept of ABC let us look at a simple example, which puts these criticisms in context.

Worked Example 9.9

Traditional Moulding Ltd manufactures two plastic fittings, the RX-L and the RX-R. Both products are produced in the Moulding2 department, which has total overheads of £5,000 for the month of March. Moulding2 uses 4,000 hours of direct labour to produce the RX-L (2,000) and RX-R (2,000). The other activities within the Moulding2 department are 10 machine set-ups (eight to produce the RX-L and two to produce the RX-R) which cost £3,200, and the processing of 90 sales orders (50 for the RX-L and 40 for the RX-R) costing £1,800.

The costs charged to each product may be determined using absorption costing on a direct labour hours basis, and alternatively they may be determined on the basis of the other activities within the department.

Absorption costing basis
Cost per labour hour = £5,000/4,000 hours = £1.25 per direct labour hour

	RX-L £	RX-R £	Total £
2,000 hours at £1.25	2,500		2,500
2,000 hours at £1.25		2,500	2,500
	2,500	2,500	5,000

Alternative activities basis

	RX-L	RX-R	Total	
Machine set-ups	8	2	10	(cost £3,200)
Sales orders	50	40	90	(cost £1,800)
				(total cost £5,000)

	RX-L £	RX-R £	Total £
Machine set-ups at £320 each	2,560	640	3,200
Sales orders at £20 each	1,000	800	1,800
	3,560	1,440	5,000

There is obviously a considerable difference between the overhead costs attributed to each of the products, depending on which basis we have used. We may question whether or not the absorption basis is fair and whether or not the activity basis provides a fairer method.

Increasing competition is a fact of life within any industry, public or private, and whatever product or service is being offered to customers in the marketplace. Globalisation has brought increased pressures of competition. Pressures on a company's profit margins inevitably follow from the increasing pace of technological change, which results in shortened life cycles of products that have been manufactured by the company as they are replaced by completely new models. Thus, the obsolescence of capital equipment is accelerated. This all means that the basis of competition has changed.

The effects on businesses are significant, and those that do not respond successfully may fail, or be acquired by other companies. Costs such as development costs and costs of capital equipment must be recovered over a shorter time period. The phases within the product life cycle must be managed more effectively and efficiently. The faster pace of business and the need for quick decisions and action mean that effective computerised information systems are required to provide relevant and timely information.

The above changes in the manufacturing business environment have led to changes in the patterns of cost behaviour. Technological and other changes have meant a lowering of the percentage of direct labour costs as a proportion of total manufacturing costs. An indication of the trend and the scale of this reduction in percentage of direct labour cost are shown in Fig. 9.6. In many industries materials and components costs have become an increasingly large proportion of total manufacturing costs. Automation and decreasing equipment life spans have led to capital equipment costs forming a higher percentage of total costs. The costs of information technology and other overhead and indirect costs have also increased as a percentage of total cost. There has therefore been increasing dissatisfaction with traditional costing and decision-making techniques and the search for other, perhaps more relevant and meaningful methods.

Traditional decision-making and control have looked at cost/volume relationships and the splitting of fixed and variable costs. The consideration of 'other characteristics' has not been emphasised. Activity based costing (ABC) was developed by Kaplan and Cooper in 1984 and was aimed to get accountants to consider 'other characteristics' in terms of the causes of cost, or what are defined as the cost drivers.

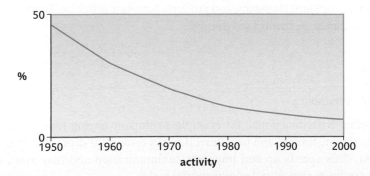

Figure 9.6 Estimated UK direct labour costs as % of manufacturing costs over the past 50 years

Kaplan and Cooper said that one cost system was not enough, and that three were needed:

- for stock valuation
- for operational control
- for product cost measurement.

Together with Cooper, Kaplan proposed ABC as a method for dealing with the latter two requirements. ABC involves the examination of activities across the entire chain of value-adding organisational processes underlying the causes, or drivers, of cost and profit. Kaplan and Cooper have defined ABC as an approach to costing and monitoring of activities which involves tracing resource consumption and costing final outputs. Resources are assigned to activities and activities to cost objects based on consumption estimates. The latter utilise cost drivers to attach activity costs to outputs.

> **Progress check 9.6** Why does traditional analysis of fixed and variable costs within a fast moving company (for example, a company that supplies computer hardware, software and helpline services) not appear to provide managers with enough information?

An activity driver is defined as a measure of the frequency and intensity of the demands placed on activities by cost objects. An example is the number of customer orders which measures the consumption of order entries by each customer. A cost driver is defined as any factor which causes a change in the cost of an activity. For example, the quality of parts received by an activity is a determining factor in the work required by that activity and therefore affects the resources required. An activity may have multiple cost drivers associated with it.

If a company produces only one product then all overheads may be allocated to that product. The unit cost of the product is then the average cost. The difficulty of allocation of overheads arises when the company produces many products using many different resources consumed in different proportions by products. It is the sharing of overheads and the feasibility of monitoring the costs that causes the difficulty.

Traditional cost allocation approaches allocate overheads, for example, on the basis of direct labour hours, or units produced. They are therefore volume driven, based on a scientific management basis of mass production with standard design, a high labour content percentage of total costs, large volumes, low fixed costs, and with demand greater than supply. This incidentally resulted in competitive advantage gained from cost leadership.

ABC starts by considering four different groups of activities giving rise to overheads: movement, production demands, quality, and design, rather than the volume of production. ABC is based on the premise that activities consume resources, and products consume activities. There is a need to identify how labour and machinery is actually used through:

- interview
- questionnaire
- observation
- process activity mapping.

Activities are often cross-functional, for example a company buying function that involves purchasing, finance, administration, and personnel (human resources) departments in the whole procurement process. This speeds up and improves communication and may avoid a great deal of unnecessary and duplicate clerical and administrative tasks.

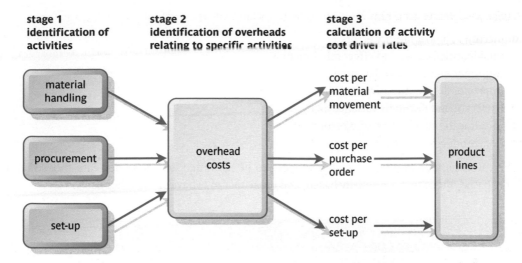

Figure 9.7 Framework of activity based costing (ABC)

ABC requires the analysis of total overhead costs into variable costs and fixed costs, with variable costs split into short-term and long-term variable costs. Within an ABC system it is assumed that fixed costs do not vary with any measure of activity volume for a given time period. Short-term variable costs – volume-based costs – are defined in the same way as traditional volume-driven variable costs – materials and direct labour. Long-term variable costs – activity based costs – are defined as those costs which vary with the level of activity, which may be non-productive, and the variation may not be instant. Examples of these are machine set-up costs, and goods receiving costs, which are driven by the activities of the number of production runs and number of customer orders, respectively.

The diagram in Fig. 9.7 represents an example of the framework of ABC. The bases of ABC are:

- it is activities that cause costs, not products
- it is activities and not costs that can be managed
- control of costs is best achieved through the management of activities
- each cost driver, or activity, is evaluated by setting up its own individual cost centre, to see if it is worth undertaking or buying in, and to see how it may be managed, reported on and evaluated.

The search for alternative methods such as ABC also highlights many weaknesses in traditional cost accounting methods. Indiscriminate use of a single performance measure can lead to misleading conclusions about profit and cost performance. Traditional cost accounting methods can lead to a failure to understand the activities that are causing costs, and a compartmentalised approach to costing which does not look at the processes and activities that cross departmental boundaries.

> **Progress check 9.7** Use an example of a media group to provide the basis for a discussion on how ABC analysis considers departmental activities as the causes of costs rather than the products that are being produced.

These weaknesses result in:

- pricing and profitability errors
- misidentified cause and effect relationships
- improper make or buy decisions
- improper design initiatives
- irrelevant and untimely variance analysis
- misallocations of capital and resources
- non-productive activities.

The ABC methodology requires all cost types to be identified and classified into those that are volume based, those that are activity based, and those that may have some other basis.

Worked Example 9.10

Let's consider how the costs of a wine-bottling process, for example, for supply to one large customer, may be classified into those that are volume based, activity based, or on some other basis.

The bottle-filling process costs may be totally volume related. The labelling and corking processes may be related to stocking and handling of materials and the set-up of the processes required to align labels and corks. Alternatively, costs may in some way be related to the different grades of product, perhaps the perceived quality of the wine as 'cheap plonk' or fine wine.

Volume-based costs are then computed on a product unit costs basis, for example, materials costs. Activity based costs are computed relative to each activity. For each product the cost of using each activity for the output level is calculated. The total costs for each product are then calculated and divided by the output volume in order to calculate the unit cost for each product.

The ABC accounting system may be used to develop an **activity based management (ABM)** system. This is a system of management, which uses activity based information for a variety of purposes including cost reduction, cost modelling and customer profitability analysis. The system involves four key operations: activity analysis; activity costings; activity costs per product; activity performance measurement and management. A good ABM system should promote more effective cross-function management.

Major companies involved with providing consumers with customer service and advice found the resources required on site were quite expensive, both in capital and management time. As a result of various experiments during the latter part of the 1990s, the UK has seen a major move towards the out-sourcing of these services to specialist call centres located in 'low cost' areas, away from 'high cost' city centres. This illustrates the ABM process applied to the customer service activity. Decisions are taken following analyses of activities and their costs, followed by the evaluation of various alternative options that might be available, their implementation and subsequent management. In a similar way, many companies have investigated the out-sourcing of a number of routine accounting functions to specialist contractors.

The activity analysis identifies all activities and analyses all inputs and outputs of each activity. Activity costings identify all relevant and important costs of all activities. The activity volume that is chosen is the one that most directly influences costs, and the total costs are expressed in terms of activity per unit of activity volume.

Next, the activity costs per product are calculated by identifying the activity, which each product consumes, and measuring the consumption rates of activities per product. Using the unit activity cost consumption rates, costs are then allocated to each product.

The final step is activity performance measurement and management. This involves evaluation of the major elements in the performance of an activity. Changes in activity levels are then evaluated and performance reviewed which may then result in re-engineering of the methods used in that activity. The results are evaluated by:

- measuring, and
- monitoring, and
- controlling the re-engineered activity.

Worked Example 9.11

Let's assume that Traditional Moulding Ltd (from Worked Example 9.9) had achieved improvements in the processes, which resulted in a reduction in the costs and number of machine set-ups required. We can calculate the revised costs that would result if the RX-L and the RX-R each required only one set-up and the total cost of set-ups was only £640.

	RX-L	RX-R	Total	
Machine set-ups	1	1	2	(cost £640)
Sales orders	50	40	90	(cost £1,800)

	RX-L	RX-R	Total
	£	£	£
Machine set-ups at £320 each	320	320	640
Sales orders at £20 each	1,000	800	1,800
	1,320	1,120	2,440

There is another considerable difference between the overhead costs attributed to each of the products. We have used the same basis as previously, but an improvement in one of the processes has brought the costs attributed to each product virtually in line with each other whereas previously one product bore almost three times the cost of the other product.

A full worked example will clarify the ABC accounting concepts we have discussed and show the results obtained using ABC compared with those using an alternative traditional absorption costing method.

Worked Example 9.12

A clothing manufacturer, Brief Encounter Ltd, manufactures two products, the Rose and the Rouge, using the same equipment and similar processes. Activities have been examined to identify the relevant cost drivers as machine hours, set-ups and customer orders. August budget data has been provided relating to the cost drivers, in addition to material, labour and overhead costs and quantities produced.

August budget ABC data	Rose	Rouge
Budgeted number of units manufactured	20,000	10,000
Direct material cost per unit	£5	£20
Direct labour hours per unit	0.5	0.5
Direct labour cost per hour	£8	£8
Machine hours per unit	2	4
Set-ups during the month	30	70
Customer orders handled in the month	40	160

Overhead costs for the month:	relating to machine activity	£300,000
	relating to set-ups of production runs	£50,000
	relating to order handling	£70,000

We can use the above data to illustrate ABC and to provide a comparison with traditional costing methods. The full production cost of each unit of the Rose and the Rouge using both a traditional absorption costing approach and an ABC costing approach may be compared and illustrated in both tabular and graphical form.

Absorption costing
Using a traditional absorption costing approach the full production cost of each unit of Rose and Rouge may be calculated:

Budget direct labour hours (20,000 units × 0.5 hours) + (10,000 units × 0.5 hours)
= 15,000 hours
Overhead absorption rate per direct labour hour

$$= \frac{\text{machine activity costs} + \text{set-up costs} + \text{order handling costs}}{\text{direct labour hours}}$$

$$= \frac{(£300,000 + £50,000 + £70,000)}{315,000 \text{ hours}} = £28 \text{ per direct labour hour}$$

Full unit production costs of the Rose and the Rouge:

		Rose		Rouge
		£		£
Direct materials		5.00		20.00
Direct labour	(0.5 hours × £8)	4.00	(0.5 hours × £8)	4.00
Factory overhead	(0.5 hours × £28)	14.00	(0.5 hours × £28)	14.00
Unit production costs		23.00		38.00

Total costs (20,000 × £23) + (10,000 × £38) = £840,000

ABC

Using an ABC costing approach the full production cost of each unit of the Rose and the Rouge may be calculated:

Planned for the month of August:

Machine hours (20,000 units × 2 hours) + (10,000 × 4 hours)		= 80,000 hours
Machine costs		= £300,000
Machine rate per hour		= £3.75
Number of set-ups	(30 + 70)	= 100 set-ups
Set-up costs		= £50,000
Cost per set-up		= £500
Number of orders handled	(40 + 160)	= 200 orders
Order handling costs		= £70,000
Cost per order handled		= £350

Overhead costs per unit of the Rose and the Rouge on an ABC basis:

		Rose £		Rouge £
Machine activity	(2 hours × £3.75)	7.50	(4 hours × £3.75)	15.00
Set-ups	(30 × £500)/20,000	0.75	(70 × £500)/10,000	3.50
Order handling	(40 × £350)/20,000	0.70	(160 × £350)/10,000	5.60
Unit overhead costs		8.95		24.10

ABC unit production costs of the Rose and the Rouge:

		Rose £		Rouge £
Direct materials		5.00		20.00
Direct labour	(0.5 hours × £8)	4.00	(0.5 hours × £8)	4.00
Factory overhead		8.95		24.10
Unit production costs		17.95		48.10

Total costs (20,000 × £17.95) + (10,000 × £48.10) = £840,000

Summary of unit product costs

	Rose £	Rouge £
Full absorption cost per unit	23.00	38.00
ABC cost per unit	17.95	48.10

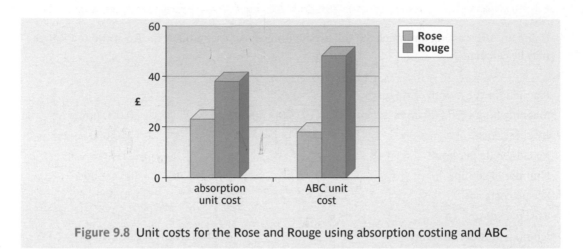

Figure 9.8 Unit costs for the Rose and Rouge using absorption costing and ABC

There are large differences between the two alternative calculations of unit costs. In practice, this can have a significant impact on pricing policies adopted by companies, and on other decision-making, for example with regard to discontinuation of apparently unprofitable products.

It can be seen from Worked Example 9.12 that all costs have been accounted for and included in the unit costs for the Rose and the Rouge using both the absorption costing and ABC methods. However, using absorption costing, the Rose has been shown to be far less profitable, and the Rouge shown to be far more profitable than by using the ABC approach. In this brief example, the ABC approach has probably shown the more correct and realistic unit costs applying to the Rose and the Rouge because it has identified the activities, the causes of costs, directly related to the manufacture of each product. The pooling of the costs associated with each activity has enabled costs to be attributed directly to each product, rather than using an estimate based on, say, direct labour costs. Therefore, a more informed approach may be taken to improving machine set-up, and order-handling performance, and their cost reduction and better pricing decisions may be made regarding both the Rose and the Rouge.

There are benefits to be gained from the use of ABC: it facilitates improved understanding of costs; it enables improvements and overhead savings to be made; it focuses on activities and not production volumes; it examines the profitability of products; it identifies loss-making products; it leads to development of activity based management systems.

However, there are also many problems associated with the implementation and use of an ABC system:

- it does not comply with statutory stock valuation requirements
- it is as subjective as absorption costing
- it is historical
- it uses cost pooling (points of focus for the costs relating to particular activities), but also requires the use of apportionment, which involves the same problems of subjectivity identified in the use of absorption costing
- it requires identification of cost drivers, the right ones; it requires the measurement of cost drivers and activity costs
- it requires the relating of activities to products

- it requires the measurement of cross-product drivers, which are factors that cause changes in costs of a number of activities and products
- there are always other consequences that ABC does not address
- there is a novelty, or flavour of the month, factor associated with ABC which is questionable
- it is an expensive and time-consuming exercise.

Despite the problems associated with the implementation of ABC, its acceptance is becoming more widespread in the UK. Nevertheless, there is as yet little evidence as to improved profitability resulting from the implementation of ABC. Dr Stephen Lyne and Andy Friedman from Bristol University carried out research into 11 companies to study the impact of activity based techniques in real-life situations over a six-year period up to 1999 (*Success and Failure of Activity Based Techniques*).

The Lyne/Friedman research involved defining exactly what was meant by success and failure, and using the researchers' criteria five companies failed, and six were deemed a partial success. Interestingly, the research highlighted some key factors that influenced the success or otherwise of implementing ABC:

- the positive and negative roles of individuals
- the degree to which ABC was an embedded system
- the degree of integration with information technology systems
- the use of consultants
- relations between accountants and operational managers.

ABC should perhaps not be regarded totally as the panacea, the answer to all the problems associated with cost accounting. ABC, no doubt, represents an enlightened approach and adds something more meaningful than traditional costing methods. Its implementation requires very large and complex data-collection exercises in which involvement of all activities throughout the whole organisation is necessary. ABC is very time-consuming and costly. Care needs to be taken in evaluation of the results of ABC. It is very useful for identification and management of the activities that cause costs. It is a useful tool to assist in product pricing decisions. It is not yet a costing method which may replace absorption costing for use in financial reporting.

> **Progress check 9.8** **Describe the activity based costing (ABC) process and in what ways it may be most effectively used.**

Throughput accounting (TA)

Another recent development in management accounting has been the introduction of throughput accounting (TA). It has its roots in the development of the production scheduling software, optimised production technology (OPT), from the mid-1970s. Through the 1980s and 1990s Eli Goldratt further developed and refined these ideas to construct the theory of constraints (TOC), which was outlined in 1984 by Goldratt and Cox in their book *The Goal* (Gower, 1984).

As part of the OPT approach, TA, developed from Goldratt's TOC, provides a new measurement system. This approach takes labour and overhead costs as given and concentrates on the flow of production through the factory. TA recognises that maybe only one or two variables limit the ability of the organisation to achieve its goal to make money. Concentration only on those specific variables, and putting the efforts where the problems are, can result in huge overall gains.

A simple definition of TA was provided by Takeo Yoshikawa in *Contemporary Cost Management* (Chapman and Hall, 1993). Throughput accounting (TA) is an approach to accounting which is largely in sympathy with the **just in time** (JIT) philosophy. In essence, TA assumes that a manager has a given set of resources available. These (fixed resources) comprise existing buildings, capital equipment, and a labour force. Using these resources, purchased materials and parts must be processed to generate sales revenue. Given this scenario the most appropriate financial objective to set for doing this is the maximisation of **throughput**.

Just in time (JIT) is a philosophy with an objective to produce or to procure products or components as they are required by a customer or for use, rather than for stock. A JIT system is a 'pull' system, which responds to demand, in contrast to a 'push' system, in which stocks act as buffers between the different elements of the system, such as purchasing, production and sales.

There is a link between TA and JIT in that throughput is not directly generated by producing for stock but only by effecting sales from finished output. TA is probably more usefully regarded as a new general approach within which a number of different measures can be constructed, rather than a new set of accounting techniques. This then needs to be supported by a change from traditional cost thinking to throughput thinking as a means of improving profitability.

TA is similar to the approach of contribution per unit of scarce resource, but whereas

$$\text{contribution} = \text{sales revenue} - \text{total variable costs}$$

throughput is defined as:

$$\text{throughput} = \text{sales revenue} - \text{direct materials cost}$$

An advantage of TA over traditional methods is that decisions made on standard costing 'efficiencies' are thus avoided. Examples of such decisions are those based on apparent improvements in labour productivity gained from manufacturing increased volumes (and build-ups of unnecessary stocks), not supported by increased customer orders. TA concentrates on identification and management of **bottlenecks** (which is in itself a process of continuous improvement) and so priority may be given to investment in bottlenecks. The concentration on throughput highlights the critical profit improvement areas of sales prices, volume, and material costs.

TA is a method of performance measurement, which relates production and other costs to throughput. The product costs calculated using TA relate to the usage of key resources by various products. As the costs of all factors other than materials are deemed fixed, the objective of maximisation of throughput will motivate management to generate the greatest profit for the business. TA is therefore an extreme form of marginal costing. The similarity can be seen in Fig. 9.9 from the example of a throughput report developed by Yoshikawa.

	£	£
Sales		x
Direct materials		(x)
Throughput		x
Direct labour	(x)	
Production overhead	(x)	
Administrative expenses	(x)	
Selling costs	(x)	
		(x)
Operating profit		x

Figure 9.9 Throughput report

In *The Goal*, Goldratt defines:

- throughput as the rate at which the system generates money through sales
- inventory is all the money that the system invests in purchasing things which it intends to sell (not to be confused with inventory as the American term for stocks)
- operational expense is all the money the system spends in order to turn inventory into throughput.

Goldratt's three measures are operationalised through a number of simple calculations:

- throughput = sales revenue − outside purchases of product-related materials and services
- inventory (in Goldratt's terminology) includes materials stocks plus machines and buildings
- operational expense covers conversion cost, including direct and indirect employee costs, operating, or idle time.

From these three measures Goldratt defines two important relationships:

$$\textbf{net profit} = \textbf{throughput} - \textbf{operational expense}$$

$$\textbf{return on investment (ROI)} = \frac{\textbf{throughput operational expense}}{\textbf{inventory}}$$
$$\textbf{(in the TA world)}$$

(Note the difference between this definition of ROI and the financial accounting definition that we looked at in Chapter 5.)

The three elements of the throughput accounting ROI ratio belong to three different 'worlds':

- throughput – the throughput world
- operational expense – the cost world, which is obsessed and involved with cost cutting
- inventory (stocks) – the just in time (JIT) world, concentrating on reducing stocks and the costs of holding stocks and with the aim of reducing waste.

Goldratt sees throughput as the priority, with inventory second, and operational expense last. This is a big change in managers' mind sets in which it is crucial for cost accounting not to interfere with the improvement of manufacturing performance. Traditional cost accounting methods may be criticised for reporting efficiency gains from longer production runs and increased volumes of production. Such efficiencies may be illusory if the result is high levels of unsold stock.

> **Progress check 9.9** Discuss the relationship between throughput and the traditional ratio of return on capital employed (ROCE) or return on investment (ROI).

Goldratt's approach broadened from a concentration on 'bottlenecks' (in production) to a general concern with constraints. A constraint may be defined as anything that prevents a system from achieving a higher performance relative to its goal. Constraints do not necessarily have to be within the production processes, but may, for example, be concerned with:

- demand
- skills
- accounting systems.

Note how in 2000 and 2001, the UK general public saw the Government attempting to solve constraint problems by allocating further funds to the health service and schools. There are four key influences on throughput, and therefore profitability:

- selling prices
- direct materials purchase costs
- direct material usage
- volume of throughput.

Progress check 9.10 Discuss the connection between TA and the electronic point of sale (EPOS) systems used by all the major supermarket chains.
   (Hint: Start the discussion by considering just in time (JIT).)

To maximise throughput it is first necessary to identify the constraints, the factors that currently limit the expansion of throughput. Constraints may be:

- the existence of uncompetitive selling prices
- the need for on-time deliveries
- the lack of product quality and reliability
- the lack of reliable materials supplies
- shortages of production resources.

Attention may then be given by managers to minimisation or elimination of these constraints.
   TA then focuses on some key activities:

- identification of bottlenecks and constraints, through profiling of processes and identification of buffer stocks
- close attention to decision making on new capital equipment investments
- project teams investigating and implementing reductions in lead times, set-up times and waiting times.

Along with its inventive approach to performance measurement and control, the overriding benefit of TA is that it forces everyone, and management in particular, to get back to understanding what is actually happening where the products and services are being provided, and to appreciate the critical need for adherence to customer schedules.

Worked Example 9.13

An aim of throughput accounting (TA) is maximisation of throughput, defined as sales revenue less direct material cost. Purchased materials and parts must be processed to generate this sales revenue.

   We may discuss how the contemporary scenario of manufacturing clothing in the Far East and selling in London's West End may generate stress within the UK managers of such a business.

   Throughput as defined by Goldratt and Cox is sales (and money) driven. Competition between the clothing retailers is severe. There is no guarantee that what is on the racks of the UK retailers will sell out, ready for the next range. Anything not sold by a certain date must be discounted for a short time or sold at a greatly reduced price to other specialist retailers. Time is of the essence as the selling seasons are fashion, weather and temperature driven. There must be careful monitoring of sales and stock levels, and continuous contact by the UK retailer managers with their Far East factories to boost production of fast sellers and reduce excess stocks and production of the slow sellers to the minimum.

> **Progress check 9.11** What is throughput and what do we mean by throughput accounting (TA)? In what ways can TA be used to improve productivity?

Life cycle costing

Life cycle costing has an ultimate aim of minimising total expenditure over the lifetime of a product, or over the lifetime of an item or a fixed asset. Life cycle costing involves the maintenance of physical asset records over the entire asset life, so that decisions concerning the acquisition, use or disposal of the asset can be made in a way that achieves the optimum assets usage at the lowest possible cost to the business.

With a focus on maximising reliability and minimising maintenance and repair costs, acquisition of machinery or equipment involves an examination of the original cost and the support cost of the asset over the number of years of its expected lifetime. Depending on the type of equipment, support costs may range from 10 to 100 times the cost of acquisition. The approach may be applied to smaller items such as computer hardware and software, and vehicles, to very large equipment like buildings and aircraft. The construction industry has become increasingly aware of the need to adopt an holistic approach to the design, building and disposal of structures. It has been estimated that around 60% of a typical total construction budget is spent on repair and maintenance and so there is an obvious need to design for reliability and durability, with more carefully planned maintenance and repair schedules.

As distinct from the service sector, the manufacturing environment has become more advanced in response to customer requirements for higher and higher levels of quality, durability and reliability. Such factors have to be designed into the product at the planning stage in addition to design for ease and speed of manufacture. Prototype and pre-production stages of a product's development have a significant impact on the product, and its cost over the entire life of the product. Life cycle costing may be applied to the profiling of cost over a product's life, including the prototyping and pre-production stages and in terms of the life cycles of both the business and the industry.

Worked Example 9.14

Powerful IT resources are now widely available, and all types of business may benefit from their acquisition and use. Fixed asset registers used to be maintained manually or not at all. Now they can be maintained with ease on a computer. A large plc, for example, can benefit from maintaining its fleet of company cars (say 100 vehicles) on a computer system, using a spreadsheet that may cost no more than £100.

Any spreadsheet can easily hold all the records relating to 100 cars.

The records should include acquisition cost, date of acquisition, supplier, specification, insurance, maintenance, mileages, market values (from external sources), and depreciation.

The spreadsheet should be robust enough to last several years and be able to be exported to other IT packages for report and update purposes.

Managers should be able to interrogate the data to make decisions on the future management of their fleet, and expansion of the system and retrieval of data should be available at all times.

> **Progress check 9.12** **How can life-cycle costing achieve its aims of improving reliability and minimising costs?**

Target costing

Management accounting traditionally supported pricing decisions based on, for example, the calculation of the selling price required to be charged for a product or service that covered total costs plus a margin for profit for the business. Such an approach took no account of the price which the market might accept for the particular product or service. Neither did this approach encourage the objective of total cost minimisation. In fact, one could argue that such an approach encouraged costs to be increased since the higher the cost, the higher was the level of total profit. Increased pressures on businesses to provide higher and higher specifications and levels of quality at more competitive prices has prompted changes to traditional approaches to the costing of products and services.

Target costing policies have been developed from wide usage in Japan based on the principle that a product must have a target price that will succeed in winning a share of the market. A target cost is a product cost estimate (for example, a car at £12,000) derived by subtracting a desired profit margin (for example, £2,000) from a competitive market price (for example £14,000), determined through customer analysis and market research. The target cost may be less than the planned initial product cost (which may have been say £13,500). The cost reduction (in this case £1,500) will be expected to be achieved by the time the product reaches the mature production stage, through continuous improvement and replacement of technologies and processes.

Target costing has also been described as a structured approach to determining the cost at which a proposed product with specified functionality and quality must be produced in order to generate the desired level of profitability at the product's anticipated selling price. Target costing focuses on reducing the cost of a product through design changes.

The traditional Western approach of 'cost plus' involved the setting of a target selling price by adding an expected margin to expected costs. If actual costs were more than expected then the selling price would be higher. Using target costing, in the long run, costs must come down to below the target price for the product to be worth manufacturing. This is saying that market prices determine product costs and not *vice versa*.

Target costs are determined by setting specific goals. Better performance then emerges from specific, challenging goals rather than a company's general goal of merely doing its best. Over many years, car manufacturers have been replacing metal with composites, and upgrading vehicle specifications without increasing prices. Many examples of this can now be seen from car advertisements appearing in the UK press.

Worked Example 9.15

UK computer buyers continue to see major improvements to the specification of PCs, costing around £1,000 or less. We may consider how the marketplace needs to react regarding the functionality of a PC.

Computer technology changes very quickly indeed. Products using the latest technology command very high prices. A high volume demand for older models (over 6 months old!) may be stimulated by offering consumers competitive target selling prices. High throughput then enables the suppliers of PCs, and peripherals, to meet such target prices by using economies of scale to drive down unit prices. DVD drives have followed printers, scanners and CD writers. The majority of PCs that are sold for around £1,000 or less in the UK usually include, as standard, integrated DVD drives and CD rewriters. Most retailers and dealers also include printers and scanners in their promotional deals. The consumer normally prefers to buy this type of package off the shelf from one source at the lowest price, whereas the PC dealer aims to maintain the unit price as high as possible.

There are three factors that affect the structure of a target-costing system:

- type of product – complex, capital-intensive products that have a long development time tend to require more sophisticated target costing systems that are closely linked to the use of value engineering techniques

- the market – where goods are supplied to the general public, the target costing system is based on a heavier bias towards consumer analysis and a focus on functionality; examples were apparent in UK press advertisements during 2001, where PCs were offered with CD writers, whereas earlier advertisements would have offered merely a CD player

- influence over suppliers – the target costing system creates a downward pressure on supplier prices, assuming that the customer company has greater power and is more important than the supplier company; in the UK during 2000, many manufacturers found themselves being pressurised by the major retailers to hold or reduce their prices in the electrical goods sector, for example, which reflected 'target costing' by those retailers.

Worked Example 9.16

Over the past few years, two companies in the UK called Time and Tiny selling PCs both advertised in the same national daily newspapers, with advertisements promoting packages comprising a computer with printer, camera, scanner, and a range of software, and with very similar prices.

The two companies were able to exert some pressure on suppliers of DVD drives and CD rewriters.

Neither company should let the other company drive down prices unilaterally. One of the key ways of remaining competitive is to examine 'ways and means' of reducing the number of constituent parts of the package and unit prices from various individual sources. Almost certainly both companies may have alternative sources, to enable them to play one off against the other, which is really standard buyer practice.

Worked Example 9.17

In the late 1990s there were many articles in the business press on how Marks and Spencer plc was working with suppliers as a 'partnership' at the factory floor level. These suppliers were all aware of other suppliers making the same products for Marks and Spencer plc, but Marks and Spencer plc was still able to put pressure on its suppliers.

There may always be several potential manufacturers that can supply a garment or a food product, for example, to a retailer. The national retailers are aware of this and may use these circumstances to negotiate volumes, prices, quality and deliveries. There will always be such 'tension' between the retailer and manufacturer.

Worked Example 9.18

Nissan operates in the automotive market where functionality continues to increase at a quite rapid pace. Nissan also uses a target costing system.

Nissan's target costing system would tend to be determined by market factors, using the following process:

- identification of the major characteristics of the car model, its engine, air conditioning system, etc.
- determination of current costs
- calculation of the 'allowable cost' of each function
- assessment of the level of cost reductions required
- use of an iterative process looking at costs and possible reductions in levels of functionality, in consultation with the marketing department
- assessment of first draft target costs achievable using value engineering
- detailed review of target costs to assess feasibility
- acceptance of draft target costs to be implemented in product development
- implementation of target costs using value engineering as appropriate.

After products are in production, costs are constantly monitored against targets. If costs are not in line with target costs then further cost reduction exercises are introduced to achieve targets.

Target costs may be used to exert pressure on suppliers to reduce costs. However, target costing creates a great deal of pressure within the organisation and the targets set must be achievable. It is not a method of cost control in the traditional sense, but rather provides a goal and a focus for cost reduction. Target costing is something that must be applied at the design stage of new product development, and cross-functional support and co-operation are absolute requirements for its success. The cross-functional support might involve:

- the designer wanting to change from one material used in manufacture to another
- the buyer sourcing materials or components from a new supplier
- the factory floor agreeing that the new product will cause no problems during assembly.

> **Progress check 9.13** Outline what is meant by target costing and why it has become increasingly popular for large manufacturers of consumer products.

Benchmarking

Benchmarking is the establishment, through data gathering, of targets and comparators, through whose use relative levels of performance (and particularly areas of under-performance) can be identified. Through the adoption of identified best practices it is hoped that performance will improve.

The performance of other companies should be continually benchmarked. This should look at, for example, design, quality, cost, and delivery, and is known as internal benchmarking, which is a method of comparing one operating unit or function with another within the same industry.

Benchmarking need not be restricted to companies with similar products or companies in the same industry. Lessons may be learned and costs reduced by comparing the company's processes with processes in other non-related companies or industries. Functional benchmarking (also known as operational, or generic benchmarking), compares internal functions with those of the best external practitioners of those functions, regardless of the industry they are in. A well-known airline achieved such improvements from benchmarking a photocopier manufacturer.

Competitive benchmarking compares performance from information gathered about direct competitors, through techniques such as reverse engineering. Reverse engineering relates to the decomposition and analysis of competitors' products in order to determine how they are made, their costs of production and the way in which future development may proceed. This is a technique favoured by Japanese manufacturers who have used it to advantage to copy and improve on quality and reliability of competing products and to manufacture at lower cost. Another type of competitive benchmarking is strategic benchmarking, which is aimed at strategic action and organisational change.

Benchmarking is a very useful tool that companies may use to develop suitable performance measures and also targets for improvement in each part of their business. A number of further techniques and concepts may be adopted to achieve such improvements, for example:

- value analysis/value engineering
- concurrent engineering
- cost of quality
- kaizen.

We will look at two of most important of these concepts and techniques, kaizen, and cost of quality (COQ), in the next two sections.

> **Progress check 9.14 What is benchmarking and how can it be used in support of business performance improvement?**

Kaizen

Change management is sometimes considered an oxymoron by many people, who say that change is usually, by its very nature, unplanned and independent of human purpose and is therefore unmanageable. However, the management of change was for many years one of the fundamental sources of competitive advantage that Japanese businesses had over their Western counterparts. The management of change is the basis of the concept of kaizen, which simply means improvement. It was a concept so natural and obvious to most Japanese managers that they often did not realise they possessed it.

The tools of kaizen were introduced to Japan in the 1950s from the USA by Deming and Juran.

However, the concept continued to be rejected for a long time in the West until the Japanese postwar 'economic miracle' began to be studied more seriously and the techniques applied to achieve the same improvements in productivity.

Kaizen means continuous improvement involving everyone, including both managers and operators – the people actually doing things. The *kaizen* philosophy assumes that everyone's way of life, whether it is working life, social life, or home life, deserves to be constantly improved. *Kaizen* signifies small continuous improvements to the *status quo* as a result of constant efforts rather than drastic investment/improvement programmes.

In his book *Kaizen* (McGraw-Hill, 1986), Imae described *kaizen* as an umbrella concept (see Fig. 9.10), covering most of those 'uniquely Japanese' practices that have achieved such worldwide fame.

Kaizen teams are small multi-disciplined groups that are brought together to brainstorm and develop improvement ideas. A prerequisite for *kaizen* is a culture within the organisation that is conducive to change – from top to bottom. Two of the fundamentals of total quality control (TQC), policy deployment and cross-function management, provide an important framework in which *kaizen* may operate. Policy deployment is a process of internalising improvement policies throughout the company from translation of customer requirements, through each process of specification, design, etc. to final manufacturing and delivery. *Kaizen* usually involves first line maintenance becoming the responsibility of operators in what is termed total productive maintenance (TPM).

An organisation that has a cross-functional structure has a horizontal, cross-departmental organisation as opposed to the traditional vertical, functional, chimney organisation of separate departments or functions. This allows for improved communication and team-working, and develops better relationships and quicker decision-making.

It is always beneficial for a business to have at least one continuous improvement team running at any one time to look at:

KAIZEN

customer orientation
total quality control (TQC)
robotics
quality control circles
suggestion system
automation
workplace discipline
total productive
  maintenance (TPM)

kanban
quality improvement
just in time (JIT)
zero defects
small group activities
co-operative operator/
  management relations
productivity improvement
new product development

Figure 9.10 The *kaizen* umbrella

- products
- materials
- processes
- purchasing
- logistics
- any of the support functions.

The make-up of the *kaizen* teams should be changed frequently and the process should ensure that employees are involved in assessing, and auditing, departments and tasks other than their own departments.

> **Progress check 9.15 What does *kaizen* mean in terms of business performance?**

Lean accounting

In 1990 we were introduced for the first time to the terms 'lean production' and 'lean enterprise', which were coined by Dan Jones and Jim Womack in their landmark business book *The Machine That Changed The World* (Macmillan, 1990). Since that time the term 'lean' has become a generally-accepted part of business-speak: lean design; lean organisation; lean management; lean supply; lean customer relations, etc. Lean anything means using less of everything to provide more, and in greater variety. Getting more from less is very much about the control and elimination of waste in all its forms (see more about this in the section about stocks management in Chapter 15); lean accounting provides the relevant information and measurements to support this and to encourage lean thinking throughout the organisation.

Lean accounting includes the use of target costing (as we have seen) to drive the business from a customer value perspective rather than from a cost perspective. It also includes value stream cost analysis, which looks at costs and capacity in every process (from the basic supply of materials and other resources through to final delivery to the customer), in order to provide an understanding of the bottlenecks and constraints to operations, as we saw when we considered throughput accounting. We have already discussed *kaizen*, one of the tools of lean management, which aims to provide the improvements required to create customer value at the lowest cost.

A lean enterprise should be operating at a level at which the need for many of the traditional accounting and control mechanisms, like for example stock records, is unnecessary. Such mechanisms were only really necessary because processes were out of control. Instead, in the lean enterprise, processes may be managed and controlled primarily through lean accounting performance measurement. The strategic emphasis of lean accounting is on performance measurement that focuses on the elimination of waste and creation of capacity, rather than short-term cost-cutting, which results in an improved longer-term financial performance of the business. It should be noted that although many disciples of lean methods claim major savings from its implementation, the use of lean accounting may not be a simple and straightforward task. As with any improvement technique, the costs and benefits of its use should be carefully evaluated.

In the next two sections we will discuss some aspects of lean accounting that deal with the management of quality costs, and the increasingly important area of the non-financial performance measurement.

Cost of quality (COQ)

Quality, once a deviation from the 'normal' product by providing extra 'luxury' and more features, is now a given. Quality means doing what the customer wants every time at the lowest internal cost. It involves:

- getting it right
- getting it right first time
- only doing the right things and doing them right
- doing the right things better.

In many businesses that have no quality systems, or neglected quality systems, the cost of quality is usually in excess of 20% of turnover. Within service industries this cost may be 40% or more! Organisations that have implemented well-developed quality systems may be able to reduce the cost of quality down to below 20% and perhaps as low as 2% of turnover.

Cost of quality (COQ) is a technique that is used to measure the difference between the actual costs incurred within each of the processes of manufacture and/or supply of goods, and services, and the equivalent costs if there were no failures within each of those processes. It may be defined as the additional cost incurred in non-added-value activities and events in a business in fully satisfying customers' agreed requirements for products and services delivered. It is the cost of both not doing the right things and not doing things right first time.

Worked Example 9.19

Amazon.com was set up to be able to take orders in the UK for books and CDs through the Internet. If a customer complained regarding poor delivery, the order would be re-sent by courier, even if Amazon were sure that the original had been despatched, if there was a reasonable excuse for the delay.

A simple internal report could have been used to reveal to the managers of Amazon whether or not they were delivering a quality service.

The managers of Amazon could obtain, at any time, reports in detail or summary of deliveries by courier, because of the availability of their powerful IT resources. The reports should identify causes of delay and identify whether these are within or outside the control of Amazon. The managers may then accept the reasonable excuses for delay to customers (snow or earthquake?), or take the appropriate corrective action regarding their operations.

In the UK, the Department of Trade and Industry (DTI) quality standard BS6143 (1990) defines quality costs using four categories:

- two types of cost of achieving quality
  - prevention costs
  - appraisal costs
- two costs of not achieving quality
  - internal failure costs
  - external failure costs.

In addition, there are two further important categories, which are the costs of exceeding requirements, and the cost of lost opportunities.

These six costs of quality are fertile areas for cost reduction and performance improvement.

Quality costs

- Prevention costs – costs of activities that prevent failure from occurring
  - training employees
  - quality awareness programmes
  - planning and continuous improvement teams
  - costs of supplier assurance
  - costs of calibration, test and control equipment.

- Appraisal costs – costs incurred to determine conformance with quality standards
  - inspection
  - checking
  - auditing or expediting parts or documentation
  - performance testing
  - costs of stock evaluation and storage records (e.g. traceability).

Non-quality costs

- Internal failure costs – costs of correcting products or services which do not meet quality standards prior to delivery to customers
  - scrap
  - rework
  - design changes after process implementation
  - obsolete inventory
  - absenteeism
  - costs of downtime.

- External failure costs – costs incurred to correct products and services after delivery to customers
  - customer credits
  - replaced products
  - customer invoice errors and adjustments
  - unplanned field service costs
  - costs of complaints
  - warranty claims
  - concessions (deviations from specification)
  - product liability.

- Cost of exceeding requirements – costs incurred providing information or services which are unnecessary or unimportant, or for which no known requirement has been established
  - excess stocks
  - redundant copies of documents
  - reports which are not read
  - detailed analytical effort when simple estimates would suffice.

- Cost of lost opportunities – lost revenues resulting from the loss of existing customers, the loss of potential customers and the loss of business growth arising from the failure to deliver products and services at the required quality standards
  - cancellations due to inadequate service response times
  - ordering of competitors' products because the company's products are not available
  - wrong products offered for the specific customer's application.

Worked Example 9.20

We will use Flatco plc as an example and look at its cost of quality for the year 2005. In the year 2005 Flatco plc's sales turnover was £3.5m, and its profit before tax was £590,000. Flatco plc has calculated the following costs of quality for 2005, which have been categorised as:

- PR prevention
- AP appraisal
- ER exceeding requirements
- IF internal failure
- EF external failure.

Flatco plc
Costs of quality

Department	Description	Cost £000	Category
Logistics	Unnecessary storage space	12	IF
Management	Ineffective meetings	10	IF
Production	Scrap	10	IF
Finance	Computer maintenance records	15	PR
Purchasing	Order errors	13	IF
Human resources	Health and Safety and environmental costs	20	PR
Human resources	Unplanned absenteeism	30	IF
Quality	Customer warranty returns	55	EF
Logistics	Excess stocks	14	ER
Quality	Costs of inspection equipment	14	AP
Management	Training in problem solving	7	PR
Production	Unused production floor space	9	ER
Human resources	Training in skill improvement	32	PR
Purchasing	Inefficient scheduling	19	IF
Design and development	Design changes	21	IF
Design and development	Project overruns	31	IF
Total		312	

The costs of quality were first identified in each of the departments in the company and then a cost and a category allocated to them. Excess stocks of £14,000, for example, were calculated from an average of £35,000 surplus stock through the year, which was unusable stocks with no value, multiplied by 40%, its stock carrying costs (space, handling, funding, etc.). The purchasing department employed a person, costing £20,000 per annum, who was employed for two thirds of her time on correction of purchase orders, therefore costing £13,000. The total cost of quality at £312,000 can be seen to be 8.9% of sales of £3.5m. Whilst not perhaps at disastrous levels this is nevertheless a big number at 53% of profit before tax. The analysis of costs of quality shows prevention costs £74,000; appraisal costs £14,000; and analysis of costs of non-quality shows internal failure costs £146,000; external failure £55,000; costs of exceeding requirements £23,000. The total quality costs of £88,000 are incurred to maintain a high level of quality. The balance of £224,000 non-quality costs is incurred as a result of low quality. These costs should be prioritised for inclusion in a cost-reduction plan to minimise or eliminate. This may involve spending on additional quality costs but would result in significant profit improvement.

The traditional view of quality was to consider it as an inevitable cost (see Fig. 9.11). Improvements in quality were considered as expensive and the increased cost was reflected in higher-priced products having greater levels of quality than 'standard' products, for example 'luxury' or 'gold-plated' models. The culture within businesses having a traditional approach to quality was reactive to problems rather than trying to anticipate and prevent them. Quality problems were usually considered as being the fault of operators. 'Acceptable' levels of quality costs were established as the norm. Resources were committed to the checking and detection of faults and defects at 'acceptable' levels of costs of quality.

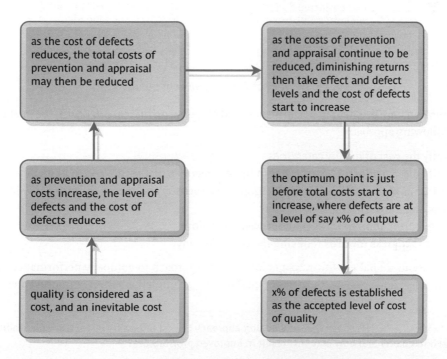

Figure 9.11 The traditional view of quality costs

The total quality approach to quality costs is illustrated in Fig. 9.12. It considers that quality will pay for itself. There are no 'standard' and 'luxury' products. The highest quality at the lowest cost is required for all products and services. The culture of businesses having a total quality approach to quality is pre-emptive, aiming to identify the root causes of problems and eliminating them so that they do not reoccur. It is a culture that requires quality to be the responsibility of everyone in the organisation to ensure that all processes are 'right first time'. The aim of the total quality organisation is to become defect free through the effective implementation of continuous improvement.

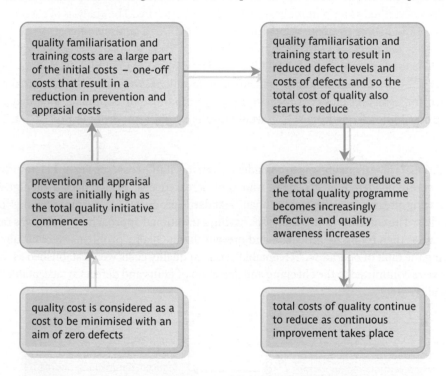

Figure 9.12 The total quality view of quality costs

To achieve an improvement in performance, and therefore an increase in profit, the business must take the following approach:

- identify the cost of quality categories
- identify the activities and events within these categories that result in cost of quality
- prioritise as high, medium, low to categorise each activity and specify the cost of quality category to determine areas of high opportunity
- use the information to focus on improvement actions
- monitor progress towards reducing the cost of quality.

This represents a total quality management (TQM) approach to company performance by raising quality awareness and reducing the costs of quality through implementation of improvement actions.

> Progress check 9.16 **How does the total quality approach to cost of quality differ from the traditional approach to quality and how may this result in improved profitability?**

Non-financial performance indicators

The externally published financial reports and internal financial information do not give a full picture of what is actually happening in an organisation. Such financial information is necessarily historical, and is open to manipulation and interpretation within the scope of the various accounting standards, practices and current legislation. The numbers presented are invariably the numbers the organisation wishes to be seen, and usually to present a favourable impression, while ignoring problems and areas for improvement.

Financial reporting does not tell us, for example, how well the company is meeting its delivery schedules or how satisfied its customers really are with its products and after sales service. Although in themselves these and other such performance indicators are not given a value that is shown on the balance sheet, they certainly have significant value in terms of the underlying strength of the company and its ability to create sustained increases in shareholder wealth in the future.

The use of non-financial performance indicators is assuming increasing importance. These are measures of performance based on non-financial information, which may originate in and be used by operating departments to monitor and control their activities without any accounting input. Non-financial performance measures may give a more timely indication of the levels of performance achieved than do financial ratios, and may be less susceptible to distortion by factors such as uncontrollable variations in the effect of market forces on operations.

Some examples of non-financial performance indicators are:

Customer service quality	■ number of customer complaints ■ % of repeat orders ■ customer waiting time ■ number of on-time deliveries ■ % customer satisfaction index ■ number of cut orders
Manufacturing performance	■ % waste ■ number of rejects ■ set-up times ■ output per employee ■ material yield % ■ adherence to production schedules ■ % of rework ■ manufacturing lead times
Purchasing/logistics	■ number of suppliers ■ number of days stock held ■ purchase price index
Customer development	■ number of new accounts ■ number of new orders ■ % annual sales increase ■ % level of promotional activity ■ % level of product awareness within company
Marketing	■ market share trends ■ growth in sales volume ■ sales volume actual versus forecast

	■ number of customers
	■ customer survey response information
New product development	■ number of new products developed
	■ number of on-time new product launches
	■ % new product order fulfilment
Human resources/ Communications/ Employee involvement	■ staff turnover
	■ absenteeism days and %
	■ accident/sickness days lost
	■ training days per employee
	■ training spend % to sales
	■ % of employees having multi-competence
	■ % of employees attending daily team briefings
Information technology	■ number of PC breakdowns
	■ number of IT training days per employee
	■ % system availability
	■ number of hours lead time for queries/problem solving

> **Progress check 9.17 Explain, giving some examples, what are meant by non-financial performance measures and what they may add to our understanding of business performance.**

The balanced scorecard

In 1990 David Norton and Robert Kaplan were involved in a study of a dozen companies that covered manufacturing and service, heavy industry and high technology to develop a new performance measurement model. The findings of this study were published in the *Harvard Business Review* in January 1992 and gave birth to an improved measurement system, the **balanced scorecard**.

The balanced scorecard concept had evolved by 1996 from a measurement system to a core management system. *The Balanced Scorecard*, published by Kaplan and Norton in 1996, illustrates the importance of both financial and non-financial measures incorporated into performance measurement systems; these are included not on an *ad hoc* basis but are derived from a **top-down process** driven by the company's **mission** and strategy.

An example of a balanced scorecard is shown in Fig. 9.13. It provides a framework for translating a strategy into operational terms.

The balanced scorecard includes headings covering the following four key elements:

■ financial
■ internal business processes
■ learning and growth
■ customer.

From Fig. 9.13 it can be seen that although:

■ objectives
■ measures
■ targets
■ initiatives

to succeed financially, how should we appear to our shareholders?

to achieve our vision, how should we appear to our customers?

to satisfy our shareholders and customers what business processes must we excel at?

to achieve our vision, how will we sustain our ability to change and improve?

Figure 9.13 An example of a balanced scorecard

are implied within each of the elements, the financial element represents only one quarter of the total.

How the company appears to its shareholders is an important underlying factor of the balanced scorecard approach. But it is interesting to see that the measures that are considered by the company in satisfying shareholders go much further than just financial ones:

- to satisfy our shareholders and customers, what business processes must we excel at?
- to achieve our vision, how will we sustain our ability to change and improve?
- to achieve our vision, how should we appear to our customers?

Norton and Kaplan comment on the dissatisfaction of investors who may see only financial reports of past performance. Investors increasingly want information that will help them forecast future performance of companies in which they have invested their capital. In 1994 the American Certified Public Accountants (CPA) Special Committee on Financial Reporting in New York reinforced this concern with reliance on financial reporting for measuring business performance. 'Users focus on the future while today's business reporting focuses on the past. Although information about the past is a useful indicator of future performance, users also need forward-looking information.'

The CPA committee was concerned on how well companies are creating value for the future and how non-financial measurement must play a key role. 'Many users want to see a company through the eyes of management to help them understand management's perspective and predict where management will lead the company. Management should disclose the financial and non-financial measurements it uses in managing the business that quantify the effects of key activities and events.'

The subject of non-financial performance measures and techniques like the balanced scorecard have been introduced in this book as an illustration and to provide some balance against the dominance of financial-based measures that are used to measure and evaluate performance in most businesses. It also serves to highlight the recognition that the accountancy profession itself has given to these wider business issues and the way in which professional accounting bodies in particular have led the thinking away from their narrowly focused beginnings.

> **Progress check 9.18** **Describe the framework of the balanced scorecard approach and explain what you think it tries to achieve.**

Summary of key points

- Cost/volume/profit (CVP) analysis may be used to determine the break-even position of a business and provide sensitivity analyses on the impact on the business of changes to any of the variables used to calculate break-even.

- There are a great many limitations to CVP analysis, whether it is used to consider break-even relationships, decision-making or sales pricing.

- The more recently developed techniques of activity based costing (ABC) and throughput accounting (TA) are approaches that attempt to overcome the problem of allocation and apportionment of overheads.

- Life cycle costing uses maintenance of cost records over entire asset lives so that decisions regarding acquisition or disposal may be made in a way that optimises asset usage at the lowest cost to the business.

- A target cost is a product cost estimate (that may be less than the planned initial product cost but which will be expected to be achieved by the time the product reaches the mature production stage through continuous improvement and replacement of technologies and processes), derived by subtracting a desired profit margin from a competitive market price, determined through customer analysis and market research.

- Benchmarking processes of the best performing organisations within the industry, or within any other industry, can identify best practice, the adoption of which may improve performance.

- *Kaizen*, an 'umbrella' concept covering most of the 'uniquely Japanese' practices, is a technique used for continuous improvement of all aspects of business performance.

- Cost of quality (COQ) is used to identify areas for improvement and cost reduction within each of the processes throughout the business.

- The use of non-financial indicators is important in the evaluation of business performance.

- Both financial and non-financial measures are now incorporated into performance measurement systems such as the balanced scorecard.

Questions

Q9.1   How may cost/volume/profit (CVP) analysis be used to determine the break-even point of a business?

Q9.2   Are the assumptions on which CVP analysis is based so unrealistic that the technique should be abandoned?

Q9.3   (i)   What are the principles on which activity based costing (ABC) is based?

   (ii)   How does ABC differ from traditional costing methods?

Q9.4   (i)   Is throughput accounting (TA) an alternative to traditional costing methods?

   (ii)   What may be some of the real benefits from the use of TA?

Q9.5   Describe the process of life cycle costing, together with some examples that illustrate its aims and benefits.

Q9.6   (i)   Describe the various approaches to target costing.

   (ii)   Critically evaluate the differences between target costing approaches and traditional cost plus pricing.

Q9.7   The *kaizen* philosophy includes a wide range of practices and techniques concerned with achievement of continuous improvement. Describe the role of three of these and how you think they may support the implementation of *kaizen* in a business within a service industry.

Q9.8   How may benchmarking add value to a business?

Q9.9   (i)   Describe what is meant by cost of quality, giving examples within each of the categories of cost of quality you have outlined.

   (ii)   Explain how quality costing may be used to achieve business performance improvement.

Q9.10   (i)   What does financial performance not tell us about the health of a business?

   (ii)   Give examples, from each of the key areas of business activity, of non-financial measures that may fill these gaps.

Q9.11   (i)   Why has the balanced scorecard become such an essential part of so many business management toolkits in recent years?

   (ii)   How can the balanced scorecard be used to achieve improved business performance?

Discussion points

D9.1 Is activity based costing (ABC) a serious contender to replace the traditional costing methods? What are some of the drawbacks in implementing this?

D9.2 'Many companies benchmark every element of every process, at great cost, but seem to lose sight of what they are trying to achieve.' Discuss.

D9.3 '*Kaizen* is probably the Japanese business tool that has had the most significant impact on performance improvement in the West.' Why should that be so?

D9.4 The balanced scorecard is a recently developed technique, but it also appears to be the grouping together of a number of well-established principles and techniques. In what ways does it represent a new technique?

Exercises

Solutions are provided in Appendix 4 to all exercise numbers highlighted in colour.

Level I

E9.1 *Time allowed – 15 minutes*

Break-even sales	£240,000
Marginal cost of sales	£240,000
Sales for January	£320,000

What is the profit?

E9.2 *Time allowed – 15 minutes*

Sales for January	£120,000, on which profit is £10,000
Fixed cost for January	£30,000

What is the break-even point?

E9.3 *Time allowed – 15 minutes*

Selling price	£15
Marginal cost	£9
Fixed cost for January	£30,000
Sales for January	£120,000

What is the break-even point and what is the profit?

E9.4 *Time allowed – 30 minutes*

Seivad Ltd plans to assemble and sell 20,000 novelty phones in 2005 at £30 each.
Seivad's costs are as follows:

Variable:

materials	£10	per phone
labour	£7	per phone
overheads	£8	per phone
Fixed	£70,000 for the year	

You are required to calculate:

(i) **Seivad Ltd's planned contribution for 2005.**

(ii) **Seivad Ltd's planned profit for 2005.**

(iii) **The break-even sales value.**

(iv) **The break-even number of phones sold.**

(v) **The margin of safety for 2005 in sales value.**

(vi) **The margin of safety for 2005 in number of phones sold.**

and

(vii) **If fixed costs were increased by 20% what price should be charged to customers for each phone to enable Seivad Ltd to increase the profit calculated in (ii) above by 10%, assuming no change in the level of demand?**

E9.5 *Time allowed – 60 minutes*

Atlas plc, a large UK manufacturer and supplier of business equipment, had a total turnover for 2005 of £50m. Its profitability has suffered over the past couple of years through competition, lack of innovation, high stock levels, slow introduction of new products, and high levels of rework in production. The managing director has proposed the implementation of a quality costing system to identify the problems in each department and to develop action plans for improvement.

In the sales and marketing department a number of areas have been identified for action. A reduction in the volume of sales orders has revealed that £4m of sales has been lost to competitors' products. The budget had been based on earning a profit before tax of 12% of sales, but the actual profit for the past year was 4% of sales, due to higher costs. The marketing department has discovered that competitors on average have been able to price products at an average premium of 10% over Atlas due to superior quality and the fact that Atlas have been forced to reduce prices to maintain sales levels. 15% of sales orders completed by Atlas salesmen have errors (that does not please the customers at all) resulting in delivery delays, invoicing, pricing and quantity errors. Delays in payments from customers have resulted in debtor levels increasing by £2.5m mainly because of invoicing errors resulting from incorrect sales orders.

We are told that costs of production are 65% of sales, and the number of people in the sales team is 84 and the average annual gross cost per person is £27,000. Rework and error correction costs have been estimated at 25% of original costs, and Atlas's borrowing costs are 9% per annum.

(i)   **Based on the information provided, what is the total cost of quality for the sales and marketing department in value and as a percentage of total sales, and**

(ii) **in which quality cost categories do they fall?**

(iii) **What actions would you recommend to provide a significant reduction to these costs?**

Level II

E9.6 *Time allowed – 45 minutes*

It is a morning in February and Marsha Ighodaro picks up the keys of her brand new Mini from the Rover dealer in a town situated some 29 miles from the village in which she lives. She drives away in the car she has dreamt about since finally choosing and ordering it five weeks earlier (she has very quickly rationalised her acceptance of the red model instead of the British racing green she originally wanted). It's a cold morning and so she moves the heater control lever to the left and switches on the fan. Alas, nothing happens! The heater doesn't work.

Fortunately, these days, such failures rarely occur. But how may a manufacturing company ensure that the complete product offering, such as a Mini, provides the required level of quality and delivery on each of the assemblies making up the product to meet the expectations of the customer, at a cost he/she is willing to pay?

E9.7 *Time allowed – 45 minutes*

The managing director of Flatco plc has agreed with his budget committee that a 20% profit before tax to sales should be achievable for 2006. The sales and marketing department have already agreed to a target of 10% increase in sales for 2006 over 2005. The managing director has suggested that a percentage improvement should be targeted for costs in all areas of the company that will provide a 20% profit before tax. (The Flatco plc profit and loss account for the year 2005 is shown in Fig. 5.4 in Chapter 5, p. 156.)

(i)   Calculate the required percentage cost reduction on the assumption that the same percentage is applied throughout the company.

(ii)   How fair do you think this is as a method of target setting?

(iii) How may each department assess whether such targets are achievable or not?

(iv)   What impacts may such targets have on the effectiveness of each of the departments within Flatco?

E9.8 *Time allowed – 60 minutes*

Abem Ltd produces three products, using the same production methods and equipment for each. The company currently uses a traditional product costing system. Direct labour costs £8 per hour. Production overheads are absorbed on a machine hour basis and the rate for the period is £25 per machine hour. Estimated cost details for the next month for the three products are:

	Hours per unit		Materials per unit	Volumes (units)
	Labour hours	Machine hours	£	
Product A	$\frac{1}{2}$	$1\frac{1}{2}$	20	750
Product B	$1\frac{1}{2}$	1	10	1,975
Product C	1	3	25	7,900

An ABC system is being considered by Abem Ltd, and it has been established that the total production overhead costs may be divided as follows:

	%
Costs relating to set-ups	35
Costs relating to machinery	20
Costs relating to materials handling	15
Costs relating to inspection	30
	100

The following activity volumes are associated with the production for the period:

	Number of set-ups	Number of movements of materials	Number of inspections
Product A	70	10	150
Product B	120	20	180
Product C	480	90	670
	670	120	1,000

Required:

(i)   Calculate the cost per unit for each product using the traditional method of absorption costing.

(ii)   Calculate the cost per unit for each product using ABC principles.

(iii) Comment on any differences in the costs in your answers to (i) and (ii).

10

Decision-making

Contents

Learning objectives

Completion of this chapter will enable you to:

- explain the scope and importance of decision-making to an organisation
- outline the decision-making process
- explain the significance of the concept of relevant costs
- apply marginal costing techniques to decision-making
- evaluate shut-down or continuation decisions
- critically compare make or buy alternatives
- consider the problem of product mix, scarce resources and limiting factors
- consider the wide range of sales pricing options
- use a decision tree to determine expected values of alternative outcomes.

Introduction

In Chapter 9 we looked at the relationship between costs, activity levels, contribution and profit. This chapter will further develop these ideas and introduce some additional ways of looking at costs. One of the most important uses of accounting and financial information is as an aid to decision-making. There are many categories of business decisions. The costs and benefits that result from each type of decision may be very different and so it is useful to identify the different categories of decisions. Broadly, decisions are to do with:

- problem solving
- planning
- control
- investment.

This chapter begins by outlining what decision-making means and considers the different types of decision that may be assisted by various accounting techniques. A later chapter has been devoted to the whole area of capital investment decision-making.

We will outline the various types and levels of decision and the process of decision-making. The concept of relevant costs is explored in some detail and we will consider its significance in assessing the information that should be used in calculations to support decision-making.

This chapter will look at the following specific types of decision:

- whether or not to shut down a factory or a department, in a manufacturing or service environment
- whether to buy a component or part used in manufacturing from an outside supplier or to make it internally
- decisions on product or service mix and the constraints of limiting factors
- pricing policy and the alternative sales pricing options available to an entity
- decisions in which risk is a key factor, and the use of decision trees.

The scope of decision-making

The management accountant is involved with providing financial and non-financial information and analysis to enable managers to evaluate alternative proposals and to determine which courses of action they should take. However, decisions are made by managers, not by the management accountant, and the levels of authority within the management hierarchy are determined by company policy. Companies normally establish limits at each management level for each type of decision, and the level of expenditure allowed. The approval of one or more directors is normally required for all capital expenditure. Strategic decision-making is carried out at board level. Operational decisions are normally made at the middle manager level, and tactical decisions made at the junior manager level.

There are obviously different levels of decision-making and different levels and types of decisions. The decision by the chairman of Corus (formerly British Steel) about whether he should wear a blue tie or a red tie is of less significance (although perhaps not to tie-makers) than his decision on whether or not to shut down a steel-producing plant. Indeed, decisions on factory closures by Corus and many other companies have unfortunately been all too common in the UK over the past 20 or 30 years (see the Royal Doulton press extract below) as the manufacturing sector of the economy has shrunk to a fraction of its former size.

Royal Doulton has followed the closures of many other potteries in the areas around Stoke-on-Trent over the past few years. The impact of these factory closures is wider than on just the companies themselves, having much wider economic and social consequences for both the immediate areas in which the potteries are located and for UK manufacturing in general.

The scope of decision-making includes the areas of problem solving, planning, control, and investment (see Fig. 10.1).

Problem solving decisions

Decision-making relating to problem solving considers relevant costs (and revenues) which are the costs (and revenues) appropriate to a specific management decision. These include incremental or

Closing down a factory

Royal Doulton is to close its last remaining major UK factory with the loss of 525 jobs – 17pc of the group's workforce.

The loss-making fine china group will transfer work from its Nile Street factory in Stoke-on-Trent to a site in Indonesia as part of a restructuring programme.

However, production of Royal Doulton's high-value items, such as the collectable figurines, will continue at a new smaller factory and visitor centre in Festival Park, Stoke-on-Trent.

About 50 staff will transfer to the new facility, with the remaining 525 facing redundancy 'in stages' before June 2005.

The cost of the closure, redundancies and new site is expected to be reflected in an £8.5m exceptional charge in the group's 2004 accounts. Royal Doulton made a £5m pre-tax loss last year.

Geoff Bagnall, general secretary of The Ceramic and Allied Trades Union, claimed the management had broken every assurance made to the union and called for them to resign.

End of an era for Royal Doulton, by Tessa Thorniley

© *Daily Telegraph*, 27 March 2004

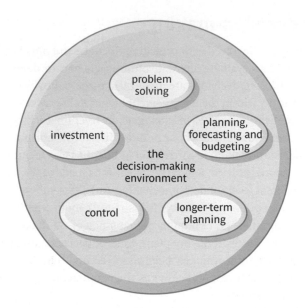

Figure 10.1 The scope of decision-making

➡ **differential costs** and benefits, and opportunity costs. They are represented by future cash flows whose magnitude will vary depending upon the outcome of the management decision made. If stock is sold to a retailer, the relevant costs used in the determination of the profitability of the transaction would be the cost of replacing the stock, not its original purchase price, which is a sunk cost. Sunk costs, or irrecoverable costs, are costs that have been irreversibly incurred or committed to prior to a decision point and which cannot therefore be considered relevant to subsequent decisions.

An opportunity cost is the value of the benefit sacrificed when one course of action is chosen in preference to an alternative. The opportunity cost is represented by the forgone potential benefit from the best of the alternative courses of action that have been rejected.

Planning, forecasting and budgeting decisions

Planning, forecasting and budgeting decisions require best estimates of costs and the use of cost/volume/profit (CVP) analysis.

Long-term planning decisions

Longer-term planning decisions assume that in the long run all costs are variable and that scarce resources, and over- or under-capacity, are problems that can be overcome.

Control decisions

Control decisions use historical information and comparisons such as variance analysis and actual/budget comparisons.

Investment decisions

Investment decisions tend to be longer term, and cash flow and the time value of money are important appraisal factors.

Decision-making is a crucially important process within any organisation. It is used to select, hopefully, the correct future course of action in, for example:

- whether to make or buy equipment
- levels of order quantities and stock holding
- whether or not to replace an asset
- determination of selling prices
- contract negotiation.

Decisions also have to be made as to whether or not to invest in capital projects and on choices between investments in alternative projects, which are competing for resources. Such decisions will be examined in Chapter 12 which deals with capital investment decisions.

Routine planning decisions, including budgeting, commonly analyse fixed and variable costs, together with revenues, over one year. These costs are often estimated and may support the use of cost/volume/profit (CVP) analysis. The usefulness of the analysis will almost certainly be enhanced by the speed and sophistication of IT spreadsheets. An example may be seen from special offers and weekend breaks seen within the UK hotel sector. Spreadsheet 'what-ifs' linked to current bookings suggest the capacity available to be offered at a special rate for specific periods (note the Travelodge 'book by 23 January 2001 – stay by 15 February 2001' offer).

Decisions on short-run problems are of a non-recurring nature, where costs are incurred and benefits are obtained all within a relatively short period. An example is whether or not a contract should be accepted or rejected. These types of decision need identification of incremental or differential costs and revenues and a distinction between sunk costs and opportunity costs.

Investment and disinvestment decisions, such as whether to buy a new machine, or shut down a department, often have long-term consequences, and so ideally the time value of money should be allowed for, using **discounted cash flow (DCF)** techniques. The long-term consequences may span several accounting periods and the economies of more than just one country may be involved, for example international motor manufacturers with plants established throughout the world.

Longer-range decisions are made once and reviewed infrequently. They are intended to provide a continuous solution to a continuing or recurring problem. They include decisions about selling and distribution policies, for example whether to sell direct to customers or through an agent. In the long run all costs are variable. In the short-term, fixed costs, or resource and capacity problems that may be encountered, can be changed or overcome over time.

Such changes may be determined by the board of directors at the strategic level, where the priorities of the business may be changed, or at the operational and tactical levels where change may be achieved through, for example, bottom-up continuous improvement initiatives. The process may therefore take several months or even years (especially, for example, when trying to sell a site or a building). The timespan may however be shorter; for example, UK retailers are able to announce the impact of their Christmas trading results very early in January, which suggests that analyses of variances are undertaken on a daily, or even perhaps an hourly, basis.

Control decisions involve deciding whether or not to investigate disappointing performance, and expected benefits should exceed the costs of investigation and control. Historical information such as comparison of costs, revenues or profits to budget, is used to carry out variance analysis to indicate what control decisions need to be taken. Variance analysis can be used to look at just one factory, or several factories. Manufacturers will often locate new plant and equipment in subsidiaries where there are few 'disappointing performances'.

Worked Example 10.1

The UK motor manufacturer Vauxhall began producing police cars and rally cars based on its 'family saloons'.

Let's consider the short-term problems that may have been encountered by Vauxhall during the decision-making process relating to these products.

The specification of the police car was customer driven and the changes to the standard saloons could be costed in order that a price could be proposed to the customer. The operatives on the production line could easily modify the existing model to the new specification.

The rally car was almost certainly going to create problems because the specification may need to change throughout the season. Production-line disruptions would inevitably ensue. The rally car would probably require specialists amongst the work force to design and produce it.

Progress check 10.1 **Why is decision-making so important to any organisation and what types of decision do they face?**

The decision-making process

We have seen that it is possible to analyse decisions into five main categories:

- short-term problem decisions
- routine planning decisions
- long-range decisions
- control decisions
- investment and disinvestment decisions.

This is useful because the relevant costs and benefits are likely to differ between each type of decision. The decision-making process comprises the seven steps outlined in Fig. 10.2.

First, the objectives, either long-term or short-term, need to be identified. Short-term objectives may be financial, such as:

- profit maximisation
- loss avoidance
- profit growth
- sales growth

or non-financial, such as:

- improved product quality
- customer service
- employee welfare
- environmental friendliness.

Figure 10.2 The seven steps of the decision-making process

Long-term objectives may be more to do with:

- the financial risk of the company
- long-term growth
- debt/equity financing
- dividend growth
- the relationships between these factors.

Second, alternative opportunities must be identified which might contribute to achieving the company's objectives. The ability to identify opportunities, or things to do which might help the company reach its objectives, is a major test of how good management is. Failure to recognise opportunities that exist may result in decisions not taken and/or opportunities missed.

Third, the relevant data about each of the alternatives must be collected and analysed. For example, this may relate to decisions on whether to manufacture or buy from an external supplier, or to use an existing site or establish a new site.

Fourth, the decision must then be made and the expected outcome stated. If a board of directors, for example, makes a decision, then the minute of that decision should formally refer back to the various documentation, forecasts, etc. that are an integral part of that decision.

company may have to be weeded out. Therefore, the company will have to forgo current benefits as a result of culling a profitable product.

The UK motor industry has several examples of product options that were dropped in favour of others. The German motor industry has seen two products dropped, only for them to reappear: the Beetle (VW) car and Boxer (BMW) motor cycle. In these cases, management decided to forgo the benefit of producing the products in favour of new models. Eventually they had to change their minds as the benefits forgone needed to be reassessed and updated versions were eventually brought back.

Sunk costs, committed costs and notional costs

None of these costs are relevant. They include, for example, costs of dedicated fixed assets and development costs already incurred.

Worked Example 10.6

A company bought a computer system two years ago for £57,000. After allowing for depreciation its book value is now £19,000. Because computer technology moves so quickly, resulting in obsolescence and price reductions, this equipment has no resale value. Although the company may continue to use the computer system for another year, with the limited facilities it provides, it would prefer to scrap it now and replace it with a much enhanced system providing many more functions.

Let us consider the implications of the company's decision to replace its computer system.

The original computer system initial cost of £57,000, which now has a net book value of £19,000, is a sunk cost, and therefore ignored in terms of decisions made to replace the computer system. The money has been spent and the asset has no alternative use.

Fixed costs

Fixed costs are not relevant costs, unless they are a direct consequence of the decision. For example, the cost of employing an extra salesman would normally be categorised as a fixed cost. Conceptually, fixed costs stay at the same level irrespective of the changes in level of activity. In practice, management needs to make decisions regarding future fixed costs. Longer-term forecasts and budgets may indicate that changes in activity levels require changes to levels of fixed costs. For example, if higher education in the UK saw the falling-off of student numbers in certain courses then that might result in the universities cutting back on their fixed overheads, such as premises and staff numbers.

Worked Example 10.7

The UK saw two attractions open in London in 2000: the Millennium Dome and the London Eye. What should we consider to be the fixed costs of the two attractions?

One basic difference between the two attractions is that the Dome was to remain open for one year and the London Eye would remain open for a number of years. Obviously the majority of the Dome's fixed costs would cease with its closure, but charges like insurance would need to continue to be paid. The London Eye became popular and fully booked very quickly. Unlike the

Dome, its capacity is limited to the number of passengers each gondola can hold. In the Eye's case an analysis of the fixed costs should reveal that the costs are indeed genuinely fixed and there will be little 'movement' from year to year, whereas the headlines during 2000 would suggest that most of the Dome's expenses were varying throughout the year!

Variable costs

Variable costs are generally relevant costs but care must be taken with regard to the provisos outlined above. Variable costs may be non-relevant costs in some circumstances, for example where a variable cost is also a committed cost.

Worked Example 10.8

A company is planning a small new project that requires 1,000 hours of direct labour, costing £9 per hour. However, the company pays its direct labour workforce a fixed wage of £342 per person for a 38-hour week.

The company has a 'no redundancy' agreement, and has enough spare capacity to meet the additional hours required for the project.

What should we consider are the relevant costs relating to the new project?

The direct labour cost for accounting purposes is regarded as a variable cost of £9 per hour. But it is really a committed cost, and therefore a fixed cost of £342 per week. The relevant cost of the new project for direct labour is therefore zero.

It should be noted that the company may similarly treat depreciation of say £2.40 per hour as an accounting variable cost. However, for decision-making, depreciation is never considered as a relevant cost. It is a past cost, and therefore not a cash flow to be incurred in the future.

Attributable costs

We may consider fixed costs as comprising divisible fixed costs, and indivisible fixed costs. A fixed cost is divisible if significant changes in activity volumes require increases or decreases in that cost.

An **attributable cost** is the cost per unit that could be avoided, on average, if a product or function were discontinued entirely without changing the supporting organisational structure. An attributable cost consists of:

- short-run variable costs
- divisible fixed costs
- only those indivisible fixed costs that are traceable.

Worked Example 10.9

A company employs 55 people, who are paid fixed monthly wages, within four departments in its factory. Each department is headed by a departmental manager who is paid a salary.

How should each of the staff costs be regarded in a decision relating to the possible shutdown of one of the departments?

The direct labour costs of the 55 operators are divisible fixed costs (if there were only one operator, then the direct labour cost would be an indivisible fixed cost).

Each departmental manager's salary is an indivisible fixed cost that is traceable to their department. This is because if a department were to be shut down, the manager would no longer be required and therefore no cost would be incurred.

Scarce resources

The relevant cost of a scarce resource to be included in a decision-making calculation is the benefit forgone (the opportunity cost) in using the resource in another way, in addition to the direct cost of purchasing the resource. Let us look at an example.

Worked Example 10.10

Mr and Mrs Green are willing to pay £22,000 to Steamy Windows Ltd to build a conservatory. The general manager of Steamy Windows estimates that the job requires the following materials:

Material	Total units required	Units in stock	Book value of units in stock £/unit	Realisable value £/unit	Replacement cost £/unit
A	1,000	0	0.0	0.0	6.0
B	1,000	600	2.0	2.5	5.0
C	1,000	700	3.0	2.5	4.0
D	200	200	4.0	6.0	9.0

B is regularly used by Steamy Windows Ltd and if it is required for this job it needs to be replaced to meet other production demands.

C and D are in stock because of previous overbuying, and have restricted use. No other use can be found for C, but D could be used as a substitute for 300 units of E, which currently costs £5/unit and Steamy Windows Ltd currently has none in stock.

Steamy Windows Ltd needs to determine the relevant costs of the project to assist the company in its decision on whether or not it should take the job.

Relevant costs:

		£	
A	1,000 × £6/unit	6,000	replacement cost because these materials have not yet been purchased
B	1,000 × £5/unit	5,000	replacement cost because these materials are used regularly and so the stock items would have to be replaced

C	(300 × £4/unit) + (700 × £2.50/unit)	2,950	300 must be bought at the replacement cost of £4/unit 700 will not be replaced but could have been sold for £2.50 per unit
D	(300 E × £5/unit)	1,500	200 could be sold for £6/unit, but this is less than the opportunity cost of substitution of E
		15,450	

The relevant costs of the job are £15,450. If the difference of £6,550 is an acceptable level of profit to Steamy Windows Ltd, before allowing for labour and overhead costs, then the job should be accepted.

> **Progress check 10.3** **Outline three examples of costs that are usually relevant, and three costs that are not usually relevant in decision-making.**

Figure 10.3 Practical areas of decision-making

We will now look at examples of four specific areas of decision-making, outlined in Fig. 10.3.

Marginal costing and shut-down or continuation decisions

We have already discussed the importance of the marginal costing technique as an aid to costing and break-even decision-making. In the UK, during December 2000 a major car manufacturer decided that production of cars would cease at its Luton (Bedfordshire) plant. The company explained that over-capacity forced it to cut back on production. The employees on the second shift were sent home on full pay in February 2001 since there was no point in producing cars that would not sell. It was quite obvious from the public announcements that the company had carried out many 'what-ifs' on the corporate spreadsheets. However, it was apparently unable to justify continuation of production at the Luton site, despite its presence in the town for the past 90 years or so. The following example looks at the use of marginal costing in a decision regarding the possible closure of an apparent loss-making activity.

Worked Example 10.11

Ron G Choice Ltd has three departments: C chairs; D desks; T tables, manufacturing three separate ranges of office furniture. Choice Ltd's sales manager, Jim Brown, has just started a course on cost accounting and has reviewed the company's accounts for last year with renewed interest.

	C	D	T
	£	£	£
Sales	60,000	80,000	40,000
Variable costs	40,000	60,000	34,000
Fixed costs allocated	6,000	10,000	8,000

It appeared to Jim that all was not well with the table department T. He was about to recommend to the managing director that department T should be closed down because it appeared to be making a loss. However, Jim felt he should first run his ideas past the company's accountant, Tony White, to check his figures and gain some support.

Jim provided the following analysis, using an absorption costing basis:

	C	D	T	Total
	£	£	£	£
Sales	60,000	80,000	40,000	180,000
Total costs	46,000	70,000	42,000	158,000
Profit/(loss)	14,000	10,000	(2,000)	22,000

On this basis, Jim said, department T was making a loss and should be closed.

Tony asked Jim if he had considered the position using a marginal costing basis. Jim said he had not and so Tony provided the following analysis:

	C	D	T	Total
	£	£	£	£
Sales	60,000	80,000	40,000	180,000
Variable costs	40,000	60,000	34,000	134,000
Contribution	20,000	20,000	6,000	46,000
less: Fixed costs				24,000
Profit				22,000

Tony explained to Jim that the profit for the company was the same using both techniques because there is no closing-stock adjustment involved.

However, Tony said that the way in which the fixed costs had been allocated to each department was fairly arbitrary and so perhaps they could consider the position of Choice Ltd following the closure of department T on a marginal costing basis.

The result was as follows:

	C	D	T	Total
	£	£	£	£
Sales	60,000	80,000	–	140,000
Variable costs	40,000	60,000	–	100,000
Contribution	20,000	20,000	–	40,000
less: Fixed costs				24,000
Profit				16,000

Jim could see that closure of the tables department T would result in a reduction in total company profit by £6,000 to £16,000, compared with the original £22,000. Tony explained that this was caused by the loss of contribution of department T.

Jim thanked Tony for helping him avoid an embarrassing visit to the managing director's office. He would now also be better prepared for the next part of his costing course – on marginal costing!

This simple example shows that despite what the absorption costing approach indicated, department T should be kept open because it yields a contribution towards covering the fixed costs.

The marginal costing approach, as we have seen previously, focuses on the variable costs which are affected by the decision and separates them from the fixed costs which are unaffected by the decision and are therefore irrelevant to it. In Worked Example 10.11, the closure of department T would not save any of the allocated fixed costs – they would then have to be shared amongst departments C and D. If the fixed costs had been directly attributable to each department rather than allocated then there would have been an £8,000 saving by closing department T. Since that is higher than the department's contribution of £6,000, then Jim's advice would have been correct to close department T.

Progress check 10.4 **In what way is marginal costing useful in shut-down decisions?**

Make versus buy

Make versus buy decisions are made when a component used in one of the manufacturing processes to produce a product may either be bought in from outside suppliers or manufactured within the factory. It would seem that the choice is simply a straightforward comparison between the extra cost to make the component, the marginal cost, and the price charged by suppliers. In fact, the decision involves consideration of a number of other factors, for example:

- cost price sensitivity to changes in volumes
- accuracy of data

- reliability of bought-in and/or self-manufactured components
- supplier switching costs
- reliability of suppliers in terms of delivery and financial stability
- length of time the cost price will be held
- opportunity cost.

If the component were not made in-house what activities would be carried out using the relevant facilities? If other manufacturing activities have to be forgone so as to make the component in-house then there is a loss of the contribution that this work would otherwise have earned. The contribution sacrificed is the opportunity cost of not carrying out the alternative activities. The opportunity cost must be added to the marginal cost of making the component to compare with suppliers' prices in making a make versus buy decision. The technique usually used to determine loss of contribution is contribution per unit of a key factor (limiting factor) of production.

Worked Example 10.12

Procrastinate Ltd makes a product A, which takes 30 hours using the Dragon machine. Its marginal cost and selling price are £1,400 and £2,000 respectively. Component X, which is used in the manufacture of product A, could be made on the Dragon machine in five hours with a marginal cost of £400. The best outside supplier price for one component X is £450.

Procrastinate have to decide whether to make or buy component X.

Contribution of product A	= £2,000 − £1,400 = £600
Contribution per hour of use of the Dragon machine	= £600/30 = £20

If component X is made in five hours then 5 × £20, or £100 contribution would be lost. Opportunity cost plus marginal cost = £100 + £400 = £500, which is greater than the best outside supplier price of £450 so component X should be bought rather than made in-house.

In this example, we have assumed that the Dragon machine is working at full capacity in order to calculate the opportunity cost of lost production. If this were not so and the Dragon machine were idle for a significant amount of time then there would be no loss of contribution. The only cost of making component X would then be its marginal cost of £400 which, being less than the best supplier price of £450, would indicate a decision to make in-house rather than buy.

Progress check 10.5 **Illustrate the process used to make a make/buy decision.**

Product mix decisions and limiting factors

An organisation may not have access to an unlimited supply of resources to allow it to exploit every opportunity to continue indefinitely to increase contribution. Such scarce resources, for example may be:

- labour hours
- levels of labour skills

- machine capacity
- time
- market demand
- components
- raw materials
- cash
- credit facilities.

A limiting factor, or key factor, is anything that limits the activity of the organisation. The organisation has to decide what mix of products or services to provide, given the restricted resources available to it, with its volume of output constrained by the limited resources rather than by sales demand. It can do this by seeking to maximise profit by optimising the benefit it obtains from the limiting factor. Machine time would be an example of a limiting factor for a company if all the machines in the company were operating at full capacity without being able to provide the output required to meet all the sales demand available to the company.

The technique used for decisions involving just one scarce resource assumes that the organisation is aiming to maximise profit. This further assumes that fixed costs are unchanged by the decision to produce more or less of each product. The technique therefore is to rank the products in order of their contribution-maximising ability per unit of the scarce resource. The following two examples illustrate this technique. The first example assumes that product demand is unlimited, whilst the second example assumes given levels of product demand.

Worked Example 10.13

Need The Dough, a small village bakery, makes only two types of loaf, small and large. There is unlimited demand for this bread and both products use the same skilled labour of bakers, which is in short supply. The product data are as follows:

	Small	Large
Sales price per loaf	£0.71	£0.85
Variable cost per loaf	£0.51	£0.61
Contribution per loaf	£0.20	£0.24
Minutes of skilled labour per loaf	20	30

We can determine the contribution-maximising strategy for Need The Dough.

If we consider the contribution per unit of scarce resource, one hour of skilled labour, we can see that the contribution for each loaf per hour is:

| Small loaves earn | £0.60 per labour hour | [60/20 × 20p] |
| Large loaves earn | £0.48 per labour hour | [60/30 × 24p] |

So even though large loaves generate a larger unit contribution of 24p compared to 20p earned by small loaves, the contribution-maximising strategy for Need The Dough is to bake and sell as many small loaves as possible which generate a contribution of 60p, compared with 48p for large loaves, per each hour of scarce labour.

Worked Example 10.14

Felinpot Ltd are potters who make only two products, two ornamental pots called the Bill and the Ben. The product data are as follows:

	Bill	Ben
Contribution per pot	£5	£7.20
Volume of special blue clay per pot	1 kg	2 kg
Monthly demand	470	625

In one month the maximum amount of specialist blue clay available is 1,450 kg.

We can determine the contribution-maximising strategy for Felinpot Ltd.

For each pot the contribution per unit of blue clay is:

Bill   £5/1 kg   =   £5   per kg
Ben   £7.20/2 kg =   £3.60   per kg

The contribution-maximising strategy for Felinpot Ltd should therefore be to make Bill pots in preference to Ben pots, even though the unit contribution of a Ben is greater than a Bill.

   Output of Bill pots should be maximised to meet the monthly demand of:

470 pots, using 1 kg × 470 = 470 kg   contribution = 470 × £5   = £2,350

The balance of 980 kg of clay (1,450 kg less 470 kg) should be used to make Ben pots

980 kg/2 kg = 490 pots   contribution = 490 × £7.20   = £3,528
                            total contribution   = £5,878

Worked Example 10.14 showed that because special blue clay was in short supply, every endeavour should be made to maximise the contribution to Felinpot Ltd for every kilogram of clay used. Regardless of the high level of demand for the other product, the product with the highest contribution per kilogram of special clay used is the one which should be produced to its maximum demand level. All the clay left over from that should then be used to produce the 'less profitable' product in terms of its return per kilogram of special clay.

   More complex actual scenarios may be encountered. For example, there may be limited product demand with one scarce resource. The same technique applies whereby the factors are ranked in order of their contribution per unit of scarce resource. Optimum profit is earned from the decision to produce the top-ranked products up to the limit of demand.

   Many situations occur where there are two or more scarce resources. The technique of ranking items in order of contribution per unit of limiting factor cannot be used in these situations. In these cases linear programming techniques need to be used – the graphical method or the simplex (algebraic) method – which are beyond the scope of this book.

Progress check 10.6   What are limiting factors and how do they impact on decisions related to product mix?

Sales pricing

Pricing policy is just one of the four categories of decision-making included in the 'marketing mix'. The others are the product, place (where sold and how distributed), and promotion (selling, advertising and promotion). Pricing decisions must have some regard for cost, in order to ensure that the selling price exceeds the average unit cost in order to make a profit. Pricing decisions must also recognise the importance of the range of factors that comprise the general heading of 'demand'.

Worked Examples 10.15 to 10.19 look at various sales pricing methods that are concerned solely with cost, and assuming unlimited demand, that may be used to achieve a break-even position or a targeted profit. These methods illustrate both the marginal and full absorption costing approach.

Worked Example 10.15

Chip Pendale's company Pendale Ltd has a maximum production output of 500 chairs. It has been asked to tender for a contract to supply 300 chairs.

The costing information for Pendale Ltd for 300 chairs (or units) is as follows:

	£
Assembly cost centre costs:	
Wages for 300 units	1,500
Materials – timber and glue	300
Direct costs	1,800
Production overheads absorbed:	
Machine maintenance	150
Machine depreciation	250
Supervision	100
	2,300
General overheads absorbed:	
Factory rent, rates	100
Administrative expenses	100
Heating and lighting	130
Total costs	2,630

Initially, we may assume a selling price of £11 per chair.

We will calculate the unit cost of a chair at output levels of 300 and 500 chairs, using:

(i)   absorption costing
(ii)   marginal costing

and

(iii)   compare the profits of both methods at output levels of 200, 300 and 500 chairs.

Calculation of the unit cost of a chair at output levels of 300 and 500 chairs:

		Output			
		300 chairs unit costs		**500 chairs** unit costs	
		£		£	
Wages	(£1,500/300 units)	5.00	(£1,500/300 units)	5.00	
Materials	(£300/300 units)	1.00	(£300/300 units)	1.00	
Variable cost per chair,		6.00		6.00	
unchanged on changes in output					
Production overhead	(£500/300 units)	1.67	(£500/500 units)	1.00	
General overhead	(£330/300 units)	1.10	(£330/500 units)	0.66	
Full cost per chair		8.77		7.66	

Although total fixed costs remain unchanged, the unit costs of £8.77 and £7.66 are different due to costs being based on output of either 300 or 500 units.

On an absorption costing basis:
Assuming a full cost of £8.77 per chair on output of 300 units, we can consider sales volumes for 200, 300, and 500 chairs:

Chairs	**200**	**300**	**500**
	£	£	£
Sales revenue at £11 per unit	2,200	3,300	5,500
Total costs at £8.77 per unit	1,754	2,630	4,385
(volume × full cost per unit)			
Net profit	446	670	1,115

On a marginal costing basis:

Chairs	**200**	**300**	**500**
	£	£	£
Sales revenue at £11 per unit	2,200	3,300	5,500
Variable costs at £6.00 per unit	1,200	1,800	3,000
Contribution	1,000	1,500	2,500
Fixed costs (the same regardless of output):			
Production overheads	500	500	500
General overheads	330	330	330
Profit	170	670	1,670

The differences in profit between the
two approaches   (276)   –   555

are due to the under- or over-charge of the fixed cost element being £8.77 – £6.00 =
£2.77 × (−100 or +200), the volume difference against 300 chairs.
   It should be noted that there may be small rounding differences in the above calculations.

Worked Example 10.16

Using the data from Worked Example 10.15 Pendale Ltd may consider the pricing approach of
minimum pricing at specified volumes of 300 and 500 chairs.

Minimum pricing at specified volumes:
If we assume 300 units
Total revenue   = total costs which   = £2,630 [(300 × £6.00) + £500 + £330]
The break-even price   = £2,630/300 units = £8.77 per unit
At 500 units the break-even price = [(500 × £6.00) + £500 + £330]/500 units
                                 = £3,830/500 units = £7.66 per unit

Worked Example 10.17

Using the data from Worked Example 10.15 Pendale Ltd may consider the pricing approach of
break-even volume at specified prices of £11 and £13 per chair.

Break-even volume at specified prices:
If we assume that the selling price is £11 per unit:
Contribution   = revenue − direct costs = £11 − £6 = £5 per unit
The break-even volume $= \dfrac{\text{total fixed costs}}{\text{contribution per unit}} = \dfrac{£830}{£5} = 166$ units

If we assume that the selling price is £13 per unit
Contribution   = revenue − direct costs = £13 − £6 = £7 per unit
The break-even volume $= \dfrac{\text{total fixed costs}}{\text{contribution per unit}} = \dfrac{£830}{£7} = 119$ units

Cost plus pricing

The technique of full cost plus pricing requires the assessment of the total cost of a product or
service, which is then marked up with a percentage, or an absolute sum, to achieve the required level
of profit.
   Price-taking companies have little control over the prices of their services or products, for example
commodities. They may also be small companies, of which there are many in their market sector, and

where there may be little to tell the difference between one product and another. Cost information is therefore very important for price takers in deciding on levels of output and product mix because they cannot do anything to influence price and so their profits are totally dependent on costs.

Price-setting companies are companies that are able to influence selling prices and may exercise discretion over the setting of prices for their products or services. These are companies that may have highly differentiated or customised products, and are market leaders. Cost information is also very important for price setters in making their pricing decisions. This is because the prices they set will be influenced by their costs, together with the actions of their competitors and their customers' perceived value of their products.

Companies may sometimes be price setters and sometimes be price takers, or they may be price setters for some products or services and price takers for others. Regardless of which they are, we can see that cost is of paramount importance.

Inaccurate cost information can result in over- or under-costing and therefore impact directly on profit, selling prices, and demand. Under-costing may result in the acceptance of unprofitable business, and over-costing may result in the loss of profitable business. As we have seen in Chapter 9, inaccurate costing of products and services is most likely to result from the way in which overheads are allocated to products and services.

For stock valuation purposes (SSAP 9), products are required to be valued on an absorption costing basis. However, cost assignment for pricing should be based on direct cost tracing or cause-and-effect cost assignment, that is to say activity based costing (ABC). Some arbitrary cost allocations based on direct labour or machine hours are inevitable, for items such as general administrative costs and property costs, but an ABC approach will provide more accurate product costs. ABC also provides a better understanding of cost behaviour, which provides a sounder basis for negotiation with customers around selling price and order size.

Cost plus pricing is widely used by companies for a number of reasons:

- it is simple to use and on the face of it looks factual and precise
- it may encourage price stability if all companies in the industry use it
- the impact on demand can be taken into account to some extent by adjusting mark-ups
- if a company manufactures and/or markets hundreds of products or services there may be difficulties in adopting more sophisticated pricing approaches that use expensive market research and complicated pricing calculations
- cost plus pricing may be applied only to selected and relatively minor revenue items, for example on a **Pareto analysis** 80/20 basis
- cost plus pricing may be used for guidance in price setting whilst also taking other factors into account such as levels of demand and competition.

But why use cost-plus pricing if it is likely to be changed? Well, cost-plus pricing does provide an initial approximation although it should be by no means the only information that is used for the final pricing decision. However, there are also many criticisms of cost plus pricing because:

- it is not demand-based, ignoring competition and the relationships between demand and price; cost and demand are not related
- it does not necessarily ensure that total sales will be greater than total costs
- it does not necessarily maximise profit
- it can lead to wrong decisions if for example costs are based on budgeted levels of activity
- selecting a suitable basis for overhead absorption, and the apportionment of shared costs where a business produces more than one product, can be difficult

- it may ignore the distinction between variable, fixed and opportunity costs
- some estimate of demand is needed to estimate the fixed costs per unit of a product or service. But how can the price be set until the volume of demand is known so as to calculate the fixed cost absorption rates? This is a vicious circle: a full cost plus price cannot be calculated without a knowledge of demand and demand cannot be estimated without a knowledge of price

and perhaps most importantly:

- it encourages waste and a failure to control costs, because it assumes that any cost increases or overspends will be paid for by the customer – the higher the cost, the higher the selling price (but not necessarily higher profits).

The following two worked examples illustrate the use of cost-plus pricing. You should also take a look at Case Study VI that follows Chapter 16, which considers an approach to cost-plus pricing that is based on achievement of a required ROI.

Worked Example 10.18

Using the data from Worked Example 10.15 Pendale Ltd may consider the pricing approach of cost plus pricing at outputs of 300 and 500 chairs.

Cost plus pricing:

This method uses the full cost per unit plus a mark up:

If we assume 300 units
Full cost per unit   = £8.77
plus 25% mark-up
New selling price   = £11.00 (rounded up)

If we assume 500 units
Full cost per unit   = £7.66
plus 25% mark-up
New selling price   = £9.60 (rounded up)

Worked Example 10.19

Using the data from Worked Example 10.15 Pendale Ltd may consider the pricing approach of volume required to achieve a target profit of £1,000 at a selling price of £11 per chair, and of £1,200 at a selling price of £13 per chair.

Volume required to achieve a target profit:

If we assume that the target profit is £1,000
And assume that the selling price is £11 per unit
Contribution = £11 − £6 = £5 per unit

$$\text{Therefore required volume} = \frac{\text{total fixed costs} + \text{required profit}}{\text{contribution per unit}} = \frac{(£830 + £1,000)}{£5}$$
$$= 366 \text{ units}$$

If we assume that the target profit is £1,200
And assume that the selling price is £13 per unit
Contribution = £13 − £6 = £7 per unit

$$\text{Therefore required volume} = \frac{\text{total fixed costs} + \text{required profit}}{\text{contribution per unit}} = \frac{(£830 + £1,200)}{£7}$$
$$= 290 \text{ units}$$

In considering each of the pricing methods we have considered so far we need to ask ourselves:

- which selling price is most appropriate, and
- which cost base is most appropriate?

The prices we have calculated in the worked examples have had no relationship with market demand. Neither has there been an identification of profit potential at different output or market demand levels, and there has been no attempt to maximise profit. The cost-based approach is not market based.

> **Progress check 10.7** Outline four methods of sales pricing that do not make use of market data.

Maximum contribution using market data

The final sales pricing option we shall consider looks at a range of selling prices per unit and uses a graphical representation of profits and losses at various volume levels to determine the maximum contribution, and therefore maximum profit level (see Worked Example 10.20).

There is difficulty in estimating a demand curve but certain practical steps can be taken to reach a pricing decision based on demand analysis as follows:

- establish the variable cost per unit and the fixed costs for the period, and using a number of different prices construct a profit line for each price on a profit/volume (PV) chart
- make a rough estimate of demand at each price and calculate the profit at this level of demand, and plot this profit on the profit lines on the PV chart, a different profit value for each selling price
- join up the profit values for each selling price and so construct a contribution curve to determine the highest point on the contribution curve which is the highest contribution and highest profit and so the approximate price that the company should consider.

> **Progress check 10.8** How may a business use market data to price its product in order to maximise contribution?

Worked Example 10.20

Turning again to Pendale Ltd, let us assume the following price and market information for its one product – its chair:

	p1 £11	p2 £12	p3 £13	p4 £14
Selling price per unit	p1 £11	p2 £12	p3 £13	p4 £14
Sales volume units demand	500	420	300	250
Variable cost per unit	£6	£6	£6	£6
Contribution per unit	£5	£6	£7	£8
Total contribution	£2,500	£2,520	£2,100	£2,000

Directly attributable fixed costs are assumed to be £1,830

We will use a profit/volume (PV) chart contribution curve to determine a selling price at which profit may be maximised.

The PV chart shown in Fig. 10.4 shows profit lines for each selling price plotted as p1, p2, p3, p4.

The expected profit at each price is plotted at points A, B, C and D.

Selling price per unit			Profit	(contribution – fixed costs)
p1	£11	A	£670	£2,500 – £1,830
p2	£12	B	£690	£2,520 – £1,830
p3	£13	C	£270	£2,100 – £1,830
p4	£14	D	£170	£2,000 – £1,830

The line drawn through A, B, C and D is the contribution curve which shows how contribution is maximised at or around point B and at a price of £12.

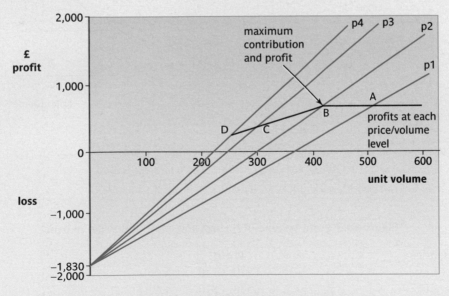

Figure 10.4 Profit volume (PV) chart and contribution curve

Since demand estimates at any price are likely to be approximate it may be useful to show bands of profit rather than single numbers, illustrated in Worked Example 10.21.

Worked Example 10.21

We may take the concept introduced in Worked Example 10.20 a step further. Assume a band of demands around each of the estimated demands, for example:

a range of 480 to 520 around the estimate of 500 units
a range of 400 to 440 around the estimate of 420 units, and so on.

Selling price per unit		Contribution per unit	Demand units	Contribution £	Profit £
p1	£11	£5	480–520	2,400–2,600	570–770
p2	£12	£6	400–440	2,400–2,640	570–810
p3	£13	£7	280–320	1,960–2,240	130–410
p4	£14	£8	230–270	1,840–2,160	10–330

We will draw the contribution curve as a band to illustrate the selling price at which profit may be maximised.

The PV chart will then show the contribution curve as a band, as shown in Fig. 10.5.

Figure 10.5 Profit volume (PV) chart and contribution curve band

Selling price			Profit
p1	£11	A	£570–£770
p2	£12	B	£570–£810
p3	£13	C	£130–£410
p4	£14	D	£10–£330

This indicates an optimal price of around £12.

We have assumed a strong relationship in the above examples between demand and price. However, it should also be remembered that demand is influenced by other factors besides price.

Risk analysis and sales pricing

The model we have used to consider market data may be further refined by providing a simple **risk analysis** by looking at the likely probabilities of demand at each selling price level. The end result of risk analysis in practice can be seen in the pricing of various computer peripherals, for example scanners and printers, where the prices are continually changing. In the PC software market during 2000/2001 major supermarkets and other retailers were stocking formerly 'sold out' software at much reduced prices.

   Probabilities of occurrences may be used to weight the various estimated levels of demand at each price (and hence contribution) level to calculate **expected values**. The total expected values at each price level may then be compared. The optimum selling price is the one having the highest total expected value. This technique is demonstrated in Worked Example 10.22.

Worked Example 10.22

We will consider the sensitivity over the selling price range £11 to £12 per unit in Worked Example 10.21. The probability of actual demand volumes for chairs may in practice be determined from market research. For this example, we may assume the following probability distribution to provide an illustration of the principle. Note that the total of each of the probabilities of volumes of demand at each price totals one. This means that demand is assumed to be certainly at one of the volume levels, but we do not know with certainty which one.

Price £11		Price £11.50		Price £12	
Demand estimate Units	Probability	Demand estimate Units	Probability	Demand estimate Units	Probability
480	0.1	410	0.3	400	0.4
490	0.2	420	0.5	420	0.4
500	0.3	430	0.2	440	0.2
510	0.3				
520	0.1				
	1.0		1.0		1.0

The profit maximising price may then be estimated on the basis of this risk analysis, the optimum price being the price that gives the highest total expected value.

Price £11 Cont./unit £5				Price £11.50 Cont./unit £5.50				Price £12 Cont./unit £6			
Est. demand	Cont.	Prob.	Exp. value	Est. demand	Cont.	Prob.	Exp. value	Est. demand	Cont.	Prob.	Exp. value
Units	£		£	Units	£		£	Units	£		£
480	2,400	0.1	240	410	2,255	0.3	677	400	2,400	0.4	960
490	2,450	0.2	490	420	2,310	0.5	1,155	420	2,520	0.4	1,008
500	2,500	0.3	750	430	2,365	0.2	473	440	2,640	0.2	528
510	2,550	0.3	765								
520	2,600	0.1	260								
		1.0	2,505			1.0	2,305			1.0	2,496

This risk analysis would point to an optimum selling price of around £11 per unit, having the highest total expected value at £2,505.

Pricing policy

We have seen that the traditional approach to sales pricing policy is full cost plus pricing. There are some compelling reasons for its use but it also has many disadvantages. We have looked at other cost-based models like minimum pricing and we have seen that the company will maximise profits where marginal cost equals marginal revenue. We have further considered sales pricing using market data and taking account of risk and uncertainty. To complete our discussion of pricing policy three other important factors should also be considered:

■ **price elasticity**: the percentage change in the quantity demanded arising from a percentage change in price
  – elastic demand is where a fall or rise in price will increase or reduce demand such that total revenue will be higher or lower than at the current price
  – inelastic demand (for example cigarettes) is the converse
■ price discrimination occurs when an organisation sells the same products at different prices in two or more different markets (note the extensive use of this practice by the oil companies which sell petrol at a range of prices throughout their garages' distribution outlets in different locations)
■ pricing decisions should always take account of **competitive pricing**.

In real-life business situations many further factors may impact on the company's pricing policy, for example scarcity of production resources and limiting factors of production. Profit-maximising budgets may be established through the ranking of products in order of contribution earned per unit of the scarce resource or limiting factor. However, as we have previously discussed, very often there are two or more limiting factors, in which case a linear programming model would need to be used to determine optimum solutions. Such approaches are beyond the scope of this book.

> **Progress check 10.9** Describe how sensitivity analysis may be used to evaluate alternative sales pricing policies.

Decision trees

A decision tree is a pictorial method of showing a sequence of interrelated decisions and their expected outcomes. Decision trees can incorporate both the probabilities of, and values of, expected outcomes.

Worked Example 10.23

The sales department of Billy Ardtable Ltd has the opportunity to promote a new children's toy, which will provide a unit contribution of £20. Market research has indicated that if the promotion is undertaken at a cost of £50,000, there is a 60% chance of selling 50,000 units, and a 40% likelihood of selling 30,000 units. Market research has also shown that if the product is not promoted then there is a 50/50 chance of selling either quantity.

The sales manager is unsure about what he should do and has asked for advice about whether it is worthwhile promoting the product.

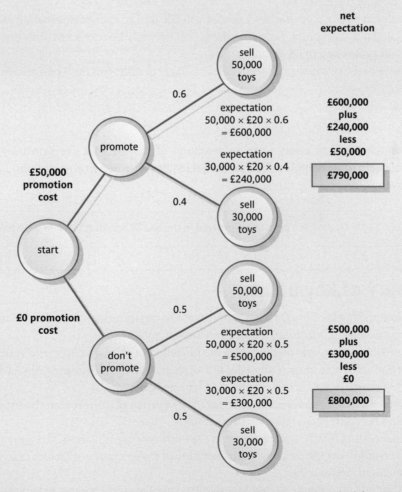

Figure 10.6 Billy Ardtable Ltd sales department's promotion decision tree

We first need to draw a decision tree, which shows the start point and the two alternatives of promoting or not promoting the product (see the decision tree diagram in Fig. 10.6).

The branch of the tree indicating that Ardtable should promote is labelled with the cost of that activity, £50,000.

The branch of the tree indicating that Ardtable should not promote is labelled with the cost of that activity, £0.

The next step is to label the probabilities of occurrences (sales volumes in this example) on the branches following the decision to promote, being 0.6 (60%) for sales of 50,000 toys and 0.4 (40%) for sales of 30,000 toys.

The same thing is done on the branches following the decision not to promote, being 0.5 (50%) for sales of 50,000 toys and 0.5 (50%) for sales of 30,000 toys. The expectations of contributions are then calculated by multiplying sales volumes by unit contribution and probability.

The contribution expectation following no promotion is
£500,000 + £300,000 = £800,000

The contribution expectation following the promotion is
£600,000 + £240,000 = £840,000

but the promotion option also involves a cost of £50,000 and so the net expectation is £790,000.

The £790,000 net expectation following the promotion may be compared with the net expectation from not promoting of £800,000.

On the above basis we should advise the sales manager of Billy Ardtable Ltd not to promote the sales of toys.

Worked Example 10.23 is a very simple illustration of the use of a decision tree in decision-making. In practice, a more complex situation would require trees bearing many alternative branches and probability branches to solve the problem.

> **Progress check 10.10** Outline the principles involved in the use of decision trees in decision-making.

Summary of key points

- Decision-making is of fundamental importance to organisations, for example in the areas of problem solving, planning, control and investment.
- The decision-making process includes identification of relevant costs, and starts with the identification of objectives. Following the implementation of decisions, the process ends with the comparison of actual results with expected outcomes.
- Relevant costs, or incremental or differential costs, arise as a direct consequence of a decision, and may differ between alternative options.
- Marginal costing may be used to assist in shut-down or continuation decisions.
- Make versus buy decisions involve consideration of a wider range of factors than simply the differences in the basic cost.
- Organisations do not have access to unlimited supplies of resources, for example, labour

hours, levels of labour skills, machine capacity, time, market demand, components and raw materials, cash – a limiting factor is the lack of any resource which limits the activity of the organisation.

■ Product mix decisions are influenced by the scarcity of resources and the availability of limiting factors.

■ There are a number of reasons why cost plus sales pricing is one of the most widely used methods to determine selling price, but there are also many disadvantages in its use and it does encourage waste and may result in a failure to control costs.

■ Sales pricing policy is just one of the four categories of decision included in the marketing mix of price, product, place, and promotion, and is based on cost and market factors that influence demand for the product.

■ Decision trees enable a sequence of interrelated decisions, and their expected outcomes, to be reported pictorially.

Questions

Q10.1   Why is decision-making so important to organisations?

Q10.2   What are short- and long-range decisions, and control decisions?

Q10.3   What are the seven steps used in the decision-making process?

Q10.4   Use some examples to illustrate, and explain what are meant by relevant costs, sunk costs, and opportunity costs.

Q10.5   In what ways may marginal costing provide a better approach to decision-making than absorption costing?

Q10.6   What are the key factors that should be considered in make versus buy decisions?

Q10.7   How should limiting factors be considered if a business is seeking to maximise its profits?

Q10.8   (i)   What are scarce resources?

        (ii)   What factors does an entity need to consider to make optimising decisions related to product mix?

Q10.9   Outline the five main approaches to sales pricing decisions.

Q10.10 How may risk analysis be applied to sales pricing decisions?

Q10.11 What is a decision tree and what is its relevance as an aid to decision-making?

Discussion points

D10.1 'What is all the fuss about decision-making? Surely it's simply a question of adding up a few numbers and the decision makes itself.' Discuss.

D10.2 The selling price of a product is the amount that the average customer will pay. Discuss.

E10.5 *Time allowed – 60 minutes*

Ceiling Zero plc has manufactured six CZ311 aircraft for a customer who has now cancelled the order. An alternative buyer, Coconut Airways, would be prepared to accept the aircraft if certain agreed modifications were completed within one month. The CZ contracts manager has prepared a costs schedule as a basis for establishing the minimum price that should be charged to Coconut Airways:

	£000	£000
Original cost of manufacture of 6 CZ311 aircraft		
Based on direct costs + 100% overheads charge		6,400
less: Deposit retained when order cancelled		1,000
		5,400
Costs of modification		
Direct materials	520	
Direct labour	200	
		720
Fixed overheads at 75% of direct costs of modification [0.75 × 720]		540
Administration costs at 25% of direct costs [0.25 × 720]		180
Total costs		6,840
The contracts manager has suggested an additional mark up of 25%		1,710
Suggested minimum price to Coconut airways		8,550

Two types of material were used in the original aircraft manufacture:

Melunium could be sold as scrap for reuse for £400,000, but it would take 60 hours of labour at £100 per hour to prepare the melunium for sale. The department required to carry out this work is particularly slack at the moment.

Polylindeme could be sold for £300,000 and would also require 60 hours' preparation by the same department at the same rate per hour. Alternatively, polylindeme could be kept for a year and used on another contract instead of metalindeme which would cost £400,000. To do this, a further 120 hours of labour at £150 per hour would be required in addition to the 60 hours above.

The materials used in the modifications for Coconut Airways were ordered last year at a cost of £840,000. The delivery was late and the realisable value fell to £200,000. Because of this the suppliers of the materials have given CZ a discount of £320,000. CZ cannot use this material on any other contracts.

The direct labour for the modifications is a temporary transfer from another department for four weeks. That department usually contributes £1,000,000 per week to overhead and profits. 75% of that level could be maintained if a special piece of equipment were hired at a one-off cost of £300,000 to compensate for the reduction in labour force.

If the aircraft were not sold, the specifications, plans and patents could be sold for £350,000.

Additional interim managers would need to be hired at £180,000 for the modifications, included in overhead costs. The fixed overhead rate included straight line depreciation (included in overheads at £140,000), staff expenses and lighting. Hand tools will be used for the modifications. No other overheads are affected by the modifications.

CZ's normal profit mark-up is 50%. The contracts manager has reduced this to 25% because it is felt that this is probably what Coconut Airways would be willing to pay.

You are required to redraft the contract manager's schedule to give a more meaningful price and to explain all assumptions and alterations.

E10.6 *Time allowed – 60 minutes*

Use the data for Muckraker Ltd from Exercise E10.4 to calculate the most profitable combination of output of peats A, B, C and D from subcontracting 2,000 kg of one of the products at a price of 80% of its selling price and producing extra quantities of another product up to Muckraker's total capacity.

You should assume that demand for Muckraker's products will be sufficient to meet the extra output, and that Muckraker's levels of quality and delivery performance will be maintained.

E10.7 *Time allowed – 90 minutes*

Mr Threefingers Ltd manufactures three DIY tools, the Rimbo, the Cutzer, and the Brazer. The numbers for the financial year just ended are as follows:

	Rimbo £	Cutzer £	Brazer £	Total £
Sales	100,000	80,000	120,000	300,000
(units)	(10,000)	(4,000)	(10,000)	
Variable costs	60,000	50,000	70,000	180,000
Contribution	40,000	30,000	50,000	120,000
Fixed costs	34,000	36,000	40,000	110,000
Profit/(loss)	6,000	(6,000)	10,000	10,000

£10,000 of the fixed costs of producing Cutzers are costs which would be saved if their production ceased.

Mr Threefingers Ltd is considering a number of options:

(a) Cease production of Cutzers.
(b) Increase the selling price of Cutzers by 15%.
(c) Reduce the selling price of Cutzers by 10%.
(d) Resurrect a tool which was popular 10 years ago, the Thrad, on the following basis:
   – use the resources released by ceasing production of Cutzers
   – incur variable costs of £48,000 and extra fixed costs of £12,000, for sales of 20,000 units
   – sales of 20,000 Thrads, according to market research, could be made at a price of £5 each.

(i) Evaluate the options (a) to (d), stating any assumptions that are made to support your calculations.
(ii) What other factors should be considered by Mr Threefingers Ltd in its decision on which option(s) to adopt?
(iii) Which option(s) would you recommend and why?

Case Study III

MOULDAL LTD

Mouldal Ltd is a fourth tier automotive components supplier. All of its aluminium casting output is supplied, via third and second tier suppliers, to be used ultimately on the bodies of cars produced by one major automotive manufacturer, Resmedec plc. Mouldal's annual turnover is a little over £7m, and it currently employs 60 direct operators and 10 staff.

The directors of Mouldal Ltd are concerned that in their existing traditional costing system there may under- or over-costing of their products, and are considering refinements to the system through the implementation of activity based costing (ABC).

Mouldal Ltd's current costing system

Mouldal Ltd produces castings for the exterior bodywork of cars. The castings are made using aluminium casting in the company's foundry. The casting operation consists of first melting aluminium ingots, and the molten aluminium is then injected into pre-heated dies that provide moulds of the required shapes. Each separate die contains moulds for each part design. The dies are cooled to allow the molten aluminium to solidify. The parts, when cooled, are removed from the moulds and checked. Any excess bits of aluminium are snipped off by hand, and these together with any rejects are re-used by melting with new ingots. The moulded aluminium parts are then processed through sandblasting machines to give them a very high gloss finish, as required. After a final inspection, the castings are then carefully wrapped and packed into batches by hand for despatch to the customer. Any rejects are re-used and melted down with new ingots.

Under its supply contract, Mouldal makes two types of casting: a large complex casting, the LMB2; and a smaller simple casting, the SMB10. The complex casting is larger and has a more detailed shape (squiggles, curves and fins). Manufacturing the larger casting is more complex because of the more detailed features. The simple casting is smaller and has few special features.

The design, production and distribution processes at Mouldal Ltd

The following processes are used to design, produce and distribute castings, whether they are complex or simple:

1. *Design of products and processes.* Each year Resmedec plc specifies some modifications to both the complex and simple castings. Mouldal's design department specifies the design of the tools and dies, from which initial prototypes and then the final castings will be made. It also defines the required manufacturing operations.

2. *Tools and dies manufacture.* The tools and dies used in the casting process are manufactured by a number of small local toolmakers. The cost of tools and dies, and sales of product protoypes are recovered from Resmedec plc on the basis of cost plus 15%, which includes internal costs of sampling and approval and tooling design costs. This is usually recovered as a single invoiced sum (or may sometimes be amortised as an element of the piece part

selling price). Prototype samples are charged to Resmedec plc plus handling charges plus a 15% uplift.

3. *Manufacturing operations.* The parts are cast in moulds, as described earlier, finished, cleaned and inspected.

4. *Shipping and distribution.* Finished castings are packed, batched and despatched to the customer.

Mouldal is operating at capacity and incurs very low marketing costs. Because of its high-quality products, Mouldal has minimal customer service costs. But Mouldal's business environment is very competitive with respect to the simple castings. At a recent meeting, Resmedec's purchasing director indicated that a new competitor, who makes only simple castings, was offering to supply the SMB10 casting at a price of around £215, which was below Mouldal's price of £235. Unless Mouldal lowers its selling price, it will be in jeopardy of losing the Resmedec business for the simple casting, similar to SMB10, for the next model year. Mouldal's directors are very concerned about this development. The same competitive pressures do not exist for the complex casting, the LMB2, which Mouldal currently sells at a price of £420 per casting.

Mouldal has years of experience in manufacturing and distributing simple castings, and the directors have investigated and found that their technology and processes are very efficient in manufacturing and distributing the simple SMB10 casting. Because Mouldal often makes process improvements, the directors are confident that their technology and processes for making simple castings are similar to or better than their competitors'.

However, the directors were less certain about Mouldal's capabilities in manufacturing and distributing complex castings like the LMB2. Mouldal had only recently started making this particular casting. Although the directors were pleasantly surprised to learn that Resmedec plc considered the price of the LMB2 casting to be very competitive, they were puzzled that, even at that price, it earned such large margins. Mouldal's directors were surprised that the margins were so high on this newer, less-established product, and yet low on the SMB10 product where the company had strong capabilities. Since Mouldals were not deliberately charging a low price for the SMB10, the directors wondered whether the costing system overcosts the simple SMB10 casting (assigning excessive costs to it) and undercosts the complex LMB2 casting (assigning too little costs to it).

Mouldal's directors have various options that they may consider:

- give up the Resmedec business in simple castings if it really is unprofitable
- reduce the price on the simple casting and accept a lower margin
- reduce the price on the simple casting and drastically cut costs.

First, the directors needed to understand what it actually costs to make and sell the SMB10 and LMB2 castings. For sales pricing decisions, Mouldal assigns all costs, both manufacturing and non-manufacturing, to the SMB10 and LMB2 castings. (Had the focus been on costing for stock valuation, they would only assign manufacturing costs to the castings.)

In a year, Mouldal plc works to full capacity and makes 20,000 simple SMB10 castings, and 6,000 complex LMB2 castings. The costs of direct materials and direct manufacturing labour are as follows:

	SMB10	LMB2
Direct materials	£1,270,000	£750,000
Direct production labour	£880,000	£300,000

Most of the indirect costs of £2,915,000 consist of salaries paid to supervisors, engineers, manufacturing support and maintenance staff that support direct manufacturing labour. Mouldal currently uses direct manufacturing labour-hours as the only allocation base to allocate all indirect costs to the SMB10 and LMB2. In a year, Mouldal uses 87,800 total direct manufacturing labour-hours to make the small simple SMB10 castings and 28,800 direct manufacturing labour-hours to make the larger complex LMB2 castings.

Mouldal's directors were quite confident about the accuracy of the direct materials and direct manufacturing labour costs of the castings. This was because those costs could be traced directly to each of the castings. They were less certain about the accuracy of the costing system in measuring the overhead resources used by each type of casting. The directors considered that a refined costing system would provide a better measurement of the non-uniformity in the use of the overhead resources of the business.

Second, therefore, the directors decided to investigate the refining of its costing system and consider the implementation of an ABC system at Mouldal, and to identify the activities that may help explain why Mouldal incurs the costs that it currently classifies as indirect. To investigate these activities, Mouldal organised a cross-functional ABC team from design, manufacturing, distribution, and accounting and administration.

Refinement of the costing system by the Mouldal Ltd ABC team

The ABC team used the following three guidelines to refine its costing system:

1. *Use of direct cost tracing*, to classify as many of the total costs as possible as direct costs, and reduce the amount of costs classified as indirect.
2. *Identification of indirect cost pools*, to expand the indirect cost pool into a number of homogeneous pools. In an homogeneous cost pool all the costs would have the same or a similar cause-and-effect relationship with the cost-allocation base.
3. *Determination of cost allocation bases*, to identify an appropriate cost-allocation base for each indirect cost pool.

The ABC team looked at the key activities by mapping all the processes needed to design, manufacture and distribute castings, and identified seven major activities:

(i)   *design products and processes*
(ii) *set up the machinery to melt the aluminium ingots, align the dies and cast the moulds, and sandblast the parts*
(iii) *operate the machines to manufacture castings*
(iv) *clean and maintain the moulds after the parts have been cast*
(v)   *prepare batches of finished castings for shipment*
(vi) *despatch the castings to Resmedec plc*
(vii) *administer and manage all the processes at Mouldal.*

[It should be noted that for the sake of simplicity the processes relating to the melting of aluminium ingots, casting of the moulds, and sandblasting, have been combined into one activity. In practice, of course, these are three distinctly separate processes, which would have individual cost attributes and cost-allocation bases.]

The ABC team then separated its original single overhead cost pool into seven activity-related cost pools. For each activity-cost pool, a measure of the activity performed was used as the cost-allocation base. The costs in each cost pool have a cause-and-effect relationship with the cost-allocation base. For example, Mouldal defined set-up hours as a measure of machine set-up activity and cubic metres of packages moved as a measure of distribution activity. Because each activity-cost pool related to a narrow and focused set of costs (e.g. set-up or distribution), the cost pools are homogeneous. At Mouldal, over the long run, set-up hours is a cost driver of machine set-up costs, and cubic metres of packages moved is a cost driver of distribution costs.

The Mouldal plc ABC team used a four-part cost hierarchy (defined by Cooper, who, together with Kaplan developed ABC in the 1980s). This is commonly used in ABC systems to facilitate the allocating of costs to products. It categorises costs into different cost pools on the basis of the different types of cost driver (or cost-allocation base) or different degrees of difficulty in determining cause-and-effect (or benefits-received) relationships:

(a) *Unit-level activity costs*, which are resources sacrificed on activities performed on each individual unit of a product. Manufacturing operations costs (such as electricity, depreciation of machinery and equipment, and repairs) that are related to the activity of running the machines are unit-level costs, because the cost of this activity increases with each additional unit of output produced (or machine-hour).

(b) *Batch-level activity costs*, which are resources sacrificed on activities that are related to a group of units of product rather than to each individual unit of product. Purchasing costs, which include the costs of placing purchase orders, receiving materials, and paying suppliers, are batch-level costs because they are related to the number of purchase orders placed rather than to the quantity or value of materials purchased.

(c) *Product-sustaining activity costs*, which are resources sacrificed on activities undertaken to support individual products. Examples may be design costs for each type of product, which depend largely on the time spent by designers on designing and modifying the particular product, and processes, and engineering costs incurred to change product designs.

(d) *Facility-sustaining activity costs*, which are resources sacrificed on activities that cannot be traced to individual products but which support the organisation as a whole. General administration costs (for example, rent and security costs) are facility-sustaining costs, where it is usually difficult to find cause-and-effect relationships between the costs and a cost-allocation base. Because of the lack of a cause-and-effect relationship, these costs may be deducted from operating profit rather than allocated to products. Alternatively, if the business believes that all costs should be allocated to products, facility-sustaining costs may be allocated to products on a basis of, for example, direct manufacturing labour-hours. Allocating all costs to products becomes particularly important when the business wants to set selling prices on a cost basis that embraces all costs.

The ABC team then set out to explain the cause-and-effect relationships and decide on the different types of cost driver relationships for each activity, and their cost allocation base. In some cases, costs in an indirect cost pool may be traced directly to products, rather than being considered as indirect costs and dealt with on an allocation basis.

In its current system, Mouldal classifies mould-cleaning and maintenance costs as indirect costs and allocates them to products using direct manufacturing labour-hours. However, the ABC team found that these costs could be traced directly to a casting because each type of casting can only be produced from a specific mould. Because mould-cleaning and maintenance costs consist of operators' wages for cleaning moulds after each batch of castings is produced, these costs are direct batch-level costs. Complex castings incur more cleaning and maintenance costs than simple castings because the moulds of complex castings are more difficult to clean, and because Mouldal produces more batches of complex castings than simple castings (see Table 1 below).

Table 1

	LMB2	SMB10	Total
Number of castings	6,000	20,000	
Castings per production batch	10	40	
Number of production batches	600	500	
Set-up time per production batch	2.3 hours	0.9 hours	
Total set-up hours	1,375 hours	450 hours	1,825 hours

Therefore, the £330,000 of the total indirect costs that were for mould-cleaning and maintenance were identified as relating directly to products. £147,000 related to the production of 20,000 SMB10 castings, and £183,000 relating to production of 6,000 LMB2 castings. For each of the remaining six activities the ABC team identified the indirect costs associated with each activity for the balance of the total indirect costs (£2,915,000 less £330,000 now treated as direct costs). The cost identified for each activity, together with the cost allocation base and overhead allocation rate, is shown in Table 2 below. The table also includes an explanation of cause-and-effect relationships that supported the decisions on the choice of allocation base.

The ABC team carried out extensive observation and measurement of each process and identified the amount of each activity required by each of the products LMB2 and SMB10, which is shown in Table 3 below.

Table 2

Activity	Cost category	Total costs	Cost allocation base	Overhead allocation rate	Cause-and-effect basis of allocation base
Design	Product-sustaining	£550,000	110 parts-square metres	£5,000 per parts-square metres	Complex moulds require more design resources
Machine set-up	Batch level	£365,000	1,825 set-up hours	£200 per set-up hour	Set-up overheads increase as set-up hours increase
Manufacturing operations	Unit level	£780,000	7,800 machine hours	£100 per machine hour	Production overhead to support the machines increases with machine usage
Shipments	Batch level	£99,000	200 shipments	£495 per shipment	Costs of preparing shipment batches increase
Distribution	Unit level	£478,500	30,000 cubic metres	£15.95 per cubic metre	Distribution overheads increase with the cubic metres of packages shipped
Administration	Product-sustaining	£312,500	116,600 direct labour hours	£2.68 per direct labour hour	Administrative resources support direct labour hours because they increase with direct labour hours

Table 3

Activity	LMB2	SMB10	Total
Design	77 parts-square metres	33 parts-square metres	110 parts-square metres
Machine set-up	1,375 set-up hours	450 set-up hours	1,825 set-ups
Manufacturing operations	2,300 machine hours	5,500 machine hours	7,800 machine hours
Shipments	100 shipments	100 shipments	200 shipments
Distribution	10,000 cubic metres	20,000 cubic metres	30,000 cubic metres
Administration	28,800 direct labour hours	87,800 direct labour hours	116,600 direct labour hours

Required

(i)   Use Mouldal Ltd's current traditional costing system to calculate the costs and profit margins in total for the company and each of its products, the SMB10 and the LMB2.

(ii) Use the data provided from the study by the Mouldal plc ABC team to calculate the costs and profit margins in total for the company and each of its products, the SMB10 and the LMB2, using activity based costing (ABC).

(iii) Compare the detailed total and unit cost information from (i) and (ii) above to identify the differences, if any, and discuss what action Mouldal plc may consider with regard to its pricing of the SMB10 and the LMB2.

11

Planning and budgeting

Contents

Learning objectives

Completion of this chapter will enable you to:

- identify budgeting as one part of the strategic management process
- define a budget, its purpose and uses
- recognise the importance of forecasting within the budget process
- outline how a business may apply the budgeting process in practice
- explain the preparation of budgets for planning purposes
- prepare the elements of an operating budget and a financial budget to derive the master budget
- describe the system of responsibility accounting and identify the four different types of responsibility centre
- outline the advantages and disadvantages of ways in which divisional performance may be measured
- appreciate the motivational and behavioural aspects of budgeting
- explain the preparation of budgets for control purposes and how performance against budget may be evaluated
- identify the potential problems that may be encountered during budget preparation.

Introduction

Chapter 10 looked at decision-making as one application of the management accounting roles of problem solving and attention directing. This chapter looks at a further application of those roles and is concerned with how businesses attempt to plan their activities for the year ahead, or for a shorter period, to enable them to plan and maintain control of the business. Budgeting is the part of the strategic management of the business to do with planning and control. In this chapter we will consider the budget for planning and control purposes.

This chapter considers the role of forecasting in the budget process, and looks at the budget-setting process in detail. The budgeting process will be used to construct a simple budget for a company based on its organisational objectives, and its best estimates of future activities.

We return to the use of budgets for control purposes in discussing the motivational aspects of budgeting and how performance against budget may be evaluated, and consider the use of return on investment (ROI) and residual income (RI) in the measurement of divisional performance. The chapter closes by identifying some of the important conflicts and problems encountered in the budgeting process.

Budgeting, planning and control

Many companies believe that the traditional annual budgeting system is unsuitable and irrelevant in rapidly changing markets. Further, they believe that budgets fail to deal with the most important drivers of shareholder value such as intangible assets like brands and knowledge. Some of these companies, like Volvo, Ikea, and Ericsson, have already revised their need for annual budgets as being an inefficient tool in an increasingly changing business environment. Volvo abandoned the annual budget 10 years ago. Instead, they provide three-month forecasts and monthly board reports, which include financial and non-financial indicators. These forecasts and reports are supplemented with a 2-year rolling forecast, updated quarterly, and four- and ten-year strategic plans updated yearly. It should also be noted that many of the dot.com companies that failed during the 1990s and early 2000s also felt that traditional budget methods were a little old-fashioned and irrelevant.

The budgeting process is questioned in the following article reproduced from *Accountancy Age*, with particular emphasis on the time spans over which budgets may be realistic and therefore useful. This article, based on a survey of 258 finance directors, considers whether budgets for large projects like the Olympics can be realistic when they are prepared so many years ahead of the events.

There are clearly different views as to whether or not the budget is an effective and essential business tool. However, the majority of the world's most successful companies have attributed a large part of their success to their reliance on traditional formal budgeting systems. The long-term (strategic) and short-term (budget) planning processes are core management tasks that are critically important to the future survival and success of the business. The budget prepared for planning purposes, as part of the strategic planning process, is the quantitative plan of management's belief of what the business's costs and revenues will be over a specific future period. The budget prepared for control purposes, even though it may have been based on standards that may not be reached, is used for motivational purposes to influence improved departmental performance. Monitoring of actual performance against the budget is used to provide feedback in order to take the appropriate action necessary to reach planned performance, and to revise plans in the light of changes.

The following Worked Examples 11.1 and 11.2 illustrate the importance of the preparation of business plans and what can result if there is a lack of preparation for unexpected future events.

The accuracy of budgets

We asked FDs two questions: Is the UK and London in particular capable of hosting the 2012 Olympic Games? AND Are budgets drawn up now unrealistic for an event to be held eight years later?

More than three-quarters of finance directors believe it is unrealistic for the 2012 London Olympic finance team to draw up budget plans eight years in advance of the event taking place.

As bid FD Neil Wood prepares the capital and operating budgets as part of the 600-page bid document to be submitted on 14 November, just 16% of the 258 FDs polled in the latest *Accountancy Age*/Reed Accountancy Big Question survey saw any value in doing this now.

Paresh Samat, finance director of Croner Consulting, said the bid team should 'learn the lessons from the rebuilding of the Wembley Stadium. The figures will end up 30% to 40% higher than estimates. Maybe we should go to Japan and learn from their experiences of building an infrastructure from the last World Cup,' he said.

Another FD was even less convinced: 'Whatever you budget for now you need to double the figure that you ask for.'

FDs were, however, more supportive of the UK's and London's ability to host the 2012 Games, with more than two-thirds believing the capital will be able to stage the event. One FD said: 'Having hosted the Commonwealth Games successfully, I do not see why we should not host the Olympics.'

London 2012 says it will have access to £2.2bn of public funds if the bid succeeds – with £1.4bn coming from the National Lottery, £581m from London residents via a local tax and the rest coming from the London Development Agency.

FDs claim Olympic budgeting now is 'unrealistic', by Larry Schlesinger

© *Accountancy Age*, 3 June 2004

Worked Example 11.1

A business, which was involved in providing marquees and hospitality facilities for business entertaining and private parties, began to face a gradual economic downturn. The effect of this was that demand from companies started to decrease as they cut back their entertaining and hospitality budgets. The business had previously been doing very well and the proprietor felt confident of being able to continue to meet overhead payments even with a reduced sales level, because a reasonable bank balance had been built up. The proprietor did not quantify the change in position in a revised financial plan. After a few months the business needed overdraft facilities and began to delay its payments to creditors. The bank manager was not sympathetic since he had received no prior warning of the potential problem. Goodwill with creditors began to diminish. The business failed, but may not have if the proprietor had:

- attempted to quantify the effect of the economic downturn on profit and cash flow
- warned the bank of the problem
- tried to negotiate the overdraft facility
- negotiated favourable terms with creditors.

The careful preparation, and regular revision, of financial plans is vital to be prepared against the risk of unexpected events and changes in circumstances.

Worked Example 11.2

The managing director of a company that manufactured and sold solid wood kitchen and dining room furniture wanted to increase the turnover of the business by 30% in the coming year. She had identified the requirements necessary to fulfil this increase:

- spare capacity in existing retail outlets
- additional new equipment
- one extra employee.

However, the managing director had failed to recognise the cost of financing the increased turnover:

- cash outflow for additional raw materials before cash flowed in from increased sales
- financing costs of additional equipment
- additional wages.

The managing director had focused only on the positive aspects of the expansion:

- increased sales (although sales prices remained constant)
- increased cash flowing into the business.

The business ran into cash flow problems because it did not inform its bankers of its expansion plans and therefore did not submit a business plan (projected profit and loss account and cash flow) or negotiate a new overdraft facility. For any business it is crucial that any major change, whether expansion or diversification, must be quantified financially in revised business plans. Smaller businesses are particularly vulnerable and should prepare projections more frequently than on an annual basis incorporating realistic expectations for existing activities and plans for any changes in the business in order to:

- alert the business owner to risks and difficulties which may arise
- allow time for remedial action to be taken.

The broad picture of planning and control includes budgeting, strategic planning, management control, and operations control. The process involves:

- identification of objectives, involving factors such as profit, market share, value, etc.
- identification of potential strategies using facts as well as opinion
- evaluation of options, including a selection of courses of action and preparation of forecasts
- implementation of long-term plans, and finalising the planning before going on to provide control
- monitoring of actual outcomes, which will highlight whether the budget was too easy or unachievable
- provision of responses regarding actual outcomes against plans through feedback.

Strategic planning

Strategic planning is the process of deciding:

- on the objectives of the organisation
- on changes in these objectives
- on the resources used to attain these objectives
- on the policies that are to govern the acquisition, use and disposition of these resources.

It is not correct to assume that strategic planning is just an extension of budgeting, but there is a close relationship between these processes. A budget is a quantified statement, for a defined period of time, which may include planned revenues, expenses, assets, liabilities and cash flows. A budget provides a focus for the organisation, aids the co-ordination of activities, and facilitates control.

The way in which a typical strategic planning process may be carried out in an organisation is best illustrated in the flow charts in Figs 11.1 and 11.2. The chart in Fig. 11.1 shows how analysis is used to develop strategies and actions. The chart in Fig. 11.2 shows the sequences of each step in the process and the relationship between strategic planning and budgeting.

Figure 11.1 The strategic planning process

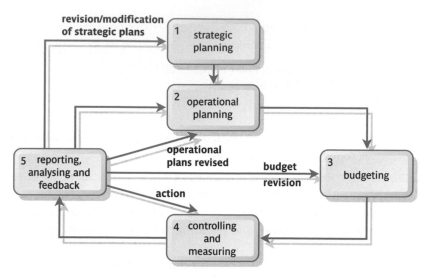

Figure 11.2 The strategic planning relationship with budgeting

Budgeting

The broad purposes of budgeting include:

- planning and control, through
  - exception reporting of financial and non-financial indicators, which
  - economises on managerial time, and
  - maximises efficiency
- co-ordination, which
  - assists goal congruence
- communication, through
  - the feedback process, which should
  - reduce or prevent sub-optimal performance
- motivation and alignment of individual and corporate goals, through
  - participation of many people in the budget-setting process
- evaluation of performance, to
  - facilitate control.

Budgetary control establishes a basis for internal audit by regularly evaluating departmental results. The budget process should ensure that scarce resources are allocated in an optimal way, and so enable expenditure to be controlled. Management is forced to plan ahead so that long-term goals are achieved.

The budget provides a yardstick for performance rather than rely on comparisons with past periods, since when conditions and expectations will have changed. Areas of efficiency and inefficiency are identified through reporting of variances, and variance analysis will prompt remedial action where necessary. Part of the budget process should identify the people responsible for items of cost and revenue so that areas of responsibility are clearly defined.

Planning

Planning and control are two of the most visible ways that financial and non-financial information may be used in the management control process. This is done by:

- setting standards of performance and providing feedback, and therefore
- identifying areas for improvement, by means of
- variance reports (a subject to which we shall return in more detail in Chapter 12).

Planning is the establishment of objectives and the formulation, evaluation and selection of the policies, strategies, tactics and action required to achieve them. Planning comprises long-term/strategic planning, and short-term operational planning. The latter usually refers to a period of one year. With regard to a new retail product, the strategic (long-term) plan of the business, for example, may include the aim to become profitable, and to become a market leader within three years. The short-term operational plan may be to get the product stocked by at least one leading supermarket group within 12 months.

Control

Control and monitoring are the continuous comparison of actual results with those planned, both in total, and for the separate divisions within the organisation, and taking appropriate management action to correct adverse variances and to exploit favourable variances. The UK has seen the growth of 'call centres', and the press have exposed the constant monitoring by management as unpleasantly intrusive. There appears to be a high turnover of staff in these new hi-tech businesses, where they are regarded as cheap labour but do not necessarily meet management targets.

Management control is the process by which managers assure that resources are obtained and used effectively and efficiently in the accomplishment of the organisation's objectives. The UK company Railtrack plc found itself forced into diverting extra resources into rail maintenance during the autumn months of 2000, as it was felt that it was not achieving the basic objective of safety of passengers and employees.

Operational control is concerned with day-to-day activities of organisations, and is the process of assuring that specific tasks are carried out effectively and efficiently. For example, the UK Government decided in the year 2000 to allocate further funds to hospitals for the recruitment of more nurses, to enable the hospitals to carry out specific tasks 'effectively and efficiently'.

Whereas planning is achieved by means of a fixed master budget, control is generally exercised through the comparison of actual costs with a flexible budget. A flexible budget is a budget which, by recognising different cost behaviour patterns, is designed to show changes in variable costs as the volume of activity of the organisation changes. Over the short time-spans that budgets normally cover (one year or six months), fixed costs are assumed to remain unchanged. The mobile telephone market in 2000/2001 is probably one of the best illustrations of a 'high profile' market having the need for flexible budgeting, as the number of units sold in successive periods continued to make the headlines in the media.

> **Progress check 11.1 What is budgeting, and how does it fit into the overall strategic planning process?**

Forecasting and planning

The budget is a plan. The planning activity of the budget process should reflect real beliefs of each company's management, reflecting what they think will happen, flexible to changes in circumstances, and providing feedback.

A forecast is not a budget but a prediction of future environments, events, and outcomes. Forecasting is required in order to prepare budgets. This should start with projected sales volumes/market share of current and new products. Examples of forecasts by product, or sector, can be found regularly in the press, for example car sales and mobile telephone sales.

Large companies need to be very sensitive to trends and developments within their forecasting process as mistakes can prove very expensive. For example, a major UK chocolate manufacturer made too many eggs for Easter 2000, which did not sell; its forecasts and therefore its budgets were proved to be very wide of the mark, and the impact on the business was extremely costly.

In order to highlight more clearly some of the issues around forecasting it may be useful to consider it in the context of budgeting in terms of large group plcs, comprising many companies that may be either diversified or within the same industrial sector.

Sales volume projections are required to evaluate turnover and product margins. Marketing policy may or may not be centralised. Centralised marketing information may not always be congruent with individual company expectations and may allow little scope for negotiation.

Sales prices are usually negotiated by individual companies with their customers, to ensure that group margin targets are met. However, in the case of large group companies, relationships with major customers may mean that this is not always an autonomous process, resulting in inevitable acceptance of group agreements in many cases. Whilst this may achieve corporate goals, it may conflict with individual company objectives in trying to meet targeted gross margins. Conversely, commercial managers may try to set sales budgets that may be too easily achievable through understatement of price increase expectations.

Increased market share through new innovation is commonly a primary objective of individual companies. However, new product development, financed out of internally generated funds, involves very large investments and long lead times. This creates competition for resources, and difficulties whilst also trying to achieve group targets for return on investment (ROI). Resources may come off second best, but without any relaxation in product development objectives.

The production manager forecasts production resource requirements, materials and labour, based on sales forecasts, stock-holding policies, and performance improvement targets. The production manager may have an easier job in an expanding rather than a declining market.

Many companies within large groups may be suppliers and customers within the group. The prices to be charged between companies within large groups, transfer prices, are usually set by the parent company and based on pre-determined formulae. Some companies within the group may lose and some companies may gain, the objective being that the group is the overall winner. As a consequence, transfer pricing may provide prices that are disagreed and cause disputes, which rarely result in acceptable outcomes for individual companies. Optimal pricing for the group must take precedence over individual company requirements to meet group profitability objectives (despite the impact on individual company profit performance bonuses!).

There are groups of companies where materials or components may be supplied from group-nominated suppliers, or certainly from suppliers where unit price is the dominant procurement criterion. Purchase indices are an important performance measure of the purchasing function, but may not relate to total procurement cost. Group purchasing performance objectives may therefore subvert those of the individual companies, which seek to minimise total costs, on which delivery costs, for example, and the impact of foreign currency exchange rate fluctuations may have a significant impact.

The above examples illustrate some important conflicts at the forecasting stage, arising from policy decisions where group goals inevitably dominate individual company goals, which in turn may also lack congruence with individual goals. Quite frequently a subsidiary company must comply with a group instruction, which may result in an apparently successful local product being dropped, in favour of a group-wide product. An example of this was seen in the year 2001 where the group goals of General Motors (USA) were not appreciated by a wide cross-section of the UK community, because so many lost their jobs (and businesses) as a result of Vauxhall cutbacks initiated by the group board of directors.

Forecasting usually relies on the analysis of past data to identify patterns used to describe it. Patterns may then be extrapolated into the future to prepare a forecast. There are many forecasting methods, qualitative and quantitative, with no one best model. It is usually a question of fitting the pattern of historical data to the model that best fits. It could be argued that it is easier to forecast the sales of ice-cream than the sales of CDs by a new band. Apparently, the major music-based groups have also found this a mystery over the years.

> **Progress check 11.2 What is the role of forecasting in budgeting?**

Qualitative forecasting

Qualitative forecasting uses expert opinion to predict future events and includes:

- the Delphi method – use of a panel of recognised experts
- technological comparisons – independent forecasters predicting changes in one area by monitoring changes in another area
- subjective curve fitting – for example, similar product life cycles for similar products like CD players and DVD players.

Quantitative forecasting

Quantitative forecasting uses historical data to try to predict the future, and includes univariate models and causal models. Univariate models predict future values of time series when conditions are expected to remain the same, for example exponential smoothing and the use of moving averages.

Causal models involve the use of the identification of other variables related to the variable being predicted. For example, linear regression may be used to forecast sales, using the independent variables of:

- sales price
- advertising expenditure
- competitors' prices.

The major UK retailers have been seen to be highly pro-active in revising their sales prices and their advertising activities (and expenditure) as a result of changes in the marketplace.

Whichever method is used it is important that the basis and the methodology of the forecasting is understood. All assumptions made and the parameters of time, availability of past data, costs, accuracy required, and ease of use must be clearly stated to maintain any sort of confidence in the forecasts.

> **Progress check 11.3 Give examples of some of the techniques used to forecast the demand for a product.**

The budget process

The budgeting process normally aims to:

- identify areas of efficiency/inefficiency
- allow people participation
- allocate responsibility to enable performance evaluation through exception reporting of actual versus budget.

Whilst participation may be encouraged, insufficient attention may be given to managers' differing motivational tendencies either to achieve success or to avoid failure. The budget process therefore may not always achieve desired results, nor provide the appropriate rewards for success.

We will use Supportex Ltd in Worked Examples 11.1 to 11.7 to illustrate a step-by-step approach to the budget preparation process.

Sales and gross margin budget

The complete budget preparation process is outlined in Fig. 11.3. Once the sales forecast has been prepared the budgeted gross margin may be calculated. The budgeted gross margin is derived from estimated:

- sales volumes, and prices
- materials usage, and prices
- direct labour hours, and rates
- overhead costs.

> **Progress check 11.4 What are the decisions to be made and the policies established by a business before embarking on the budget preparation process?**

Worked Example 11.3

Supportex Ltd manufactures three only specialist types of lintels: Small; Medium; Large. Supportex has received sales forecasts prepared by its sales manager, Ms Crystal Ball. Taking account of trends in the building industry and an analysis of competitive performance, Crystal has used a linear regression computer model to forecast demand for Supportex's products and

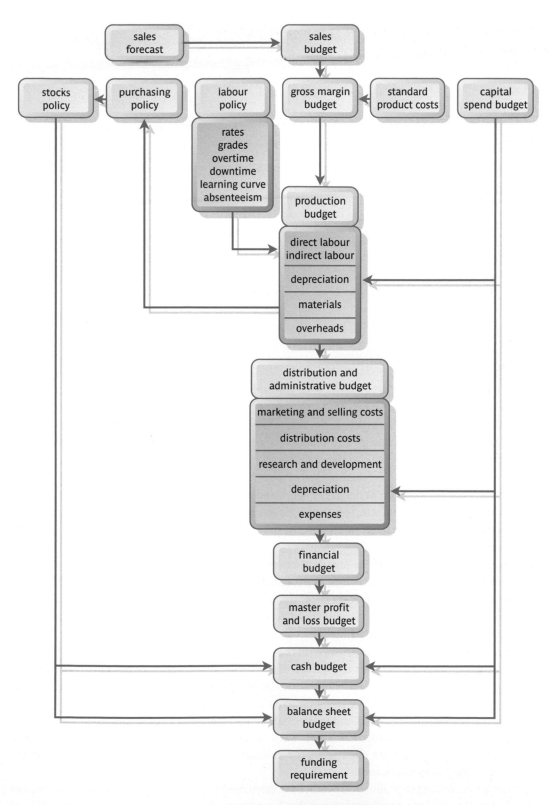

Figure 11.3 Budget preparation flow diagram

sales prices for the year from 1 April 2005. Crystal Ball's sales forecast data are as follows:

Lintel	Demand	Price
Small	5,000	£20
Medium	8,000	£30
Large	6,000	£40

These data will be used to prepare an unphased sales budget for the year ended 31 March 2006.

Sales budget

Lintel	Demand	Price	£ sales
Small	5,000	£20	100,000
Medium	8,000	£30	240,000
Large	6,000	£40	240,000
			580,000

Production budget

The production budget may be prepared by allowing for expected stock movements in the period, based on company policy and targets for improvement. Budgeted materials requirements are based on a **bill of materials (BOM)**, which is the 'list of ingredients and recipe' for each product. The purchasing function ensures that the right materials, components and packaging are procured in the right quantities, at the right time to the right location, in line with production and stockholding requirements.

Budgeted labour requirements are based on standard labour hours required for each product. Conflicts arise between manufacturing and engineering in respect of estimates of standard hours. Engineering changes may be made continuously, but may not always be reflected in up-to-date bills of materials.

In practice, the calculation of the standard hours required to manufacture each product is not a straightforward process. There is always much debate between managers with regard to how standard labour hours are adjusted in respect of, for example, absenteeism, downtime, training, efficiency, and the extent to which they should be reflected in the standard labour rate. These factors have an obvious impact on the manufacturing director's requirements for direct labour resources for given levels of production, inevitably conflicting with the human resources director's headcount objectives.

Many companies have structures comprised of business units, each with responsibility for production areas relating to specific products/customers. Responsibility for estimating budget production overheads and indirect labour requirements is devolved to business unit managers, the remaining above-the-line overheads and indirect labour requirements being provided by quality, purchasing, logistics and maintenance managers. Each manager may also submit his/her capital expenditure requirements, which are then used for subsequent calculation of depreciation, and the assessment of cash flow implications.

Depreciation charged to production overhead is calculated based on existing plant and equipment and the plans for new plant and equipment that have been submitted by managers responsible for production and production support activities. It must be emphasised that the method of determining the depreciation charge is highly subjective, and the marketplace has seen many products last much longer than the most extreme original estimates made by managers. An example has been the Rover Mini car, which was not expected to be in production for over 40 years!

Worked Example 11.4

The purchasing manager of Supportex Ltd, Mr Daley, has obtained what he believes are the most competitive prices for materials used to make and package Supportex's products. Supportex's cost prices and the standard quantities used in each product for the budget year are as follows:

Materials

	Labels	Packaging	Rubbers	Steels
Cost prices	£1	£2	£3	£6
Standard quantities				
Small	2	1	1	0.5
Medium	1	1	2	1
Large	2	2	1	1

Material handlers and operators are employed to make the Supportex products. The company's production manager, Ben Drools, has provided the following hourly rates and the standard times used in production:

	Material handlers	Operators
Hourly rates	£6	£7.50
Standard minutes		
Small	5	12
Medium	5	20
Large	10	40

Production overheads are forecast at £38,000, which are absorbed into product costs on the basis of direct labour hours.

At 31 March 2005 stock levels have been estimated by Arthur Daley at:

Finished product	Quantity	Materials	Quantity
Small	1,000	Labels	15,000
Medium	1,500	Packaging	10,000
Large	1,000	Rubbers	15,000
		Steels	10,000

The Managing Director has set Ben a target of a 20% reduction in component stocks by 31 March 2006 and the company expects finished goods stock to be up by 10% by the same time.

Unphased budgets for the year ended 31 March 2006 may be prepared for the following:

(i) Production
(ii) Direct labour
(iii) Unit gross margin
(iv) Materials usage and purchases.

(i) Production budget

	Sales units	Stock increases	Production units
Small	5,000	100	5,100
Medium	8,000	150	8,150
Large	6,000	100	6,100

(ii) Direct labour budget

	Production units	Material handlers hours	Operators hours	
Small	5,100	425	1,020	
Medium	8,150	679	2,717	
Large	6,100	1,017	4,067	
Direct labour hours		2,121	7,804	Total 9,925 hours
Direct labour rates		£6/hour	£7.50/hour	
Direct labour cost		£12,726	£58,530	Total £71,256

(iii) Unit gross margin budget

Unit product costs

	Small £	Medium £	Large £
Materials:			
Labels	2	1	2
Packaging	2	2	4
Rubbers	3	6	3
Steels	3	6	6
(a)	£10	£15	£15
Direct labour:			
Material handlers	0.5 [5 × £6/60]	0.5 [5 × £6/60]	1 [10 × £6/60]
Operators	1.5 [12 × £7.50/60]	2.5 [20 × £7.50/60]	5 [40 × £7.50/60]
(b)	£2	£3	£6

Total production
overheads
£38,000 ÷ 9,925

= £3.8287 per hour	**(c)**	£1.0848	£1.5953	£3.1906
Total unit				
production costs				
(a + b + c)	**(d)**	£13.0848	£19.5953	£24.1906
Sales prices				
Unit gross	**(e)**	£20	£30	£40
margins (e − d)		£6.9152	£10.4047	£15.8094
rounded to		£6.92	£10.40	£15.81

(iv) Materials usage budget

Units	Labels	Packaging	Rubbers	Steels
Small	10,200	5,100	5,100	2,550
Medium	8,150	8,150	16,300	8,150
Large	12,200	12,200	6,100	6,100
Total usage	30,550	25,450	27,500	16,800
Stocks 31 March 2005	15,000	10,000	15,000	10,000
Stocks reduction by 31 March 2006 targeted at 20% of 31 March 2005 levels	3,000	2,000	3,000	2,000

Materials purchases budget

Units	Labels	Packaging	Rubbers	Steels	
Total usage	30,550	25,450	27,500	16,800	
Stock decrease	3,000	2,000	3,000	2,000	
Purchase requirements	27,550	23,450	24,500	14,800	
Unit costs	£1	£2	£3	£6	Total
Purchase requirements	£27,550	£46,900	£73,500	£88,800	£236,750

Distribution and administrative budget

The non-production costs of:

- marketing and selling
- distribution
- administration
- research and development

and also planned capital expenditure, are provided by managers responsible for departments such as:

- commercial and marketing
- information technology
- administration
- human resources
- engineering
- product development.

Financial budget

Costs of financing and/or interest receivable from the investment of surplus funds may be estimated for the first draft budget. As the phased profit and loss accounts, capital expenditure, and cash budget become finalised the financial budget can be refined with a little more accuracy.

Master profit and loss budget

The master budget is prepared by pulling together each of the elements outlined above to provide a budgeted:

- trading account
- manufacturing account
- profit and loss account

for the year.

These may then be phased to show expected month-by-month results. The ways in which the various items within the budget are phased are determined by the type of revenue or cost. Some items may be related to the volume of sales, or production levels, whilst others may be spread evenly on a monthly, weekly or daily basis.

The budget preparation procedure described above is usually a negotiation process between budget holders and the budget committee. Conflicts may arise as budgets are very often seen as 'finance' budgets, perceived as a pressure device, with a corresponding demotivating effect on personnel.

Problems ensue due to lack of information, ignorance, and misunderstanding of the budget process (probably through a lack of training), which may result in generally inflated budgets. Judgement is required to identify whether apparently inflated budgets reflect real needs, or some degree of 'padding' due to a fear of cutbacks. Padding relates to the overestimation of budgeted costs (or underestimation of budgeted revenues) by managers with the expectation that their budgets may be cut, so that their final agreed budgets may be at levels that they feel are achievable.

Further conflicts arise between departments within a company, through competition for resources, and also poor communication, resulting in duplication in cost budgets or padding. Examples of costs omitted, or duplicated, are health and safety costs (human resources or manufacturing?), training costs (human resources or decentralised into the operational departments?), and the question of centralised/decentralised costs generally. This often results in each department blaming the other if services are not provided, or if cost targets are not achieved.

Padding may occur where budget holders are allowed to be excessively prudent regarding costs and expenses or achievement of sales. If the company or a sector of its business is expanding, the padding may be tolerated. When competition is fierce or the industry is in decline, then the padding could prove quite harmful and lead to decisions being based on an incorrect cost base. It is inevitable that managers may be prudent when constructing their budgets, and this can take the form of putting a little extra into expense categories that may be difficult to verify, or a little less into certain categories of sales.

The budget preparation process is a continuous process of:

- setting objectives
- forecasting
- draft budget preparation
- evaluation
- feedback
- forecast and budget revisions.

Within most organisations this process continues, limited by budget preparation timetable constraints, until an acceptable final budget has been achieved.

During the budget process, cost reductions are inevitably requested from all areas within the organisation. This poses obvious dilemmas for all managers. Whilst wanting to co-operate in meeting profitability objectives, they must still maintain the same levels of service for both internal and external customers.

Worked Example 11.5

Supportex Ltd have budgeted selling and administrative costs of £80,000 for the following year. The overheads and selling and administrative costs include total depreciation budgeted for the year of £23,569. There are not expected to be any financing costs over the coming year.

We will prepare an unphased profit and loss account budget, using absorption costing, for the year ended 31 March 2006.

Profit and loss account master budget

	Small		Medium		Large		Total
	Total	**Unit**	**Total**	**Unit**	**Total**	**Unit**	**Total**
Sales units	5,000		8,000		6,000		
	£		£		£		£
Sales	100,000	£20	240,000	£30	240,000	£40	580,000
Cost of sales (derived from sales less gross margin)	65,400		156,800		145,140		367,340
Gross margin	34,600	£6.92	83,200	£10.40	94,860	£15.81	212,660
Using unit gross margins from Worked Example 11.4 (iii)							
Selling and administrative costs							80,000
Profit							132,660

Cash budget

Cash flow is an extremely important element in the budget preparation process. The master profit and loss budget, together with the planned capital expenditure, the outflow of cash on fixed asset acquisitions and investments, may then be used to prepare an initial cash budget. This will also include the impact of the operating cycle:

- materials purchases become stock items held for a period before use, and creditors to be paid out of cash at a later date
- production uses up stock to generate sales which become debtors to be received into cash at a later date
- the more immediate payment of staff costs and other operational expense.

The final cash budget, phased to show monthly cash surpluses or cash requirements, will also include the effect of non-operational events such as cash raised through the issue of shares and loans, and cash paid in respect of taxation and dividends to shareholders.

Worked Example 11.6

Supportex Ltd have prepared an estimated balance sheet for 31 March 2005 as follows:

	£	£
Fixed assets	362,792	
Stocks	206,669	
Trade debtors	46,750	
Cash and bank	2,432	618,643
Trade creditors	35,275	
Share capital	200,000	
Retained earnings	383,368	618,643

Trade debtors all pay in the month following the month of sale and Arthur Daley has negotiated trade creditors' payments in the second month following the month of purchase. Direct labour, production overheads, and selling and administrative costs are all paid in the month they are incurred. There is no planned capital expenditure for the budget year and trading is expected to be evenly spread over the 12 months, except for month 12 when the changes in stock levels are expected to occur.

We can use this to prepare an unphased cash budget for the year ended 31 March 2006.

Cash budget

Cash inflows from customers:	£	Cash outflows to suppliers:	£
Trade debtors at 31/3/05	46,750	Trade creditors at 31/3/05	35,275
Sales 2005/06	580,000	Purchases 2005/06	236,750
less: Trade debtors at 31/3/06	(48,333)	less: Trade creditors at 31/3/06	(39,458)
(1 month sales)	578,417	(2 months purchases)	232,567

Cash outflows for overheads:		Cash outflow for capital:	zero
Production overheads	38,000	Cash outflow for tax:	zero
Sales and administration	80,000	Cash outflow for dividends:	zero
less: Depreciation	(23,569)	Cash outflow for direct labour:	71,256
	94,431	Cash inflow for shares/loans:	zero

	£	
Inflows from customers	578,417	
Outflows to suppliers	(232,567)	
Outflows for overheads	(94,431)	
Outflow for direct labour	(71,256)	
Budgeted cash flow 2005/06	180,163	[see Worked Example 11.7]
Forecast cash and bank 31/3/05	2,432	
Budgeted cash and bank 31/3/06	182,595	

The calculation of the budgeted cash flow statement, shown in Worked Example 11.6, was carried out by preparing a direct cash flow statement (see Chapter 4). This may be checked by the preparation of a more conventional indirect cash flow statement, as shown in Worked Example 11.7.

Worked Example 11.7

An unphased budgeted indirect cash flow statement may be prepared for Supportex Ltd for the year ended 31 March 2006.

Cash flow statement

	£	
Budgeted operating profit 2005/06	132,660	
plus: Depreciation	23,569	
plus: Decrease in stocks	21,334	[206,669 − 185,335]
		See Worked Example 11.8
less: Increase in debtors	(1,583)	[48,333 − 46,750]
		See Worked Example 11.6
plus: Increase in creditors	4,183	[39,458 − 35,275]
Budgeted cash flow 2005/06	180,163	See Worked Example 11.6
Forecast cash and bank 31/3/05	2,432	
Budgeted cash and bank 31/3/06	182,595	

The budgeted cash flow figure of £180,163 can be seen to agree with the budgeted cash flow calculated in Worked Example 11.6.

Balance sheet budget

The budget balance sheet may be prepared with reference to:

- information relating to sales, costs, etc., from the master profit and loss budget
- the capital expenditure budget
- operating cycle assumptions on stock days, debtor days, creditor days
- the cash budget.

As with the profit and loss budget and cash budget, the balance sheet budget may be phased to show the expected month-by-month financial position of the organisation.

Worked Example 11.8

Using the information from the last four Worked Examples 11.4 to 11.7 we can now prepare an unphased balance sheet budget for Supportex Ltd as at 31 March 2006.

Stock valuations at 31 March 2006

	Quantity	£ unit price (see Worked Example 11.4)	£
Finished product			
Small	1,100	13.0848	14,393
Medium	1,650	19.5953	32,332
Large	1,100	24.1906	26,610
Total			73,335
Materials			
Labels	12,000	1.00	12,000
Packaging	8,000	2.00	16,000
Rubbers	12,000	3.00	36,000
Steels	8,000	6.00	48,000
Total			112,000
Budgeted stocks at 31 March 2006			185,335
Fixed assets			
Fixed assets at 31 March 2005			362,792
Budgeted depreciation 2005/06			(23,569)
Budgeted fixed assets at 31 March 2006			339,223
Retained earnings			
Retained earnings at 31 March 2005			383,368
Budgeted profit 2005/06 (see Worked Example 11.5)			132,660
Budgeted retained earnings at 31 March 2006			516,028

Using the budgeted stocks, fixed assets, and retained earnings calculations above, and the budgeted cash and bank balance, trade debtors and trade creditors calculated in Worked Example 11.6, we now have the complete information to construct the budgeted balance sheet as at 31 March 2006:

Balance sheet:

	£	£
Fixed assets	339,223	
Stocks	185,335	
Trade debtors	48,333	
Cash and bank	182,595	755,486
Trade creditors	39,458	
Share capital	200,000	
Retained earnings	516,028	755,486

The budget balance sheet as at 31 March 2006 shown in Worked Example 11.8 has been prepared by calculating:

- the effect on fixed assets of depreciation for the year 2005/06
- the closing valuation of stocks at 31 March 2006
- the closing valuation of trade debtors at 31 March 2006
- the cash and bank balance at 31 March 2006
- the closing valuation of trade creditors at 31 March 2006
- the addition to retained earnings, the budgeted profit for the year 2005/06.

There is an alternative way of deriving the balance sheet that may be used in practice, which also clarifies the links between stock movements and the profit and loss account and its links with the balance sheet. This method requires a calculation of the materials cost of products actually sold (compared with the materials used in production in Worked Example 11.4). It also requires a calculation of the direct labour and production overheads cost of products actually sold (compared with the cash paid out in Worked Example 11.6). The cash paid out for direct labour and overheads in the budget year will be absorbed into the valuation of stock of finished product. Not all that finished product will be sold in the period. Some will have been left in stock at 31 March 2006. The same situation applied at 31 March 2005.

Therefore finished product stocks at 31 March 2006 will need to be adjusted by the amount of direct labour and overheads in their valuation that relates to the difference in the finished goods stock level between 31 March 2005 and 31 March 2006. The balance of what is paid out for direct labour and overheads in the budget year is charged to the profit and loss account.

Worked Example 11.9

The budget balance sheet for Supportex Ltd at 31 March 2006 can be derived by plotting the expected movements for the budget year 2005/06 relating to each type of activity, and totalling across each line from the starting balance sheet 31 March 2005. This is an alternative approach to Worked Example 11.8, which also shows the relationship between sales, costs, cash and the balance sheet.

Materials cost of goods sold

Units	Labels		Packaging		Rubbers		Steels	
Small	[5,000 × 2]	10,000	[5,000 × 1]	5,000	[5,000 × 1]	5,000	[5,000 × 0.5]	2,500
Med.	[8,000 × 1]	8,000	[8,000 × 1]	8,000	[8,000 × 2]	16,000	[8,000 × 1]	8,000
Large	[6,000 × 2]	12,000	[6,000 × 2]	12,000	[6,000 × 1]	6,000	[6,000 × 1]	6,000
Total		30,000		25,000		27,000		16,500
Unit costs		£1		£2		£3		£6
Materials cost of sales		£30,000		£50,000		£81,000		£99,000

Total = £260,000

Direct labour in finished stock increase 31 March 2006

	Stock increases	Direct labour/unit £	Stock adjustment £
Small	100	2	200
Medium	150	3	450
Large	100	6	600
			1,250

Production overhead in finished stock increase 31 March 2006

	Stock increases	Production overhead/unit (see Worked Example 11.4) £	Stock adjustment £
Small	100	1.0848	108
Medium	150	1.5953	239
Large	100	3.1906	319
			666

Sales, materials purchases, depreciation, cash receipts, and cash payments have previously been calculated (see Worked Examples 11.3 to 11.7).

Balance sheet

Figures in £	31/03/05	Sales	Cash recs.	Purchases	Cash pays.	Depn.	Materials cost of sales	Direct labour	Production overheads	31/03/06
Fixed assets	362,792					(23,569)				339,223
Stocks	206,669			236,750			(260,000)	1,250	666	185,335
Trade debtors	46,750	580,000	(578,417)							48,333
Cash and bank	2,432		578,417		(232,567)			(71,256)	(94,431)	182,595
	618,643									755,486
Trade creditors	35,275			236,750	(232,567)					39,458
Share capital	200,000									200,000
Retained earnings	383,368	580,000				(23,569)	(260,000)	(70,006)	(93,765)	516,028
	618,643									755,486

> Progress check 11.5 **Describe a typical budget preparation process.**

Funding requirements

The final budget should not be accepted until the projected financial position of the business has been reviewed in terms of the adequacy, or otherwise, of funding. The budget for the forthcoming period may have been based on higher or lower activity than the previous period, or it may include new product development, or other major new projects. Risk analysis and risk assessment is essential to be carried out on each of the uncertain areas of the budget, to determine any requirement for additional funding and to safeguard the future of the business.

Additional funding may be by way of extended overdraft facilities, loans or additional share capital. The appropriate funding decision may be made and matched with the type of activity for which funding is required. For example, major capital expenditure projects would not normally be funded by an overdraft; the type of longer-term funding generally depends on the nature of the project.

Worked Example 11.10

Magic Moments have planned to sell fluffy puppies between October and December to meet the Christmas demand. They have forecast the following sales at £20 each to be received in cash in the month of sale.

	Oct	Nov	Dec	Total
Units	500	750	1,500	2,750

Magic Moments have contracted to buy fluffy puppies at £12 each. They will have to buy 300 in September. Month-end stocks are planned to be:

October 30% of November sales
November 20% of December sales
December zero

Magic Moments must pay for fluffy puppies in the month following purchase.

We will prepare:

- a schedule of opening stocks, purchases, and closing stocks in units for September to December

- a direct cash flow forecast phased for October to January

and then consider how Magic Moments have funded their activities.

Stocks and purchases:

Units	Sep	Oct	Nov	Dec
Opening stock	–	300	225	300
Purchases (derived)	300	425	825	1,200
Sales	–	500	750	1,500
Closing stock	300	225	300	–

Cash flow:

Figures in £		Oct		Nov		Dec		Jan
Opening balance		–		6,400		16,300		36,400
Cash inflow	(500 × £20)	10,000	(750 × £20)	15,000	(1,500 × £20)	30,000		–
Cash outflow	(300 × £12)	3,600	(425 × £12)	5,100	(825 × £12)	9,900	(1,200 × £12)	14,400
Closing balance		6,400		16,300		36,400		22,000

Magic Moments have funded their business through managing their operating cycle. Effectively, their creditors have financed the business.

Regardless of whether higher or lower activity is expected and budgeted for future periods, it is absolutely essential that the company's bankers are kept fully informed of expectations. Bankers do not like surprises. The corporate graveyard is littered with small businesses in particular who have ignored this basic requirement.

Performance evaluation and control

The many uses of budgeting may be summarised as follows:

- a system for optimal allocation of scarce resources, for example a factory capable of a specific process like plate glass manufacture
- a yardstick for performance, better than past performance, since conditions may have changed
- people participation to provide motivation for improved performance and alignment of individual and corporate goals
- improved communication to enable co-ordination of various parts of the business and so avoid sub-optimisation
- thinking ahead to achieve long-term goals and identify short-term problems
- a system of authorisation and for clear identification of responsibility
- internal audit by evaluating efficiency and effectiveness of departmental performance for prompt remedial action as necessary
- a system of control and management by exception reporting.

Prior to budget preparation, targets may be issued, for example, for:

- sales
- gross margin
- return on investment
- stock days
- debtor collection days
- creditor payment days.

Whilst the responsibility for the budget usually rests with a budget committee, for the budget to achieve its aims, it is important for relevant managers to have full participation in the process and receive communication of the guidelines. Uncertainties, limiting factors and constraints, along with all assumptions, must be made available to all managers with budget responsibility.

It is by ensuring that full communication and participation take place that the most effective use may be made of budgeting as a tool of control. Actual departmental results may then be regularly reported against control budgets that have had full acceptance by the relevant managers and are based on up-to-date and realistic standards of performance. The budget is used as a tool for control of the business by monitoring actual performance and comparing how closely it is in line with the plan. For this purpose the overall budget plan is broken down into the individual elements, representing the areas of responsibility of each of the budget holders, which are called responsibility centres.

Responsibility centres

As part of the budgetary process, in order to co-ordinate an organisation's activities, responsibility is assigned to managers who are accountable for their actions. Each manager therefore is in charge of a responsibility centre. A responsibility centre is a department or organisational function whose performance is the direct responsibility of a specific manager. Responsibility accounting is the system used to measure and compare actual results against budget for each centre. Costs are traced to the activities causing them, or to the individuals knowledgeable about why they arose, and who authorised them.

There are four main types of responsibility centre, and within each type, the responsibilities of the manager of each centre are defined in a different way:

- cost centre is a production or service location, function, activity or item of equipment for which costs are accumulated – the manager is accountable for costs only
- revenue centre is a centre devoted to raising revenue with no responsibility for costs, for example, a sales centre – the manager is responsible for revenues only (revenue centres are often used in not-for-profit organisations)
- profit centre is a part of the business that is accountable for both costs and revenues – the manager is responsible for revenues and costs
- investment centre is a profit centre with additional responsibilities for capital investment and possibly for financing, and whose performance is measured by its return on investment – the manager is responsible for investments, revenues and costs.

Responsibility must be matched with control, otherwise a manager is more likely to be demotivated. The manager must be able to influence the costs in question over specific time spans. Problems may also arise when costs may be influenced by more than one manager. Many very large businesses have pursued the policy of devolving spending responsibility down through the organisation. Employees are frequently motivated by being given spending responsibility and fully accepting control, which may be supported by sophisticated IT techniques as hardware and software has become more economic, by, for example, file sharing or remote interrogation of files.

Budget holders can only be responsible for controllable costs or revenues within their areas of responsibility. For example, a production manager may be responsible for ensuring that he/she does not exceed the number of direct labour hours allowed within their area of responsibility for a given level of output. Uncontrollable costs, for example the level of depreciation on the machines and equipment used within the production manager's department, may appear within budget holders' areas of activity but cannot realistically be used to measure performance. Further examples of such costs may be business taxes, or rents on property that may have been the subject of long-term agreements.

In a similar way, a budget holder may be responsible for controlling costs of a department that relate to sales volumes or other variable activities. The costs of that department, the variable costs and possibly the fixed costs, will vary according to the level of activity that takes place. For this reason, the budget for control purposes is flexed in line with actual levels of activity to provide more realistic levels of expected costs against which to measure performance.

> **Progress check 11.6** Outline the system of responsibility accounting in its various forms and describe what it aims to achieve.

For control purposes, therefore, the master budget needs to be:

- phased by reporting period – usually by week, calendar month, or four-week periods
- broken down to provide a separate budget for each responsibility centre
- flexed to show the costs (or revenues) expected as a result of changes in activity levels from those planned within the master budget.

We will look at the mechanics of flexed budgets in Chapter 12, together with the method of comparison with actual performance. We shall look at the way in which standards are used for this purpose in budget preparation to enable meaningful exception reporting to be provided for analysis of differences, or variances, to the budget plan.

Divisional performance measurement

For cost control and performance measurement purposes it is necessary to measure performance at frequent intervals. Managers may be evaluated on a short-term basis monthly, quarterly or even yearly. As we discussed in Chapter 5, the measures used to consider a company's economic performance may not be the most appropriate to evaluate divisional performance of managers. Responsibility centres may be business units, divisions of a company or even companies within a group. The performance of managers of responsibility centres may be considered using the divisional performance measures of return on investment (ROI) and residual income (RI). Such short-term performance measures focus only on the performance for the particular control period.

ROI is calculated as a percentage by dividing operating profit by the investment (or net assets, which are usually averaged – see Chapter 5). It is therefore a relative measure of profitability rather than an absolute measure of profit. RI is calculated by deducting a notional interest charge for capital invested from profit before tax, and is therefore an absolute measure.

Worked Example 11.11

Consider two divisions, A and B, of a company with the following results for 2004:

	Division A	Division B
Operating profit	£1m	£2m
Average net assets (investment)	£4m	£20m

The ROI for division A is 25% and for division B is 10%. Division B earns higher profits but A is more profitable.

Divisional managers may, for example, be rewarded via a remuneration package, which is linked to an ROI performance measure. Since ROI tends to be low in the early stages of an investment project, managers are likely to take a short-term view in appraising investment proposals because they will be anxious to maintain their level of earnings. Managers may therefore reject proposals for such investment projects even though they may provide a satisfactorily high ROI over the longer term. The owners of the business, the shareholders, will of course be more interested in the longer-term ROI over the entire life of an investment project.

The divergence between the two points of view occurs because divisional managers and shareholders are each using different assessment criteria. The views of divisional managers and the shareholders may be brought into line if they both used the same criteria. This would mean abandoning the practice of linking a manager's remuneration directly to short-term ROI because it is likely to encourage short-term thinking.

It is sometimes claimed that RI is more likely to encourage goal congruence, but a similar lack of goal congruence to that resulting from the use of ROI may occur if divisional managers' performance is measured using RI. If divisional manager performance is based on RI then managers may decide to

Worked Example 11.12

Let's consider two divisions within a company that have an opportunity to invest in projects that both have an initial cost of £10m. The overall cost of capital for the company is 15% per annum. The expected operating profits from each investment and the current returns earned by the divisions are shown below:

	Division X	Division Y
Investment projects available cost	£10m	£10m
Expected operating profit	£2m	£1.3m
ROI of divisions at present	25%	9%

The expected returns from each proposed project are 20% for division X and 13% for division Y. The manager of division X would not be motivated to invest in the new project because 20% is less than the current ROI. The manager of division Y would be motivated to invest in the project because 13% is greater than the current ROI. However, both decisions are incorrect for the company as a whole. This is because the division Y project returns 2% less, and the division X project returns 5% more, than the average cost of capital for the company of 15%.

Worked Example 11.13

Let's consider two divisions within a company that have an opportunity to invest in projects that both have an initial cost of £10m. The overall cost of capital for the company is 15% per annum. The expected operating profits from each investment are shown below:

	Division R	Division S
Proposed investment	£10.0m	£10.0m
Expected profit before tax	£2.0m	£1.3m
Cost of capital charge (15%)	£1.5m	£1.5m
Residual income (loss)	+£0.5m	−£0.2m

The manager of division R will be motivated to invest and the manager of division S will not be motivated not to invest.

replace old equipment (resulting in lower ROI and worsened cash flow) to increase profit and therefore increase RI. The reduction in ROI may therefore result in a sub-optimisation decision for the company as a whole. Alternatively, if divisional manager performance is based on ROI then managers may decide to make do with old equipment, resulting in a higher ROI and improved cash flow, but which may result in a reduced RI. There have been many case studies based on UK manufacturers which showed that the age of their plant was much older than that used by overseas competitors, which may be as a direct result of the type of divisional performance measure being used.

If a great deal of stress is placed on managers to meet short-term performance measurement targets, there is a danger that they will take action that will improve short-term performance but that will not maximise long-term profits. For example, by skimping on expenditure on advertising, customer services, maintenance, and training and staff development costs, it is possible to improve short-term performance. However, such actions may not maximise long-term profits.

It is probably impossible to design performance measures which will ensure that maximising the short-run performance measure will also maximise long-term performance. Some steps, however, can be taken to improve the short-term performance measures so that they minimise the potential conflict. For example, during times of rising prices, short-term performance measures can be distorted if no attempt is made to adjust for the changing price levels.

ROI and RI represent single summary measures of performance. It is virtually impossible to capture in summary financial measures all the variables that measure the success of a manager. It is therefore important that accountants broaden their reporting systems to include additional non-financial measures of performance that give clues to future outcomes from present actions (see the sections on non-financial performance indicators, and the balanced scorecard in Chapter 5). For example, obtaining feedback from customers regarding the quality of service encourages managers not to skimp on reducing the quality of service in order to save costs in the short term. Other suggestions have focused on refining the financial measures so that they will reduce the potential for conflict between actions that improve short-term performance at the expense of long-term performance.

The use of ROI as a divisional performance measure has a number of deficiencies. For example, it encourages managers to accept only those investments that are in excess of their current ROI, leading to the rejection of profitable projects. Such actions may be reduced by replacing ROI with RI as the performance measure. However as we have seen, merely changing from ROI to RI may not eliminate the short term versus long-term conflicts. RI does enable different cost of capital percentages to be applied to different investments that have different levels of risk. It should be noted that if RI is used as the measure of divisional performance then it should be compared with budgeted/target levels of RI, which reflect the size of the divisional investment. However, empirical evidence indicates that RI is not widely used.

Ideally, performance measures ought to be based on future results that can be expected from a manager's actions during a period. This would involve a comparison of the present value of future cash flows at the start and end of the period, and a manager's performance would be based on the increase in present value during the period. Such a system may not be totally feasible, given the difficulty in predicting and measuring future outcomes from current actions. A variation on RI is economic value added (EVA^{TM}), which is discussed in more detail in Chapter 14. EVA aims to provide a performance measure that is highly correlated with both shareholder wealth and divisional performance. EVA is calculated by deducting from profit after tax a financial charge for the use of the company's net assets. The net assets figure reported in the accounts is usually adjusted (in a variety of different ways) to reflect as realistic a valuation as possible of the company's net assets. The basis for the financial charge is usually the average cost of the capital used by the company.

Motivation and the behavioural aspects of budgeting

We have discussed the importance of participation and communication in the budget process and so it can be seen that key aspects of budgeting are behavioural. One of the main objectives is to influence the behaviour of the people in the organisation so that efficiency is maximised and corporate goals are attained. It is important therefore that the evaluation of performance does not degenerate into a blame culture. It follows then that motivation is an important underlying factor in ensuring that achievable budgets are set and that the managers with the responsibility for each of the elements of the budget have a very good chance of achieving their objectives.

The question of motivation is a very large subject in its own right. It is sufficient for our purposes to outline some of the many motivational factors without going into much further detail. Key motivational factors include:

- pay
- bonuses
- feedback of information
- communication and discussion of control reports
- success, and reward for target achievement
- training in the budget process
- the identification of controllable and uncontrollable costs
- the setting of fair, achievable standards
- the avoidance of short-term wins at the expense of long-term considerations, leading to dysfunctional decision-making
- flexibility in meeting the requirements of the budgeting system
- performance appraisal using budgets flexed to actual activity levels
- inclusion of non-financial performance indicators.

Many writers, including Hopwood, Argyris, Hofstede, McGregor, Becker and Green, have identified the various motivational problems which may be encountered in budgeting. The ways they have suggested these problems can be alleviated, and how motivation can be enhanced, is beyond the scope of this book, and may be followed up with further reading.

> **Progress check 11.7** As Supportex Ltd's purchasing manager, Arthur Daley is responsible for negotiating the best deals with suppliers. For planning purposes the budget that was prepared for 2005/06 used current materials' prices and suppliers' credit terms that were negotiated by Arthur. Within a control budget, give examples of the type of performance targets that may have been set for Arthur and how these targets may have been set and monitored.

Problems in budgeting

Within most companies budgeting is a high-profile, formal process, prepared on either a yearly or half-yearly basis. The budget is prepared within the context of a company's strategic management process, and includes current year performance projections. It should ideally emphasise the strategies and priorities of the company and focus on both financial and non-financial performance.

Information provided from the budget process generally falls into the following main categories:

- sales, relating to
  - customers
  - demand volumes
  - market share
  - price index expectations
- product margins
- purchase price index expectations

- overheads
- headcount
- new product development
- capital investment
- working capital
- cash
- non-financial performance indicators, in areas such as
  - product quality
  - staff development
  - delivery performance
  - customer satisfaction.

Many companies have developed dynamic budgeting models, using packaged IT solutions that may link financial and non-financial performance measures.

The major purposes of budgeting may be identified as:

- compelling planning and forcing management to look ahead by
  - setting targets
  - anticipating problems
  - giving the organisation purpose and direction
- formalising the communication of ideas and plans to all appropriate individuals
- co-ordinating activities of different business units and departments
- establishing a system of control, by
  - allocating responsibility
  - providing a plan against which actual performance may be measured and evaluated
- motivating improved performance of personnel.

It may be seen from many job advertisements how motivation is recognised as being extremely important in providing a vital link with individual performance, which in turn links with achievement of corporate budget targets.

The emphasis given to each budget purpose varies, and is very much dependent upon:

- company policy
- the way in which information is provided/received and by whom
- the negotiating skills of each manager with the company's budget team.

Problems of conflict arise out of actual and perceived fulfilment of each of the purposes of the budget. Each area is a minefield of potential problems of conflict. For example, it was revealed in 2005 that the chief executive of a major UK retailer only wanted to hear good news about the company's position in the marketplace. The managers were afraid to give him bad news.

There are basic problems within the process of setting targets. Organisations can be very unforgiving when targets are not achieved. The budget preparation process has become easier to manage with the introduction of powerful IT resources; but it has also resulted in more accuracy required within the estimates and also within a shorter time-frame.

During the budget-setting process, it is essential that individual budget holders 'buy in' to their budgets to enable subsequent meaningful monitoring and evaluation of actual performance. Their budgets, while representing difficult-to-meet targets, must also be achievable to provide the necessary motivation to reach their goals.

Responsibility must be matched with control. Costs that should be considered uncontrollable may not necessarily be treated as such in evaluating individual performance, resulting in discontent and demotivation. Similar conflicts arise if there is insufficient clarification, or if costs are controlled by more than one person; for example, special transport costs incurred to meet production needs through supplier non-performance – a manufacturing or purchasing responsibility?

Performance against budgeted costs at the operating level should be flexed to reflect current activity. This may not always happen, resulting in unfair appraisal of individual performance and misrepresentation of company performance. It is quite obvious that managers have no influence on the basic 'health' of their company's industrial sector; note the examples of mobile telephones (expanding in the UK) and coal (declining in the UK), seen in the latter part of the twentieth century.

Budgeted levels of training, particularly operator quality training, must be evaluated considering short-term profitability performance objectives and longer-term goals of zero defects. The aim must be of course to achieve both! A well-known UK car manufacturer used the pressure of telephone calls from customers direct to the factory floor, to reduce defects in the finished motor cars, especially those going into the export markets. Another UK manufacturer of motor cars required the engines to be signed for by the appropriate engineer, so that the customer could identify who was responsible for that particular engine.

Many materials may be procured in foreign currency. Should the performance of the purchasing department (responsible for supplier selection) reflect the impact of any resultant currency rate variances? Or should performance be measured using standard exchange rates prevailing at the outset, with, say, the finance department (usually responsible for hedging activities) bearing the cost of currency movements?

Major conflicts arise out of management of the operating cycle, the objective being its minimisation, through reduced debtor and stock days and extended creditor days. The company treasurer must respect this objective, while maintaining good relationships with customers and suppliers, and ensuring no threat to operations. The purchasing and manufacturing directors must ensure low stock days, while maintaining buffer stocks to cover disasters and ensuring that schedules are met, through perhaps the use of JIT processes.

When extremely tight time constraints are imposed for the budget-setting process (which is invariably the case in practice) this may conflict with the degree of accuracy possible in reporting. It also means that top management commitment is critical in providing timely:

- direction
- communication
- feedback

required for the budget process.

The final budget is inevitably a quantitative representation of future plans and targets, and the ways in which each company will reach its short-term goals. Whilst increasing attention is now paid to non-financial measures, the focus remains on performance in financial terms. That being so, traditional cost allocation methods continue to distort the way in which product profitability is reported. This, together with the short-term emphasis of the budgeting activity, therefore provides potentially misleading results. It may also have a demotivating effect on managers involved in both commercial and manufacturing activities, which may result in poor performance.

The problems encountered in the budgeting process may be summarised to include:

- the need for good planning
- difficulties with attitudes including lack of motivation, trust and honesty

- the problems in gathering information
- timeliness of the information
- the amount of detail required
- responsibility for the budget and the key performance areas within the budget.

This outline of some of the problems that may be encountered in the budgeting process may appear to give a negative perspective to its use as an instrument of planning and control. However, the conflicts, by their very nature, ideally serve to highlight the important issues and ensure that budgeting is not just a mechanical exercise carried out once or twice a year but a dynamic part of the strategic planning process contributing to successful management of the business.

> **Progress check 11.8** **What are the key aims of budgeting and what sort of problems are encountered that may prevent those aims being met?**

Summary of key points

- A budget is a plan and budgeting is one part of the strategic planning process, which is concerned with planning and control.
- Planning budgets are management's belief of what the business's costs and revenues will be over a specified future time period, the budget period.
- Control budgets are used for management motivational purposes and are used in this way to influence improved departmental performance.
- Forecasts are not plans but predictions of the future, which are required as an important prerequisite to the budget process.
- Prior to budget preparation, in addition to forecasting, decisions must be made and policies formulated regarding stock days and purchasing, debtor and creditor days, staff costs, capital expenditure, and standard costs.
- The master profit and loss budget is prepared from each of the elements of the operating budget: sales; production; distribution and administration; and the financial budget.
- The master budget is comprised of the profit and loss budget, cash budget, and balance sheet budget.
- Risk assessment and risk analysis should be applied to the master budget, and it must be closely reviewed in terms of additional funding requirements.
- As part of the control function of the budget, the system of responsibility accounting is used to measure actual results against budget for each of the various types of responsibility centre.
- Control budgets are usually flexed to reflect actual activity levels, and performance against budget provided from exception reporting is evaluated so that corrective actions may be implemented as appropriate.
- The preparation of budgets for planning and control purposes needs the involvement of people to provide realistic plans and the motivation for performance targets to be achieved.
- One aim of the use of economic value added (EVA) as a measure of performance is to overcome the lack of goal congruence with the whole organisation that may result from the use of ROI and RI as divisional performance measures.

> ■ There are usually many conflicts and problems associated with the budget preparation process in most organisations, the majority of which are concerned with the 'softer' human resources issues of managers' behaviour.

Questions

Q11.1   **(i)**   Why do businesses need to prepare budgets?

            (ii)   What are they used for?

Q11.2   If there are differences between budgets prepared for planning purposes and budgets prepared for control purposes, what are these differences?

Q11.3   Describe and illustrate the differences between qualitative and quantitative forecasting techniques.

Q11.4   **(i)**   Give some examples of the forecasts that are required to be able to prepare the complete master budget.

            (ii)   What are the most suitable techniques for each of these forecasts?

Q11.5   Draw a flow diagram to illustrate the budget preparation process.

Q11.6   Explain and illustrate the way in which a business may approach the strategic management process.

Q11.7   **(i)**   What are the internal and external sources of funding for a business?

            (ii)   How may a business use the budget process to assess its future funding requirements?

Q11.8   How does the assignment of individual budget responsibility contribute to improved organisational performance?

Q11.9   Discuss the ways in which a budget may be used to evaluate performance.

Q11.10   Outline some of the major problems that may be encountered in budgeting.

Q11.11   Performance is frequently measured using residual income (RI) and return on investment (ROI). However, these measures are often criticised for placing too great an emphasis on short-term results, with the possible effect of damaging longer-term performance.

            (i)   Discuss the issues involved in the long-term/short-term conflict referred to above.

            (ii)   Suggest some of the ways in which these issues may be reconciled.

Discussion points

D11.1 'Once I know what the forecast sales are for next year I can tell you how much profit we will make within five minutes, so there's no need for this annual time-wasting and costly budgeting ritual.' Discuss.

D11.2 'The area of budgeting is a minefield of potential problems of conflict.' How can these problems be usefully used as a learning experience to ultimately improve the performance of the business?

D11.3 You are the general manager of a newly formed subsidiary company. The group managing director has declared that he has targeted your company to make a profit of £250,000 in its first year.

What assumptions, decisions and policies are concerned with preparing a budget by working backwards from a starting point of budgeted profit?

Exercises

Solutions are provided in Appendix 4 to all exercise numbers highlighted in colour.

Level I

E11.1 *Time allowed – 15 minutes*

Earextensions plc set up a new business to assemble mobile phones from kits. They planned to make and sell one model only and expected to sell 441,200 units between January and June in their first year of trading. February, March, and April volumes were each expected to be 20% above the preceding month and May, June, and July volumes were expected to be the same as April. The selling price was £50 each.

Cost prices for the parts used in making a phone were as follows:

Electronic assembly	Keypad	Case
£23.30	£1	£2

Operators and assemblers were employed to make the phones with the following hourly rates and standard times used in production:

	Assemblers	Operators
Hourly rate	£10	£8
Standard minutes	3	1.5

Production overheads were forecast at £4.1m, which was incurred on an equal monthly basis and absorbed into product costs on the basis of direct labour hours.

At 31 December the numbers of units in stock were estimated at:

Finished product	Quantity		Quantity	
	zero	**Materials**		
		Electronic		
		assembly	10,000	
		Keypad	30,000	} purchased in December
		Case	20,000	

Materials stock levels at the end of each month were planned to be 50% of the following month's usage. Finished product stock levels at the end of each month were planned to be 20% of the following month's sales.

Earextensions plc have budgeted selling and administrative costs of £4.5m for the six months. The first three months were evenly spread at 60% of the total and the second three months evenly spread at 40% of the total. Production overheads included total depreciation of £50,000 budgeted for 6 months. Financing costs over the 6 months were expected in line with sales at 0.2% of sales value.

Earextensions plc prepared an estimated balance sheet for its new subsidiary at 31 December as follows:

	£	£
Fixed assets	495,000	
Stocks	303,000	
Trade debtors	–	
Cash and bank	355,000	1,153,000
Trade creditors	303,000	
Loans	450,000	
Share capital	400,000	
Retained earnings	–	1,153,000

Trade debtors were expected to pay in the second month following the month of sale and trade creditors were planned to be paid in the third month following the month of purchase. Direct labour, production overheads, and selling and administrative costs are all paid in the month in which they are incurred. There was no further planned capital expenditure during the first six months.

You are required to prepare a phased sales budget in units and values for the six months January to June.

E11.2 *Time allowed – 30 minutes*
Using the information from Exercise E11.1 prepare a phased finished product stocks and a phased production budget in units for the six months January to June.

Level II

E11.3 *Time allowed – 30 minutes*
Using the information from Exercise E11.1 prepare a unit gross margin budget and a phased direct labour budget for the six months January to June.

E11.4 *Time allowed – 30 minutes*
Using the information from Exercise E11.1 prepare a phased materials stocks, materials usage and purchases budget in units and values for the six months January to June.

E11.5 *Time allowed – 30 minutes*
Using the information from Exercise E11.1 prepare a phased selling and administrative costs budget, and financial budget for the six months January to June, and a phased profit and loss account budget, using absorption costing, for the six months January to June.

E11.6 *Time allowed – 30 minutes*
Using the information from Exercise E11.1 prepare a finished product valuation budget for the six months January to June.

E11.7 *Time allowed – 30 minutes*

An extract of the financial results for 2004 for three of the operating divisions of Marx plc is shown below:

Division	Chico	Groucho	Harpo
Average net operating assets	£7.5m	£17.5m	£12.5m
Operating profit	£1.5m	£1.4m	£2.0m
Administrative expenses	£0.8m	£0.3m	£0.65m
Divisional cost of capital per annum	7%	5%	10%

Required:

(i)   Calculate the ROI for each division for 2004.

(ii) Calculate the RI for each division for 2004.

(iii) Each division is presented with an investment opportunity that is expected to yield a return of 9%.

   (a) Which division(s) would accept and which division(s) would reject the investment opportunity if divisional performance is measured by ROI, and why?
   (b) Which division(s) would accept and which division(s) would reject the investment opportunity if divisional performance is measured by RI, and why?

E11.8 *Time allowed – 60 minutes*

Using the information from Exercise E11.1 prepare a creditors' budget and a debtors' budget, and a phased cash budget for the six months January to June.

E11.9 *Time allowed – 60 minutes*

Using the information from Exercise E11.1 prepare a phased balance sheet budget for the six months January to June.

12

Budgetary control

Contents

Learning objectives

Completion of this chapter will enable you to:

- use standard costing in the budget process
- use standard costing in performance evaluation and control
- identify the use of flexible budgeting in performance evaluation and control
- prepare flexed budgets in line with changes in activity levels
- explain what is meant by a variance between actual and standard performance
- appreciate the importance of variance analysis in exception reporting
- calculate the individual variances used to explain differences between actual and standard performance
- summarise variances in the form of standard cost operating statements
- explain the reasons for variances between actual and standard performance
- appreciate the differences between planning and operational variances.

Introduction

In Chapter 11 we illustrated the budget preparation process with the construction of budgets using:

- forecast volumes
- forecast prices
- policy decisions relating to capital expenditure and working capital
- unit product costs.

This chapter will explore in greater detail how the costs of units of a product or a process are determined. We will look at how standards may be used in the budgeting process to cost each unit or process. The budgeted unit or process cost is called its standard cost.

This chapter will explain the technique of standard costing and the ways in which actual performance may be measured and compared with the budget through the use of variance analysis. We will look at how, using standard costs, the budget may be flexed to reflect actual levels of activity, and then used to calculate individual variances. Individual variances may then be investigated to explain the reasons for the differences between actual and expected performance.

The process of explaining significant variances from standard continues to be considered as a powerful management tool. This chapter closes by introducing a further refinement to variance analysis through the use of planning and operational variances.

Variance analysis is almost exclusively concerned with the comparison of performance against short-term budget targets. Short-term performance is very important. However the achieving, or exceeding, of short-term targets should not be considered in isolation, which may ignore or be to the detriment of longer-term objectives (see the extract from *Accountancy Age* below).

The Homer Simpson approach to budgetary control

The business world lost one of its most colourful characters when the board of directors at Rentokil Initial dumped chairman Sir Clive Thompson after more than 20 years with the nation's leading ratcatcher. Once known as 'Mr 20%' for his ability to grow the group's earnings by that amount every year, the senior independent director Sir Brian McGowan let it be known that Sir Clive had recently become too obsessed with meeting short-term targets and had failed to invest in long-term growth.

Now admittedly John Maynard Keynes said that in the long run we're all dead (though someone else once added,'Yes, but not all at the same time!').

Seventies entrepreneur Jim Slater used to say that a long-term investment was a short-term investment that has gone wrong. And, of course, we've all seen project plans that have 'year four' hockey stick projections.

So an overemphasis on the long-term at the expense of keeping on top of the day-to-day business can be just as fatal – but judging by a recent report, that's not the way businesses appear to work. A US study by two universities and the National Bureau of Economic Research demonstrates quite conclusively that senior executives trade off long-term economic value so as to meet short-term earnings targets to satisfy investors. This finding comes two years after PricewaterhouseCoopers castigated companies, saying that many businesses 'confuse short-term shareholder appeasement with effective cost control'.

The bizarre thing is, many businesses know this is going on – surplus cash gets committed before the year-end on a use-it-or-lose-it approach to budgeting, good projects get deferred till a period that has some slack in it – but no one does anything about it. Homer Simpson put it best: 'Marge,' he exclaimed, 'if you're going to get mad at me every time I do something stupid then I'm going to have to stop doing stupid things.' Maybe we could start by encouraging everyone – from line managers to FDs to institutional investors – to regularly ask, 'What stupid things have been done in order to make the company look really clever?'

Management lessons from Homer Simpson, by Andrew Sawers

© *Accountancy Age*, 1 June 2004

Standard costing

Although forecasting and budgeting systems should reflect realistic expectations, it is inevitable that differences will arise between actual and expected performance. It is extremely important that the planning and budgeting process includes control systems that enable accurate feedback of actual performance at the right time to the appropriate people within the organisation. Budgetary control systems should ensure that information is regularly communicated and evaluated by key decision-makers in an organisation, so that appropriate action may taken as necessary. Budgetary control systems must provide:

- fast reporting of performance
- quick response in the implementation of remedial actions
- timely revision of forecasts.

As part of the budgeting process, or at any other time when actual costs need to be compared with planned costs, a basis for comparison must be established. Standard costing provides such a basis through the setting of predetermined cost estimates.

A standard cost is defined as the planned unit cost of the products, components or services produced in a period, and it may be determined using many alternative bases. The main uses of standard costs are:

- measurement of business performance
- control of processes
- valuation of stocks
- establishment of selling prices.

Standards may be defined as benchmark measurements of resource usage, set in defined conditions, and can be set on a number of bases:

- on an *ex ante* (before the event) estimate of expected performance
- on an *ex post* (after the event) estimate of attainable performance
- on a prior level of performance by the same organisation
- on the level of performance achieved by comparable organisations
- on the level of performance required to meet organisational objectives.

Standards may also be set at attainable levels which assume efficient levels of operation, but which include allowances for normal loss, waste and machine downtime, or at ideal levels, which make no allowance for the above losses, and are only attainable under the most favourable conditions.

Budgeted costs and standard costs are sometimes used to mean the same thing but this is not always so. All amounts in a budget are budgeted amounts, but not all budgeted amounts are standard amounts. Budgeted costs are usually used to describe the total planned costs for a number of products. Standard amounts relate to a series of specific processes. For example, one of the processes included in production of a bottle of beer, the sticking of the label on to the bottle, is a process that includes the time and the cost of the label.

A standard product specification is a statement containing a full breakdown of the cost elements, which are included in the standard cost of a product or service. For each cost element (direct labour, direct material, overhead) a standard input quantity and standard unit input cost are shown as well as standard cost per unit of output produced.

A bill of materials is a detailed specification, for each product produced, of the sub-assemblies, components and materials required, distinguishing between those items that are purchased externally and those which are manufactured in-house. Having established the quality and other specifications of materials required, the purchasing department estimates costs based on suppliers' prices, inflation and the availability of bulk discounts, in order to establish direct material unit costs.

The standard direct labour cost is the planned average cost of direct labour, based on the standard time for the job and standard performance. A standard hour is the amount of work achievable, at standard efficiency levels, in an hour. Work study and analysis of the learning curve are techniques that may be used to assist in determining standard hours. The standard time for a job is the time in which a task should be completed at standard performance.

Standard performance is the level of efficiency, which appropriately trained, motivated and resourced employees can achieve in the long run. Initially, the time taken to produce a specific level of output is longer than the time taken after 'normal' employees have been adequately trained and have gained experience of the process. Time taken to achieve specific levels of output will reduce over time, but the amount of the reductions in time will also reduce over time until almost negligible. This is called the learning curve effect, and when time reductions have virtually ceased the curve becomes horizontal. It is that level, where the long-term time for the particular activity has been established, that may be considered standard performance for the activity. The standard direct labour cost is then calculated by multiplying a standard direct labour hour by a standard hourly rate. Direct labour rates per hour are determined with reference to the type of skills to be used, union agreements, inflation and market rates.

> **Progress check 12.1** **What is meant by the standard cost of a product and what type of specifications and analyses are required prior to being able to calculate a standard cost?**

A typical standard cost for a unit of a product may be illustrated in the following worked example.

Worked Example 12.1

Applejack Ltd manufactures drums of high grade apple pie filling that uses two types of material, apples and sugar, and requires one grade of direct labour. The company additionally incurs some variable and fixed production overheads, which are absorbed into the unit costs of the product. The standard cost for a drum (one unit) of the product may be represented as follows, where overheads have been absorbed on the basis of direct labour hours:

		£
Direct materials		
Sugar	1 kilo at £2 per kilo =	2
Apples	2 kilos at £3 per kilo =	6
		8
Direct labour		
1 hour at £8 per hour		8
Variable production overhead		
1 hour at £2 per hour		2
Fixed production overhead		
1 hour at £3 per hour		3
Standard full production cost per drum		21

Advantages of standard costs

There are several advantages in using a standard costing system:

- it is a basis for budget preparation
- it may be used in planning and control
- it can be used to highlight areas of strength and weakness
- it can be used in evaluation of performance by comparing actual costs with standard costs and so assisting in implementation of responsibility accounting
- it should result in the use of the best resources and best methods and so increase efficiency
- it may be used as a basis for stock valuation
- it can be used as a basis for pay incentive schemes
- it can be used for decision-making in its estimation of future costs

- it fits in with management by exception, whereby only significant variances (differences between actual and expected results) are investigated, so making effective use of management time
    - control action is immediate because, for example, as soon as materials are issued from stores into production they can be compared with the standard materials which should be required for actual production
    - transfer prices (the prices at which goods or services are transferred from one process or department to another or from one company in the group to another) may be based on standard rather than actual costs to avoid inefficiencies in the form of excess costs.

Disadvantages of standard costs

There are also a number of disadvantages in using a standard costing system, not least of which is the difficulty in the establishment of the standard fixed overhead rate if standard absorption costing is used as opposed to standard marginal costing.

Standard costing requires a great deal of input data, which can prove time-consuming and expensive, as can the maintenance of the cost database. The amount of detail required, together with a lack of historical detail, and lack of experience and further training requirements all add to this administrative burden.

Standard costing is usually used in organisations where the processes or jobs are repetitive. It is important to set accurate standards or else evaluation of performance will be meaningless. If the standard is weak then the comparison is of little value. However, it is difficult to strike a balance in setting accurate standards so that they both motivate the workforce and achieve the organisation's goals. There may be difficulties in determining which variances against standard are significant, and too narrow a focus on certain variances may exclude other useful information.

If performance evaluation is linked to management by exception, which assumes actual equals standard unless variances contradict that, there may be attempts by managers to cover up negative results. Morale may suffer if reprimands follow poor results and managers are not praised for positive results.

Further adverse impacts on behaviour may occur if managers and supervisors feel that they do not have an overall view and are involved only in limited areas, seeing only a small part of the big picture. Responsibility accounting must also ensure that controllable and non-controllable variances are separately identified.

Operating difficulties and frustration may be encountered through, for example, technological and environmental factors, assessment of standards of performance, departmental interdependence, variances reported at the wrong levels, the timing of revisions to standards, over-reaction to results, and the constant need to estimate. It is important to remember that there is a great deal of uncertainty in setting standards costs. This can arise due to inflation, economic and political factors. Standards therefore need to be continually updated and revised – once a year is usually not often enough.

> **Progress check 12.2 To what extent do the advantages of the use of standard costing outweigh its disadvantages?**

Types of standard

In addition to current costs there are three types of standard that may be used as the basis for a standard costing system. The use of current standards by definition relates to current circumstances with regard to performance levels, wastage and inefficiencies. It may be observed from the following explanations that 'standard costing' can be seen to be flexible and dynamic. It should not be seen as a straitjacket.

➡ Basic standards are those that remain unchanged since the previous period and probably many previous periods. They may be used for comparison but are likely to be out of date and irrelevant. As business circumstances may change dramatically in the marketplace, so the original basic standard will not reflect the current situation.

➡ Ideal standards are the results expected from perfect performance under perfect conditions. They assume no wastage, or inefficiencies. However, although they may be aimed for they will be impossible to achieve and therefore provide a poor motivational tool.

➡ Attainable standards are the results expected under normal operating conditions, having some allowances for wastage and a degree of inefficiency. Attainable standards should be set to be difficult but not impossible to achieve; they may therefore provide the most challenging targets and give the greatest motivation for achievement.

> **Progress check 12.3** **What are the different types of standard that may be used as the basis for standard costing and which one may be the most appropriate?**

Flexed budgets

We discussed flexible budgeting in Chapter 11. Control budgets need to be revised in line with actual levels of activity to provide more realistic levels of expected costs against which to measure performance. Such a revised budget is called a flexed budget which shows the costs (and revenues) expected as a result of changes in activity levels from those planned within the master budget.

The standards chosen for use in the budget preparation are also used in the revised flexed budget to provide a method of comparison with actual performance. This method allows comparison of costs on a like-for-like basis and so enables meaningful exception reporting of the analysis of variances.

➡ This system of management control uses a closed-loop system. This is a system which allows corrective action using a feedforward or a feedback basis. A feedback control system is shown in Fig. 12.1 and provides the measurement of differences between planned outputs and actual outputs and the modification of subsequent actions or plans to achieve future required results. Figure 12.2 illustrates a feedforward control system which forecasts differences between actual and planned outcomes and implements action before the event to avoid such differences.

Normally, fixed overheads by definition are fixed over the short term regardless of changes in the level of activity, for example units sold, units produced, number of invoices. Equally, direct labour and direct materials costs may be assumed to vary directly with sales. In practice, there is usually a wide band of activity over which direct labour costs may not vary.

Care should be taken in using the above assumptions but we may consider that they hold true for the purpose of illustration of flexed budgets and variance analysis. The variance analysis can be routine but decisions resulting from the interpretation can be far-reaching. Consider how, following

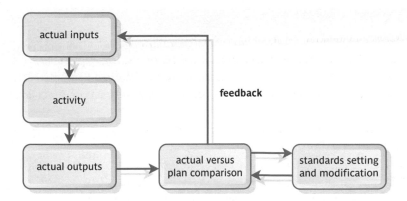

Figure 12.1 Feedback control system

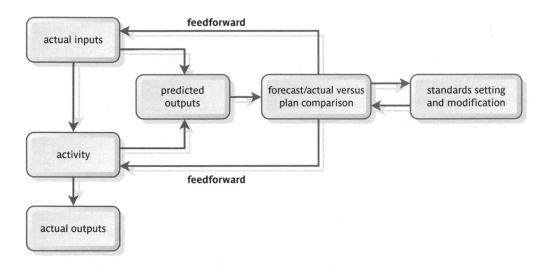

Figure 12.2 Feedforward control system

the public's reaction to buying products originating from genetically modified foodstuffs (soya or maize), many UK supermarkets publicly announced they would cease stocking them.

> **Progress check 12.4** Describe the way in which flexed budgets are used in a management control system.

The worked example that follows shows how a straight comparison of actual with budgeted performance may be refined through the preparation of a revised budget flexed in line with the actual activity level.

If we compare the total manufacturing cost from the flexed budget shown in Worked Example 12.2 with the total actual cost for the month, the performance looks even better than the comparison with the total budgeted cost; the total cost is £1,447 [£13,650 − £12,203] less than expected at that level of output. However, whilst the comparison of total cost is favourable, this does not tell us anything about individual performance within each element of the budget; the impacts of

Worked Example 12.2

Applejack Ltd planned to produce 600 drums of pie filling during September. The budget for September was prepared using the standard costs shown in Worked Example 12.1. Fixed overheads are budgeted at £1,800 for September and absorbed on the basis of direct labour hours.

Budget costs for September

Production	600 units
	£
Direct materials	
Sugar 600 kilos at £2 per kilo =	1,200
Apples 1,200 kilos at £3 per kilo =	3,600
	4,800
Direct labour	
600 hours at £8 per hour	4,800
Variable production overhead	
600 hours at £2 per hour	1,200
Fixed production overhead	
600 hours at £3 per hour	1,800
Total production cost	12,600

600 drums of filling were planned to be produced in the month at a manufacturing cost of £12,600.

At the end of September the actual output turned out to be 650 drums as follows:

Actual costs for September

Production	650 units
	£
Direct materials	
Sugar 610 kilos at £2.10 per kilo =	1,281
Apples 1,210 kilos at £3.20 per kilo =	3,872
	5,153
Direct labour	
500 hours at £9 per hour	4,500
Variable production overhead	
500 hours at £1.50 per hour	750
Fixed production overhead	
500 hours at £3.60 per hour	1,800
Total production cost	12,203

650 drums of filling were actually produced in the month at a manufacturing cost of £12,203.

The above data can be used to prepare a flexed budget for September as the basis for subsequent variance analysis.

A flexed budget for Applejack Ltd must be prepared for 650 drums output. The flexed budget will use the standard costs shown in Worked Example 12.1 to show what the costs would have been if the budget had been based on 650 drums instead of 600 drums.

Flexed budget costs for September

Production	650 units
	£
Direct materials	
Sugar 650 kilos at £2 per kilo =	1,300
Apples 1,300 kilos at £3 per kilo =	3,900
	5,200
Direct labour	
650 hours at £8 per hour	5,200
Variable production overhead	
650 hours at £2 per hour	1,300
Fixed production overhead	
650 hours at £3 per hour	1,950
Total production cost	13,650

If 650 drums of filling had been planned to be produced in the month the standard manufacturing cost would be £13,650.

the differences between the actual and the flexed budget with regard to:

- amounts of materials used
- materials prices
- direct labour hours
- direct labour rates
- overheads.

The analysis of the detailed variances in respect of each cost can identify each element making up the cost, the unit costs and the unit quantities, and tell us something about whether the individual cost performances were good or bad. From the year 2000 to date the UK has seen an amazing upward demand for mobile telephones and a decline in the demand for university places (as a percentage of available places). Both sectors would have carried out an 'analysis of the detailed variances' during that year to assist in the determination of conclusions regarding cost performance.

> **Progress check 12.5 In what ways does a flexed budget provide a more realistic measure of actual performance than comparison with the original budget?**

Variance analysis

A variance is the difference between a planned, budgeted or standard cost and the actual cost incurred. The same comparisons may be made for revenues. Variance analysis is the evaluation of performance by means of variances, whose timely reporting should maximise the opportunity for managerial action. These variances will be either favourable variances (F) or adverse variances (A). Neither should occur if the standard is correct and actual performance is as expected. A favourable variance is not necessarily good – it may be due to a weak standard. Management by exception assumes that actual performance will be the same as the standard unless variances contradict this.

Detailed variances can identify each difference within the elements making up cost or revenue by looking at unit prices and unit quantities. Variances may be due to:

- measurement errors
- use of standards that are out of date
- operations that are out of control
- random factors.

When variances occur it must then be considered as to whether these variances should be investigated or not. The variances may not be material, or it may not be cost effective to carry out such an investigation.

Calculation of variances

Let's look at the individual variances that occurred for the month of September in Applejack's manufacture of apple pie filling. We will analyse each of the variances and provide a detailed, line-by-line comparison of actual versus budget performance of each of the items that comprise the total actual to budget favourable variance of £397. The simplest way to start to examine the differences is to present the original budget, flexed budget and actual results in three columns for further analysis.

Worked Example 12.3

We saw from Worked Example 12.2 that on the face of it Applejack's performance for September was very good – higher than budget output (650 versus 600 units) at lower than budget costs (£12,203 versus £12,600).

Is it a good performance? If it is, how much of a good performance is it?

To determine how good Applejack's performance was for September we need to provide an analysis of variances to explain the favourable total cost variance of £397 against budget (£12,600 – £12,203).

Applejack Ltd's budget, actual and flexed budget (from Worked Example 12.2) for the production of apple pie filling for the month of September may be summarised as follows:

	Budget	Flexed	Actual	Difference Actual–Flexed
Units	600	650	650	–

	£		£		£	£

Direct materials

Sugar	(600 × £2)	1,200	(650 × £2)	1,300	(610 × £2.10)	1,281	19
Apples	(1,200 × £3)	3,600	(1,300 × £3)	3,900	(1,210 × £3.20)	3,872	28
		4,800		5,200		5,153	47

Direct labour

| | (600 × £8) | 4,800 | (650 × £8) | 5,200 | (500 × £9) | 4,500 | 700 |

Variable production overhead

| | (600 × £2) | 1,200 | (650 × £2) | 1,300 | (500 × £1.50) | 750 | 550 |

Fixed production overhead

| | (600 × £3) | 1,800 | (650 × £3) | 1,950 | (500 × £3.60) | 1,800 | 150 |
| **Total cost** | | **12,600** | | **13,650** | | **12,203** | **1,447** |

Figure 12.3 Applejack Ltd's actual and flexed budget costs for September

The above graphical representation of each of the cost elements and the total of actual costs compared with the flexed budget for output of 650 units gives a broad picture of Applejack Ltd's good performance.

Let us look at the detailed variances.

We have prepared a flexed budget, which in effect gives us a new starting point against which to compare actual performance more realistically. We have therefore already built in a variance, arising out of the change in volume from 600 drums to 650 drums. At a unit cost of £21 the total of this difference, or variance, is an adverse volume variance of £1,050 (50 × £21).

Volume:

Variance 650 drums less 600 drums at a total unit cost of £21 per drum   £1,050A

We also need to consider the individual cost element variances, between actual costs and the flexed budget costs.

Materials:	
Sugar usage was 40 kilos less than it should have been at a standard cost of £2 per kilo	£80F
The sugar price was 10p more per kilo than standard for the 610 kilos used	£61A
Apples usage was 90 kilos less than it should have been at a standard cost of £3 per kilo	£270F
The apple price was 20p more per kilo than standard for the 1,210 kilos used	£242A
Total materials variance actual versus flexed budget	£47F
Direct labour:	
Hours worked were 150 hours less than they should have been at a standard rate of £8 per hour	£1,200F
The labour rate was £1 more per hour than standard for the 500 hours worked	£500A
Total direct labour variance actual versus flexed budget	£700F
Variable production overhead:	
Hours worked were 150 hours less than they should have been at a standard rate of £2 per hour	£300F
The overhead rate was 50p less per hour than standard for the 500 hours worked	£250F
Total variable production overhead variance actual versus flexed budget	£550F
Fixed production overhead:	
Hours worked were 150 hours less than they should have been at a standard rate of £3 per hour	£450F
Hours worked were 100 less (at £3 per hour) than required to absorb total fixed costs	£300A
Total fixed production overhead variance actual versus flexed budget	£150F
Total variances [£1,050A + £47F + £700F + £550F + £150F] =	£397F
Budget total costs	£12,600
Actual total costs	£12,203
Total variance (favourable)	£397

Several variances are calculated to quantify the difference in activity or volume. Most of the other variances show the impact of:

- differences in prices
  - price variances
  - rate variances
  - expenditure variances

and

- differences in quantities

- usage variances
- efficiency variances

between those prices and quantities actually incurred and those which should have been expected at the actual level, or volume of output. The exception to this is the fixed production overhead variance, which is comprised of a fixed production overhead expenditure variance (budget minus actual cost) and a fixed production overhead volume variance.

The total fixed production variance is the difference between:

■ the actual cost

and

■ the cost shown in the flexed budget.

The two components of the total fixed production volume variance are:

■ the fixed production overhead efficiency variance
  - a 'normal' one that calculates the difference between actual and flexed hours at the standard overhead absorption rate
■ the fixed production overhead capacity variance
  - calculates the difference between actual and budgeted hours at the standard overhead absorption rate
  - measures the amount by which overheads have been under- or over-absorbed (under-absorbed in the Applejack example), caused by the actual hours worked differing from the hours originally budgeted to be worked.

In the Applejack example we have used the absorption costing approach to calculate unit standard costs for the product and therefore in the calculation of variances. Marginal costing may also be used to calculate unit standard costs for the product and calculation of variances. Some of the differences between the variances that are calculated are as one would expect, using contribution instead of profit. Another difference is in respect of production fixed costs, which of course are not absorbed into unit marginal product costs. The fixed production overhead variance using marginal costing is simply the difference between the actual and the budgeted cost.

> **Progress check 12.6 What does variance analysis tell us about actual performance that a direct analysis of differences to budget cannot tell us?**

The hierarchy of variances in Figs. 12.4 and 12.5 show variances using marginal costing principles and variances using absorption costing principles respectively.

A non-accountant will not usually be called upon to calculate variances. However, as a manager, it is important to appreciate clearly the way in which variances are calculated, to be better able to:

■ consider their materiality
■ investigate the reasons for their occurrence if necessary
■ take the appropriate corrective actions.

Explanation of variances is usually part of the day-to-day responsibilities of most budget holding managers. Unless there is knowledge of exactly what a variance represents it is virtually impossible to begin to determine the reason why such a variance occurred. Figures 12.6 and 12.9 include the detailed formulae for the calculation of variances, on a marginal costing basis. Figures 12.10 and

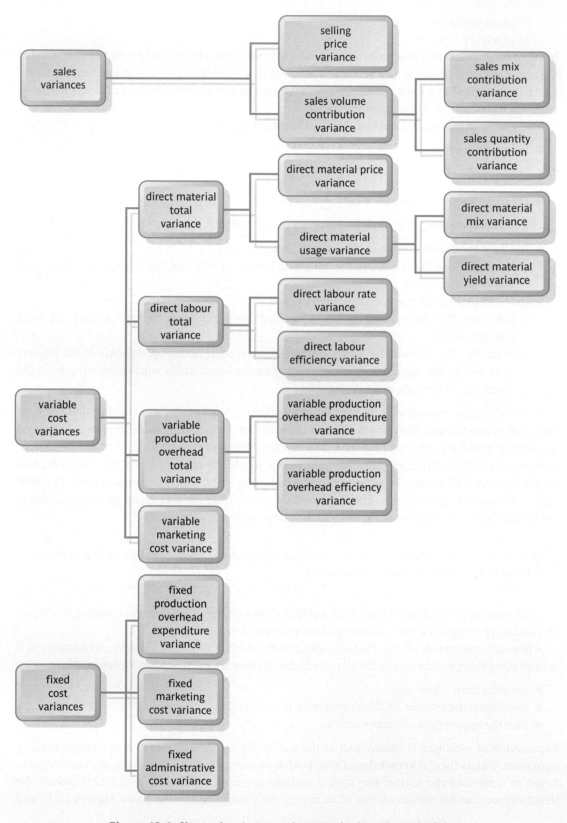

Figure 12.4 Chart of variances using marginal costing principles

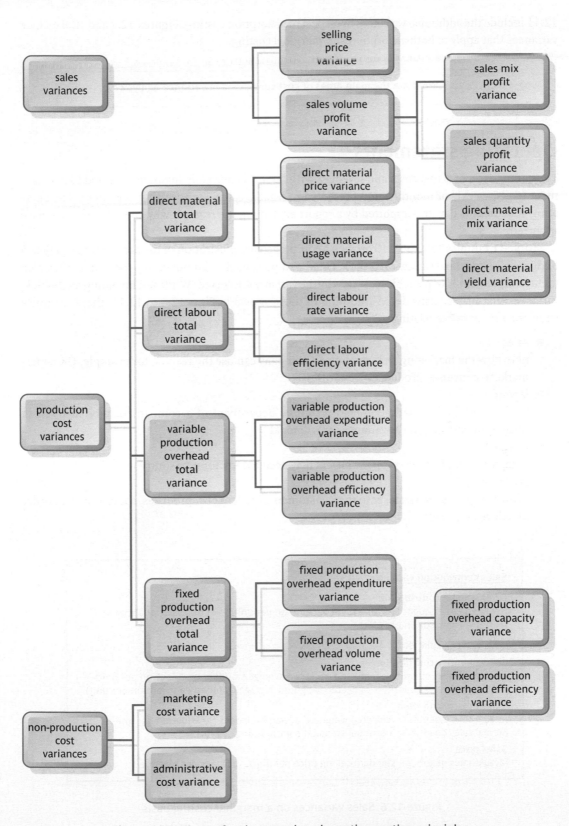

Figure 12.5 Chart of variances using absorption costing principles

12.11 include the additional variances in respect of absorption costing. Figures 12.7 and 12.8 include variances that apply to both absorption and marginal costing.

> Progress check 12.7 **What are the main areas of cost considered in variance analysis?**

Operating statements

The comparison of actual costs and revenues with budget is normally regularly reported to management (daily, weekly or monthly) and presented in what is called an operating statement. The operating statement is usually supported by a report explaining the reasons why specific variances have occurred.

Worked Examples 12.4 to 12.10 provide a comprehensive illustration of the preparation of a flexed budget and show how variances are calculated and presented in an operating statement. They also include explanations of possible reasons why the variances occurred. While not including all possible variances that may be considered according to those shown in Figs. 12.4 to 12.11, these examples show the key variances relating to:

- sales
  note how the marketing department of a company can use the results, for example, UK supermarkets' consumer products special offers
- labour
  note, for example, how the human resources department of a company may be involved in further investigation if the variances are material
- materials
  note, for example, how company buyers may need to look for new sources
- overheads
  many companies move closer to their customers or to low-cost premises, for example, in order to reduce overheads.

Sales contribution variances

Sales volume contribution
(budgeted sales quantity × standard contribution per unit) − (actual sales quantity × standard contribution per unit)

Which can be split into:

Sales quantity contribution
(budgeted sales quantity × budgeted weighted average standard contribution per unit) − (total actual sales quantity × budgeted weighted average standard contribution per unit)

Sales mix contribution
(actual sales quantity × budgeted weighted average standard contribution per unit) − (actual sales quantity × individual standard contribution per unit)

Sales price
(actual sales quantity × standard selling price per unit) − actual sales revenue

---

Figure 12.6 Sales variances on a marginal costing basis

Materials variances

Direct material price
(actual quantity of material purchased × standard price) – actual cost of material purchased

Direct material usage
(standard quantity for actual production × standard material cost per unit) – (actual material quantity used × standard cost per unit)

Which can be split into:

Direct material mix
(actual input quantity – standard material input quantity for the output produced) × (standard weighted average cost per input unit – standard cost per input unit)

Direct material yield
(actual material input quantity – standard material input quantity for the output produced) × standard weighted average cost per unit of material input
Or
(actual material input quantity × standard cost per unit) – (total actual material input in standard proportions × standard cost per unit)

Figure 12.7 Direct materials variances

Labour variances

Direct labour rate
(actual hours paid × standard direct labour rate per hour) – (actual hours paid × actual direct labour rate per hour)

Direct labour efficiency
(actual production in standard hours × standard direct labour rate per hour) – (actual direct labour hours worked × standard direct labour rate per hour)

Figure 12.8 Direct labour variances

Overhead variances

Variable production overhead expenditure
actual cost incurred – (actual hours worked × standard variable production overhead absorption rate per hour)

Variable production overhead efficiency
(actual hours worked × standard variable production overhead absorption rate per hour) – (actual production in standard hours × standard variable production overhead absorption rate per hour)

Fixed production overhead expenditure
budgeted fixed production overhead – actual fixed production overhead

Figure 12.9 Overheads variances on a marginal costing basis

Sales profit variances

Sales volume profit
(budgeted sales quantity × standard profit per unit) – (actual sales quantity × standard profit per unit)

Which can be split into:

Sales quantity profit
(budgeted sales quantity × budgeted weighted average standard profit per unit) – (total actual sales quantity × budgeted weighted average standard profit per unit)

Sales mix profit
(actual sales quantity × budgeted weighted average standard profit per unit) – (actual sales quantity × individual standard profit per unit)

Figure 12.10 Sales variances on an absorption costing basis

Overheads variances

Fixed production overhead volume
(actual production in standard hours × standard fixed production overhead absorption rate per hour) – budgeted fixed production overhead

Which can be split into:

Fixed production overhead efficiency
(actual hours worked × standard fixed production overhead absorption rate per hour) – (actual production in standard hours × standard fixed production overhead absorption rate per hour)

Fixed production overhead capacity
(actual hours worked × standard fixed production overhead absorption rate per hour) – (budgeted hours to be worked × standard fixed production overhead absorption rate per hour)

Figure 12.11 Overheads variances on an absorption costing basis

Worked Example 12.4

Dymocks Ltd manufactures large ornamental garden pots, called the El Greco, the standards for which are as follows:

Direct labour	1 hour at £4 per hour
Direct materials	2 kgs at £7.50 per kg
Variable overheads	£3 per direct labour hour
Selling price	£50 per unit

Fixed overheads are budgeted at £4,000 and absorbed on a direct labour hours basis. Dymocks have budgeted to produce and sell 800 Grecos in the month of July.

Using standard costs, the budget for El Grecos for July was:

		£
Sales	800 × £50 per unit	40,000
Direct labour	800 × 1 hour × £4 per hour per unit	(3,200)
Direct materials	800 × 2 kg × £7.50 per kg per unit	(12,000)
Variable overheads	800 × 1 hour × £3 per direct labour hour	(2,400)
Fixed overheads	800 × 1 hour × £5 per direct labour hour	(4,000)
Budgeted profit for July		18,400

The standard profit per unit used in the budget $= \dfrac{£18,400}{800 \text{ units}} = £23$ per unit

Actual results for July were:

		£
Sales	900 × £48	43,200
Direct labour	850 hours × £3.50 per hour	(2,975)
Direct materials	1,400 kgs × £8 per kg	(11,200)
Variable overheads	Actual	(2,750)
Fixed overheads	Actual	(5,000)
Actual profit for July		21,275

The flexed budget for July, prepared from this data, can be used to give a summary that compares the actual results for July with the budget and the flexed budget.

The flexed budget for July for sales of 900 units is:

		£
Sales	900 × £50 per unit	45,000
Direct labour	900 × 1 hour × £4 per hour per unit	(3,600)
Direct materials	900 × 2 kg × £7.50 per kg per unit	(13,500)
Variable overheads	900 × 1 hour × £3 per direct labour hour	(2,700)
Fixed overheads	900 × 1 hour × £5 per direct labour hour	(4,500)
Flexed budgeted profit for July		20,700

The July results for Dymocks Ltd may be summarised as follows:

	£ Budget	£ Actual	£ Flexed	£ Difference Actual – Flexed
Sales	40,000	43,200	45,000	(1,800)
Direct labour	(3,200)	(2,975)	(3,600)	625
Direct materials	(12,000)	(11,200)	(13,500)	2,300
Variable overheads	(2,400)	(2,750)	(2,700)	(50)
Fixed overheads	(4,000)	(5,000)	(4,500)	(500)
Profit	18,400	21,275	20,700	575

The variance or the difference between the budget and the flexed budget of £2,300(F) (£20,700 – £18,400) is only due to volume. The profit variance for sales volume is the only one that will need to be considered between the flexed budget and the budget. All other variances are between actual results and the flexed budget.

Worked Example 12.5

Using the summary of results for Dymocks Ltd for July from Worked Example 12.4 we can prepare an analysis of sales variances, and provide an explanation of why these variances might have occurred.

Sales variances
Sales volume profit

(budgeted sales quantity × standard profit per unit) – (actual sales quantity × standard profit per unit)

measuring the effect of changing sales volumes on profit

$(800 \times £23) - (900 \times £23) = £2,300$ (F)   (the profit variance of £2,300 noted in Worked Example 12.4)

Sales price

(actual sales quantity × standard selling price per unit) – actual sales revenue

measuring the effect of selling prices different to those budgeted

$(900 \times £50) - £43,200 = £1,800$ (A)   (see Worked Example 12.4 summary)

Possible reasons for the above variances:

- selling prices are likely to affect sales volumes
- external factors such as economic recession, changes in demand, or increased competition
- prices not achievable perhaps due to lack of market research or bad planning.

Worked Example 12.6

Using the summary of results for Dymocks Ltd for July from Worked Example 12.4 we can prepare an analysis of materials variances, and provide an explanation of why these variances might have occurred.

Materials variances
Direct material price

(actual quantity of material purchased × standard price) – actual cost of material purchased

$(1,400 \times £7.50) - £11,200 \qquad = £700$ (A)

Direct material usage

(standard quantity for actual production × standard material cost per unit) − (actual material quantity used × standard cost per unit)

$(1,800 \times £7.50) - (1,400 \times £7.50)$ $= £3,000$ (F)

Total materials variances   £2,300 (F)   (see Worked Example 12.4 summary)

Possible reasons for the above variances:

- market conditions have changed
- foreign currency exchange rates may have changed (if applicable)
- supplier discounts have been reduced
- changes in the quality levels of materials used
- there may be a supplier invoicing error
- stock control has improved
- the skills of the labour force have changed
- production methods have changed.

Note that materials price variances occur at two points: standard price compared to receipt of goods price; receipt of goods price compared to invoiced price.

Worked Example 12.7

Using the summary of results for Dymocks Ltd for July from Worked Example 12.4 we can prepare an analysis of direct labour variances, and provide an explanation of why these variances might have occurred.

Direct labour variances

Direct labour rate

(actual hours paid × standard direct labour rate per hour) − (actual hours paid × actual direct labour rate per hour)

$(850 \times £4) - (850 \times £3.50)$ $= £425$ (F)

Direct labour efficiency

(actual production in standard hours × standard direct labour rate per hour) − (actual direct labour hours worked × standard direct labour rate per hour)

$(900 \times £4) - (850 \times £4)$ $= £200$ (F)

Total direct labour variances   £625 (F)   (see Worked Example 12.4 summary)

Possible reasons for the above variances:

- wage rate negotiations
- changes in the skills of the labour force
- better than expected impact of the effect of the learning curve
- impact of machinery efficiency, levels of maintenance, or use of different materials, with changed levels of quality.

Worked Example 12.8

Using the summary of results for Dymocks Ltd for July from Worked Example 12.4 we can prepare an analysis of variable overhead variances, and provide an explanation of why these variances might have occurred.

Variable overhead variances
Variable production overhead expenditure

    actual cost incurred − (actual hours worked × standard variable production overhead absorption rate per hour)

    £2,750 − (850 × £3.50)   = £225 (A)

Variable production overhead efficiency

    (actual hours worked × standard variable production overhead absorption rate per hour) − (actual production in standard hours × standard variable production overhead absorption rate per hour)

    (850 × £3.50) − (900 × £3.50)   = £175 (F)

Total variable overhead variances   £50 (A)   (see Worked Example 12.4 summary)

Possible reasons for the above variances may be:

- related to the direct labour variances
- due to a number of individual variances within total variable overheads
- changes in the overhead rate with different levels of activity.

Worked Example 12.9

Using the summary of results for Dymocks Ltd for July from Worked Example 12.4 we can prepare an analysis of fixed overhead variances, and provide an explanation of why these variances might have occurred.

Fixed overhead variances
Fixed production overhead expenditure

    budgeted fixed production overhead − actual fixed production overhead

    £4,000 − £5,000   = £1,000 (A)

Fixed production overhead volume

    (actual production in standard hours × standard fixed production overhead absorption rate per hour) − budgeted fixed production overhead

    (900 × £5) − £4,000   = £500 (F)

    Total fixed overhead variances £500 (A) (See Worked Example 12.4 Summary)

Possible reasons for the above variances:

- due to a number of individual variances within total fixed overheads.

> **Progress check 12.8** What are the main differences between variance analysis using marginal costing and variance analysis using absorption costing?

Worked Example 12.10

Using the variances calculated for Dymocks Ltd for July we can prepare an operating statement that reconciles the actual profit for July to the budgeted profit for July.

The actual profit for July may be reconciled with the budgeted profit by summarising the variances:

Operating statement

	£	£	£
Budget profit (Worked Example 12.4)			18,400
Sales variances			
Sales volume (Worked Example 12.5)	2,300 (F)		
Sales price (Worked Example 12.5)	1,800 (A)	500 (F)	
Direct materials variances			
Materials price (Worked Example 12.6)	700 (A)		
Materials usage (Worked Example 12.6)	3,000 (F)	2,300 (F)	
Direct labour variances			
Labour rate (Worked Example 12.7)	425 (F)		
Labour efficiency (Worked Example 12.7)	200 (F)	625 (F)	
Variable overheads variances			
Expenditure (Worked Example 12.8)	225 (A)		
Efficiency (Worked Example 12.8)	175 (F)	50 (A)	
Fixed overheads variances			
Expenditure (Worked Example 12.9)	1,000 (A)		
Volume (Worked Example 12.9)	500 (F)	500 (A)	
			2,875 (F)
Actual profit (Worked Example 12.4)			21,275

The reasons for variances

Although not an exhaustive list of possible causes, the following provides the reasons for most of the common variances encountered in most manufacturing and service businesses:

- direct material price: skills of purchasing department, quality of materials, price inflation, supplier discounts, foreign currency exchange rate fluctuations, invoicing errors

- direct material usage: quality of materials, labour efficiency, pilfering, stock control, quality control
- direct labour rate: use of higher or lower skilled labour than planned, wage inflation, or union agreement
- direct labour efficiency: use of higher or lower skilled labour than planned, quality of materials, efficiency of plant and machinery, better or worse than expected learning curve performance, inaccurate time allocation – employees have to learn a new process and then repeat that process for real many times, within times established during the learning curve evaluation
- overhead expenditure: inflation, wastage, resource usage savings, changes in services – many companies are outsourcing basic in-house services, for example accounting
- overhead efficiency: labour efficiency, efficiency of plant and machinery, technological changes
- overhead capacity: under- or over-utilisation of plant capacity, idle time.

> **Progress check 12.9** **Most of the reasons for materials variances may be identified so that the appropriate corrective actions can be taken. What are the types of action that may be taken?**

Without exploring the detail, we have also already mentioned materials mix and yield variances that show the effects on costs of changing the mix of materials input, and of materials input yielding either more or less output than expected.

Planning and operational variances

The above discussion has necessarily focused on the description, calculation and understanding of the most common variances that one may come across on a day-to-day basis in a manufacturing or service environment. Regarding each resource, such variances are normally based on the questions:

- what did it cost?

and

- what should it have cost?

or

- how long did it take?

and

- how long should it have taken?

Further light may be shown on the reasons for differences between actual and planned performance through taking variance analysis to a greater level of sophistication than that outlined in the charts and examples above.

There are inevitably problems with traditional variance analyses, which are invariably due to:

- failure to distinguish variances due to an incorrect standard from those that are real operational variances
- failure to indicate which variances are controllable and which are uncontrollable
- failure to identify responsibility for variances
- lack of updating standards to current efficiency levels.

It is sufficient for our purposes to be aware of *ex post* variance analysis, which distinguishes between planning and operational variances. Planning variances are due to inaccuracies in the original (*ex ante*) budget. The variances between the new budget that is drawn up to reflect actual conditions during the budget (the *ex post* budget) can then be compared with actual performance to show operational variances.

There are a number of variance investigation decision models:

- the percentage rule, which prompts investigation if variances are greater than a certain percentage of the standard
- statistical significance rule, which investigates variances that are 'unusual' occurrences using a normal distribution
- statistical control charts, which provide warning limits and action limits.

It is useful for non-financial managers to be aware of some of these further uses of variances, even though the detail of these is outside the scope of this book.

Summary of key points

- Standard costing can be used to calculate costs of units or processes that may be used in budgeted costs.
- Not all budgeted amounts are standard amounts, as the latter will be precise by nature, unlike budgeted amounts.
- Standard costing provides the basis for performance evaluation and control from comparison of actual performance against budget through the setting of predetermined cost estimates.
- A flexed budget reflects the costs or revenues expected as a result of changes in activity levels from those planned in the master budget.
- A flexed budget provides a more realistic basis for comparison of actual performance.
- Flexed budgets enable comparison of actual costs and revenues on a like-for-like basis through the calculation of differences, or variances.
- Variances are the difference between planned, budgeted or standard costs (or revenues) and actual costs incurred and may be summarised in an operating statement to reconcile budget with actual performance.
- Variances between actual and standard performance may be investigated to explain the reasons for the differences through preparation of a complete analysis of all variances, or alternatively through the use of exception reporting that highlights only significant variances.
- Inaccuracies in original budgets may be identified through planning variances, and actual performance may then be compared with a subsequently revised budget to show operational variances.

Questions

Q12.1   How is standard costing used in the preparation of budgets?

Q12.2   **(i)**   What are the benefits of using standard costing?

           (ii)   What type of standard may best ensure that those benefits are achieved?

          (iii)   How are standards used to achieve those benefits?

Q12.3   Describe and illustrate the technique of flexible budgeting.

Q12.4   **(i)**   What is management by exception?

           (ii)   How is variance analysis used to support this technique?

Q12.5   **(i)**   Outline the main variances that may be reported using the bases of absorption costing and marginal costing.

           (ii)   What do these variances tell us about direct labour, direct materials, and overhead costs?

Q12.6   Describe the main reasons why usage and efficiency variances may occur and illustrate these with some examples.

Q12.7   What are mix and yield variances?

Q12.8   **(i)**   Explain some of the problems associated with traditional variance reporting.

           (ii)   What are planning and operational variances?

Discussion points

D12.1   'We set the budget once a year and then compare the actual profit after the end of the financial year. If actual profit is below budget, then everyone needs to make more effort to ensure this doesn't happen the following year.' Discuss.

D12.2   'The standard-setting process is sometimes seen as management's way of establishing targets that demand better and better manufacturing performance.' To what extent do you think that is true, and if it is true how effectively do you think the standard-setting process achieves that objective?

D12.3   To what extent do you think that the techniques of flexed budgets and variance analysis complicate the otherwise simple process of comparing the various areas of actual performance against budget?

D12.4   'Traditional variance analysis tends to focus on cutting costs and increasing output in a way that is detrimental to product and service quality, and the longer term viability of the business.' Discuss.

Exercises

Solutions are provided in Appendix 4 to all exercise numbers highlighted in colour.

Level I

E12.1   *Time allowed – 60 minutes*

Nilbog Ltd makes garden gnomes. It uses standard costs and has budgeted to produce and sell 130,000 Fishermen (their top of the range gnome) in 2005. Nilbog's budget for the year is phased over 13 four-week periods, and production and sales are spread evenly in the budget.

Budgeted standards costs and selling prices for the Fisherman are:

		£
Direct materials	3 cu. yds at £3.60	10.80
Direct labour	2 hours at £6.60 per hour	13.20
Variable overheads	2 hours at £2.40 per hour	4.80
Fixed overheads	2 hours at £4.80 per hour	9.60
Standard cost of one Fisherman		38.40
Standard profit		9.60
Standard selling price		48.00

The actual results for period 5, a four-week period, were:

Sales	9,000 Fishermen at £48 each
Production	9,600 Fishermen
Purchase of direct materials	30,000 cu. yards at a cost of £115,200
Direct materials usage	28,000 cu. yards
Direct labour cost	£142,560 over 22,000 hours
Variable overhead	£44,000
Fixed overhead	£100,000

There was no work-in-progress at the start or at the end of period 5. Finished goods and materials stocks are valued at standard cost.

You are required to prepare a flexed budget and an operating statement for Nilbog Ltd for period 5, showing the profit for the period and all standard variances with their detailed calculations, together with an explanation of their likely causes.

E12.2 *Time allowed – 90 minutes*

Cyclops plc is an electronics business that manufactures television sets, and uses a standard costing system. The TV cabinets division of Cyclops manufactures, for sale within the company, the plastic cases for one of their most popular models, the F24. The results for the F24 for October 2004 were as follows:

	Actual	Budget
Sales units	61,200	40,800
	£	£
Sales	348,840	244,800
Direct labour	133,280	81,600
Direct materials	114,240	81,600
Variable overheads	27,200	16,320
Contribution	74,120	65,280
Fixed overheads	25,000	20,400
Profit	49,120	44,880

The budget had been finalised for 2004 using standard costs for that year.

Sales volumes were increasing and just prior to October the TV cabinets division expected around 50% increase in sales volumes for the month. The division had unused capacity to take up this expected increase in volume. Vimla Patel had recently been appointed as commercial manager and she proposed a 30p selling price reduction per unit, which was effective from 1 October.

Melanie Bellamy, Cyclops' purchasing manager, had negotiated a 4% discount on the standard price of raw materials purchased and used from October. The production manager Graham Brown had been having problems with quality due to the learning curve and some operators who were still receiving training. Training had been completed by the end of September. This meant some increase in operator pay rates but the planned productivity rate was maintained and there was less materials wastage in October. The variable costs of utilities increased in October, primarily due to electricity and gas price increases.

Graham Brown was able to keep stock levels of materials and finished product at the same level at the start and end of October.

You are required to:

(i)   **prepare an operating statement that provides an analysis of the variances between actual and budget for October on a marginal costing basis, highlighting the performance of each of the managers**

(ii)   **give full explanations of why the variances may have occurred**

(iii) **and (iv) prepare the same analysis and explanations as (i) and (ii) above using absorption costing**

(v)   **explain whether absorption costing provides the best basis for assessment of manager performance.**

Level II

E12.3 *Time allowed – 90 minutes*

White Heaven Ltd manufactures a bathroom basin, the Shell, and uses standard costing based on a monthly output of 50,000 units. White Heaven uses two types of direct labour and two items of raw material.

Variable costs include:

- indirect labour costs of materials handlers and stores persons
- maintenance labour costs
- general production overheads.

Fixed costs include:

- supervisory salaries
- other overheads such as
  - factory rent
  - electricity standing charges
  - gas standing charges.

The **ideal** standard cost of a Shell is as follows:

Direct labour	1 hour at £7.20 per hour	grade A
	0.75 hours at £6.00 per hour	grade B
Direct materials	5 kgs at £2 per kg clay	
	3 kgs at £4 per kg glaze	
Indirect labour	0.25 hours at £5.00 per hour	
Maintenance	0.05 hours at £10.00 per hour	

Variable overheads	15% of direct materials cost, plus
	10% of direct labour cost
Supervisory salaries	£95,000 per month
Other fixed overheads	£109,000 per month

In June 2005 adjustments were agreed as the basis for the following month's **attainable** standard costs:

Grade A labour rates increased by 40p, grade B by 30p and indirect and maintenance labour by 20p

Grade B labour hours increased by 0.05 hours because of process delays due to a tool change problem

Turnover of operators has meant recruiting some inexperienced, untrained operators

10% of grade A operators with 50% efficiency

25% of grade B operators with 60% efficiency

The clay is to be upgraded in quality with the supplier imposing a 10% surcharge

The glaze will be purchased in larger batches with a 12.5% discount but resulting in an increase in variable overheads to 20% of materials cost for this type of material.

For the July output of 49,000 Shells you are required to calculate:

(i)   the ideal standard cost for a Shell

(ii)   the attainable standard cost for a Shell for July 2005

(iii) the total variance between the ideal and attainable standards.

E12.4 *Time allowed – 90 minutes*

White Heaven Ltd (see Exercise E12.3) actually produced 49,000 Shells during July 2005 and the actual costs for the month were as follows:

Direct labour	52,000 hours at £7.60 per hour	grade A
	43,500 hours at £6.30 per hour	grade B
Direct materials	247,000 kgs at £2.16 per kg	clay
	149,000 kgs at £3.60 per kg	glaze
Indirect labour	12,000 hours at £5.20 per hour	
Maintenance	2,250 hours at £10.20 per hour	
Variable overheads	£251,000	
Supervisory salaries	£97,000	
Other fixed overheads	£110,000	

You are required to:

(i)   calculate the variances between actual costs for July 2005 and the attainable standard

(ii)   prepare an operating statement that summarises the variances

(iii) reconcile the actual cost for July with the expected total attainable cost

(iv)   comment on the likely reasons for each of the variances.

E12.5 *Time allowed – 90 minutes*

Millennium Models Ltd manufactured an ornamental gift for the tourist trade. The standard variable cost per unit was:

Materials price	£0.85 per kg
Unit material usage	2 kgs
Direct labour rate	£4.20 per hour
Standard labour per unit	42 minutes
Selling price per unit	£5.84

Fixed overhead is recovered on the basis of units produced at the rate of £0.82 per unit and Millennium planned to sell 4,300 units in November 2004.

In November 2004 Millennium' s actual performance was:

Units manufactured and sold	4,100
Sales	£24,805
Materials used	6,600 kgs at £0.83
	1,900 kgs at £0.89
Direct labour paid	2,975 at £4.50 per hour
Overheads incurred	£3,800

You are required to:

    (i)   **prepare a budget to actual profit reconciliation for November 2004 including an analysis of sales, materials, and labour variances**

    (ii)   **calculate the fixed overhead expenditure variance and fixed overhead volume variances for November 2004.**

E12.6 *Time allowed – 90 minutes*

Using the information about Millennium Models Ltd from Exercise E12.5:

    (i)   **explain what you think are the advantages and disadvantages of the implementation of a standard costing system by Millennium Models Ltd**

    (ii)   **explain how the analyses of variances may have helped Millennium Models Ltd control the business**

    (iii) **prepare a report that explains the variance analysis you have carried out in Exercise E12.5 above and provides explanations of Millennium's performance.**

E12.7 *Time allowed – 90 minutes*

The Stables is a small holiday-let business in Wales. The standard variable cost for each holiday-let unit (HLU) for one holiday is:

	£
Direct materials (food, cleaning materials and repairs)	120
Direct labour 15 hours at £10 per hour	150
Variable overhead 5 hours at £1 per hour	5

Budgeted costs and sales for the 2004 season are:

Number of holidays	50
Price per holiday	£400
Fixed costs	£2,080

The actual outcome for one HLU for 2004 was:

Number of holidays	52
Total sales revenue	£19,760
Direct materials	£5,928
Direct labour (780 hours at £9 per hour)	£7,020
Variable overhead	£260
Fixed overhead	£1,950

You are required to:

(i)   Prepare a budgeted profit and loss account for one HLU for 2004.

(ii) Prepare an actual profit and loss account for one HLU for 2004.

(iii) Prepare a flexed budget for one HLU that reflects the amount of actual business for 2004.

(iv) Prepare a detailed variance analysis for one HLU that gives possible reasons for each of the variances.

(v)   Summarise the variances in an operating statement that reconciles the difference between the budgeted profit and the actual profit achieved by one HLU in 2004.

(vi) Outline some of the problems with traditional variance analysis and explain how the identification of planning variances may assist in more accurate reporting of operational variances.

ARTHURSTONE

During the 1990s, Sir William Kiloshake began work on a project that had been a dream he had wished to realise for many years.

Bill was a keen botanist and environmentalist and had been brought up close to a large country house called Arthurstone, which stood in a 500-acre estate in which there had once been extensive gardens. The house had long since gone into disrepair and the gardens had been untended for around 50 years.

Bill had brought together a consortium of experts to investigate how Arthurstone could be developed into a national educational and tourist facility.

After many years of feasibility studies, market research, soil analyses, and Government grant applications, the project became a reality by 2001. The project would cost £35m to restore the building and re-establish the gardens. This was supported by a National Lottery grant of £17m. It was expected that around 350,000 people would visit Arthurstone every year, mostly during the summer months.

The net project cost investment of £18m (£35m total cost less £17m grant) had been obtained from sponsorship from the private sector. However, the project needed to be self-financing from its first day of opening to the public, which was 1 May 2004. The costs associated with running the house and gardens are broadly:

- variable operational costs
- fixed operational costs
- variable marketing and administrative costs
- fixed marketing and administrative costs.

The initial price for admission to Arthurstone was £6 per person.

Although market research had been carried out, there was still some uncertainty about the reliability of visitor estimates. Equally, the management of Arthurstone did not have much information about the elasticity of demand for garden attractions and were not convinced that the admission price of £6 was the optimum price. For its first year of operation there were to be no discounts for children, senior citizens, or job seekers/unemployed persons; neither were there to be volume discounts for large parties of visitors.

The following budget information relates to the first four months that Arthurstone would be open to the public.

	Month 1		Month 2		Month 3		Month 4	
	Visitors	£	Visitors	£	Visitors	£	Visitors	£
Sales	85,000	510,000	90,000	540,000	95,000	570,000	85,000	510,000
Variable operational costs		153,000		162,000		171,000		153,000
Fixed operational costs		45,000		45,000		45,000		45,000
Variable marketing and administrative costs		51,000		54,000		57,000		51,000
Fixed marketing and administrative costs		52,500		52,500		52,500		52,500

The budget for 2004/2005 was prepared on the assumption that during its first year of operation there would be no visitors during the months September to April. During that period of course no variable costs would be incurred.

Required

(i)   Prepare the budgeted profit and loss account for each of the first six months, and the total for the year to 30 April 2005, on a marginal costing basis.

(ii) Explain the reasons for the differences in profit levels between the first four months of operation (with supporting calculations).

(iii) Draw a break-even chart that shows the admission price to be charged at the break-even point for Arthurstone.

(iv) What admission price to Arthurstone should be charged to achieve a profit of 10% mark-up on full absorption costs?

(v)   What admission price to Arthurstone should be charged to achieve a target profit of £500,000 for the year May 2004 to April 2005?

(vi) What may be the possible impact of charging the prices calculated in (iv) and (v) above, and to what factors may that impact be sensitive?

(vii) At the prices calculated in (iv) and (v), by what percentage levels may the visitor numbers drop from that budgeted before Arthurstone started to make a loss?

(viii) Prepare a short report, which includes any calculations that you consider relevant, outlining the factors that may be discussed with regard to a proposal that has been made to introduce a revised pricing structure for 2005/2006 which includes discounting for children, senior citizens, job seekers/unemployed persons, and large parties of visitors.

Part III

Business finance

Part contents

Part III is about business finance, and provides an introduction to financial management. Financial management is broadly defined as the management of all the processes associated with the efficient acquisition and deployment of both short- and long-term financial resources. Businesses raise money from shareholders and lenders to invest in assets, which are used to increase the wealth of the business and its owners. The underlying fundamental economic objective of a company is to maximise shareholder wealth.

Chapter 13 considers how businesses make decisions about potential investments that may be made, in order to ensure that the wealth of the business will be increased. This is an important area of decision-making that usually involves a great deal of money and relatively long-term commitments that therefore requires techniques to ensure that the financial objectives of the company are in line with the interests of the shareholders.

Chapter 14 deals primarily with long-term, external sources of business finance for investment in businesses. This relates to the various types of funding available to business, including the raising of funds from the owners of the business (the shareholders) and from lenders external to the business. Chapter 14 also shows how the costs of the alternative sources of capital are used in the calculation of the overall cost of capital that may be used by companies as the discount rate to evaluate proposed investments in capital projects, and in the calculation of economic value added (EVA) to evaluate company performance.

In **Chapter 15** we look at one of the areas of funds management internal to the business, the management of working capital. Working capital comprises the short-term assets of the business, stock, trade debtors, and cash and claims on the business, trade creditors. This chapter deals with how these important items may be effectively managed.

Finally, in **Chapter 16** we consider the relationships between information technology, accounting and financial management. We look at how technological change has quickly evolved to meet the requirements for speedier and more accurate processing of transactions, and communication of information and data. This has resulted from an increase in the range of products and services available to us, globalisation, and increasing competition. This chapter considers the increasing links with accounting of a wide range of corporate activities, which have been influenced by their use of IT.

13

Capital investment decisions

Contents

Learning objectives

Completion of this chapter will enable you to:

- explain what is meant by an investment
- outline the key principles underlying investment selection criteria
- outline the strengths and weaknesses of the five investment appraisal criteria
- explain what is meant by discounted cash flow (DCF)
- consider investment selection using the appraisal criteria of net present value (NPV) and internal rate of return (IRR)
- explain the effects of inflation, working capital requirements, length and timing of projects, taxation, and risk and uncertainty on investment criteria calculations
- evaluate the impact of risk and the use of sensitivity analysis in decision-making
- consider the ways in which capital projects may be controlled and reviewed
- appreciate the importance of the project post-completion audit.

Introduction

We have seen in Part II how the management accountant is involved with providing financial and non-financial information and analysis to enable managers to evaluate alternative proposals and to make decisions.

In Chapter 10 we had an introduction into the ways in which accounting and financial information may be used as an aid to decision-making. This chapter looks at the specific area of decision-making that relates to investment. Such decisions may relate to whether or not to invest in a project, or choices between investment in alternative projects which are competing for resources.

We will begin by looking at exactly what an investment is, and outlining the techniques used to decide on whether or not to invest, and how to choose between alternative investments.

We shall evaluate the advantages and disadvantages of the five main investment appraisal criteria used by companies and consider examples that demonstrate their use. The most important of these are the discounted cash flow methods of net present value (NPV), and internal rate of return (IRR). The technique of discounted cash flow (DCF) will be fully explained.

In addition to the initial costs of an investment and the returns expected from it, a number of other factors usually need to be taken into account in investment decision-making. These include, for example, inflation, the need for working capital, taxation, and the length and timing of the project. We will consider the possible impact of these factors and how the effects of risk and uncertainty on the appraisal of investments may be quantified using sensitivity analysis.

Appraisal of an investment is more than an accounting exercise. An investment decision is a crucially significant and important decision for a business. It is usually a highly politically charged area in the management of an organisation, which if mismanaged is capable of destroying shareholder value. Once an investment decision has been made the project may then be planned and implemented. This chapter closes with an introduction to the ways in which capital investment projects may be controlled and reviewed.

What is an investment?

For the accountant an **investment** appears within the assets section of the balance sheet under fixed assets. For the finance director an investment is any decision that implies expenditure today with the expectation that it will generate cash inflows tomorrow.

Investment decisions are extremely important because they are invariably concerned with the future survival, prosperity and growth of the organisation. The organisation's primary objective of maximisation of shareholder wealth is a basic assumption that continues to hold true. Investments must be made not only to maintain shareholder wealth but more importantly to increase it. To meet the shareholder wealth maximisation objective it is crucial that those managing the organisation make optimal decisions that are based on the best information available and use of the most appropriate appraisal techniques.

At the corporate level, investment (in shares) relates to the amount that shareholders are willing to invest in the equity of a company in the expectation of future cash flows in the form of dividends and enhancement of share price. The level of future dividends and share price enhancement are in turn dependent on the extent to which the company is able to optimise returns on 'real' investment (investment in companies, plant, machinery, working capital) in new products, projects, new business, and so on. There is a great deal of pressure on chief executives to ensure that profitable 'real' investments are made to provide sustained dividend growth and increasing share prices.

Investment decisions faced by companies are therefore financially driven, and so if performance is deemed inadequate or unlikely to meet shareholder expectations, then the pressure becomes even greater to identify alternative, more profitable projects. Decisions are made by managers and not by the management accountant. Levels of authority within the management hierarchy are determined by company policy. Companies normally establish limits at each management level for each type of decision, and the level of expenditure allowed. The approval of one or more directors is normally required for all capital expenditure and for major projects.

Investment may appear in the balance sheet within fixed assets in line with the accountants' definition, for example land, buildings, plant, machinery, etc. It may also appear in the profit and loss account in terms of public relations, staff training, or research and development. In some cases the amount of money gained as a result of making an investment is relatively easy to measure, such as cost savings, capacity increases, etc. In other cases, it may be impossible to measure the gains – company image, education, and so on. The amount of spend may be easily forecast, for example the costs of computerisation of a process to reduce the production of non-quality products. In other projects, such as research and development, costs may be more uncertain.

Regardless, an investment decision is required before spending shareholders' and lenders' funds. The decision made needs to be one that shareholders and lenders would be happy with; it is one that is expected to provide anticipated gains in real terms that greatly exceed the funds spent today, in other words a good return on the money invested. Otherwise the investment should not be made.

> **Progress check 13.1 Describe what is meant by investment.**

Investment appraisal criteria

The five main methods used in investment appraisal are shown in Fig. 13.1:

- the **accounting rate of return (ARR)** for appraising capital investment projects is based on profits and the costs of investment; it takes no account of cash flows or the time value of money

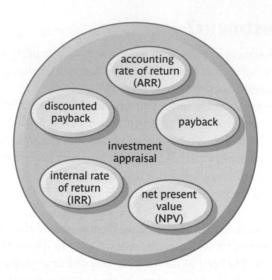

Figure 13.1 The five main investment appraisal criteria methods

➡ ■ the payback method for appraising capital investment projects is based on cash flows, but also ignores the time value of money

➡ ■ net present value (NPV) is one of the two most widely used investment decision criteria, which are based on cash flow and the time value of money

➡ ■ internal rate of return (IRR) is the second of the two most widely used investment decision criteria, which are based on cash flow and the time value of money

➡ ■ the discounted payback appraisal method is also based on cash flow and the time value of money.

We will look at examples of each of the five appraisal criteria and the advantages and disadvantages of using each of them.

Accounting rate of return (ARR)

ARR is a simple measure which is sometimes used in investment appraisal. It is a form of return on capital employed. It is based on profits rather than cash flows and ignores the time value of money.

ARR may be calculated using:

$$\frac{\textbf{average accounting profit over the project}}{\textbf{initial investment}} \times \textbf{100\%}$$

There are alternative ways of calculating ARR. For example, total profit may be used instead of average profit, or average investment may be used instead of initial investment. It should be noted that in such a case if, for example, a machine originally cost £800,000 and its final scrap value was £50,000 then the average investment is £850,000/2, or £425,000. This is because the investment at the start is valued at £800,000, and the investment at the end of the project is £50,000. The average value over the period of the project is then the addition of these two values divided by two.

It should be noted that the method of calculation of ARR that is selected must be used consistently. However, ARR although simple to use is not recommended as a primary appraisal method. The method can provide an 'overview' of a new project but it lacks the sophistication of other methods (see the following explanations and methods). The impact of cash flows and time on the value of

Worked Example 13.1

Alpha Engineering Ltd is a company that has recently implemented an investment appraisal system. Its investment authorisation policy usually allows it to go ahead with a capital project if the accounting rate of return is greater than 25%. A project has been submitted for appraisal with the following data:

	£000	
Initial investment	100	(residual scrap value zero)

Per annum profit over the life of the project:

Year	
1	25
2	35
3	35
4	25

The capital project can be evaluated using ARR.

$$\text{Average profit over the life of the project} = \frac{£25,000 + £35,000 + £35,000 + £25,000}{4}$$

$$= £30,000$$

$$\text{Accounting rate of return} = \frac{£30,000}{£100,000} \times 100\% = 30\%$$

which is greater than 25% and so acceptance of the project may be recommended.

money really should be considered in investment appraisal, which we will discuss in a later section about key principles underlying investment selection criteria.

> **Progress check 13.2** **What is the accounting rate of return (ARR) and how is it calculated?**

Payback

Payback is defined as the number of years it takes the cash inflows from a capital investment project to equal the cash outflows. An organisation may have a target payback period, above which projects are rejected. It is useful and sometimes used as an initial screening process in evaluating two mutually exclusive projects. The project that pays back in the shortest time may on the face of it be the one to accept.

Worked Example 13.2

Beta Engineering Ltd's investment authorisation policy requires all capital projects to pay back within 3 years, and views projects with shorter payback periods as even more desirable. Two mutually exclusive projects are currently being considered with the following data:

	Project 1 £000	Project 2 £000	
Initial investment	200	200	(residual scrap value zero)

Per annum cash inflows over the life of each project:

	Project 1		Project 2	
Year	Yearly cash flow £000	Cumulative cash flow £000	Yearly cash flow £000	Cumulative cash flow £000
1	60	60	100	100
2	80	140	150	250
3	80	220	30	280
4	90	310	10	290

The projects can be evaluated by considering their payback periods.

- Project 1 derives total cash inflows of £310,000 over the life of the project and pays back the initial £200,000 investment three quarters of the way into year three, when the cumulative cash inflows reach £200,000 [£60,000 + £80,000 + £60,000 (75% of £80,000)].
- Project 2 derives total cash inflows of £290,000 over the life of the project and pays back the initial £200,000 investment two thirds of the way into year two, when the cumulative cash inflows reach £200,000 [£100,000 + £100,000 (67% of £150,000)].
- Both projects meet Beta Engineering Ltd's three-year payback criteria.
- Project 2 pays back within two years and so is the preferred project, using Beta's investment guidelines.

Worked Example 13.2 shows how payback may be used to compare projects. The total returns from a project should also be considered, in addition to the timing of the cash flows and their value in real terms. As with ARR, although its use is widespread amongst companies, payback is not recommended as a primary appraisal method. This method can also provide an 'overview' but should be the primary appraisal method used in larger companies or with regard to large projects because it ignores the time value of money.

> Progress check 13.3 **What is payback and how is it calculated?**

Key principles underlying investment selection criteria: cash flow, the time value of money, and discounted cash flow (DCF)

The first two appraisal criteria we have considered are simple methods that have limitations in their usefulness in making optimal capital investment decisions. The three further appraisal criteria are NPV, IRR and discounted payback. Whichever of these three methods is used, three basic principles apply: *Cash is king, Time value of money,* and *Discounted cash flow (DCF)* (see pages 487 and 488).

In Part I of this book (Chapters 3, 4 and 5) we discussed the differences between cash flow and profit and the advantages in using cash as a measure of financial performance.

We may assume that a specific sum of money may be held in reserve for some unforeseen future need, or used:

- to earn interest in a bank or building society account over the following year
- to buy some bottles of champagne (for example) at today's price
- to buy some bottles of champagne at the price in one year's time, which we may assume will be at a higher price because of inflation.

We may assume that the bank or building society interest earned for one year, or the amount by which the price of champagne goes up due to inflation over one year is say 5%. Then we can see that £100 would be worth £105 if left in the building society for one year, and £100 spent on champagne today would actually buy just over £95 worth of champagne in one year's time because of its price increase.

Cash is king

Real funds can be seen in cash but not in accounting profit.

Interest charges become payable as soon as money is made available, for example, from a lender to a borrower, not when an agreement is made or when a contract is signed.

Time value of money

Receipt of £100 today has greater value than receipt of £100 in one year's time.

There are two reasons for this:

The money could have been invested alternatively in, say, risk-free Government gilt-edged securities – in fact, the actual rate of interest that will have to be paid will be higher than the Government rate, to include a risk premium, because neither companies nor individuals are risk-free borrowers. Generally, the higher the risk of the investment, the higher the return the investor will expect from it. Purchasing power will have been lost over a year due to inflation.

The percentage rate by which the value of money may be eroded over one year is called the discount rate. The amount by which the value of, say, £100 is eroded over one year is calculated by dividing it by what is called the discount factor

$$\frac{£100}{(1 + \text{discount rate } \%)}$$

So, for example, we could buy champagne in one year's time worth

$$£100/(1 + 5\%) \text{ or } £100/1.05 = £95.24$$

Figure 13.2 Future values of £100 using a discount rate of 5% per annum

If the £95.24 were left for another year, and assuming that prices continued to increase at 5% per annum, we could buy champagne after a further year worth

$$£95.24/(1 + 5\%) \text{ or } £95.24/1.05 = £90.70$$

The yearly buying power continues to be reduced by application of the discount factor (or using the appropriate discount factor if the discount rate has changed). If the money is not used either to earn interest or to buy something, its value therefore normally becomes less and less. The discount factor for each year obviously depends on the discount rate. The successive year-by-year impact on £100 using an unchanging discount rate of 5% per annum may be illustrated using a simple graph showing its cumulative value from the start until the end of 10 years. The graph shown in Fig. 13.2 illustrates the concept of the time value of money.

Discounted cash flow (DCF)

Whichever of the three methods of appraisal is used: NPV; IRR; or discounted payback, a technique of discounting the projected cash flows of a project is used to ascertain its **present value**. Such methods are called discounted cash flow or DCF techniques. They require the use of a discount rate to carry out the appropriate calculation.

If we consider a simple company balance sheet:

net assets = equity + financial debt

we can see that an investment is an additional asset that may be financed by equity or debt or by both.

Shareholders and lenders each require a return on their investment that is high enough to pay for the risk they are taking in funding the company and its assets. The expected return on equity will be higher than the cost of debt because the shareholders take a higher risk than the lenders. The average cost of these financial resources provided to the company is called the weighted average cost of capital (WACC). An important rule is that the return generated by a new investment undertaken by a company must be higher than the WACC, which reflects the discount rate – the rate of financing the investment. If, say, a company's WACC is 10%, an investment may be accepted if the expected rate of return is 15% or 16%. The importance of WACC and the significance of the debt/equity financial structure of a business will be examined in more detail in Chapter 14 when we look at sources of finance and the cost of capital.

Other discount rates may be used, such as a borrowing interest rate or even the accounting rate of return. However, the cost of capital – the WACC – is usually the hurdle rate, the opportunity cost of funds, that is used to evaluate new investments.

If i represents the cost of capital (the discount rate), and n the number of periods, e.g. years, these can be used to derive a

$$\text{present value discount factor, which is } 1/(1 + i)^n$$

where n may have a value from 0 to infinity.
(Note the similarity between this and the way we calculated the future values of £100 illustrated in Fig. 13.2.)

If we consider a project where the initial investment in year 0 is I, and each subsequent year's net cash flows are CF_1, CF_2, CF_3, CF_4 and so on for n years up to CF_n, and the cost of capital is i, then the

$$\text{present value of the cash flows} =$$
$$-I + CF_1/(1 + i) + CF_2/(1 + i)^2 + \cdots + CF_n/(1 + i)^n$$

The present value of the cash flows using an appropriate cost of capital, or discount rate, is called the net present value or NPV.

> **Progress check 13.4** **What do we mean by discounted cash flow (DCF) and what are the principles on which it is based?**

Net present value (NPV)

NPV is today's value of the difference between cash inflows and outflows projected at future dates, attributable to capital investments or long-term projects. The value now of these net cash flows is obtained by using the discounted cash flow method with a specified discount rate.

Worked Example 13.3

An investment of £5,000 is made in year 0. For the purpose of NPV, year 0 is regarded as being today. (The reason for this is that any number to the power of 0 is equal to unity.) The investment generates subsequent yearly cash flows of £1,000, £3,000, £3,000, and £2,000. The cost of capital is 10%.

We can evaluate the investment using an NPV approach.

NPV = $-£5,000 + £1,000/1.1 + £3,000/1.1^2 + £3,000/1.1^3 + £2,000/1.1^4$
NPV = $-£5,000 + (£1,000 \times 0.91) + (£3,000 \times 0.83) + (£3,000 \times 0.75) + (£2,000 \times 0.68)$
NPV = $-£5,000 + £910 + £2,490 + £2,250 + £1,360$
NPV = $+£2,010$ which is greater than 0, and being positive the investment should probably be made.

Such an analysis is more usefully presented in tabular form. The discount rates for each year: $1/1.1$, $1/1.1^2$, $1/1.1^3$, $1/1.1^4$, may be shown in the table as discount factor values which are calculated, or alternatively obtained from present value tables (see the extract below from the Present Value table in Appendix 2 at the end of this book).

Rate r %	1	2	3	4	5	6	7	8	9	10	11	12
After n years												
1	0.99	0.98	0.97	0.96	0.95	0.94	0.93	0.93	0.92	**0.91**	0.90	0.89
2	0.98	0.96	0.94	0.92	0.91	0.89	0.87	0.86	0.84	**0.83**	0.81	0.80
3	0.97	0.94	0.92	0.89	0.86	0.84	0.82	0.79	0.77	**0.75**	0.73	0.71
4	0.96	0.92	0.89	0.85	0.82	0.79	0.76	0.74	0.71	**0.68**	0.66	0.64
5	0.95	0.91	0.86	0.82	0.78	0.75	0.71	0.68	0.65	0.62	0.59	0.57

Tabular format of NPV analysis

Year	Cash outflows £	Cash inflows £	Net cash flow £	Discount factor	Present values £
0	−5,000		−5,000	1.00	−5,000
1		1,000	1,000	0.91	910
2		3,000	3,000	0.83	2,490
3		3,000	3,000	0.75	2,250
4		2,000	2,000	0.68	1,360
				NPV	+2,010

Progress check 13.5 **What is net present value (NPV) and how is it calculated?**

Internal rate of return (IRR)

The NPV of a capital investment project is calculated by:

- discounting, using a rate of return, discount rate, or cost of capital, to obtain
- the difference in present values between cash inflows and cash outflows.

The internal rate of return (IRR) method calculates:

- the rate of return, where
- the difference between the present values of cash inflows and outflows, the NPV, is zero.

Through this calculation, the IRR provides the exact rate of return that the project is expected to achieve. An organisation would then undertake the project if the expected rate of return, the IRR, exceeds its target rate of return.

IRR may most easily be determined through interpolation, which assumes a linear relationship between the NPVs of a capital investment project derived using different discount rates. If a project generates a positive NPV of £50,000 using a discount rate of 10% and a negative NPV of £5,000 using a discount rate of 20%, then the IRR (at which point NPV is zero) must be somewhere between 10%

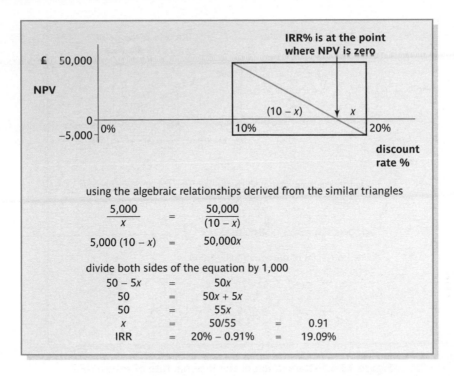

Figure 13.3 Interpolation of the internal rate of return (IRR)

and 20%. The exact rate may be determined graphically or calculated algebraically, as illustrated in Fig. 13.3.

A similar approach may be adopted if both NPVs are positive. For example, if a project generates a positive NPV of £50,000 using a discount rate of 10% and a positive NPV of £20,000 using a discount rate of 15%, then the IRR (at which point NPV is zero) may be extrapolated as shown in Fig. 13.4.

As an alternative to the graphical approach, the calculation of IRR can be carried out manually using a trial and error process, which is a quite laborious task. This may be overcome since IRR can also be determined using the appropriate spreadsheet function in Excel, for example. However, there a couple of further serious difficulties with the use of IRR.

Discount rates of return may change over the life of a project because of changes in the general level of interest rates. The IRR calculated for a project may therefore be greater than expected rates of return in some years and less in other years, which makes a decision on the project very difficult to make. Alternatively, the NPV approach may use different discount rates for each year of a project.

The cash flows of projects do not normally fall into the simple pattern of an outflow at the start of the project followed by positive cash flows during each successive year. Project cash flows may be positive at the start, or may vary between negative and positive throughout the life of a project. Such unconventional cash flow sequences through out each period may lead to a project having no IRR or multiple IRRs. Multiple IRRs makes it impossible to use IRR for decision-making.

Progress check 13.6 **What is the internal rate of return (IRR) and how is it calculated?**

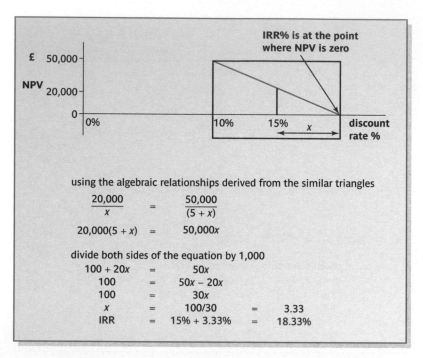

using the algebraic relationships derived from the similar triangles

$$\frac{20,000}{x} = \frac{50,000}{(5+x)}$$

$$20,000(5+x) = 50,000x$$

divide both sides of the equation by 1,000

$100 + 20x$	=	$50x$
100	=	$50x - 20x$
100	=	$30x$
x	=	$100/30$ = 3.33
IRR	=	$15\% + 3.33\%$ = 18.33%

Figure 13.4 Extrapolation of the internal rate of return (IRR)

Worked Example 13.4 illustrates the use of both NPV and IRR, using conventional cash flows.

Worked Example 13.4

Gamma plc is a diversified multinational group that wishes to acquire a computer system costing £600,000, which is expected to generate cash gains of £170,000 per year over five years. The computer system will have a residual value of zero after five years. The suggested cost of capital is 12%. For this example we may ignore taxation. Gamma has a target IRR of 15%. Gamma plc evaluates the computer system investment by considering its IRR.

Yearly cash gains
£
170,000

Year	Cash outflows £000	Cash inflows £000	Net cash flow £000	Discount factor at 12%	Present values £000
0	−600		−600	1.00	−600.0
1		170	170	0.89	151.3
2		170	170	0.80	136.0
3		170	170	0.71	120.7
4		170	170	0.64	108.8
5		170	170	0.57	96.9
				NVP	+13.7

Alternatively, using the cumulative present values in the Present Value tables, the present value of £1 at 12% over five years is £3.61, therefore

$$NPV = -£600,000 + (£170,000 \times 3.61) = +£13,700$$

The project gives a positive NPV of £13,700 over five years. If Gamma plc used NPV to appraise capital projects then acceptance of this project may be recommended because NPV is positive.

The IRR is the rate of return that would give an NPV of zero. The interpolation technique shown in Fig. 13.3 may be used to derive the internal rate of return of the project.

If we assume a rate of return of 20%, the five-year cumulative discount rate is 2.99 (from the cumulative present value of £1 in the Present Value tables in Appendix 2).

The new NPV would be:

$$-£600,000 + (£170,000 \times 2.99) = -£91,700$$

(Note that if Gamma plc used NPV to appraise capital projects then acceptance of this project would not be recommended at a cost of capital of 20% because it is negative.)

We have already calculated the positive NPV of £13,700 using a cost of capital of 12%. The IRR must be at some point between 20% and 12% (difference 8%). Using a similar calculation to that used in Fig. 13.3:

$$\frac{£91,700}{x} = \frac{£13,700}{(8-x)}$$

$$£91,700(8 - x) = £13,700x$$

$$(£91,700 \times 8) - £91,700x = £13,700x$$

$$£733,600 - £91,700x = £13,700x$$

$$£733,600 = £13,700x + £91,700x$$

$$£733,600 = £105,400x$$

$$\frac{£733,600}{£105,400} = x$$

$$x = 7.0$$

Therefore, interpolation gives us an IRR of 20% less 7%, which is 13%.

If the Gamma group uses IRR to appraise capital projects then this project may be rejected as the target rate is 15%.

NPV or IRR?

We have looked at the two main capital appraisal methods, which use the DCF technique. Which method should an organisation adopt for the appraisal of capital investment projects? Which is the better method?

IRR is relatively easy to understand, particularly for non-financial managers. It can be stated in terms that do not include financial jargon, for example 'a project will cost £1m and will return 20% per annum, which is better than the company's target of 15%'. Whereas, NPV is not quite so clear, for example 'a project will cost £1,000,000 and have an NPV of £250,000 using the company's weighted average cost of capital of 12%'. But there are major disadvantages with the use of IRR:

■ IRR is very difficult to use for decision-making where expected rates of return may change over the life of a project

- if project cash flows do not follow the usual 'outflow at the start of the project followed by inflows over the life of the project' the result may be no IRR, or two or more IRRs, which can lead to uncertainties and difficulties in interpretation
- IRR should not be used to decide between mutually exclusive projects because of its inability to allow for the relative size of investments.

IRR ignores the size of investment projects, because it is a percentage measure of a return on a project rather than an absolute cash return number. Two projects, one with a large initial investment and one with a small initial investment, may have the same IRR, but one project may return many times the cash flow returned by the other project. So, if the projects were judged solely on IRR they would seem to rank equally.

If mutually exclusive projects need to be compared then the following rules for acceptance should apply:

- is the IRR greater than the hurdle rate (usually the WACC)?

If so

- the project with the highest NPV should be chosen assuming the NPV is greater than zero.

A company may be considering a number of projects in which it may invest. If there is a limited amount of funds available then capital rationing is required. This method requires ranking the competing projects in terms of NPV per each £ of investment in each project. Investment funds may then be allocated according to NPV rankings, given the assumption that the investments are infinitely divisible.

> Progress check 13.7 **What are the disadvantages in the use of internal rate of return (IRR) in the support of capital investment appraisal decisions?**

Discounted payback

The discounted payback appraisal method requires a discount rate to be chosen to calculate the present values of cash inflows and then the payback is the number of years required to repay the original investment.

Worked Example 13.5

A new leisure facility project is being considered by Denton City Council. It will cost £600,000 and is expected to generate the following cash inflows over six years:

	£
Year	
1	40,000
2	100,000
3	200,000
4	350,000
5	400,000
6	50,000

The cost of capital is 10% per annum.
Denton City Council evaluates projects using discounted payback.

Year	Net cash flow	Cumulative net cash flow	Discount factor at 10%	Present values	Cumulative present values
	£000	£000		£000	£000
0	−600	−600	1.00	−600.0	−600.0
1	40	−560	0.91	36.4	−563.6
2	100	−460	0.83	83.0	−480.6
3	200	−260	0.75	150.0	−330.6
4	350	90	0.68	238.0	−92.6
5	400	490	0.62	248.0	155.4
6	50	540	0.56	28.0	183.4
	540			NPV +183.4	

Taking a simple payback approach we can see that the project starts to pay back at nearly three quarters of the way through year four. The discounted payback approach shows that with a cost of capital of 10% the project does not really start to pay back until just over a third of the way into year five. This method also highlights the large difference between the real total value of the project of £183,400 in discounted cash flow terms, and the arithmetic total of cash flows of

---

Progress check 13.8 **What is discounted payback and how is it calculated?**

Advantages and disadvantages of the five investment appraisal criteria

We have discussed the five capital investment criteria and seen examples of their application. The table in Fig. 13.5 summarises each of the methods and the advantages and disadvantages of their practical use in investment appraisal.

It is interesting to note that even ten years ago payback still seemed to be the most popular appraisal method within UK companies, closely followed by IRR! NPV, discounted payback and ARR appeared to be equal third sharing around the same level of popularity (*A Survey of Management Accounting Practices in UK Companies* 1993).

It should be emphasised that the whole area of capital investment appraisal is one that requires a great deal of expertise and experience. In real-life decision-making situations these types of appraisal are generally carried out by the accountant or the finance director. These sorts of longer-term decisions are concerned primarily with the maximisation of shareholder wealth, but they also impact on issues relating to the health and future development of the business. Therefore, such decisions are normally based on qualitative as well as quantitative factors.

Non-financial measures appear to be as important, if not more important, to businesses in their

$$i = \frac{1.11}{1.02} - 1 = 0.088 \text{ or } 8.8\%$$

This would normally then be rounded to say 9% and forecast cash flows that have been adjusted for inflation may then be discounted using this real cost of capital. Alternatively, if forecast cash flows have not been adjusted for inflation, then these money cash flows would be discounted using the company's actual cost of capital. The result is the same using either method.

Working capital

Any increases in working capital required for a project in addition to the normal investments need to be shown as cash outflows as necessary in one or more years, offset by cash inflows to bring the total to zero by the end of the project.

Worked Example 13.7

Delta Precision plc, a manufacturing company, has the opportunity to invest in a machine costing £110,000 that will generate net cash inflows from the investment of £30,000 for five years after which time the machine will be worth nothing. Cost of capital is 10%. We may ignore inflation and taxation in our evaluation of the project using NPV.

Year	Cash outflows £000	Cash inflows £000	Net cash flow £000	Discount factor at 10%	Present values £000
0	−110		−110	1.00	−110.0
1		30	30	0.91	27.3
2		30	30	0.83	24.9
3		30	30	0.75	22.5
4		30	30	0.68	20.4
5		30	30	0.62	18.6
				NPV	+3.7

The positive NPV of £3,700 would indicate acceptance of this investment.
Suppose that in addition to the above factors, for this project Delta required:

- £20,000 working capital in year 1
- £40,000 working capital in year 2, but then
- zero working capital in years 3, 4 and 5.

The revised cash flows would be:

Year	0	1	2	3	4	5	Total
	£000	£000	£000	£000	£000	£000	£000
Investment	−110						−110
Cash inflows		30	30	30	30	30	150
Working		−20		20			0
capital			−40	40			0
Total	−110	10	−10	90	30	30	40

The total cash flow of the project is still the same at £40,000, but the timings of the cash flows are different.

Year	Net cash flows £000	Discount factor	Present values £000
0	−110	1.00	−110.0
1	10	0.91	9.1
2	−10	0.83	−8.3
3	90	0.75	67.5
4	30	0.68	20.4
5	30	0.62	18.6
		NPV	−2.7

The need for, and the timing of, working capital gives a negative NPV of £2,700 which would now indicate rejection of this investment.

Taxation

In practice, tax must always be allowed for in any capital investment appraisal calculations. The following two examples provide an introduction to this topic, which illustrate the principles.

Worked Example 13.8

Epsilon Ltd is a company that manufactures and distributes consumer products. It is currently considering the acquisition of a machine costing £2,700,000 to market a new product.

The machine will be worth nothing after 10 years but is expected to produce 10,000 units of a product per year during that period, with variable costs of £35 per unit.

The product can be sold for £120 per unit.

Fixed costs directly attributed to this product will be £300,000 per year.

The company's cost of capital is 10%.

We may assume that all costs and revenues are paid and received during each year.

We may further assume that corporation tax is paid in the year that profit is made and calculated at 40% of profit, and that for tax purposes each year's depreciation is equal to capital allowances.

The acquisition of the machine can be evaluated using NPV.

	£000	
Sales revenue	1,200	[10,000 × £120]
Variable costs	(350)	[10,000 × £35]
Depreciation	(270)	[2,700,000 over 10-year life]
Fixed costs	(300)	
Taxable profit	280	
Corporation tax at 40%	(112)	[based on taxable profit plus depreciation less capital allowances]
Profit after tax	168	
Add back depreciation	270	[non-cash flow]
Yearly cash flow	438	

Using the cumulative Present Value tables (see Appendix 2) the present value of £1 at 10% over 10 years is £6.15, therefore:

$$NPV = -£2,700,000 + (£438,000 \times 6.15) = -£6,300$$

The NPV is less than 0 and the project is therefore not acceptable.

Corporation tax is normally payable by a company in the year following the year in which profit is earned. If a project lasts for say four years then cashflow in respect of tax must be shown in the fifth year. The length of the project is then effectively five years. Tax payable in respect of operating profit must be shown separately from cash flows in respect of capital allowances. The first investment year is normally shown as year 0 and the first tax allowance year is therefore year one.

Worked Example 13.9

Zeta plc has the opportunity to invest in a machine costing £100,000 that will generate cash profits of £30,000 per year for the next four years after which the machine would be sold for £10,000. The company's after tax cost of capital is 8% per annum.

We may assume:

- corporation tax at 30%
- annual writing down allowances in each year are on the investment reducing balance at 25%
- there will be a balancing charge or allowance on disposal of the machine.

We can consider whether the investment should be made, using an NPV approach.

Capital allowances:

Year	Opening balance	Capital allowance at 25%	Balancing allowance/ (charge)	Closing balance
	£	£	£	£
0	100,000	25,000		75,000
1	75,000	18,750		56,250
2	56,250	14,063		42,187
3	42,187	10,547		31,640
4	31,640	7,910		23,730
	23,730			
Proceeds	10,000		13,730	
Total		76,270	13,730	

Note that the totals of the capital allowances and balancing allowance equal £90,000, the net cost of the machine £100,000 less £10,000.

Next, we can calculate the taxable profit, and the tax payable.

Year	0	1	2	3	4
	£	£	£	£	£
Profits		30,000	30,000	30,000	30,000
Capital allowances	25,000	18,750	14,063	10,547	21,640
Taxable 'profit'	– 25,000	11,250	15,937	19,453	8,360
Tax receivable/ (payable) at 30%	7,500	–3,375	–4,781	–5,836	–2,508

We can now calculate the net cash flows and the present values of the project:

Year	Machine	Profits	Tax	Net cash flow	Discount factor at 8% pa	Present values
	£	£	£	£		£
0	–100,000			–100,000	1.00	–100,000
1		30,000	7,500	37,500	0.93	34,875
2		30,000	–3,375	26,625	0.86	22,897
3		30,000	–4,781	25,219	0.79	19,923
4	10,000	30,000	–5,836	34,164	0.74	25,281
5			–2,508	–2,508	0.68	–1,705
					NPV	+1,271

The positive NPV of £1,271 would indicate acceptance of this investment.

Capital investment decisions take on a wider dimension for international corporations with the consideration of a further factor, the uncertainty associated with foreign currency exchange rate fluctuations. For UK-based companies this has had a particular significance over the past few years with the uncertainty surrounding the UK's adoption of the euro. Foreign currency exchange rate risk is not discussed in this chapter but is an important topic that was introduced in Chapter 2.

> **Progress check 13.10** **Why and how should inflation and working capital be allowed for in making capital investment decisions?**

Back in 2001, Nissan's decision to build its new Micra car in Sunderland in the UK illustrated the importance of some of the additional factors that influence investment appraisal decisions. The strength of the £ sterling against the euro had damaged Sunderland's chances of winning the contract. But, the level of Government support and the flexibility of the Sunderland workforce were factors that impacted favourably on the Nissan decision, in addition to their positive initial financial appraisal of the investment. As we can see from the press extract below, the fact that UK had still not joined the euro was now threatening any future new investment in the plant.

The same press extract highlights an additional factor influencing investment decisions – the cost of labour. The labour cost differentials between UK and, for example, China and Eastern Europe have resulted increasingly in companies making new investments in countries like Poland, Czechoslovakia, and China. Despite the receipt from the UK Government of huge grants, interest-free loans and fully-subsidised staff training, Samsung has decided to re-invest in plants in the Far East and Slovakia.

The impact of high UK costs on investments by large foreign companies

Electronics group Samsung yesterday announced it was shutting down its UK manufacturing operation, resulting in the loss of 425 jobs in the north-east.

The South Korean conglomerate said UK labour costs were too high, forcing it to move all of its factories to the Far East and Slovakia.

The Department for Trade and Industry said it would decide whether Samsung should pay back £10.5m of government aid granted it when the two Billingham factories were built for £450m in 1995.

Samsung UK's deputy managing director of manufacturing, John Slider, said the closure was 'the only practical way forward'.

He said: 'It's very sad news. This factory won the gold medal for productivity in the Samsung empire, which is no mean feat. The problem is the expense of the UK. We pay £4.50 to £5.50 an hour, which is not that much over here, but, when you compare that with 50p an hour in China, and £1 an hour in Slovakia, it's clear we can't compete.'

The microwave and flat-panel monitor plant's closure – timetabled for April – threatens another 1,000 jobs with suppliers in the area. It also follows Samsung's closure in 1999 of a nearby factory making fax machines.

Yesterday's move cast further doubt on the Government's policy of attempting to lure large foreign companies to build in the UK with grants and aid. When originally announced at the end of 1994, Michael Heseltine, then President of the Board of Trade, had called the Samsung deal 'a wonderful opportunity'.

The company was promised a total of £58m in grants, provided it created 3,000 jobs in the following five years, but, because employment only reached 1,500 at its peak, it received only £10.5m.

Samsung was also offered a £13m interest-free loan and £20m worth of training provided by a combination of local authorities and quangos. It said yesterday it used £1m of this to build a training centre, and did not take up the loan.

About £11m was also invested by local authorities and English Partnerships in improving the site itself and its transport facilities.

Unions and MPs rounded on Samsung last night, demanding that the grant be repaid in full. Frank Cook, Labour MP for Stockton North, said: 'They were allocated £58m and given every kind of consideration. They had every possible convenience provided for them. They claimed they have only drawn down £10.5m as if they have done us some kind of a favour. Words fail me.'

A DTI spokesman said: 'Offers of this kind include claw-back provisions for the recovery of grant paid where projects run into difficulty or firms withdraw from an investment,' she said. 'The Government has given funding to local agencies to help those affected by today's announcement.'

Another local recipient of government aid, Nissan, has hinted that it might move production abroad. The Japanese car company was most recently awarded £3.26m to build its Micra cabriolet in Sunderland, but its president, Carlos Ghosn, last week threatened to pull the replacement for the Almera from the plant unless the UK joined the euro.

Many of those losing their jobs yesterday live in Prime Minister Tony Blair's Sedgefield constituency. Yesterday he said: 'This is part of the world economy in which we live. There will be occasions when companies close plants.'

High labour cost drives Samsung out of Britain, by Edmund Conway
© *Daily Telegraph*, 16 January 2004

Risk and uncertainty and decision-making – sensitivity analysis

In our earlier discussion on the decision-making process we talked about comparing actual results following implementation of the decision with the expected outcome. Our own experience tells us that actual outcomes usually differ considerably from expected outcomes. In terms of capital investment, the greater the timescale of the project the more time there is for more things to go wrong; the larger the investment, the greater may be the impact.

As a final step in evaluation of the investment in a project it is prudent to carry out some sort of sensitivity analysis. Sensitivity analysis may be used to assess the risk associated with a capital investment project. A project having a positive NPV may on the face of it seem viable. It is useful to calculate how much the NPV may change should there be changes to the factors used in the appraisal exercise. These factors are shown in Fig. 13.6.

Sensitivity may be evaluated through numerical analysis, which is illustrated in Worked Examples 13.10 to 13.14. Sensitivity may also be shown graphically:

- NPV may be plotted on the y vertical axis
- the percentage change in the variable factors, used in the appraisal, may be plotted on the x horizontal axis.

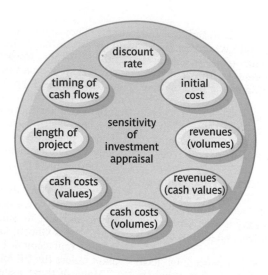

Figure 13.6 Project appraisal factors used in sensitivity analysis

This process may be carried out for each variable, for example:

- sales
- cost savings
- investment
- scrap value.

The most sensitive variable is the one with the steepest gradient.

Worked Example 13.10

Theta Ltd has the opportunity to invest in a project with an initial cost of £100,000 that will generate estimated net cash flows of £35,000 at the end of each year for five years. The company's cost of capital is 12% per annum. For simplicity we can ignore the effects of tax and inflation.

The sensitivity of the initial investment in the project can be evaluated using an NPV approach.

The cumulative present value tables show us the annuity factor over five years at 12% per annum at 3.61 (see Appendix 2).

Therefore the NPV of the project is:

$$-£100,000 + (£35,000 \times 3.61)$$
$$= -£100,000 + £126,350$$
$$NPV = +£26,350$$

The positive NPV of £26,350 would indicate going ahead with the investment in this project.

We can consider the sensitivity analysis of the project to changes in the initial investment.

Initial investment

The NPV of the project is £26,350. If the initial investment rose by £26,350 to £126,350 (£100,000 + £26,350) the NPV would become zero and it would not be worth taking on the project. This represents an increase of 26.4% on the initial investment.

Worked Example 13.11

Using the data from Worked Example 13.10 we can evaluate the sensitivity of the annual cash flows from the project, using an NPV approach.

We can consider the sensitivity analysis of the project to changes to the annual cash flows.

Annual cash flow

If we again consider what needs to happen to bring the NPV to zero

then $$\text{NPV} = 0 = -£100,000 + (a \times 3.61)$$

where a is the annual cash flow

$$a = £100,000/3.61$$
$$a = £27,700$$

which is a reduction of 20.9% from the original per annum cash flow of £35,000.

Worked Example 13.12

Using the data from Worked Example 13.10 we can evaluate the sensitivity of cost of capital on the project for Theta Ltd, using an NPV approach.

We can consider the sensitivity analysis of the project to changes in the cost of capital.

Cost of capital

When the NPV is zero the internal rate of return (IRR) is equal to the cost of capital. If the cost of capital is greater than the IRR then the project should be rejected.

In this example we therefore first need to calculate the cumulative discount factor at which the NPV is zero.

$$\text{NPV} = 0 = -£100,000 + (£35,000 \times d)$$

Where d is the cumulative discount factor for five years

$$d = £100,000/£35,000$$
$$d = 2.857$$

The cumulative present value tables show us that the annuity factor over five years of 2.86 represents an interest rate of 22%.

The IRR is therefore approximately 22%, which is an 83.3% increase over the cost of capital of 12%.

Worked Example 13.13

Using the data from Worked Example 13.10 we can evaluate the sensitivity of the length of the project for Theta Ltd, using an NPV approach.

We can consider the sensitivity analysis of the project to changes to the length of project.

Length of project

The original project was five years for which we calculated the NPV at £26,350. We may consider what would be the effect if the project ended after say four years or three years.

If the project was four years, the cumulative discount factor (from the tables) is 3.04 so the NPV of the project is:

$$-£100,000 + (£35,000 \times 3.04)$$
$$= -£100,000 + £106,400$$
$$\text{NPV} = +£6,400$$

The positive NPV of £6,400 still indicates going ahead with the investment in this project.

If the project was three years the cumulative discount factor (from the tables) is 2.40 so the NPV of the project is:

$$-£100,000 + (£35,000 \times 2.40)$$
$$= -£100,000 + £84,000$$
$$\text{NPV} = -£16,000$$

The negative NPV of £16,000 indicates not going ahead with the investment in this project if the length of the project drops below four years, which is the year in which NPV becomes negative. This is a change of 20% (that is a drop from five years to four years).

Worked Example 13.14

Each of the sensitivities that have been calculated in Worked Examples 13.10 to 13.13 may be summarised and we can draw some conclusions about the sensitivity of the project that are apparent from the summary.

The sensitivity analysis that we have carried out is more usefully summarised to show each of the factors we have considered, to show:

- the values used in the original appraisal
- the critical values of those factors
- the percentage change over the original values that they represent.

Factor	Original value	Critical value	% change
Initial investment	£100,000	£126,350	26.4
Annual cash flow	£35,000	£27,700	−20.9
Cost of capital	12%	22%	83.3
Length of project	5 years	4 years	−20.0

We may draw the following conclusions from our sensitivity analysis:

- none of the factors used in the appraisal was critical, their critical values all being +/− 20%
- cost of capital is the least critical factor at 83.3%, which is useful to know since the accuracy of the calculation of cost of capital may not always be totally reliable.

The same technique of sensitivity analysis may be used as an early warning system before a project begins to show a loss. It can be seen from the factors outlined in this section that a board of directors should request a sensitivity analysis on major projects. In the UK, the 5 years up to 2000 saw several projects concerned with the manufacture of chips for computers become very unprofitable, with timing of cash flows critical to their viability.

However, there are limitations to the use of sensitivity analysis. In the worked examples we have considered we have looked at the effect of changes to individual factors in isolation. In reality two or more factors may change simultaneously. The impact of such changes may be assessed using the more sophisticated technique of linear programming. A further limitation may be the absence of clear rules governing acceptance or rejection of the project and the need for the subjective judgement of management.

When we looked at risk and sales pricing in Chapter 10 we saw that we may apply probabilities to estimated demand estimates at different pricing levels to derive expected values. In the same way, cash flows from investments may be weighted by their probabilities of occurrence to calculate an expected NPV.

Worked Example 13.15

Kappa plc has the opportunity of engaging in a two-year project for a specific client. It would require an initial investment in a machine costing £200,000. The machine is capable of running three separate processes. The process used will depend on the level of demand from the client's final customers. Each process will therefore generate different yearly net cash flows, each with a different likelihood of occurrence. The company's cost of capital is 15% per annum.

The forecast probabilities and net cash flows for each year are:

Process	Probability of occurrence	Per annum cash flow
Process 1	0.5	£150,000
Process 2	0.1	£15,000
Process 3	0.4	£90,000
	1.0	

The total of the probabilities is 1.0, which indicates that one of the options is certain to occur. Even though one process will definitely be used should Kappa take on the project?

We first need to use the probabilities to calculate the weighted average of the expected outcomes for each year.

Process	Cash flow	Probability	Expected cash flow
	£		£
1	150,000	0.5	75,000
2	15,000	0.1	1,500
3	90,000	0.4	36,000
Expected per annum cash flows			112,500

To calculate the expected NPV of the project we need to discount the expected annual cash flows using the discount rate of 15% per annum.

Year	Expected cash flow	Discount rate	Expected present value
	£		£
1	112,500	0.87	97,875
2	112,500	0.76	85,500
Total	225,000		183,375
Initial investment (year 0)			200,000
Expected NPV			−16,625

The negative expected NPV of £16,625 indicates that Kappa plc should reject investment in this project.

Although the technique of expected net present value is a clear decision rule with a single numerical outcome there are caveats:

- this technique uses an average number which in the above example is not actually capable of occurrence
- use of an average number may cloud the issue if the underlying risk of outcomes worse than the average are ignored
- if the per annum cash flow from process 1 had been £300,000 and the expected NPV had been positive consider the impact on Kappa if, for example, the client had actually required the use of process 2.

Progress check 13.11 **Risk and uncertainty increasingly impact on investment decisions. What are these risk factors, and how may we evaluate their impact?**

Control of capital investment projects

Once a project has been appraised and a sensitivity analysis carried out and the approval has been given at the relevant level in the organisation, project controls must be established and then post-project completion audits carried out. The controls cover the three main areas of:

- capital spend – note the number of subjective areas where things can go wrong
- project-timing – delays appear to be 'routine' in many major projects as evidenced almost daily in the financial press
- benefits – evidenced almost as frequently in the financial press, this is another area where things may not turn out as planned.

Capital spending limits are usually put in place by most organisations with levels of spend requiring authorisation at the appropriate managerial level. Capital expenditure proposals should be documented to show:

- project details, including costs, benefits and the life of the project
- appraisal calculations and comparisons with the organisation's targets
- assumptions
- names of the project manager and the project team
- name(s) and signature(s) of the manager(s) authorising the project
- the period(s) in which expenditure should take place.

Material delays in capital spend or in the progress of the project should prompt a resubmitted proposal together with the reasons for delay. A good project manager with the appropriate level of responsibility and authority should ensure that projects run to plan.

Benefits from projects are not easy to control because they are usually derived over many years. The importance of having a good project manager in place cannot be overemphasised. He/she should ensure that expected benefits actually materialise and are as large in value as anticipated. The project manager should also ensure that costs are kept in line with expectation.

Post-implementation audits should be carried out for all projects if possible. Although after the event corrective action cannot usually be taken, variances may be analysed to use the project as an information and learning tool:

- to appraise manager performance
- to identify strengths and weaknesses in the forecasting and estimating techniques
- to identify areas of improvement in the capital investment process
- to advertise the fact that both project and manager performance are being monitored.

> **Progress check 13.12 In what ways can we ensure that capital investment projects are adequately controlled?**

Summary of key points

- An investment requires expenditure on something today that is expected to provide a benefit in the future.

- The decision to make an investment is extremely important because it implies the expectation that expenditure today will generate future cash gains in real terms that greatly exceed the funds spent today.
- '£1 received today is worth more than £1 received in a year's time' is an expression of what is meant by the 'time value of money'.
- The principles underlying the investment appraisal techniques that use the DCF method are cash flow (as opposed to profit), and the time value of money.
- Five main criteria are used to appraise investments: accounting rate of return (ARR); payback; net present value (NPV); internal rate of return (IRR); and discounted payback – the last three being discounted cash flow (DCF) techniques.
- The technique of discounted cash flow discounts the projected net cash flows of a capital project to ascertain its present value, using an appropriate discount rate, or cost of capital.
- Additional factors impacting on investment criteria calculations are: the effect of inflation on the cost of capital; working capital requirements; length of project; taxation; risk and uncertainty.
- There may be a number of risks associated with each of the variables included in a capital investment appraisal decision: estimates of initial costs; uncertainty about the timing and values of future cash revenues and costs; the length of project; variations in the discount rate.
- Sensitivity analysis may be used to assess the risk associated with a capital investment project.
- To establish the appropriate levels of control, the appointment of a good project manager with the appropriate level of responsibility and authority, together with regular project reviews, are absolute essentials to ensure that projects run to plan.
- The techniques of capital investment appraisal require a great deal of expertise and experience, and further training should be received before attempting to use them in real life decision-making situations.

Questions

Q13.1 (i)   What is capital investment?

(ii) Why are capital investment decisions so important to companies?

Q13.2 Outline the five main investment appraisal criteria.

Q13.3 Describe the two key principles underlying DCF investment selection criteria.

Q13.4 What are the advantages in the use of NPV over IRR in investment appraisal?

Q13.5 What are the factors that impact on capital investment decisions?

Q13.6 (i)   What is meant by risk with regard to investment?

(ii) How does sensitivity analysis help?

Q13.7 Describe how capital investment projects may be controlled and reviewed.

Discussion points

D13.1 'I know that cash and profit are not always the same thing but surely eventually they end up being equal. Therefore, surely we should look at the likely ultimate profit from a capital investment before deciding whether or not to invest?' Discuss.

D13.2 'This discounted cash flow business seems like just a bit more work for the accountants to me. Cash is cash whenever it's received or paid. I say let's keep capital investment appraisal simple.' Discuss.

D13.3 'If you don't take a risk you will not make any money.' Discuss.

Exercises

Solutions are provided in Appendix 4 to all exercise numbers highlighted in colour.

Level I

E13.1 *Time allowed – 30 minutes*

Global Sights & Sounds Ltd (GSS) sells multi-media equipment and software through its retail outlets. GSS is considering investing in some major refurbishment of one of its outlets, to enable it to provide improved customer service, until the lease expires at the end of four years. GSS is currently talking to two contractors, Smith Ltd and Jones Ltd. Whichever contractor is used, the improved customer service has been estimated to generate increased net cash inflows as follows:

Year	£
1	75,000
2	190,000
3	190,000
4	225,000

Smith:
The capital costs will be £125,000 at the start of the project, and £175,000 at the end of each of years 1 and 2.

Jones:
The capital costs will be the same in total, but payment to the contractor can be delayed. Capital payments will be £50,000 at the start of the project, £75,000 at the end of each of years one, two and three, and the balance of capital cost at the end of year four. In return for the delayed payments the contractor will receive a 20% share of the cash inflows generated from the improved services, payable at the end of each year. In the interim period, the unutilised capital will be invested in a short-term project in another department store, generating a cash inflow of £60,000 at the end of each of years one, two and three.

It may be assumed that all cash flows occur at the end of each year.

The effects of taxation and inflation may be ignored.

You are required to advise GSS Ltd on whether to select Smith or Jones, ignoring the time value of money, using the appraisal basis of:

    (i)   **accounting rate of return (ARR), and**

    (ii)   **comment on the appraisal method you have used.**

E13.2 *Time allowed – 30 minutes*

Using the information on Global Sights & Sounds Ltd from Exercise E13.1, you are required to advise GSS Ltd on whether to select Smith or Jones, ignoring the time value of money, using the appraisal basis of:

(i)   payback, and

(ii)   comment on the appraisal method you have used.

E13.3 *Time allowed – 60 minutes*

Rainbow plc's business is organised into divisions. For operating purposes, each division is regarded as an investment centre, with divisional managers enjoying substantial autonomy in their selection of investment projects. Divisional managers are rewarded via a remuneration package, which is linked to a return on investment (ROI) performance measure. The ROI calculation is based on the net book value of assets at the beginning of the year. Although there is a high degree of autonomy in investment selection, approval to go ahead has to be obtained from group management at the head office in order to release the finance.

Red Division is currently investigating three independent investment proposals. If they appear acceptable, it wishes to assign each a priority in the event that funds may not be available to cover all three. The WACC (weighted average cost of capital) for the company is the hurdle rate used for new investments and is estimated at 15% per annum.

The details of the three proposals are as follows:

	Project A £000	Project B £000	Project C £000
Initial cash outlay on fixed assets	60	60	60
Net cash inflow in year 1	21	25	10
Net cash inflow in year 2	21	20	20
Net cash inflow in year 3	21	20	30
Net cash inflow in year 4	21	15	40

Taxation and the residual values of the fixed assets may be ignored.

Depreciation is straight line over the asset life, which is four years in each case.

You are required to:

(i)   give an appraisal of the three investment proposals with regard to divisional performance, using ROI and RI

(ii)   give an appraisal of the three investment proposals with regard to company performance, using a DCF approach

(iii) explain any divergence between the two points of view, expressed in (i) and (ii) above, and outline how the views of both the division and the company can be brought into line.

Level II

E13.4 *Time allowed – 30 minutes*

Using the information on Global Sights & Sounds Ltd from Exercise E13.1, you are required to advise GSS Ltd on whether to select Smith or Jones, using the appraisal basis of:

    (i)   net present value (NPV), using a cost of capital of 12% per annum to discount the cash flows to their present value, and

    (ii)   comment on the appraisal method you have used.

E13.5 *Time allowed – 30 minutes*

Using the information on Global Sights & Sounds Ltd from Exercise E13.1, you are required to advise GSS Ltd on whether to select Smith or Jones, using the appraisal basis of:

    (i)   discounted payback, using a cost of capital of 12% per annum to discount the cash flows to their present value, and

    (ii)   comment on the appraisal method you have used.

E13.6 *Time allowed – 45 minutes*

Using the information on Global Sights & Sounds Ltd from Exercise E13.1, you are required to advise GSS Ltd on whether to select Smith or Jones, using the appraisal basis of:

    (i)   internal rate of return (IRR), and

    (ii)   comment on the appraisal method you have used.

E13.7 *Time allowed – 45 minutes*

In Exercise E13.1 we are told that a 20% share of the improved cash inflow has been agreed with Jones Ltd.

You are required to:

    (i)   calculate the percentage share at which GSS Ltd would be indifferent, on a financial basis, as to which of the contractors Smith or Jones should carry out the work

    (ii)   outline the other factors, in addition to your financial analyses in (i), that should be considered in making the choice between Smith and Jones.

E13.8 *Time allowed – 60 minutes*

Alive & Kicking Ltd (AAK) owns a disused warehouse in which a promoter runs regular small gigs. There are currently no facilities to provide drinks. The owners of AAK intend to provide such facilities and can obtain funding to cover capital costs. This would have to be repaid over five years at an annual interest rate of 10%.

The capital costs are estimated at £120,000 for equipment that will have a life of five years and no residual value. To provide drinks, the running costs of staff, etc., will be £40,000 in the first year, increasing by £4,000 in each subsequent year. AAK proposes to charge £10,000 per annum for lighting, heating and other property expenses, and wants a nominal £5,000 per annum to cover any unforeseen contingencies. Apart from this, AAK is not looking for any profit as such from the provision of these facilities, because it believes that there may be additional future benefits from increased use of the facility. It is proposed that costs will be recovered by setting drinks prices at double the direct costs.

It is not expected that the full sales level will be reached until year three. The proportions of that level estimated to be reached in years one and two are 40% and 70% respectively.

You are required to:

(i)   calculate the sales that need to be achieved in each of the five years to meet the proposed targets

(ii)   comment briefly on four aspects of the proposals that you consider merit further investigation.

You may ignore the possible effects of taxation and inflation.

E13.9 *Time allowed – 90 minutes*

Lew Rolls plc is an international group that manufactures and distributes bathroom fittings to major building supply retailers and DIY chains. The board of Rolls is currently considering four projects to work with four different customers to develop new bathroom ranges (toilet, bidet, bath, basin, and shower).

Rolls has a limit on funds for investment for the current year of £24m. The four projects represent levels of 'luxury' bathrooms. The product ranges are aimed at different markets. The lengths of time to bring to market, lives of product and timings of cash flows are different for each product range.

The Super bathroom project will cost £3m and generate £5m net cash flows spread equally over five years.

The Superluxury bathroom project will cost £7m and generate £10m net cash flows spread equally over five years.

The Executive bathroom project will take a long time to start paying back. It will cost £12m and generate £21m net cash flows, zero for the first two years and then £7m for each of the next three years.

The Excelsior bathroom project will cost £15m and generate £10m net cash flows for two years.

For ease of calculation it may be assumed that all cash flows occur on the last day of each year.

Projects may be undertaken in part or in total in the current year, and next year there will be no restriction on investment. Lew Rolls plc's cost of capital is 10%.

You are required to:

(i)   calculate the NPV for each project

(ii)   calculate the approximate IRR for each project

(iii)   advise on the acceptance of these projects on the basis of NPV or IRR or any other method of ranking the projects.

(iv)   What are the advantages of the appraisal method you have adopted for Lew Rolls plc?

(v)   What other factors should be used in the final evaluations before the recommendations are implemented?

E13.10 *Time allowed – 90 minutes*

A UK subsidiary of a large multinational is considering investment in four mutually exclusive projects. The managing director, Indira Patel, is anxious to choose a combination of projects that will maximise shareholder wealth.

At the current time the company can embark on projects up to a maximum total of £230m. The four projects require the following initial investments:

£20m in project Doh
£195m in project Ray
£35m in project Mee
£80m in project Fah

The projects are expected to generate the following net cash flows over the three years following each investment. No project will last longer than three years.

Project	Doh	Ray	Mee	Fah
Year	£m	£m	£m	£m
1	15	45	15	20
2	30	75	25	25
3		180	60	100

The company's WACC is 12% per annum, which is used to evaluate investments in new projects. The impact of tax and inflation may be ignored.

Advise Indira with regard to the projects in which the company should invest on the basis of maximisation of shareholder wealth, given the limiting factor of the total funds currently available for investment.

14

Sources of finance and the cost of capital

Contents

Learning objectives

Completion of this chapter will enable you to:

- identify the different sources of finance available to an organisation
- explain the concept of gearing, or the debt/equity ratio
- explain what is meant by the weighted average cost of capital (WACC)
- calculate the cost of equity and the cost of debt
- appreciate the concept of risk with regard to capital investment
- outline the capital asset pricing model (CAPM), and the β factor
- analyse return on equity as a function of financial structure
- explain the use of economic value added (EVA™) and market value added (MVA) as performance measures and value creation incentives.

Introduction

This chapter begins with an outline of the types of finance available to organisations to fund their long-term capital investment and short-term requirement for working capital. Financing may be internal or external to the organisation, and either short-term (shorter than one year) or medium-to long-term (longer than one year). Short-term financing is discussed in Chapter 15, which covers working capital management.

In Chapter 13 we dealt with decisions related to capital investment. This chapter will consider a number of financing options such as leasing and Government grants, but will focus on the main sources of long-term external finance available to an entity to finance such investments: loans (or debt) and ordinary shares (or equity). We shall also discuss gearing or financial structure, which relates to the relationship between the debt and equity of the entity. The appraisal of investment projects by a company inevitably involves calculations, which use some sort of discount rate. The discount rate that is normally used is the company's cost of capital. A company's cost of capital is dependent on the financial structure of the entity, its relative proportions and cost of debt (loans) and equity capital (shares). In Chapter 5 and in Chapter 13 we introduced WACC and in this chapter we will consider its calculation and application.

We will look at how the costs of equity and debt may be determined. One of the fundamental differences between equity and debt is the risk associated with each type of financing and its impact on their cost. The capital asset pricing model (CAPM) is introduced to show how risk impacts on the cost of equity.

This chapter looks briefly at the relationship between the return on equity and the financial structure of the company. The chapter closes with an introduction to economic value added (EVA) and market value added (MVA). These measures are increasingly replacing traditional performance measures in many large companies. An outline of these recently developed techniques is considered in terms of their use as both performance measures and motivational tools.

Sources of finance

In Chapter 2 we considered some of the various types of business finance when we looked at the balance sheet. Organisations require finance for both short- and medium- to long-term requirements and the financing is usually matched with the funding requirement. Longer-term finance (longer than one year) is usually used to fund capital investment in fixed assets and other longer-term projects. Short-term finance (shorter than one year) is usually used to fund the organisation's requirement for working capital.

Both short- and long-term finance may be either internal or external to the organisation.

Internal finance may be provided from:

- retained earnings
- trade credit
- cash improvements gained from the more effective management of working capital.

Retained earnings

Retained earnings are the funds generated that are surplus to:

- the costs of adding to or replacing fixed assets
- the operational costs of running the business
- net interest charges
- tax charges
- dividend payments.

There is statistical evidence, which shows that through the 1990s the majority of capital funding of UK companies continued to be derived from internal sources of finance. However, this is not free. The profit or net earnings generated from the operations of the company belongs to the shareholders of the company. There is a cost, an opportunity cost, which is the best alternative return that shareholders could obtain on these funds elsewhere in the financial markets.

It is the shareholders who decide at the annual general meeting (AGM) how much of those earnings are distributed to shareholders as dividends, the balance being held and reinvested in the business. The retained earnings of the company are increased by net profit less any dividends payable; they are part of the shareholders' funds and therefore appear within the equity of the company. Similarly any losses will reduce the retained earnings of the company. The cost of shareholders' equity is reflected in the level of dividends paid to shareholders, which is usually dependent on how well the company has performed during the year.

Trade credit, together with the more effective management of working capital, will be discussed in Chapter 15.

The main source of external short-term funding is short-term debt.

Short-term debt

Short-term financial debts are the elements of overdrafts, loans and leases that are repayable within one year of the balance sheet date. Short-term finance tends to be less expensive and more flexible than long-term debt. Short-term debt is therefore normally matched to finance the fluctuations in levels of the company's net current assets, its working capital.

Such short-term finance represents a higher risk for the borrower. Interest rates can be volatile, and an overdraft, for example, is technically repayable on demand. The company may finance its operations by taking on further short-term debt, as levels of working capital increase. Because of the higher risk associated with short-term debt, many companies adopting a conservative funding policy may accept a reduction in profitability and use long-term debt to finance not only fixed assets, but also a proportion of the company's working capital. Less risk-averse companies may use short-term debt to finance both working capital and fixed assets; such debt provides increased profitability because of its lower cost.

We will discuss each of the other sources of external finance, which are primarily long-term, and include:

- ordinary shares (or equity shares)
- preference shares
- loan capital (financial debt that includes bank loans, debentures, and other loans)
- hybrid finance (for example, convertible loans)
- leasing
- UK Government funding
- European funding.

The two main primary sources of long-term finance available to a company, which are both external, are broadly:

- equity share capital (ordinary shares)
- debt (long-term loans and debentures).

Both types of financing have a unique set of characteristics and rights. The main ones are shown in the table in Fig. 14.1.

equity (ordinary shares)	debt (loans)
the term is unlimited, i.e. for life	the term is fixed and has a maturity date
ordinary shares have a nominal or par value	loans require security, e.g. debentures
ordinary shares have voting rights	loans have no voting rights
dividends are payable on ordinary shares, the values of which are dependent on company performance	interest is payable on loans: it may be fixed; variable; rolled over
dividends are an appropriation or a use of profits, and are therefore payable after corporation tax	interest on loans is an allowable expense for corporation tax
if a company is wound up the ordinary shareholders are the last to be considered – it is capital having the highest risk	if a company is wound up, lenders appear near the top of the list for consideration

Figure 14.1 Some of the main characteristics and rights of equity capital compared with debt capital

Share capital

The capital of a company is called share capital and may comprise ordinary shares and preference shares (although there are other classes of shares, which are not covered in this book). The company determines the maximum share capital that it is ever likely to need to raise and this level is called its authorised share capital. The amount of shares actually in issue at any point in time is normally at a level for the company to meet its foreseeable requirements. These shares are called the company's issued share capital which, when all the shareholders have paid for them, are referred to as fully paid up issued share capital. Ordinary shares represent the long-term capital provided by the owners of a company, both new and existing.

In start-up businesses the ordinary shares are usually owned by the founder(s) of the business, and possibly by family and friends, or by investors seeking a gain in their value as the business grows. As a company grows it may decide:

- to raise further equity share capital, in order to finance its growth, at levels much higher than the founders of the business and/or their friends and family are willing or able to afford, or
- to sell its shares by making them publicly available and freely traded, to realise gains in their value for the founders or other investors.

The way that such businesses action these decisions is by making what are termed **initial public offerings (IPOs)** of shares in their companies. This means that shares are offered for sale to the general public and to financial institutions and are then traded (in the UK) on the Stock Exchange or the Alternative Investment Market (AIM).

Floating on the AIM

Shearings, the holiday company and coach operator, is to join the Alternative Investment Market with a potential value of more than £100m.

The company was founded almost 100 years ago. Although it started out as a coach firm, it has expanded to include hotel breaks and cruises.

It now carries more than 500,000 holiday makers to destinations across the globe every year, specialising in customers over 55.

Shearings has been conducting a strategic review since earlier this year.

Although several trade buyers are thought to have expressed an interest, majority shareholder Bridgepoint Capital is understood to favour a stock market listing.

It is being advised by Baird, the broker.

The company is just one of a handful which said yesterday they intended to float on AIM, giving a further boost to London's junior market.

AIM has played host to 80 new admissions since the start of the year, taking the total to more than 831 companies with a market capitalisation of around £22 billion.

The exchange said it had accounted for about 60pc of new listings in Western Europe last year.

Mat Wootton, deputy head of AIM, said the past six months had seen a strong level of activity in the market, with AIM being particularly attractive because of its light regulatory burden.

It has about 25 companies in the pipeline who have expressed their intention to seek admission. AIM celebrates its ninth birthday this month and Mr Wootton said his ambition for the next year would be to improve the efficiency of the secondary market and attract more international companies to the exchange. But Garry Levin, managing director at Altium, sounded a note of caution.

He said: 'The market is not open for

opportunistic companies. The emphasis from fund managers is on quality companies with solid equity growth stories. Only if these are sensibly priced is there an appetite for it.'

Others intending to float include:

- Monkleigh, a new company seeking to develop an integrated event marketing services group
- Libertas Capital, a financial services firm
- US online bookmaker Betonsports
- Plusnet, an internet service provider focusing on broadband services
- Eurocastle Investment, a Guernsey-based investment company dealing primarily in European real estate

- Smallbone, a Devizes-based manufacturer of bespoke kitchens
- Sales technology firm XN Checkout.

However, Wagamama, the Japanese-style noodle bar chain, said it was putting its planned initial public offering on hold to pursue discussions with possible buyers. The company, controlled by private equity firm Graphite Capital, said it had already had a number of approaches.

'We will choose the route that will maximise value for shareholders,' a spokesman said.

Shearings takes fast lane to market, David Litterick

© *Daily Telegraph*, 8 June 2004

The holiday company Shearings (see the press extract above) has expanded from a coach business to a company that provides hotel breaks and cruises to become a company with a value of over £100m. The company carried out a strategic review of its business and considered that its future development may be best served by obtaining a stock market listing on the AIM. The press extract also indicates that a further 25 companies were also currently interested in obtaining an AIM listing.

Ordinary shareholders receive a dividend at a level determined usually by company performance and not as a specific entitlement. The level of dividends is usually based on the underlying profitability of the company (Tesco plc actually advised their shareholders of this relationship in the late 1990s). Preference shareholders receive a dividend at a level that is fixed, subject to the conditions of issue of the shares, and have priority over the ordinary shareholders if the company is wound up. In addition, ordinary shareholders normally have voting rights, whereas preference shareholders do not.

If a company goes into liquidation the ordinary shareholders are always last to be repaid. Ordinary shareholders are paid out of the balance of funds that remain after all other creditors have been repaid.

Additional equity capital may be raised through increasing the number of shares issued by the company through **scrip issues** and **rights issues**. A scrip issue (or bonus issue) increases the number of shares with the additional shares going to existing shareholders, in proportion to their holdings, through capitalisation of the reserves of the company. No cash is called for from the shareholders.

Rights issues

In a rights issue, the right to subscribe for new shares (or debentures) issued by the company is given to existing shareholders. The 'rights' to buy the new shares are usually fixed at a price discounted to below the current market price (see Worked Examples 14.1 and 14.2). A shareholder not wishing to take up a rights issue may sell the rights.

Worked Example 14.1

A company that achieves a profit after tax of 20% on capital employed has the following capital structure:

400,000 ordinary shares of £1	£400,000
Retained earnings	£200,000

In order to invest in some new profitable projects the company wishes to raise £252,000 from a rights issue. The company's current ordinary share price is £1.80.

The company would like to know the number of shares that must be issued if the rights price is: £1.60; £1.50; £1.40; £1.20.

Capital employed is £600,000 [£400,000 + £200,000]

Current earnings are 20% of £600,000 = £120,000

Therefore, earnings per share (eps) $= \dfrac{£120,000}{400,000} = 30\text{p}$

After the rights issue earnings will be 20% of £852,000 [£400,000 + £200,000 + £252,000], which equals £170,400.

Rights price	Number of new shares £252,000/ rights price	Total shares after rights issue	Eps £170,400/ total shares
£	£	£	pence
1.60	157,500	557,500	30.6
1.50	168,000	568,000	30.0
1.40	180,000	580,000	29.4
1.20	210,000	610,000	27.9

We can see that at a high rights issue share price the earnings per share are increased. At lower issue prices eps are diluted. The 'break-even point', with no dilution, is where the rights price equals the capital employed per share £600,000/400,000 = £1.50.

Worked Example 14.2

A company has 1,000,000 £1 ordinary shares in issue with a market price of £2.10 on 1 June. The company wished to raise new equity capital by a 1 for 4 share rights issue at a price of £1.50. Immediately the company announced the rights issue the price fell to £1.95 on 2 June. Just before the issue was due to be made the share price had recovered to £2 per share, the cum rights price.

The company may calculate the theoretical ex-rights price, the new market price as a consequence of an adjustment to allow for the discount price of the new issue.

The market price will theoretically fall after the issue

1,000,000 shares × the cum rights price of £2	£2,000,000
250,000 shares × the issue price of £1.50	£375,000
Theoretical value of 1,250,000 shares	£2,375,000

Therefore, the theoretical ex-rights price is $\dfrac{£2,375,000}{1,250,000} = £1.90$ per share

Or to put it another way

Four shares at the cum rights value of £2	£8.00
One new share issued at £1.50	£1.50
	£9.50

Therefore, the theoretical ex-rights price is $\dfrac{£9.50}{5} = £1.90$ per share

Long-term debt

Generally, companies try and match their financing with what it is required for, and the type of assets requiring to be financed:

- fixed assets
- long-term projects.

Long-term debt is usually more expensive and less flexible, but has less risk, than short-term debt. Long-term debt is therefore normally matched to finance the acquisition of fixed assets, which are long-term assets from which the company expects to derive benefits over several periods.

Long-term financial debts are the elements of loans and leases that are payable after one year of the balance sheet date. Debt capital may take many forms: loans, debentures, Eurobonds, mortgages, etc. We will look at debentures, but we will not delve into the particular attributes of every type of debt capital. Suffice to say, each involves interest payment, and capital repayment and security for the loan is usually required. Loan interest is a fixed commitment, which is usually payable once or twice a year. But although debt capital is burdened with a fixed commitment of interest payable, it is a tax-efficient method of financing.

Debentures

Debentures and long-term loans are both debt, which are often taken to mean the same thing. However, loans may be either unsecured, or secured on some or all of the assets of the company. Lenders to a company receive interest, payable yearly or half-yearly, the rate of which may vary with market conditions. A debenture more specifically refers to the written acknowledgement of a debt by a company, usually given under its seal, and is secured on some or all of the assets of the company or its subsidiaries. A debenture agreement normally contains provisions as to payment of interest and the terms of repayment of principal. Other long-term loans are usually unsecured.

Security for a debenture may be by way of a floating charge, without attachment to specific assets, on the whole of the business's assets. If the company is not able to meet its obligations the floating charge will crystallise on specific assets like debtors or stocks. Security may alternatively, at the outset, take the form of a fixed charge on specific assets like land and buildings.

Debentures are a tax-efficient method of corporate financing, which means that interest payable on such loans is an allowable deduction in the computation of taxable profit. For example, if corporation tax were at 30%, a 10% debenture would actually cost the company 7%, that is {10% − (10% × 30%)}.

Debentures, and other loans, may be redeemable in which case the principal, the original sum borrowed, will need to be repaid on a specific date.

Hybrid finance

Loans may sometimes be required by companies as they move through their growth phase, and for them to finance specific asset acquisitions or projects. Disadvantages of loans are:

- the financial risk resulting from a reduction in the amount of equity compared with debt
- the commitment to fixed interest payments over a number of years
- the requirement of a build up of cash with which to repay the loan on maturity.

Alternatively, if an increase in equity is used for this type of funding, eps (earnings per share) may be immediately 'diluted'. However, some financing is neither totally debt nor equity, but has the characteristics of both. Such hybrid finance, as it is called, includes financial instruments like convertible loans. A **convertible loan** is a 'two stage' financial instrument. It may be a fixed interest debt or preference shares, which can be converted into ordinary shares of the company at the option of the lender. Eps will therefore not be diluted until a later date. The right to convert may usually be exercised each year at a predetermined conversion rate up until a specified date, at which time the loan must be redeemed if it has not been converted. The conversion rate may be stated as:

- a conversion price (the amount of the loan that can be converted into one ordinary share), or
- a conversion ratio (the number of ordinary shares that can be converted from one unit of the loan).

The conversion price or ratio will be specified at the outset and may change during the term of the loan. Convertibles tend to pay a lower rate of interest than straight loans, which is effectively charging lenders for the right to convert to ordinary shares. They therefore provide an additional benefit to company cash flow and cost of financing.

> **Progress check 14.1** **What makes convertible loans attractive to both investors and companies?**

Leasing

Leases are contracts between a lessor and lessee for the hire of a specific asset. Why then is leasing seen as a source of long-term financing? There are two types of leases, **operating leases** and **finance leases**, and the answer to the question lies in the accounting treatment of the latter.

Under both types of leasing contract the lessor has ownership of the asset but gives the lessee the right to use the asset over an agreed period in return for rental payments.

An operating lease is a rental agreement for an asset, which may be leased by one lessee for a period, and then another lessee for a period, and so on. The lease period is normally less than the economic life of the asset, and the lease rentals are charged as a cost in the profit and loss account as they occur. The leased asset does not appear in the lessee's balance sheet. The lessor is responsible for maintenance and regular service for assets like photocopiers, cars, and PCs. The lessor therefore retains most of the risk and reward of ownership.

A finance lease relates to an asset where the present value of the lease rentals payable amounts to at least 90% of its fair market value at the start of the lease. Under a finance lease the legal title to the asset remains with the lessor, but the difference in accounting treatment, as defined by SSAP 21, Accounting for Leases and Hire Purchase Contracts, is that a finance lease is capitalised in the balance sheet of the lessee. A value of the finance lease is shown under fixed assets, based on a calculation of the present value of the capital part (excluding finance charges) of the future lease rentals payable. The future lease rentals are also shown as long- and short-term creditors in the balance sheet. The lessee, although not the legal owner, therefore takes on the risks and rewards of ownership.

The leasing evaluation process involves appraisal of the investment in the asset itself, its outright purchase or lease, and an evaluation of leasing as the method of financing. These two decisions may be made separately in either order or they may form a combined decision, and take account of a number of factors:

- asset purchase price and residual value
- the lease rental amounts and the timing of their payments
- service and maintenance payments
- tax
  - capital allowances for purchased fixed assets
  - tax allowable expenses of lease rentals
- VAT (relating to the asset purchase and the lease rentals)
- interest rates (the general level of rates of competing financing options).

Apart from this outline of the process, the evaluation of leasing as a source of finance is beyond the scope of this book.

UK Government and European funding

Businesses involved in certain industries or located in specific geographical areas of the UK may from time to time be eligible for assistance with financing. This may be by way of grants, loan guarantees, and subsidised consultancy. Funding may be on a national or a regional basis from various UK Government or European Union sources.

By their very nature, such financing initiatives are continually changing in format and their areas of focus. For example, funding assistance has been available in one form or another for SMEs, the agriculture industry, tourism, former coal and steel producing areas, and parts of Wales.

This type of funding may include support for the following:

- business start-ups
- new factories
- new plant and machinery

- research and development
- IT development.

There are many examples of funding schemes that operate currently. For example, the Government, via the DTI (Department of Trade and Industry), can provide guarantees for loans from banks and other financial institutions for small businesses that may be unable to provide the security for conventional loans. Via the various regional development agencies, they may also provide discretionary selective financial assistance, in the form of grants or loans, for businesses that are willing to invest in 'assisted areas'. The DTI and Government Business Link websites, www.dti.gov.uk and www.businesslink.gov.uk, provide up-to-date information of all current funding initiatives.

The Welsh Assembly's use of European Structural Funds (ESFs) assists businesses in regenerating Welsh communities. For example, through a scheme called match funding, depending on the type of business activity and its location, ESFs can contribute up to 50% of a project's funding. The balance of the funding is provided from the business's own resources or other public or private sector funding. Websites like the Welsh European Funding Office website, www.wefo.wales.gov.uk, provide information on this type of funding initiative.

> **Progress check 14.2** Describe what is meant by debt and equity and give some examples of each. What are the other sources of long-term, external finance available to a company?

Gearing

In Chapter 5 when we looked at financial ratios we introduced gearing, the relationship between debt and equity capital that represents the financial structure of an organisation. We will now take a look at the application of gearing and then consider worked examples that compare the use of debt capital compared with ordinary share capital.

The relationship between the two sources of finance, loans and ordinary shares, or debt and equity gives a measure of the gearing of the company. A company with a high proportion of debt capital to share capital is highly geared, and low geared if the reverse situation applies. Gearing (leverage, or debt/equity) has important implications for the long-term stability of a company because of, as we have seen, its impact on financial risk.

Companies closely monitor their gearing ratios to ensure that their capital structure aligns with their financial strategy. Various alternative actions may be taken by companies, as necessary, to adjust their capital structures by increasing/decreasing their respective levels of debt and equity. An example of one of the ways in which this may be achieved is to return cash to shareholders. In May 2004 Marshalls plc, the paving stone specialist that supplied the flagstones for the newly-pedestrianised Trafalgar Square in London, announced that they were planning to return £75m to shareholders through a capital reorganisation. The reason the company gave for this was that it expected a more efficient capital structure as a result. The company was geared at only 6%, and had generated £5.3m cash in its previous financial year, after dividends and £40m capital expenditure, which its chairman said had reflected its success in growing shareholder value and generating cash.

The extent to which the debt/equity is high or low geared has an effect on the earnings per share (eps) of the company:

- if profits are increasing, then higher gearing is preferable
- if profits are decreasing, then lower gearing or no gearing is preferred.

Similarly, the argument applies to the riskiness attached to capital repayments. If a company goes into liquidation, lenders have priority over shareholders with regard to capital repayment. So, the more highly geared the company the less chance there is of ordinary shareholders being repaid in full.

The many types of short- and long-term capital available to companies leads to complexity, but also the expectation that overall financial risks may be reduced through improved matching of funding with operational needs. The gearing position of the company may be considered in many ways depending on whether the long-term capital structure or the overall financial structure is being analysed. It may also be analysed by concentrating on the income position rather than purely on the capital structure.

Financial gearing relates to the relationship between a company's borrowings, which includes debt, and its share capital and reserves. Concerning capital structure, gearing calculations may be based on a number of different capital values. All UK plcs disclose their net debt to equity ratio in their annual reports and accounts.

The two financial ratios that follow are the two most commonly used (see also Chapter 5). Both ratios relate to financial gearing, which is the relationship between a company's borrowings, which includes both prior charge capital and long-term debt, and shareholders' funds (share capital plus reserves).

$$\text{gearing} = \frac{\text{long-term debt}}{\text{equity} + \text{long-term debt}}$$

$$\text{debt equity ratio, or leverage} = \frac{\text{long-term debt}}{\text{equity}}$$

Worked Example 14.3 illustrates the calculation of both ratios.

Worked Example 14.3

Two companies have different gearing. Company A is financed totally by 20,000 £1 ordinary shares, whilst company B is financed partly by 10,000 £1 ordinary shares and a £10,000 10% loan. In all other respects the companies are the same. They both have assets of £20,000 and both make the same profit before interest and tax (PBIT).

	A	B
	£	£
Assets	20,000	20,000
less 10% loan	–	(10,000)
	20,000	10,000
Ordinary shares	20,000	10,000

$$\text{Gearing} = \frac{\text{long-term debt}}{\text{equity} + \text{long-term debt}} \qquad \frac{0}{20,000 + 0} = 0\% \qquad \frac{10,000}{10,000 + 10,000} = 50\%$$

$$\text{Debt equity ratio} = \frac{\text{long-term debt}}{\text{equity}} \qquad \frac{0}{20,000} = 0\% \qquad \frac{10,000}{10,000} = 100\%$$

Company B must make a profit before interest of at least £1,000 to cover the cost of the 10% loan. Company A does not have any PBIT requirement because it has no debt.

Company A is lower geared and considered less risky in terms of profitability than company B which is a more highly geared company. This is because PBIT of a lower geared company is more likely to be sufficiently high to cover interest charges and make a profit for equity shareholders.

As we have seen, gearing calculations can be made in a number of ways, and may also be based on earnings/interest relationships in addition to capital values. For example:

$$\text{dividend cover (times)} = \frac{\text{earnings per share (eps)}}{\text{dividend per share}}$$

This ratio indicates the number of times the profits attributable to the equity shareholders covers the actual dividends paid and payable for the period. Financial analysts usually adjust their calculations for any exceptional or extraordinary items of which they may be aware.

$$\text{interest cover (times)} = \frac{\text{profit before interest and tax}}{\text{interest payable}}$$

This ratio calculates the number of times the interest payable is covered by profits available for such payments. It is particularly important for lenders to determine the vulnerability of interest payments to a drop in profit. The following ratio determines the same vulnerability in cash terms.

$$\text{cash interest cover} = \frac{\text{net cash inflow from operations} + \text{interest received}}{\text{interest paid}}$$

> **Progress check 14.3** **What is gearing? Outline some of the ways in which it may be calculated.**

Worked Example 14.4

Swell Guys plc is a growing company that manufactures equipment for fitting out small cruiser boats. Its planned expansion involves investing in a new factory project costing £4m. Chief Executive, Guy Rope, expects the 12-year project to add £0.5m to profit before interest and tax each year. Next year's operating profit is forecast at £5m, and dividends per share are forecast at the same level as last year. Tax is not expected to be payable over the next few years due to tax losses that have been carried forward.

Swell Guys last two years' results are as follows:

	Last year £m	Previous year £m
Profit and loss account for the year ended 31 December		
Sales	18	15
Operating costs	16	11
Operating profit	2	4
Interest payable	1	1
Profit before tax	1	3
Tax on ordinary activities	0	0
Profit after tax	1	3
Dividends	1	1
Retained profit	0	2

Balance sheet as at 31 December

Fixed assets	8	9
Current assets		
Stocks	7	4
Debtors	4	3
Cash	1	2
	12	9
Creditors due within one year		
Bank overdraft	4	2
Trade creditors	5	5
	9	7
Net current assets	3	2
Total assets less current liabilities	11	11
less		
Long-term loans	6	6
Net assets	5	5
Capital and reserves		
Share capital (25p ordinary shares)	2	2
Profit and loss account	3	3
	5	5

Swell Guys is considering two options:

(a) Issue of £4m 15% loan stock repayable in five years' time

(b) Rights issue of 4m 25p ordinary shares at £1 per share after expenses
     For each of the options the directors would like to see:
     (i)   how the retained profit (derived from operating profit) will look for next year
     (ii) how earnings per share will look for next year
     (iii) how the capital and reserves will look at the end of next year
     (iv) how long-term loans will look at the end of next year
     (v)   how gearing will look at the end of next year.

(i) Swell Guys plc forecast profit and loss account for next year ended 31 December

Operating profit £5m + £0.5m from the new project

		New debt	New equity
		£m	£m
Operating profit		5.5	5.5
Interest payable	[1.0 + 0.6]	1.6	1.0
Profit before tax		3.9	4.5
Tax on ordinary activities		0.0	0.0

Profit after tax	3.9	4.5
Dividends	1.0	1.5
Retained profit	2.9	3.0

(ii) Earnings per share

$$\frac{\text{Profit available for ordinary shareholders}}{\text{Number of ordinary shares}} \qquad \frac{£3.9m}{8m} = 48.75p \qquad \frac{£4.5m}{12m} = 37.5p$$

(iii) Capital and reserves

	As at 31 December		
	New debt		**New equity**
	£m		**£m**
Share capital			
(25p ordinary shares)	2.0	(8m shares)	3.0 (12m shares)
Share premium account	0.0		3.0
Profit and loss account	5.9		6.0
	7.9		12.0

(iv) Long-term loans [6 + 4]   10.0   6.0

(v) Gearing

$$\frac{\text{long-term debt}}{\text{equity + long-term debt}} \qquad \frac{£6m + £4m}{£7.9m + £6m + £4m} = 55.9\% \qquad \frac{£6m}{£12m + £6m} = 33.3\%$$

> **Progress check 14.4 Explain how a high interest cover ratio can reassure a prospective lender.**

The weighted average cost of capital (WACC)

The weighted average cost of capital (WACC) may be defined as the average cost of the total financial resources of a company, i.e. the shareholders' equity and the net financial debt.

If we represent shareholders equity as E and net financial debt as D then the relative proportions of equity and debt in the total financing are:

$$\frac{E}{E + D} \quad \text{and} \quad \frac{D}{E + D}$$

The cost of equity is the expected return on equity, the return the shareholders expect from their investment. If we represent the return on shareholders' equity as e and the return on financial debt as d, and t is the rate of corporation tax, then we can provide a formula to calculate WACC. As we saw in Chapter 10, the return on shareholder equity comprises both cash flows from dividends and increases in the share price. We will return to how the cost of equity may be derived in a later section in this chapter.

Interest on debt capital is an allowable deduction for purposes of corporate taxation and so the cost of share capital and the cost of debt capital are not properly comparable costs. Therefore this tax relief on debt interest ought to be recognised in any discounted cash flow calculations. One way would be to include the tax savings due to interest payments in the cash flows of every project. A simpler method, and the one normally used, is to allow for the tax relief in computing the cost of debt capital, to arrive at an after-tax cost of debt. Therefore the weighted average cost of capital is calculated from:

$$\text{WACC} = \left\{ \frac{E}{(E+D)} \times \boldsymbol{e} \right\} + \left\{ \frac{D}{(E+D)} \times \boldsymbol{d(1-t)} \right\}$$

The market value of a company may be determined by its WACC. The lower the WACC then the higher the net present values of its future cash flows and therefore the higher its market value. The determination of the optimum D/E ratio is one of the most difficult tasks facing the finance director.

Worked Example 14.5

Fleet Ltd has the following financial structure:

$e =$	15%	return on equity (this may be taken as given for the purpose of this example)
$d =$	10%	lower risk, so lower than the return on equity
$t =$	30%	rate of corporation tax
$\dfrac{E}{E+D} =$	60%	equity to debt plus equity ratio
$\dfrac{D}{E+D} =$	40%	debt to debt plus equity ratio

We can calculate the WACC for Fleet Ltd, and evaluate the impact on WACC of a change in capital structure to equity 40% and debt 60%.

Calculation of WACC for Fleet Ltd with the current financial structure:

$$\text{WACC} = \left\{ \frac{E}{(E+D)} \times e \right\} + \left\{ \frac{D}{(E+D)} \times d(1-t) \right\}$$

$$\text{WACC} = (60\% \times 15\%) + \{40\% \times 10\% \, (1-30\%)\} = 11.8\%$$

If the company decides to change its financial structure so that equity is 40% and debt is 60% of total financing, then WACC becomes:

$$(40\% \times 15\%) + \{60\% \times 10\% \, (1-30\%)\} = 10.2\%$$

So it appears that the company has reduced its WACC by increasing the relative weight from 40% to 60% of the cheapest financial resource, debt, in its total financing. However, this is not true because as the debt/equity ratio of the company increased from 0.67 (40/60) to 1.50 (60/40) the company's risk has also increased. Therefore the providers of the financial resources will require a higher return on their investment. There is a well-established correlation between risk and return. So, it is not correct to calculate the WACC using the same returns on equity and debt, as both will have increased.

One of the consequences of this is the problem of calculating an accurate WACC for a company, which is based on its relative proportions and costs of debt and equity capital.

The risks and costs associated with debt capital and equity capital are different and subject to continual change, and may vary from industry to industry and between different types of business. Measurement of the D/E ratio may therefore not be a straightforward task, particularly for diversified groups of companies. Companies in different markets and indeed diversified companies that have trading divisions operating within different markets and producing different products face different levels of risk. If division A operates with a higher risk than division B then the required rate of return of A's investments should be higher than the hurdle rate of return of B's investments. The difference is 'paying' for the difference in risk. This is an important principle but very difficult to implement in practice.

In a later section, we will look at ways in which both the cost of equity and the cost of debt to the company may be determined.

There are many arguments for and against the use of WACC for investment appraisal. Its use is argued on the basis that:

- new investments must be financed by new sources of funds – retained earnings, new share issues, new loans, and so on
- the cost of capital to be applied to new project evaluation must reflect the cost of new capital
- the WACC reflects the company's long-term future capital structure, and capital costs; if this were not so, the current WACC would become irrelevant because eventually it would not relate to any actual cost of capital.

It is argued that the current WACC should be used to evaluate projects, because a company's capital structure changes only very slowly over time; therefore, the marginal cost of new capital should be roughly equal to the WACC. If this view is correct, then by undertaking investments which offer a return in excess of the WACC, a company will increase the market value of its ordinary shares in the long run. This is because the excess returns would provide surplus profits and dividends for the shareholders.

The arguments against the use of WACC are based on the criticisms of the assumptions made that justify the use of WACC:

- new investments have different risk characteristics from the company's existing operations therefore the return required by investors may go up or down if the investments are made, because their business risk is perceived to be higher or lower
- finance raised to fund a new investment
  - may substantially change the capital structure and perceived risk of investing in the company
  - may determine whether debt or equity used to finance the project will change the perceived risk of the entire company, which
  - must be taken into account in the investment appraisal
- many companies raise floating rate debt capital as well as fixed rate debt capital, having a variable rate that changes every few months in line with current market rates; this is difficult to include in a WACC calculation, the best compromise being to substitute an 'equivalent' fixed debt rate in place of the floating rate.

> **Progress check 14.5 What is WACC and why is it so important?**

Cost of debt and equity capital

We have introduced the concept of risk and its correlation with returns on investments. The relationship between risk and return is also one of the key concepts relating to determination of the cost of debt and equity capital. It is an important concept and so we will briefly explore risk a little further, with regard to investments in companies. We shall discuss the cost of debt based on future income flows, that is, interest. We shall similarly discuss the cost of equity based on future income flows, that is, dividends. This will also provide an introduction to the beta factor and the capital asset pricing model (CAPM).

The cost of servicing debt capital, as we have discussed, is the yearly or half yearly interest payment, which is an allowable expense for tax. The cost of repayment of a loan, or debt, depends on the type of loan. Loan capital, a debenture for example, may be irredeemable and traded, with a market value. The cost of capital for a redeemable loan may be calculated using a quite complicated formula.

For our purposes, to demonstrate the principle, we can look at the cost of irredeemable loan capital to a company that may be calculated as follows:

$$d = \frac{i \times (1 - t)}{L}$$

where

d = cost of debt capital
i = annual loan interest rate
L = the current market value of the loan
t = the rate of corporation tax.

By rearranging the formula it can be seen that market value of the debt is dependent on the level of future returns, the interest rate paid, which is determined by the level of risk associated with the investment, and the rate of corporation tax:

$$L = \frac{i \times (1 - t)}{d}$$

Worked Example 14.6

Owen Cash plc pays 12% interest (i) per annum on an irredeemable debt of £1m, with a nominal value of £100. The corporation tax rate (t) is currently 50%. The market value of the debt (L) is currently £90.

What is Owen Cash plc's cost of debt?

$$d = \text{cost of debt capital}$$

$$d = \frac{i \times (1 - t)}{L} = \frac{12\% \times (1 - 50\%)}{90}$$

$$d = \frac{12\% \times 50\%}{90} = 6.7\%$$

In a similar way, the cost of equity to a company may be determined by looking at future income flows. In the case of equity or ordinary shares this future income is dividends. A difference between this method and the method applied to debt is that there is no tax relief for dividend payments.

The value of an ordinary share may be simply expressed as the present value of its expected future dividend flows.

$$S = v_1/(1 + e) + v_2/(1 + e)^2 + v_3/(1 + e)^3 \ldots v_n/(1 + e)^n$$

where

e = cost of equity capital
v = expected future dividends for n years
S = the current market value of the share

If dividends are expected to remain level over a period of time the formula may be simplified to:

$$S = \frac{v}{e}$$

Therefore, the cost of equity to the company would be:

$$e = \frac{v}{S}$$

Dividends payable on a particular share rarely stay constant from year to year. However, they may grow at a regular rate. This so-called dividend growth model approach to the cost of equity may then be used with the above formula revised as:

$$S = v/(e - G)$$

where G = the expected future dividend growth rate.

The cost of equity may then be stated as:

$$e = \frac{v}{S} + G$$

Worked Example 14.7

Cher Alike plc has 3m ordinary shares in issue that currently have a market price (S) of £2.71. The board have already recommended next year's dividend (v) at 17p per share. The chairman, Sonny Daze, is forecasting that dividends will continue to grow (G) at 4.2% per annum for the foreseeable future.

What is Cher Alike plc's cost of equity?

$$e = \text{cost of equity capital}$$
$$e = \frac{v}{S} + G = \frac{0.17}{2.71} + 4.2\%$$
$$e = 0.063 + 0.042 = 10.5\%$$

The interest rate paid on a loan is known almost with certainty. Even if the debt carries a variable interest rate it is far easier to estimate than expected dividend flows on ordinary shares.

The cost of equity to a company may alternatively be derived using the capital asset pricing model (CAPM). We will look at this approach to risk, and at how some risk may be diversified away by using a spread (or portfolio) of investments.

> Progress check 14.6 **In broad terms how are the costs of debt and equity determined?**

Cost of equity and risk, CAPM and the β factor

Whenever any investment is made there will be some risk involved. The actual return on investment in ordinary shares (equity capital) may be better or worse than hoped for. Unless the investor settles for risk-free securities a certain element of risk is unavoidable.

However, investors in companies or in projects can diversify their investments in a suitably wide portfolio. Some investments may do better and some worse than expected. In this way, average returns should turn out much as expected. Risk that can be diversified away is referred to as unsystematic risk.

Some investments are by their very nature more risky than others. This is nothing to do with chance variations in actual compared with expected returns, it is inherent risk that cannot be diversified away. This type of risk is referred to as systematic risk or market risk. The investor must therefore accept this risk, unless he/she invests entirely in risk-free investments. In return for accepting systematic risk an investor will expect to earn a return which is higher than the return on risk-free investment.

The amount of systematic risk depends, for example, on the industry or the type of project. If an investor has a balanced portfolio of shares he/she will incur exactly the same systematic risk as the average systematic risk of the stock market as a whole. The capital asset pricing model (CAPM) is mainly concerned with how systematic risk is measured and how systematic risk affects required returns and share prices. It was first formulated for investments in shares on the stock exchange, but is now also used for company investments in capital projects.

Systematic risk is measured using what are known as beta factors. A beta factor is the measure of the volatility of a share in terms of market risk. The CAPM is a statement of the β principles outlined above. An investor can use the beta factor β in such a way that a high factor will automatically suggest a share is to be avoided because of considerable high risk in the past. Consider the impact in January 2001 on the beta factor of Iceland plc caused by the resignation from the board of the major shareholder together with the issue of a profits warning by the company.

The CAPM model can be stated as follows:

the expected return from a security = the risk-free rate of return, plus a premium for market risk adjusted by a measure of the volatility of the security

If

Rs	is the expected return from an individual security
β	is the beta factor for the individual security
Rf	is the risk-free rate of return
Rm	is the return from the market as a whole
(Rm – Rf)	is the market risk premium

$$Rs = Rf + \{\beta \times (Rm - Rf)\}$$

There are many analysts that specialise in the charting of the volatility of shares and markets, and their findings may regularly be found in the UK financial press.

A variation of the above β relationship may be used to establish an equity cost of capital to use in project appraisal. The cost of equity e equates to the expected return from an individual security Rs, and the beta value for the company's equity capital βe equates to beta factor for the individual security β.

So

| the return expected by ordinary shareholders, or the cost of equity to the company | = | the risk-free rate of return plus a premium for market risk adjusted by a measure of the volatility of the ordinary shares of the company |

$$e = Rf + \{\beta e \times (Rm - Rf)\}$$

Worked Example 14.8

Bittaboth plc has ordinary shares in issue with a market value four times the value of its debt capital. The debt is considered to be risk free and pays 11% (Rf) before tax. The beta value of Bittaboth's equity capital has been estimated at 0.9 (βe) and the average market return on equity capital is 17% (Rm). Corporation tax is at 50% (t).

We can calculate Bittaboth plc's WACC.

e = cost of equity capital
$e = Rf + \{\beta e \times (Rm - Rf)\} = 11\% + \{0.9 \times (17\% - 11\%)\}$
$e = 0.11 + (0.9 \times 0.06) = 0.164 = 16.4\%$
d = cost of debt capital
which after tax is i $\times$ (1 – t) or 11% $\times$ 50% = 5.5%

Any capital projects that Bittaboth may wish to consider may be evaluated using its WACC, which may be calculated as:

{equity/(debt + equity) ratio $\times$ return on equity} + {debt/(debt + equity) ratio $\times$ after tax cost of debt}
(4/5 $\times$ 16.4%) + (1/5 $\times$ 5.5%) = 14.2%
14.2% is Bittaboth's weighted average cost of capital (WACC).

It should be remembered that the CAPM considers systematic risk only, and is based on an assumption of market equilibrium.

β factors may be calculated using market and individual companies' information. β values are also obtainable from a variety of sources and are published quarterly by the London Business School.

Progress check 14.7 **Describe what is meant by systematic risk and unsystematic risk.**

Return on equity and financial structure

The important formula that follows shows the return on equity (ROE) as a function of return on investment (ROI) and the financial structure, leverage or gearing of the company, where:

D = debt capital

E = equity capital

t = corporation tax rate

i = interest rate on debt

ROI = return on investment

$$\text{ROS} = \text{return on sales} = \frac{\text{profit after tax}}{\text{total investment}}$$

$$\textbf{ROE} = \{\textbf{ROI} \times (\textbf{1} - \textit{t})\} + \{(\textbf{ROI} - \textit{i}) \times (\textbf{1} - \textit{t}) \times \textbf{D/E}\}$$

Worked Example 14.9 illustrates the use of this relationship and also gives a general rule derived from it.

Worked Example 14.9

A hospital equipment manufacturing company, Nilby Mouth plc, makes an operating profit (PBIT) of £10m on sales of £100m and with a total investment of £60m. The investment is financed by equity (E) of £40m and debt (D) of £20m with an interest rate (i) of 10%. Assume the corporation tax rate (t) is 50%.

We will calculate:

(i)   the current return on equity (ROE)

(ii)   the ROE if financing were changed so that debt was £40m and equity was £20m

(iii)   the current ROE if operating profit were reduced to £4m

(iv)   the ROE if operating profit were reduced to £4m and if financing were changed so that debt was £40m and equity was £20m.

Figures in £m

(i) Calculation of return on equity (ROE)

Profit before interest and tax, or operating profit PBIT = 10

Profit before tax PBT = $10 - (20 \times 10\%) = 8$

Profit after tax PAT = $8 \times (1 - 50\%) = 4$

Return on sales ROS = $4/100 = 4\%$

Return on investment ROI (pre interest and tax) = $10/60 = 16.7\%$

Debt/equity ratio D/E = $20/40 = 50\%$

ROE = $\text{ROI} \times (1 - t) + \{(\text{ROI} - i) \times (1 - t) \times \text{D/E}\}$

Return on equity ROE = $\{16.7\% \times (1 - 50\%)\} + \{(16.7\% - 10\%) \times (1 - 50\%) \times 50\%\}$

$\qquad\qquad = 0.10025 \text{ or } 10\%$

(ii) Calculation of ROE if financing is changed so that debt is £40m and equity is £20m

PBIT = 10   PBT = $10 - (40 \times 10\%) = 6$ PAT = $6 \times (1 - 50\%) = 3$

ROS = $3/100 = 3\%$

ROI (pre interest and tax) = 10/60 = 16.7%

D/E = 40/20 = 200%

ROE = {16.7% × (1 − 50%)} + {(16.7% − 10%) × (1 − 50%) × 200%}

   = 0.15050 or 15.1%

Return on sales has reduced, whereas return on equity has increased.

(iii) Calculation of ROE if the operating profit were reduced to £4m

PBIT = 4   PBT = 4 − (20 × 10%) = 2   PAT = 2 × (1 − 50%) = 1

ROS = 1/100 = 1%

ROI (pre interest and tax) = 4/60 = 6.7%

D/E = 20/40 = 50%

ROE = {6.7% × (1 − 50%)} + {(6.7% − 10%) × (1 − 50%) × 50%} = 0.02525 or 2.53%

(iv) Calculation of ROE if financing is changed so that debt is £40m and equity is £20m

PBIT = 4   PBT = 4 − (40 × 10%) = 0   PAT = 0 × (1 − 50%) = 0

ROS = 0/100 = 0%

ROI (pre interest and tax) = 4/60 = 6.7%

D/E = 40/20 = 200%

ROE = {6.7% × (1 − 50%)} + {(6.7% − 10%) × (1 − 50%) × 200%} = 0.00050 or 0.05%

Return on sales has reduced and return on equity has also reduced.

The general rule apparent from the relationships outlined in Worked Example 14.10 is:

- when ROI is greater than i   the higher the D/E, the higher the ROE
- when ROI is less than i   the higher the D/E, the lower the ROE.

However, even if the ROI is greater than the debt interest the company's bankers may not automatically allow the D/E to increase indefinitely. The company's risk increases as the D/E or leverage increases, in terms of its commitment to high levels of interest payments, and bankers will not tolerate too high a level of risk; they will also be inclined to increase the debt interest rate as D/E increases. Shareholders will have the same reaction – they are happy with an increase in ROE but realise that they also have to face a higher risk.

For a high growth company, to limit the shareholders' investment, the company will have a tendency to increase D/E and therefore ROE, but also the financial risk. The press (for example Questor in the *Daily Telegraph*) usually comments when a plc is seen to embark on a policy of increased borrowings and increasing its gearing ratio, which alerts the reader to 'increased financial risk'. Plcs are usually prepared and ready for such comments in order to respond with their 'defence' of such a policy.

Progress check 14.8 Discuss why bankers may refuse additional lending to a company as its debt/equity ratio increases.

Growth of a company may be looked at using profit and loss account horizontal analyses. Use of this technique, which was covered in Chapter 6, presents all numbers in the profit and loss account as a percentage using a base year, which is 100, for year-on-year comparison. Financial commentators usually begin articles on the performance of plcs by comparing the current year performance with the previous year, and then attempt a forecast of future performance. This is an example of a basic horizontal analysis that focuses on turnover and profits. Only a few companies actually succeed in growing year on year, over an extended period (for example, 10 years).

Economic value added (EVA™) and market value added (MVA)

Maximisation of shareholder wealth continues to be the prime objective with which managers of companies are charged. We have considered various ways in which managers may measure financial performance (see Chapter 11). The extent to which success in particular performance measures aligns with shareholder wealth is particularly relevant. Equally important are the ways in which managers are motivated to maximise shareholder wealth. As we saw in Chapter 11, in most organisations managerial remuneration provides the link between the measures of financial performance and shareholder value.

Financial performance measures such as a company's share price are commonly used to indicate how well the company is doing. However, it may be questioned as to how directly the share price reflects decisions that have been taken by management. In the context of managers' performance against budget targets, and the company's overall financial performance, we have previously discussed the merits and otherwise of other performance measures such as profit after tax, earnings per share, dividends, return on capital employed, and cash flow, etc. Each has its limitations, but cash flow based measures are now becoming accepted as perhaps better indicators than profit related measures.

During the mid-1980s, Rappaport developed shareholder value analysis, from which the American firm Stern Stewart Management Services evolved concepts known as economic value added (EVA), which we introduced in Chapter 11, and market value added (MVA). Through EVA, Stern Stewart attempted to reconcile the need for a performance measure correlated with shareholder wealth, and a performance measure which was also responsive to actions taken by managers. By the mid-1990s over 200 global companies had been in discussion with Stern Stewart with regard to adoption of EVA; Lucas Varity in the UK and Coca Cola in the USA were already successful users of EVA.

If we assume that the organisation's objective is to maximise shareholder wealth then this will be achieved if new projects are taken on and existing projects are allowed to continue only if they create value. Investment in capital projects may be made only on the basis of choosing those with a positive net present value (NPV). However, NPV cannot be applied to remuneration schemes because it is a summary measure based on projected cash flows and not realised performance.

Companies usually turn to company earnings and cash flow (which are termed flow measures) for management remuneration schemes. EVA supports the same sort of recommendations that NPV provides at the project level, but also provides a better measure of management performance because it rewards for earnings generated, whilst also including charges for the amount of capital employed to create those earnings.

If profit after tax = PAT
Weighted average cost of capital = WACC
Net assets = adjusted book value of net capital = NA
Then we may define EVA as:

$$\textbf{EVA} = \textbf{PAT} - (\textbf{WACC} \times \textbf{NA})$$

Worked Example 14.10 will illustrate the calculation of EVA and its relationship with NPV.

Worked Example 14.10

A manager has to choose between three mutually exclusive projects. The company may invest:

£50,000 in project A, or
£110,000 in project B, or
£240,000 in project C

Project A is expected to generate incremental profits after tax (PAT) of £50,000 in year one, £40,000 in year two (total £90,000), after which the project is terminated.

Project B is expected to generate incremental PATs of £45,000 in year one, £70,000 in year two, £70,000 in year three (total £185,000), after which the project is terminated.

Project C is expected to generate incremental PATs of £55,000 in year one, £75,000 in year two, £80,000 in year three (total £210,000), after which the project is terminated.

The company's WACC is 10% per annum. Capital levels may be assumed to be maintained throughout the life of each project. That is, each year's new capital investment equals depreciation in that year.

Capital items are sold at their book value in the final year of each project, so free cash flow (operating cash flow less capital expenditure) will be equal to PAT each year except the final years when the capital costs are recovered.

We will assess which project the manager will choose if:

(i)   his/her remuneration is tied to the NPV of the project
(ii)   his/her remuneration is based on IRR
(iii)   his/her remuneration is based on project earnings
(iv)   his/her remuneration is based on EVA.

Using a discount rate of WACC at 10% per annum, we first calculate the NPVs of each project.

Year	Cash outflows	Cash inflows		Net cash flow at 10%	Discount factor	Present values
	£000	£000		£000		£000
Project A						
0	−50			−50	1.00	−50.0
1		50		50	0.91	45.5
2		90	[40 + 50]	90	0.83	74.7
3		0		0	0.75	0.0
Total	−50	140		90		+70.2
Project B						
0	−110			−110	1.00	−110.0
1		45		45	0.91	40.9
2		70		70	0.83	58.1
3		180	[70 + 110]	180	0.75	135.0
Total	−110	295		185		+124.0

Project C

0	−240			−240	1.00	−240.0
1		55		55	0.91	50.0
2		75		75	0.83	62.3
3		320	[80 + 240]	320	0.75	240.0
Total	−240	450		210		+112.3

The IRR is the rate of return that would give an NPV of zero.

The interpolation/extrapolation techniques covered in Chapter 13 may be used to derive the internal rate of return of each project.

For project C, if we assume a discount rate of 30%, we may calculate a revised NPV as follows:

Year	Cash outflows	Cash inflows	Net cash flow	Discount factor at 30%	Present values
	£000	£000	£000		£000
0	−240		−240	1.00	−240.0
1		55	55	0.77	42.4
2		75	75	0.59	44.3
3		320	320	0.46	147.2
Total	−240	450	210		−6.1

We have already calculated the positive NPV for project C of £112,300 using a cost of capital of 10%. The IRR of project C must be at some point between 30% and 10% (difference 20%).

Using a similar calculation to that used in Fig. 13.3 (Chapter 13):

$$\frac{£6,100}{x} = \frac{£112,300}{(20-x)}$$

$(£6,100 \times 20) - £6,100x = £112,300x$

$£122,000 = £118,400x$

$$x = \frac{£122,000}{£118,400}$$

$x = 1.03$

Therefore, interpolation gives us an IRR of 30% less 1.03%, which equals 28.97% and may be rounded to 29%.

The IRRs of projects A and B may be calculated in the same way.

The cash flows, NPVs and IRRs of the three projects may be summarised as:

Project	PAT			Cash out	Cash in			Total cash flow	IRR	NPV
	Year 1	Year 2	Year 3		Year 1	Year 2	Year 3			
	£000	£000	£000	£000	£000	£000	£000	£000	%	£000
A	50	40		−50	50	90 [40 + 50]		90	93	70.2
B	45	70	70	−110	45	70	180 [70 + 110]	185	53	124.0
C	55	75	80	−240	55	75	320 [80 + 240]	210	29	112.3

(i)   Based on the highest NPV, project B at £124,000 is best for the company shareholders.

(ii)   But if the manager's remuneration is based on IRR then he/she will choose project A at 93%.

(iii)   If the manager is remunerated on total project earnings then he/she will choose project C at £210,000.

(iv)   We can calculate the EVA for each project, which equals profit after tax for each period, less capital employed at the start of each period multiplied by the weighted average cost of capital.

Year	Project A		Project B		Project C	
		EVA		EVA		EVA
	£000	£000	£000	£000	£000	£000
1	$50 - (50 \times 10\%)$	45	$45 - (110 \times 10\%)$	34	$55 - (240 \times 10\%)$	31
2	$40 - (50 \times 10\%)$	35	$70 - (110 \times 10\%)$	59	$75 - (240 \times 10\%)$	51
3			$70 - (110 \times 10\%)$	59	$80 - (240 \times 10\%)$	56
Total		80		152		138

We may also calculate the NPV of the EVAs of each project, the present values of the EVAs:

Year	Discount factor at 10%	Project A Cash flow £000	Project A NPV £000	Project B Cash flow £000	Project B NPV £000	Project C Cash flow £000	Project C NPV £000
1	0.91	45	41.0	34	30.9	31	28.2
2	0.83	35	29.1	59	48.9	51	42.3
3	0.75			59	44.2	56	42.0
Total		80	+70.1	+152	+124.0	138	+112.5

This illustrates that EVAs actually equate to cash flows because their present values are the same as the NPV of each project. The small differences between the totals calculated for Project A and Project C are as a result of rounding differences.

We have seen from Worked Example 14.10 that earnings-based remuneration schemes may result in over-investment of capital whereas return on net assets will result in under-investment of capital. Use of EVA as a basis for management remuneration takes account of the fact that the use of capital is charged for by using WACC; additionally, at the project level, the present value of the EVAs gives the same result as NPVs derived from free cash flows. Compare the results in the project NPV tables with the NPVs of the EVAs of each project in Worked Example 14.10.

Although the free cash flow NPVs give the same result as the present values of the EVAs, EVA is more appropriate for remuneration schemes because, as well as being fundamentally related to shareholder value, it is a flow measure of performance. The reason is that flow measures of performance are needed for periodic remuneration because remuneration is designed to provide a flow of rewards. The other flow measure is cash flow. EVA is a better measure than that because it takes into account the cost of capital invested in the project.

Worked Example 14.11

We will compute the EVA for 2002, 2003 and 2004 for a major plc from the following information.

Group cost of capital		5%
		£m
Adjusted net assets	2004	750
	2003	715
	2002	631
Profit after tax	2004	550
	2003	526
	2002	498
Equity	2004	100
	2003	48
	2002	115
Net debt	2004	800
	2003	802
	2002	546

Year	Profit after tax	Adjusted net assets	5% cost of capital × net assets	EVA	EVA % of net profit
	£m	£m	£m	£m	
2004	550	750	37.50	512.50	93%
2003	526	715	35.75	490.25	93%
2002	498	631	31.55	466.45	94%

Note how the profits are being earned using borrowed funds to finance the group. The plc can earn a very high EVA by using borrowed funds.

We have talked about EVA in respect of projects, and that the present value of future EVAs equals the NPV derived from future free cash flows. At a company level, the present value of EVAs equals the market value added (MVA) of a business. This is defined as the difference between the market value of the company and the adjusted book values of its assets.

EVA is a good financial performance measure because it answers the question of how well has the company performed in generating profits over a period, given the amount of capital tied up to generate those profits. However, the capital base is a difficult element to estimate in calculating EVA. The total net assets value on a balance sheet is not an accurate representation of either the liquidation value or the replacement cost value of the business. Stern Stewart consider more than 250 possible

Worked Example 14.12

We will compute the MVA for 2003 and 2004 from the following extracts from the annual report and accounts of a major plc, using the unadjusted value of net assets.

	2004	**2003**
Number of shares (5p)	950.2m	948.9m
Share price	278p	268p
Net assets	£1,097m	£1,437m

	2004	**2003**
Net assets	£1,097m	£1,437m
Market value	£2,641m	£2,543m
MVA	£1,544m	£1,106m

accounting adjustments to a balance sheet to arrive at a valuation of the company's assets. In practice most organisations find that no more than a dozen or so adjustments are truly significant, for example stocks, depreciation, goodwill, deferred tax, and closure costs.

> **Progress check 14.9 What is economic value added (EVA) and what is it used for?**

EVA probably does not change or add anything to the conclusions reached on the basis of conventional cash flow based valuation analysis. EVA is primarily a behavioural tool that corrects possible distortions. However, along with most other financial measures, it fails to measure on an *ex post* basis. EVA is undoubtedly a very useful concept for measuring and evaluating management and company performance. It is not a cure for poor management and poor investment decisions but it raises the profile and the awareness of the costs of capital involved in undertaking projects and in running the business.

Summary of key points

- Sources of finance internal to a company are its retained earnings, extended credit from suppliers, and the benefits gained from the more effective management of its working capital.
- Short-term, external sources of finance include overdrafts and short-term loans.
- The two main sources of long-term, external finance available to a company are equity (ordinary shares), preference shares and debt (loans and debentures).
- Other sources of long-term, external finance available to UK companies include hybrid finance, leasing, and UK Government and European funding.
- Gearing, or the debt/equity ratio, is the relationship between the two sources of finance,

loans and ordinary shares – a company having more debt capital than share capital is highly geared, and a company having more share capital than debt capital is low geared.

■ The weighted average cost of capital (WACC) is the average cost of the total financial resources of a company, i.e. the shareholders' equity and the net financial debt, that may be used as the discount rate to evaluate investment projects, and as a measure of company performance.

■ Both the cost of debt and the cost of equity are based on future income flows, and the risk associated with such returns.

■ A certain element of risk is unavoidable whenever any investment is made, and unless a market investor settles for risk-free securities, the actual return on investment in equity (or debt) capital may be better or worse than hoped for.

■ Systematic risk may be measured using the capital asset pricing model (CAPM), and the β factor, in terms of its effect on required returns and share prices.

■ The return on equity may be considered as a function of the gearing, or financial structure of the company.

■ The recently developed techniques of economic value added (EVA) and market value added (MVA) are widely becoming used in business performance measurement and as value creation incentives.

Questions

Q14.1 (i) What are the main sources of long-term, external finance available to an organisation?

(ii) What are their advantages and disadvantages?

Q14.2 What are the advantages and disadvantages of convertible loans?

Q14.3 Why may leasing be considered as a long-term source of finance?

Q14.4 What are the implications for a company of different levels of gearing?

Q14.5 What are the advantages and disadvantages for a company in using WACC as a discount factor to evaluate capital projects?

Q14.6 Describe the ways in which the costs of debt and equity capital may be ascertained.

Q14.7 How does risk impact on the cost of debt and equity?

Q14.8 What is the β factor, and how may it be related to WACC?

Q14.9 How may a company's return on equity (ROE) be related to its financial structure?

Q14.10 In what way is company growth of such interest to shareholders?

Q14.11 Business performance may be evaluated to determine ways in which it can be improved upon. If managers are capable of delivering improved performance how can EVA be used to support this?

Discussion points

D14.1 The ex-owner/manager of a private limited company recently acquired by a large plc, of which he is now a board member, said: 'This company has grown very quickly over the past few years so that our turnover is now over £20m per annum. Even though we expect our turnover to grow further and double in the next two years I cannot see why we need to change our existing financing arrangements. I know we need to make some large investments in new machinery over the next two years but in the past we've always operated successfully using our existing overdraft facility, which has been increased as required, particularly when we've needed new equipment. I don't really see the need for all this talk about additional share capital and long-term loans.' Discuss.

D14.2 The marketing manager of a large UK subsidiary of a multinational plc: 'Surely the interest rate that we should use to discount cash flows in our appraisal of new capital investment projects should be our bank overdraft interest rate. I don't really see the relevance of the weighted average cost of capital (WACC) to this type of exercise.' Discuss.

D14.3 In the long run does it really matter whether a company is financed predominantly by ordinary shares or predominantly by loans? What's the difference?

D14.4 'Economic value added (EVA) is nothing more than just flavour of the month.' Discuss.

Exercises

Solutions are provided in Appendix 4 to all exercise numbers highlighted in colour.

Level I

E14.1 *Time allowed – 30 minutes*
A critically important factor required by a company to make financial decisions, for example the evaluation of investment proposals and the financing of new projects, is its cost of capital. One of the elements included in the calculation of a company's cost of capital is the cost of equity.

(i) **Explain in simple terms what is meant by the 'cost of equity capital' for a company.**

The relevant data for Normal plc and the market in general is given below.

Normal plc

Current price per share on the London Stock Exchange	£1.20
Current annual dividend per share	£0.10
Expected average annual growth rate of dividends	7%
β beta coefficient for Normal plc's shares	0.5

The market

Expected rate of return on risk-free securities	8%
Expected return on the market portfolio	12%

(ii) **Calculate the cost of equity capital for Normal plc, using two alternative methods:**
　　(a) the Capital Asset Pricing Model (CAPM)
　　(b) a dividend growth model of your choice.

E14.2 *Time allowed – 30 minutes*

Normal plc pays £20,000 a year interest on an irredeemable debenture, which has a nominal value of £200,000 and a market value of £160,000. The rate of corporation tax is 30%.

You are required to:

    (i)   calculate the cost of the debt for Normal plc

    (ii)   calculate the weighted average cost of capital for Normal plc using the cost of equity calculated in Exercise E14.1 (ii) if Normal plc has only ordinary capital of £300,000

    (iii) comment on the impact on a company's cost of capital of changes in the rate of corporation tax

    (iv) calculate Normal plc's WACC if the rate of corporation tax were increased to 50%.

Level II

E14.3 *Time allowed – 30 minutes*

Lucky Jim plc has the opportunity to manufacture a particular type of self-tapping screw, for a client company, that would become indispensable in a particular niche market in the engineering field.

Development of the product requires an initial investment of £200,000 in the project. It has been estimated that the project will yield cash returns before interest of £35,000 per annum in perpetuity.

Lucky Jim plc is financed by equity and loans, which are always maintained as two thirds and one third of the total capital respectively. The cost of equity is 18% and the pre-tax cost of debt is 9%. The corporation tax rate is 40%.

If Lucky Jim plc's WACC is used as the cost of capital to appraise the project, should the project be undertaken?

E14.4 *Time allowed – 30 minutes*

You are required to compute the MVA for 2002, 2003 and 2004 from the estimated information for a large supermarket group.

	2004	2003	2002
Number of shares	6.823m	6.823m	6.770m
Share price	261p	169p	77p
Adjusted net assets	£5,000m	£4,769m	£4,377m

E14.5 *Time allowed – 60 minutes*

Yor plc is a fast growing, hi-tech business. Its profit and loss account for the year ended 30 September 2004 and its balance sheet as at 30 September 2004 are shown below. The company has the opportunity to take on a major project that will significantly improve its profitability in the forthcoming year and for the foreseeable future. The cost of the project is £10m, which will result in large increases in sales, which will increase profit before interest and tax by £4m per annum. The directors of Yor plc have two alternative options of financing the project:

The issue of £10m of 4% debentures at par, or a rights issue of 4m ordinary shares at a premium of £1.50 per share (after expenses).

Regardless of how the new project is financed, the directors will recommend a 10% increase in the dividend for 2004/2005. You may assume that the effective corporation tax rate is the same for 2004/2005 as for 2003/2004.

Yor plc
Profit and loss account for the year ended 30 September 2004

Figures in £m

PBIT	11.6
Interest payable	(1.2)
Profit before tax	10.4
Tax on profit on ordinary activities	(2.6)
Profit on ordinary activities after tax	7.8
Retained profit 1 October 2003	5.8
	13.6
Dividends	(3.0)
Retained profit 30 September 2004	10.6

Yor plc
Balance sheet as at 30 September 2004

Figures in £m

Fixed assets	
Tangible	28.8
Current assets	
Stocks	11.2
Debtors	13.8
Cash and bank	0.7
	25.7
Current liabilities (less than one year)	
Creditors	9.7
Dividends	1.6
Taxation	2.6
	13.9
Net current assets	11.8
Total assets less current liabilities	40.6
less	
Long-term liabilities (over one year)	
6% loan	20.0
Net assets	20.6
Capital and reserves	
Share capital (£1 ordinary shares)	10.0
Profit and loss account	10.6
	20.6

The directors of Yor plc would like to see your estimated profit and loss account for 2004/2005, and a summary of share capital and reserves at 30 September 2005, assuming:

    (i)   the new project is financed by an issue of the debentures

    (ii)   the new project is financed by the issue of new ordinary shares

To assist in clarification of the figures, you should show your calculations of:

  (iii)   eps for 2003/2004
  (iv)   eps for 2004/2005, reflecting both methods of financing the new project
  (v)   dividend per share for 2003/2004
  (vi)   dividend per share for 2004/2005, reflecting both methods of financing the new project

Use the information you have provided in (i) and (ii) above to:

  (vii)   calculate Yor plc's gearing, reflecting both methods of financing the new project, and compare with its gearing at 30 September 2004
  (viii)   summarise the results for 2004/2005, recommend which method of financing Yor plc should adopt, and explain the implications of both on its financial structure.

E14.6 *Time allowed – 90 minutes*

Sparks plc is a large electronics company that produces components for CD and minidisk players. It is close to the current year end and Sparks is forecasting profits after tax at £60m. The following two years' post-tax profits are each expected to increase by another £15m, and years four and five by another £10m each.

The forecast balance sheet for Sparks plc as at 31 December is as follows:

	£m
Fixed assets	500
Current assets	
Stocks	120
Debtors	160
	280
Creditors due within one year	
Trade creditors	75
Overdraft	75
	150
Net current assets	130
Long-term loans	150
	480
Capital and reserves	
Share capital (£1 ordinary shares)	220
Share premium	10
Profit and loss account	250
	480

Sparks plc has a large overdraft of £75m on which it pays a high rate of interest at 15%. The board would like to pay off the overdraft and obtain cheaper financing. Sparks also has loan capital of £150m on which it pays interest at 9% per annum. Despite its high level of debt Sparks is a profitable organisation. However, the board is currently planning a number of new projects for the next year, which will cost £75m. These projects are expected to produce profits after tax of £8m in the first year and £15m a year ongoing for future years.

The board has discussed a number of financing options and settled on two of them for further consideration:

1.   a 1 for 4 rights issue at £3.00 a share to raise £150m from the issue of 50m £1 shares
2.   a convertible £150m debenture issue at 12% (pre tax) that may be converted into 45m ordinary shares in two years' time.

The equity share index has risen over the past year from 4,600 to the current 5,500, having reached 6,250. Sparks plc's ordinary shares are currently at a market price of £3.37. Gearing of companies in the same industry as Sparks plc ranges between 25% and 45%. In two years' time it is expected that all Sparks debenture holders will convert to shares or none will convert.

The rate of corporation tax is 50%. Repayment of the overdraft will save interest of £5.625m a year after tax.

The board requires some analysis of the numbers to compare against the current position:

(i)   **if they make the rights issue**
(ii)   **if they issue debentures**
(iii)   **if the debentures are converted.**

The analysis should show:

(a)   **the impact on the balance sheet**
(b)   **the impact on the profit after tax**
(c)   **earnings per share**
(d)   **gearing**
(e)   **which option should be recommended to the board and why.**

Case Study V

COMPUTACORE LTD

Computacore Ltd produces and sells a range of computer systems. After-sales service work is carried out by local subcontractors, approved by Computacore Ltd. The managing director is considering Computacore carrying out all or some of the work itself and has chosen one area in which to experiment with the new routine.

Some of the computer systems are so large that repair or service work can only be done on site at customers' premises. Others are small enough for subcontractors to take back to their local repair workshops, repair them, and re-deliver them to the customer. If the company does its own after-sales service, it proposes that customers would bring these smaller items for repair to a local company service centre which would be located and organised to deal with visitors.

There is a list price to customers for the labour content of any work done and for parts used. However, the majority of the after-sales service work is done under an annual service contract taken out by customers on purchasing a computer system; this covers the labour content of any service work to be done, but customers pay for parts used.

Any labour or parts needed in the first six months are provided to the customer free of charge under Computacore's product guarantee, and subcontractors are allowed by the company a fixed sum of 2.5% of the selling price of each appliance to cover this work. These sums allowed have proved to be closely in line with the work needed over the past few years.

The price structure is as follows.

Parts
The price to the subcontractor is the Computacore Ltd cost plus 15%.
The price to customer is the subcontractor price plus 30%.

Labour
The price to the subcontractor is:
80% of list price for work done under a service contract
75% of list price for work not done under a service contract.

Records show that 70% by value of the work has to be carried out at customers' premises, whilst the remainder can be done anywhere appropriate.

The annual income Computacore Ltd currently receives from subcontractors for the area in which the experiment is to take place is as follows:

Parts
Under service contract	£360,000
Not under service contract	£120,000

Labour
Under service contract	£600,000
Not under service contract	£240,000
	£1,320,000

The company expects the volume of after-sales work to remain the same as last year for the period of the experiment.

Computacore Ltd is considering the following options:

(a)   setting up a local service centre at which it can service small computer systems only – work at customers' premises would continue to be done under subcontract
(b)   setting up a local service centre to act only as a base for its own employees who would only service appliances at customers' premises – servicing of small computer systems would continue to be done under subcontract
(c)   setting up a local combined service centre plus base for all work – no work would be sub-contracted.

If the company were to undertake service work, it has estimated that annual fixed costs would be budgeted as follows:

Option	(a)	(b)	(c)
	£000	£000	£000
Staff costs			
Managers	180	100	200
Stores	90	70	100
Repair and service	310	1,270	1,530
Rent, rates and lighting	350	100	900
Van and car hire, and transport costs	70	460	470

Required

(i)   Prepare an appropriate financial analysis to evaluate each of the alternative options, compared with the current position.
(ii)   Recommend which of the three options Computacore Ltd should adopt on the basis of your financial analysis.
(iii) Identify and comment on the non-financial factors, relevant to your recommendation, which might favourably or adversely affect the customer.
(iv)   Outline the factors that may be discussed if Computacore Ltd were to propose the establishment of a 'call centre' within or outside the UK, to deal with after-sales service and organisation and scheduling of repair and service work.

15

Management of working capital

Contents

Learning objectives

Completion of this chapter will enable you to:

- explain what is meant by working capital and the operating cycle
- describe the management and control of the working capital requirement
- outline some of the working capital policies that may be adopted by companies
- implement the systems and techniques that may be used for the management and control of stocks, and optimisation of stock levels
- outline a system of credit management and the control of debtors
- consider the management of creditors as an additional source of finance
- use the operating cycle to evaluate a company's working capital requirement performance
- consider the actions and techniques to achieve short-term and long-term cash flow improvement.

Introduction

Chapters 13 and 14 have been concerned with the longer-term elements of the balance sheet, investments and the alternative sources of funds to finance them. This chapter turns to the shorter-term elements of the balance sheet, the net current assets (current assets less current liabilities) or working capital, which is normally supported with short-term financing, for example bank overdrafts. The chapter begins with an overview of the nature and purpose of working capital.

An emphasis is placed on the importance of good management of the working capital requirement (WCR) for the sustained success of companies. The techniques that may be used to improve the management of stocks, debtors (accounts receivable), and creditors (accounts payable) are explored in detail.

Regular evaluation of the operating cycle may be used to monitor a company's effectiveness in the management of its working capital requirement. Minimisation of working capital is an objective that reduces the extent to which external financing of working capital is required. However, there is a fine balance between minimising the costs of finance and ensuring that sufficient working capital is available to adequately support the company's operations.

This chapter will close by linking working capital to the effective management of cash and by considering some of the ways that both long-term and short-term cash flow may be improved.

Working capital and working capital requirement

The balance sheet is sometimes presented showing assets on the one side and liabilities on the other. This may be said to be a little unsatisfactory since the various categories of assets and liabilities are very different in nature. Cash, for example, is a financial asset and has very different characteristics to fixed assets and stocks.

If we consider the following relationship:

$$\text{assets} = \text{equity} + \text{liabilities}$$

it may be rewritten as

$$\text{fixed assets} + \text{stocks} + \text{debtors} + \text{prepayments} + \text{cash}$$
$$=$$
$$\text{equity} + \text{financial debt} + \text{creditors} + \text{accruals}$$

This may be further rewritten to show homogeneous items on each side of the = sign as follows:

$$\text{equity} + \text{financial debt} - \text{cash}$$
$$=$$
$$\text{fixed assets} + \text{stocks} + \text{debtors} - \text{creditors} - \text{accruals} + \text{prepayments}$$

Therefore

$$\textbf{equity}$$
$$=$$
$$\textbf{fixed assets} + \textbf{stocks} + \textbf{debtors} - \textbf{creditors} - \textbf{accruals} + \textbf{prepayments} - \textbf{financial debt} + \textbf{cash}$$

Financial debt comprises two parts:

- long-term debt (payable after one year, in accounting terms)
- short-term debt (payable within one year, in accounting terms)

and so from substitution and rearranging the equation we can see that:

$$\text{equity} + \text{long-term debt}$$
$$=$$
$$\text{fixed assets} + \text{stocks} + \text{debtors} - \text{creditors} - \text{accruals} + \text{prepayments} - \text{short-term debt} + \text{cash}$$

Therefore, equity plus long-term financial debt is represented by fixed assets plus, as we saw in Chapter 2, working capital (WC)

$$\textbf{WC} = \textbf{stocks} + \textbf{debtors} - \textbf{creditors} - \textbf{accruals} + \textbf{prepayments}$$
$$- \textbf{short-term financial debt} + \textbf{cash}$$

Stocks, of course, comprise raw materials, finished product and work in progress (including their share of allocated and apportioned production overheads).

Progress check 15.1 Explain briefly the main components of working capital, using an example of a UK plc.

The need for working capital – the operating cycle

The interrelationship of each of the elements within working capital may be represented in the operating cycle (Fig. 15.1), which was introduced in Chapter 2 when we looked at the balance sheet.

The operating cycle includes:

- acquisition of raw materials and packaging, which are at first stored in warehouses prior to use, are invoiced by suppliers and recorded by the company in trade creditors (or accounts payable), and then normally paid for at a later date

Figure 15.1 The operating cycle

- use of materials and packaging in the manufacturing process to create partly completed finished goods, work in progress, stored as stock in the company's warehouses
- use of materials, packaging, and work in progress to complete finished goods, which are also stored as stock in the company's warehouses
- despatch of finished goods from the warehouses and delivery to customers, who accept the products for which they will pay
- recording as sales by the company its deliveries to customers, which are included in its trade debtors (or accounts receivable) and normally paid by customers at a later date
- use of cash resources to pay overheads, wages and salaries
- use of cash resources to pay trade creditors for production overheads and other expenses
- use of cash resources to pay trade creditors for raw materials.

Worked Example 15.1

We can identify which of the following categories may be included within a company's operating cycle:

- plant and machinery
- trade creditors
- investments in subsidiaries
- cash
- work in progress
- patents
- accounts receivable
- fixtures and fittings

Fixed assets are not renewed within the operating cycle. The following items extracted from the above list relate to fixed assets:

plant and machinery   patents
investments in subsidiaries   fixtures and fittings

The remaining categories therefore relate to the operating cycle, as follows:

trade creditors   cash
work in progress   accounts receivable (trade debtors)

The company therefore uses some of its funds to finance its stocks, through the manufacturing process, from raw materials to finished goods, and also the time lag between delivery of the finished goods or services and the payments by customers of accounts receivable. Short-term funds, for example bank overdrafts, are needed to finance the working capital the company requires as represented in the operating cycle. Many companies use the flexibility of the bank overdraft to finance fluctuating levels of working capital.

> **Progress check 15.2 How is a company's need for investment in operations explained by the operating cycle?**

Working capital requirement (WCR)

We have seen that

$$\text{equity} + \text{long-term debt}$$
$$=$$
$$\text{fixed assets} + \text{stocks} + \text{debtors} - \text{creditors} - \text{accruals} + \text{prepayments}$$
$$- \text{short-term debt} + \text{cash}$$

From this equation we can see that the total financial resources of the company are equity plus long- and short-term financial debt minus cash. This represents the total money invested in the company, and is called the total investment. Therefore

total investment
=
fixed assets + stocks + debtors − creditors − accruals + prepayments

The total investment in the company can therefore be seen to comprise broadly two elements:

- investment in fixed assets
- investment in operations

where the investment in operations is

stocks + debtors − creditors − accruals + prepayments

which is called the working capital requirement (WCR).

Stated in words, the WCR is telling us something very important: the company has to raise and use some of its financial resources, for which it has to pay, to invest in its operating cycle. These financial resources are specifically for the company to purchase and create stocks, while it waits for payments from its customers. The impact of this is decreased by the fact that suppliers also have to wait to be paid. Added to this is the net effect of accruals and prepayments. Prepayments may be greater than accruals (requiring the use of funds) or accruals may be greater than prepayments (which is a source of funds).

In most manufacturing companies the WCR is positive. The smaller the WCR, the smaller are the total financial resources needed, and the stronger is the company. Some businesses, for example supermarkets, may have limited stocks and zero accounts receivable, but high accounts payable. In such cases WCR may be negative and these companies are effectively able to finance acquisition of fixed assets with funds payable to their suppliers.

Worked Example 15.2

From the balance sheet of Flatco plc for 2005 and the comparatives for 2004, we may calculate the working capital requirement for 2005 and the working capital requirement for 2004.

Figures in £000
Working capital requirement:
WCR = stocks + debtors − creditors − accruals + prepayments
WCR for 2005 = 311 + 573 − 553 − 82 + 589 = 838
WCR for 2004 = 268 + 517 − 461 − 49 + 617 = 892

We will use the financial statements of Flatco plc, an engineering company, shown in Figs 15.2 and 15.3, throughout this chapter to illustrate the calculation of the key working capital ratios. The profit and loss account is for the year ended 31 December 2005 and the balance sheet is as at 31 December 2005. Comparative figures are shown for 2004.

> Progress check 15.3 **What is meant by working capital requirement (WCR)?**

Working capital (WC)

Working capital (WC) is normally defined as:

$$\text{current assets} - \text{current liabilities}$$
$$\text{or}$$
$$\text{WC} = \text{stocks} + \text{debtors} - \text{creditors} - \text{accruals} + \text{prepayments} - \text{short-term debt} + \text{cash}$$

Therefore   **WC = WCR − short-term debt + cash**

The difference between WC and WCR can be seen to be cash less short-term financial debt.

The financial analyst considers the definitions of long- and short-term in a different way to the accountant, thinking of long-term as 'permanent' or 'stable' and so will consider WC in an alternative way by calculating the difference between the stable financial resources of the company and its long-term use of funds, its fixed assets.

Since

$$\text{equity} + \text{short-term debt} + \text{long-term debt} - \text{cash}$$

$$=$$

$$\text{fixed assets} + \text{stocks} + \text{debtors} - \text{creditors} - \text{accruals} + \text{prepayments}$$

and

$$\text{WC} = \text{stocks} + \text{debtors} - \text{creditors} - \text{accruals} + \text{prepayments}$$
$$- \text{short-term financial debt} + \text{cash}$$

an alternative representation of working capital is

$$\textbf{WC} = \textbf{equity} + \textbf{long-term debt} - \textbf{fixed assets}$$

Flatco plc Balance sheet as at 31 December 2005		
Figures in £000		
	2005	**2004**
Fixed assets		
Intangible	416	425
Tangible	1,884	1,921
Financial	248	248
	2,548	2,594
Current assets		
Stocks	311	268
Debtors	573	517
Prepayments	589	617
Cash	327	17
	1,800	1,419
Current liabilities (less than one year)		
Financial debt	50	679
Creditors	553	461
Taxation	50	44
Dividends	70	67
Accruals	82	49
	805	1,300
Net current assets	995	119
Total assets		
less current liabilities	3,543	2,713
less		
Long-term liabilities		
Financial debt	173	–
Creditors	154	167
	327	167
less		
Provisions	222	222
Net assets	2,994	2,324
Capital and reserves		
Capital	1,200	1,000
Premiums	200	200
Profit and loss account	1,594	1,124
	2,994	2,324

Figure 15.2 Flatco plc balance sheet as at 31 December 2005

As a general rule, except in certain commercial circumstances WC should always be positive in the long run because if it were negative then the company would be financing its (long-term) fixed assets with short-term debt. Renewal of such debt represents a major liquidity risk. It is the same thing as, say, financing one's house purchase with an overdraft. Since WC has to be positive and the aim should be for WCR to be as small as possible, or even negative, there is a dilemma as to the acceptability of either positive or negative cash. The answer really depends on the quality of the WCR.

If net cash is negative then short-term debt is higher than the cash balance and so WCR is financed partly with short-term debt. So the question may be asked 'will the company suffer the same liquidity risk as with a negative WC?' If stocks are of high quality champagne, the value of which will probably rise year by year, or if the debtors (accounts receivable) are, say, blue chip companies with no credit risk, then a bank is likely to finance such WCR with no restrictions. If the quality of the WCR is poor the bank is unlikely to finance the WCR with short-term debt. The management and control of each of the elements of WCR: stocks; debtors; creditors, which we will look at in the following sections, must be considered in terms of both their quality and their level.

Flatco plc
Profit and loss account for the year ended 31 December 2005

Figures in £000

		2005		2004
Turnover				
Continuing operations		3,500		3,250
Discontinued operations		–		–
		3,500		3,250
Cost of sales		(2,500)		(2,400)
Gross profit		1,000		850
Distribution costs	(300)		(330)	
Administrative expenses	(155)		(160)	
Other operating costs				
Exceptional items: redundancy costs	(95)		–	
		(550)		(490)
Other operating income		100		90
Operating profit				
Continuing operations	550		450	
Discontinued operations	–		–	
		550		450
Income from other fixed asset investments		100		80
Profit before interest and tax		650		530
Net interest		(60)		(100)
Profit before tax		590		430
Tax on profit on ordinary activities		(50)		(44)
Profit on ordinary activities after tax		540		386
Dividends		(70)		(67)
Retained profit for the financial year		470		319

Figure 15.3 Flatco plc profit and loss account for the year ended 31 December 2005

> **Progress check 15.4** What is meant by working capital (WC)? How may it differ in a manufacturing company compared with a supermarket retailer?

Working capital policy

The financing of its investment in operations, its working capital requirement (WCR), offers a number of options to a company. Choices may be made between internal and external finance. The external financing of WCR is usually provided by bank overdraft. This is because of its flexibility in accommodating the fluctuating nature of net current assets.

Nevertheless, the servicing costs of bank overdrafts, and other short-term funding, are not insignificant and so it is of obvious benefit for companies to maintain their overdraft facility requirements at minimum levels. Such requirements may be reduced by the adoption of appropriate policies with regard to the level of investment in working capital that a company chooses to operate.

The working capital policy adopted will be dependent on individual company objectives that may often be influenced by the type of business and the commercial or industrial sector in which it operates. The choice of objective inevitably presents a conflict between the goals of profitability and liquidity. Working capital policies range between aggressive policies and conservative policies. The former increase profitability through holding low levels of cash and stocks, but run the risk of potential cash shortages and stock-outs. The latter provide greater flexibility, with higher levels of cash and stocks, which provide lower risk at the expense of reduced profitability.

Regardless of the policies adopted, improved management of working capital may have a significant impact on the level of requirement for external financing. Reductions in levels of WCR reduce the requirement for external financing and its associated costs. Maintenance of optimal, and therefore more manageable, levels of WCR increase levels of efficiency and effectiveness and so additionally contribute to increased profitability and a reduction in the requirement for external financing.

Working capital is the 'lubricant' of the investment in operations, enabling the investment in fixed assets to be most effectively exploited. Under-utilised fixed assets can produce extra stocks which then add to the working capital requirement. Good management of their working capital requirement by companies can therefore be seen to be crucially important to both their short- and long-term success.

> **Progress check 15.5** Why is the good management of the working capital requirement (WCR) crucial to company success?

Stocks management

In Chapter 9 we discussed how lean accounting can provide the relevant information and measurements to support and encourage lean thinking throughout an organisation. The lean enterprise uses less of everything to provide more, which results from the control and elimination of waste in all its forms. The Japanese quality expert Taiichi Ohno identified seven main areas of waste (called *muda* by Ohno), which relate to stocks to a large extent in terms of their handling, their movement, and their storage, in addition to the levels held and the proportion of defective and obsolete stocks (see *The Toyota Production System*, Productivity Press, 1988). These areas of waste emphasise the importance for companies to identify and take the appropriate action for improvement in this aspect of the management of working capital.

Overproduction

- The most serious, which discourages the smooth flow of goods/services and inhibits quality, productivity, communication and causes increases in stocks
- leads to excessive lead and storage times
- lack of early detection of defects
- product deterioration
- artificial work rate pressures
- excessive work in progress
- dislocation of operations and poorer communications
- encourages push of unwanted goods through the system, for example, through the use of bonus systems
- **pull systems** and *kanban* provide opportunities to overcome overproduction.

Waiting

- Occurs when there is no moving or work taking place
- affects materials, products, and people
- waiting time should be used for training, maintenance or *kaizen* but not overproduction.

Transportation

- Unnecessary movement and double-handling
- may result in damage and deterioration – for example, in 1999 and 2000 the UK car manufacturers Rover and Vauxhall found themselves with unsold or excess stocks being stored for too long in the open air, and were then forced to cut back production because of storage and damage problems
- increased distance means slower communication or feedback of poor quality, therefore slower corrective action.

Inappropriate processing

- Complex solutions to simple procedures
- large inflexible machines instead of small flexible ones – this encourages overproduction to recoup investment, and poor layout leading to excessive transportation and poor communications – the ideal is the smallest machine for the required quality located next to the preceding and succeeding operations
- results from insufficient safeguards, for example, *poka yoke* and *jidoka* – the lack of these lead to poor quality.

Unnecessary stocks

- Leading to increased lead time, space, and costs
- prevents rapid identification of problems
- discourages communication

- all leads to hidden problems, found only by reducing stocks
- results in high storage costs.

Unnecessary motion

- Refers to the importance of ergonomics for quality and productivity
- quality and productivity ultimately affected by operators stretching unnecessarily, bending, and picking up, leading to undue exertion and tiredness.

Product defects

- A direct money cost
- and an opportunity to improve, therefore an immediate kaizen activity target.

An example of the problems of overproduction resulting in excessive stocks can be seen from the Matalan press extract below. Its immediate effect is to increase the length of the operating cycle and increase the need for further funding, the cost of which has a negative impact on profitability. The other further effects of high stock levels have an additional downward impact on profit from the cost of increased waste in the ways we have examined above.

The result of Matalan being unable to clear its excess stocks following a disastrous Christmas 2004, was fear of a cut in the dividend paid to its shareholders. Many financial analysts downgraded their 2005 profit forecasts for Matalan, and the company saw a large drop in its share price.

Stock levels should be optimised so that neither too little is held to meet orders nor too much is held so that waste occurs. The forecasting of stock requirements must be a part of the management process. In addition, stock level optimisation requires the following:

- establishment of robust stock purchase procedures
- appropriate location and storage of stocks
- accurate and timely systems for the recording, control and physical checks of stocks
- monitoring of stock turnover performance
- implementation of effective stock management and reorder systems.

Progress check 15.6 **Briefly explain how electronic point of sales (EPOS) provides a system of monitoring stock turnover performance.**

The problem of too much stock

Matalan came under pressure yesterday after a leading broker cut its profit forecasts in the light of a year-end round-up meeting with the discount retailer.

After a disastrous Christmas, Matalan warned the City last month that it would make profits of only between £60m and £70m in the year ended February 28.

Yesterday, German bank Dresdner Kleinwort Wasserstein moved its estimate to the lower end of that range, citing concerns that Matalan had been unable to clear excess stock despite heavy discounting.

Dresdner said it had cut its pre-tax profit forecast by 8% to £60.4m and had advised clients to switch into JJB Sports, off 2.5p at 294.

'On our revised estimates, the stock trades on 13.9 times 2005 earnings. This looks expensive relative to the rest of the sector and we therefore maintain our reduce recommendation,' Dresdner said. The bank said it was concerned that the company might have to cut its dividend. Last year Matalan paid a dividend of 8.1p.

Other analysts were not so gloomy. Nick Bubb at Evolution Beeson Gregory said that although he had reduced his profit forecast by a couple of million pounds Matalan had made a good start to the new season. He believes it is possible that he will be upgrading his 2005 forecast when the company reports the full-year figures in May.

Matalan shares closed 7.25p lower at 164p – one of the biggest fallers in the FTSE 250.

Matalan given a dressing down, by Neil Hume

© *The Guardian*, 26 February 2004

Stock purchase

For cash flow (and operational efficiency) purposes it is crucial that efficient and effective sales order, materials procurement and stock control systems are in place and operated by highly trained staff. Authority levels for the appropriate purchasing and logistics managers must be established for both price and quantities, for initial orders and reorders.

Stock location

A variety of options exist for the location of stocks and the ways in which they may be stored. Related items of stocks may be grouped together, or they may be located by part number, or by frequency of pick, or located based on their size or weight.

Stock recording and physical checks

Ideally, all stock transactions should be recorded simultaneously with their physical movement. Stock turnover must be regularly reviewed so that damaged, obsolete and slow moving stock may be disposed of, possibly at discounted sales prices or for some scrap value.

In cash terms, holding on to unsaleable stocks is a 'waste' of the highest order. It uses up valuable space and time and needs people to manage it. It clogs up the system and reduces efficient order fulfilment and represents money tied up in assets of little or no value. Businesses need to move on and dispose of old, obsolete and slow-moving stocks.

> **Progress check 15.7** **What are the ways in which improvements in a company's management of stocks may contribute to achievement of optimisation of its level of working capital requirement (WCR)?**

It is inevitable that stocks will be required to be physically counted from time to time, to provide a check against stock records. This may be by way of a complete physical count two or three times a year, with one count taking place at the company's financial year end. Alternatively, physical cycle counts may take place continuously throughout the year. This system selects groups of stocks to be counted and checked with stock records in such a way that all stocks are checked two, three, four or more times up to maybe 12 times a year, dependent on such criteria as value or frequency of usage.

Stock ratios

You may recall from the sections in Chapter 5 about financial ratios that one of the efficiency ratios related to stock turnover is a measure used to monitor stock levels:

$$\text{stock days} = \frac{\text{stock value}}{\text{average daily cost of sales in period}}$$

Stock turnover (or stock days) is the number of days that stocks could last at the forecast or most recent usage rate. This may be applied to total stocks, finished goods, raw materials, or work in progress. The weekly internal efficiency of stock utilisation is shown in the following ratios:

$$\frac{\text{finished goods}}{\text{average weekly despatches}} \qquad \frac{\text{raw materials}}{\text{average weekly raw material usage}} \qquad \frac{\text{work in progress}}{\text{average weekly production}}$$

Stock ratios are usually calculated using values but may also be calculated for individual stock lines using quantities where appropriate:

$$\text{stock weeks} = \frac{\text{total stock units}}{\text{average weekly units cost of sales}}$$

Financial analysts usually only have access to published accounts and so they often calculate the stock weeks ratio using the total closing stocks value in relation to the cost of sales for the year.

Worked Example 15.3

From the balance sheet and profit and loss account of Flatco plc for 2005 and the comparatives for 2004, we may calculate the stock turnover for 2005 and the stock days (stock turnover) for 2004.

$$\text{Stock days 2005} = \frac{\text{stock value}}{\text{average daily cost of sales in period}} = \frac{£311}{£2,500/365}$$

$$= 45 \text{ days (6.5 weeks)}$$

$$\text{Stock days 2004} = \frac{£268}{£2,400/365} = 41 \text{ days (5.9 weeks)}$$

The performance for 2004, 2005 and future years may be more clearly presented in a trend analysis. If 2004 was the first year in the series, then 41 days may be expressed as the base of 100. The 45 days for the year 2005 is then expressed as 110 [$45 \times 100/41$], and so on for subsequent years. Comparison of 110 with 100 more clearly shows its significance than the presentation of the absolute numbers 45 and 41.

ABC and VIN analysis

The appropriate level of control of stocks may be determined through assessment of the costs of control against the accuracy required and the potential benefits. Use of a Pareto analysis (80/20 analysis) allows selective levels of control of stocks through their categorisation into A items, B items, and C items. The ABC method uses Pareto to multiply the usage of each stock item by its value, ranking from the highest to the lowest and then calculating the cumulative result at each level in the ranking.

A items, for example, may be chosen so that the top five stock items make up 60% of the total value. Such items would then be continuously monitored for unit-by-unit replenishment. B items, for example, may be chosen from say 60% to 80% of the total value. Such items would be subject to auto-mated systematic control using cycle counts, with levels of stocks replenished using economic order quantities (see below). C items, for example, may be identified as the 20% of stocks remaining – 'the trivial many' in financial terms. These stocks may be checked by sample counting; because of their low value, more than adequate levels may be held.

Other important factors impact on the choice of stock levels. Total acquisition costs must be considered rather than simply the unit purchase price. There may be requirements to provide items of stock using a just-in-time approach (see the section dealing with JIT later in this chapter). The cost of not having a particular item in stock, even though it may itself have a low cost, may be significant if it is an integral part within a process. Consequently, in addition to ABC categories, stocks are usually allocated vital/important/nice to have (VIN) categories, indicating whether they are:

- vital (V) – out of stock would be a disaster
- important (I) – out of stock would give significant operational problems or costs
- nice to have (N) – out of stock would present only an insignificant problem.

> **Progress check 15.8** **Describe how stock turnover may be regularly monitored.**

Economic order quantity (EOQ)

A simplistic model called EOQ, or the 'economic order quantity' model, aims to reconcile the problem of the possible loss to a business through interruption of production, or failure to meet orders, with the cost of holding stocks large enough to give security against such loss. EOQ may be defined as the most economic stock replenishment order size, which minimises the sum of stock ordering costs and stockholding costs. EOQ is used in an 'optimising' stock control system.

If

P = the £ cost per purchase order
Q = order quantity of each order in units
N = annual units usage
S = annual £ cost of holding one unit

Then the annual cost of purchasing

= cost per purchase order × the number of orders to be placed in a year
(annual usage divided by quantity ordered per purchase)
Or $P \times N/Q$
Or PN/Q

The annual cost of holding stock

= annual cost of holding one unit in stock × average number of units held in stock
= $0.5Q \times S$ or $QS/2$

The minimum total cost occurs when the annual purchasing cost equals the annual holding cost,

Or $PN/Q = QS/2$

Cross multiplication gives

$$2PN = Q^2 S$$

Or $Q^2 = 2PN/S$

Therefore when the quantity ordered is the economic order quantity:

EOQ $= \sqrt{2PN/S}$

Let's look at a simple example.

Worked Example 15.4

E.C.O. Nomic & Sons, the greengrocers, buy cases of potatoes at £20 per case.

£ cost of one purchase order	$P = £5$ per order
Number of cases turned over in a year	$N = 1,000$ cases (units)
Annual £ cost of holding one case	$S = 20\%$ of purchase price
Then, $S = 20\% \times £20 = £4$	
	$EOQ = \sqrt{2PN/S} = \sqrt{2 \times 5 \times 1,000/4}$
	$EOQ = \sqrt{2,500}$
The economic order quantity	$EOQ = 50$ cases of potatoes per order

EOQ illustrates the principle of stock ordering and stock holding optimisation but it is extremely limited. In practice, significant divergences from the EOQ may result in only minor cost increases:

- the optimum order quantity decision may more usually be dependent on other factors like storage space, storage facilities, purchasing department resources, logistical efficiency, etc.
- costs of purchasing and holding stock may be difficult to quantify accurately so the resultant EOQ calculation may be inaccurate
- in periods of changing prices, interest rates, foreign currency exchange rates, etc., continual recalculation is required that necessitates constant updates of all purchasing department and warehouse records of purchases and stocks – computerised systems can assist in providing the answers to some of the financial 'what-ifs' presented by changes in the business environment.

The emphasis over the past couple of decades on stock minimisation or stock elimination systems through the implementation of, for example, JIT, *kanban*, and **vendor managed inventory (VMI)** has reinforced the disadvantages of holding large stocks. High stock levels reduce the risk of disappointing customers, but it is a costly process not only in the inherent cost of the stock itself, but in the cost resulting from the 'wastes' identified by Shingo and Ohno.

> **Progress check 15.9** Outline the basic conflict that might arise between the marketing department and the finance department when discussing the practical application of an economic order quantity (EOQ) system.

Just in time (JIT), materials requirement planning (MRP), and optimised production technology (OPT)

Just in time (JIT)

Just in time (JIT) is sometimes incorrectly referred to as a stock reduction or a zero stock system. JIT is a philosophy that is a response to two key factors: the reduction in product life cycles; the increase in levels of quality required from demanding customers.

JIT is a management philosophy that incorporates a 'pull' system of producing or purchasing components and products in response to customer demand. In a JIT system products are pulled through the system from customer demand back down through the supply chain to the level of materials and components. The consumer buys, and the processes manufacture the products to meet this demand. The consumer therefore determines the schedule.

The JIT system contrasts with a 'push' system where stocks act as buffers between each process within and between purchasing, manufacturing, and sales. In a push system, products are produced to schedule, and the schedule may be based on:

- a 'best guess' of demand
- last year's sales
- intuition.

Some of the key principles and techniques of waste elimination, which in turn support improved stock management, are embraced within the implementation of the JIT process:

- total quality control (TQC), which embraces a culture of waste elimination and 'right first time'
- *kanban* which is a system of signals used to control stock levels and smooth the rate of production, for example using cards to prompt top-up of materials or components driven by demand from the next process
- set-up time reduction for reduced manufacturing batch sizes
- *heijunka*, which is the smoothing of production through levelling of day-to-day variations in schedules in line with longer-term demand
- *jidoka*, or autonomation, where operators are empowered to stop the line if a quality problem arises, avoiding poor quality production and demanding immediate resolution of the problem
- improved production layout
- *poka yoke* (mistake proofing) fail-safe devices, supporting *jidoka* by preventing parts being fitted in the wrong way, so that poor quality is not passed to the next stage in the production process
- employee involvement including self-quality and operator first-line maintenance
- multi-skilling of employees for increased flexibility
- supplier development for higher quality and greater reliability of supply – in the UK, M&S, for example, have publicised their adoption of this practice.

Two other approaches to stock management:

- materials requirement planning (MRP), its development into manufacturing resource planning (MRPII), and
- optimised production technology (OPT)

are sometimes seen as alternatives to JIT, but in fact may be used to complement JIT systems.

> **Progress check 15.10** Explain briefly what benefits might be gained by both supplier (manufacturer) and customer (national retailer) if they work jointly on optimisation of stock levels and higher quality levels.
>
> (Hint: Research *Daily Telegraph* website www.telegraph.com, Marks and Spencer plc and Bairds plc 1999 and 2000.)

Materials requirement planning (MRP)

MRP is a set of techniques, which uses the bill of materials (BOM), stock data and the master production schedule to calculate future requirements for materials. It essentially makes recommendations to release material to the production system. MRP is a 'push' approach that starts with forecasts of customer demand and then calculates and reconciles materials requirements using basic mathematics. MRP relies on accurate BOMs and scheduling algorithms, EOQ analyses and allowances for wastage and shrinkage.

Optimised production technology (OPT)

OPT is a philosophy, combined with a computerised system of shop-floor scheduling and capacity planning, that differs from a traditional approach of balancing capacity as near to 100% as possible and then maintaining flow. It aims to balance flow rather than capacity. Like JIT, it aims at improvement of the production process and is a philosophy that focuses on factors such as:

- manufacture to order
- quality
- lead times
- batch sizes
- set-up times

and has important implications for purchasing efficiency, stock control and resource allocation.

OPT is based on the concept of throughput accounting (TA), which was outlined in Chapter 8, developed by Eli Goldratt and vividly portrayed in his book *The Goal* (Gower, 1984). The aim of OPT is to make money, defined in terms of three criteria: throughput (which it aims to increase), and inventory and operating expense, which should at the same time both be reduced. It does this by making better use of limited capacity through tightly controlled finite scheduling of bottleneck operations, and use of increased process batch sizes, which means producing more of a high priority part once it has been set up on a bottleneck machine.

> **Progress check 15.11** In the UK there are several low volume car manufacturers. Make an attempt to relate the optimised production technology (OPT) philosophy to their operations.
>
> (Hint: Research Morgan Cars of Malvern and TVR of Blackpool.)

Factory scheduling is at the root of OPT and the critical factor in OPT scheduling is identification and elimination or management of bottlenecks. OPT highlights the slowest function. This is crucially important in OPT: if one machine is slowing down the whole line then the value of that machine at that time is equivalent to the value of the whole production line. Conversely, attention paid to improving the productivity of a non-bottleneck machine will merely increase stocks.

> **Progress check 15.12** What are some of the systems and techniques that may be used to optimise the levels of stocks held by a manufacturing company?

Debtors and credit management

All companies that sell on credit to their customers should maintain some sort of system of credit control. Improved debt collection is invariably an area that produces significant, immediate cash flow benefits from the reduction of debtor balances. It is therefore an area to which time and resources may be profitably devoted.

Cash flow is greatly affected by the policies established by a company with regard to:

- the choice of customers
- the way in which sales are made
- the sales invoicing system
- the speedy correction of errors and resolution of disputes
- the means of settlement
- the monitoring of customer settlement performance
- the overdue accounts collection system.

These are all areas that can delay the important objective of turning a sale into a debtor and a debtor into cash in the shortest possible time. Each area of policy involves a cost. Such costs must be weighed against the levels of risk being taken.

Customers and trading terms

Sales persons are enthusiastic to make sales. It is important that they are also aware of the need to assess customer risk of the likelihood of slow payment or non-payment. If risks are to be taken then this must be with prior approval of the company and with an estimate of the cost of the risk included within the selling price. Similar limits and authorisations must be in place to cover credit periods, sales discounts, and the issue of credit notes.

Credit checks should always be made prior to allowing any level of credit to a potential new customer. Selling on credit with little hope of collection is a way of running out of cash very quickly and invariably resulting in business failure. The procedure for opening a new account must be a formal process that shows the potential customer that it is something that the organisation takes seriously. Many risky customers may thus be avoided.

Before a new account is agreed to be opened, at least three references should be obtained: one from the customer bank and two from high profile suppliers with whom the customer regularly does business. It is important that references are followed up in writing with requests as to whether there are any reasons why credit should not be granted. A credit limit should be agreed that represents minimum risk, but at a level that the customer can service. It should also be at a level within which the customer's business may operate effectively.

A copy of the latest annual and interim accounts of a potential customer should be requested from the Registrar of Companies. These will indicate the legal status of the company, who the owners are, and its financial strength. These accounts are by their nature historical. If large volumes of business are envisaged then details of future operations and funding may need to be discussed in more detail with the potential customer. If such large contracts involve special purchases then advance payments should be requested to reduce any element of risk.

Having established relationships with creditworthy customers a number of steps may be taken to further minimise risk associated with ongoing trading:

- sale of goods with reservation of title (Romalpa clause) – the goods remain in the ownership of the selling company until they are paid for, and may be recovered should the customer go into liquidation
- credit insurance cover in respect of customers going into liquidation and export risk
- passing of invoices to a factoring company for settlement; the factoring company settles the invoices, less a fee for the service, which therefore provides a type of insurance cover against non-payment – a factoring company can be used as a source of finance enabling short-term funds to be raised on the value of invoices issued to customers.

The measures adopted should be even more rigorous in their application to the supply of goods or services to businesses abroad. This is because of the inevitable distance, different trading conditions, regulations, currencies and legislation.

> **Progress check 15.13** **What are the ways in which improvements in the management of debtors and credit management may contribute to achievement of optimal levels of working capital requirement (WCR)?**

Settlement methods

Payment collection methods should be agreed with all customers at the outset. The use of cheques, though still popular, is becoming a costly and ineffective collection method. Cash, credit card receipts, and automated electronic transfers are the main methods used by retailers and regular speedy banking is the cornerstone of efficient use of funds. Bankers drafts are the next best thing to cash but should be avoided because of the risk involved through their potential for accidental or fraudulent loss. Electronic mail transfers are frequently used for settlement by overseas companies. These tend to be costly and have been known to 'get lost' in the banking systems. Letters of credit together with sight drafts are frequently used for payments against large contracts.

Extreme care needs to be taken with letters of credit, which are a minefield of potential problems for non-settlement. Letters of credit must be completed providing full details and with the requisite numbers of copies of all supporting documentation. The conditions stipulated must be fully complied with and particularly regarding delivery of goods at the right time at the right location and in the quantity, quality and condition specified.

Electronic collection methods continue to increase in popularity. Direct debit payments are an option where settlement may be made on presentation of agreed sales invoices to the bank. Personal banking is now a feature of the Internet. As its use and level of sophistication continues to be developed, corporate banking transactions conducted through the Internet will inevitably become a major feature. Absolute control is required over both sales and purchase ledger transactions, and all businesses benefit from the strict adherence to administrative routines by the staff involved. Successful control of cash and cheques requires well-thought-out procedures. Examples may be seen in the formal recording that takes place in the systems adopted in high volume businesses.

One of the most acceptable methods is payment through BACS, the bankers' automated clearing services. The BACS method requires customers to register as BACS users and to specify the type of payment pattern they wish to adopt for settlement of their creditor accounts (or payroll). Every week, or two weeks or every month, companies supply details of payments to be made – names of payees and amounts. These are then settled by BACS exactly on the day specified and with only one payment transaction appearing on the bank statement. This means that the problems of cost of individual cheques and the uncertainty of not knowing when each payment will be cleared are avoided.

Cash takings must be strictly controlled in terms of a log and the issue of receipts. Regular physical counts must be carried out and cash banked twice daily or at least once daily. Cheques may be lost in the post, or bear wrong dates, or wrong amounts, or the customer may have forgotten to sign. One person should be nominated to receive and bank cash and cheques. A separate person should maintain the sales ledger in order to maintain internal control.

Sales invoices

The sales invoicing system must ensure that prompt, accurate invoices are submitted to customers for all goods and services that are provided. A control system needs to be implemented to prevent supply without a subsequent sales invoice being issued. An invoicing delay of just one day may result in one month's delay in payment. Incorrect pricing, VAT calculations, invoice totalling, and customer names and addresses may all result in delay. A customer is unlikely to point out an undercharged invoice.

Sales invoices may be routinely followed up with statements of outstanding balances. The credit period offered to customers should obviously be as short as possible. Care should be taken in offering cash discounts for immediate or early payment. This is invariably a disadvantage. Many customers will take the discount but continue to take the extended credit. This is something that may not even be spotted by staff responsible for checking and processing receipts from customers, which effectively results in an unauthorised cost being incurred by the business.

Debtor ratios

Another of the efficiency ratios from the sections in Chapter 5 about financial ratios relates to debtor days, which is a measure used to monitor customer settlement performance.

$$\text{debtor days} = \frac{\text{accounts receivable} \times 365}{\text{sales}}$$

Debtor days indicate the average time taken, in calendar days, to receive payment from credit customers. Adjustment is needed if the ratio is materially distorted by VAT or other taxes. Currently, UK sales for exports to countries abroad are not applicable for VAT. Other forms of sales tax may be applicable to sales in those countries.

Worked Example 15.5

From the balance sheet and profit and loss account of Flatco plc for 2005, and the comparatives for 2004, we may calculate the debtor days for 2005 and the debtor days for 2004.

$$\text{Debtor days 2005} = \frac{\text{accounts receivable} \times 365}{\text{sales}} = \frac{£573 \times 365}{£3,500} = 60 \text{ days}$$

$$\text{Debtor days 2004} = \frac{£517 \times 365}{£3,250} = 58 \text{ days}$$

A similar trend analysis to that described in Worked Example 15.3 may be used for greater clarification of performance.

If in 2004, 58 days = 100, then the year 2005 debtor days would = 103.

Progress check 15.14 **Describe how customer settlement performance may be regularly monitored.**

Collection policy

As a great many experienced businessmen may confirm, perhaps the key factor underlying sustained, successful collection of accounts receivable is identification of 'the person' within the customer organisation who actually makes things happen and who can usually speed up the processing of a payment through the company's systems. Payments are usually authorised by the finance director and/or managing director or the accountant. However, 'the person' is the one who prepares payments and pushes them under the nose of the appropriate manager for signature. Cultivation of a good relationship with 'the person' within each customer organisation is an investment that usually pays massive dividends.

The benefit of issue of regular monthly statements of account to customers may be questioned. Most companies pay on invoice and so a brief telephone call to confirm that all invoices have been received, to check on the balance being processed for payment, and the payment date, usually pays greater dividends. Issue of a statement is usually of greater benefit as an *ad hoc* exercise to resolve queries or when large numbers of transactions are involved.

A routine should be established for when settlement of invoices becomes overdue. This process should include having a member of staff who has the specific responsibility for chasing overdue accounts – a credit controller. Chasing overdue accounts by telephone is usually the most effective method. It allows development of good working relationships with customers to enable problems to be quickly resolved and settled.

It is absolutely essential that accurate debtor information is available, up-to-date in terms of inclusion of all invoices that have been issued and allowing for all settlements received, before calling a customer to chase payment. It is also imperative that immediately errors are identified, for example errors in invoicing, they are corrected without delay. These are two of the commonest areas used by customers to stall payment and yet the remedy is within the hands of the company!

An indispensable information tool to be used by the credit controller should be an up-to-date **aged debtors report** giving full details of all outstanding invoices (see Fig. 15.4). This shows the totals of accounts receivable from all customers at a given date and also an analysis of the outstanding invoices in terms of the time between the date of the report and the dates on which the invoices were issued.

In addition, it is useful to have available the full details of each customers' payment record showing exactly what has been paid and when, going back perhaps one year. To provide an historical analysis and assist in resolving possible customer disputes, computerised systems may be used to hold customer data going back many years, for future retrieval. The friendly agreement of the facts on a customer account on the telephone usually goes a very long way towards obtaining settlement in accordance with agreed terms.

Perhaps one of the most effective methods of extracting payment from an overdue account is a

	Hannagan plc				
Aged debtors		**As at 30 September 2005**			
		·············· **ageing** ························			
Customer name	total balance	up to 30 days	over 30, up to 60 days	over 60, up to 90 days	over 90 days
	£	£	£	£	£
Alpha Chemicals Ltd	16,827	7,443	8,352	635	397
Brown Manufacturing plc	75,821	23,875	42,398	6,327	3,221
Caramel Ltd	350,797	324,776	23,464	2,145	412
*	*	*	*	*	*
*	*	*	*	*	*
*	*	*	*	*	*
*	*	*	*	*	*
Zeta Ltd	104,112	56,436	43,565	3,654	457
Total	**4,133,714**	**2,354,377**	**1,575,477**	**184,387**	**19,473**
% ageing		**56.96%**	**38.11%**	**4.46%**	**0.47%**

Figure 15.4 Example of an aged debtors report

threat to stop supply of goods or services. If a debt continues to be unpaid then the next step may be a chasing letter that shows that the organisation means business and will be prepared to follow up with legal action. Prior to sending any such letter the facts should be checked and double-checked – people and computers make mistakes! This letter should clearly explain what is expected and what the implications may be for non-compliance with agreed terms. A solicitor's letter should probably be considered, as a rule of thumb, not before an invoice is, say, 60 days overdue from its expected settlement date.

The last resort is to instruct a solicitor to take action against a customer for non-payment. Small debts may be recovered through the small claims court. The costs are low and the services of a solicitor are not necessarily required. Large debts may be recovered by suing the customer for non-payment. This is an expensive and very time-consuming business. The use of the last resort measures that have been outlined should be kept to a minimum. Their use may be avoided through a great deal of preliminary attention being paid to the recruitment of excellent staff, and the establishment of excellent systems, robust internal controls, and a formal credit control system.

> **Progress check 15.15 What are some of the ways in which the settlement of accounts receivable from customers may be speeded up?**

Creditors management

The balance sheet category of creditors payable within one year comprises taxes, National Insurance, VAT, etc. and accounts payable to suppliers of materials, goods and services provided to the company (trade creditors). Payments to the Government are normally required to be made promptly, but trade creditors are sometimes considered a 'free' source of finance. This really is not the case, and accounts payable are not free debt as the following example illustrates.

Worked Example 15.6

A supplier may offer Justin Time Ltd payment terms of 90 days from delivery date. If Justin Time Ltd alternatively proposes to the supplier payment terms of 60 days from delivery date the supplier may, for example, offer 1% (or 2%) discount for settlement 30 days earlier.

Annual cost of discount:

At 1% discount $\dfrac{365 \times 1\%}{30}$ = 12.2% per annum

At 2% discount $\dfrac{365 \times 2\%}{30}$ = 24.3% per annum

A discount of 1% for settlement one month early is equivalent to over 12% per annum (and a discount of 2% is over 24% per annum). Consequently, it becomes apparent that the supplier's selling price must have included some allowance for financial charges; accounts payable are therefore not a free debt.

Many companies habitually delay payments to creditors, in order to enhance cash flow, either to the point just before relationships break down or until suppliers refuse further supply. Creditors may be paid slower than the agreed terms to gain a short-term cash advantage but even as a short-term measure this should only be regarded as temporary. It is very short-term thinking and obviously not a strategy that creates an atmosphere conducive to the development of good supplier relationships. A more systematic approach to the whole purchasing/payables system is the more ethical and professional means of providing greater and sustainable benefits. This is an approach followed by the majority of UK plcs, which is now supported by changes in legislation that were introduced during 1999/2000.

With regard to suppliers, overall business effectiveness and improved control over cash flow may be better served by establishment of policies, in much the same way as was suggested should apply to customers, with regard to:

- the choice of suppliers
- the way in which purchases are made
- the purchase invoicing system
- the speedy correction of errors and resolution of disputes
- the means of settlement
- the monitoring of supplier payment performance.

Progress check 15.16 **Explain whether or not trade creditors are a 'free' or even a cheap source of finance for a company, and why.**

Suppliers and trading terms

New suppliers should be evaluated perhaps even more rigorously than customers with particular regard to quality of product, quality and reliability of distribution, sustainability of supply, and financial stability. Appropriate controls must be established to give the necessary purchasing authority to the minimum of managers. This requires highly skilled buyers who are able to source the right quality product for the job at the best total acquisition price (base price, delivery, currency risk, etc.), in the delivery quantities and frequencies required and at the best possible terms. Their authority must be accompanied by rules governing:

- which suppliers may be dealt with
- acceptable ranges of product
- purchase volumes
- price negotiation
- discounts
- credit terms
- transaction currencies
- invoicing
- payment methods
- payment terms.

Terms of trading must be in writing. Most companies print their agreed terms on their purchase orders.

Payment methods

Payments to suppliers should be made in line with terms of trading, but advantages may be gained from cheaper payment methods and better control than the issue of cheques. For example, the payables system may automatically prepare weekly payment schedules and trigger automated electronic payments (for example, BACS) directly through the bank. Alternatively, submission of correct supplier invoices directly to the company's bank may also be used to support automatic payment in line with agreed terms. Provided that adequate controls are put in place to check and monitor such transactions these methods provide a cost-effective method of controlling cash outflows and may be an invaluable aid to cash planning.

Purchase invoices

Integrated purchase order, stock control and payables systems, preferably computerised, should be used to control approval of new suppliers, trading terms, prices, etc. When supplier invoices are received by the organisation they must match completely with goods or services received and be matched with an official order. An efficient recording system should allow incorrect deliveries or incorrect invoices to be quickly identified, queried and rectified. The recording system should verify the credit terms for each invoice.

> **Progress check 15.17** What are some of the ways in which payments to suppliers may be improved to the mutual benefit of the company and its suppliers?

Creditor ratios

Another of the efficiency ratios, from the sections in Chapter 5 about financial ratios, relates to creditor days, which is a measure used to monitor supplier payment performance.

$$\text{creditor days} = \frac{\text{accounts payable} \times \textbf{365}}{\text{cost of sales}} \quad \textbf{(or purchases)}$$

Creditor days indicate the average time taken, in calendar days, to pay for supplies received on credit. Adjustment is needed if the ratio is materially distorted by VAT or unusual trading terms.

Worked Example 15.7

From the balance sheet and profit and loss account of Flatco plc for 2005, and the comparatives for 2004, we may calculate the creditor days for 2005 and the creditor days for 2004.

$$\text{Creditor days } 2005 = \frac{\text{accounts payable} \times 365}{\text{cost of sales}} = \frac{£553 \times 365}{£2,500} = 81 \text{ days}$$

$$\text{Creditor days } 2004 = \frac{£461 \times 365}{£2,400} = 70 \text{ days}$$

A trend analysis may also be calculated in the same way as discussed in Worked Examples 15.3 and 15.5.

Payment policy

The priority for the accounts payable manager must be to maintain the level of payables and cash outflows in line with company policy, but at all times ensuring absolutely no interruption to any manufacturing processes or any other operations of the business. Fundamental to this is the development of good working relationships with suppliers so that problems may be quickly resolved and settled, thus avoiding any threats to supply.

The accounts payable manager must have accurate accounts payable information that is up-to-date in terms of all invoices received, invoices awaited and payments made. In the same way as the credit controller deals with customer queries it is also imperative that the accounts payable manager requests corrections of invoice errors, immediately errors are identified. The accounts payable manager should have access to an up-to-date aged creditors report (see Fig. 15.5). This shows the totals of accounts payable to all suppliers at a given date and also an analysis of the balances in terms of the time between the date of the report and the dates of the invoices from suppliers.

The accounts payable manager should also have available detailed reports of all unpaid invoices on each account, and full details of each supplier's payment record showing exactly what has been paid and when, going back perhaps one year. The availability for use of correct, up-to-date information goes a long way to ensuring the avoidance of the build-up of any potential disputes.

> **Progress check 15.18** **Describe how supplier payment performance may be regularly monitored.**

Hannagan plc

Aged creditors   As at 31 December 2005

·············· ageing ····························

Customer name	total balance	up to 30 days	over 30, up to 60 days	over 60, up to 90 days	over 90 days
	£	£	£	£	£
Ark Packaging plc	9,800	4,355	2,555	455	2,435
Beta Plastics plc	45,337	32,535	12,445	144	213
Crown Cases Ltd	233,536	231,213	2,323	*	*
*	*	*	*	*	*
*	*	*	*	*	*
*	*	*	*	*	*
*	*	*	*	*	*
Zonkers Ltd	89,319	23,213	21,332	12,321	32,453
Total	3,520,811	2,132,133	1,142,144	123,213	123,321
% ageing		60.56%	32.44%	3.50%	3.50%

Figure 15.5 Example of an aged creditors report

Operating cycle performance

The operating cycle, or working capital cycle, which was illustrated in Fig. 15.1, is the period of time which elapses between the point at which cash begins to be expended on the production of a product and the collection of cash from the customer. It determines the short-term financing requirements of the business. For a business that purchases and sells on credit the cash operating cycle may be calculated by deducting the average payment period for suppliers from the average stock turnover period and the average customer's settlement period.

operating cycle (days) = stock days + debtor days − creditor days

The operating cycle may alternatively be calculated as a percentage using:

$$\text{operating cycle \%} = \frac{\text{working capital requirement (stocks + debtors − creditors)}}{\text{sales}}$$

Worked Example 15.8

From the working capital requirement calculated in Worked Example 15.2 and the stock days, debtor days, and creditor days calculated in Worked Examples 15.3, 15.5, and 15.7, we may calculate the operating cycle in days and % for Flatco plc for 2005 and 2004.

Operating cycle days:

Operating cycle 2005 = stock days + debtor days − creditor days

= 45 + 60 − 81 = 24 days

Operating cycle 2004 = 41 + 58 − 70 = 29 days

Operating cycle %:

$$\text{Operating cycle \% 2005} = \frac{\text{working capital requirement}}{\text{sales}}$$

$$= \frac{(\pounds311 + \pounds573 - \pounds553) \times 100\%}{\pounds3,500} = 9.5\%$$

$$\text{Operating cycle \% 2004} = \frac{(\pounds268 + \pounds517 - \pounds461) \times 100\%}{\pounds3,250} = 10.0\%$$

From this example we can see that Flatco plc's operating cycle has improved by five days from 2004 to 2005, an improvement of 0.5%. The deterioration in debtor days and stock turnover in this example has been more than offset by the increase in creditor days. Despite the overall improvement, this must be a cause for concern for the company who should therefore set targets for improvement and action plans to reduce its average customer collection period and reduce its number of stock days.

Overtrading

We have seen how important to a company is its good management of WCR. Personal judgement is required regarding choice of optimal levels of working capital appropriate to the individual company and its circumstances. This generally leads to the quest for ever-reducing levels of working capital. However, there is a situation called overtrading which occurs if the company tries to support too great a volume of trade from too small a working capital base.

Overtrading is a condition of a business which enters into commitments in excess of its available short-term resources. This can arise even if the company is trading profitably, and is typically caused by financing strains imposed by a lengthy operating cycle or production cycle. Overtrading is not inevitable. If it does occur then there are several strategies that may be adopted to deal with it:

- reduction in business activity to consolidate and give some breathing space
- introduction of new equity capital rather than debt, to ease the strain on short-term resources
- drastically improve the management of working capital in the ways which we have outlined.

This chapter has dealt with working capital, and the working capital requirement (WCR). We have looked specifically at management of the WCR. The appreciation by managers of how working capital operates, and its effective management, are fundamental to the survival and success of the company. Cash and short-term debt are important parts of working capital, the management of which we shall consider in the section that follows.

> **Progress check 15.19** How may a company's investment in operations, its operating cycle, be minimised? What are the potential risks to the company in pursuing an objective of minimisation?

Cash improvement techniques

We have already discussed how profit and cash flow do not mean the same thing. Cash flow does not necessarily equal profit. However, all elements of profit may have been or will be at some time reflected in cash flow. It is a question of timing and also the quality of each of the components of profit:

- day-to-day expenses are usually immediately reflected in an outflow of cash
- fixed assets may have been acquired with an immediate outflow of cash, but the cost of these assets is reflected in the profit and loss account through depreciation which is spread over the life of the assets
- sales of products or services are reflected as revenue in the profit and loss account even though cash receipts by way of settlement of sales invoices may not take place for another month or two or more
- some sales invoices may not be paid at all even though the sales revenue has been recognised and so will subsequently be written off as a cost to bad debts in the profit and loss account
- purchases of materials are taken into stock and may not be reflected in the profit and loss account as a cost for some time after cash has been paid to creditors even though credit terms may also have been agreed with suppliers.

Cash flow is therefore importantly linked to business performance, or profit, which may fluctuate from period to period. There is also a significant impact from non-profit items, which may have a more permanent effect on cash resources.

The non-profit and loss account items that affect short-term and long-term cash flow may be iden- tified within each of the areas of the balance sheet (see Fig. 15.6).

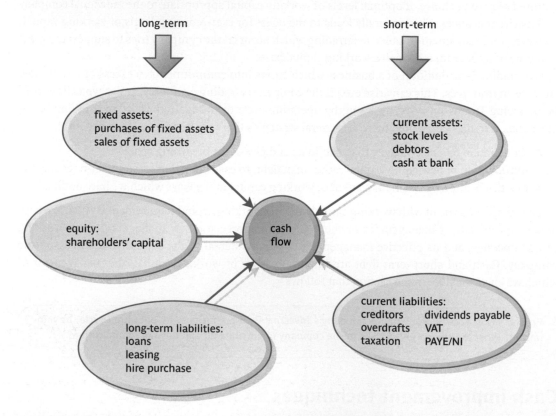

Figure 15.6 Non-profit and loss account balance sheet items that impact on short-term and long-term cash flow

The short-term cash position of a business can be improved by:

- reducing current assets
- increasing current liabilities.

The long-term cash position of a business can be improved by:

- increasing equity
- increasing long-term liabilities
- reducing the net outflow on fixed assets.

We shall consider each of these actions for improvement in the cash position of the business.

> **Progress check 15.20** **Profit and cash do not always mean the same thing. In what way therefore does profit impact on cash flow?**

Short-term cash flow improvement

Stock levels

Stock levels should be optimised so that neither too little is held to meet orders nor too much held so that waste occurs. It is a fine balance that requires planning, control and honesty. Many companies either hide or are prepared to turn a blind eye to stock errors, overordering or overstocking because managers do not like to admit their mistakes, and in any case the higher the stock then the higher the reported profit!

For cash flow (and operational efficiency) purposes it is crucial to put in place:

- efficient sales order systems
- materials procurement systems
- stock control systems

operated by highly trained staff.

Stock turnover must be regularly reviewed so that damaged, obsolete and slow-moving stock may be disposed of at discounted sales prices or for some scrap value if possible. In cash terms, hanging on to unsaleable stocks is a 'waste' of the highest order. It uses up valuable space and time and needs people to manage it. It clogs up the system, hinders efficient order fulfilment and represents money tied up in assets of little value.

Debtors

Debtors arise from sales of products or services. The methods employed in making sales, the sales invoicing system, the payment terms, and the cash collection system are all possible areas that can delay the important objective of turning a sale into cash in the shortest possible time.

Cash at bank

Whichever method is used for collection from customers, debts will ultimately be converted into a balance in the bank account. It is important to recognise that the balance shown on the bank statement is not the 'real' balance in the bank account. The bank statement balance does not represent 'cleared' funds. Cleared funds are funds that have actually been cleared through the banking system and are available for use. It is this balance, if overdrawn, which is used to calculate overdraft interest. There are software packages which routinely monitor bank charges and many users have obtained a refund from their bank.

The difference between the bank statement balance and the cleared balance is the 'float' and this can very often be a significant amount. The cleared balance information should be received from the bank and recorded so that it can be monitored daily. Cash requirements should be forecast in some detail say six months forward and regularly updated. Cleared funds surplus to immediate requirements should be invested. This may be short-term, even overnight, into, say, an interest-bearing account, or longer-term into interest-bearing investments or the acquisition of capital equipment or even other businesses.

Creditors

Creditors may be paid more slowly than the agreed terms to gain a short-term cash advantage, but even as a short-term measure this should only be regarded as temporary. A more systematic approach to the whole purchasing/payables system is a more ethical and professional approach that may provide greater and sustainable benefits.

Ordering anything from a third party by any individual within the organisation is a commitment to cash leaking out at some time in the future. Tight controls must be in place to give such authority to only the absolute minimum of employees. This authority must be accompanied by rules governing:

- which suppliers may be dealt with
- acceptable ranges of product
- purchase volumes
- price negotiation
- discounts
- credit terms
- transaction currencies
- invoicing
- payment methods
- payment terms.

A tightly-controlled and computerised system of:

- integrated purchase order
- stock control
- payables

must also feature countersigned approval of, for example:

- new suppliers
- terms
- price ranges.

When supplier invoices are received by the organisation they must match absolutely with goods or services received and be matched with an official order. The recording system should verify the credit terms for each invoice. If payment is made by cheque, these should always bear two signatures as part of the control systems.

Cash improvements may be gained from the purchasing and creditors' system in a number of ways. The starting point must be a highly skilled buyer or buyers who are able to source the right quality product for the job at the best total acquisition price (base price plus delivery costs plus allowance for currency risk, for example), in the delivery quantities and frequencies required and at the best possible terms.

Further gains may be achieved from efficient recording systems that allow incorrect deliveries or incorrect invoices to be quickly identified, queried and rectified. Payments should be made in line with terms but advantages may be gained from less costly payment methods and better control than the issue of cheques. For example, the payables system may automatically prepare weekly payment schedules and trigger automated electronic payments directly through the bank.

Alternatively, submission of correct supplier invoices directly to the company's bank may also be used to support automatic payment in line with agreed terms. Provided that adequate controls are put in place to check and monitor such transactions they provide a cost-effective method of controlling cash outflows and cash planning.

Overdrafts

If an overdraft facility is a requirement then the lowest possible interest rate should be negotiated. As with the purchase of any service, it pays to shop around to obtain the best deal. Bank interest charges should be checked in detail and challenged if they look incorrect – all banks make mistakes. Software packages are available to routinely monitor bank charges.

A bank statement should be received routinely by the company weekly, or daily, and should always be thoroughly checked. A detailed monthly schedule of bank charges should be requested from the bank and checked very carefully. These charges should be strictly in line with the tariff of charges agreed at the outset with the bank. In the same way as interest charges, bank charges should be challenged if they look incorrect.

At all times minimisation of both bank interest and bank charges must be a priority. This can be achieved by cash-flow planning and optimisation of the methods of receipts into and payments out of the bank account. If several bank accounts are held they should be seriously reviewed and closed unless they are really essential and add value to the business.

Taxation

Taxation on corporate profit is a complicated and constantly changing area. Tax experts may be engaged to identify the most tax efficient ways of running a business. At the end of the day, if a business is making profits then tax will become payable. Obvious cash gains may be made from knowing when the tax payment dates are and ensuring they are adhered to. Penalties and interest charges for late and non-payment are something to avoid.

VAT

Value added tax (VAT) is probably an area that is even more complicated than corporate taxation. VAT does not impact on the profit of the business. Businesses are unpaid collectors of VAT. If a business is registered for VAT (currently mandatory for businesses with a turnover of £58,000 or more) it is required to charge VAT at the appropriate rate on all goods and services that are vatable. Accurate records must be maintained to account for all such VAT. Such VAT output tax, as it is called, must be paid over to Her Majesty's Customs and Excise every three months or every month, whichever has been agreed.

VAT charged by suppliers, or input tax, may be offset against output tax so that the net is paid over monthly or quarterly. If input tax exceeds output tax, the VAT is refunded by HM Customs and Excise. It is important to note that VAT offices look very carefully at trends on VAT returns. A return that is materially different to the trend will usually result in a visit from a VAT inspector who will carry out an extremely rigorous audit of all accounting records.

It may benefit an organisation to choose to account either monthly or quarterly for VAT. In the same way as corporate taxation, great care must be taken to submit correct VAT returns, and pay VAT on the correct date to avoid any penalties or interest charges.

PAYE/NI

Pay As You Earn (PAYE) taxation and National Insurance (NI) contributions must be deducted at source from payments to employees. Salaries net of PAYE and NI are paid to employees, and the PAYE and NI and a further contribution for employer's NI is then paid to the Inland Revenue. Employees may be paid weekly or monthly and then PAYE and NI is paid over to the Inland Revenue by the 19th of the following month. In exceptional circumstances the IR may allow an odd day's delay. However, as with all other taxes, payment on the due date without fail is the best advice to avoid unnecessary outflows of cash in penalties and interest for non-compliance.

Dividends payable

Dividends are payable to shareholders by companies as a share of the profits. They are not a cost or a charge against profits but are a distribution of profits. There are some factors for consideration regarding cash flow. The timing of dividend payments is within the control of the company. Dividends may therefore be paid on dates that are most convenient in terms of cash flow and it is important to remember to include them in cash planning.

> **Progress check 15.21** **Which areas within the profit and loss account, and the balance sheet may be considered to identify improvements to the short-term cash position of a company?**

Worked Example 15.9

An extract from Flatco plc's balance sheet as at 31 December 2005 and 2004 is shown below. From it we can see that trade debtors at 31 December 2004 were £517,000. Sales were £3,250,000 and so debtor days for 2004 were 58 days. Trade debtors at 31 December 2005 were £573,000, sales were £3,500,000 and debtor days for 2005 had worsened to 60 days. Although new cash collection procedures and a reinforced credit control department were introduced in the latter part of 2005, it was too early to see an improvement by December 2005. A report published on the industry for 2004 indicated that the average time customers took to pay was 35 days, with the highest performing companies achieving 25 days.

We will calculate the range of savings that Flatco would expect if it were to implement the appropriate measures to achieve average performance, or if it improved enough to match the best performers. We may assume that sales are more or less evenly spread throughout the year. Flatco's profit before tax for 2004 was £430,000. The average bank interest paid/earned by Flatco plc was 9% per annum.

Flatco plc
Extract of the balance sheet as at 31 December 2005

	2005 £000	2004 £000
Current assets		
Stocks	311	268
Debtors	573	517
Prepayments	589	617
Cash	327	17
	1,800	1,419

	Flatco	Average (derived)		Best (derived)	
Debtors	£517,000		£312,000		£223,000
Sales	£3,250,000		£3,250,000		£3,250,000
Debtor days	58		35		25
Gain per annum		[517 − 312]	£205,000	[517 − 223]	£294,000
Interest saved/ earned at 9% per annum			£18,450		£26,460
Improvement to profit before tax		[£18,450 × 100/£430,000]	+4.3%	[£26,460 × 100/£430,000]	+6.2%

Assuming that Flatco plc's new credit control procedures become effective, at current trading levels it should result in a profit improvement for 2006 of between £25,000 and £37,000 per annum.

Long-term cash flow improvement

Shareholders' capital

Shareholders' capital has many advantages in providing a means of improving long-term cash flow. Provision of additional equity by the shareholders immediately strengthens the balance sheet. It also indirectly strengthens the profit position because equity (ordinary shares) does not bear a commitment to pay interest. Additional equity is an investment in future business, which will ultimately result in dividends payable from successful trading.

When owners of the organisation provide additional equity, a personal cost is imposed on them in that the funding is from their own capital. It also may dilute their own stake or percentage of the business. New shareholders or professional risk capitalists may be another source of equity. This carries the same advantages but also the expectation of rewards is much higher than those from interest-bearing loans.

Loans

Long-term loans have certain advantages, particularly for the acquisition of fixed assets, even though they carry a commitment to regular interest payments which may bear a fixed or variable rate. The period of the loan may be matched with the life of the asset and the agreed repayment schedule may be included in the cash flow plan with reasonable certainty.

Borrowing is always a big decision regardless of the amount. It has a cost and always has to be repaid. The ability to service any borrowing and the ability to repay must be assessed before making the decision to borrow. The real payback on borrowing for investment in fixed assets and working capital should be calculated and cheaper alternatives such as:

- re-use of equipment
- renovation of equipment
- renegotiated terms of trading

fully explored before borrowing.

A disadvantage of long-term loans is that they will invariably need to be secured by lenders on fixed assets to be acquired, or existing, or on other long-term or short-term assets. This reduces some flexibility for the organisation and may limit future short-term or long-term borrowing requirements.

If a company needs to acquire land and buildings in order to trade it has a choice of purchasing leasehold or freehold, or renting. Purchase of premises additionally takes an organisation immediately into the property business. While property prices are rising, this speculation may appear attractive. However, it does represent some risk to the organisation – property speculation has proved disastrous to many companies in the past – and it may result in a lack of flexibility. If a company needs to expand or relocate it may not be able to achieve this quickly and may be hampered by the fixed cost of owning a property.

Renting or short leases may present lower risk and greater opportunities in terms of location and flexibility and with regular payments that may be included in the cash flow plan. It also gives the organisation further financing opportunities, by not having a fixed liability of a loan secured on property.

Leasing and hire purchase

Leasing or hire purchase may be used for financing acquisitions of fixed assets. These two sources of finance require a slightly different accounting treatment. Hire purchase requires a large initial deposit and has VAT included in repayments. Hire purchase and leasing incur interest charges and depreciation, which are charged against profits. The term of either hire purchase or leasing can be matched with the expected life of the assets acquired. Cash flow may be planned in advance whichever method is chosen.

Purchases of fixed assets

The acquisition of fixed assets may represent an immediate outflow of cash. Cash-rich organisations may see advantages in outright purchases. However, the majority of organisations generally need to seek alternative funding. The sources of such funding may be from shares, loans or leasing, either within the UK or from overseas.

The use of an overdraft facility is not usually appropriate for acquisition of fixed assets. Fixed assets by definition have a long life and may be permanent in nature. An overdraft is repayable on demand, which is suitable for working capital requirements but is a risk if used to finance, for example, some machinery which may have an expected life of say 15 years.

Sales of fixed assets

Sales of fixed assets are an obvious means of raising funds. However, the opportunity cost of disposal of an asset must be considered prior to disposal and this should be considered in real terms using discounted cash flows with some allowance for inflation and taxation. An alternative may be to consider the sale of the asset to a leasing company, which then leases it back to the company.

Cash management

Any cash improvement exercise should include the factors we have discussed, which should also be regularly reviewed. However, in order to maintain control over cash flow it is crucial that a cash flow plan or statement is prepared on a month-by-month or week-by-week basis for, say, six months ahead.

The phased cash flow plan should be updated weekly or monthly. It may be continually reviewed and revised in the light of actual performance, and for advantage to be taken of opportunities for improvement through savings and rephasing as a result of consideration of the factors we have discussed above.

The recruitment of honest and reliable staff to deal with the control of cash and working capital is extremely important. Insufficient attention to this point together with a lack of frequent, appropriate training in credit control and cash management is a common occurrence, much to the cost of many companies. Many customers may detect a weak system of credit control and take advantage, resulting in considerable delays in payment of invoices.

Effective, integrated, computerised purchasing, stock control, order processing and sales invoicing systems are the tools necessary for trained and motivated staff to optimise the use of cash resources and safeguard the company's assets. It should be appreciated that until a customer has paid an invoice it remains an asset, which is effectively under the direct control of another business.

> Progress check 15.22 **Which areas within the profit and loss account and the balance sheet may be considered to identify improvements to the long-term cash position of a company?**

Cash shortage is a common reason for business failure. However, businesses that are cash-rich may also fail to take full advantage of opportunities to maximise the return on capital employed in the business. Such opportunities may include:

- acquisition of new businesses
- investment in research and development
- investment in new products
- lending to gain the most tax-efficient returns.

All investments should, as a matter of company policy, be appraised using one of the recognised discounted cash flow techniques. A realistic company cost of capital should be used to determine whether each project is likely to pay back an acceptable return.

If surplus funds are to be invested for short-term returns, the most tax-efficient investments should be sought. An understanding of the relationship between risk and reward is a prerequisite.

High-risk investment strategies should only be undertaken if the downside risk is fully understood, and the consequences are what the business could bear and survive should the worst happen. In both the UK and USA there have been some high profile failures of deposit-takers, resulting in massive losses by the depositors (note the collapse of BCCI in the UK).

Good banking relationships should be maintained at all times, with regular meetings and the provision of up-to-date information on company performance and new initiatives. The bank should ensure that information is provided to the company as frequently as is required on loans, interest and bank charges detail, bank statements, and daily cleared balance positions, so that they may be thoroughly checked as part of the daily routine. All slow-moving or inactive accounts, particularly, for example, old currency accounts opened for one-off contracts, should be closed to avoid incurring continuing account maintenance charges.

Summary of key points

- The operating cycle of working capital (WC), the net of current assets less current liabilities, is the period of time which elapses between the point at which cash begins to be expended on the production of a product or service, and the collection of cash from the customer.
- The difference between working capital (WC) and working capital requirement (WCR) is cash less short-term financial debt (bank overdraft).
- The working capital requirement is normally financed by bank overdraft because of its flexibility in accommodating the fluctuating nature of net current assets, and the generally lower cost of short-term financing.
- Effective management and control of stock requires its appropriate location and storage, establishment of robust stock purchase procedures and reorder systems, and accurate and timely systems for recording, control and physical check of stocks.
- Effective management and control of debtors requires establishment of appropriate policies covering choice of the way in which sales are made, the sales invoicing system, the means of settlement, and the implementation of a credit management and overdue accounts collection system.
- Although not free, trade creditors provide the company with an additional source of finance.
- Effective management and control of creditors requires the establishment of appropriate policies covering choice of suppliers, the way in which purchases are made, the purchase invoicing system, and the means of settlement.
- Regular measurement of the operating cycle, which determines the short-term financing requirements of the business, enables the company to monitor its working capital performance against targets and identify areas for improvement.
- The short-term cash position of an organisation may be improved by reducing current assets, and/or increasing current liabilities.
- The long-term cash position of an organisation may be improved by increasing equity, increasing long-term liabilities, and reducing the net outflow on fixed assets.

Questions

Q15.1 Describe how a company's financing of its investment in operations may be different from its financing of its investment in fixed assets.

Q15.2 (i) Explain the differences between working capital (WC) and working capital requirement (WCR).

  (ii) What are the implications for companies having either negative or positive WCs or WCRs?

Q15.3 Outline the policy options available to a company to finance its working capital requirement (WCR).

Q15.4 Outline the processes and techniques that may be used by a company to optimise its stock levels.

Q15.5 (i) Explain what is meant by economic order quantity (EOQ).

  (ii) Describe some of the more sophisticated stock management systems that the EOQ technique may support.

Q15.6 Describe the areas of policy relating to the management of its customers on which a company needs to focus in order to minimise the amount of time for turning sales into cash.

Q15.7 Outline the processes involved in an effective collections and credit management system.

Q15.8 Describe the policies and procedures that a company may implement for effective management of its suppliers.

Q15.9 (i) What is meant by overtrading?

  (ii) What steps may be taken by a company to avoid the condition of overtrading?

Q15.10 Describe

  (i) a review of the operating cycle, and

  (ii) an appropriate action plan that may be implemented to improve the short-term cash position of a business.

Q15.11 (i) For what reasons may some companies require increases in long-term cash resources?

  (ii) What sources are available to these companies?

Discussion points

D15.1 If working capital is the 'lubricant' of a company's investment in its operations that enables its investment in fixed assets to be most effectively exploited, how does the company choose the best method of lubrication and how often should this oil be changed?

D15.2 'Management of working capital is simply a question of forcing suppliers to hold as much stock as we require for order and delivery at short notice, and extending payment as far as possible to the point just before they refuse to supply, and putting as much pressure as possible on customers by whatever means to make sure they pay within 30 days.' Discuss.

D15.3 'A manufacturing company that adopts a policy of minimising its operating cycle may achieve short-term gains in profitability and cash flow but may suffer longer-term losses resulting from the impact on its customer base and its ability to avoid disruption to its production processes'. Discuss.

Exercises

Solutions are provided in Appendix 4 to all exercise numbers highlighted in colour.

Level I

E15.1 *Time allowed – 30 minutes*

Oliver Ltd's sales budget for 2005 is £5,300,000. Oliver Ltd manufactures components for television sets and its production costs as a percentage of sales are:

	%
Raw materials	40
Direct labour	25
Overheads	10

Raw materials, which are added at the start of production, are carried in stock for four days and finished goods are held in stock before sale for seven days. Work in progress is held at levels where products are assumed to be 25% complete in terms of labour and overheads.

The production cycle is 14 days and production takes place evenly through the year. Oliver Ltd receives 30 days' credit from suppliers and grants 60 days' credit to its customers. Overheads are incurred evenly throughout the year.

What is Oliver Ltd's total working capital requirement?

E15.2 *Time allowed – 45 minutes*

Coventon plc's profit and loss account for the year ended 30 June 2004, and its balance sheet as at 30 June 2004 are shown below. The chief executive of Coventon has set targets for the year to 30 June 2005, which he believes will result in an increase in PBT for the year. The marketing director has forecast that targeted debtor days of 60 would result in a reduction in sales of 5% from 2004 but also a £30,000 reduction in bad debts for the year. The same gross profit percentage is expected in 2005 as 2004 but stock days will be reduced by 4 days. The CEO has set further targets for 2005: savings on administrative and distribution costs of £15,000 for the year; creditor days to be rigidly adhered to at 30 days in 2005. One third of the loan was due to be repaid on 1 July 2004 resulting in a proportionate saving in interest payable. (Note: Coventon plc approximates its creditor days and stock days using cost of sales at the end of the year rather than purchases for the year.)

Coventon plc
Profit and loss account for the year ended 30 June 2004

Figures in £000

Turnover	2,125
Cost of sales	(1,250)
Gross profit	875
Distribution and administrative costs	(300)
Operating profit	575
Interest payable	(15)

Profit before tax	560
Tax on profit on ordinary activities	(125)
Profit on ordinary activities after tax	435
Retained profit 1 July 2003	515
	950
Proposed dividends	(125)
Retained profit 30 June 2004	825

Coventon plc
Balance sheet as at 30 June 2004

Figures in £000

Fixed assets

Intangible	100
Tangible	1,875
	1,975

Current assets

Stocks	125
Debtors	425
Prepayments	50
Cash and bank	50
	650

Current liabilities (less than one year)

Overdraft	50
Creditors	100
Accruals	150
Dividends	125
Taxation	125
	550
Net current assets	100

Total assets less current liabilities	2,075
less	
Long-term liabilities (over one year)	
Loan	250
Net assets	1,825

Capital and reserves

Share capital	1,000
Profit and loss account	825
	1,825

You are required to calculate the following:

(i)   operating cycle days for 2003/2004
(ii) operating cycle days for 2004/2005
(iii) the expected value of stocks plus debtors less creditors as at 30 June 2005
(iv) the PBT for 2004/2005.

E15.3 *Time allowed – 45 minutes*

Trumper Ltd has recently appointed a new managing director who would like to implement major improvements to the company's management of working capital. Trumper's customers should pay by the end of the second month following delivery. Despite this they take on average 75 days to settle their accounts. Trumper's sales for the current year are estimated at £32m, and the company expects bad debts to be £320,000.

The managing director has suggested an early settlement discount of 2% for customers paying within 60 days. His meetings with all the company's major customers have indicated that 30% would take the discount and pay within 60 days; 70% of the customers would continue to pay within 75 days on average. However, the finance director has calculated that bad debts may reduce by £100,000 for the year, together with savings of £20,000 on administrative costs.

Trumper Ltd has an overdraft facility to finance its working capital on which it pays interest at 12% per annum.

The managing director would like to know how Trumper may gain from introducing early settlement discounts, if it is assumed that sales levels would remain unchanged. The managing director would also like suggestions as to how the company may reduce its reliance on its overdraft, perhaps through better management of its debtors, and whether the overdraft is the best method of financing its working capital.

Level II

E15.4 *Time allowed – 45 minutes*

Josef Ryan Ltd has experienced difficulties in getting its customers to pay on time. It is considering the offer of a discount for payment within 14 days to its customers, who currently pay after 60 days. It is estimated that only 50% of credit customers would take the discount, although administrative cost savings of £10,000 per annum would be gained. The marketing director believes that sales would be unaffected by the discount. Sales for 2006 have been budgeted at £10m. The cost of short-term finance for Ryan is 15% per annum.

What is the maximum discount that Josef Ryan Ltd may realistically offer?

E15.5 *Time allowed – 45 minutes*

Worrall plc's sales for 2004 were £8m. Costs of sales were 80% of sales. Bad debts were 2% of sales. Cost of sales variable costs were 90% and fixed costs were 10%. Worrall's cost of finance is 10% per annum. Worrall plc allows its customers 60 days' credit, but is now considering increasing this to 90 days' credit because it believes that this will increase sales. Worrall plc's sales manager estimated that if customers were granted 90 days' credit, sales may be increased by 20%, but that bad debts would increase from 2% to 3%. The finance director calculated that such a change in policy would not increase fixed costs, and neither would it result in changes to creditors and stock.

Would you recommend that Worrall plc increase customer credit to 90 days?

E15.6 *Time allowed – 45 minutes*

Chapman Engineering plc has annual sales of £39m, which are made evenly throughout the year. At present the company has an overdraft facility on which its bank charges 9% per annum.

Chapman Engineering plc currently allows its customers 45 days' credit. One third of the customers pay on time, in terms of total sales value. The other two thirds pay on average after 60 days. Chapman believes that the offer of a cash discount of 1% to its customers would induce them to pay within 45 days. Chapman also believes that two-thirds of the customers who now take 60 days to pay would pay within 45 days. The other third would still take an average of 60 days. Chapman estimates that this action would also result in bad debts being reduced by £25,000 a year.

(i)   What is the current value of debtors?

(ii)   What would the level of debtors be if terms were changed and 1% discount was offered to reduce debtor days from 60 days to 45 days?

(iii) What is the net annual cost to the company of granting this discount?

(iv)   Would you recommend that the company should introduce the offer of an early settlement discount?

(v)   What other factors should Chapman consider before implementing this change?

(vi)   Are there other controls and procedures that Chapman could introduce to better manage its debtors?

E15.7 *Time allowed – 60 minutes*

Sarnico Ltd, a UK subsidiary of a food manufacturing multinational group, makes sandwiches for sale by supermarkets. The group managing director, Emanuel Recount, is particularly concerned with Sarnico's cash position. The financial statements for 2005 are as follows:

Profit and loss account for the year ended 30 September 2005

	£m	£m
Sales		49
less: Cost of sales		
Opening stock	7	
add: Purchases	40	
	47	
less: Closing stock	10	37
Gross profit		12
Expenses		(13)
Net loss for the year		(1)

Balance sheet as at 30 September 2005

	£m	£m	£m
Fixed assets			15
Current assets:			
Stock		10	
Debtors		6	
		16	
less			
Creditors due within one year			
Trade creditors	(4)		
Bank overdraft	(11)	(15)	1
			16
less			
Creditors due after one year			
Loans			(8)
			8
Capital and reserves			
Ordinary share capital			3
Retained profit			5
			8

We may assume that debtors and creditors were maintained at a constant level throughout the year.

(i)   Why should Emanuel Recount be concerned about Sarnico's liquidity?

(ii)   What is the 'operating cycle'?

(iii)   Why is the operating cycle important with regard to the financial management of Sarnico?

(iv)   Calculate the 365-day operating cycle for Sarnico Ltd.

(v)   What actions may Sarnico Ltd take to improve its operating cycle performance?

E15.8 *Time allowed – 60 minutes*

Refer to the balance sheet for Flatco plc as at 31 December 2005, and its profit and loss account for the year to 31 December 2005 shown at the beginning of Chapter 15.

A benchmarking exercise that looked at competing companies within the industry revealed that on average debtor days for 2005 were 33 days, average creditor days were 85 days, and average stock days were 32 days. The exercise also indicated that in the best performing companies in the industry the time that customers took to pay was 24 days, with creditor days at 90 days and stock days at 18 days. **You are required to calculate the range of values of savings that Flatco may achieve in 2006 (assuming the same activity levels as 2005) if it were to implement the appropriate measures to achieve average performance or if it improved enough to match the best performers.**

You may assume that sales are more or less evenly spread throughout the year. The average bank interest paid/earned by Flatco plc is 9% per annum.

16

Information technology and accounting, and e-business

Contents

Learning objectives

Completion of this chapter will enable you to:

- outline the ways in which information technology (IT) has been used to change and improve the ways in which accounting and financial data is recorded, processed, stored, retrieved, and reported
- explain the ways in which IT has impacted on traditional payroll and accounting systems
- describe the ways in which computer systems have been developed to include all the operational areas of a business, for example manufacturing, distribution and quality management
- explain how businesses have been able to achieve the full integration of their applications software through the implementation of enterprise resource planning (ERP) systems
- illustrate the ways in which spreadsheets have taken the place of the traditional accountants' analysis pad and simplified and speeded up the most complicated and sophisticated financial calculations and analyses
- describe the use of databases for the storage, retrieval and reporting of wide ranges of related data
- explain how graphics tools and groupware have enhanced and improved the ways in which accounting information, ideas, and concepts may be shared and presented using computer projections and the Internet
- discuss the range of additional accounting-related software systems that have been developed for personal and business use
- outline the key data protection principles contained in the Data Protection Act 1998
- outline some of the changes in accounting following the emergence of the 'new economy' through the latter part of the twentieth century and the start of the twenty-first century
- explain the broad concept of e-business and its various elements, for example e-commerce, email and websites, and their impact on accounting systems.

Introduction

This chapter considers the important impact that computers increasingly continue to have not only on virtually every aspect of modern life, but on business organisations in particular. The development of the use of computers specifically and information technology (IT) in general has a huge influence on how organisations operate and on changes in the way accounting and financial management is able to support them.

The development of IT has been fuelled not only by the tremendous increase in the pace of technological change but also to a great extent by the vast increase in the range of products and services available to us all, increasing globalisation, and breadth of competition. Increasing competition is a fact of life within any industry, public or private, and whatever product or service is being offered to customers in the marketplace. Globalisation has brought increased pressures of competition. Pressures on a company's profit margins inevitably follow from the increasing pace of technological change, which results in shorter life cycles of products as completely new models are being developed at a much quicker rate. Thus, the obsolescence of capital equipment is accelerated. This all means that the basis of competition has changed.

The effects on businesses are significant (and those that do not respond successfully may fail, or be acquired by other companies):

- costs such as development costs and costs of capital equipment must be recovered over a shorter time period
- the phases within the product life cycle must be managed more effectively and efficiently
- the faster pace of business and the need for quick decisions and action mean that effective computerised information systems are required to provide relevant and timely information.

This has all resulted in the requirement for speedier and more accurate communication of information and data, delivery of products and services, and processing of transactions.

Business processes and IT

The use of computers by business organisations began with payroll applications and was developed to cover a wide range of general accounting applications. The early days, from the 1940s up until the 1970s, saw a growth in the use of large mainframe computers for payroll, sales ledger, purchase ledger, general ledger, and financial reporting systems (see the example in Fig. 16.1). As the technology advanced the size of mainframes decreased as their capacity and memories increased.

However, the early mainframe systems required:

- manual preparation of batches of large amounts of data for subsequent input to the computer system
- validation of data entry, and
- recording and processing of the data.

Figure 16.1 One of the earliest mainframe computer systems installed by HSBC (formerly Midland Bank) in 1962 at its West End Computer Centre in London

The whole process was very tedious and time-consuming and involved long delays between the recording of data and the provision of reports based on that data.

In the early 1980s the emergence of personal computers (PCs) – starting with computers like the Sinclair ZX81, Apple and BBC Acorn, through to IBM, Compaq and Hewlett Packard – provided the springboard for the revolution in ways that data could be recorded, analysed and reported on. Personal computers also opened up the paths along which many other applications could proceed. However, PCs did not make mainframe computers obsolete.

Mainframe computer systems increasingly continue to be used for the processing of extremely high volumes of transactions such as, for example, large payrolls, automated payment systems, and pay as you earn (PAYE) taxation. Mainframe software like Peoplesoft and SAP is also still used by some large organisations for their accounting, ordering and invoicing, purchasing, manufacturing, and distribution systems. These systems may or may not be linked with the PC systems used in such organisations. Since the 1990s there has been a move by the larger businesses to smaller computers. This has resulted in the development of what are called client-server computer systems, which are cheaper in terms of their initial cost, and maintenance, and require lower levels of staffing. Small to medium sized enterprises (SMEs) use either standalone or networked PCs, and client-servers for applications similar to those run on the larger mainframe systems.

Application software includes accounting software, which is used to record, process, store, retrieve and report on transactions and produce financial statements and other reports. Decision support software (DSS) is used in the decision-making process to analyse data and predict the outcome of decisions in order to assist in choosing between alternatives. Executive information systems (EIS) provide internal and external information to managers, usually at a consolidated and summarised level but with a facility to drill down to transaction level.

This chapter will look at examples of the accounting software that is run on PC systems. It will also look at some of the other associated applications that have been developed over the past 20 years or so, for example:

- computer-aided design and computer-aided manufacturing (CAD/CAM)
- computer-aided engineering (CAE)
- computer-integrated manufacturing (CIM)
- just in time (JIT) and *kanban*
- materials requirements planning (MRP)
- manufacturing resource planning (MRPII)
- quality management
- enterprise resource planning (ERP)
- spreadsheets and modelling
- database management systems (DBMS)
- communication and presentation of information
- VAT audits
- year end statutory accounts audits
- risk management
- knowledge management.

The chapter will conclude with an introduction to the emergence of new economy businesses, e-business, and how businesses are increasingly using website resources, electronic mail (or email) and e-commerce in the further development of their organisations, and their accounting systems.

It is important to appreciate that there may be many advantages to be gained from the close involvement of accounting in each of the areas discussed above, some of which at first glance seem completely unrelated, like CAD/CAM. Note, for example, the article in the June 2004 of *Financial Management*, 'Draft Excluders', where it was observed that 'When management accountants get closely involved in the process of designing new products and services, the results tend to be highly beneficial. But this message doesn't seem to have got through to many designers.'

The development of computerised accounting systems

Up until the 1970s many businesses continued to use manual, paper-based systems for maintaining accounting records and reporting financial information. Traditionally, batches of source accounting data were prepared by entering details of transactions on analysis sheets for sales invoices, purchase invoices, cash receipts, and cash payments. These data were then entered either in detail or summary into the sales and purchase ledgers, to maintain records of amounts owed by/to customers/suppliers; the general ledger, to maintain records of sales and costs; the cash book, to maintain records of the cash position. Various other books of account, or ledgers, were in the same way maintained manually relating to information on product costs, special projects, fixed assets, etc.

Throughout the 1970s increasing numbers of organisations began to take their first steps along the computerisation path. The first main use of computers in the finance function was the recording and processing of payroll information. This enabled details of gross pay and deductions (pay as you earn tax (PAYE), national insurance (NI) contributions, pension contributions, etc.) to be held for individual employees and the total for the whole organisation. Payroll systems are used to print individual pay slips in support of net pay paid to each employee, and to provide reports for the organisation relating to employee costs, and amounts payable to their pension schemes, and payable to the Inland Revenue for PAYE and NI. Computerised payroll systems were either run for organisations by external agencies or run within and by the organisations themselves.

Computerised payroll applications were quickly followed by the development of computerised accounting ledger systems. These systems used batches of transactions similar to those used in the manual systems. The batches were prepared so that they could be uniquely identified and have the data verified and validated. The data were then input by computer department staff dedicated to transferring the data onto punched cards for each transaction. In the earliest punched card systems the punched cards were read by a card reader and then sorted appropriately for specific reports to be produced on a printer. The next development was the use of punched cards, which were similarly read by a card reader, from which information was processed by the computer system and the records held on magnetic tape. The data on the tapes could then subsequently be used to provide printed reports. Tape was soon replaced as the storage medium by computer discs, but back-ups were still maintained on tape for some time, until disc technology had advanced to a stage that made tapes obsolete.

Punched card systems were subsequently replaced with screen-based systems, which enabled individual transactions to be keyed directly into the computer system. The transition to screen-based input by individuals led to the demise of the large data processing departments that had grown within companies as their use of computerisation increased. Instead, transaction data could be input directly by user departments, primarily the accounting and finance departments. Initially, the reporting from these systems for the user departments continued to be relatively slow, with delays between data input and the reporting of information, and remained under the control of the data processing, or IT, department. Driven by user requirements for faster reporting of information, systems were soon developed that allowed complete control of data input and output reporting of information by user departments, and with much faster response times in terms of data entry and reporting.

Payroll and human resources management (HRM) software

As we have already seen, application software to run payrolls either within the organisation by its own staff, or by using specialist agencies, was the first area of computerisation of an 'accounting' process. The basics of these systems were not substantially different from the manual payroll processes. As with manual payrolls, very tight authorisation and control procedures are essential in support of computerised payroll systems to ensure absolute accuracy and dependability, and to prevent fraud.

A payroll system maintains details of all employees with regard to name and address, PAYE tax coding, gross pay, payment frequency, payment method, pension, and other additions and deductions. This is to ensure that employees are always paid the correct net pay, on the right date, and in the right place. It also ensures that employers account appropriately for income tax, NI contributions, pension contributions, and any other deductions. In addition, payroll systems maintain employee details relating to their department, cost centre, and/or project codes so that total employee costs of gross pay, employer's NI, employer's pension contributions, and any other costs are properly accounted for and charged to the appropriate expense codes and departments.

Payrolls were traditionally the responsibility of the accounting or finance departments in most organisations. As payroll systems were developed and enhanced to encompass personnel or human resources processes, the responsibility became blurred as to whether these systems should be controlled by the finance department or the human resources department. An important issue arises here relating to the adequacy of internal control within the organisation. Should the department responsible for authorisation of additions and changes to the payroll/human resource management system (the personnel or human resources department) also have responsibility for the processing of the data and the generation of the payments from the system? Segregation of responsibilities is required to provide an adequate level of internal control. This control is provided when the payroll processing/payments functions are carried out by a department (i.e. the finance department) separate from the department responsible for authorisation of additions/changes to the system (i.e. the personnel or the human resources department).

A fully-integrated HRM (human resources management) system provides the fundamental payroll processes and the links with the accounting and planning systems. It also provides much more. It maintains data relating to departmental budgets in terms of numbers of employees in particular roles and grades. A complete HRM system maintains individual employee details about age, sex, ethnic origin, skills, qualifications, experience, training, promotion progression, retirement and pension details, grievance and disciplinary issues, and the results of staff appraisals. This data provides the basis for the information required for HR planning and succession planning, implementation of HR policy, and control and evaluation of performance. HRM software continues to be developed to assist in the effective management of the entire range of human resources available to an organisation.

Currently, the most recent development in HRM systems is 'employee self-service'. This is a term that is used to describe the way in which employees may have direct access to their organisation's HRM system to input their hours worked (if they are paid on an hours worked basis) and also their expenses claims for travel, hotel accommodation, etc. The results of employees' input is then routed to their managers for approval and acceptance by the system for electronic payment into their bank accounts, and automatic recording of the costs in the accounting system.

> **Progress check 16.1 In what ways has the computerisation of payrolls improved the recording of accounting information?**

Accounting software

A variety of operating systems have been developed on which to run application software. Operating system software is a group of computer programs that manage the basic operations of the computer by communicating with and instructing the hardware components of the computer. Operating software tells the computer how to execute application programs and manage the storage of data.

Mainframe operating systems were developed like the IBM S/390 and the VSE/VM, and used in very large organisations with huge volumes of transactions. Currently the market leaders include companies like SAP, PeopleSoft, JD Edwards, and Oracle. PC-based operating systems were developed in parallel with their mainframe brothers and included, for example, various versions of MS DOS that ran software like Pegasus, Sun, and Sage accounting software. As an alternative, many organisations chose to write their own accounting software using business systems programming languages like Cobol.

The development of the Windows operating system saw the emergence of other software that may have been developed using MS DOS and then modified to run on the Windows operating system. Such accounting software, of which Sage is currently the market leader, runs on PC standalone or networked systems, primarily for use by smaller and medium sized companies with a relatively small volume of transactions (although these volumes are also actually very large). The use of graphics technology enabled users to use a mouse or a pointer to click on icons rather than using a keyboard for inputting text instructions. The use of GUI (graphic user interfaces) has made IT much more accessible and easy to operate.

As we have already discussed, the use of mainframe computers for accounting packages has gradually been replaced by smaller centralised systems on large server PCs. These servers are linked to desktop PCs, which are then called clients, and which gives the systems their name of client-servers. As the use of mainframes diminished the accounting packages that were run on them were modified to run on client-server systems.

PCs may be used standalone or may be linked into networks. They may be linked in a local area network (LAN) to allow common use of hard disc drives, printers, scanners, modems, etc. Modems may be telephone modems, which transmit at 56 kilobytes per second, and which are usually used for computer connections for transmission via telephone lines; they may also be cable modems, which transmit data at much higher speeds (from 1 to 3 or megabytes or more) and may additionally provide television access to the Internet. Wide area networks (WANs) allow geographically more diverse network links between users on a worldwide basis. Accounting and other data may then be collected from such diverse locations and communicated to other sites for maintenance and analysis.

Operating system software is used to drive application programs like accounting systems software. The early computerised accounting systems based on traditional methodology may be criticised because of their narrow focus and their inability to extend across all other business functions. At the centre of such systems was the general ledger or nominal ledger. As its name implies, this held summary totals of transactions under each account heading, which does not facilitate detailed reporting. Additionally, these systems did not record and process data in real time; there were usually considerable time gaps between when transactions took place and when they were recorded, when they were processed, and when they could be reported on. Many systems were developed in parallel with general ledger systems like sales ordering, purchase ordering, fixed assets records, stocks management, personnel records, and so on. However, these were largely run as separate and independent systems with little integration.

General ledger, sales ledger and purchase ledger

The general ledger (GL) or nominal ledger was one of the first accounting software applications to be developed. Manual maintenance of GLs was very time-consuming and costly in terms of the staff required to carry out this function. GL software automates most of the features of the traditional manual bookkeeping approach and makes the process more efficient and reliable; it reduces the time spent in collecting transaction data and preparing financial statements.

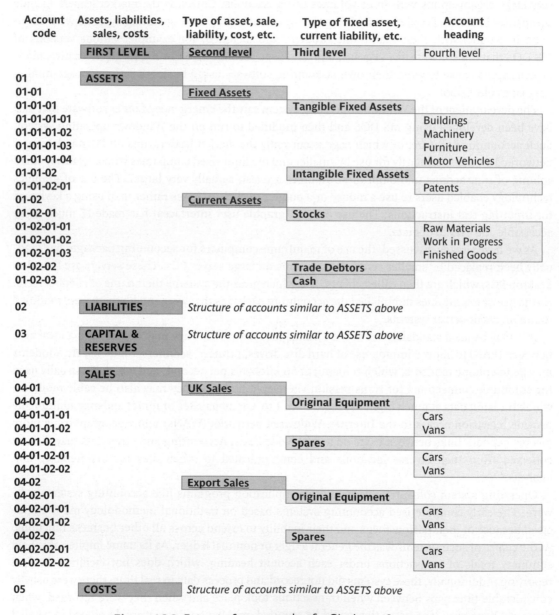

Account code	Assets, liabilities, sales, costs	Type of asset, sale, liability, cost, etc.	Type of fixed asset, current liability, etc.	Account heading
	FIRST LEVEL	Second level	Third level	Fourth level
01	ASSETS			
01-01		Fixed Assets		
01-01-01			Tangible Fixed Assets	
01-01-01-01				Buildings
01-01-01-02				Machinery
01-01-01-03				Furniture
01-01-01-04				Motor Vehicles
01-01-02			Intangible Fixed Assets	
01-01-02-01				Patents
01-02		Current Assets		
01-02-01			Stocks	
01-02-01-01				Raw Materials
01-02-01-02				Work in Progress
01-02-01-03				Finished Goods
01-02-02			Trade Debtors	
01-02-03			Cash	
02	LIABILITIES	*Structure of accounts similar to ASSETS above*		
03	CAPITAL & RESERVES	*Structure of accounts similar to ASSETS above*		
04	SALES			
04-01		UK Sales		
04-01-01			Original Equipment	
04-01-01-01				Cars
04-01-01-02				Vans
04-01-02			Spares	
04-01-02-01				Cars
04-01-02-02				Vans
04-02		Export Sales		
04-02-01			Original Equipment	
04-02-01-01				Cars
04-02-01-02				Vans
04-02-02			Spares	
04-02-02-01				Cars
04-02-02-02				Vans
05	COSTS	*Structure of accounts similar to ASSETS above*		

Figure 16.2 Extract of an example of a GL chart of accounts

A computerised GL requires the development of a chart of accounts, which is a coding scheme that uses numbers or letters to represent an account. For example, a range of numbers may be used for assets, liabilities, capital and reserves, sales and costs. A further range of numbers may relate to the different categories of assets, liabilities, etc., for example fixed assets, and current liabilities. A further range of numbers may relate to different types of fixed assets, current liabilities, etc., for example tangible fixed assets, and intangible fixed assets. A further range of numbers may relate to the different headings within tangible assets, and intangible assets, etc., for example land and buildings, and patents.

An example of this type of chart of accounts may, at the highest level, define assets as 01, liabilities as 02, capital and reserves as 03, sales as 04, and costs as 05. The further codings may then be cascaded down through the second, third, and fourth levels (and possibly more) of the chart of accounts, as shown in Fig. 16.2. The hierarchical coding structure enables ease of analysis.

Cash transactions, receipts and payments, were usually recorded in one or two accounts in the GL that were created for a bank account or overdraft. The details of these accounts showing the opening and closing balances, at the start and end of each accounting period, and the receipts and payments within each period were also recorded in a separate book of account, the cash book. On a regular basis it was necessary to manually reconcile each of the cash book balances with the balances on the accounts that represented them in the GL to ensure that there were no differences.

Alongside the general ledger, most of the early accounting software suites included subsidiary ledgers: sales ledgers (SL), which recorded all sales transactions with, and cash received from, customers; and purchase ledgers (PL), which recorded all purchase transactions with, and cash paid to, suppliers. These early SL and PL systems were not integrated with the GL but maintained separately (see Fig. 16.3). In the same way as with the cash book, this meant that their total balances at any one time required manual reconciliation with their respective control accounts in the GL. Within the sales and purchase ledgers, codings were required to uniquely identify customers and suppliers. For example, SL or AR may denote the sales ledger (or accounts receivable) and similarly PL or AP may denote the purchase ledger (or accounts payable). Therefore, for example, AR001, AR002, AR003 may define customers Abbott, Adams, and Alan, and PL001, PL002, PL003, for example, may define suppliers Abrahams, Appleby, and Ascot, and so on.

Fully integrated GL, SL and PL systems were soon developed which facilitated the recording of each transaction in the SL or PL, but at the same time simultaneously recording each sale, purchase and cash receipt and payment transaction in summary or in detail within the GL. This eliminated the need for the manual reconciliation of control account balances with the total balances of the subsidiary ledgers (SL and PL). Such fully-integrated accounting systems also included many other ledgers and books of account (see Fig. 16.4). An example of a fully-integrated computerised accounting system is Sage Sterling, which is distributed by the Sage Group plc.

Sage accounting software provides input forms for each module in the system, which are all screen-based, and which are completed using the computer mouse. The Sage modules also provide a screen-based numeric pad that enables simple calculations to be made at the appropriate points in the entry of transactions. At its basic level the Sage accounting software includes the following fully-integrated modules:

- sales ledger
- purchase ledger
- general ledger
- cash book
- stock control
- sales order processing and invoicing
- purchase order processing

- supplier invoice matching
- fixed assets register.

Figure 16.3 Traditional standalone computerised accounting systems

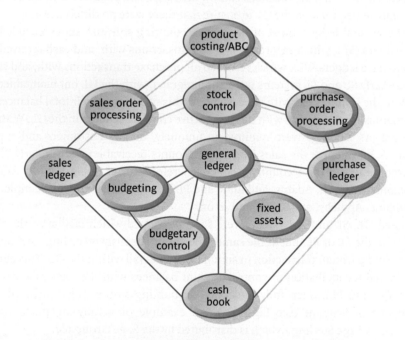

Figure 16.4 An integrated computerised accounting system

In addition, Sage Sterling provides audit trail reports and standard transaction and balance reports from each of the modules, as well as VAT reports, financial statement reporting of the profit and loss account and balance sheet, and a budgeting facility.

Stock control and distribution software

A stock control system is another subsidiary ledger like the sales ledger. Stock control software deals with the acquisition, storage, control, and movement of stocks:

- materials and components
- work in progress
- finished goods.

As with the SL and PL, such systems began as standalone systems that were not integrated with the GL, but were soon developed to allow the simultaneous recording of each transaction in stock control at the same time as recording each transaction in summary or in detail within the GL.

Many businesses have implemented even more sophisticated stock control systems that are also integrated with purchasing and manufacturing systems. This is to provide a higher level of control with the aim of ensuring that precise quantities of stocks are available in the right place at the right time without allowing any build up of unnecessary stocks. Such systems may, for example, involve the use of just in time (JIT), materials requirement planning (MRP), and manufacturing resource planning systems (MRPII), which are discussed later.

Warehousing and distribution systems have been developed to include much more than the recording of items in and out of warehouses. Bar coding systems allow individual stock items to be stamped with individual codings. The codings may be used to check items into the warehouse using fixed or remote scanners, and facilitate the checking of quantities of items held in various locations at any point in time. Bar coding systems may also be used to enable tracking systems to follow the movement of stocks out of one location and throughout their journey to their final destination.

Bar codings are also now widely used in the retail business. They may be used to check items into each store and also to record sales more efficiently and reliably by scanning items out as they are purchased by customers. In this way, these electronic point of sale (EPOS) systems as they are called, support the stock control systems but also provide important sales data that enable the business to develop a valuable information resource database. EPOS systems:

- provide the immediate updating of stock records so that stock-outs are avoided
- enable trends in sales of products to be identified, which is an extremely useful marketing tool
- enable consumer profiles and buying activities to be identified linking types of items sold with types of customer through links with customer store loyalty cards – another extremely useful marketing tool.

> **Progress check 16.2 What are the main aims of computerised stock control systems?**

Sales order processing and invoicing software

Sales order processing (SOP) software is used to process customer orders. Such systems are linked to the stock control system to provide details on numbers of stock items held and their availability. SOP systems are also supported by lists of the complete product range supplied by the business together with their selling prices, and customer account information, so that invoices may be produced for goods supplied and allowing for any special discounts given to specific customers. SOP systems are also linked with SL systems to enable sales invoices that have been produced from sales orders to be recorded within the relevant customer accounts and for the sales and VAT values of invoices to be recorded within the GL, via the SL. The SOP link with the stock control system ensures that sales of an item simultaneously reduce the stock numbers of that item.

Purchase order processing and supplier invoice matching software

Purchase order processing (POP) software is used to create and process orders for goods and services from suppliers. Such systems are linked to the stock control system to provide details on numbers of items already held and possibly their requirement in the foreseeable future. POP systems are also supported by lists of the complete range of items purchased by the business together with their con-, tracted purchase prices, allowing for any trade discounts. When goods are received by the business they are booked into stock and their quantities checked against purchase orders. Invoice matching systems are used to match invoices with goods received and to check that correct prices have been charged by suppliers. These systems are also used to register suppliers' invoices and record them on the PL in the appropriate suppliers account, and for the costs of stock (and non-stock) items and VAT values of invoices to be recorded within the GL, via the PL. The POP link with the stock control system ensures that purchases of an item simultaneously increase the stock numbers of that item.

> **Progress check 16.3** **With which other parts of an integrated accounting system should the sales order processing and purchase order processing software be linked and why?**

Product costing systems software

Generally, product costs may be assembled to meet the following three requirements:

- stock valuation and internal and external profit measurement, by allocating costs between products sold and fully and partly completed products that are unsold
- provision of relevant information to help managers make better decisions, for example profitability analysis, product pricing, make or buy (or outsourcing), product mix and discontinuation
- provision of information for planning, control and performance measurement, for example long-term planning and short-term planning (budgeting), periodic performance reports for feedback control, and performance reports which are widely used to evaluate managerial performance.

Product costing software is used to maintain data relating to the complete range of finished and partly-completed products or services created and/or sold by the business, using a hierarchical coding system for materials, components, work-in-progress and finished products. Such systems may be linked to the SOP and POP systems and the stock control system to provide a valuation of these items of stock at any time in terms of cost or sales value. They may be linked to budgeting systems and systems used for the reporting of actual versus budget performance, and also to modelling and decision-making systems used for product sales pricing and other decision-making.

Activity based costing (ABC) software

ABC was discussed in some detail in Chapter 9. ABC software systems require the identification of the major processes or activities that take place in the organisation. The activities chosen should be at a reasonable level of aggregation based on cost/benefit criteria. The choice of activities is influenced by the total cost of the activity centre and the ability of a single cost driver to provide a satisfactory determinant of the cost of the activity. Costs are assigned to cost pools/cost centres for each activity. Costs assigned to activity cost pools include direct and indirect costs.

In the same way as traditional product costing, ABC software is used to maintain data relating to the complete range of finished and partly-completed products or services created and/or sold by the business. Such systems may be linked to budgeting systems and systems used for the reporting of actual versus budget performance, and also to modelling and decision-making systems used for product sales pricing and other decision-making. ABC may also be linked to the stock control system to provide a valuation of stock items.

> **Progress check 16.4** **Discuss the benefits of a computerised ABC system compared with a traditional product costing system.**

Fixed assets register software

The fixed assets register is effectively another subsidiary ledger like the sales ledger. In the same way as the GL, SL, PL, and product costing/stock control systems, fixed assets software requires a coding system to define each category of asset, type of asset within categories and a unique code to identify each individual asset. The category and type codes may be linked to similar codes used within the GL. Fixed assets registers record the acquisition and disposal of fixed assets. They provide the facility to calculate depreciation values for each month and year of the asset's life (using whichever depreciation method may be appropriate) and calculate profits or losses arising when fixed assets are disposed of. As with the SL and PL, fixed assets register systems began as standalone systems that were not integrated with the GL, but were soon developed to allow the simultaneous recording of each transaction in the fixed asset register (acquisition, proceeds of disposal, depreciation, profit/loss on disposal) at the same time as recording each transaction in summary or in detail within the GL.

> **Progress check 16.5** **Discuss the main features of a computerised fixed assets register and its many advantages over a manually prepared register.**

Budgeting and budgetary control software

Most software packages have a budgeting facility that is linked to the GL or a part of the GL, using the same coding structures as the GL and providing the same sort of reporting including the financial statements. Some budgeting packages allow budget data to be input for the budget period at the level of individual elements of cost, sale, asset, and liability, for each department of the business, and possibly for a number of companies within a group. Alternatively, departmental managers may use spreadsheets (see later) to prepare their individual, detailed sales and cost budgets, and details of their planned fixed asset additions/disposals and possibly their working capital requirements for the budget period.

The preparation of a master budget for the business, which provides a budgeted profit and loss account, balance sheet and cash flow statement for the budget period, may then be produced from the budgeting software either directly from input of budget data or from input or downloads of departmental spreadsheets.

After the budgeting process has been completed it is necessary to compare actual performance against the plan and a basis for comparison is usually established through the setting of predetermined cost estimates, for example using standard costing. Budgetary control software calculates and reports differences, or variances, between a planned, budgeted or standard cost or sale and the actual cost or sale, whose timely reporting should maximise the opportunity for managerial action. Variance analysis is the evaluation of performance by means of variances, which are either favourable variances (F) or adverse variances (A), and neither will occur if the standard is correct and actual performance is as expected.

The use of computers in the budget preparation process has made it much easier to manage. The resulting shorter budget preparation timeframes has also required much greater accuracy in estimating the data going into the budget. Many companies have developed dynamic budgeting models, using packaged IT solutions that may link both financial and non-financial performance measures.

> **Progress check 16.6** What have been the main advantages and disadvantages for businesses from the computerisation of budget preparation and budgetary control systems?

Consolidation software

Software packages have been developed to provide reporting at the highest level on a budget and actual basis for businesses that are comprised of a very large number of departments, divisions, or companies. Such software is rarely used for reporting totals below the departmental total level. Consolidation packages like Hyperion are primarily used in this way to consolidate, or accumulate, the financial results of a number of companies within a large group for specified accounting periods. Such software can make the consolidation adjustments that are necessary when combining the financial results of two or more companies within a group. This software is particularly useful for consolidating the results of companies, whose financial statements are denominated in a variety of different currencies, into the one common currency adopted for group reporting.

> **Progress check 16.7** What is consolidation software and how is it used by businesses?

Accounting software, and GL systems in particular, has been criticised for a number of reasons:

- the lack of real-time processing of data
- the narrow focus on financial data to the exclusion of important non-financial data
- the emphasis only on specific areas of the business's processes
- the summarisation of data
- the exclusion of much of the data surrounding a transaction (focusing primarily on dates and values)
- the focus primarily on one stakeholder perspective, namely the shareholder.

As a result, GL systems continue to be developed as organisations search for new methods for recording and reporting transaction data. Consequently, GL software is becoming a smaller percentage of the total of software applications. Very often, data from computerised manufacturing systems and other processes' systems are interfaced with GL packages.

Manufacturing and other processes

The development of accounting software over recent years has been extended to include the operational areas of design and development, engineering, manufacturing, and quality management. This area of IT has had a significant impact on organisations in the area of production management. Production processes may be evaluated and planned using production management system software.

These may also assist organisations in their design and implementation of more effective operational processes. The extensive use of IT assists organisations involved in such diverse industries as food, automotive manufacture, construction, and publishing, in their aim of minimising manufacturing costs whilst maintaining the highest levels of quality. IT now provides decision-makers with greater volumes of higher quality information with which to better manage such processes.

Organisational productivity tools are available which may be used to enhance processes and improve productivity. An example is the use of workflow software, which graphically represents, documents, and defines business processes. The software may then be used to analyse and automate business processes. Other examples of software development relating to operational processes, which have accounting implications, are:

- computer-aided design and manufacturing (CAD/CAM)
- computer-integrated manufacturing (CIM)
- computer-aided engineering (CAE)
- just in time (JIT)
- materials requirement planning (MRP)
- manufacturing resource planning (MRPII)
- quality management.

These areas of software development are important to the accounting function for a number of reasons, for example:

- appraisal of investments in manufacturing systems software requires an appreciation of their true costs and the benefits that may be derived
- an understanding of how such systems operate is necessary to develop the appropriate links with accounting and other systems
- appropriate performance measurement systems must be installed to evaluate the economic and managerial performance of such tools.

Progress check 16.8 Why do you think that the use of IT has been extended to include manufacturing and other operational processes?

Computer-aided design and manufacturing (CAD/CAM) software

Computer-aided design (CAD) is a general term referring to software applications and the method used in art, architecture, engineering and manufacturing to design and provide precision drawings for objects such as buildings, machinery, components and other items, using a computer. Computer-aided manufacturing (CAM) is the use of computers for managing manufacturing processes. The standardisation of CAD/CAM systems now enables the interchange of design and manufacturing information between organisations, for example suppliers and customers.

Worked Example 16.1

It is possible for a designer and manufacturer of a seating system for a car manufactured by General Motors to ensure that it provides compatibility and a perfect fit for the vehicle in which it is intended.

The seating system supplier may exchange a three-dimensional CAD/CAM file that contains the detailed drawing of a seat with GM, who are then able to integrate it with their CAD/CAM system relating to the entire vehicle. Both GM and the seating system supplier may then ensure complete compatibility and fit with the intended vehicle. Both supplier and customer may then use this technology to ensure compliance with the original specification or to discuss and implement agreed deviations from it. The benefits from improved project management and the cost savings derived from the use of CAD/CAM systems are immense.

Computer-aided engineering (CAE) software

Computer-aided engineering (CAE) is the broad term used by the electronic design automation (EDA) industry for the use of computers to design, analyse, and manufacture products and processes, and includes computer-aided design (CAD – the use of a computer for drafting and modelling designs) and computer-aided manufacturing (CAM).

Computer-integrated manufacturing (CIM) software

Computer-integrated manufacturing (CIM) is the use of computers to give instructions that automatically set up and run manufacturing equipment. The costs involved in the setting up of a production process and the calibration of equipment have traditionally been very high. Reduction in set-up times is a key objective in most manufacturing organisations that can result in significant ongoing cost savings. Additionally, the use of robotic plant and equipment provides computer software to monitor the manufactured product and directly control processes, which ensures high quality manufacturing output that is defect-free.

There is extensive use of robotics in the automotive industry, the result of which has been to significantly reduce the amount of labour employed in manufacturing. Apart from the design and support of the software systems, manufacturing labour becomes increasingly focused on the areas of manufacturing engineering and maintenance of plant and equipment.

Just in time (JIT) software

Another key objective of most manufacturing businesses these days is to significantly reduce the amount of stocks required to be held in their warehouses and so reduce their operating costs. Coordination of shipments of goods to and from internal and external suppliers and customers can ensure that stocks are produced and/or delivered no sooner and no later than exactly when they are needed in exactly the right quantities required. The necessary level of coordination requires the use of sophisticated IT systems.

Just in time (JIT) software systems are sometimes referred to merely as stock reduction or zero stock systems. JIT is actually a management philosophy that has been developed in response to two key factors:

- the reduction in product life cycles
- the increase in levels of quality required from demanding customers.

Materials requirement planning (MRP), and its development into manufacturing resource planning (MRPII), are sometimes seen as alternatives to JIT, but in fact can be used to complement JIT systems.

Materials requirement planning (MRP) software

MRP software converts a production schedule into a listing of the materials and components required to meet that schedule, so that adequate stock levels are maintained and items are available when needed. MRP is a set of techniques, which uses the bill of materials (BOM), stock data and the master production schedule to calculate future requirements for materials. The master production schedule is a computerised time-phased statement of how many items are to be produced in a given period (like a giant timetable), based on customer orders and demand forecasts.

MRP software essentially makes recommendations to release material to the production system. MRP is a 'push' down approach that starts with forecasts of customer demand and then calculates and reconciles using basic mathematics. MRP relies on accurate BOMs and scheduling algorithms, EOQ (economic order quantity) analyses and allowances for wastage and shrinkage.

In a later section of this chapter on electronic data interchange (EDI) we will discuss how suppliers and customers may communicate using Internet technology. Increasing numbers of businesses now allow suppliers and customers to link into their systems via the Internet. For example, supply chain software modules enable companies to run their MRP systems in such a way that they may create purchase orders in the order processing systems of their suppliers.

Manufacturing resource planning (MRPII) software

MRPII software is effectively an expansion of material requirements planning (MRP) to give a broader approach than MRP to the planning and scheduling of resources, embracing areas of the business such as finance, logistics, engineering and marketing.

Quality management software

The most effective way of achieving the highest levels of quality is to design this into the products, through the use of CAD/CAM and techniques like FMEA (failure mode and effect analysis). FMEA may be used in the design and development stage of a product to examine the various ways in which a product or service may fail and what the effect of each mode of failure will be. This technique leads to the identification of the most important possible modes of failure so that action may be taken to reduce the risks of those occurrences. FMEA is a Pareto analysis technique that focuses on the 'vital few' failure modes that relate to the majority of failures.

If it has not been possible to design total quality into the product then the safety net is the implementation of quality measurement systems that enable problems to be prevented or if they cannot be prevented then detected, or identified, and rectified so that they do not recur. In the area of manufacturing, computerised systems that use SPC (statistical process control) software aim at achieving the highest quality during manufacture through prevention rather than detection. SPC is used to control the processes used in making products. SPC computer software provides charts on which the performance of the process is plotted. If the process goes out of control then it can be stopped before many (if any) defective products are produced.

The cost of quality (COQ) was discussed in Chapter 9. It is used to measure the difference between the actual costs incurred within each of the processes of manufacture and/or supply of goods, and services, and the equivalent costs if there were no failures within each of those processes. Standalone software systems may be used to analyse cost of quality, or these systems may be linked to the traditional costing systems so that costs may be linked to their appropriate COQ categories:

- costs of achieving quality – prevention costs and appraisal costs

- costs of not achieving quality – internal failure costs and external failure costs
- cost of exceeding requirements
- cost of lost opportunities.

> **Progress check 16.9 Explain how a computerised COQ system may help to achieve a large increase in the profitability of a business.**

Enterprise resource planning (ERP) systems software

We have discussed the ways in which standalone accounting software systems such as the general ledger and sales ledger have been integrated, and then further integrated with for example sales order processing, sales invoicing and stock control.

We have also seen how software has been developed to encompass the whole range of organisational processes beyond payroll and accounting to include for example design, manufacturing, and quality management. Software is now available that provides full integration of an organisation's systems. Full integration of an organisation's systems may be achieved through the installation and implementation of enterprise resource planning (ERP) software. ERP systems provide software that is focused on processes spanning across functional boundaries, which are totally integrated, but at the same completely flexible. These processes include all of the software systems that we have discussed above.

The earliest ERP systems began with implementation by only the largest companies, but ERP packages are now also being installed by an increasing number of SMEs. These ERP packages comprise a number of individual modules, supporting a range of processes internal to the organisation including:

- supply chain management
- stocks management
- logistics
- human resource management
- finance
- accounting
- manufacturing planning
- sales
- distribution.

➡ ERP systems can facilitate the use of Internet and intranet resources, and also support processes external to the organisation that may facilitate information flows and global operations between the organisation and its trading partners, suppliers, and customers. ERP systems are provided by software providers like, for example, PeopleSoft, SAP, Oracle, and JD Edwards.

Unfortunately, due to the complexity of ERP systems it is often necessary for organisations to adapt the way in which they operate to meet the system requirements rather than receive a system that is tailored to their needs. This may provide benefits to the organisation from changing its business processes in line with 'best practice' rather than continuing with organisational methods that may be out of date and no longer appropriate. Another advantage of this is the lower cost of the software and its implementation.

From the outset, computerised accounting systems have provided great benefits from the fact that data are only required to be entered, or input once and then used in many ways. The verification and validation checks provided by the systems mean that there are fewer errors and corrections made, and greater accuracy in the recorded data. This compares with the manual systems in which data may have been entered many times into their various sub-systems, and with a high likelihood of error.

A further benefit of computerised accounting systems is achieved from the facility to 'close the books' if not at the end of the last day of an accounting period then very soon afterwards. Most ERP systems are real time systems and so monthly, weekly, and even daily reporting is possible, which is a great aid to decision-making and provides a further justification for the cost of ERP implementation and development.

> **Progress check 16.10** **What are the benefits of ERP systems, which may be weighed against their costs of implementation and support?**

Spreadsheets

At the start of the 1980s PC technology really took off because of the interest of home users in computer games and the interest of business users in word processing and spreadsheets. The spreadsheet replicated the accountant's paper analysis pad of rows and columns, which was used for numbers and text. The computerised spreadsheet additionally has a calendar, and a calculator and a host of accounting, mathematical, statistical and scientific functions used for quite complex calculations and to enable ease of handling and manipulation of data.

The ground-breaking Sinclair Spectrum computer even had a very simple spreadsheet application. But it was the spreadsheet called VisiCalc that ran on the Apple II computer, which paved the way for the future development of spreadsheet technology. VisiCalc, which was created and developed by Mitch Kapor at VisiCorp, really captured the imagination of the business world by showing how simple 'what-if' scenarios could be provided by changing one or more variables within the spreadsheet. Mitch Kapor soon left VisiCorp to set up the Lotus Development Corporation which then released Lotus 123 ™ to be run on the newly developed IBM PCs.

The success of Lotus 123 ™ was astronomical and led the way for yet further development of spreadsheet technology. By the late 1980s Microsoft Excel, which included all the features of Lotus and more, became extremely popular and has long since eclipsed the early success of Lotus 123 ™. Microsoft Excel has now replaced Lotus 123 ™ as the leading spreadsheet software and is used in a wide variety of ways for analysis and support for decision-making.

The additional features that have taken spreadsheets on to a level that is far higher than that of the first computerised spreadsheets include:

- the use of graphics for enhancement of analytical presentations
- the vast range of mathematical, statistical and financial functions for increasingly complex calculations
- macros to enable automation of many calculation processes
- the ability to link and 'layer' spreadsheets, making them effectively three-dimensional
- the ability to link spreadsheets and embed spreadsheets in other application software like word processing and presentations.

The Excel spreadsheet software is now currently so successful that most modern ERP systems include automatic downloads of any report into Excel. Some ERP packages actually have Excel embedded within their systems to take care of their reporting requirements.

In the area of accounting and finance, the spreadsheet is now used in so many useful ways that makes it an indispensable tool. Indeed, it is easy to forget a world without spreadsheets and how tedious were the tasks, which could only be carried out manually.

Some of the key areas of use of spreadsheets in accounting and finance are:

- depreciation, including for example
  - straight line depreciation
  - reducing balance depreciation
- break-even analysis, including for example
  - break-even sales volume calculations
  - break-even sales value calculations
  - margin of safety calculations
  - sensitivity analysis, for example the impact on the break-even point of changes in selling price, changes in variable costs, changes in volumes, changes in fixed costs
- budgeting, including for example
  - extensions of selling prices and sales volumes to produce a sales budget
  - extensions of product costs and production volumes to produce a production budget
  - preparation of a company profit and loss account budget from detailed departmental budgets of sales and costs
  - budgeted balance sheet using data from the budgeted profit and loss account, capital expenditure, financing, and working capital relationships
  - sensitivity analysis, for example the impact on profit of changes in sales prices or demand volumes
  - three-dimensional spreadsheets for modelling, and consolidation of multi-company organisations into group budgets
  - flexed budgets
  - variance analysis
- financing, including for example
  - interest calculations
  - lease amortisations
- capital investment appraisal, including for example
  - net present values (NPV)
  - internal rate of return (IRR)
  - sensitivity analysis, for example the impact on NPV on changes in investment values and lives, discount rates, and cash flows.

> **Progress check 16.11** Explain, giving examples, in what ways spreadsheet technology has been developed over the past 30 years to provide the indispensable accountants' tool it has now become.

You may find it useful to re-visit some of the Worked Examples in earlier chapters of this book to see how the solutions may be simplified through use of the appropriate spreadsheet features. The following Worked Examples 16.2, 16.3, 16.4, and 16.5 illustrate the use of Excel spreadsheets in depreciation calculations, break-even analysis, budgeting, and capital investment appraisal.

Worked Example 16.2

Please refer to Chapter 3 Depreciation, Worked Example 3.6.

Castle Ltd purchases an item of equipment for £16,000 and estimates its residual value, at the end of its useful economic life of five years, at £1,000. At the start of year one the net book value (NBV) is the acquisition cost of the asset £16,000.

The different net book values may be calculated from using the appropriate spreadsheet functions (see Fig. 16.5) for each of the alternative depreciation methods of:

- straight line
- reducing balance.

	A	B	C	D	E	F	G
1	**straight line depreciation**						
2	@SLN(cost, residual value, useful life of asset)						
3	cost		£16,000				
4	useful life of asset		5	years			
5	residual value		£1,000				
6							
7	depreciation per year	=	@SLN(+C3, +C5, +C4)				
8		=	@SLN(16000, 1000,5)		=	£3,000	per month
9	total depreciation	=	+F8*C4	+3000*5	=	£15,000	

	A	B	C	D	E	F	G
1	**reducing balance depreciation**						
2	@DB(cost, residual value, useful life of asset, year, months in first year)						
3	cost		£16,000				
4	useful life of asset		5	years			
5	residual value		£1,000				
6	months in first year		12				
7							
8	depreciation 1st year	=	@DB(+C3, +C5, +C4, 1, +C6)				
9		=	@DB(16000, 1000,5, 1, 12)		=	£6,816.00	
10	depreciation 2nd year	=	@DB(+C3, +C5, +C4, 2, +C6)				
11		=	@DB(16000, 1000,5, 2, 12)		=	£3,912.38	
12	depreciation 3rd year	=	@DB(+C3, +C5, +C4, 3, +C6)				
13		=	@DB(16000, 1000,5, 3, 12)		=	£2,245.71	
14	depreciation 4th year	=	@DB(+C3, +C5, +C4, 4, +C6)				
15		=	@DB(16000, 1000,5, 4, 12)		=	£1,289.04	
16	depreciation 5th year	=	@DB(+C3, +C5, +C4, 5, +C6)				
17		=	@DB(16000, 1000,5, 5, 12)		=	£739.91	
18	total depreciation	=	+F9+F11+F13+F15+F17		=	£15,003.04	
19			or approximately			£15,000	

Figure 16.5 Castle Ltd straight line and reducing balance depreciation Excel model

The spreadsheet solution to Worked Example 16.2 may be downloaded from the OLC that supports this book (www.mcgraw-hill.co.uk/textbooks/davies). It also provides alternative spreadsheet solutions to the following worked three examples (featured also in earlier chapters of this book).

Worked Example 16.3

Please refer to Chapter 9 Break-even Analysis, Worked Example 9.1.

		£
Sales	(1,000 units)	10,000
Variable costs (direct materials and direct labour)		6,000
Contribution		4,000
Fixed costs		2,000
Profit		2,000

A spreadsheet may be used to calculate the break-even point in number of units and the sales value.

Worked Example 16.4

Please refer to Chapter 11 Budgeting, Worked Example 11.7.

The budget balance sheet for Supportex Ltd at 31 March 2006 may be derived using a spreadsheet by plotting the expected movements for the budget year 2005/06 relating to each type of activity, and totalling across each line from the starting balance sheet 31 March 2005.

Worked Example 16.5

Please refer to Chapter 13 Capital Investment Appraisal, Worked Example 13.3.

An investment of £5,000 is made in year 0, and it generates yearly cash flows of £1,000, £3,000, £3,000, and £2,000. The cost of capital is 10%.
   The investment can be evaluated using the appropriate NPV spreadsheet functions.

Databases

Relational database management systems (DBMS) have been developed to set up relationships between different kinds of data. A DBMS system like Microsoft Access enables different types of data to be linked from which reports may be generated.

   Relational databases organise and store data in two-dimensional tables of rows and columns. The rows are called records, which may contain a number of columns or fields. Each row is divided into cells that contain a single piece of data. Fields separate the different types of data. When a table is created, the fields are required to be named and with a designation of what type of data they contain.

The type of data establishes the amount of storage reserved for the field content and specifies the types of formatting and mathematical or logical operations that can be performed on the data.

Data may be text, numbers, dates, times, or currency. For example:

- a sales invoicing table may list
  - invoice numbers
  - invoice dates
  - customer names
- a customer table may list
  - customer names
  - telephone numbers
- a product table may list
  - product codes
  - product descriptions
  - unit selling prices
- a product sales table may list
  - invoice numbers
  - product codes
  - numbers of products sold.

Each of the above examples is shown in tabular format in Fig. 16.6.

A database may be individually updated and used to provide reports. It may also be linked with many other different external databases. A relational DBMS is very powerful because it can maintain several tables of related information that can be accessed by several different users in several different ways. The data items from the various tables shown in Fig. 16.6 can be used to provide reports like the examples shown in Figs. 16.7 and 16.8.

It can be seen from the reports in Figs. 16.7 and 16.8 that data has been linked from each of the tables to produce the reports, and additional data created by using database instructions or functions. In the examples, the multiplication and addition functions have been used to create calculated columns for total balance, and total sales, and the report totals in both reports.

A disadvantage of a relational DBMS is that its *ad hoc* search ability uses a large amount of the computer's resources. This may result in an increasing loss of computer efficiency as the number of data tables increases.

Customer

Name	Phone Number
Bloggs	01564239989
Rabbit	02453548990

Sales Invoicing

Invoice Number	Invoice Date	Customer Name
1234	01Apr2004	Bloggs
2345	05Apr2004	Rabbit

Product

Product Code	Product Description	Unit Selling Price
AGR	fridge	£200
GMK	oven	£250

Product Sales

Invoice Number	Product Code	Numbers Sold
1234	AGR	12
2345	GMK	10

Figure 16.6 Example of relational DBMS tables

Customer Total Balances at 30 April 2004		
Customer Name	**Phone Number**	**Total Balance**
Bloggs	01564239989	£2,400
Rabbit	02453548990	£2,500
Total		**£4,900**

Figure 16.7 Example of a customer total balance report

Customer Sales During April 2004						
Customer Name	**Product Code**	**Product Description**	**Unit Selling Price**	**Number Sold**	**Total Sales**	**Invoice Number**
Bloggs	AGR	fridge	£200	12	£2,400	1234
Rabbit	GMK	oven	£250	10	£2,500	2345
Total					**£4,900**	

Figure 16.8 Example of a sales report by customer

> **Progress check 16.12 What is a database? Discuss how a database may be used effectively by an organisation and the circumstances when it may cease to be an effective tool.**

Communicating and presenting information

IT can be seen to have made a tremendous contribution to the recording, processing and analysis of accounting and financial data. IT has simplified accounting tasks and provided greater accuracy and speed in the processing and reporting of information. In parallel with the development of accounting and operations software, databases, and spreadsheets, there has been an increasing additional requirement to communicate accounting and financial information to people through speeches, presentations, lectures, seminars, workshops, etc. Powerful graphics tools have been developed to present ideas and concepts to people either directly using computer projections or via websites. These tools have made accounting information easier to understand and more accessible to a much wider audience, in areas like employee communication, training, and education.

An example of a presentation graphics program is Microsoft PowerPoint, which enables the creation of computerised slide shows that include text, numbers, pictures, and sound effects, using a range of designs, layouts and formats. Graphics programs like PowerPoint may also be enhanced though the integration of multimedia effects including music, clip art, and video. Wider audiences may be reached using broadcasting to an intranet either live or for later viewing. Even wider audiences may be reached through the delivery of web-based presentations.

Software developers like Lotus and Microsoft have enhanced and adapted some of their products to provide what is called groupware such as Lotus Notes and Microsoft Exchange, which enables organisational tasks to be worked on and completed using a team approach. Such software may be adopted by users who work individually, or in groups or teams, to coordinate efforts and collaborate on various tasks and projects, and may support collaborative decision-making. Groupware activities may also incorporate interactive group meetings and videoconferencing.

Other applications

There are a number of further areas in accounting and finance on which IT has an impact.

Personal income tax

Since self-assessment was introduced for personal income taxation by the Inland Revenue a few years ago there has been an increasing endeavour to persuade individuals to complete and process their self-assessment returns online.

Value added tax (VAT)

Businesses which are registered for VAT complete VAT returns either monthly or quarterly and either pay/receive the balance on their VAT account to/from HMCE (Her Majesty's Customs and Excise) depending on whether their input VAT is less than or greater than their output VAT for the period. HMCE inspectors visit VAT registered businesses periodically to carry out audits of their VAT records and accounts. HMCE are now able to access most organisations' computer systems directly to read the appropriate files and provide an audit and analysis of transactions using their own VAT audit software.

Annual accounts audit

An annual audit of their accounts is a statutory requirement for all limited companies, except for those currently having an annual turnover of less than £5.6 million and a balance sheet total of less than £2.8 million. For firms of accountants that are appointed by the shareholders of companies to carry out the annual audits this was traditionally a very labour intensive and time-consuming task. Their task was particularly onerous before accounting software was introduced by companies to replace their manual accounting systems. However, since accounting systems began to be computerised the focus of the audit has changed. Traditionally, the audit involved the testing of large samples of accounting transactions to verify their accuracy and authenticity and the ticking of transactions against their entries in the ledgers and books of account.

   The introduction of computerised accounting systems has resulted instead in audit firms auditing the computer systems to ensure they provide accurate processing and adequate controls, together with reviews of much smaller samples of transactions to verify their accuracy and correct processing. In addition, audit firms have developed their own audit system software that is able to access companies computer systems directly to read the appropriate files and provide an audit of a company's computer systems and analyses of transaction samples.

Risk management

In an increasingly uncertain world the management of risk is becoming a very high profile responsibility with which company accountants and finance directors are particularly concerned. Consultancy firms that specialise in risk assessment and risk management use software that enables them, for example, to analyse areas of risk in terms of their likelihood or probability of occurrence and the significance or the impact of their occurrence on the business. Risk analysis may then identify the appropriate actions a business may implement to minimise its exposure.

Knowledge management

We have seen how accounting systems software (and other personal and business software with which it is associated) that were initially developed as standalone have increasingly become integrated – note ERP systems and groupware. At the same time, the unprecedented growth in IT in the areas of computerisation and communications has overwhelmed both individuals and organisations with the volume of data and information available from seemingly limitless sources. This presents a new challenge in how to ensure that useful information is easily accessible and how effectively it may be used. Effective use of useful information increasingly becomes more important than simply producing more information. To this end what is termed knowledge management software has become very important.

Knowledge management emerged as a discipline in the mid-1990s primarily as a response to the destruction by business process engineering (BPR) of accumulated knowledge and experience, informal networks and rules of thumb that enable organisations to function effectively. Its focus has now moved to include human capital as well as intellectual capital. The aim of knowledge management systems software is to identify and locate the useful knowledge that may be gleaned from the mass of information that individuals and organisations are now able to produce. Knowledge management promises better access to the knowledge and experience of individuals leading to greater innovation and protection against the risk of loss of vital business information. Knowledge management fails if there is a breakdown in information-sharing and interpretation, and if there is information overload.

> **Progress check 16.13 Discuss the benefits that may be achieved both by their clients and from audit firms as a result of their implementation of computerised audit systems.**

The new economy

Accountants and accounting systems have needed to change as technological development has created the basis for the emergence of the 'new economy'. Any new economy occurs when the normal progress of the economy is disturbed to the extent that there is a fundamental change in its structure. We have seen this in the past in the invention of the wheel, the industrial revolution, and the development of steam power and of electricity. The current 'new economy' has emerged throughout the latter part of the twentieth century and the start of the twenty-first century from the advances in IT, particularly in the development of the computer chip, telecommunications, and the Internet, and their impact on the economic environment in which organisations operate.

E-business

E-business (electronic business) is generally considered to relate to the ways in which the Internet impacts on organisations. It is normally used to broadly describe the ways in which technology has changed the economic environment and the ways in which businesses operate. The impact of the development of IT in e-business is seen in communication, new product development, sales and marketing, manufacturing, quality management, customer service, and the various service functions that support the operations of the organisation.

The use of e-business requires new skills to be acquired by managers of organisations. Accounting and financial techniques have in the past traditionally focused on the internal aspects of the organisation. E-business requires a shift of emphasis to include the external relationships between the organisation and its customers and suppliers, and other business partners.

E-commerce

Organisations may provide internal networks, or intranets, that use Internet technologies so that their users, for example employees, may find, use and share documents and webpages. They may also use extranets in a similar way to communicate both privately and selectively with their customers. An extranet is really a part of the organisation's intranet that is extended to users outside the organisation.

E-commerce (electronic commerce) is a term that is normally used with regard to the parts of e-business that are concerned with the use of IT for business-to-business transactions (as distinct from business-to-customer transactions) between an organisation and its suppliers and customers. E-commerce includes the sharing and transfer of information between the organisation and its suppliers and customers, for example details, specifications and prices about products and services. E-commerce includes the use of IT in the commercial transactions of selling and buying products and services. The major advantages of e-commerce can be seen in the way that it enables:

- information, goods and service transactions to be made 24 hours a day, 365 days a year
- expansion of the scope of business to encompass global markets.

E-commerce transactions include much business-sensitive and confidential information. It is therefore of paramount importance that all parties to e-commerce transactions are confident that they are properly controlled in terms of security, accuracy and reliability. It is essential that the Internet service providers (ISPs) that facilitate e-commerce transactions ensure its availability with acceptable response times on a 24/7 basis.

The key tools of e-commerce are websites, electronic data interchange (EDI), electronic funds transfer (EFT) and electronic mail (email).

Websites

A website is a related collection of World Wide Web (www) computer files with a unique reference address or url (uniform resource locator). Organisations have created and developed their websites with increasing creativity. This has enabled them to present and advertise themselves and the products and services they can offer in ways that are informative and attention-grabbing.

In the early days of website development, their success was seen in the number of 'hits' or visits to the website by individuals or organisations using the Internet. This measure gave an indication of the level of awareness about the organisation and the level of potential interest in what it had to offer. Websites remain a rich source of information. Examples include the very useful government information websites like www.ukonlineforbusiness.gov.uk and www.dti.gov.uk, professional websites like www.cimaglobal.com and www.icaew.co.uk, and news information and journals websites like www.businessweek.com and www.reuters.com.

Websites are also a valuable marketing tool for advertising and promotion and facilitate communication to markets on both a national and a global level. In addition, and increasingly, websites have become the vehicle for consumer-to-business transactions. One of the first uses was sale of books (e.g. Amazon on www.amazon.com). Online book sales was quickly followed by other businesses, for example the banking industry, which introduced online banking (e.g. the HSBC bank on www.hsbc.co.uk) and the tourism industry for online accommodation bookings (e.g. the Wales Tourist Board www.wtbonline.gov.uk).

There were initial problems in the early days of selling online by dot.com businesses, mainly due to the enthusiasm and eagerness to be first in the marketplace. Many dot.com businesses had the front ends of their systems developed by web designers as standalone applications. This meant that potential customers saw what looked like fully-integrated web-linked order, invoice, delivery and payment systems, but in fact they were front-end systems only, which were supported by armies of clerks employed to re-key data into the support systems. The heavy staffing requirements probably contributed in some way to the many dot.com failures in the late 1990s and the early part of the twenty-first century.

Videoconferencing

Videoconferencing has been a business communications tool that has been in use since the early 1980s. Its increase in sophistication and ease of use has been matched by its greatly reduced cost to now make it a viable alternative to the high cost of air travel and accommodation and the logistical problems of arranging meetings, for example, to resolve problems or to present financial or other information.

The early days of videoconferencing involved the use of dedicated videoconference suites, very expensive hardware and dedicated communications lines. It is now possible to obtain very cheap kit that uses standard telecommunications connections to provide high quality videoconference facilities almost anywhere and at any time. The accounting implications, particularly for large multinational companies, include the huge cost savings achieved from fewer face-to-face meetings. They also include the vast savings in time and cost in situations, for example, where technical staff who are based in many different locations may all be working on a major project; design and engineering problems can be speedily resolved so that project costs are reduced and the project lead times cut to an absolute minimum.

Electronic data interchange (EDI)

Electronic data interchange (EDI) is a form of e-commerce that is used to improve the relationships between sellers and buyers. EDI enables transmission of data between or within organisations in structured formats that allow it to be retrieved by their computer systems and may be used for sales order processing and invoicing, purchase order processing, cash payments, and cash receipts. It is different from fax or simple text email messages, which are not in structured formats. EDI data is usually presented in batches for transmission between businesses compared with the interactive customer/business transactions that currently take place via websites.

A key feature of EDI systems is the disappearance of the need for paper trails for sales and purchase order, invoice, delivery, and receipt transactions, and the need for EDI-specific computer hardware and software. The structured transmission formats comply with standards like, for example, EDIFACT (Electronic Data Interchange for Administration, Commerce, and Transport), which therefore allow the transmission and receipt of data between different configurations of hardware and software within the user organisations. The application software of the user organisations then enables EDI data to be input and processed by the appropriate systems. EDI users may communicate directly or via third party providers that enable connectivity between the various users.

EDI appears to rely on complicated behind-the-scenes activities, but the development of Internet processes has simplified EDI usage and its implementation. This has resulted in a number of major advantages gained from the use of EDI from:

- reduction in errors
- reduction in the use of paper documentation
- reduction in mail and telephone costs
- considerable reduction in costs of transactions.

As well as large corporations, EDI may be used to advantage by even the smallest businesses with a minimum investment. The major benefits of EDI can be classified as business benefits and also supply chain benefits. Business benefits include:

- more efficient purchasing, production scheduling, stock control and order fulfillment resulting in reduced ordering costs, labour costs and stockholding costs and increased customer satisfaction
- increased competitiveness from better product availability and pricing information, reduced lead times, more reliable and accurate delivery, and the passing on of internal savings to customers, and a reduction in out-of-stock items
- reduction of human error since there is no re-keying of data
- time saved from automation of routine tasks such as ordering time for ordering staff to be engaged in other functions
- a reduction in the operating cycle from production to final cash inflow, resulting in lower costs and improved cash flow.

Supply chain benefits include:

- expansion of potential markets through global trading 24 hours a day, 365 days a year
- increased trust between partners in the supply chain built from a commitment to share information and to work collaboratively through the EDI links
- greater speed and accuracy enabling EDI to support the implementation of just in time (JIT) systems
- a broadening of the trading base through links with existing supply chains that are already using EDI, and may insist on it as a requirement for doing business with them.

A note of caution should be mentioned with regard to the implementation of EDI systems. The risks arising out of the EDI systems' ability to guarantee the transmission of complete and accurate data together with its verification of their authenticity, must be considered by the system designers. It is crucial that user organisations also put in place appropriate procedures for limiting authorised access to the EDI systems and for error detection and correction.

Electronic funds transfer (EFT)

Electronic funds transfer (EFT) is a system used by banks for the movement of funds between accounts and for the provision of services to the customer. EFT uses a different set of standards for the control of transmission of financial data. The bankers automated clearing services (BACS) system was one of the earliest EFT systems to be developed in the UK. It is an electronic bulk clearing system used by banks and building societies for low value and/or repetitive items such as standing orders, direct debits and automated payments such as salary and suppliers payments made by their customers.

EFT methods have the same risks as EDI but with the additional risk of possible fraudulent transfers of funds. However, EFT transfers do reduce human involvement with cash if customers pay directly into the selling organisation's bank account, and if the organisation pays directly into a supplier or employee bank account.

Electronic mail (email)

Electronic mail, or email, enables any person with Internet access to send and receive written messages, together with attached files of text and numeric data and both still and moving images, to and from any other person with Internet access, anywhere in the world, and almost instantaneously.

Over recent years, there has been a massive increase in the volume of electronic exchanges involving commercial and legal transactions, documents, funds, and the whole range of text and numeric data. This has necessitated a requirement for greater emphasis on security of information against unauthorised access, hackers (malicious intruders) and the receipt of spam or unwanted emails.

Information security is critical to business organisations (as well as home users) and so security software packages are now an essential element in the management and control of this area of risk. The different types of information security devices include, for example, physical controls, encryption, intrusion detection software, firewalls, and anti-virus software.

Computer security

Unauthorised access to computers is a serious, major problem, from which even the largest organisations and most sophisticated systems are not immune. The mighty Microsoft Corporation, for example, has had its computer security attacked (see the press extract below which shows that even Bill Gates has protection problems).

Microsoft security protection problems

IN OCTOBER 2000 MICROSOFT called in the FBI to investigate one of the most embarrassing breaches of computer security in corporate history. Hackers were reported to have copied the source code blueprints of the latest versions of its flagship Windows and Office products, which are installed on 90 per cent of the world's personal computers.

The break-in was discovered when security employees detected passwords being sent to an email account in St Petersburg while electronic footprints showed that the passwords had been used to transfer source code outside Microsoft's campus at Redmond, near Seattle.

The company had been frequently castigated for the security of its own products, so the news came as little surprise within the computer industry, but the feeling remains that if the world's largest software company can be breached, then it must be easy to get into smaller businesses.

The area of security has remained a hot topic since, despite it being shrouded in secrecy with most companies trying to hush up any breaches. But essentially the aims remain the same: to protect against internal and external threats.

According to Paul King, a senior consultant at Cisco, securing a business begins not with technology, but by setting out the ground rules. 'A security policy is where it starts,' says Mr King. 'If you haven't got one it all breaks down.'

For example, a company may provide its staff with Internet access. But does it allow uncensored use or does it control the sites its employees visit? 'The bigger problem is not just having a policy, but making sure your employees know about it,' adds Mr King.

'If you're a small 30-user software development company in California you may allow unrestricted access to do what they like. But you could be a big law firm and there might be legal risks to that stance. You might say 'our policy is that we allow access to the Internet but don't go to non-business sites'.

Everyone understands that. On top of the policy you might have URL logging where you say you'll record the sites people are visiting and go through the logs, or you could block sites and hope the software is good enough.'

Another policy might outline how staff access the internal network. If they are sitting inside the company, most staff will probably be allowed access without using encryption, a code which only allows those authorised to unscramble the message.

However, if someone is working from home, say, the policy most companies will have is that the employee can only access the network through an encrypted virtual private network (VPN), more of which later.

It is on top of these basic rules that the rest of the security system is based and it takes on many levels. This process is known as 'defence in depth' which sounds like a catchphrase that George Graham might once have used but Tom Scholtz, an analyst with technology researcher the Meta Group, explains: 'It is best practice [within large companies] to develop a policy and then implement different layers of security technology. But in the case of small companies, defence in depth is often more than they need.'

The level of security a company requires depends on how much confidential information it holds and the value of the transactions it conducts online, Mr Scholtz says. Because smaller companies often will not have security experts internally they will typically buy products as part of a bundle from their existing network supplier. 'Small businesses need to make sure they understand what this entails because otherwise they end up with inappropriate products being pushed on them,' he adds. 'Too many products and it will cost too much. Nothing comes for free.'

Still, most smaller companies will begin with perimeter security which is generally seen as the first line of defence. One of the most common technologies used is the fire wall – which is essentially a fence which sits between the internal and external network and prevents and detects any security attacks.

On top of that, anti-virus software on PCs will detect intrusions from trojans (a piece of code which appears to be harmless but allows an outsider to access a network or PC). This is the most common way hackers penetrate systems and was the method successfully employed by the Microsoft hackers.

But despite the front page news when a system is broken, it is estimated that up to 80% of crimes are committed by insiders. The same principle of layered security applies within a company.

Employees will have different requirements depending on their status. For example, only the human resources department should be able to alter salary details, but a manager may need to see the details before an appraisal.

Most commonly a company makes sure the right people have access through a username and a password, but this method has its weaknesses as users can easily forget them or they can be intercepted.

The next level identifies users not only by what they know (username and password) but also by what they have, for example a key fob which generates a one-off pin number each time they log on.

If that method is not secure enough, companies can employ an even more sophisticated method called biometrics, which includes eye and fingerprint scanning. However, this is currently far too costly for most businesses.

For added security information is often encrypted as it is sent and received. This is particularly true for access to the system from outside the company and, with the current trend towards employees working from outside the office, the most common solution is to set up a VPN.

A VPN is essentially a private network that uses the Internet, thereby avoiding the costs of leasing a private line. To maintain privacy VPNs use access control and encryption, so they can exchange information privately.

The final security layer usually contains

monitoring software, which checks the network for faults and reports on any breaches. However, these products need interpreting and therefore can be costly for smaller companies to deploy.

Still, cost should not be an inhibitor to securing a small business. According to a recent white paper by technology researcher Ovum, throwing lots of money at security is no answer. 'The key to successful security is planning and assessment,' it states. 'Many of the most effective steps you can take do not require expensive products, although some will be needed within a comprehensive strategy.'

Safety begins with rules, not technology, by Simon Goodley

© *Daily Telegraph*, 13 January 2004

Security covers many aspects of computer hardware, software and communications. It relates to the physical security of the computer hardware itself, and the risk of it being easily stolen or damaged. Security relates to ensuring that regular back-ups of data are regularly and frequently carried out and securely stored away from the premises where the business normally operates. Security relates to control of the ways in which confidential information may be copied on to removable disks and CDs, or downloaded on to laptops, all of which may easily be stolen. Encryption technology may be used to secure data in the case of physical theft.

Encryption is one of the best ways to protect highly confidential and sensitive information from being stolen. Encryption is a process, which is used to encode data that is entered into a system, and storing or transmitting the data in coded form, and then decoding the data when it arrives at its destination. Encryption therefore provides security through preventing unauthorised access to data while it is being stored or transmitted and before it reaches its required destination.

Public key encryption is widely used to ensure privacy and protect data in the e-business environment. The users who are communicating each have a key, one of which is publicly known and the other of which is private. The relationship between the keys is such that if one key locks data then the other key must be used to unlock it. Encryption may be used for securing files of data and also for data handled via the Internet.

Physical information security controls relate to how a company or an individual's computer system is accessed. Such controls are concerned with access to computer resources. It is essential that only those people who are authorised to do so have access to, and are able to communicate via, the computers and servers that hold sensitive information. Access may be controlled using unique user IDs and **passwords** at a number of levels:

- computer rooms housing the computers and peripheral equipment
- computer hardware
- operating software
- application software
- e-business resources, such as email, EFT and EDI software.

Passwords are most effective if they contain a random set of alphanumeric characters, and not names, places or dates of birth, although these may not be so easy for users to remember. Passwords should be changed on a regular basis and never disclosed by one user to another.

Intrusion detection software packages are designed to detect intrusion of entrance to systems. They monitor the entire computer system continuously and notify users if the system has been entered without authorisation or if the system is being used inappropriately. In a business environment pre-defined levels of management may be alerted if the systems for which they are responsible, for example, have received many unsuccessful attempts at access, or have had orders processed with zero or non-standard selling prices. Intrusion detection software may also be reactive in limiting the access of a possible intruder to the system and by the immediate locking of the system. The system is then only unlocked after the problem has been resolved by the network administrator.

Firewall software applications are designed to block unauthorised access to files, directories and networks. Firewalls are a must for e-business users and are used extensively in both the business and home use environment. Firewalls are extremely effective but may only provide security if they are correctly configured; many businesses that use firewalls may still be exposed to unauthorised access. Firewalls are also vulnerable to hackers (malicious intruders to computer systems). Hackers may find a way into a system that may be password deficient in just one area, and then gain entry to try and access and transfer funds or change numbers or text in accounts, email or other electronic transactions. The firewall itself then becomes completely ineffective.

Computer **viruses** are software programs that may infect computer files in a number of ways. Viruses may infect the system that boots up the computer system and runs its operating software; they may also infect the files of the operating software itself. Both types of virus may create virus files by changing file extensions like .exe or .com and making new files with the same names but different file extensions. Computer viruses are designed to replicate themselves and to spread from one location to another without the knowledge of the users; they may spread within a standalone computer system, or throughout a network or from one system to many external systems via the Internet. Virus-infected files are used to instruct computer systems to change, reformat, or delete important programs or data. Computer **worms** are the same as computer viruses except that they do not replicate themselves. Worms are created to change or delete data within a system.

It is essential for both commercial and home use of electronic communications and e-business to protect themselves by installing anti-virus and anti-worm software, and/or intrusion detection software. However, there are tens of thousands of computer viruses or worms currently in existence and the number is always increasing with new viruses and worms being discovered each day. Consequently, computer users are never one 100% protected from all viruses and worms, and therefore protection software must be frequently and regularly updated. A number of software companies provide such software updates that may be freely downloaded from their websites. Examples are Grisoft Incs AVG anti-virus software and McAfee Stinger software, which detects and removes specific viruses that may exist within a computer system.

Data protection

The use of data and information has been discussed in various parts of this book, particularly with regard to decision-making. Some information relates to data about individuals. The Data Protection Act 1998, effective from 1 March 2000, is designed to protect personal information held about individuals who are alive, and is used to regulate the processing of that data.

This Act implements part of the European Convention on Human Rights. It applies only to data and information about an individual (called a data subject) that all companies and organisations may record and store, either manually or electronically, for example name; address; personal reference number. The Act applies to personal details about employees, clients, customers and other third parties, but does not apply to non-personal data, such as data and information relating to other businesses.

There are eight principles within the Data Protection Act 1998, which are based on three key concepts:

- data held only for a clear purpose
- fairness
- transparency.

The principles state that personal data must:

1. be processed fairly and lawfully
2. be obtained only for one or more specified and lawful purposes
3. be adequate, relevant and not excessive
4. be accurate and kept up-to-date where necessary
5. not be kept for longer than necessary
6. be processed in accordance with the rights of data subjects under the Act, for example right of access, and the right to prevent processing for the purposes of direct marketing
7. be protected by appropriate measures against unauthorised or unlawful processing, accidental loss, destruction, or damage
8. not be transferred outside the European Economic Area unless the rights and freedoms of data subjects are maintained.

The rights of individuals are probably the most significant parts of the Data Protection Act 1998. It is important that companies are aware of the potential of individuals to seek compensation through the courts for any breach.

The impact of IT and e-business on accounting

Traditional accounting systems, as we have already seen, were totally supported by paper transactions and records. These provided a paper trail, which enabled transactions to be followed through from their inception to their recording and subsequent reporting. Such audit trails, as they are called, provided the fundamental basis on which their authenticity and accuracy could be verified.

As accounting systems became increasingly computerised, accounting records enhanced and to a large extent replicated the manual recording systems. Transactions were still supported by paper trails and their verification continued as with traditional systems, but they were increasingly supported by the use of audit software.

As yet, e-commerce systems like EDI have not impacted greatly on accountants and accounting recording systems within the organisations, which are engaged in the buying and selling transactions. This is because sales and purchase order, invoice, delivery, and receipt transactions, whether provided manually or totally electronically, nevertheless provide transaction records within the relevant computer accounting systems together with their appropriate cost and revenue analysis codings. However, in terms of provision of information for decision-making, computerised accounting systems supporting e-commerce are able to provide much more detailed and informative reporting faster and more reliably than traditional systems.

Verification of the authenticity and accuracy of transactions and records is an area of great concern with regard to internal and external auditors. E-commerce transactions are likely to be supported by little or no paper trails. The focus of verification or audit of such transactions therefore necessarily moves away from the method of checking samples of transactions to assurance that the e-commerce systems are properly controlled in terms of their operation and their security and that they ensure that transactions are created and recorded accurately and reliably and that the data are complete.

> **Progress check 16.14** **Discuss the major impacts of e-commerce on accounting systems.**

The decisions that businesses have to make with regard to investment in IT require the use of the appropriate appraisal techniques in the same way as any other capital project. However, the justifications for IT investment are usually more far reaching than those of other investments since they normally impact on the whole organisation and its trading partners for a very long time into the future. Nevertheless, the costs must generally be more than offset by the overall benefits to the business and as with any other project an investment in IT should not be made unless it is expected to add value to the business for its shareholders.

As with the majority of technological developments, over the past few years the costs of computer hardware and software have reduced significantly. This has resulted from the huge increases in demand, and technological development of more effective ways of providing increasingly sophisticated systems with enhanced functionality. The standardisation of the technology used to connect the various PC systems particularly via the Internet has also resulted in reduced costs, and ease of communication of data between a variety of different computer configurations that may have been installed to meet the specific local needs of the users. Information on the Internet is accessed or navigated through the use of **browsers**, programs which present text and numeric data, still and moving images, sound and other information.

Further cost savings are being achieved through the development of faster and cheaper communication systems. **Integrated services digital networks (ISDN)** provide digital data services over traditional analogue telephone lines enabling both data and voice transmission over the same lines. However, the use of ISDN has been matched by the development of the **asymmetric digital subscriber line (ADSL)**, which is potentially 40 times faster than a 56 kilobyte modem (see glossary for the definition of kilobytes, **megabytes**, **gigabytes**, **bytes** and **bits**), and has enabled **broadband** transmission on existing telephone networks. Broadband systems provide much faster ways of connecting computers to the Internet than conventional dial-up systems.

One of the aims of this chapter has been to provide an insight into the extent of the use of computers in business organisations. It has also aimed to provide a practical context for many of the accounting and finance topics covered in this book, and how they are inextricably linked to all other business disciplines, for example manufacturing, human resources management, and distribution. The role of the accountant can be seen to have changed as IT systems have eliminated the need for tasks such as the verification of data and the reconciliation of control account balances. Accountants are now more involved with analysis and evaluation of information, and the use of techniques in support of business decision-making. However, it should be borne in mind that the subject of IT soon becomes out of date; by its very nature IT continues to change the ways in which things are done, and continues to develop at an ever-increasing pace.

Summary of key points

- Information technology (IT) over the past 20 or 30 years has been used to vastly change and improve the ways in which accounting and financial data is recorded, processed, stored, retrieved, and reported.
- IT has had a significant impact on traditional payroll and accounting systems.

- Computer systems have been developed in a number of ways to include all the operational areas of a business, for example manufacturing, distribution and quality management.
- Businesses are now able to achieve the full integration of their applications software through the implementation of enterprise resource planning (ERP) systems.
- Spreadsheets have revolutionised accounting and financial analysis, having taken the place of the traditional accountant's analysis pad and simplified and speeded up the most complicated and sophisticated financial calculations and analyses.
- Databases are now extensively used for the storage, retrieval and reporting of wide ranges of related data.
- Graphics tools and groupware have enhanced and improved the ways in which accounting information, ideas, and concepts may be shared and presented using computer projections and the Internet.
- There is a wide range of additional accounting-related software systems that have been developed for personal and business use.
- In the same way as its predecessors the invention of the wheel, and the industrial revolution, the IT-based new economy has emerged through the latter part of the twentieth century and the start of the twenty-first century.
- The broad concept of e-business and its various elements, such as e-commerce, email and websites, have had a significant impact on accounting systems.
- There are eight principles contained in the Data Protection Act 1998, aimed to protect the rights of individuals with regard to their personal data that is stored by organisations.

Questions

Q16.1   Explain how IT has improved the running of payroll systems and outline the enhancements that have resulted from the development of payroll processing software into fully-integrated HRM systems. What are the internal control implications of these developments?

Q16.2   Explain the ways in which integrated accounting software packages have overcome some of the criticisms of earlier computerised accounting systems.

Q16.3   Why were enterprise resource planning (ERP) systems developed and what have they achieved?

Q16.4   Spreadsheet and database packages were developed primarily for dealing with accounting and financial information. In what ways have they also become indispensable tools for the non-accountant?

Q16.5   Describe the 'new economy' and how it has changed the ways in which organisations conduct their business.

Q16.6   What is e-business and how has it impacted on manufacturing and service functions that support the operations of an organisation?

Q16.7   Outline some of the problems faced by computerised accounting and e-commerce systems and how these are being addressed.

Discussion points

D16.1 'As the use of IT in businesses has increased so has the number of accounting scandals,' Discuss.

D16.2 'The accountants' analysis pad provided everything and more than a spreadsheet such as Excel.' Discuss.

D16.3 'Traditional annual audits of companies were very labour intensive, but more effective than the current computerised audits.' Discuss.

Exercises

The following exercises appear in other chapters of this book (see cross-references to the original exercises), or in the Additional Exercises section of the book's accompanying website. Excel model solutions to each exercise are provided in the OLC accompanying this book (www.mcgraw-hill.co.uk/textbooks/davies).

Level I

E16.1 *Time allowed – 30 minutes (E5.1)*
The information below relates to Priory Products plc's actual results for 2004 and 2005 and their budget for the year 2006.

Figures in £000	2004	2005	2006
Cash at bank	100	0	0
Overdraft	0	50	200
Loans	200	200	600
Ordinary shares	100	200	400
Profit and loss account	200	300	400

Use a spreadsheet to calculate the following financial ratios for Priory Products for 2004, 2005, and 2006:

(i)   **debt/equity ratio (net debt to equity)**
(ii) **gearing (long-term loans to equity and long-term loans).**

E16.2 *Time allowed – 30 minutes (E9.4)*
Seivad Ltd plans to assemble and sell 20,000 novelty phones in 2005 at £30 each.
Seivad's costs are as follows:

Variable:
materials	£10	per phone
labour	£7	per phone
overheads	£8	per phone
Fixed	£70,000 for the year	

Use a spreadsheet to make the following calculations:

(i)   **Seivad Ltd's planned contribution for 2005.**
(ii) **Seivad Ltd's planned profit for 2005.**
(iii) **The break-even sales value.**

(iv)   The break-even number of phones sold.

(v)   The margin of safety for 2005 in sales value.

(vi)   The margin of safety for 2005 in number of phones sold.

(vii)   If fixed costs were increased by 20% what price should be charged to customers for each phone to enable Seivad Ltd to increase the profit calculated in (ii) above by 10%, assuming no change in the level of demand?

E16.3 *Time allowed – 45 minutes (E2.4)*

The following information relates to Major plc at 31 December 2005, and the comparative numbers at 31 December 2004.

	2004 £000	2005 £000
Accruals	800	1,000
Bank overdraft		16,200
Cash at bank	600	
Plant and machinery at cost	17,600	23,900
Debentures (interest at 15% per annum)	600	750
Plant and machinery depreciation	9,500	10,750
Proposed dividends	3,000	6,000
Ordinary share capital	5,000	5,000
Preference share capital	1,000	1,000
Prepayments	300	400
Profit and loss account	3,000	10,100
Stocks	5,000	15,000
Taxation	3,200	5,200
Trade creditors	6,000	10,000
Trade debtors	8,600	26,700

Use a spreadsheet to prepare a balance sheet in the format adopted by most of the leading UK plcs showing the previous year comparative figures.

E16.4 *Time allowed – 45 minutes (E3.5)*

Tartantrips Ltd, a company in Scotland, operates several ferries and has a policy of holding several in reserve, due to the weather patterns and conditions of various contracts with local authorities. A ferry costs £5 million and has an estimated useful life of 10 years, at which time its realisable value is expected to be £1 million.

Use the appropriate spreadsheet functions to calculate three methods of depreciation available to the company:

(i)   sum of the digits

(ii)   straight line

(iii)   reducing balance.

E16.5 *Time allowed – 60 minutes (E3.6)*

From the following profit and loss information that has been provided by Lazydays Ltd, for the year ended 31 March 2005 (and the corresponding figures for the year to 31 March 2004), use a spreadsheet to construct a profit and loss account, using the format adopted by the majority of UK plcs, including comparative figures.

	2005	2004
	£	**£**
Administrative expenses	22,000	20,000
Depreciation	5,000	5,000
Closing stock	17,000	15,000
Distribution costs	33,000	30,000
Dividends paid	32,000	30,000
Dividends received from non-related companies	5,000	5,000
Interest paid	10,000	10,000
Interest received	3,000	3,000
Opening stock	15,000	10,000
Purchases	99,000	90,000
Redundancy costs	5,000	
Sales	230,000	200,000
Taxation	25,000	24,000

(a) Depreciation is to be included in the administrative expenses

(b) Redundancy costs are to be regarded as an exceptional item

E16.6 *Time allowed – 60 minutes (E4.3)*

Jaffrey Packaging plc have used the following information in the preparation of their financial statements for the year ended 31 March 2005:

	£000
Dividends paid	25
Issue of a debenture	200
Reduction in stocks	32
Corporation tax paid	73
Interest paid	28
Operating profit for the year	450
Bank and cash balance 31 March 2005	376
Purchase of factory equipment	302
Dividends payable at 31 March 2005	25
Interest received	5
Depreciation charge for the year	195
Purchase of a new large computer system	204
Sale of a patent (intangible fixed asset)	29
Increase in trade debtors	43
Reduction in short-term creditors	62
Bank and cash balance 1 April 2004	202

You are required to use spreadsheets to prepare a cash flow statement in compliance with the provisions of FRS 1, together with the appropriate supporting schedules and reconciliations.

E16.7 *Time allowed – 60 minutes (OLC Additional Exercise E13.13)*

An automotive components manufacturing group, Lubosh plc, supplies parts to all the main UK motor vehicle manufacturers. The group is considering a £40m investment in tooling and plant for a new vehicle (codename Mondino) for one of its customers. The project is expected to have a three-year life. In each of the years one, two, and three the incremental cash inflows are expected to be £50m and the cash outflows £30m in each year. The initial investment is stated in money terms, but all other cash flows include the effects of inflation. The inflation rate is 8% per annum with regard to cash outflows and 7% per annum with regard to cash inflows. Lubosh's cost of capital is 17%.

Lubosh normally expects projects to pay back within 18 months, with a discounted payback of less than two years. Use appropriate spreadsheet functions to determine whether the Mondino project will meet those criteria.

Level II

E16.8 *Time allowed – 60 minutes (E3.8)*
From the trial balance of Retepmal Ltd at 31 March 2004 use spreadsheets to prepare a profit and loss account for the year to 31 March 2004 and a balance sheet as at 31 March 2004 using the vertical formats used by most UK companies.

	£
Premises (net book value)	95,000
Trade debtors	75,000
Purchases of stocks	150,000
Retained earnings at 31 March 2003	130,000
Stocks at 31 March 2003	15,000
Furniture and fixtures	30,000
Sales	266,000
Distribution costs and administrative expenses	90,000
Trade creditors	54,000
Motor vehicles (net book value)	40,000
Cash and bank	35,000
Share capital	80,000

Additional information:

(a) Stocks at 31 March 2004 were £25,000.
(b) Dividend proposed for 2004 was £7,000.
(c) An accrual for expenses of £3,000 was required at 31 March 2004.
(d) A prepayment of expenses of £5,000 was required at 31 March 2004.
(e) Corporation tax estimated to be payable on 2003/2004 profits was £19,000.
(f) Annual depreciation charges on premises and motor vehicles for the year to 31 March 2004 are included in administrative expenses and distribution costs respectively, and in the cumulative depreciation provisions used to calculate the net book values of £95,000 and £40,000, shown in the trial balance at 31 March 2004.

The furniture and fixtures balance of £30,000 relates to purchases of assets during the year to 31 March 2004. The depreciation charge to administrative expenses and the corresponding depreciation provision are not included in the trial balance at 31 March 2004. They are required to be calculated for a full year to 31 March 2004, based on a useful economic life of eight years and an estimated residual value of £6,000.

Case Study VI

OAK LTD

Oak Ltd is a UK manufacturing company that assembles one product called the Acorn. Oak Ltd bases its pricing policy on the pricing policy of the General Motors Corporation, outlined in an article by Albert Bradley back in the 1920s (see below).

The data that follow relate to the operations of Oak Ltd during the forthcoming year:

Investment in plant and other fixed assets	£1m
Required return on investment (ROI)	20% before tax
Annual capacity	400,000 Acorns
Factory and selling costs per Acorn:	
Materials	£3.75
Assembly labour	£0.60
Overhead	£1.90
Total	£6.25

The factory and selling costs have been determined as being 60% fixed costs and 40% variable costs.

Working capital comprises stocks of raw materials, work in progress, and finished product, debtors, and cash, which are all assumed to be in direct proportion to factory and selling costs and in total are turned over on average five times a year.

On 1 January 1927 in the USA, Albert Bradley published an article in the *National Association of Cost Accountants (NACA) Bulletin*, which described the General Motors Corporation (GM) pricing policy. At the time of writing the article, Mr Bradley was the general assistant treasurer of GM. He later became its vice-president, then executive vice-president, and then chairman of the board of directors. The following notes are a summary of the main points from Mr Bradley's article.

General policy

Return on investment is the basis of the General Motors policy with regard to the pricing of product. The return on investment is the highest average long-term rate of return over a protracted period of time that can be expected, consistent with a healthy growth of the business.

The necessary rate of return on capital will vary as between separate sectors of industry as a result of differences in their economic situations, and within each industry primarily because of the relatively greater efficiency of certain producers.

The fundamental policy with regard to pricing product and expansion of the business requires a decision as to the normal average rate of plant operation. The relationship between assumed normal average rate of operation and practical annual capacity is known as standard volume.

The basis of GM pricing policy is standard volume and required return on investment.

Standard volume

Costs of production and distribution per unit of product vary with fluctuation in volume because of the fixed or non-variable nature of some of the expense items. Productive materials and productive labour may be considered costs which are 100% variable, since within reasonable limits the aggregate varies directly with volume, and the cost per unit of product therefore remains uniform.

Among the items classified as manufacturing burden (overhead) there exist varying degrees of fluctuation with volume. Manufacturing expenses include 100% fixed expenses such as depreciation, since within the limits of plant capacity the aggregate will not change, but the amount per unit of product will vary in inverse ratio to the output.

Manufacturing expenses also include 100% variable expenses, such as inspection and material handling, since the amount per unit of the product is unaffected by volume. Between the classes of 100% fixed and 100% variable is a large group of expense items that are partially variable, such as light, heat, power, and salaries.

In the General Motors Corporation, standard burden rates are developed for each burden centre, so that there will be included in costs a reasonable average allowance for manufacturing expense. In order to establish this rate, it is first necessary to obtain an expression of the estimated normal average rate of plant operation.

The rate of plant operation is affected by such factors as general business conditions, extent of seasonal fluctuation in sales, policy relating to stocks levels, and plant capacity. Each factor should be carefully considered before making additions to existing plants, in order that there may be a logical relationship between assumed normal average rate of plant operation and practical annual capacity. The percentage accepted by GM as its policy with regard to the relationship between assumed normal rate of plant operation and practical annual capacity is referred to as standard volume.

A standard burden rate is then developed, which represents the proper absorption of burden in costs at standard volume. In periods of low volume, the unabsorbed manufacturing expense is charged directly against profits as unabsorbed burden, while in periods of high volume, the overabsorbed manufacturing expense is credited to profits, as overabsorbed burden.

Return on investment

Before an enterprise can be considered successful and worthy of continuation or expansion, however, still another element of cost must be reckoned with. This is the cost of capital including an allowance for profit.

Thus, the calculation of standard prices of products necessitates the establishment of standards of capital requirement as well as expense factors, representative of the normal operating condition. The standard for capital employed in fixed assets is expressed as a percentage of factory cost, and the standards for working capital are expressed in part as a percentage of sales, and in part as a percentage of factory cost.

The amount tied up in working capital items should be directly proportional to the volume of business. For example, raw materials on hand should be in direct proportion to the manufacturing requirements – so many days supply of this material, so many days supply of that material, and so on – depending on the condition and location of sources of supply, transportation conditions, etc. Work in process should be in direct proportion to the requirements of finished production, since it is dependent on the length of time required for the material to pass from the raw to the finished state, and the amount of labour and other charges to be absorbed in the process.

Finished product should be in direct proportion to sales requirements. Accounts receivable should be in direct proportion to sales, being dependent on terms of payment and efficiency of collections.

Conclusion

The basic pricing policy stated in terms of the economic return attainable is a policy, and it does not absolutely dictate the specific price. At times, the actual price may be above, and at other times below, the standard price. The standard price calculation affords a means not only of interpreting actual or proposed prices in relation to the established policy, but at the same time affords a practical demonstration as to whether the policy itself is sound. If the prevailing price of product is found to be at variance with the standard price other than to the extent due to temporary causes, it follows that prices should be adjusted; or else, in the event of conditions being such that prices cannot be brought into line with the standard price, the conclusion is necessarily drawn that the terms of the expressed policy must be modified.

You are required to use the same pricing technique for Oak Ltd, as that outlined by Albert Bradley for GM, to:

   (i)   **calculate the standard selling price of an Acorn**
   (ii)   **calculate the standard selling price of an Acorn if production was at only 75% of capacity.**

You should also:

   (iii) **outline the assumptions on which this pricing policy is made, and some of its limitations**
   (iv)   **explain the possible impacts on Oak Ltd of production at less than full capacity.**

Appendices

Contents

Outline of Appendices

Appendix 1 is about the system used to record accounting transactions and accounting data and provides the fundamental basis for the further analysis and reporting of financial information. It provides an introduction to double-entry bookkeeping. Bookkeeping is a process that records accounting data in such a way that allows subsequent preparation of financial reports in appropriate formats which inform shareholders and others about the financial position and the financial performance of the business. The topics covered may or may not be required by you in order to use the rest of this book. Alternatively, this appendix may be used as a learning aid in support of study of the topics covered in Chapters 1 to 16.

Appendix 2 provides discounted cash flow tables, which show the present value of £1 on both a yearly and a cumulative year basis, up to 15 years for discount rates from 1% up to 50% per annum.

Appendix 3 includes schedules of all Statements of Standard Accounting Practice (SSAPs) and Financial Reporting Standards (FRSs) currently in use in the UK. It also includes schedules of current International Accounting Standards (IASs) and International Financial Reporting Standards (IFRSs), for which with effect from 1 January 2005 there is mandatory application for all listed companies in the European Union. Additions, changes and withdrawals to these standards may be found on the book's accompanying website, which is regularly updated.

Appendix 4 contains solutions to around one half of the chapter-end exercises, which include a mix of both Level I and Level II exercises. They refer to the chapter-end exercise numbers which are highlighted in colour. This allows you to attempt the exercises at the end of each chapter and then check on your understanding of the key points and how well you have been able to apply the various learning topics and techniques. Further exercises are included on the book's accompanying website.

Appendix 1

Double-entry – the basics

Contents

Learning objectives

Completion of this appendix will enable you to:

- explain the convention of double-entry bookkeeping
- describe what is meant by 'debit' and '*credit*'
- write up business transactions into accounts
- account for closing stocks and other accounting adjustments
- explain the balancing of accounts
- extract a trial balance from a company's accounts
- prepare a profit and loss account, balance sheet and cash flow statement from a trial balance
- appreciate the concepts of accrual accounting and cash accounting
- explain and account for payments in advance (prepayments) and charges not yet received (accruals)
- appreciate the importance of accounting periods

Introduction

This appendix begins by explaining what is sometimes referred to as the dual aspect rule. This rule recognises that for all transactions there is a two-sided effect within the entity. A manager in a non-accounting role may not be expected to carry out the recording of transactions in this way, but an appreciation of how accounting data has been recorded will be extremely helpful in the interpretation of financial information. We will go on to describe the processes that deal with the two sides of each transaction, the 'debits' and 'credits' of double-entry bookkeeping.

Don't worry if at first these topics seem a little difficult and confusing. They will become clearer as we follow through some transactions step-by-step into the accounts of a business and show how these accounts are kept in balance.

The appendix continues with an introduction to the way in which each of the accounts are held in what are termed the books of account and ledgers of the business. The balances on all the accounts in an entity are summarised in what is called a trial balance. The trial balance may be adjusted to allow for payments in advance, charges not yet received, and other adjusting entries. From this information we will show how to prepare a simple profit and loss account, balance sheet, and cash flow report.

This appendix refers to some of the accounting concepts introduced in Chapter 1. In that context we will look at the time period chosen by a business, to which the financial reporting relates – the accounting period.

Theory and practice of double-entry bookkeeping

Double-entry bookkeeping has a long history, having been created by the father of modern accounting, the Franciscan monk Luca Pacioli in Italy in the late fifteenth century. His publication, *Summa de Arithmetica, Geometria, Proportioni et Proportionalita* (Everything About Arithmetic, Geometry and

Proportion), published in 1494, was the first printed work dealing with algebra and also contained the first text on **bookkeeping**, entitled *De Computis et Scripturis*. Bookkeeping then spread throughout the world by a series of plagiarisms and imitations of Pacioli's work.

It is important to remember that the idea of double-entry is a convention. There are two main objectives of bookkeeping: to have a permanent record of transactions; to show the effect of each transaction and the combined effect of all the transactions on the financial position of the entity.

The fundamental idea of double-entry bookkeeping is that all business transactions of a business entity, for example, cash and invoices, should be recorded twice in the entity's business records. It is based on the principle that every financial transaction involves the simultaneous receiving and giving of value, and is therefore recorded twice. Transactions of course involve both services and goods. We shall find out later in this appendix that there are other accounting entries which do not result directly from invoice or cash transactions but which also result in double-entry records being created. These **accounting adjustment** entries relate, for example, to accounting for **depreciation**, **bad debts**, and **doubtful debts**.

The convention of double-entry assumes that in all business transactions equal and opposite values are exchanged. For example, if a company purchases materials for £1,000 for cash it adds to its stock of materials to the value of £1,000, but reduces its cash balance also to the value of £1,000. The convention uses two terms for convenience to describe the two aspects of each transaction. These terms are debit and credit.

There is sometimes confusion in the use of the terms of debit and credit used in bookkeeping when they are compared with the same terms used on bank statements. Bank statements traditionally refer to receipt of cash as a credit, whereas receipt of cash in bookkeeping terms is referred to as a debit. The reason for this is that customer accounts are presented from the bank's point of view; as far as the bank is concerned, account holders are creditors, to whom the bank will eventually have to repay any money deposited by them.

Debits and credits

The explanation of debits and credits in terms of value received and value given respectively is not perhaps one that provides the clearest understanding. Neither is the explanation that debits are in the left-hand column and credits are in the right-hand column, or debits are on the side of the room closest to the window!

Debits and credits do represent certain types of account, as we will see later, in both the **balance sheet**: **assets** and **liabilities**, and the **profit and loss account**: **costs** and **sales**. However, for the purpose of clarity of explanation we shall propose a couple of basic assumptions with which to work from as we go through some elementary accounting entries.

If we initially consider all business transactions as either goods or services then it is reasonable to assume (unless we are in a barter society) that all these transactions will ultimately end up with cash (or cash equivalents, such as cheques, bank transfers, etc.) changing hands. We can also assume that all these transactions will involve a document being raised, as a record of the transaction and an indication of the amount of cash that will change hands, namely an invoice. A **purchase invoice** records a purchase from a third party and so it represents an account to be payable at some time. A **sales invoice** records a sale to a third party and so it represents an account to be receivable at some time.

Business entities themselves have a separate identity from the owners of the business. When we consider double-entry we will now assume that all the entries we are discussing relate to those of the business entity, in whatever form the entity takes: sole trader; partnership; limited company; public limited company (see Chapter 1).

For the business entity, we shall define the following business transactions:

Transaction		Accounting entries	
CASH RECEIPT	=	DEBIT CASH	and credit something else
CASH PAYMENT	=	CREDIT CASH	and debit something else
PURCHASE INVOICE	=	CREDIT PAYABLES	and debit something else
SALES INVOICE	=	DEBIT RECEIVABLES	and credit something else

These are definitions within the convention of double-entry bookkeeping, which may be usefully remembered as a basis for establishing whether all further subsequent transactions are either debits or credits. It is suggested that the above four statements are kept filed in permanent memory, as a useful aid towards the understanding of further accounting entries.

> **Progress check A1.1** **Outline what is meant by double-entry bookkeeping.**

An elementary method of representing and clarifying double-entry is known as the T account. We shall use this method to demonstrate double-entry in action using a simple example. (Note that in the UK there are many computerised accounting packages that automate the double-entry for a business, for example Sage. The purpose of this extensive worked example is to illustrate how such transactions take place).

Worked Example A1.1

Mr Bean decides to set up a wholesale business, Ayco, on 1 January 2005. He has his own cash resources available for the purpose of setting it up and has estimated that an initial £50,000 would be required for this purpose. During the first month in business, January 2005, **Ayco** (as distinct from Mr Bean) will enter into the following transactions:

	£
Receipt of cheque from Mr Bean	50,000
Purchase for cash the freehold of a shop	30,000
Purchase for cash the shop fittings	5,000
Cash expenses on printing and stationery	200
Purchases of stock, from Beeco, of Aymen toys, payable two months later	12,000
(12,000 toys at £1 each)	
Sales of Aymen toys to Ceeco for cash (1,000 toys at £2 each)	2,000
Sales of Aymen toys to Deeco, receivable one month later	16,000
(8,000 toys at £2 each)	

We shall consider each of these transactions in detail and subsequently represent them in T account format for clarity, with debits on the left and credits on the right of the middle line of the T. We will repeatedly refer to the earlier four key double-entry definitions in order to establish the entries required for each transaction.

Receipt of cheque from Mr Bean £50,000 – transaction 1
Ayco will have needed to open a bank account to pay in the money received from Mr Bean. This

represents a receipt of cash of £50,000 to Ayco, and so

Debit cash account	£50,000	and credit what?

This money represents the capital that Mr Bean, as the sole investor in the business, has invested in Ayco and so the account is called the capital account. So:

Debit cash account	£50,000
Credit capital account	£50,000

Worked Example A1.2

Purchase for cash the freehold of a shop £30,000 – transaction 2
This represents a cash payment for the purchase of a shop, something which is called a fixed asset: an asset acquired for retention by the entity for the purpose of providing a service to the business, and not held for resale in the normal course of trading.

Credit cash account	£30,000	and debit what?

A payment of cash of £30,000 is a credit to the cash account, and so:

Credit cash account	£30,000
Debit fixed assets – shop account	£30,000

Worked Example A1.3

Purchase for cash the shop fittings £5,000 – transaction 3
This represents a cash payment for the shop fittings, which are also fixed assets, but a different category of fixed assets from the freehold shop.

A payment of cash of £5,000 is a credit to the cash account, and so:

Credit cash account	£5,000
Debit fixed assets – fittings account	£5,000

Worked Example A1.4

Cash expenses on printing and stationery £200 – transaction 4
This represents a payment of cash of £200 by Ayco in the month, and so:

Credit cash account	£200	and debit what?

This money was paid out on day-to-day expenses that have been made to support the business, and is a charge for printing and stationery expenses. So:

Credit cash account	£200
Debit printing and stationery expenses account	£200

Worked Example A1.5

Purchases of stock, from Beeco, of Aymen toys, payable two months later £12,000 – transaction 5
This represents a purchase on credit from Beeco. An invoice is assumed to have been received from Beeco along with the receipt of stock. The invoice from Beeco is a purchase invoice for £12,000 to Ayco, and so:

Credit creditors (accounts payable) account	£12,000	and debit what?

This represents a purchase of stock which are goods held for resale, and so

Credit creditors account	£12,000
Debit stock account	£12,000

A purchase of stock may alternatively be initially debited to a purchases account and then subsequently transferred to a stocks account.

Worked Example A1.6

Sales of Aymen toys to Ceeco for cash £2,000 – transaction 6
This represents a sale for cash to Ceeco. An invoice will be issued by Ayco to Ceeco along with the delivery of stock. The invoice to Ceeco is a sales invoice for £2,000 from Ayco, and so:

Debit debtors (accounts receivable) account	£2,000	and credit what?

This represents sales of stock which are called sales, revenue or turnover, and so:

Debit debtors account	£2,000
Credit sales account	£2,000

But as a cash sale this sales invoice is being paid immediately with a cash receipt of £2,000, so:

Debit cash account	£2,000	and credit what?

This £2,000 is immediately paying the receivables, and so:

Debit cash account	£2,000
Credit debtors account	£2,000

which means that on this transaction the net balance of the receivables (debtors) account is zero.

This transaction may be short cut by directly crediting the sales account and debiting the cash account. However, it is normally recorded in the way described in order to create and record a VAT sales invoice.

Worked Example A1.7

Sales of Aymen toys to Deeco, receivable one month later £16,000 – transaction 7
This represents sales on credit to Deeco. An invoice will be issued by Ayco to Deeco along with the delivery of stock.

The invoice to Deeco is a sales invoice for £16,000 from Ayco, and so as above:

Debit debtors account   **£16,000**
Credit sales account   **£16,000**

This is different from the transaction in Worked Example A1.6 because the receivables will not be paid until the following month.

Closing stocks adjustment

In the Ayco example, one further accounting entry needs to be considered, which relates to stocks of toys sold during the period. It is called a **closing stocks** adjustment, which is illustrated in Worked Example A1.8.

Worked Example A1.8

We represented the purchase of 12,000 toys into the stock of Ayco as a debit of £12,000 to the stock account. Ayco sold 1,000 toys for cash and 8,000 toys on credit. The physical stock of 12,000 toys at 31 January 2005 has therefore been reduced to only 3,000 (12,000 – 1,000 – 8,000). We may value these units that are left in stock at cost, for the purpose of this example, at 3,000 × £1, or £3,000. Ayco sold a total of 9,000 units during January at a selling price of £2 per unit. These 9,000 units cost £1 each and so these sales have cost Ayco £9,000: cost of sales £9,000. A double-entry accounting transaction is necessary to represent this for two reasons: to show the cost of the 9,000 toys that matches the sale of 9,000 toys; to ensure that the stock account represents only the physical toys that are actually held in stock.

The entries for the original purchase of stock were:

Credit creditors account   **£12,000**
Debit stock account   **£12,000**

We know that the stock account should now be £9,000 less than the original £12,000, representing the £9,000 cost of sales. Therefore we need to credit the stock account to reduce it and debit something else. The something else is the cost of sales account.

Transaction 8
Credit stock account   **£9,000**
Debit cost of sales account   **£9,000**

Accounting adjustments

The diagram in Fig. A1.1 includes all the main types of accounting transactions that may be recorded in an accounting system. The shaded items represent the prime entries (the first record of transactions) and cash entries. The non-shaded items are the five main accounting adjustment entries.

The closing stocks adjustment, illustrated in Worked Example A1.8, is one of the five main accounting adjustment entries not normally incorporated into the trial balance (although they sometimes may be in practice), shown in Fig. A1.2.

Accounting adjustments are made prior to preparation of the profit and loss account and balance sheet. The other four adjusting entries are accruals and prepayments (covered later in this appendix), depreciation, and bad and doubtful debts and the doubtful debt provision (which are covered together with further detail on closing stocks in Chapter 3).

Each of the T accounts in Fig. A1.3 shows the detailed movement through the month and each account represents the balance on each account at 31 January 2005, the end of the first month of trading.

> **Progress check A1.2 Explain broadly what is meant by accounting adjustment entries.**

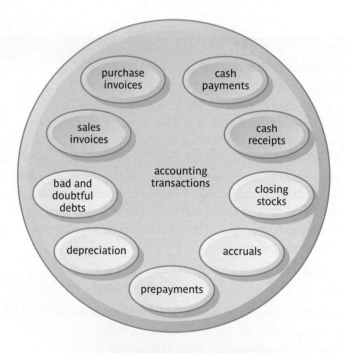

Figure A1.1 Accounting transactions

Books of account and the ledgers in action

We saw in the previous section how the principle of double-entry bookkeeping operates to record the detail of transactions. We represented these records in T accounts to provide some clarity in seeing how each entry has been made and the interrelation of the entries. In practice, accounting records are

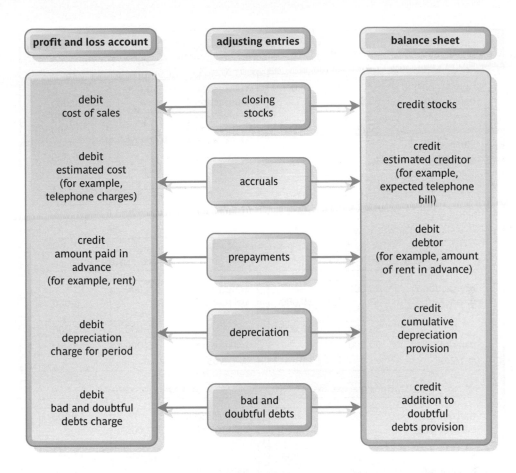

Figure A1.2 The five accounting adjustments and their impact on the profit and loss account and the balance sheet

kept along the same lines but in books of account and ledgers rather than T accounts on a piece of paper. The old-fashioned manually prepared ledgers maintained by companies have long since been superseded by computerised accounting systems. Nevertheless, the same principles apply and the same books of account and ledgers are maintained albeit in an electronic format.

The chart shown in Fig. A1.4 shows the relationship between the main ledger, the general ledger (or nominal ledger) and the other books of account, and subsidiary ledgers:

- cash book (receipts and payments)
- purchase invoice daybook and purchase ledger (or accounts payable)
- sales invoice daybook and sales ledger (or accounts receivable).

It also shows the main sources of data input for these ledgers and the basic reporting information produced out of these ledgers and books of account.

General ledger

In smaller businesses, wages and salaries data are usually recorded in the cash books and subsequently posted to the general ledger. In larger companies, wages and salaries usually have their own ledgers and control accounts in the general ledger.

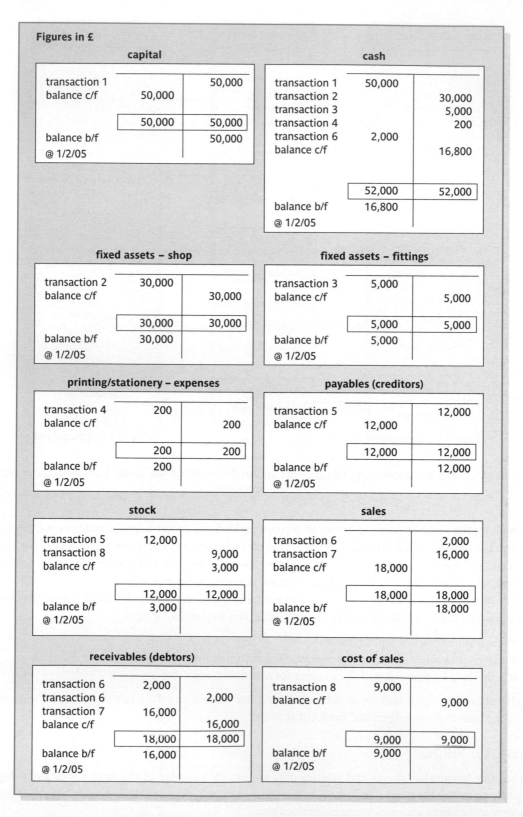

Figure A1.3 T account representation of the January 2005 transactions of Ayco

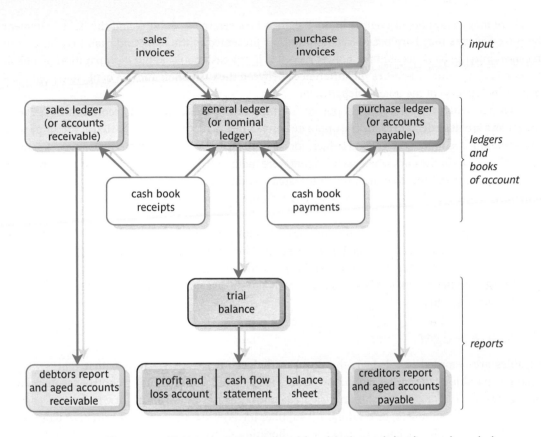

Figure A1.4 The general ledger and its relationship with the cash book, purchase ledger and sales ledger

The main ledger of any company, in which the results of all transactions made by the entity are recorded, is called the **general ledger** or nominal ledger. This ledger is set up to include all accounts whether they are assets, liabilities, sales (or revenues), or costs (or expenses). The detail of every transaction finds its way to this ledger, or is posted to it (to use the technical term), in much the same way as we saw in the T accounts. The general ledger may be said to be the collection of every T account within the entity.

Within the general ledger one account or more will be established to represent cash transactions (including cheques, drafts, bank transfers, etc.). These entries are posted to the general ledger from the analysis of entries made into the cash book. The cash book is a book of original entry maintained to show the detail of all receipts and payments made by the entity; it records the dates, values and unique references of all receipts and payments, and what they are for. These include, for example, payment of salaries, receipts from customers, purchase of fixed assets, etc.

Cash book

The cash book is a book of account that in theory should match exactly with the regular statements issued by the entity's bank. In practice, the cash book is prepared partly from company internally generated **cash payment** information and available information relating to **cash receipts**. Some transactions may appear in the bank account without prior notification, for example bank charges, and so the cash book may also be partly prepared from the bank statement.

There may always be differences in the balances between the cash book and the bank statement because cheques may have been issued but not yet presented to the bank and cash may have been received into the bank account but not yet recorded in the cash book. Regular preparation of a **bank reconciliation**, which identifies the differences between the cash book and the bank statement, is a necessary function of the finance department.

Each payment and each receipt is posted from the cash book to the cash account in the general ledger as a credit or debit to cash. The opposite entry, either debit or credit, is posted at the same time to its relevant account in the general ledger, for example, payables, printing and stationery expenses, receivables, etc. In the days when such ledgers were maintained manually such postings were made weekly or monthly. With computerised, integrated accounting systems postings may be made simultaneously to the cash book and the general ledger from the same source but avoiding any duplication of effort.

It is most important that the balance on the cash book, the net of all receipts and payments, at all times equals the balance of the cash book represented in the cash account within the general ledger, and that all the opposite entries have also been posted to their relevant accounts. In this way, the equality of total debits and total credits is maintained. The use of computerised accounting systems should guarantee this.

Purchase ledger

Payables are recorded in a ledger, the purchase ledger (or accounts payable) that represents all accounts payable by the entity. Within the general ledger one account or more (control accounts) will be established to represent payables transactions, the purchases by the entity for which invoices have been rendered by suppliers, or vendors. All supplier invoices are recorded in a purchase ledger and analysed into the various items of expense by allocating them to a specific general ledger account. These entries are debited to the appropriate general ledger accounts from the analysis of invoices made in the purchase ledger. The totals of these entries are credited to the account(s) representing accounts payable in the general ledger.

The purchase ledger is maintained to show the detail of all invoices received from suppliers. In addition to the purchase ledger's function of posting the totals of invoices to the accounts payable account in the general ledger, and the analysis of what the invoices represent to the appropriate accounts in the general ledger, it analyses all invoices and groups them by supplier.

Payments made to suppliers from the cash book which have been credited to the cash account and debited to the payables account in the general ledger are also recorded in detail by amount, date and supplier within the purchase ledger. In this way it can be seen that the total balances at any one time of all accounts in the purchase ledger equal the balance on the payables account in the general ledger.

Sales ledger

Receivables are recorded in another ledger – the sales ledger (or accounts receivable) which represents all accounts receivable by the entity. Within the general ledger one account or more will be established (control accounts) to represent receivables transactions – the sales by the entity for which invoices have been issued to customers. All customer invoices are recorded in a sales ledger and analysed into the various items of sale or revenue by allocating them to a specific general ledger account. These entries are credited to the appropriate general ledger accounts from the analysis of invoices made in the sales ledger. The totals of these entries are debited to the account(s) representing accounts receivable in the general ledger.

The sales ledger is maintained to show the detail of all invoices issued to customers. The totals of customer invoices are posted to the accounts receivable account in the general ledger. The analyses of what the invoices represent are posted to the appropriate accounts in the general ledger. The sales ledger may also enable each invoice to be analysed and grouped by customer.

Receipts from customers from the cash book which have been debited to the cash account and credited to the receivables account in the general ledger are also recorded in detail by amount, date and customer within the sales ledger. In this way the total balances at any one time of all accounts in the sales ledger equal the balance on the receivables account in the general ledger.

The cash accounts, payables and receivables accounts in the general ledger are referred to as control accounts because they provide control over the same transactions which are also represented in some further detail, and which must agree in total, in what are termed the books of account and subsidiary ledgers; the cash book, accounts payable (purchase ledger), and accounts receivable (sales ledger).

> Progress check A1.3 What are the usual books of account and ledgers you would expect to be used in a company's accounting system?

The trial balance

A trial balance is a list of account balances in a double-entry system. If the records have been correctly maintained, the sum of the debit balance accounts will be equal and opposite to the sum of the credit balance accounts, although certain errors such as omission of a transaction or erroneous entries will not be apparent in the trial balance.

Worked Example A1.9

If we turn again to the Ayco example, we can that see that each of the T accounts we have prepared represents the general (or nominal) ledger balances of the entity. These balances may be listed to form a trial balance for Ayco as at 31 January 2005.

The trial balance for Ayco as at 31 January 2005

	Debit £	Credit £
Capital		50,000
Cash	16,800	
Fixed assets – shop	30,000	
Fixed assets – fittings	5,000	
Printing and stationery expenses	200	
Payables		12,000
Stock	3,000	
Sales		18,000
Receivables	16,000	
Cost of sales	9,000	
	80,000	80,000

> From this simple trial balance it is possible to derive three reports that tell us something about the business: the profit and loss account (or income statement); the balance sheet; the cash flow statement.

How do we know which items in the trial balance are balance sheet items and which are profit and loss items? Well, if an item is not a cost (expense) or a sales (revenue) item, then it must be an asset or a liability. The expenses and revenues must appear in the profit and loss account and the assets and liabilities must appear in the balance sheet. Even a computerised accounting system must be told the specific classification of a transaction.

Worked Example A1.10

Let's examine each of the items in the Ayco trial balance as at 31 January 2005.

	Debit £	Credit £
Capital		50,000
This represents the original money that the investor Mr Bean put into Ayco – not revenue/expense		
Cash	16,800	
This represents the total cash that Ayco has at its disposal at 31 January, an asset – not revenue/expense		
Fixed assets – shop	30,000	
This represents assets purchased out of cash to help run the business – not revenue/expense		
Fixed assets – fittings	5,000	
This represents assets purchased out of cash to help run the business – not revenue/expense		
Printing and stationery expenses	200	
This represents costs incurred on disposable items used in running the business through January – expense		
Payables		12,000
This represents debts which Ayco must pay in the next two months, a liability – not revenue/expense		
Stock	3,000	
This represents items held in stock to sell to customers over future periods, an asset – not revenue/expense		

Sales This represents the value of toys delivered to customers in January – revenue		18,000
Receivables This represents debts which Ayco will receive payment for next month, an asset – not revenue/expense	16,000	
Cost of sales This represents the cost of toys delivered to customers in January – expense	9,000	
	80,000	80,000

> **Progress check A1.4 What is a trial balance?**

Profit and loss account

The profit and loss account shows the profit or loss generated by an entity during an accounting period by deducting all costs from total sales. Within the trial balance we may extract the balances on the costs (expenses) and sales (revenues) accounts in order to construct the profit and loss account. The total sum of these accounts will then result in a balance which is profit or a loss, and which may be inserted back into a restated trial balance in summary form in place of all the individual profit and loss items which comprise that balance.

Worked Example A1.11

The expense and revenue items, or the profit and loss account items, may be extracted from Ayco's trial balance and summarised as follows:

	Debit £	Credit £
Sales		18,000
Cost of sales	9,000	
Printing and stationery expenses	200	
Balance representing a profit for January	8,800	
	18,000	18,000

Although the £8,800 is shown in the debit column to balance the account, it is in fact a credit balance that is carried forward, that is a balance resulting from £18,000 less debits of £9,200.

Ayco profit and loss account for January 2005

	£
Sales	18,000
less	
Cost of sales	9,000
Gross margin (gross profit)	9,000
Printing and stationery expenses	200
Net profit for January 2005	8,800

> **Progress check A1.5** **Outline what a profit and loss account tells us about a company.**

Balance sheet

The balance sheet of an entity discloses the assets (debit balances) and liabilities, and shareholders' capital (credit balances), and gains or losses as at a given date. A gain or profit is a credit balance, and a loss is a debit balance. The revised trial balance, which includes the net balance of profit or loss, then forms the basis for the balance sheet. The balance sheet may then be constructed by rearranging the balances into an established format.

Worked Example A1.12

The profit is a credit balance of £8,800, and if we substitute this back into Ayco's trial balance for the individual revenue and expense items we have:

	Debit £	Credit £
Capital		50,000
Cash	16,800	
Fixed assets – shop	30,000	
Fixed assets – fittings	5,000	
Payables (or creditors)		12,000
Stock	3,000	
Receivables (or debtors)	16,000	
Profit for January		8,800
	70,800	70,800

To construct a balance sheet this needs to be rearranged into a more usual sort of format:

Ayco balance sheet as at 31 January 2005

	£	£		£	£
Assets			**Liabilities**		
Fixed assets		35,000	**Owner's investment**		
			Capital	50,000	
			Profit and loss account	8,800	
					58,800
Current assets			**Short-term liabilities**		
Debtors	16,000		Creditors		12,000
Stock	3,000				
Cash	16,800				
		35,800			
		70,800			70,800

> **Progress check A1.6 Outline what a balance sheet tells us about a company.**

Cash flow statement

The final report, the cash flow statement, is simply a report on the detail of the movement within the cash account in Ayco's trial balance. This starts with the opening balance, shows the receipts and payments during the accounting period and results in the closing balance.

Worked Example A1.13

The final report, the cash flow report, may be constructed by looking at the elements that are included in Ayco's cash T account, that is the elements which make up the total movements in the cash account in the general ledger:

	Debit	Credit
	£	£
Cash balance at 1 January 2005	–	
Receipt from Mr Bean – capital for business	50,000	
Payment for freehold shop		30,000
Payment for shop fittings		5,000
Payment for printing and stationery expenses		200
Receipt from customers	2,000	
Cash balance at 31 January 2005		16,800
	52,000	52,000

The £16,800 debit balance carried forward represents a positive cash position of £16,800.

The aim of the last few sections has been to explain the basics of double-entry bookkeeping, the sources of accounting data, and to provide an introduction to the accounting ledgers and books of account. This begins to show how the information from double-entry records may be usefully used. The inclusion of the rudimentary financial statements shown above illustrates the importance of the:

- accuracy
- timeliness
- completeness

of the financial data included in the double-entry system.

> **Progress check A1.7 Outline what a cash flow statement tells us about a company.**

Accrual accounting and cash accounting

We have already covered a number of important accounting ideas and concepts, one of which is that profit does not necessarily equal cash. This was apparent from the Ayco example. The net cash movement in that example for the month of January was an inflow, a positive of £16,800. However, the profit and loss account showed a gain, a positive of £8,800. The reason that they were not identical was first (as shown in the cash flow report) due to cash items other than those associated with trading, for example receipt of the original capital, and expenditure on fixed assets. Second, the trading or operational transactions were not all converted into cash within the month of January; they were held as accounts payable, stocks, and accounts receivable.

The approach that we took in the Ayco example demonstrated compliance with the **accruals concept**, or matching concept, the principle that revenue and costs are:

- recognised as they are earned or incurred
- matched with one another
- dealt with in the profit and loss account of the period to which they relate, irrespective of the period of receipt or payment.

> **Progress check A1.8 In what way does a company's profit and loss account differ from the movements on its cash account during an accounting period?**

Accruals

It may be that an expense has been incurred within an accounting period, for which an invoice may or may not have been received. For example, electricity used, telephone charges incurred, or stationery supplies received and used. We have talked about the concept of matching costs with sales, or revenues. Costs not necessarily related to sales cannot be matched in that way. Such charges must be matched to the **accounting period** to which they relate, and therefore an estimate of the cost (an accrual) must be made and included as an accounting adjusting entry in the accounts for that period.

Figure A1.5 shows an invoice dated 15 April 2005 received by a company from its communications provider for charges of £2,000 for the period January to March 2005. At the end of April 2005 the company had not yet received its bill for the next quarter even though it had use of telephone lines and had incurred call charges. We may assume that the company's accounting year runs from January to

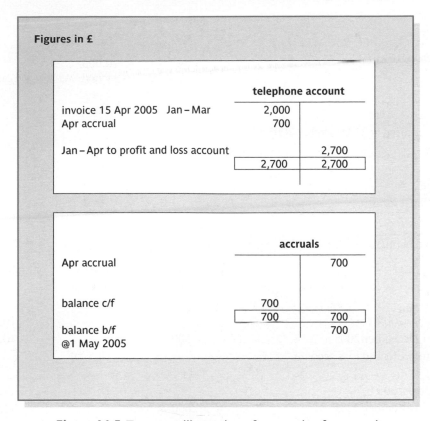

Figures in £

	telephone account	
invoice 15 Apr 2005 Jan – Mar	2,000	
Apr accrual	700	
Jan – Apr to profit and loss account		2,700
	2,700	2,700

	accruals	
Apr accrual		700
balance c/f	700	
	700	700
balance b/f		700
@1 May 2005		

Figure A1.5 T account illustration of accounting for accruals

December. Therefore, before finalising its profit and loss account for January to April the company needed to estimate its telephone costs for April, which are shown as £700.

The estimate of £700 has been charged, or debited, to telephone costs in the profit and loss account, and a temporary creditor, an accrual, credited in the balance sheet for £700. The total telephone costs charged to the profit and loss account for January to April 2005 are therefore £2,700. The accrual carried forward at the end of April would normally be reversed and the position assessed again at the end of May, and the same procedure followed at the end of June. By the end of July the bill would normally be expected to have been received covering the period April to June and so no accrual will be necessary. However, an accrual will be required for the month of July.

Worked Example A1.14

From the following information we are required to prepare three-column accounts (in an Excel spreadsheet or in a Word table) to reflect the current balances on each account, which are then required to be adjusted for the accruals at 31 December 2005 to show the total transfer to the profit and loss account. We are also required to show a summary of the accruals as at 31 December 2005.

	£
Current balances at 31 December 2005	
Electricity	10,000
Gas	11,000
Telephone	5,000
Interest on overdraft	6,000
Accruals required at 31 December 2005	
Electricity	500
Gas	600
Telephone	500
Interest on overdraft	600

Accruals adjustments at 31 December 2005:

	Debit £	Credit £	Balance £
Electricity			
31 December 2005			10,000
Accrual 31 December 2005	500		10,500
Transfer to profit and loss account		(10,500)	0
Gas			
31 December 2005			11,000
Accrual 31 December 2005	600		11,600
Transfer to profit and loss account		(11,600)	0
Telephone			
31 December 2005			5,000
Accrual 31 December 2005	500		5,500
Transfer to profit and loss account		(5,500)	0
Interest payable on overdraft			
31 December 2005			6,000
Accrual 31 December 2005	600		6,600
Transfer to profit and loss account		(6,600)	0
Accruals 31 December 2005			
Electricity		(500)	(500)
Gas		(600)	(1,100)
Telephone		(500)	(1,600)
Interest payable on overdraft		(600)	(2,200)

The same sort of exercise is carried out within a company for all of the categories of expense for which accruals are likely to be required. Worked Example A1.15 explains how accruals may have been dealt with in Ayco.

Worked Example A1.15

The accruals concept could have been further illustrated in the Ayco scenario by the introduction of a number of additional factors. Assume, for example, that Ayco had used more than £200 of stationery in the month, say £1,000. We know that Ayco had been invoiced for and paid for £200 worth of stationery.

If £500 worth of the additional stationery had been used, and an invoice had been received but not processed through the ledgers, what would be the impact on Ayco? If £300 worth of the additional stationery had been used, and an invoice had not yet been received but was in the mail what would be the impact on Ayco?

The answer is that both would have to be debited to printing and stationery expenses for a total of £800, and credited not to payables but to accruals.

Accruals are treated in a similar way to payables but the invoices for these charges have not yet been processed by the entity. They are charges which are brought into the period because, although goods (or services) have been provided, they have not yet been included in the supplier's accounts.

Expense recognition is an important concept. Expenses should be recognised immediately they are known about. Ayco knew they had used stationery for which there was a cost even though an invoice may not have been processed. On the other hand revenues or profits should not be recognised until they are earned.

The net impact of the above on Ayco would have been a reduction in profit, a debit of £800 and an increase in liabilities, a credit of £800 to accruals. The accruals entries would need to be exactly reversed at the beginning of the following month to avoid a doubling up since the actual transactions will also be processed.

Prepayments

It may be that an expense has been incurred within an accounting period that related to future period(s). For example, business rates, rents, or vehicle licence fees paid in advance. As with accruals, these costs are not necessarily related to sales and cannot be matched with sales. Such charges must also be matched to the period to which they relate and therefore the proportion of the charges that relate to future periods (a prepayment) must be calculated and included as an adjustment in the accounts for that period. Figure A1.6 shows a charge of £6,000 that has been incurred by a company from its landlord on 1 January 2005 for rent for the period January to June 2005. At the end of April 2005 the company had paid rent not only for January to April, but rent in advance for May and June. Therefore, before finalising its profit and loss account for January to April the company needed to calculate the rent in advance for May and June, which is shown as £2,000.

The rent in advance of £2,000 has been credited to the rent account and a temporary debtor, a prepayment, created in the balance sheet for £2,000. The total rent costs charged to the profit and loss account for January to April 2005 are therefore £4,000. The prepayment carried forward at the end of April would normally be reversed and the position assessed again at the end of May, and the same procedure followed at the end of June. By the end of July a charge would normally be expected to have been received covering the period July to December and so a prepayment will be necessary at the end of July for the period August to December.

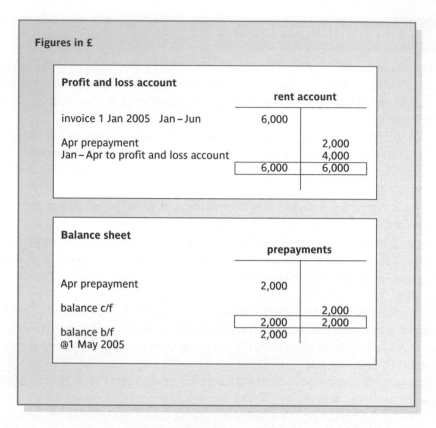

Figure A1.6 T account illustration of accounting for prepayments

Worked Example A1.16

From the following information we are required to prepare three-column accounts (in an Excel spreadsheet or in a Word table) to reflect the current balances on each account, which are then required to be adjusted for the prepayments, deferred income, and accrued income at 31 December 2005, to show the total transfer to the profit and loss account. We are also required to show a summary of the prepayments and accrued income, and accruals and deferred income as at 31 December 2005.

                                                                   £

Current balances at 31 December 2005
Rent payable   12,000
Business rates   13,000
Interest receivable   7,000 (credit)
Rent receivable   8,000 (credit)
Prepayments, accrued income, and deferred income required at 31 December 2005
Rent payable   700 (normally paid in advance)
Business rates   800 (normally paid in advance)
Interest receivable   700 (normally received in arrears)
Rent received   800 (normally received in advance)

Prepayments adjustments at 31 December 2005

	Debit £	Credit £	Balance £
Rent payable			
31 December			12,000
Prepayment 31 December 2005		(700)	11,300
Transfer to profit and loss account		(11,300)	0
Business rates			
31 December			13,000
Prepayment 31 December 2005		(800)	12,200
Transfer to profit and loss account		(12,200)	0
Interest receivable			
31 December			(7,000)
Accrued income 31 December 2005		(700)	(7,700)
Transfer to profit and loss account	7,700		0
Rent receivable			
31 December			(8,000)
Deferred income 31 December 2005	800		(7,200)
Transfer to profit and loss account	7,200		0
Prepayments and accrued income			
31 December 2005			0
Rent payable	700		700
Business rates	800		1,500
Interest receivable	700		2,200
Accruals and deferred income			
31 December 2005			0
Rent receivable		(800)	(800)

The same sort of exercise is carried out within a company for all of the categories of expense for which prepayments are likely to be required. Worked Example A1.17 explains how prepayments may have been dealt with in Ayco.

Worked Example A1.17

Assume, for example, that Ayco had received an invoice for £2,000 for advertising in January to be paid in March, but the advertising was not taking place until February. An invoice may have been received and processed through the ledgers, but what would be the impact on Ayco?

The answer is that payables would have been credited with £2,000 and advertising expenses debited with £2,000 in the month of January. However, because the advertising had not taken place, the charge of £2,000 would be considered as being in advance, or to use its technical term, a prepayment. The payables entry remains as a credit of £2,000, but an additional entry is required to credit advertising expenses with £2,000 and debit prepayments with £2,000.

A prepayment is expenditure on goods (or services) for future benefit, which is to be charged to future operations. Such amounts are similar to debtors and are included in current assets in the balance sheet.

The net impact of the above on Ayco would have been no charge to profit. The prepayment entry would need to be exactly reversed at the beginning of the following month.

> **Progress check A1.9** **What are accruals and prepayments and why are such adjusting entries needed?**

Accounting periods

In the Ayco worked examples we were introduced to the idea of an accounting period. An accounting period is that covered by the accounting statements of an entity. Different periods may be chosen within the financial year, for example 13 periods of four weeks, 12 periods using a four, four, five week quarter basis, or 12 calendar periods. The Ayco example assumed 12 periods on a calendar basis. Once an accounting period basis has been chosen, consistency must be maintained. This is an example of both the periodicity concept and the consistency concept (see Chapter 1).

> **Progress check A1.10** **What is an accounting period?**

Summary of key points

- Double-entry bookkeeping is a convention, the two main objectives of which are to have a permanent record of transactions, and to show the effect of each transaction and the combined effect of all the transactions upon the financial position of the entity.
- Double-entry bookkeeping data are recorded as transactions described as 'debits' and 'credits'.
- The meaning of a debit and a credit may most usefully be remembered using the following rule, applying to entries reflected in the accounts of a company:

Cash receipt	=	debit cash account	and credit another account
Cash payment	=	credit cash account	and debit another account
Purchase invoice	=	credit accounts payable	and debit another account
Sales invoice	=	debit accounts receivable	and credit another account

- The main ledger held within the accounting system of a company is called the general ledger, or nominal ledger, in which the results of all transactions made by the company are recorded either in summary or in detail.
- The original books of account, and subsidiary ledgers: cash book (receipts and payments); purchase invoice daybook and purchase ledger (or accounts payable); sales invoice daybook and sales ledger (or accounts receivable), hold the details of transactions that are reflected in the general ledger.

- Wages and salaries data are recorded in the cash books and posted to the general ledger.
- Adjusting accounting entries, such as those relating to closing stock valuations, are made to the accounts prior to preparation of the profit and loss account and balance sheet.
- There are five main accounting adjustments that are made prior to preparation of the profit and loss account and balance sheet:
  - closing stocks
  - accruals: charges not yet received
  - prepayments: payments in advance (and income accrued)
  - depreciation
  - bad and doubtful debts.
- The balances on the individual accounts recorded within the general ledger may be summarised in a trial balance, the total of the debit balances being equal to the total of the credit balances.
- The profit and loss account of an entity shows the profit or loss generated by the entity during an accounting period by deducting all expenses from all revenues.
- The balance sheet of an entity discloses the assets (debit balances) and liabilities, and shareholders' capital (credit balances), and gains (credits) or losses (debits) as at a given date.
- The cash flow statement is a report on the detail of the movement within the cash account in the trial balance, starting with the opening balance and adding the receipts and deducting the payments during the accounting period, resulting in the closing balance.
- The accounting period chosen by a business is the period covered by its accounting statements.

Questions

QA1.1   What are the four basic business transactions and what are their corresponding debit and credit accounting entries under the convention of double-entry bookkeeping?

QA1.2   **(i)**   Name each of the books of account and ledgers in an accounting system.
(ii)   What are they used for?

QA1.3   Describe the use and purpose of the five main accounting adjusting entries.

QA1.4   **(i)**   At a specific point in time, what does a company's trial balance show?
(ii)   What may the trial balance not show?

QA1.5   How may the financial performance of a company be ascertained from its trial balance?

QA1.6   How may the financial position of a company be ascertained from its trial balance?

QA1.7   How may the cash position of a company be ascertained from its trial balance?

QA1.8   Why is the profit made during an accounting period not necessarily equal to the cash flow during that period?

QA1.9 In what ways do businesses adjust their accounts for accruals and prepayments?

QA1.10 What is the relevance of the accounting period?

Discussion points

DA1.1 'Managers who are non-accounting specialists don't need to learn about bookkeeping, debits and credits, etc.' Discuss.

DA1.2 Computerised accounts and information systems have speeded up the recording of accounting data and the presentation of information. What are the other advantages over manual accounting systems and what are the disadvantages?

Exercises

Solutions are provided in Appendix 4 to all exercise numbers highlighted in colour.

Level I

EA1.1 *Time allowed – 30 minutes*
Extracts from the ledgers of Hall Ltd have provided the following information for 2003 and 2004.

	£
Sales 2003	11,000
Sales 2004	12,000
Purchases 2003	7,100
Purchases 2004	8,300
Expenses 2003	2,500
Expenses 2004	2,800
Stock 1 January 2003	600
Stock 31 December 2003	700
Stock 31 December 2004	800
Obsolete stock in 31 December 2004 stock	200

You are required to prepare a basic profit and loss account for the years ended 31 December 2003 and 2004.

EA1.2 *Time allowed – 30 minutes*

  (i)   Explain why there are always problems at the year end in the assessment of the costs associated with electricity, gas and telephone.
  (ii) Using the information below, prepare the appropriate year-end accounting entries.

Electricity charges account balance at 15 December 2004: £10,000
Gas charges account balance at 20 December 2004: £5,000
Estimated consumption
Electricity 16 December to 31 December 2004: £300
Gas 21 December to 31 December 2004: £150

EA1.3 *Time allowed – 30 minutes*

Arthur Moment set up a table-making business, Forlegco, on 1 July 2005. He had £10,000 available to invest, which is the amount he estimated was required for setting up costs. In the first month of trading Forlegco entered into the following transactions:

	£
£10,000 from Arthur Moment	10,000
Purchase of hand tools for cash	2,000
Purchase of lathe, power saw and drill on one month's credit	6,000
Purchase of printing and stationery – invoice received for half the order	100

The total order is £200, and it was all delivered in July and used

Purchase of advertising flyers for cash 2,000 at 50p each, of which 1,000 will
  be used in July, and 500 in August and September

Purchases of timber, glue and varnish, from Woodco, payable within the
  month £1,500 – half of this stock will be on hand at 31 July 2005

Sales of tables to Gardenfurnco for settlement one month later (10 tables at
  £700 each)

You are required to present these transactions in T account format, and then prepare a trial balance for Forlegco for 31 July 2005.

EA1.4 *Time allowed – 30 minutes*

From the trial balance for Forlegco for 31 July 2005 (Exercise EA1.3):

(i)   **Prepare a simple profit and loss account for the month of July 2005.**

(ii)   **Has Forlegco made a profit in July?**

(iii)   **If Forlegco has not made a profit, why not?**

EA1.5 *Time allowed – 30 minutes*

From the trial balance for Forlegco for 31 July 2005 (Exercise EA1.3) prepare a simple balance sheet at that date.

EA1.6 *Time allowed – 30 minutes*

From the trial balance for Forlegco for 31 July 2005 (Exercise EA1.3) prepare a simple cash flow statement for the month of July 2005.

EA1.7 *Time allowed – 30 minutes*

You are required to prepare the appropriate correcting entries in a company's accounts at 31 December 2004 for the following:

(i)   **A cheque paid for rent amounting to £2,400 has been entered into the car hire account in error.**

(ii)   **A cheque for £980 was received from a customer in full settlement of a balance of £1,000, but no accounting entry for the discount has been made.**

(iii)   **A cheque paid for insurance on the company cars amounting to £1,200 has been entered in the cost of motor cars account in error.**

(iv)   **An invoice from a builder for £3,500 has been entered in the buildings cost account, but in fact it related to redecoration of the reception area of the office and should be treated as a building repair.**

Level II

EA1.8 *Time allowed – 60 minutes*

David (Dai) Etcoak decided to set up a drinks wholesale business, Etcoakco, on 1 December 2004. He had £100,000 available to invest, which is the amount he felt was required to set up the business. In the first month of trading Etcoakco entered into the following transactions:

	£
£100,000 from Dai Etcoak	100,000
Purchase for cash the freehold of a shop	50,000
Purchase for cash the shop fittings	7,000
Purchase of a labelling machine payable one month later	20,000
Cash expenses on printing and stationery	400
Purchases of stock, from Gasco, of bottles of pop, payable three months later (25,000 bottles at £1.25 each)	31,250
Sales of bottles of Etcoak to Boozah for settlement one month later (10,000 bottles at £2.30 each)	23,000
Sales of bottles of Etcoak to Disco30, receivable in the month (12,000 bottles at £2.30 each)	27,600

You are required to:

(i)   look at these transactions in detail and then present them in T account format, and

(ii)   state any assumptions you have made particularly relating to how you have valued stock transactions.

Also:

(iii)   Do you think £100,000 was enough money or too much to invest in the business?

(iv)   What alternative courses of action are open to Dai?

Appendix 2

Present value tables

Present value of £1

The table shows the value of £1 to be received or paid, using a range of interest rates (r) after a given number of years (n). The values are based on the formula $V_n r = (1 + r)^{-n}$

Rate r % After n years	1	2	3	4	5	6	7	8	9	10	11	12
1	0.99	0.98	0.97	0.96	0.95	0.94	0.93	0.93	0.92	0.91	0.90	0.89
2	0.98	0.96	0.94	0.92	0.91	0.89	0.87	0.86	0.84	0.83	0.81	0.80
3	0.97	0.94	0.92	0.89	0.86	0.84	0.82	0.79	0.77	0.75	0.73	0.71
4	0.96	0.92	0.89	0.85	0.82	0.79	0.76	0.74	0.71	0.68	0.66	0.64
5	0.95	0.91	0.86	0.82	0.78	0.75	0.71	0.68	0.65	0.62	0.59	0.57
6	0.94	0.89	0.84	0.79	0.75	0.70	0.67	0.63	0.60	0.56	0.53	0.51
7	0.93	0.87	0.81	0.76	0.71	0.67	0.62	0.58	0.55	0.51	0.48	0.45
8	0.92	0.85	0.79	0.73	0.68	0.63	0.58	0.54	0.50	0.47	0.43	0.40
9	0.91	0.84	0.77	0.70	0.64	0.59	0.54	0.50	0.46	0.42	0.39	0.36
10	0.91	0.82	0.74	0.68	0.61	0.56	0.51	0.46	0.42	0.39	0.35	0.32
11	0.90	0.80	0.72	0.65	0.58	0.53	0.48	0.43	0.39	0.35	0.32	0.29
12	0.89	0.79	0.70	0.62	0.56	0.50	0.44	0.40	0.36	0.32	0.29	0.26
13	0.88	0.77	0.68	0.60	0.53	0.47	0.41	0.37	0.33	0.29	0.26	0.23
14	0.87	0.76	0.66	0.58	0.51	0.44	0.39	0.34	0.30	0.26	0.23	0.20
15	0.86	0.74	0.64	0.56	0.48	0.42	0.36	0.32	0.27	0.24	0.21	0.18

Rate r % After n years	13	14	15	16	17	18	19	20	30	40	50
1	0.88	0.88	0.87	0.86	0.85	0.85	0.84	0.83	0.77	0.71	0.67
2	0.78	0.77	0.76	0.74	0.73	0.72	0.71	0.69	0.59	0.51	0.44
3	0.69	0.67	0.66	0.64	0.62	0.61	0.59	0.58	0.46	0.36	0.30
4	0.61	0.59	0.57	0.55	0.53	0.52	0.50	0.48	0.35	0.26	0.20
5	0.54	0.52	0.50	0.48	0.46	0.44	0.42	0.40	0.27	0.19	0.13
6	0.48	0.46	0.43	0.41	0.39	0.37	0.35	0.33	0.21	0.13	0.09
7	0.43	0.40	0.38	0.35	0.33	0.31	0.30	0.28	0.16	0.09	0.06
8	0.38	0.35	0.33	0.31	0.28	0.27	0.25	0.23	0.12	0.07	0.04
9	0.33	0.31	0.28	0.26	0.24	0.23	0.21	0.19	0.09	0.05	0.03
10	0.29	0.27	0.25	0.23	0.21	0.19	0.18	0.16	0.07	0.03	0.02
11	0.26	0.24	0.21	0.20	0.18	0.16	0.15	0.13	0.06	0.02	0.01
12	0.23	0.21	0.19	0.17	0.15	0.14	0.12	0.11	0.04	0.02	0.008
13	0.20	0.18	0.16	0.15	0.13	0.12	0.10	0.09	0.03	0.013	0.005
14	0.18	0.16	0.14	0.13	0.11	0.10	0.09	0.08	0.03	0.009	0.003
15	0.16	0.14	0.12	0.11	0.09	0.08	0.07	0.06	0.02	0.006	0.002

Cumulative present value of £1

The table shows the present value of £1 per annum, using a range of interest rates (r), receivable or payable at the end of each year for n years.

Rate r % After n years	1	2	3	4	5	6	7	8	9	10	11	12
1	0.99	0.98	0.97	0.96	0.95	0.94	0.94	0.93	0.92	0.91	0.90	0.89
2	1.97	1.94	1.91	1.89	1.86	1.83	1.81	1.78	1.76	1.74	1.71	1.69
3	2.94	2.88	2.83	2.78	2.72	2.67	2.62	2.58	2.53	2.49	2.44	2.40
4	3.90	3.81	3.72	3.63	3.55	3.47	3.39	3.31	3.24	3.17	3.10	3.04
5	4.85	4.71	4.58	4.45	4.33	4.21	4.10	3.99	3.89	3.79	3.70	3.61
6	5.80	5.60	5.42	5.24	5.08	4.92	4.77	4.62	4.49	4.36	4.23	4.11
7	6.73	6.47	6.23	6.00	5.79	5.58	5.39	5.21	5.03	4.87	4.71	4.56
8	7.65	7.33	7.02	6.73	6.46	6.21	5.97	5.75	5.54	5.34	5.15	4.97
9	8.57	8.16	7.79	7.44	7.11	6.80	6.52	6.25	6.00	5.76	5.54	5.33
10	9.47	8.98	8.53	8.11	7.72	7.36	7.02	6.71	6.42	6.15	5.89	5.65
11	10.37	9.79	9.25	8.76	8.31	7.89	7.50	7.14	6.81	6.50	6.21	5.94
12	11.26	10.58	9.95	9.39	8.86	8.38	7.94	7.54	7.16	6.81	6.49	6.19
13	12.13	11.35	10.64	9.99	9.39	8.85	8.36	7.90	7.49	7.10	6.80	6.42
14	13.00	12.11	11.30	10.56	9.90	9.30	8.75	8.24	7.79	7.37	6.98	6.63
15	13.87	12.85	11.94	11.12	10.38	9.71	9.11	8.56	8.06	7.61	7.19	6.81

Rate r % After n years	13	14	15	16	17	18	19	20	30	40	50
1	0.89	0.88	0.87	0.86	0.85	0.85	0.84	0.83	0.77	0.71	0.67
2	1.67	1.65	1.63	1.61	1.59	1.57	1.55	1.53	1.36	1.22	1.11
3	2.36	2.32	2.28	2.25	2.21	2.17	2.14	2.11	1.81	1.59	1.41
4	2.97	2.91	2.86	2.80	2.74	2.69	2.64	2.59	2.17	1.85	1.61
5	3.52	3.43	3.35	3.27	3.20	3.13	3.06	2.99	2.44	2.04	1.74
6	4.00	3.89	3.78	3.69	3.59	3.50	3.41	3.33	2.64	2.17	1.82
7	4.42	4.29	4.16	4.04	3.92	3.81	3.71	3.61	2.80	2.26	1.88
8	4.80	4.64	4.49	4.34	4.21	4.08	3.95	3.84	2.93	2.33	1.92
9	5.13	4.95	4.77	4.61	4.45	4.30	4.16	4.03	3.02	2.38	1.95
10	5.43	5.22	5.02	4.83	4.66	4.49	4.34	4.19	3.09	2.41	1.97
11	5.69	5.45	5.23	5.03	4.83	4.66	4.49	4.33	3.15	2.44	1.98
12	5.92	5.66	5.42	5.20	4.99	4.79	4.61	4.44	3.19	2.46	1.99
13	6.12	5.84	5.58	5.34	5.12	4.91	4.71	4.53	3.22	2.47	1.99
14	6.30	6.00	5.72	5.47	5.23	5.01	4.80	4.61	3.25	2.48	1.99
15	6.46	6.14	5.85	5.58	5.32	5.09	4.88	4.68	3.27	2.48	2.00

Appendix 3

FRSs, SSAPs, IASs and IFRSs

Financial Reporting Standards (FRSs) in force in the year 2005

FRS 1	Cash flow statements
FRS 2	Accounting for subsidiary undertakings
FRS 3	Reporting financial performance
FRS 4	Capital instruments
FRS 5	Reporting the substance of transactions
FRS 6	Acquisitions and mergers
FRS 7	Fair values in acquisition accounting
FRS 8	Related party disclosures
FRS 9	Associates and joint ventures
FRS 10	Goodwill and intangible assets
FRS 11	Impairment of fixed assets and goodwill
FRS 12	Provisions, contingent liabilities and contingent assets
FRS 13	Derivatives and other financial instruments: disclosures
FRS 14	Earnings per share
FRS 15	Tangible fixed assets
FRS 16	Current tax
FRS 17	Retirement benefits
FRS 18	Accounting policies
FRS 19	Deferred tax
FRS 20	Share-based payment
FRS 21	Events after the balance sheet date
FRS 22	Earnings per share
FRS 23	The effects of changes in foreign currency rates
FRS 24	Financial reporting in hyperinflationary economies
FRS 25	Financial instruments: disclosure and presentation
FRS 26	Financial instruments: measurement
FRSSE	Financial reporting standard for smaller entities

Statements of Standard Accounting Practice (SSAPs) in force in the year 2005

SSAP 4	Accounting for government grants
SSAP 5	Accounting for value added tax
SSAP 9	Stocks and long-term contracts
SSAP 13	Accounting for research and development
SSAP 19	Accounting for investment properties
SSAP 21	Accounting for leases and hire purchase contracts
SSAP 24	Accounting for pension costs
SSAP 25	Segmental reporting

International Accounting Standards (IASs) in force in the year 2005

IAS 1	Presentation of financial statements
IAS 2	Inventories
IAS 7	Cash flow statements
IAS 8	Accounting policies, changes in accounting estimates, and errors
IAS 10	Events after the balance sheet date
IAS 11	Construction contracts
IAS 12	Income taxes
IAS 14	Segment reporting
IAS 15	Information reflecting the effects of changing prices
IAS 16	Property, plant and equipment
IAS 17	Leases
IAS 18	Revenue
IAS 19	Employee benefits
IAS 20	Accounting for Government grants and disclosure of Government assistance
IAS 21	The effects of changes in foreign exchange rates
IAS 23	Borrowing costs
IAS 24	Related party disclosures
IAS 26	Accounting and reporting by retirement benefit plans
IAS 27	Consolidated and separate financial statements
IAS 28	Investments in associates
IAS 29	Financial reporting in hyperinflationary economies
IAS 30	Disclosures in the financial statements of banks and similar financial institutions
IAS 31	Interests in joint ventures
IAS 32	Financial instruments: disclosure and presentation
IAS 33	Earnings per share
IAS 34	Interim financial reporting
IAS 36	Impairment of assets
IAS 37	Provisions, contingent liabilities and contingent assets
IAS 38	Intangible assets
IAS 39	Financial instruments: recognition and measurement
IAS 40	Investment property
IAS 41	Agriculture

International Financial Reporting Standards (IFRSs) in force in the year 2005

Preface to	International financial reporting standards
IFRS 1	First-time adoption of international financial reporting standards
IFRS 2	Share-based payment
IFRS 3	Business combinations
IFRS 4	Insurance contracts
IFRS 5	Non-current assets held for sale and discontinued operations

Appendix **4**

Solutions to selected exercises

Solutions are provided for the chapter-end exercise numbers highlighted in colour.

Chapter 2

E2.3 Trainer

Trainer plc Balance sheet as at 31 December 2005

	£000	£000
Fixed assets		
Land and buildings		320
Plant and machinery		
Cost	200	
Depreciation	80	120
Current assets		
Stocks	100	
Debtors	100	
Bank	73	
	273	
Current liabilities		
Trade creditors	130	
Accruals	5	
Taxation	20	
	155	118
		558
Capital and reserves		
Ordinary shares		320
Profit and loss account		238
		558

Working	£000
Sales	1,000
Cost of sales	600
Gross profit	400
Expenses	(120)
Bad debt	(2)
Depreciation	(20)
Profit before tax	258
Taxation (also a short-term creditor within *Current liabilities*)	(20)
Net profit	238

E2.6 Gorban

Gorban Ltd
Balance sheet as at 31 December 2004

£

Fixed assets						
Tangible assets	235,000		29,368			264,368
Less: depreciation provision	30,165					30,165
	204,835					234,203
Current assets						
Stocks	51,420		48,000			99,420
Debtors	42,500				(10,342)	32,158
Doubtful debts provision	(1,725)			(1,870)		(3,595)
Bank and cash	67,050	(20,000)	(29,368)	50,000		67,682
	159,245					195,665
Current liabilities						
Creditors	35,112					35,112
Accruals		1,173				1,173
	35,112					36,285
Net current assets	124,133					159,380
Total assets less current liabilities	328,968					393,583
less						
Long-term liabilities						
Loan	20,000	(20,000)				
Net assets	308,968					393,583
Capital and reserves						
Share capital	200,000			50,000		250,000
Profit and loss account	108,968	(1,173)	48,000	(1,870)	(10,342)	143,583
	308,968					393,583

E2.7 Pip

Pip Ltd
Balance sheet as at 31 December 2005

	£000	£000	Working
Fixed assets			
Land and buildings	100,000		
Plant and equipment	100,000		[150,000 – 50,000]
		200,000	
Current assets			
Stocks	45,000		[50,000 – 5,000]
Debtors	45,000		[50,000 – 5,000]
Cash in hand and at bank	11,000		[10,000 + 1,000]
	101,000		

Current liabilities

Bank overdraft	10,000	
Trade creditors	81,000	
	91,000	
Net current assets		10,000
		210,000

Capital and reserves

Ordinary shares (issued)		100,000
Profit and loss account		110,000
		210,000

Note that the intangible assets, brands worth £10,000 in the opinion of the directors, have not been included in the balance sheet on the assumption that they are not purchased brands. Under FRS 10 only brand names that have been purchased may be capitalised and included in the balance sheet.

Chapter 3

E3.3 CDs

Overview

Stocks are regulated by the revised SSAP 9. Stocks should be valued at the lower of cost and net realisable value. Retailers can (and do) take the retail value of their stocks (by category) and deduct the gross profit (by category) as an estimate of cost.

(i)   This stock should be valued at £5,000 (cost) as the stock is selling consistently.

(ii)   This stock should not be in the balance sheet at any value, as it will not generate any cash in the future.

(iii)   As in (i) above this stock can be valued at £1,000 (cost) for balance sheet purposes. As there are more risks associated with holding single artist CDs the stock levels should be continually reviewed.

(iv)   In this situation the selling pattern has changed and the posters have stopped selling. The posters must not appear in the balance sheet as they will not generate any future cash.

E3.4 Partex

	2002 £	2003 £	2004 £
(i) **Balance sheet as at 31 December – Debtors**			
Debtors including debts to be written-off	88,000	110,000	94,000
Write-off of debts to profit and loss account (1)	(4,000)	(5,000)	(4,000)
	84,000	105,000	90,000
Doubtful provision at 4% of debtors (2)	–	3,360	4,200
	(3,360)	(4,200)	(3,600)
Debtors at end of year	80,640	104,160	90,600

(ii)   Profit and loss account year ended 31 December – Bad and doubtful debts

Bad debts written-off (1)	4,000	5,000	4,000
Doubtful debt provision at 4% of debtors (2)	–	(3,360)	(4,200)
	3,360	4,200	3,600
Bad and doubtful debts charge for year	7,360	5,840	3,400

E3.5 Tartantrips

(i) Sum of the digits depreciation

The company needs to decide the economic life of the asset (say 10 years in this example) and its estimated residual value at the end of its life (£1m in this example).

Cost		£5,000,000
Residual value		£1,000,000
Amount to be written-off over 10 years		£4,000,000
Over 10 years the digits 10 + 9 + 8 … 2 + 1 add up to 55		
Depreciation in year 1 is 10/55 × £4,000,000	=	£727,272
Depreciation in year 2 is 9/55 × £4,000,000	=	£654,545
Depreciation in year 3 is 8/55 × £4,000,000	=	£581,818
and so on until		
Depreciation in year 9 is 2/55 × £4,000,000	=	£145,546
Depreciation in year 10 is 1/55 × £4,000,000	=	£72,727
Total depreciation for 10 years		£4,000,000

(ii) Straight line depreciation

This method is very simple to operate. The company needs to decide on the economic life of the asset and its residual value at the end of its life (as above). The annual depreciation will be:

Depreciation per year is £4,000,000 divided by 10 years = £400,000 per year

It can be seen that there is a constant charge to the annual profit and loss account for each of the ten years for 'wear and tear' of the fixed asset.

(iii) Reducing balance depreciation

This method is quite different to the straight line method because the depreciation charge is much higher in the earlier years of the life of the asset. The same sort of estimates are required: economic life, residual value, which are used in a reducing balance formula to calculate each year's depreciation.

The reducing balance formula where d is the percentage depreciation to charge on the written down value of the asset at the end of each year is:

$d = 1 - \sqrt[10]{1,000,000/5,000,000} = 14.9\%$ (which may also be calculated using the Excel DB function)

Depreciation in year 1 is 14.9% of £5,000,000	=	£745,000
Depreciation in year 2 is 14.9% of £4,255,000	=	£633,995
Depreciation in year 3 is 14.9% of £3,621,005	=	£539,530
and so on until year 10		
The total depreciation for 10 years is		£4,000,000

E3.8 Retepmal

Retepmal Ltd
Profit and loss account for the year ended 31 March 2004

		£	£
Sales			266,000
Cost of Sales			
	Opening stock 31 March 2003	15,000	
plus	Purchases	150,000	
less	Closing stock 31 March 2004	(25,000)	140,000
Gross profit			126,000
Distribution costs and administrative expenses			
[90,000 + 3,000 − 5,000 + 3,000]			91,000
Profit before tax			35,000
Tax			19,000
Profit after tax			16,000
Dividend			7,000
Net profit for the year			9,000

Balance sheet as at 31 March 2004

	£	£
Fixed assets [95,000 + 40,000 + 30,000 − 3,000]		162,000
Current assets		
Stocks	25,000	
Debtors	75,000	
Prepayments	5,000	
Cash and bank	35,000	
	140,000	
Current liabilities		
Trade creditors	54,000	
Accruals	3,000	
Taxation	19,000	
Dividend	7,000	
	83,000	
Net current assets		57,000
Net assets		219,000
Capital and reserves		
Ordinary share capital		80,000
Profit and loss account [130,000 + 9,000]		139,000
		219,000

Chapter 4

E4.1 Candyfloss

(i) Candyfloss cash flow 6 months to 30 June 2005 using the direct method

	£000	£000
Operating cash flow		76.0
Receipts from customers		
Payments		
Flowers suppliers	59.5	
Employees	5.0	
Other overheads		
Rent	4.0	
Operating expenses	7.0	75.5
Cash inflow from operations		0.5
Investing activities		
Purchase of lease	15.0	
Lease fees	1.0	
	16.0	
Purchase of van	14.5	(30.5)
Net cash outflow before financing		(30.0)
Financing		
Loan	3.0	
Issue of shares	18.0	21.0
Net cash outflow for period		(9.0)

(ii) Candyfloss profit and loss account for 6 months to 30 June 2005

	£000	£000	
Sales		84.0	[76.0 + 8.0]
Cost of flowers	54.0		[59.5 + 4.0 − 9.5]
Operating expenses	8.0		[7.0 + 1.0]
Wages	5.0	(67.0)	
Gross profit		17.0	
Overheads			
Rent	2.0		
Depreciation	1.5		[(14.5 − 2.5)/4 × 50% for the half year]
Bad debts	1.5	(5.0)	
Net profit for period		12.0	

(iii) The difference between the cash flow and profit for the period is
− £9,000 − £12,000 = −£21,000

Both cash and profit give an indication of performance.
   The profit of £12,000 may be compared with the cash inflow from operations of £500.

	Profit	Operating Cash	Differences
	£000	**£000**	
Sales/receipts	84.0	76.0	sales 8 not yet paid by customers
Bad debts	(1.5)		sales assumed will never be paid
Flowers	(54.0)	(59.5)	9.5 in stock and 4 not yet paid for
Wages	(5.0)	(5.0)	
Operating expenses	(8.0)	(7.0)	1 not yet paid
Rent	(2.0)	(4.0)	2 rent paid in advance
Depreciation	(1.5)		1.5 not cash
	12.0	0.5	

(iv) A number of items in the profit and loss account are subjective and open to various different methods of valuation:

Bad debts	1.5	different subjective views as to whether customers may pay or not
Stocks	9.5	different valuation methods
Depreciation	1.5	different bases may be used

- additionally cash flow shows how much was paid out for the lease and for the van and what financing was obtained

- cash flow gives a clear picture of the financial performance, looked at alongside the balance sheet which shows the financial position at a point in time

- looking at the profit and loss account from period to period it is difficult to compare performance and with that of similar businesses because of different approaches to asset valuation.

E4.4 Medco

Medco Ltd
Cash flow statement for the year ended 31 December 2004
Reconciliation of operating profit to net cash flow from operating activities

	£
Operating profit	2,500
Depreciation charges	2,000
Loss on sale of fixed assets	500
Increase in stocks	(1,000)
Increase in debtors	(1,000)
Decrease in creditors	(2,000)
Net cash inflow from operating activities	1,000

Cash flow statement

	£
Net cash inflow from operating activities	1,000
Interest paid	(100)
Taxation paid	(400)
Capital expenditure	(10,500)
	(10,000)
Equity dividend paid	(750)
Management of liquid resources	(2,100)
Financing	6,000
Decrease in cash	(6,850)

Reconciliation of net cash flow to movement in net debt/funds

	£
Decrease in cash for the period	(6,850)
Cash inflow from increase in loans	(1,000)
Change in net debt	(7,850)
Net funds 1 January 2004	2,000
Net debt 31 December 2004	(5,850)

Note 1 to the cash flow statement – gross cash flows

	£	£
Returns on investments and servicing of finance		
Interest paid		(100)
Capital expenditure		
Payments to acquire tangible fixed assets	(12,500)	
Receipts from sales of tangible fixed assets	2,000	
		(10,500)
Financing		
Issue of ordinary shares	5,000	
Increase in loans	1,000	
		6,000

Note 2 to the cash flow statement – analysis of change in net debt

	At 1 Jan 2004	Cash flows	At 31 Dec 2004
	£	£	£
Cash and bank	5,000	(2,850)	2,150
Overdraft	(2,000)	(4,000)	(6,000)
Loans	(1,000)	(1,000)	(2,000)
Total	2,000	(7,850)	(5,850)

E4.6 Victoria

(i)

(a)

	£000
Increase in profit and loss account 2004 over 2003 from balance sheet	500
Add tax	320
Add dividends	480
Therefore profit before tax is	1,300

(b)

	£000
Profit before tax	1,300
Add debenture interest	100
Therefore operating profit is	1,400

(ii)

Victoria plc
Cash flow statement for the year ended 30 June 2004
Reconciliation of operating profit to net cash flow from operating activities

	£000
Operating profit	1,400
Depreciation	200
Increase in stocks	(1,400)
Increase in debtors	(680)
Decrease in creditors	(200)
Net cash outflow from operating activities	(680)

Cash flow statement

	£000
Net cash outflow from operating activities	(680)
Interest paid	(100)
Taxation paid (in respect of year 2003)	(300)
Capital expenditure	(2,100)
	(3,180)
Equity dividend paid	(360)
Financing: issue of ordinary shares	2,740
Decrease in cash	(800)

Note 2 to the cash flow statement – analysis of change in net debt

	At 30 Jun 2003 £000	Cash flows £000	At 30 Jun 2004 £000
Cash and bank	200	(200)	–
Overdraft	–	(600)	(600)
Debentures	(1,000)	–	(1,000)
Total	(800)	(800)	(1,600)

E4.7 Sparklers

Sparklers plc
Cash flow statement for the year ended 31 October 2004
Reconciliation of operating profit to net cash flow from operating activities

	£m
Operating profit	41.28
Depreciation charges	10.10
Loss on sale of fixed assets	1.40
Increase in stocks	(20.00)
Increase in debtors	(36.40)
Increase in creditors	8.40
Net cash inflow from operating activities	4.78

Cash flow statement

	£m
Net cash inflow from operating activities	4.78
Returns on investments and servicing of finance (note 1)	(0.48)
Taxation – corporation tax paid	(6.40)
Capital expenditure (note 1)	(21.60)
	(23.70)
Dividends paid	(10.20)
	(33.90)
Financing (note 1)	0.30
Decrease in cash	(33.60)

Reconciliation of net cash flow to movement in net debt (note 2)

	£m
Decrease in cash for the period	(33.60)
Cash flow from increase in debenture	(0.30)
Change in net debt	(33.90)
Net debt 1 November 2003	–
Net debt 31 October 2004	(33.90)

Note 1 to the cash flow statement – gross cash flows

	£m	£m
Returns on investments and servicing of finance		
Interest received	0.08	
Interest paid	(0.56)	
		(0.48)
Capital expenditure		
Payments to acquire tangible fixed assets	(23.60)	
Receipts from sales of tangible fixed assets	2.00	
		(21.60)

Financing

Increase in debentures   0.30

Note 2 to the cash flow statement – analysis of change in net debt

	At 1 Nov 2003 £m	Cash flows £m	At 31 Oct 2004 £m
Cash and bank	1.20	(1.20)	–
Overdraft	–	(32.40)	(32.40)
Debentures	(1.20)	(0.30)	(1.50)
Total	–	(33.90)	(33.90)

Working

	£m	£m
Depreciation		
Depreciation 31 October 2004		21.50
Depreciation at 31 October 2003	19.00	
Depreciation on assets sold in 2004	(7.60)	(11.40)
Charge for the year 2004		10.10
Loss on sale of assets		
Proceeds on sale		2.00
Net book value: cost	11.00	
depreciation	(7.60)	(3.40)
Loss on sale		(1.40)

Dividends paid

Dividends payable at 31 October 2003	6.00
Dividends declared for 2004: preference	0.20
ordinary interim	4.00
ordinary final	12.00
	22.20
Less dividends payable at 31 October 2004	12.00
Dividends paid during 2004	10.20

Purchase of fixed assets

	£m	£m
Fixed assets balance 31 October 2004		47.80
Fixed assets balance 31 October 2003	35.20	
Cost of fixed assets sold	(11.00)	(24.20)
Fixed assets purchased		23.60

You should refer to the relevant sections in Chapter 4 to check your assessment of the reasons for the increased overdraft.

Chapter 5

E5.1 Priory

(i) Net debt to equity

	2004	2005	2006
Net debt	100	250	800
Equity	300	500	800
Debt/equity (%)	33%	50%	100%

(ii) Long-term loans to equity and long-term loans

	2004	2005	2006
Long-term loans	200	200	600
Equity + long-term loans	500	700	1,400
Gearing (%)	40%	29%	43%

E5.2 Freshco

Profitability ratios for Freshco plc for 2005 and the comparative ratios for 2004

Gross margin, GM

$$\text{Gross margin \% 2005} = \frac{\text{gross margin}}{\text{sales}} = \frac{£204 \times 100\%}{£894} = 22.8\%$$

$$\text{Gross margin \% 2004} = \frac{£166 \times 100\%}{£747} = 22.2\%$$

Profit before interest and tax, PBIT (or operating profit)

$$\text{PBIT \% 2005} = \frac{\text{operating profit}}{\text{sales}} = \frac{£103 \times 100\%}{£894} = 11.5\%$$

$$\text{PBIT \% 2004} = \frac{£87 \times 100\%}{£747} = 11.6\%$$

Net profit, PAT (return on sales, ROS)

$$\text{PAT \% 2005} = \frac{\text{net profit}}{\text{sales}} = \frac{£56 \times 100\%}{£894} = 6.3\%$$

$$\text{PAT \% 2004} = \frac{£54 \times 100\%}{£747} = 7.2\%$$

Return on capital employed, ROCE (return on investment, ROI)

$$\text{ROCE \% 2005} = \frac{\text{operating profit}}{\substack{\text{total assets} - \text{current liabilities} \\ \text{(average capital employed)}}} = \frac{£103 \times 100\%}{(£233 \times £233)/2} = \frac{£103 \times 100\%}{£233} = 44.2\%$$

$$\text{ROCE \% 2004} = \frac{\pounds 87 \times 100\%}{(\pounds 233 + \pounds 219)/2} = \frac{\pounds 87 \times 100\%}{\pounds 226} = 38.5\%$$

Return on equity, ROE

$$\text{ROE \% 2005} = \frac{\text{PAT}}{\text{equity}} = \frac{\pounds 56 \times 100\%}{\pounds 213} = 26.3\%$$

$$\text{ROE \% 2004} = \frac{\pounds 54 \times 100\%}{\pounds 166} = 32.5\%$$

Capital turnover

$$\text{Capital turnover 2005} = \frac{\text{sales}}{\text{average capital employed in year}} = \frac{\pounds 894}{\pounds 233} = 3.8 \text{ times}$$

$$\text{Capital turnover 2004} = \frac{\pounds 747}{\pounds 226} = 3.3 \text{ times}$$

Report on the profitability of Freshco plc

Sales for the year 2005 increased by 19.7% over the previous year, but it is not clear whether from increased volumes, new products, or higher selling prices.

Gross margin improved by 0.6% to 22.8% of sales, possibly from increased selling prices and/or from lower costs of production.

Operating profit dropped by 0.1% to 11.5% of sales despite the improvement in gross margin, because of higher levels of distribution costs and administrative expenses.

ROCE improved from 38.5% to 44.2%, indicating a more effective use of funds by Freshco.

Return on equity dropped by 6.2% to 26.3%. This was because profit after tax remained fairly static but equity was increased through an issue of shares and increases in general reserves and retained earnings.

Capital turnover for 2005 increased to 3.8 times from 3.3 in 2004, reflecting the significant increases in sales levels in 2005 over 2004.

E5.4 Freshco

Liquidity ratios for Freshco plc for 2005 and the comparative ratios for 2004

Current ratio

$$\text{Current ratio 2005} = \frac{\text{current assets}}{\text{current liabilities}} = \frac{\pounds 208}{\pounds 121} = 1.7 \text{ times}$$

$$\text{Current ratio 2004} = \frac{\pounds 191}{\pounds 107} = 1.8 \text{ times}$$

Acid test (quick ratio)

$$\text{Quick ratio 2005} = \frac{\text{current assets} - \text{stocks}}{\text{current liabilities}} = \frac{\pounds 208 - \pounds 124}{\pounds 121} = 0.7 \text{ times}$$

$$\text{Quick ratio 2004} = \frac{\pounds 191 - \pounds 100}{\pounds 107} = 0.8 \text{ times}$$

Defensive interval

$$\text{Defensive interval 2005} = \frac{\text{quick assets}}{\text{average daily cash from operation}} = \frac{£208 - £124}{(£80 + £894 - £70)/365} = 34 \text{ days}$$

$$\text{Defensive interval 2004} = \frac{£191 - £100}{(£60 + £747 - £80)/365} = 46 \text{ days}$$

Report on the liquidity of Freshco plc

The current ratio and the quick ratio have both dropped slightly to 1.7 times and 0.7 times respectively. However, the defensive interval has dropped significantly from 46 days to 34 days at which level the company could potentially survive if there were no further cash inflows.

Net cash flow from operations improved from £7m in 2004 to £8.1m in 2005. Investments in fixed assets were at lower levels in 2005 and matched by a reduction in long-term financing (debentures).

E5.8 Laurel

(i)

Profitability ratios for Hardy plc for 2005 and the comparative ratios for 2004 and 2003

Gross margin, GM

$$\text{Gross margin \% 2005} = \frac{\text{gross margin}}{\text{sales}} = \frac{£161 \times 100\%}{£456} = 35.3\%$$

$$\text{Gross margin \% 2004} = \frac{£168 \times 100\%}{£491} = 34.2\%$$

$$\text{Gross margin \% 2003} = \frac{£142 \times 100\%}{£420} = 34.0\%$$

Profit before interest and tax, PBIT (or operating profit)

$$\text{PBIT \% 2005} = \frac{\text{operating profit}}{\text{sales}} = \frac{£52 \times 100\%}{£456} = 11.4\%$$

$$\text{PBIT \% 2004} = \frac{£61 \times 100\%}{£491} = 12.4\%$$

$$\text{PBIT \% 2003} = \frac{£50 \times 100\%}{£420} = 11.9\%$$

Net profit, PAT (return on sales, ROS)

$$\text{PAT \% 2005} = \frac{\text{net profit}}{\text{sales}} = \frac{£20 \times 100\%}{£456} = 4.4\%$$

$$\text{PAT \% 2004} = \frac{£28 \times 100\%}{£491} = 5.7\%$$

$$\text{PAT \% 2003} = \frac{£25 \times 100\%}{£420} = 6.0\%$$

Return on capital employed, ROCE (return on investment, ROI)

$$\text{ROCE \% 2005} = \frac{\text{operating profit}}{\text{total assets} - \text{current liabilities}} = \frac{£52 \times 100\%}{(£284 + £292)/2} = \frac{£52 \times 100\%}{£288} = 18.1\%$$

$$\text{ROCE \% 2004} = \frac{£61 \times 100\%}{(£237 + £284)/2} = \frac{£61 \times 100\%}{£260.5} = 23.4\%$$

ROCE % 2003 is not available because we do not have the capital employed figure for 31 March 2002.

Return on equity, ROE

$$\text{ROE \% 2005} = \frac{\text{PAT}}{\text{equity}} = \frac{£20 \times 100\%}{£223} = 9.0\%$$

$$\text{ROE \% 2004} = \frac{£28 \times 100\%}{£215} = 13.0\%$$

$$\text{ROE \% 2003} = \frac{£25 \times 100\%}{£200} = 12.5\%$$

Capital turnover

$$\text{Capital turnover 2005} = \frac{\text{sales}}{\text{average capital employed in year}} = \frac{£456}{£288} = 1.6 \text{ times}$$

$$\text{Capital turnover 2004} = \frac{£491}{£260.5} = 1.9 \text{ times}$$

Capital turnover 2003 is not available because we do not have the capital employed figure for 31 March 2002.

Report on the profitability of Hardy plc

Sales for the year 2005 were 7.1% lower than sales in 2004, which were 16.9% above 2003. It is not clear whether these sales reductions were from lower volumes, fewer products, or changes in selling prices.

Gross margin improved from 34.0% in 2003 to 34.2% in 2004 to 35.3% in 2005, possibly from increased selling prices and/or from lower costs of production.

Operating profit to sales increased from 11.9% in 2003 to 12.4% in 2004 but then fell to 11.4% in 2005, despite the improvement in gross margin, because of higher levels of distribution costs and administrative expenses.

ROCE dropped from 23.4% to 18.1%, reflecting the lower level of operating profit. Return on equity increased from 12.5% in 1998 to 13.0% in 2004 but then fell sharply in 2005 to 9.0%. This was because of the large fall in profit after tax in 2005.

Capital turnover for 2005 was reduced from 1.9 times in 2004 to 1.6 in 2005, reflecting the fall in sales levels in 2005 over 2004.

Efficiency ratios for Hardy plc for 2005 and the comparative ratios for 2004 and 2003

Debtor days

$$\text{Debtor days 2005} = \frac{\text{trade debtors} \times 365}{\text{sales}} = \frac{£80 \times 365}{£456} = 64 \text{ days}$$

$$\text{Debtor days 2004} = \frac{£70 \times 365}{£491} = 52 \text{ days}$$

$$\text{Debtor days 2003} = \frac{£53 \times 365}{£420} = 46 \text{ days}$$

Creditor days

$$\text{Creditor days 2005} = \frac{\text{trade creditors} \times 365}{\text{cost of sales}} = \frac{£38 \times 365}{£295} = 47 \text{ days}$$

$$\text{Creditor days 2004} = \frac{£38 \times 365}{£323} = 43 \text{ days}$$

$$\text{Creditor days 2003} = \frac{£26 \times 365}{£277} = 34 \text{ days}$$

Stock days (stock turnover)

$$\text{Stock days 2005} = \frac{\text{stock value}}{\text{average daily cost of sales in period}} = \frac{£147}{£295/365} = 182 \text{ days (26.0 weeks)}$$

$$\text{Stock days 2004} = \frac{£152}{£323/365} = 172 \text{ days (24.5 weeks)}$$

$$\text{Stock days 2003} = \frac{£118}{£277/365} = 155 \text{ days (22.2 weeks)}$$

Operating cycle days

Operating cycle 2005 = stock days + debtor days − creditor days = 182 + 64 − 47 = 199 days
Operating cycle 2004 = 172 + 52 − 43 = 181 days
Operating cycle 2003 = 155 + 46 − 34 = 167 days

Operating cycle %

$$\text{Operating cycle \% 2005} = \frac{\text{working capital requirement}}{\text{sales}}$$

$$= \frac{(£147 + £80 - £38) \times 100\%}{£456} = 41.4\%$$

$$\text{Operating cycle \% 2004} = \frac{(£152 + £70 - £38) \times 100\%}{£491} = 37.5\%$$

$$\text{Operating cycle \% 2003} = \frac{(£118 + £53 - £26)}{£420} = 34.5\%$$

Asset turnover

Asset turnover 2005 $= \dfrac{\text{sales}}{\text{total assets}} = \dfrac{£456}{£385} = 1.18$ times

Asset turnover 2004 $= \dfrac{£491}{£374} = 1.31$ times

Asset turnover 2003 $= \dfrac{£420}{£303} = 1.39$ times

Report on the working capital performance of Hardy plc

Average customer settlement days worsened successively over the years 2003, 2004 and 2005 from 46 to 52 to 64 days. This was partly mitigated by some improvement in the average creditors settlement period which increased from 34 to 43 to 47 days over the same period. The average stock turnover period worsened from 155 to 172 to 182 days over 2003, 2004, and 2005. Therefore, mainly because of the poor debt collection performance and increasingly high stock levels, the operating cycle worsened from 167 days in 2003 to 181 days in 2004 and to 199 days in 2005 (operating cycle 34.5% to 37.5% to 41.4%). Asset turnover reduced from 1.39 to 1.31 times from 2003 to 2004 and then to 1.18 in 2005, reflecting the degree to which sales had dropped despite increasing levels of total assets.

Liquidity ratios for Hardy plc for 2005 and the comparative ratios for 2004 and 2003

Current ratio

Current ratio 2005 $= \dfrac{\text{current assets}}{\text{current liabilities}} = \dfrac{£253}{£93} = 2.7$ times

Current ratio 2004 $= \dfrac{£251}{£90} = 2.8$ times

Current ratio 2003 $= \dfrac{£197}{£66} = 3.0$ times

Acid test (quick ratio)

Quick ratio 2005 $= \dfrac{\text{current assets} - \text{stocks}}{\text{current liabilities}} = \dfrac{£253 - £147}{£93} = 1.1$ times

Quick ratio 2004 $= \dfrac{£251 - £152}{£90} = 1.1$ times

Quick ratio 2003 $= \dfrac{£197 - £118}{£66} = 1.2$ times

Defensive interval

Defensive interval 2005 $= \dfrac{\text{quick assets}}{\text{average daily cash from operations}}$

$= \dfrac{£253 - £147}{(£70 + £456 - £80)/365} = 87$ days

Defensive interval 2004 $= \dfrac{£251 - £152}{(£53 + £491 - £70)/365} = 76$ days

The defensive interval for 2003 is not available because we do not have the trade debtors figure for 31 March 2002.

Report on the liquidity of Hardy plc

The current ratio and the quick ratio have both dropped over the 3 years from 3.0 to 2.7 times, and 1.2 times to 1.1 times respectively. The defensive interval has increased from 76 days to 87 days at which level the company could potentially survive if there were no further cash inflows.

(ii) There are a number of areas that require further investigation. The following five ratios may be particularly useful to assist this investigation:

- Return on capital employed, ROCE
- Debtor days
- Creditor days
- Stock days
- Current ratio.

(iii) The relevant information has not been provided to enable the following investment ratios to be calculated for Hardy plc, which would have improved the analysis of Hardy plc's performance:

Earnings per share, eps

Cannot be calculated because we do not have details of the number of ordinary shares in issue.

Dividend per share

Cannot be calculated because we do not have details of the number of ordinary shares in issue.

Dividend cover

Cannot be calculated because we have not been able to calculate earnings per share, eps, and dividend per share.

Dividend yield %

Cannot be calculated because we have not been able to calculate dividend per share, and we do not have the market prices of the company's shares.

Price/earnings ratio, P/E

Cannot be calculated because we have not been able to calculate earnings per share, and we do not have the market prices of the company's shares.

Capital expenditure to sales %

Cannot be calculated because we do not have details of capital expenditure.

Capital expenditure to gross fixed assets %

Cannot be calculated because we do not have details of capital expenditure.

Chapter 6

E6.11 Guinness

Guinness plc five-year profit and loss account

Horizontal analysis

	Year 5	Year 4	Year 3	Year 2	Year 1
Turnover	108.4	107.3	107.5	106.9	100.0
Gross profit	93.9	92.2	93.5	91.7	100.0
Other investment income	(470.8)	(195.8)	(370.8)	200.0	100.0
Profit before interest and tax (operating profit)	107.5	99.1	104.6	89.1	100.0
Net interest	48.5	55.9	63.7	92.2	100.0
Profit before tax	122.6	110.2	115.1	88.3	100.0
Tax on profit on ordinary activities	107.0	103.7	100.4	102.1	100.0
Profit on ordinary activities after tax	129.5	113.0	121.5	82.3	100.0
Minority interests	106.9	103.4	106.9	75.9	100.0
Profit for the financial year	130.7	113.5	122.3	82.6	100.0
Dividends	124.5	127.4	117.7	108.9	100.0
Retained profit	135.9	102.1	126.1	61.0	100.0
Earnings per share	124.9	104.6	113.2	81.5	100.0
Interest cover	220.4	177.6	163.3	95.9	100.0
Dividend cover	95.7	87.0	100.0	78.3	100.0

Guinness plc five-year profit and loss account

Vertical analysis

	Year 5	Year 4	Year 3	Year 2	Year 1
Turnover	100.0	100.0	100.0	100.0	100.0
Gross profit	20.3	20.1	20.4	20.1	23.4
Other investment income	2.4	1.0	1.9	(1.0)	(0.6)
Profit before interest and tax (operating profit)	22.7	21.1	22.3	19.1	22.9
Net interest	(2.1)	(2.4)	(2.8)	(4.0)	(4.7)
Profit before tax	20.6	18.7	19.5	15.1	18.2
Tax on profit on ordinary activities	(5.5)	(5.4)	(5.2)	(5.3)	(5.5)
Profit on ordinary activities after tax	15.1	13.4	14.3	9.8	12.7
Minority interests	(0.7)	(0.6)	(0.7)	(0.5)	(0.7)
Profit for the financial year	14.5	12.7	13.7	9.3	12.0
Dividends	(6.2)	(6.5)	(5.9)	(5.5)	(5.4)
Retained profit	8.2	6.3	7.7	3.8	6.6

Sales

The horizontal analysis shows an increase in sales of 8.4% over the five years, most of which was gained from year two over year one. Since year two, sales have not increased materially.

Gross profit

The horizontal analysis shows a drop in gross profit of 6.1% of sales over the five years. The vertical analysis shows that gross profit at 23.4% of sales in year one has dropped to 20.3% of sales in year five. The group may have been suffering from increased competition as its brands failed to continue to maintain their profitability.

Operating profit

The horizontal analysis shows an increase in operating profit of 7.5% of sales over the five years, despite the drop in gross profit levels. This is due to the extremely large gains in investment income. The vertical analysis shows that operating profit has been maintained fairly level over the five years at 22.9% of sales in year one to 22.7% of sales in year five.

Interest payable

The horizontal analysis shows a drop in interest payable by year five to less than half the level in year one. The vertical analysis bears this out, showing interest payable of 2.1% of sales in year five compared with 4.7% of sales in year one. The group's borrowings were probably significantly reduced as little expansion has taken place, indicated by a reliance on mature markets and a lack of new ideas. The increased interest cover confirms the loan repayments.

Profit for the financial year

The horizontal analysis reflects a small increase in profit levels from 12.0% of sales in year one to 14.5% of sales in year five. The vertical analysis shows a steady increase in profit over the years except for a drop in year two, because of the negative investment income and high interest payments in that year.

Dividends

The level of dividends has been up and down over the years but year five is slightly higher at 6.2% of sales than year one which was 5.4% of sales, as shown in the vertical analysis. Dividend cover has been maintained at around two times.

Earnings per share

The horizontal analysis shows an increase of almost 25% in earnings per share in year five compared with year one, having recovered from a dip in earnings in year four.

Chapter 7

E7.1 Share options

Past governments have made employer/employee share option schemes tax efficient and therefore schemes are now very common amongst plcs.

Many plcs have found that their share prices react to specific management policies and decisions, for example takeovers and disposals of businesses. Users of financial information can assess these decisions, knowing of the options awarded to the directors.

Many plcs have found that they can only keep/attract high calibre managers by including share options in their remuneration packages.

Investing institutions demand more and more information regarding directors' remuneration. This can influence their basic hold/buy/sell decisions. The financial press frequently includes criticism of specific companies.

E7.2 Perks

Directors do not necessarily own the company they work for; the shareholders do.

Any monies (expenses) that a director takes from the company will affect the annual profit.

Annual dividends are paid from the annual profits. The shareholders approve the accounts at the AGM, which includes remuneration of the directors.

If the directors hide information regarding their remuneration and benefits from the shareholders, then that part of the accounts may not show a true and fair view of the situation.

E7.3 Contracts

Before the new corporate governance code was introduced, shareholders found that their directors had powers that were increasing, especially regarding length of contract and compensation for loss of office.

The Cadbury and Greenbury committees recommended that directors' contracts should be no longer than (first) three years (Cadbury) and then one year (Greenbury). These committees had looked at the evidence presented to them. Hampel (1998) provided that the contracts should be one year or less.

The financial press regularly comments on the compensation paid to a director, where company performance has been acknowledged to be poor. There is always reference to the length of outstanding directors' contracts.

Shareholders can decide whether to hold/buy/sell shares if they have advance information on the type of contracts being awarded to the executive directors of their company.

UK financial institutions have also become pro-active regarding the length of directors' contracts issue. They have noted that in the past too many highly paid directors were awarding themselves contracts in which compensation for loss of office was very expensive to pay. Currently it often costs companies potentially over £1m to buy out a chief executive from just a one-year contract.

E7.7 Tomkins

Equity shareholders are the owners of the company, and the level of their dividends usually varies with levels of profits earned by the company.

Directors are appointed by the shareholders, and remunerated for their efforts. Major multinational companies are difficult to manage successfully over a long period of time. The remuneration of directors should reflect that difficulty.

The information that has been given about Tomkins plc shows that there was an executive director who earned a basic salary of just below £1 million a year, an amount which most shareholders would like to see disclosed in the accounts and discussed at the AGM.

The bonus of £443,000 would also have generated some interest amongst the institutions and individual shareholders. Institutions (and the UK Government) are seen to put pressure on directors if they feel pay awards are excessive.

The consultancy agreement for a non-executive director may also have been of interest to the various users of the notes to the accounts.

Chapter 8

E8.1 Bluebell Woods

(i) Absorption costing

$$\text{Overhead absorption rate} = \frac{\text{budgeted fixed production cost}}{\text{budgeted units of production}} = \frac{£3,526}{4,300} = £0.82 \text{ per unit}$$

		£
Selling price per unit		5.84

Total production costs per unit

		£
Direct material	[£0.85 × 2 kg]	1.70
Direct labour	[42 × £4.20/60]	2.94
Variable production overhead		0.12
Variable production cost		4.76
Fixed production overhead		0.82 see above
Full production cost per unit		5.58

Four-week standard profit statement

		£
Sales	[4,300 × £5.84]	25,112
Cost of sales		
Direct material	[4,300 × £1.70]	7,310
Direct labour	[4,300 × £2.94]	12,642
Variable production overhead	[4,300 × £0.12]	516
Fixed production overhead	[4,300 × £0.82]	3,526
		23,994
Profit for the period		1,118

(ii) Marginal costing

		£
Selling price per unit		5.84

Variable production costs per unit

		£
Direct material	[£0.85 × 2 kg]	1.70
Direct labour	[42 × £4.20/60]	2.94
Variable production overhead		0.12
Variable production cost		4.76

Four-week standard profit statement

		£
Sales	[4,300 × £5.84]	25,112
Variable cost of sales	[4,300 × £4.76]	20,468
Contribution		4,644
Fixed production overhead		3,526
Profit for the period		1,118

E8.4 Rocky

Profit and loss accounts for July and August on an absorption costing basis

	Per unit £	July Units	July £	July £	August Units	August £	August £
Sales	10.00	4,400		44,000	5,000		50,000
Production costs:							
Variable	7.50	5,300	39,750		4,400	33,000	
Fixed	0.50	5,300	2,650		4,400	2,200	
		5,300	42,400		4,400	35,200	
Opening stock	8.00	0	0		900	7,200	
		5,300	42,400		4,400	35,200	
Closing stock	8.00	900	7,200		300	2,400	
Cost of sales	8.00	4,400		35,200	5,000		40,000
Gross profit	2.00	4,400		8,800	5,000		10,000
Selling/ administrative costs			7,200			7,200	
(Under)/over absorption of fixed production costs	0.50		350			800	
				7,550			8,000
Net profit				1,250			2,000

E8.5 Rocky

Profit and loss accounts for July and August on a marginal costing basis

	Per unit £	July Units	£	£	August Units	£	£
Sales	10.00	4,400		44,000	5,000		50,000
Production costs:							
Variable	7.50	5,300	39,750		4,400	33,000	
Opening stock	7.50	0	0		900	6,750	
		5,300	39,750		4,400	33,000	
Closing stock	7.50	900	6,750		300	2,250	
Marginal cost of sales	7.50	4,400		33,000	5,000		37,500
Contribution	2.50	4,400		11,000	5,000		12,500
Fixed costs							
Production costs			3,000			3,000	
Selling/administrative costs			7,200	10,200		7,200	10,200
Net profit				800			2,300

Chapter 9

9.1 Profit

Contribution for January = sales − variable costs
= £320,000 − £240,000
= £80,000

$$\text{Contribution to sales ratio \%} = \frac{£80,000 \times 100\%}{£320,000} = 25\%$$

$$\text{£ sales value at break-even point} = \frac{\text{fixed costs}}{\text{contribution to sales ratio \%}}$$

£240,000 = fixed costs/25%
Fixed costs = £60,000
Profit for January = contribution − fixed costs
= £80,000 − £60,000
= £20,000

E9.2 Break-even

Contribution for January = profit + fixed costs
= £10,000 + £30,000
= £40,000

$$\text{Contribution to sales ratio \%} = \frac{£40,000 \times 100\%}{£120,000} = 33.3\%$$

$$\textbf{£ sales value at break-even point} = \frac{\text{fixed costs}}{\text{contribution to sales ratio \%}}$$

$$= \pounds30{,}000/33.3\%$$
$$= \pounds90{,}000$$

E9.3 Break-even and profit

Selling price   = £15
Marginal cost   = £9
Contribution   = £6

Contribution to sales ratio % $= \dfrac{\pounds6 \times 100\%}{\pounds15} = 40\%$

£ sales value at break-even point $= \dfrac{\text{fixed costs}}{\text{contribution to sales ratio \%}}$

$$= \pounds30{,}000/40\%$$
$$= \pounds75{,}000$$

Profit for January   = contribution − fixed costs
$$= (40\% \times \pounds120{,}000) - \pounds30{,}000$$
$$= \pounds48{,}000 - \pounds30{,}000$$
$$= \pounds18{,}000$$

E9.4 Seivad

(i)
Unit contribution   = selling price − variable costs
$$= \pounds30 - (\pounds10 + \pounds7 + \pounds8)$$
$$= \pounds5$$
Planned contribution for 2005 $= 20{,}000 \times \pounds5$
$$= \pounds100{,}000$$

(ii)
Profit   = contribution − fixed costs
Planned profit for 2005 $= \pounds100{,}000 - \pounds70{,}000$
$$= \pounds30{,}000$$

(iii)
Planned sales for 2005 $= 20{,}000 \times \pounds30$
$$= \pounds600{,}000$$
Planned contribution for 2005 $= \pounds100{,}000$

Contribution to sales ratio % $= \dfrac{\pounds100{,}000}{\pounds600{,}000} \times 100\% = 16.67\%$

£ sales value at break-even point $= \dfrac{\text{fixed costs}}{\text{contribution to sales ratio \%}}$

$$= \pounds70{,}000/16.67\%$$
$$= \pounds419{,}916$$

(iv)

Number of units at break-even point	= £419,916/£30
	= 13,998 units

(It should be noted that the correct break-even point is £420,000 sales and 14,000 units – £419,916 and 13,998 units are the result of using a rounded-up contribution ratio of 16.67%.)

(v)

Margin of safety (sales value)	= planned sales value – break-even sales value
	= £600,000 – £419,916
	= £180,084

(vi)

Margin of safety (sales units)	= planned sales units – break-even sales units
	= 20,000 – 13,998
	= 6,002 units

(vii)

Revised profit for 2005	= (20,000 × unit contribution) – (£70,000 + 20%)
(£30,000 + 10%)	= (20,000 × unit contribution) – (£70,000 + 20%)
(20,000 × unit contribution)	= (£30,000 + 10%) + (£70,000 + 20%)
	= £33,000 + £84,000
	= £117,000
Unit contribution	$= \dfrac{£117,000}{20,000}$
	= £5.85
Selling price	= unit contribution + unit variable costs
	= £5.85 + £25
	= £30.85

E9.8 Abem

(i) Cost per unit using conventional methods:

	Product A	Product B	Product C
	£	£	£
Direct labour ($\frac{1}{2}$, $1\frac{1}{2}$, 1 hours × £8)	4.00	12.00	8.00
Direct materials	20.00	10.00	25.00
Prime cost	24.00	22.00	33.00
Overhead ($1\frac{1}{2}$, 1, 3 hours × £25)	37.50	25.00	75.00
Cost per unit	61.50	47.00	108.00

(ii) Total overhead may be calculated from multiplying total machine hours by the overhead absorption rate per machine hour.

Total machine hours (750 × $1\frac{1}{2}$) [Product A] + (1,975 × 1) [Product B] + (7,900 × 3) [Product C]
= 26,800 hours. Total overhead is therefore (26,800 × £25) = £670,000.

This may be apportioned to activities using the percentages given:

Activity	%	Apportionment (£)	Cost driver
Set-ups	35	234,500	Set-ups
Machining	20	134,000	Machine hours
Materials handling	15	100,500	Movements
Inspection	30	201,000	Inspections
		670,000	

The relevant cost driver for each activity is taken from the question.

$$\text{Absorption rate per set-up} = \frac{\text{Budgeted set-up cost}}{\text{Number of set-ups}} = \frac{£234,500}{670} = £350$$

$$\text{Absorption rate per machine hour} = \frac{\text{Budgeted machine cost}}{\text{Number of machine hours}} = \frac{£134,000}{26,800} = £5$$

$$\text{Absorption rate per movement} = \frac{\text{Budgeted handling cost}}{\text{Number of movements}} = \frac{£100,500}{120} = £837.50$$

$$\text{Absorption rate per inspection} = \frac{\text{Budgeted inspection cost}}{\text{Number of inspections}} = \frac{£201,000}{1,000} = £201$$

	Product A £	Product B £	Product C £
Set-up costs:			
70, 120, 480 set-ups × £350	24,500	42,000	168,000
divided by 750, 1,975, 7,900 units	32.67	21.27	21.27
Machine costs: $1\frac{1}{2}$, 1, 3 hours × £5	7.50	5.00	15.00
Materials handling costs:			
10, 20, 90 movements × £837.50	8,375	16,750	75,375
divided by 750, 1,975, 7,900 units	11.17	8.48	9.54
Inspection costs:			
150, 180, 670 inspections × £201	30,150	36,180	134,670
divided by 750, 1,975, 7,900 units	40.20	18.32	17.05

Cost per unit	Product A £	Product B £	Product C £
Prime cost (from (i))	24.00	22.00	33.00
Overhead: Set-up cost	32.67	21.27	21.27
Machine cost	7.50	5.00	15.00
Handling cost	11.17	8.48	9.54
Inspection cost	40.20	18.32	17.05
Cost per unit	115.54	75.07	95.86

(iii) Comparative cost per unit	Product A £	Product B £	Product C £
Using machine hour rate	61.50	47.00	108.00
Using ABC	115.54	75.07	95.86
Difference	54.04	28.07	(12.14)

These are very significant differences. If the cost driver information is reasonably accurate, then the existing absorption rate causes the high-volume product (C) to heavily subsidise the other two, which have lower volumes. Product costs may therefore be inaccurate, with implications for stock valuation and profit. Also, to the extent that they are based on cost, selling prices may be too low for A and B, while being too high for C. A and B may thus be selling at a loss, whereas C's sales volume may be depressed by an artificially high price.

Chapter 10

E10.1 Eifion

(i)

A limiting factor is anything which limits the activity of a business. Examples of limiting factors, or key factors, are a shortage of supply of a resource or a restriction on sales demand at a particular price. A business should seek to optimise the benefit it obtains from the limiting factor. If a company has a short-term capacity constraint then its product mix should be based on maximising its contribution per limiting factor.

(ii)

Existing capacity	$= (12,000 \times 7) + (24,000 \times 3.5)$
	$= \underline{168,000 \text{ machine hours}}$
Fixed cost per unit	$= £1,680,000/168,000$
	$= \underline{£10 \text{ per machine hour}}$

	A £	B £
Total cost per unit	93.50	126.00
Fixed cost per unit	70.00 (7 × £10)	35.00 (3.5 × £10)
Variable cost per unit	23.50	91.00
Selling price per unit	107.50	175.00
Contribution per unit	84.00	84.00
Contribution per machine hour	12.00 (£84/7)	24.00 (£84/3.5)

Machine hours are fully utilised at the existing production level. Therefore, demand is in excess of current capacity. Profits will be maximised by concentrating on B, since this yields the larger contribution per machine hour. In order to meet the maximum demand for B, 105,000 (30,000 × 3.5) machine hours will be required. The remaining capacity of 63,000 hours (168,000 – 105,000) should be allocated to producing 9,000 (63,000/7) units of A. The total profit for this output level is as follows:

		£
A (9,000 × £84 contribution per unit)	=	756,000
B (30,000 × £84 contribution per unit)	=	2,520,000
		3,276,000
less Fixed costs		1,680,000
Profit		1,596,000

(iii)

You should refer to the relevant section in Chapter 10 to check on the limitations of cost-plus pricing.

In practice, one solution to the problems of cost-plus pricing is to estimate likely demand (which should be known from past experience in the case of established products) and calculate an absorption rate on this assumed volume of output. Provided that actual volume equals or exceeds the estimated volume of sales, the company will achieve (or exceed) its target profit.

Another solution is to set a price on the basis of a budgeted production volume and allow stocks to build up for a time if demand is below production volume at this price. A price review can be made when demand conditions are known better, and either of the following actions could be taken.

A price reduction could be made to stimulate demand if this seems appropriate.

Production volumes could be reduced and prices raised if necessary in recognition of the lack of demand for the product at the original budgeted volumes.

E10.2 Phil Atterley

(i)

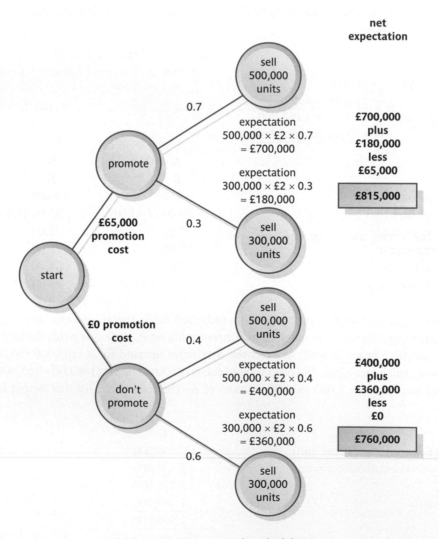

Phil Atterley Ltd promotion decision tree

The branch of the tree indicating that Phil Atterley Ltd should promote is labelled with the cost of that activity £65,000.

The branch of the tree indicating that Phil Atterley Ltd should not promote is labelled with the cost of that activity £0.

The probabilities of occurrences are labelled on the branches following the decision taken to promote, being 0.7 (70%) for sales of 500,000 units and 0.3 (30%) for sales of 300,000 units.

Similarly, the same thing is done on the branches following the decision not to promote, being 0.4 (40%) for sales of 500,000 units and 0.6 (60%) for sales of 300,000 units.

(ii)

The expectations of contributions are then calculated by multiplying sales volumes by unit contribution and probability.

The contribution expectation following no promotion is:

£400,000 + £360,000 = £760,000

The contribution expectation following the promotion is:

£700,000 + £180,000 = £880,000

but, the promotion option also involves a cost of £65,000 and so the net expectation is £815,000.

The £815,000 net expectation following the promotion may be compared with the net expectation from not promoting of £760,000.

On the above basis we can recommend to Stan to advise the company to promote the sales of its new product.

(iii)

There are a number of further factors that Phil Atterley Ltd may consider when making this decision, for example:

- accuracy of market research information
- cost of obtaining market research information
- cost of getting perfect information
- risk analysis
- sensitivity analysis
- working capital requirements
- return on investment
- opportunity costs
- demand for competing products
- prices of competing products
- product life cycle.

(iv)

Information may be usefully obtained about the years in which sales may be achieved and the possible different probabilities of these occurring in each year. Use of an appropriate cost of capital would enable calculation of the net present values of the expected outcomes of each decision. This may provide a more realistic comparison, particularly if the timing of cash flows was significantly different following whether or not promotion was undertaken or if the cost of capital was significantly high.

E10.3 Hurdle

(i)

In view of the scarcity of labour, labour hours are obviously a key factor. Since any new work undertaken by the company will entail diverting labour from the standard product (for which there is a heavy demand) the first thing that must be done is to find a contribution per hour of the key factor.

Standard product

	£	£
Selling price		28
Marginal cost:		
Materials	10	
Labour 0.5 hours × £10 per hour	5	15
Contribution		13
Contribution per labour hour (£13 ÷ 0.5 hours)		26

Make-versus-buy decision for the special component
Making the component

		£
Materials cost		100
Labour cost	4 hours at £10 per hour	40
Opportunity cost	4 hours at £26 per hour	104
Total cost to make special component		244

Since the component can be purchased for only £220 then it is cheaper for the company to buy it rather than make it.

(ii)

The contract costs can now be calculated assuming that the special component may be purchased.

		£
Materials cost		600
Special component		220
Labour cost	100 hours at £10 per hour	1,000
Opportunity cost	100 hours at £26 per hour	2,600
Total cost of contract		4,420

The contract may be accepted by the company if the contract price is greater than £4,420.

(iii)

If a 20% mark-up is required by the company then the contract price should be £4,420 plus 20%, which is £5,304.

Chapter 11

E11.1 Earextensions

Sales price   £50

	Jan	Feb	Mar	Apr	May	Jun	Total
Sales budget							
Units	50,000	60,000	72,000	86,400	86,400	86,400	441,200
£	2,500,000	3,000,000	3,600,000	4,320,000	4,320,000	4,320,000	22,060,000

E11.2 Earextensions

	Jan	Feb	Mar	Apr	May	Jun	Total
Production budget (units)							
Opening stock	0	12,000	14,400	17,280	17,280	17,280	0
Production	62,000	62,400	74,880	86,400	86,400	86,400	458,480
Sales	50,000	60,000	72,000	86,400	86,400	86,400	441,200
Closing stock	12,000	14,400	17,280	17,280	17,280	17,280	17,280

E11.3 Earextensions

Production overheads

Direct labour hours

Assemblers	3.0 × 458,480	1,375,440 minutes	=	22,924 hours
Operators	1.5 × 458,480	687,720 minutes	=	11,462 hours
Total	4.5 × 458,480	2,063,160 minutes	=	34,386 hours

Total production overheads   £4,100,000

$$\text{Production overheads per direct labour hour} \quad \frac{£4,100,000}{34,386} = £119.235 \text{ per hour} = £1.987 \text{ per minute}$$

Unit gross margin budget

			£	£	£
Sales price					50.000
Unit cost					
Direct labour	Assemblers	3 minutes @ £10 per hour	0.5000		
	Operators	1.5 minutes @ £8 per hour	0.2000		
				0.7000	
Materials	Electronic assembly		23.3000		
	Keypad		1.0000		
	Case		2.0000		
				26.3000	
Overheads	4.5 minutes @ £1.987 per minute			8.9426	
					35.9426
Unit gross margin					14.0574

	Jan	Feb	Mar	Apr	May	Jun	Total
Direct labour budget (£)							
Production units							
× £0.70 per unit	43,400	43,680	52,416	60,480	60,480	60,480	320,936

E11.4 Earextensions

	Jan	Feb	Mar	Apr	May	Jun	Total
Materials purchases and usage budget (units)							
Electronic assembly							
Opening stock	10,000	31,200	37,440	43,200	43,200	43,200	10,000
Purchases	83,200	68,640	80,640	86,400	86,400	86,400	491,680
Usage	62,000	62,400	74,880	86,400	86,400	86,400	458,480
Closing stock	31,200	37,440	43,200	43,200	43,200	43,200	43,200
Keypad							
Opening stock	30,000	31,200	37,440	43,200	43,200	43,200	30,000
Purchases	63,200	68,640	80,640	86,400	86,400	86,400	471,680
Usage	62,000	62,400	74,880	86,400	86,400	86,400	458,480
Closing stock	31,200	37,440	43,200	43,200	43,200	43,200	43,200
Case							
Opening stock	20,000	31,200	37,440	43,200	43,200	43,200	20,000
Purchases	73,200	68,640	80,640	86,400	86,400	86,400	481,680
Usage	62,000	62,400	74,880	86,400	86,400	86,400	458,480
Closing stock	31,200	37,440	43,200	43,200	43,200	43,200	43,200

Materials purchases and usage budget (£)							
Electronic assembly £23.30 per unit							
Opening stock	233,000	726,960	872,352	1,006,560	1,006,560	1,006,560	233,000
Purchases	1,938,560	1,599,312	1,878,912	2,013,120	2,013,120	2,013,120	11,456,144
Usage	1,444,600	1,453,920	1,744,704	2,013,120	2,013,120	2,013,120	10,682,584
Closing stock	726,960	872,352	1,006,560	1,006,560	1,006,560	1,006,560	1,006,560
Keypad £1.00 per unit							
Opening stock	30,000	31,200	37,440	43,200	43,200	43,200	30,000
Purchases	63,200	68,640	80,640	86,400	86,400	86,400	471,680
Usage	62,000	62,400	74,880	86,400	86,400	86,400	458,480
Closing stock	31,200	37,440	43,200	43,200	43,200	43,200	43,200
Case £2.00 per unit							
Opening stock	40,000	62,400	74,880	86,400	86,400	86,400	40,000
Purchases	146,400	137,280	161,280	172,800	172,800	172,800	963,360
Usage	124,000	124,800	149,760	172,800	172,800	172,800	916,960
Closing stock	62,400	74,880	86,400	86,400	86,400	86,400	86,400

E11.5 Earextensions

	Jan	Feb	Mar	Apr	May	Jun	Total
Overheads, selling, administrative, financial costs budget (£)							
Production overheads (£4,100,000 less depreciation £50,000)	675,000	675,000	675,000	675,000	675,000	675,000	4,050,000
Selling and administrative costs	900,000	900,000	900,000	600,000	600,000	600,000	4,500,000
Interest (0.2% of sales)	5,000	6,000	7,200	8,640	8,640	8,640	44,120
Profit and loss account budget							
Sales units	50,000	60,000	72,000	86,400	86,400	86,400	441,200
Figures in £							
Sales	2,500,000	3,000,000	3,600,000	4,320,000	4,320,000	4,320,000	22,060,000
Cost of sales	1,797,130	2,156,556	2,587,866	3,105,440	3,105,440	3,105,440	15,857,872
Gross margin	702,870	843,444	1,012,134	1,214,560	1,214,560	1,214,560	6,202,128
Selling/administrative/ interest costs	905,000	906,000	907,200	608,640	608,640	608,640	4,544,120
Profit/(loss)	(202,130)	(62,556)	104,934	605,920	605,920	605,920	1,658,008
Cumulative profit and loss account	(202,130)	(264,686)	(159,752)	446,168	1,052,088	1,658,008	

E11.6 Earextensions

	Jan	Feb	Mar	Apr	May	Jun	Total
Finished product stock valuation budget @ £35.9426/unit							
	£431,311	£517,573	£621,088	£621,088	£621,088	£621,088	
Over (under) absorption of production overheads units	76,413	76,413	76,413	76,413	76,413	76,413	458,480
	62,000	62,400	74,880	86,400	86,400	86,400	458,480
	14,413	14,013	1,533	(9,987)	(9,987)	(9,987)	0
@ £8.9426/unit	£128,893	£125,316	£13,712	£(89,307)	£(89,307)	£(89,307)	£0
Cumulative stock adjustment	£128,893	£254,208	£267,920	£178,614	£89,307	£0	
Total finished goods stock	£560,204	£771,782	£889,008	£799,702	£710,395	£621,088	

E11.7 Marx

(i)

	Chico	Groucho	Harpo
Average net operating assets	£7.5m	£17.5m	£12.5m
Operating profit	£1.5m	£1.4m	£2.0m
ROI%	20%	8%	16%
Ranking of ROI%	1	3	2

(ii)

	Chico	Groucho	Harpo
Average net operating assets	£7.5m	£17.5m	£12.5m
Divisional WACC	7%	5%	10%
Operating profit	£1.5m	£1.4m	£2.0m
Administrative expenses	£0.80m	£0.30m	£0.65m
	£0.70m	£1.10m	£1.35m
Notional financial charge			
(WACC × average net operating assets)	£0.525m	£0.875m	£1.250m
RI	£0.175m	£0.225m	£0.100m
Ranking of RI	2	1	3

(iii)

(a) The ROI % of each division is currently above its WACC with Chico being by far the best performer, followed by Harpo and then Groucho.

Chico and Harpo would be reluctant to pursue an investment opportunity that is expected to yield a return of 9% because they both currently earn 20% and 16% respectively.

In the case of Chico this represents a lost opportunity for Marx plc because taking on the investment would add value since Chico's WACC is 2% lower than the project's 9%.

Harpo's decision not to take on the investment is in the best interest of Marx plc since Harpo's WACC is 7% above the project's 9%.

Groucho would be keen to pursue an investment opportunity that is expected to yield a return of 9% because it currently earns only 8%.

Groucho's decision to take on the investment is also in the best interest of Marx plc since Groucho's WACC is 4% below the project's 9%.

(b) The current RI of Groucho is the highest, followed by Chico and then Harpo.

If performance is measured using RI, then Chico and Groucho would take on an investment opportunity that yields 9% because even after capital charges on net operating assets at 7% and 5% respectively it would add to their residual incomes.

If performance is measured using RI, Harpo would not take on an investment opportunity that yields 9% because after the capital charge on net operating assets at 10% there would be a reduction to residual income.

E11.8 Earextensions

Trade debtors budget (£)

Sales		Jan	Feb	Mar	Apr	May	Jun
	2,500,000	2,500,000	2,500,000				
	3,000,000		3,000,000	3,000,000			
	4,320,000			3,600,000	3,600,000		
	4,320,000				4,320,000	4,320,000	
	4,320,000					4,320,000	4,320,000
	4,320,000						4,320,000
Total debtors		2,500,000	5,500,000	6,600,000	7,920,000	8,640,000	8,640,000

Trade creditors budget (£)

Materials purchases	Jan	Feb	Mar	Apr	May	Jun
303,000	303,000	303,000				
2,148,160	2,148,160	2,148,160	2,148,160			
1,805,232		1,805,232	1,805,232	1,805,232		
2,120,832			2,120,832	2,120,832	2,120,832	
2,272,320				2,272,320	2,272,320	2,272,320
2,272,320					2,272,320	2,272,320
2,272,320						2,272,320
Total creditors	2,451,160	4,256,392	6,074,224	6,198,384	6,665,472	6,816,960

Cash flow budget (£)

Customer	Jan	Feb	Mar	Apr	May	Jun	Total
receipts	0	0	2,500,000	3,000,000	3,600,000	4,320,000	13,420,000
Supplier							
payments	0	0	303,000	2,148,160	1,805,232	2,120,832	6,377,224
Direct labour	43,400	43,680	52,416	60,480	60,480	60,480	320,936
Overheads	675,000	675,000	675,000	675,000	675,000	675,000	4,050,000
Selling and administrative							
costs	900,000	900,000	900,000	600,000	600,000	600,000	4,500,000
Interest	5,000	6,000	7,200	8,640	8,640	8,640	44,120
Total							
payments	1,623,400	1,624,680	1,937,616	3,492,280	3,149,352	3,464,952	15,292,280
Cash flow	(1,623,400)	(1,624,680)	562,384	(492,280)	450,648	855,048	(1,872,280)
Opening							
balance	355,000	(1,268,400)	(2,893,080)	(2,330,696)	(2,822,976)	(2,372,328)	355,000
Closing							
balance	(1,268,400)	(2,893,080)	(2,330,696)	(2,822,976)	(2,372,328)	(1,517,280)	(1,517,280)

E11.9 Earextensions

Balance sheet budget (£)

	Dec	Jan	Feb	Mar	Apr	May	Jun	Depreciation per month
Fixed assets	495,000	486,666	478,332	470,000	461,666	453,333	445,000	8,333
Stocks	303,000	1,380,764	1,756,454	2,025,168	1,935,862	1,846,555	1,757,248	
Trade debtors	0	2,500,000	5,500,000	6,600,000	7,920,000	8,640,000	8,640,000	
Cash and bank	355,000	(1,268,400)	(2,893,080)	(2,330,696)	(2,822,976)	(2,372,328)	(1,517,280)	
	1,153,000	3,099,030	4,841,706	6,764,472	7,494,552	8,567,560	9,324,968	
Trade creditors	303,000	2,451,160	4,256,392	6,074,224	6,198,384	6,665,472	6,816,960	
Loans	450,000	450,000	450,000	450,000	450,000	450,000	450,000	
Share capital	400,000	400,000	400,000	400,000	400,000	400,000	400,000	
Retained earnings	0	(202,130)	(264,686)	(159,752)	446,168	1,052,088	1,658,008	
	1,153,000	3,099,030	4,841,706	6,764,472	7,494,552	8,567,560	9,324,968	

Chapter 12

E12.1 Nilbog

Flexed budget

		Budget		Flexed		Actual
Units (Fishermen)						
Opening stock finished goods		0		0		0
Unit production		10,000		9,600		9,600
Unit sales		10,000		9,000		9,000
Closing stock finished goods		0		600		600
Cubic yards (materials)						
Opening stock materials		0		0		0
Materials purchases		30,000		30,800		30,000
Materials usage		30,000		28,800		28,000
Closing stock materials		0		2,000		2,000

Figures in £							**Actual to Flexed Budget Variances**	
Sales	$(10,000 \times 48)$	480,000	$(9,000 \times 48)$	432,000	$(9,000 \times 48)$	432,000	sales price	0
Opening stock								
Finished goods		0		0		0		
Materials		0		0				
Materials purchased $(10,000 \times 3 \times 3.6)$		(108,000)	$((9,600 \times 3 + 2,000) \times 3.6)$	(110,880)	$(30,000 \times 3.84)$	(115,200)	materials price	$(7,200)\ 30,000 \times (3.6 - 3.84)$
							materials quality	$2,880\ (30,800 - 30,000) \times 3.6$
Direct labour	$(10,000 \times 2 \times 6.6)$	(132,000)	$(9,600 \times 2 \times 6.6)$	(126,720)	$(22,000 \times 6.48)$	(142,560)	labour rate	$2,640 \times 22,000 \times (6.6 - 6.48)$
							labour efficiency	$(18,480)\ (19,200 - 22,000) \times 6.6$
Variable overhead	$(10,000 \times 2 \times 2.4)$	(48,000)	$(9,600 \times 2 \times 2.4)$	(46,080)	$(22,000 \times 2.0)$	(44,000)	overhead spend	$8,800 \times 22,000 \times (2.4 - 2.0)$
							overhead efficiency	$(6,720)\ (19,200)\ 22,000 \times 2.4$
Fixed overhead	$(10,000 \times 2 \times 4.8)$	(96,000)		(96,000)		(100,000)	overhead spend	$(4,000)\ 96,000\ 100,000$
Closing stock:								
Finished goods			(600×38.4)	23,040	(600×38.4)	23,040		
Materials			$(2,000 \times 3.6)$	7,200	$(2,000 \times 3.6)$	7,200		
Net profit		96,000		82,560		60,480		(22,080)
Net profit £ per unit		9.60		9.17		6.72		

Flexed budget to budget variances

Sales volume $(9,600)\ (10,000 - 9,000) \times 9.6$

Fixed overhead volume

  $(3,840)\ (10,000 \times 2) \times 4.8 - (9,600 \times 2) \times 4.8$

Total variances $(35,520)$ actual minus budget profit

Operating statement for period 5 in 2005 (4 weeks)

			£
Budget sales	$10,000 \times £48$		480,000
Standard cost of sales	$10,000 \times £38.4$		384,000
Budgeted profit			96,000
Variances		Favourable £	Unfavourable £
Sales volume			9,600
Materials			
Price			7,200
Quantity		2,880	
Direct labour			
Rate		2,640	
Efficiency			18,480

Variable overhead

Expenditure	8,800		
Efficiency		6,720	

Fixed overhead

Expenditure		4,000	
Volume		3,840	
	14,320	49,840	(35,520)
Actual profit			60,480

Stock is valued at standard cost at each month end so that a true month activity is reported, not previous inadequacies.

Variances	Favourable £	Unfavourable £	Likely causes of variances
Sales volume		9,600	An extra 1,000 units had been planned for period 5 at £9.60/unit standard profit.
Materials			
Price		7,200	Factors may be economic, currency fluctuations or poor standards.
Quantity	2,880		Low defects, better quality, better stock control, different production methods, improved labour training.
Direct labour			
Rate	2,640		Lower grade, union negotiation, less overtime.
Efficiency		18,480	Machine breakdowns, rework (but not apparent from materials quantity).
Variable overhead			
Expenditure	8,800		Poor standard, tighter cost control.
Efficiency		6,720	Machine breakdowns, rework (but not apparent from materials quantity).
Fixed overhead			
Expenditure		4,000	
Volume		3,840	Under-recoveries of fixed overhead because of low volumes.
	14,320	49,840	

E12.2 Cyclops

(i)	Budget	Flexed	Actual		Variances
Units	40,800	61,200	61,200		
	£	£	£		£
Sales	244,800	367,200	348,840	sales price	
	40,800 × £6.00		61,200 × £5.70	61,200 × £0.30	18,360A
Materials	81,600	122,400	114,240	materials	
	40,800 × £2.00		61,200 × £1.87	61,200 × £0.13	8,160F

Labour	81,600	122,400	133,280	labour	
	40,800 × £2.00		61,200 × £2.18	61,200 × £0.18	10,880A
Overhead	16,320	24,480	27,200	overhead	
	40,800 × £0.40		61,200 × £0.44	£24,480 − £27,200	2,720A
Contribution	65,280	97,920	74,120		23,800A
Contribution/unit	£1.60				
	£65,280/40,800				

Volume variance

	65,280	97,920	sales	
	budget profit − flexed budget	=	£1.60 × (40,800 − 61,200)	32,640F
			Total variances	8,840F

		£	£
Budget contribution			65,280
Sales variances			
Price	(30p price reduction)	18,360A	
Volume	(50% increase)	32,640F	14,280F
Materials			
Price	(4% discount)	4,896F	
Quantity	(savings on wastage)	3,264F	8,160F
Labour	(use of more highly paid and skilled staff)		10,880A
Overhead	(higher electricity and gas supplies)		2,720A
Actual contribution			74,120

(ii)
You should refer to the relevant section in Chapter 12 to check your solution.

(iii)	**Budget**	**Flexed**	**Actual**		**Variances**
Units	40,800	61,200	61,200		
	£	£	£		£
Contribution	65,280	97,920	74,120	as above	23,800A
Fixed overhead	20,400	20,400	25,000	spend	4,600A
Profit	44,880	77,520	49,120		
Profit per unit	£1.10				
	£44,880/40,800				

Volume variance

	44,880	77,520	sales	
			£1.10 × (61,200 − 40,800)	22,440F
	budget profit − flexed budget	=	fixed overhead	
			£0.50 × (61,200 − 40,800)	10,200F
			Total variances	4,420F

		£	£
Budget profit			44,880
Sales variances			
Price	(30p price reduction)	18,360A	
Volume	(as above)	22,440F	4,080F
Materials			
Price	(4% discount)	4,896F	
Quantity	(savings on wastage)	3,264F	8,160F
Labour	(use of more highly paid and skilled staff)		10,880A

		£	
Variable overhead	(higher electricity and gas supplies)		2,720A
Fixed overhead			
Spend	(£20,400 − £25,000)	4,600A	
Volume	(as above)	10,200F	5,600F
Actual profit			49,120

(iv)

You should refer to the relevant section in Chapter 12 to check your solution.

(v)

Using absorption costing the sales volume variance now becomes £22,440F, based on profit rather than contribution. The difference of £10,200 is shown as a favourable volume variance due to increased recovery of fixed overheads due to the higher volume of sales.

The spend variance for fixed overheads is £4,600 and may be due to a number of reasons: poor budgeting; operations out of control; unforeseen cost price increases, etc.

It may be argued that fixed overheads should not be included in performance reports because they are fixed and therefore uncontrollable by nature. However, as we can see in the example of Cyclops in actuality some responsibility and accountability should be assigned to them.

If absorption costing is used it goes some way to ensuring that all costs are covered in pricing decisions. However, in situations of spare capacity it may mean that products are overpriced in tendering for new business which may then be lost. If a marginal basis were used a contribution may be provided towards meeting those fixed overheads.

E12.3 White Heaven

(i) Ideal standard cost per Shell

		£	£
Direct materials			
Clay	5 kg × £2.00	10.00	
Glaze	3 kg × £4.00	12.00	
			22.00
Direct labour			
Grade A	1 hour × £7.20	7.20	
Grade B	0.75 hours × £6.00	4.50	
			11.70
Indirect labour	0.25 hours × £5.00	1.25	
Maintenance	0.05 hours × £10.00	0.50	
Variable overhead			
Direct materials	15% × £22.00	3.30	
Direct labour	10% × £11.70	1.17	
			6.22
Total variable costs			39.92
Fixed overhead cost			
Supervisors' salaries	£95,000/50,000	1.90	
Other	£109,000/50,000	2.18	
			4.08
Ideal standard cost per Shell			44.00

(ii)

Grade A direct labour

Originally 1 operator working for 1 hour made 1 Shell

Or, 10 operators each working for 1 hours made 10 Shells

Now 1 operator working for 1 hour makes 0.5 Shells

And 9 operators each working for 1 hour make 9 Shells

So 10 operators each working for 1 hour make 9.5 Shells

So 1 Shell takes $\dfrac{10}{9.5}$ hours = 1.053 hours

The rate is now £7.20 + £0.40 or £7.60 per hour

Therefore 1 Shell costs 1.053 hours × £7.60 = £8.00 direct labour

Grade B direct labour

Originally 1 operator working for 0.75 hours made 1 Shell

Or, 10 operators each working for 0.75 hours made 10 Shells

Now 1 operator working for 0.80 hours would ideally make 1 Shell

Or, 10 operators each working for 0.80 hours would ideally make 10 Shells

But 2.5 operators working for 0.80 hours only make 0.6 Shells each or 1.5 Shells

And 7.5 operators each working for 0.80 hours make 1 Shell each or 7.5 Shells

So 10 operators each working for 0.80 hours make 9 Shells

So 1 Shell takes $\dfrac{8}{9}$ hours = 0.889 hours

The rate is now £6.00 + £0.30 or £6.30 per hour

Therefore 1 Shell costs 0.889 hours × £6.30 = £5.60 direct labour

Attainable standard cost per Shell

		£	£
Direct materials			
Clay	£10.00 + 10%	11.00	
Glaze	£12.00 − 12.5%	10.50	
		———	21.50
Direct labour			
Grade A	see workings	8.00	
Grade B	see workings	5.60	
		———	13.60
Indirect labour	0.25 hours × £5.20	1.30	
Maintenance	0.05 hours × £10.20	0.51	
Variable overhead			
Direct material			
Clay	15% × £11.00	1.65	
Glaze	20% × £10.50	2.10	
Direct labour	10% × £13.60	1.36	
		———	6.92
Total variable costs			42.02

Fixed overhead cost

Supervisors' salaries	£95,000/50,000	1.90
Other	£109,000/50,000	2.18
		4.08

Attainable standard cost per Shell   46.10

(iii)

Ideal standard cost per Shell	= £44.00 × 49,000 units = £2,156,000
Attainable standard cost per Shell	= £46.10 × 49,000 units = £2,258,900
Variance	= £2.10 × 49,000 units = £102,900

E12.5 Millennium

	Budget	Flexed	Actual		Variances
Units	4,300	4,100	4,100		
	£	£	£		£
Sales	25,112	23,944	24,805	price	
	4,300 × £5.84	4,100 × £5.84	4,100 × £6.05	4,100 × (£5.84 − £6.05)	861F
Materials	7,310	6,970	7,169	price	
	4,300 × 2 × £0.85	4,100 × 2 × £0.85	(6,600 × £0.83)	8,500 × (£0.8434 − £0.85)	56F
			+ (1,900 × £0.89)	quantity	
				£0.85 × (8,500 − 8,200)	255A
Labour	12,642	12,054	13,387.50	rate	
	4,300 × 0.7 × £4.20	4,100 × 0.7 × £4.20	2,975 × £4.50	2,975 × (£4.50 − £4.20)	892.50A
				efficiency	
				£4.20 × (2,870 − 2,975)	441A
Contribution	5,160	4,920	4,248.50		
Fixed	3,526	3,526	3,800	spend	
overhead	4,300 × £0.82			£3,526 − £3,800	274A
Profit	1,634	1,394	448.50		
Profit per unit	£0.38				
	£1,634/4,300				
Volume					
variance					
	1,634	1,394		sales	
	budget profit − flexed budget		=	£0.38 × (4,100 − 4,300)	76A
				fixed overhead	
				£0.82 × (4,100 − 4,300)	164A
Total variances					1,185.50A

	£	£
Budget profit		1,634
Sales variances		
Price	861F	
Volume	76A	785F
Materials variances		
Price	56F	
Quantity	255A	199A
Labour variances		
Rate	892.50A	
Efficiency	441A	1,333.50A
Fixed overhead variances		
Spend	274A	
Volume	164A	438A
Actual profit		448.50

Chapter 13

E13.3 Rainbow

(i)

From a divisional point of view

Divisional managers are rewarded via a remuneration package which is linked to an ROI performance measure. Therefore they are likely to take a short-term view in appraising the investment proposals because they will be anxious to maintain their earnings. They would be interested in the short-term effect on ROI and perhaps on residual income.

Project A

	Year			
	1	**2**	**3**	**4**
	£000	**£000**	**£000**	**£000**
NBV of asset at beginning of year	60	45	30	15
Net cash inflow	21	21	21	21
Depreciation	15	15	15	15
Operating profit	6	6	6	6
Imputed interest at 15%	9	7	5	2
Residual income	(3)	(1)	1	4
ROI %	(6/60) 10.0	(6/45) 13.3	(6/30) 20.0	(6/15) 40.0

Project B

	Year			
	1	**2**	**3**	**4**
	£000	**£000**	**£000**	**£000**
NBV of asset at beginning of year	60	45	30	15
Net cash inflow	25	20	20	15
Depreciation	15	15	15	15
Operating profit	10	5	5	–
Imputed interest at 15%	9	7	5	2
Residual income	1	(2)	–	(2)
ROI %	16.7	11.1	16.7	–

Project C

	Year			
	1	**2**	**3**	**4**
	£000	**£000**	**£000**	**£000**
NBV of asset at beginning of year	60	45	30	15
Net cash inflow	10	20	30	40
Depreciation	15	15	15	15
Operating profit	(5)	5	15	25
Imputed interest at 15%	9	7	5	2
Residual income	(4)	(2)	10	23
ROI %	(8.3)	11.1	50.0	166.7

Red Division is likely to reject project A because of the potential adverse effect on the manager's remuneration in year one.

Similarly, project C is also likely to be rejected due to adverse results in the early years, despite the long-term profitability of the project.

Project B is the most likely to be accepted if the manager takes a short-term view to protect his or her remuneration in the coming year, although the decision will be affected by the division's current level of ROI.

(ii)
From a company point of view
The company is likely to appraise the projects using discounted cash flow techniques.

	15% discount factor	Project A		Project B		Project C	
Year		Cash flow	Present value	Cash flow	Present value	Cash flow	Present value
		£000	£000	£000	£000	£000	£000
1	0.87	21	18.27	25	21.75	10	8.70
2	0.76	21	15.96	20	15.20	20	15.20
3	0.66	21	13.86	20	13.20	30	19.80
4	0.57	21	11.97	15	8.55	40	22.80
	2.86		60.06		58.70		66.50
Initial investment			60.00		60.00		60.00
Net present value			0.06		(1.30)		6.50

From the company point of view project A may be acceptable although the NPV is very small and there is no room for possible error in the estimates and the risk of a negative return would be very great. The final decision will depend, among other things, on the risk premium built into the cost of capital.

Project B would be unacceptable whereas project C would be acceptable from a company point of view.

(iii)
Probable decision

Project	Division	Company
A	Reject	Accept
B	Accept	Reject
C	Reject	Accept

The table shows that there is unlikely to be goal congruence between the company and the manager of Red Division.

The divergence between the two points of view has occurred because they are each using different assessment criteria. The views of the division and the company can be brought into line if they both use the same criteria in future. This would mean abandoning the practice of linking a manager's remuneration directly to short-term ROI because this is likely to encourage short-term thinking since ROI tends to be low in the early stages of an investment.

On the other hand it would be difficult to link remuneration to the net present value of individual projects because of the problems of disentanglement and the length of time before all the costs and benefits arise.

The specific problem with project A could be overcome through the use of annuity depreciation instead of the straight line method. The constant cash flows will then result in a smoother ROI profile over the life of the project. The manager would then be more likely to make the same decision as the company, although it depends to an extent on the division's current level of ROI.

The company may consider introducing the use of economic value added (EVA) as a measure of performance, which may be suitable for both divisional and economic performance.

E13.8 AAK

(i)

Year	Equipment £000	Running costs £000	Lighting, heating, etc. £000	Total outflow £000	10% discount rate	Present value £
0	120			120	1.00	120,000
1		40	15	55	0.91	50,050
2		44	15	59	0.83	48,970
3		48	15	63	0.75	47,250
4		52	15	67	0.68	45,560
5		56	15	71	0.62	44,020
Present value						355,850

We can assume that the annual sales at the full level is S. We first need to calculate the present value of each year's expected sales.

Year	Sales	10% discount rate	Present value
1	0.4S	0.91	0.364S
2	0.7S	0.83	0.581S
3	1.0S	0.75	0.750S
4	1.0S	0.68	0.680S
5	1.0S	0.62	0.620S
Present value			2.995S

Contribution = sales − variable costs

Because the prices of drinks are to be set at double their direct (variable) costs then half of the total present value of sales 2.995S must represent direct costs and the other half must represent contribution.

$$\text{Therefore contribution} = \frac{2.995S}{2}$$

$$= 1.4975S \text{ which is the present value}$$
of the contribution from the drinks

To break even at an annual interest rate of 10% the present value of the contribution from drinks must equal the present value of the total outgoings, which is £355,850.

$$1.4975S = £355,850$$
$$S = £237,629$$

Therefore the required sales of drinks in each year are:

Year		£
1	£237,629 × 40%	95,052
2	£237,629 × 70%	166,341
3		237,629
4		237,629
5		237,629

(ii)

Aspects of the proposals that require further investigation:

- Can the facilities be used outside normal opening hours for alternative uses in order to increase the contribution?
- Has market research been carried out to support the belief that there will be additional future benefits?
- Will the proposed cost plus drinks pricing methods result in competitive prices?
- Perhaps there is a better way for this project to utilise the space and the capital, and perhaps food may be an option.

E13.9 Lew Rolls

(i)

	10%	20%		Super			Superlux			Exec			Excel	
				10%	20%		10%	20%		10%	20%		10%	20%
Year	DF	DF	CF	DCF	DCF	CF	DCF	DCF	CF	DCF	DCF	CF	DCF	DCF
			£m	£m	£m	£m	£m	£m	£m	£m	£m	£m	£m	£m
0	1.00	1.00	−3	−3	−3	−7	−7	−7	−12	−12	−12	−15	−15	−15
1	0.91	0.83	1	0.91	0.83	2	1.82	1.66	0	0	0	10	9.10	8.30
2	0.83	0.69	1	0.83	0.69	2	1.66	1.38	0	0	0	10	8.30	6.90
3	0.75	0.58	1	0.75	0.58	2	1.50	1.16	7	5.25	4.06	0	0	0
4	0.68	0.48	1	0.68	0.48	2	1.36	0.96	7	4.76	3.36	0	0	0
5	0.62	0.40	1	0.62	0.40	2	1.24	0.80	7	4.34	2.80	0	0	0
Total			2	0.79	−0.02	3	0.58	−1.04	9	2.35	−1.78	5	2.40	0.20

(ii)

Calculation of IRR

From the table above calculate the IRR for each of the projects using interpolation/extrapolation as shown in Figs. 13.3 and 13.4 in Chapter 13 to obtain:

	Super	Superlux	Exec	Excel
IRR	19.8%	13.6%	15.7%	20.9%
Ranking of projects	2	4	3	1
(highest IRR ranked 1st)				

(iii)

Net present value

	Super	Superlux	Exec	Excel
NPV of each project	£790,000	£580,000	£2,350,000	£2,400,000
NPV/£ invested	£0.263	£0.083	£0.196	£0.160
Ranking	1	4	2	3

NPV per £ invested is the more reliable evaluation method for appraisal of this project therefore, given the £24m total investment constraint, the decision should be to invest:

	£m	NPV per £ invested	NPV £
Super	3	£0.263	790,000
Exec	12	£0.196	2,350,000
Excel	9	£0.160	1,440,000
Superlux	0	£0.083	0
Optimum total NPV			£4,580,000

If IRR rankings were used to make the investment decision:

	£m	NPV per £ invested	NPV £
Excel	15	£0.160	2,400,000
Super	3	£0.263	790,000
Exec	6	£0.196	1,175,000
Superlux	0	£0.083	0
Total NPV			£4,365,000
			which is not optimal

(iv) and (v)

You should refer to the relevant sections in Chapter 13 to check your solutions.

Chapter 14

E14.3 Lucky Jim

If shareholders' equity is E and the net financial debt D then the relative proportions of equity and debt in the total financing are:

$$\frac{E}{E+D} \text{ and } \frac{D}{E+D}$$

$$\frac{E}{E+D} = 2/3$$

$$\frac{D}{E+D} = 1/3$$

Cost of equity e = 18%
Return on financial debt d = 12%
WACC = (2/3 × 18%) + (1/3 × 12%) = 12% + 4% = 16%

The present value of future cash flows in perpetuity $= \dfrac{\text{annual cash flows}}{\text{annual discount rate\%}}$

$$= \frac{£35,000}{0.16} = £218,750$$

Net present value, NPV = £218,750 − £200,000 = £18,750

Using WACC to discount the cash flows of the project, the result is a positive NPV of £18,750 and therefore the project should be undertaken.

E14.4 Supermarket

	2004	2003	2002
Adjusted net assets	£5,000m	£4,769m	£4,377m
Market value	£17,808m	£11,531m	£11,995m
MVA	£12,808m	£6,762m	£7,618m

E14.5 Yor

(i)

Yor plc
Profit and loss account for the year ended 30 September 2005

Figures in £m

	Debentures	Shares
PBIT	15.6	15.6
Interest payable	(1.6)	(1.2)
Profit before tax	14.0	14.4
Tax on profit on ordinary activities	(3.5)	(3.6)
Profit on ordinary activities after tax	10.5	10.8
Retained profit at 1 October 2004	10.6	10.6
	21.1	21.4
Dividends	(3.3)	(4.6)
Retained profit at 30 September 2005	17.8	16.8

(ii)

Yor plc
Capital and reserves as at 30 September 2005

Figures in £m

	Debentures	Shares
Share capital (£1 ordinary shares)	10.0	14.0
Share premium (4m × £1.50)		6.0
Profit and loss account	17.8	16.8
	27.8	36.8
Loans	30.0	20.0

(iii)

$$\text{earnings per share 2004} = \frac{\text{profit available for ordinary shareholders}}{\text{number of ordinary shares in issue}} = \frac{£7.8m}{10m}$$
$$= 78p$$

(iv)

using debentures

$$\text{earnings per share 2005} = \frac{£10.5m}{10m} = £1.05$$

using shares

$$\text{earnings per share 2005} = \frac{£10.8m}{10m} = 77p$$

(v)

$$\text{dividend per share 2004} = \frac{\text{total dividends paid to ordinary shareholders}}{\text{number of ordinary shares in issue}} = \frac{£3.0m}{10m}$$
$$= 30p$$

(vi)

using debentures

$$\text{dividend per share 2005} = \frac{£3.3m}{10m} = 33p$$

using shares

$$\text{dividend per share 2005} = \frac{£4.6m}{14m} = 33p$$

(vii)

$$\text{gearing} = \frac{\text{long-term debt}}{\text{equity} + \text{long-term debt}}$$

	using debentures	using shares
2004	**2005**	**2005**
$\dfrac{£20.0m}{£20.6m + £20.0m} = 49.3\%$	$\dfrac{£30.0m}{£27.8m + £30.0m} = 51.9\%$	$\dfrac{£20.0m}{£36.8m + £20.0m} = 35.2\%$

(viii)

Summary of results

Figures in £m

	2004	using debentures 2005	using shares 2005
Profit after tax	7.8	10.5	10.8
Dividends	(3.0)	(3.3)	(4.6)
Retained profit for year	4.8	7.2	6.2

The use of debentures to finance the new project will increase the 2004/2005 profit after tax, and available for dividends, by £2.7m or 34.6%, whereas if shares were used the increase would be £3.0m or 38.5%. Earnings per share will be increased to £1.05 (+27p) and decreased to 77p (−1p) respectively. However, retained profit would be increased by £2.4m (50%) and £1.4m (29.2%) respectively. The difference is because the gain from the lower interest cost in using shares is more than offset by the increase in dividends.

Dividend per share will be increased from 30p to 33p per share regardless of which method of financing is used.

Gearing at 30 September 2004 was 49.3%. If debentures are used to finance the new project then gearing will increase to 51.9%, but if shares are used to finance the new project then gearing will decrease to 35.2%. This represents a higher financial risk for the company with regard to its commitments to making a high level of interest payments. The company is therefore vulnerable to a downturn in business and also the possibility of its loans being called in and possible liquidation of the company.

Chapter 15

E15.1 Oliver

Production costs

		£	
Raw materials	[40% × £5,300,000]	2,120,000	held in stock on average 4 days
Direct labour	[25% × £5,300,000]	1,325,000	finished goods held in stock
Overheads	[10% × £5,300,000]	530,000	on average 7 days
		3,975,000	

The production cycle is 14 days

Working capital requirement

			£		£
Raw materials	[£2,120,000 × 4/365]			=	23,233
Work in progress					
Raw materials	[£2,120,000 × 14/365]	=	81,315		
Direct labour	[£1,325,000 × 14/365 × 25%]	=	12,705		
Overheads	[£530,000 × 14/365 × 25%]	=	5,082		
					99,102
Finished goods	[£3,975,000 × 7/365]			=	76,233
Debtors	[£5,300,000 × 60/365]			=	871,223
Creditors	[£2,120,000 × 30/365]			=	(174,247)
Total working capital requirement					895,544

E15.5 Worrall

Cost of sales is 80% of sales

Variable cost of sales	80% × 90%	=	72% of sales
Therefore			
Contribution		=	28% of sales

Proposed debtors

Sales, increased by 20% are	120% × £8m = £9.6m		
Credit allowed increased to 90 days	£9.6m × 90/365	=	£2,367,123
Current debtors	£8m × 60/365	=	£1,315,068
Increase in debtors		=	£1,052,055
Gains			
Increase in contribution	(£9.6m − £8.0m) × 28%	=	£448,000
Losses			
Increase in bad debts	(3% × £2,367,123) − (2% × £1,315,068)	=	£44,713
Increase in financing costs	£1,052,055 × 10%	=	£105,206
Total losses per annum			£149,919
Net gain			£298,081

The net gain to Worrall Ltd is £298,081 per annum and so an increase to 90 days' credit may be recommended.

Appendix 1

EA1.1 Hall

Hall Ltd
Profit and loss account for the year ended 31 December 2004

	2004	2003
	£	£
Sales	12,000	11,000
Cost of sales	8,000	7,000
Gross profit	4,000	4,000
Expenses	3,000	2,500
Net profit	1,000	1,500

Working
2003
Cost of sales: opening stock £600 + purchases £7,100 less closing stock £700

2004
Cost of sales: opening stock £700 + purchases £8,300 less closing stock £800 less the obsolete stock of £200
Cost of sales for 2004 must exclude obsolete stock as it has not been sold
Expenses £2,800 plus the obsolete stock £200

EA1.2 Accruals

(i)

The invoices for the common utilities rarely coincide with accounting period ends. To ensure that costs up to the year end are appropriately included, an adjustment is required for the consumption between the invoice date and year end.

(ii)

	Debit £	Credit £
Profit and loss account		
Electricity to 15 December 2004	10,000	
Accruals for charges 16 to 31 December 2004	300	
Total electricity costs for the year 2004	10,300	
Gas to 20 December 2004	5,000	
Accruals for charges 21 to 31 December 2004	150	
Total gas costs for the year 2004	5,150	
Balance sheet		
Electricity accrual at 31 December 2004		(300)
Gas accrual at 31 December 2004		(150)
Total accruals at 31 December 2004		(450)

EA1.7 Correcting Entries

31 December 2004

	Debit £	Credit £
(i)		
Profit and loss account		
Rent	2,400	
Profit and loss account		
Car hire		(2,400)
Correction of account error		
(ii)		
Profit and loss account		
Discount allowed		(20)
Balance sheet		
Sales ledger control account	20	
Customer settlement discount		
(iii)		
Profit and loss account		
Car insurance	1,200	
Balance sheet		
Motor vehicle fixed assets account		(1,200)
Correction of account error		

(iv)

Profit and loss account

Building repairs	3,500

Balance sheet

Buildings fixed assets account	(3,500)

Correction of account error

EA1.8 Etcoakco

(i)

	Debit £	Credit £		Debit £	Credit £
Capital			**Cash**		
Transaction 1		100,000	Transaction 1	100,000	
Balance c/f	100,000		Transaction 2		150,000
	100,000	100,000	Transaction 3		7,000
Balance b/f		100,000	Transaction 5		400
@ 1/1/05			Transaction 10	27,600	
			Balance c/f		70,200
				127,600	127,600
			Balance b/f	70,200	
			@ 1/1/05		
Fixed assets – shop			**Fixed assets – fittings/equipment**		
Transaction 2	50,000		Transaction 3	7,000	
			Transaction 4	20,000	
Balance c/f		50,000	Balance c/f		27,000
	50,000	50,000		27,000	27,000
Balance b/f	50,000		Balance b/f	27,000	
@ 1/1/05			@ 1/1/05		
Printing/stationery expenses			**Payables**		
Transaction 5	400		Transaction 4		20,000
			Transaction 6		31,250
Balance c/f		400	Balance c/f	51,250	
	400	400		51,250	51,250
Balance b/f	400		Balance b/f		51,250
@ 1/1/05			@ 1/1/05		
Stock			**Sales**		
Transaction 6	31,250		Transaction 7		23,000
Transaction 9		27,500	Transaction 8		27,600
Balance c/f		3,750	Balance c/f	50,600	
	31,250	31,250		50,600	50,600
Balance b/f	3,750		Balance b/f		50,600
@ 1/1/05			@ 1/1/05		

	Receivables				Cost of sales	
Transaction 7	23,000			Transaction 9	27,500	
Transaction 8	27,600			Balance c/f		27,500
Transaction 10		27,600			27,500	27,500
Balance c/f		23,000		Balance b/f	27,500	
	50,600	50,600		@ 1/1/05		
Balance b/f	23,000					
@ 1/1/05						

Solutions to parts (ii), (iii) and (iv) may provide an introduction to stock valuation, cost of sales and alternative uses of funds, covered in Part I of this book.

Glossary of key terms

absorption costing A method of costing that, in addition to direct costs, assigns all, or a proportion of, production overhead costs to cost units by means of one or a number of overhead absorption rates.

accountability concept Management accounting presents information measuring the achievement of the objectives of an organisation and appraising the conduct of its internal activities in that process. In order that further action can be taken, based on this information, it is necessary at all times to identify the responsibilities and performance of individuals within the organisation.

accountancy The practice or profession of accounting.

accounting The classification and recording of monetary transactions, the presentation and interpretation of the results of those transactions in order to assess performance over a period and the financial position at a given date, and the monetary projection of future activities arising from alternative planned courses of action.

accounting adjustments Accounting entries that do not arise from the basic transactions of cash and invoices. Adjusting entries are made for depreciation, bad and doubtful debts, closing stocks, prepayments, and accruals.

accounting concepts The principles underpinning the preparation of accounting information. Fundamental accounting concepts are the broad basic assumptions which underlie the periodic financial accounts of business enterprises.

accounting period The time period covered by the accounting statements of an entity.

accounting policies The specific accounting bases selected and consistently followed by an entity as being, in the opinion of the management, appropriate to its circumstances and best suited to present fairly its results and financial position (FRS 18 and Companies Act).

accounting rate of return (ARR) Annual profit divided by investment. It is a form of return on capital employed. Unlike NPV and IRR, it is based on profits, not cash flows.

accounting standard Authoritative statement of how particular types of transaction and other events should be reflected in financial statements. Compliance with accounting standards will normally be necessary for financial statements to give a true and fair view (ASB).

Accounting Standards Board (ASB) A UK standard-setting body set up in 1990 to develop, issue and withdraw accounting standards. Its aims are to 'establish and improve standards of financial accounting and reporting, for the benefit of users, preparers and auditors of financial information'.

accounts payable Also called trade creditors, is the money owed to suppliers for goods and services.

accounts receivable Also called trade debtors, is the money owed to entities by customers.

accruals Allowances made for costs and expenses payable within one year of the balance sheet date but for which no invoices have yet been recorded.

accruals concept The principle that revenues and costs are recognised as they are earned or incurred, and so matched with each other, and dealt with in the profit and loss account of the period to which they relate, irrespective of the period of receipt or payment. Where a conflict arises, this concept is subservient to the prudence concept.

acid test Quick assets (current assets excluding stocks) divided by current liabilities measures the ability of the business to pay creditors in the short term.

activity based costing (ABC) An approach to costing and monitoring of activities which involves tracing resource consumption and costing final outputs. Resources are assigned to activities and activities to cost objects based on consumption estimates. The latter utilise cost drivers to attach activity costs to outputs.

activity based management (ABM) System of management which uses activity based cost information for a variety of purposes including cost reduction, cost modelling and customer profitability analysis.

aged creditors report The amount owed by creditors, or accounts payable, classified by age of debt.

aged debtors report The amount owed by debtors, or accounts receivable, classified by age of debt.

algorithm A process or set of rules used for a mathematical calculation.

allocation The charging to a cost centre of those overheads which result solely from the existence of that cost centre.

amortisation In the same way that depreciation applies to the charging of the cost of tangible fixed assets over their useful economic lives, amortisation is the systematic write-off of the cost of an intangible asset, relating particularly to the passage of time, for example leasehold premises (FRS 11 and FRS 15).

annual report and accounts A set of statements which may comprise a management report (in the case of companies, a directors' report), an operating and financial review (OFR), and the financial statements of the entity.

apportionment The charging to a cost centre of a fair share of an overhead on the basis of the benefit received by the cost centre in respect of the facilities provided by the overhead.

asset A right or other access to future economic benefits controlled by an entity as a result of past transactions or events (FRS 5).

asymmetric digital subscriber line (ADSL) An ADSL is the specific technology for making broadband transmissions on the existing telephone network (the main alternative for broadband transmission being cable technology). ADSL is potentially 40 times faster than a 56 kilobyte modem.

attainable standard A standard that assumes efficient levels of operation, but which includes allowances for normal loss, waste and machine downtime.

attributable cost The cost per unit that could be avoided, on average, if a product or function were discontinued entirely without changing the supporting organisational structure.

audit A systematic examination of the activities and status of an entity, based primarily on investigation and analysis of its systems, controls and records. A statutory annual audit of a company is defined by the ASB as an independent examination of, and expression of an opinion on, the financial statements of the enterprise.

Auditing Practices Board (APB) A body formed in 1991 by an agreement between the six members of the Consultative Committee of Accountancy Bodies, to be responsible for developing and issuing professional standards for auditors in the United Kingdom and the Republic of Ireland.

auditor A professionally qualified accountant who is appointed by, and reports independently to, the shareholders, providing an objective verification to shareholders and other users that the financial statements have been prepared properly and in accordance with legislative and regulatory requirements; that they present the information truthfully and fairly; and that they conform to the best accounting practice in their treatment of the various measurements and valuations.

audit report An objective verification to shareholders and other users that the financial statements have been prepared properly and in accordance with legislative and regulatory requirements; that they present the information truthfully and fairly and that they conform to the best accounting practice in their treatment of the various measurements and valuations.

BACS (bankers automated clearing services) An electronic bulk clearing system generally used by banks and building societies for low-value and/or repetitive items such as standing orders, direct debits and automated credits such as salary payments.

bad debt A debt which is considered to be uncollectable and is, therefore, written off either as a charge to the profit and loss account or against an existing doubtful debt provision.

balance sheet A statement of the financial position of an entity at a given date disclosing the assets, liabilities and accumulated funds such as shareholders' contributions and reserves, prepared to give a true and fair view of the financial state of the entity at that date.

balanced scorecard An approach to the provision of information to management to assist strategic policy formulation and achievement. It emphasises the need to provide the user with a set of information which addresses all relevant areas of performance in an objective and unbiased fashion. The information provided may include both financial and non-financial elements, and cover areas such as profitability, customer satisfaction, internal efficiency and innovation.

bank reconciliation A detailed statement reconciling, at a given date, the cash balance in an entity's cash book with that reported in a bank statement.

basic standard A standard that remains unchanged since the previous period and probably many previous periods, that may be used for comparison but is likely to be out of date and irrelevant.

benchmarking The establishment, through data gathering, of targets and comparators, whereby relative levels of performance (and particularly areas of underperformance) can be identified. By the adoption of identified best practices it is hoped that performance will improve.

beta factor (β) The measure of the volatility of the return on a share relative to the market. If a share price were to rise or fall at double the market rate, it would have a beta factor of 2. Conversely, if the share price moved at half the market rate, the beta factor would be 0.5.

bill of materials (BOM) A detailed specification, for each product produced, of the sub-assemblies, components and materials required, distinguishing between those items which are purchased externally and those which are manufactured in-house.

bit A bit is short for binary digit, either 1 or 0 in the binary number system, and is the smallest unit of information handled by a computer, represented physically by an element such as a single pulse sent through a circuit or a small spot on a magnetic disc. Bits are normally seen in groups of eight, which is termed a byte, to represent more meaningful information including the letters of the alphabet and the digits 0 to 9.

bookkeeping Recording of monetary transactions, appropriately classified, in the financial records of an entity, either by manual means or otherwise.

bottleneck An activity within an organisation which has a lower capacity than preceding or subsequent activities, thereby limiting throughput. Bottlenecks are often the cause of a build-up of work-in-progress and idle time.

break-even point The level of activity at which there is neither profit nor loss, ascertained by using a break-even chart or by calculation.

broadband The method of sending and receiving data over high speed networks which is most commonly associated with a much faster way of connecting computers to the Internet than possible via conventional dial-up. Broadband is continually operational (not tying up the telephone line) and enables quicker loading of web pages, and transfer of files and email.

browser Users generally navigate through information on the Internet with the aid of a program called a browser, or client. A browser presents text, images, sound or other information objects on a user's computer screen in the form of a page, which is obtained from a www server.

budget A quantified statement, for a defined period of time, which may include planned revenues, expenses, assets, liabilities and cash flows.

business entity concept The concept that financial accounting information relates only to the activities of the business entity and not to the activities of its owners.

byte A byte is used to represent computer information including the letters of the alphabet and the digits 0 to 9, and is a unit of information consisting of 8 bits.

cable modem A cable modem transmits data at very high speeds, typically between 1 and 3 megabytes per second (or higher) compared with a telephone modem's Internet connection at 56 kilobytes per second. A cable modem can also be used to provide a television with channels for Internet access.

Cadbury Committee Report of the Cadbury Committee (December 1992) on the Financial Aspects of Corporate Governance, set up to consider issues in relation to financial reporting and accountability, and to make recommendations on good practice, relating to:
- responsibilities of executive and non-executive directors
- establishment of company audit committees
- responsibility of auditors
- links between shareholders, directors, and auditors
- any other relevant matters.

The report established a Code of Best Practice, now succeeded by the Combined Code of Practice.

capital asset pricing model (CAPM) A theory which predicts that the expected risk premium for an individual share will be proportional to its beta, such that the expected risk premium on a share = beta × the expected risk premium in the market. Risk premium is defined as the expected incremental return for making a risky investment rather than a safe one.

capital expenditure The cost of acquiring, producing or enhancing fixed assets.

capital rationing This is a restriction on an organisation's ability to invest capital funds, caused by an internal budget ceiling being imposed on such expenditure by management (soft capital rationing), or by external limitations being applied to the organisation, for example when additional borrowed funds cannot be obtained (hard capital rationing).

cash Cash in hand and deposits repayable on demand with any bank or other financial institution. Cash includes cash in hand and deposits denominated in foreign currency (FRS 1).

cash book A book of original entry that includes details of all receipts and payments made by an entity. The details normally include transaction date, method of payment or receipt, amount paid or received, bank statement value (if different), name of payee or payer, general ledger allocation and coding.

cash flow statement A statement that summarises the inflows and outflows of cash for a period, classified under the following standard headings (FRS 1):
- operating activities
- returns on investment and servicing of finance
- taxation
- investing activities
- liquid funds
- equity dividends
- financing.

cash interest cover Net cash inflow from operations plus interest received, divided by interest paid, calculates the number of times the interest payable is covered by cash flow available for such payments.

cash payment A cash payment is the transfer of funds from a business to a recipient (for example, trade creditor or employee).

cash receipt A cash receipt is the transfer of funds to a business from a payer (for example, a customer).

cleared funds Cleared funds are funds that have actually been cleared through the banking system and are available for use. It is the cleared funds balance, if overdrawn, which is used to calculate overdraft interest.

client-server A client-server is a form of network architecture in which each computer on a network is either a client or a server. Servers are powerful computers dedicated to managing disc drives, printers or network traffic. Clients are PCs or workstations, from which users are able to run application programs. Clients rely on servers for resources such as data, devices and sometimes processing power.

closed-loop system A control system that includes a provision for corrective action, taken on either a feedback or a feedforward basis.

closing stocks All trading companies buy stock with the intention of reselling, at a profit, to a customer. At the end of each accounting period, the company will have unsold stock that will be sold during a subsequent accounting period. That unsold stock is termed 'closing stock' and is deducted from opening stock plus purchases (to derive cost of sales), and will appear in the balance sheet as stocks (within current assets).

Combined Code of Practice The successor to the Cadbury Code, established by the Hampel Committee. The code consists of a set of principles of corporate governance and detailed code provisions embracing the work of the Cadbury, Greenbury and Hampel Committees. Section 1 of the code contains the principles and provisions applicable to UK listed companies, while section 2 contains the principles and provisions applicable to institutional shareholders in their relationships with companies.

competitive pricing Setting a price by reference to the prices of competing products.

computer-aided design (CAD) CAD is a general term referring to software applications and the method used in art, architecture, engineering and manufacturing to design and provide precision drawings, for example buildings, machinery, components and other items, using a computer VDU. CAD enables the interactive design and testing of a product or component.

computer-aided engineering (CAE) CAE, the broad term used by the electronic design automation (EDA) industry for the use of computers to design, analyse, and manufacture products and processes, includes computer-aided design (CAD – the use of a computer for drafting and modelling designs), and computer-aided manufacturing (CAM).

computer-aided manufacturing (CAM) CAM relates to the use of computers for managing manufacturing processes, through software designed to control each of the tasks involved.

computer-integrated manufacturing (CIM) CIM is the use of computers to give instructions that automatically set up, run and monitor the performance of manufacturing equipment and processes. The use of robotic plant and equipment provides computer software to monitor the manufactured product and directly control processes, which ensures high quality manufacturing output of defect-free components and products.

computerised accounting system This is a system that maintains business transactions on a computer on a long-term basis.

conceptual frameworks of accounting The statements of principles, which provide generally accepted guidance for the development of new financial information reporting practices and the review of current reporting practices.

concurrent engineering A means of reducing product development time and cost by managing development processes so they can be implemented simultaneously rather than sequentially.

consistency concept The principle that there is uniformity of accounting treatment of like items within each accounting period and from one period to the next.

consolidated accounts The consolidated financial statements which present financial information for the group as a single economic entity, prepared using a process of adjusting and combining financial information from the individual financial statements of a parent undertaking and its subsidiary undertakings (FRS 2).

contingent liability A possible obligation that arises from past events and whose existence will be confirmed only by the occurrence of one or more uncertain future events not wholly within the entity's control; or

A present obligation that arises from past events but is not recognised because: it is not probable that a transfer of benefits will be required to settle the obligation; or, the amount of the obligation cannot be measured with sufficient reliability (FRS 12).

continuing operations Operations not satisfying all the conditions relating to discontinued operations (see below).

contribution Sales value less variable cost of sales, which may be expressed as total contribution, contribution per unit, or as a percentage of sales.

control The ability to direct the financial and operating policies of an entity with a view to gaining economic benefits from its activities (FRS 8).

controllability concept Management accounting identifies the elements or activities which management can or cannot influence, and seeks to assess risk and sensitivity factors. This facilitates the proper monitoring, analysis, comparison and interpretation of information which can be used constructively in the control, evaluation and corrective functions of management.

convertible loan A loan which gives the holder the right to convert to other securities, normally ordinary shares, at a pre-determined date and at a pre-determined price or ratio.

corporate governance The system by which companies are directed and controlled. Boards of directors are responsible for the governance of their companies. The shareholders' role in governance is to appoint the directors and the auditors and to satisfy themselves that an appropriate governance structure is in place.

corporate social responsibility (CSR) CSR is the decision-making and implementation process that guides all company activities in the protection and promotion of international human rights, labour and environmental standards and compliance with legal requirements within its operations and in its relations to the societies and communities where it operates. CSR involves a commitment to contribute to the economic, environmental and social sustainability of communities through the on-going engagement of stakeholders, the active participation of communities impacted by company activities and the public reporting of company policies and performance in the economic, environmental and social arenas (www.bench-marks.org).

corporation tax Tax chargeable on companies resident in the UK, or trading in the UK through a branch or agency, as well as on certain unincorporated associations (FRS 16).

cost The amount of expenditure (actual or notional) incurred on, or attributable to, a specified thing or activity. To cost something is to ascertain the cost of a specified thing or activity. Cost also relates to a resource sacrificed or forgone, expressed in a monetary value.

cost centre A production or service location, function, activity or item of equipment for which costs are accumulated and to which they are charged.

cost driver Any factor which causes a change in the cost of an activity. For example, the quality of parts received by an activity is a determining factor in the work required by that activity and therefore affects the resources required. An activity may have multiple cost drivers associated with it.

cost object The thing that we wish to determine the cost of.

cost of quality (COQ) The cost of quality may be defined as the additional cost incurred in non-added value activities and events in a business in fully satisfying customers' agreed requirements for products and services delivered. It is the cost both of not doing the right things and not doing things right first time.

cost of sales The sum of direct cost of sales, adjusted for closing stocks, plus manufacturing overhead attributable to the sales. Direct costs include the wages and salaries costs of time worked on products, and the costs of materials used in production. Manufacturing overheads include the wages and salaries costs of employees not directly working on production, and materials and expenses incurred on activities not directly used in production but necessary to carry out production. Examples are cleaning materials and electricity costs.

cost unit A unit of product or service in relation to which costs are ascertained.

creative accounting A form of accounting which, while complying with all regulations, nevertheless gives a biased (generally favourable) impression of a company's performance.

creditor A person or an entity to whom money is owed as a consequence of the receipt of goods or services in advance of payment.

creditor days Average trade creditors divided by average daily purchases on credit terms indicates the average time taken, in calendar days, to pay for supplies received on credit.

cross-function management Horizontal cross-departmental organisation as opposed to the traditional vertical, functional, chimney organisation.

cross-sectional analysis Cross-sectional analysis provides a means of providing a standard against which performance can be measured and uses ratios to compare different businesses at the same points in time (see inter-firm comparison).

current assets Cash or other assets, for example stocks, debtors and short-term investments, held for conversion into cash in the normal course of trading.

current liabilities Liabilities which fall due for payment within one year. They include that part of long-term loans due for repayment within one year.

current ratio Current assets divided by current liabilities is an overall measure of liquidity.

cycle count The process of counting and valuing selected stock items at different times, on a rotating basis, so that all stocks are counted two, three, four or more times each year.

database management system (DBMS) A database is any collection of data organised for storage in a computer memory and designed for access by authorised users. Data may be in the form of text, numbers, or encoded graphics.

debenture The written acknowledgement of a debt by a company, usually given under its seal, and normally containing provisions as to payment of interest and the terms of repayment of principal. A debenture may be secured on some or all of the assets of the company or its subsidiaries.

debt One of the alternative sources of capital for a company, also called long-term debt or loans.

debt/equity ratio A gearing ratio that relates to financial gearing, which is the relationship between a company's borrowings, which includes both prior charge capital and long-term debt, and its ordinary shareholders' funds (share capital plus reserves).

debtor days Average trade debtors divided by average daily sales on credit terms indicates the average time taken, in calendar days, to receive payment from credit customers.

debtors Money that is owed to the company by customers, usually called trade debtors.

decision tree A pictorial method of showing a sequence of interrelated decisions and their expected outcomes. Decision trees can incorporate both the probabilities of, and values of, expected outcomes, and are used in decision-making.

defensive interval Quick assets (current assets excluding stocks) divided by average daily cash from operations shows how many days a business could survive at its present level of operating activity if no inflow of cash was received from sales or other sources.

depreciation A measure of the wearing out, consumption or other reduction in the useful economic life of a fixed asset, whether arising from use, effluxion of time or obsolescence through technological or market changes (FRS 11 and FRS 15). Depreciation should be allocated so as to charge a fair proportion of the total cost (or valuation) of the asset to each accounting period expected to benefit from its use.

depreciation provision The amount of depreciation that has cumulatively been charged to the profit and loss account, relating to a fixed asset, from the date of its acquisition. Fixed assets are stated in the balance sheet at their net book value (or written down value), which is usually their historical cost less the cumulative amount of depreciation at the balance sheet date.

differential cost The difference in total cost between alternatives, calculated to assist decision-making.

direct cost A traceable cost, or expenditure which can be economically identified with and specifically measured in respect of a relevant cost object.

direct labour Labour costs which can be economically identified with and specifically measured in respect of a relevant cost object.

direct materials Materials costs which can be economically identified with and specifically measured in respect of a relevant cost object.

direct method A method of calculating cash flow as the net of operating cash receipts and payments that is summarised for inclusion in the cash flow statement. It is a time-consuming process that is not straightforward and is not widely used by UK companies.

director A person elected under the company's articles of association to be responsible for the overall direction of the company's affairs. Directors usually act collectively as a board and carry out such functions as are specified in the articles of association or the Companies Acts, but they may also act individually in an executive capacity.

discontinued operations Operations of the reporting entity that are sold or terminated and that satisfy certain criteria (FRS 3):

- the sale or termination is completed either in the period or before the earlier of three months after the commencement of the subsequent period and the date on which the financial statements are approved
- if a termination, the former activities have ceased permanently
- the sale or termination has a material effect on the nature and focus of the reporting entity's operations, and represents a material reduction in its operating facilities resulting from its withdrawal from a particular market (whether class of business or geographical) or from a material reduction in turnover in the reporting entity's continuing markets
- the assets, liabilities, results of operations and activities are clearly distinguishable physically, operationally and for financial reporting purposes.

discounted cash flow (DCF) The discounting of the projected net cash flows of a capital project to ascertain its present value, using a yield or internal rate of return (IRR), net present value (NPV) or discounted payback.

discounted payback The number of years required to repay an original investment using a specified discount rate.

dividend An amount payable to shareholders from profits or distributable reserves. Dividends are normally paid in cash, but scrip dividends, paid by the issue of additional shares, are permissible. Listed companies usually declare two dividends each year, an interim dividend based on the mid-year profits, and a final dividend based on annual profit.

dividend cover Earnings per share divided by dividend per share indicates the number of times the profits attributable to the equity shareholders cover the actual dividends payable for the period.

double-entry bookkeeping The system of bookkeeping based on the principle that every financial transaction involves the simultaneous receiving and giving of value, and is therefore recorded twice.

doubtful debt A debt for which there is some uncertainty as to whether or not it will be settled, and for which there is a possibility that it may eventually prove to be bad. A doubtful debt provision may be created for such a debt by charging it as an expense to the profit and loss account.

doubtful debt provision An amount charged against profit and deducted from debtors to allow for the estimated non-recovery of a proportion of the debts.

dual aspect concept The rule that provides the basis for double-entry bookkeeping, reflecting the practical reality that every transaction always includes both the giving and receiving of something.

earnings per share (eps) Profit after tax less preference share dividends divided by the number of ordinary shares in issue measures the return per share of earnings available to shareholders.

EBITDA Earnings before interest, tax, depreciation, and amortisation.

E-business E-business uses electronic technology to change or automate business processes and includes a range of tools and techniques such as e-commerce, business intelligence, customer relationship management, supply chain management, and enterprise planning.

E-commerce E-commerce is a more narrowly focused term, being one aspect of e-business, broadly involving the sharing of business information and performing business transactions. It may include electronic data interchange (EDI), mobile telephone technology, electronic supplier links, Internet, intranet, extranet, electronic catalogue buying, and email.

economic value added (EVA™) Profit after tax adjusted for distortions in operating performance (such as goodwill, extraordinary losses, and operating leases) less a charge for the amount of capital employed to create that profit (calculated from the adjusted book value of net assets times the company's weighted average cost of capital) (Stern Stewart).

effectiveness The utilisation of resources such that the output of the activity achieves the desired result. In other words, efficiency alone is not enough – efficiency in areas from which optimised output is what is required to be effective (to avoid being a 'busy fool').

efficiency The achievement of either maximum useful output from the resources devoted to an activity, or the required output from the minimum resource input.

electronic data interchange (EDI) EDI is the secure electronic exchange of business documents such as invoices, fund transfer requests or purchase orders between trading partners. EDI is vital for efficient e-commerce between trading partners. It allows businesses to automate routine transactions and to guarantee transaction integrity. There are several sector-specific EDI standards in use internationally. Initially, private networks were used to send and receive messages, but since the mid-1990s EDI over the Internet has been widely adopted and complexity and cost issues have been greatly reduced.

electronic funds transfer (EFT) EFT works in a similar way to EDI (which deals with the electronic transfer of documents), but with a different set of standards, and is used to transmit funds. EFT may be made between organisations and their employees, suppliers, customers, and any other third parties.

electronic point of sale (EPOS) EPOS systems process sales transactions electronically and scan and capture real-time product information at the point of sale. The systems range from networked cash registers in retail and wholesale outlets with links to business computer systems, to larger systems that link point of sale information with warehousing, suppliers ordering systems, customer databases and online web stores.

Email Electronic mail, or email, enables any person with Internet access to send and receive written messages, files, still and moving images, to and from any other person with Internet access, anywhere in the world, and almost instantaneously.

encryption Encryption is a process used to encode data that is entered into a system, and therefore provides security through preventing unauthorised access to data while it is being stored or transmitted and before it reaches its required destination.

enterprise resource planning (ERP) ERP software spans across functional boundaries. ERP packages comprise individual modules that are process-focused and supporting, for example, accounting, finance, stocks management, design, engineering, supply chain management, manufacturing, quality management, human resource management, planning, sales, and distribution. ERP packages provide flexible systems that are totally integrated and enable use of the Internet for information flows between suppliers, customers and other third parties, on a local and a global basis.

environmental reporting A statement included within the annual report and accounts that sets out the environmental policies of the company and an explanation of its environmental management systems and responsibilities. The environmental report may include reporting on the performance of the business on environmental matters in qualitative terms regarding the extent to which it meets national and international standards. It may also include a quantitative report on the performance of the business on environmental matters against targets, together with an assessment of the financial impact.

equity The total investment of the shareholders in the company, the total wealth. Equity comprises capital, premiums, and retained earnings.

ergonomics The study of the efficiency of persons in their working environment.

euro The common currency of the European Union, which came into being on 1 January 1999. Financial transactions and/or financial reporting of member states may now be undertaken in either the functional domestic currencies, or in euros.

ex ante Means before the event. An *ex ante* budget, or standard, is set before a period of activity commences, and is based on the best information available at that time on expected levels of cost, performance, etc.

exceptional items Material items which derive from events or transactions that fall within the ordinary activities of the reporting entity individually or, if a similar type, in aggregate and which need to be disclosed separately by virtue of their size or incidence if the financial statements are to give a true and fair view (FRS 3).

expected value The financial forecast of the outcome of a course of action multiplied by the probability of achieving that outcome. The probability is expressed as a value ranging from zero to 1.

ex post Means after the event. An *ex post* budget, or standard, is set after the end of a period of activity, when it can represent the optimum achievable level of performance in the conditions which were experienced. Thus the budget can be flexed, and the standards can reflect factors such as unanticipated changes in technology and in price levels.

extranet An extranet is a mechanism based on Internet and web technology for businesses to communicate both privately and selectively with their customers. It is effectively a part of the business's intranet that is extended to users outside the business.

extraordinary items Material items possessing a high degree of abnormality that arise from events or transactions that fall outside the ordinary activities of the reporting entity and which are not expected to recur. They do not include exceptional items, nor do they include prior period items merely because they relate to a prior period (FRS 3).

failure mode and effect analysis (FMEA) FMEA is used to identify the most important possible modes of failure during the design and development stage of a product so that action may be taken to reduce the risks of those occurrences.

finance director The finance director of an organisation is actively involved in broad strategic and policy-making activities involving financial considerations. The finance director provides the board of directors with advice on financing, capital expenditure, acquisitions, dividends, the implications of changes in the economic environment, and the financial aspects of legislation. The finance director is responsible for the planning and control functions, the financial systems, financial reporting, and the management of funds.

finance lease A lease is a contract between a lessor and a lessee for the hire of a specific asset. The lessor retains ownership of the asset but gives the right to the use of the asset to the lessee for an agreed period in return for the payment of specified rentals (SSAP 21). A finance lease transfers substantially all the risks and rewards of ownership of the asset to the lessee.

financial accounting Financial accounting is the function responsible for the periodic external reporting, statutorily required, for shareholders. It also provides such similar information as required for Government and other interested third parties, such as potential investors, employees, lenders, suppliers, customers, and financial analysts.

financial instrument Any contract that gives rise to both a financial asset of one entity and a financial liability or equity instrument of another entity. Financial instruments include both primary financial instruments – such as bonds, debtors, creditors and shares – and derivative financial instruments whose value derives from the underlying assets.

financial management The management of all the processes associated with the efficient acquisition and deployment of both short- and long-term financial resources. Within an organisation financial management assists operations management to reach their financial objectives.

Financial Reporting Standards (FRSs) The accounting standards of practice published by the Accounting Standards Board since 1 August 1990, and which are gradually replacing the Standard Statements of Accounting Practice (SSAPs), which were published by the Accounting Standards Committee up to 1 August 1990.

financial statements Summaries of accounts, whether to internal or external parties, to provide information for interested parties. The three key financial statements are: profit and loss account; balance sheet; cash flow statement. Other financial statements are: report of the auditors; statement of recognised gains and losses; reconciliation of movements in shareholders' funds.

financing The section of the cash flow statement that shows the long-term funds raised by or repaid by the company during the year.

finished product Finished product or finished goods are manufactured goods ready for sale or despatch.

firewall A firewall is software and/or hardware that is used to isolate a computer network from unauthorised external use.

first in first out (FIFO) Assumes that the oldest items or costs are the first to be used. It is commonly applied to the pricing of issues of materials, based on using first the costs of the oldest materials in stock, irrespective of the sequence in which actual material usage takes place. Closing stocks are therefore valued at relatively current costs.

fixed assets Any asset, tangible or intangible, acquired for retention by an entity for the purpose of providing a service to the business, and not held for resale in the normal course of trading. This includes, for example, equipment, machinery, furniture, fittings, computers, software, and motor vehicles that the company has purchased to enable it to meet its strategic objectives; such items are not renewed within the operating cycle.

fixed cost A cost which is incurred for an accounting period, and which, within certain output or turnover limits, tends to be unaffected by fluctuations in the levels of activity (output or turnover).

flexed budget The budgeted cost ascribed to the level of activity achieved in a budget centre in a control period. It comprises variable costs in direct proportion to volume achieved and fixed costs as a proportion of the annual budget.

flotation A flotation (or a new issue) is the obtaining of a listing by a company on a stock exchange, through the offering of its shares to the general public, financial institutions or private sector businesses.

forecast A prediction of future events and their quantification for planning purposes.

fraudulent trading An offence committed by persons who are knowingly party to the continuance of a company trading in circumstances where creditors are defrauded or for other fraudulent purposes. Generally, this means that the company incurs more debts at a time when it is known that those debts will not be met. Persons responsible for so acting are personally liable without limitation for the debts of the company. The offence also carries criminal penalties.

gearing Financial gearing calculations can be made in a number of ways. Gearing is generally seen as the relationship between a company's borrowings, which include both prior charge capital (capital having a right of interest or preference shares having fixed dividends) and long-term debt, and its ordinary shareholders' funds (share capital plus reserves).

general ledger Also called the nominal ledger, contains all accounts relating to assets, expenses, revenue and liabilities.

gigabyte A gigabyte or Gb is a measure of capacity equal to one billion bytes. It can often be used to mean either 1,000 megabytes or 1,024 megabytes.

going concern concept The assumption that the entity will continue in operational existence for the forseeable future.

goodwill The difference between the value of a business as a whole and the aggregate of the fair values of the separable net assets (FRS 10). Goodwill is normally recognised on the purchase of a business, when the price paid for the net assets acquired exceeds their fair values. Where the fair value of the separable net assets exceeds the value of the business as a whole, the difference is termed negative goodwill.

graphic user interface (GUI) A GUI is a development of operating systems that now enable users to command the computer by using a mouse to click on icons, rather than using the keyboard to type instructions. Icons are small pictorial representations of objects, denoting a particular function or program, which are displayed on the computer screen.

gross margin (GM) Gross margin (or gross profit) is the difference between sales and the total cost of sales.

groupware Groupware is software that allows individuals to coordinate efforts and collaborate on various tasks and projects.

hacker A hacker is a malicious intruder who has gained unauthorised access to a computer system. Hacking may occur in the systems of individuals, and in both large and small organisations by current or past employees as well as outsiders, simply to cause damage or for fraudulent purposes.

Hampel Committee The 1998 report of the Hampel Committee on Corporate Governance was set up to conduct a review of the Cadbury Code and its implications:

- review of the role of directors
- matters arising from the Greenbury Study Group on directors' remuneration
- role of shareholders and auditors
- other relevant matters.

The Hampel Committee was responsible for the corporate governance Combined Code of Practice.

heijunka The smoothing of production through the levelling of schedules. This is done by sequencing orders in a repetitive pattern and smoothing the day-to-day variations in total orders to correspond to longer-term demand.

historical cost concept A basis of accounting prescribed by the Companies Act for published accounts that uses a system of accounting in which all values are based on the historical costs incurred.

horizontal analysis (or **common size analysis**) An analysis of the profit and loss account (or balance sheet) that allows a line-by-line analysis of the accounts with those of the previous year. It may provide over a number of years a trend of changes showing either growth or decline in these elements of the accounts through calculation of annual percentage growth rates in profits, sales, stock or any other item.

hybrid finance A financial instrument that has the characteristics of both debt and equity.

ideal standard A standard that is only attainable under the most favourable conditions and makes no allowance for normal loss, waste and machine downtime.

indirect cost An indirect cost is a cost that is untraceable to particular units. It is expenditure on labour, materials or services which cannot be economically identified with a specific saleable cost unit. Such costs have to be allocated, that is, assigned to a single cost unit, cost centre, or cost account or time period. The term 'burden' used by American companies is synonymous with indirect costs or overheads.

indirect method A method of calculating cash flow which uses the starting point of operating profit, since it is the operating activities of sales and costs that normally give rise to the majority of cash inflows and cash outflows of an entity. Operating profit for the period must then be adjusted for depreciation, as well as movements in stock, debtors and creditors over the same period to derive the net cash flow from operating activities.

inflation A general increase in the price level over time. In a period of hyperinflation the rate at which the price level rises has become extremely high, and possibly out of control.

initial public offering (IPO) An IPO is a company's first public sale of its shares. Shares offered in an IPO are often, but not always, those of young, small companies seeking outside equity capital and a public market for their shares. Investors purchasing shares in IPOs generally must be prepared to accept considerable risks for the possibility of large gains.

insolvency The inability of a company, partnership or individual to pay creditors' debts in full after realisation of all the assets of the business.

intangible assets Assets, except for investments in subsidiary companies, which do not have a physical identity and include software, patents, trademarks, and goodwill (FRS 10).

integrated services digital network (ISDN) An ISDN provides digital data services over traditional analogue telephone lines in the same way as ADSL. An ISDN allows users to send and receive data at very high speeds and can carry both voice and/or data transmission on the same line. The use of ISDN appears to be declining as the use of broadband increases.

interdependency concept Management accounting, in recognition of the increasing complexity of business, must access both internal and external information sources from interactive functions such as marketing, production, personnel, procurement and finance. This assists in ensuring that the information is adequately balanced.

interest cover Profit before interest and tax divided by interest payable, calculates the number of times the interest payable is covered by profits available for such payments. It is particularly important for lenders to determine the vulnerability of interest payments to a drop in profit.

inter-firm comparison Systematic and detailed comparison of the performance of different companies generally operating in a common industry. Normally the information distributed by the scheme administrator (to participating companies only) is in the form of ratios, or in a format, which prevents the identity of individual scheme members from being identified.

internal audit An independent appraisal function established within an organisation to examine and evaluate its activities as a service to the organisation. The objective of internal auditing is to assist members of the organisation in the effective discharge of their responsibilities. To this end, internal auditing furnishes them with analyses, appraisals, recommendations, counsel and information concerning the activities reviewed (Institute of Internal Auditors – UK).

internal control As defined in the Cadbury Report, it is the whole system of controls, financial or otherwise, established in order to provide reasonable assurance of:

- effective and efficient operation
- internal financial control
- compliance with laws and regulations.

internal rate of return (IRR) The annual percentage return achieved by a project, at which the sum of the discounted cash inflows over the life of the project is equal to the sum of the discounted cash outflows.

International Accounting Standard (IAS) The international financial reporting standards issued by the IASC, which are very similar to the SSAPs and FRSs, which are used in the UK.

International Accounting Standards Board (IASB) The IASB is the body that is responsible for setting and publishing International Financial Reporting Standards (IFRSs). It was formed on 1 April 2001 and succeeded the International Accounting Standards Committee (IASC) which had been formed in 1973. The parent body of the IASB is the International Accounting Standards Committee Foundation, which was incorporated in the USA in March 2001, and was also responsible for issuing International Accounting Standards (IASs).

International Financial Reporting Standard (IFRS) The international financial reporting standards issued by the IASB, which incorporate the IASs, issued by the IASC. IASs are very similar to the SSAPs and FRSs, which are used in the UK.

Internet The Internet or the net is a worldwide system of computer networks, a network of networks in which users at any one computer can, if they have permission, exchange information with any other computer. The Internet is distinguished by its use of a set of protocols called TCP/IP, which means transmission control protocol/Internet protocol.

Internet service provider (ISP) An ISP is a company, which provides Internet access to other companies or individuals. An ISP maintains connections to other networks and ISPs, acting as a router for Internet traffic between a customer's computer and any other machine also connected to the Internet. The Internet connections are typically ADSL, cable, and dial-up.

intranet An intranet is a network within an organisation that uses Internet technologies to enable users to find, use, and share documents and web pages. Businesses also use intranets to communicate with employees. A firewall is used to isolate the network.

intrusion detection software Intrusion detection software is designed to detect intrusion or entrance to systems by monitoring the entire computer system continuously and notifying users if the system has been entered without authorisation or if the system is being used inappropriately.

investment Any application of funds which is intended to provide a return by way of interest, dividend or capital appreciation.

investment centre A profit centre with additional responsibilities for capital investment and possibly for financing, and whose performance is measured by its return on investment – the manager is responsible for investments, revenues and costs.

jidoka Autonomation, which increases productivity through eliminating the non-value adding need for operators to watch machines, thus freeing them for more productive work, for example quality assurance.

just in time (JIT) The management philosophy that incorporates a 'pull' system of producing or purchasing components and products in response to customer demand, which contrasts with a 'push' system where stocks act as buffers between each process within and between purchasing, manufacturing, and sales.

kaizen Continuous improvement in all aspects of performance, at every level within the organisation.

kanban A signal, for example a card used in JIT production to prompt top up of materials or components driven by demand from the next process.

key factor (or limiting factor) Anything which limits the activity of an entity. An entity seeks to optimise the benefit it obtains from the limiting factor. Examples are a shortage of supply of a resource or a restriction on sales demand at a particular price.

kilobyte A kilobyte or Kb is a measure of capacity equal to 1,024 bytes. For example, 15 Kb equates approximately to one A4 page of text.

knowledge management software The enormous developments in IT have resulted in the creation of unprecedented amounts of data and information that is widely and easily accessible – far more than can be realistically retrieved and used. The use of knowledge management software has become increasingly important to ensure that the information that is required may be accessed, and that the information that is really useful is obtained and used effectively.

last in first out (LIFO) Assumes that the last item of stock received is the first to be used. In the UK it is a little-used method of pricing the issue of material using the purchase price of the latest unit in stock. It is used more often in the USA as a method of valuing stock using indices to charge most recent prices against profits.

lean accounting Lean accounting is concerned with the financial performance of a company that has implemented lean processes. Lean means using less of everything to provide more, and in greater variety, through the control and elimination of waste in all its forms. It may include the organisation of costs by value stream, changes in the way that stocks may be valued, and a modification of the financial statements and the reporting of non-financial information.

leave of the court This is where the court will make a decision after hearing all the relevant information.

letter of credit A document issued by a bank on behalf of a customer authorising a third party to draw funds to a specified amount from its branches or correspondents, usually in another country, when the conditions set out in the document have been met.

liabilities An entity's obligations to transfer economic benefits as a result of past transactions or events (FRS 5).

life cycle costing The maintenance of physical asset records over the entire asset life, so that decisions concerning the acquisition, use or disposal of the asset can be made in a way that achieves the optimum assets usage at the lowest possible cost to the business. The term may be applied to the profiling of cost over a product's life, including the pre-production stage, and to company and industry life cycles.

limited company (Ltd) A Ltd company is one in which the liability of members for the company's debts is limited to the amount paid and, if any, unpaid on the shares taken up by them.

limiting factor (or key factor) Anything which limits the activity of an entity. An entity seeks to optimise the benefit it obtains from the limiting factor. Examples are a shortage of supply of a resource or a restriction on sales demand at a particular price.

linear programming The use of a series of linear equations to construct a mathematical model. The objective is to obtain an optimal solution to a complex operational problem, which may involve the production of a number of products in an environment in which there are many constraints.

liquid resources Liquid resources, or liquid assets, are cash, and other assets readily convertible into cash, for example short-term investments.

loan capital Also called debt, relates to debentures and other long-term loans to a business.

local area network (LAN) A LAN is a group of computers, printers or other hardware that are all connected in a reasonably small geographic location like an office or home, which makes it possible for the connected users to share files and applications that usually reside on a server or some type of shared computer.

management accounting The application of the principles of accounting and financial management to create, protect, preserve and increase value so as to deliver that value to the stakeholders of profit and not-for-profit enterprises, both public and private. Management accounting is an integral part of management, requiring the identification, generation, presentation, interpretation and use of information relevant to:

- formulating business strategy
- planning and controlling activities
- decision-making
- efficient resource usage
- performance improvement and value enhancement
- safeguarding tangible and intangible assets
- corporate governance and internal control.

management by exception The practice of focusing on activities which require attention and ignoring those which appear to be conforming to expectations.

management control The process by which managers assure that resources are obtained and used effectively and efficiently in the accomplishment of the organisation's objectives.

manufacturing resource planning (MRPII) An expansion of material requirements planning (MRPI) to give a broader approach than MRPI to the planning and scheduling of resources, embracing areas such as finance, logistics, engineering and marketing.

marginal costing A costing technique whereby each unit of output is charged with variable production costs. Fixed production costs are not considered to be real costs of production, but costs which provide the facilities for an accounting period that enable production to take place.

margin of safety The difference between the break-even point and an anticipated or existing level of activity above that point.

market value added (MVA) The difference between the market value of the company and the adjusted book values of its assets.

master production schedule A time-phased statement (usually computerised) of how many items are to be produced in a given period (like a giant timetable), based on customer orders and demand forecasts.

materiality Information is material if its omission or misstatement could influence the economic decisions of users taken on the basis of financial information. Materiality depends on the size of the item or error judged in the particular circumstances of its omission or misstatement.

materiality concept Information is material if its omission or misstatement could influence the economic decisions of users taken on the basis of the financial statements. Materiality depends on the size of the item or error judged in the particular circumstances of its omission or misstatement.

Thus, materiality provides a threshold or cut-off point rather than being a primary qualitative characteristic that information must have if it is to be useful.

materials requirement planning (MRP1 or MRP) A system that converts a production schedule into a listing of the materials and components required to meet that schedule, so that adequate stock levels are maintained and items are available when needed.

megabyte A megabyte or Mb is a measure of capacity equal to 1,048,576 bytes. For example, 1 Mb equates approximately to the text of an average paperback novel, and 5 Mb equates approximately to the complete works of Shakespeare.

mission The mission of an organisation, not necessarily written, is its general sense of purpose and underlying inherent beliefs, that creates and reflects a 'common thread', common values and culture throughout the organisation. An organisation's written mission statement usually includes a summary of goals and policies together with its purpose and what business it is in, what it provides and for whom its exists, its values and commitment to its employees and suppliers, its policies and behaviour standards and principles of business, quality and professionalism, and its strategy and long-term vision.

modem Modems (derived from MOdulator/DEModulator) are electronic devices for converting between serial data from a computer and an audio signal suitable for transmission over a telephone line connected to another modem, distinguished primarily by the maximum data rate they support. Data rates can range from 75 bits per second up to 56,000 bits per second and beyond, with data from the user (i.e. flowing from the local terminal or computer via the modem to the telephone line) sometimes at a lower rate than the other direction, on the assumption that the user cannot type more than a few characters per second.

money measurement concept Most quantifiable data is capable of being converted, using a common denominator of money, into monetary terms. The money measurement concept holds that accounting deals only with those items capable of being translated into monetary terms, which imposes a limit on the scope of accounting reporting to such items.

net assets The excess of the book value of assets over liabilities, including loan capital. This is equivalent to net worth, which is used to describe the paid-up share capital and reserves.

net debt The total borrowings of the company net of liquid resources. Net debt excludes non-equity shares because, although similar to borrowings, they are not actually liabilities of the entity. Net debt excludes debtors and creditors because, whilst they are short-term claims on and sources of finance to the entity, their main role is as part of the entity's trading activities.

net present value (NPV) The difference between the sums of the projected discounted cash inflows and outflows attributable to a capital investment or other long-term project.

net profit (or profit after tax) Profit before tax (PBT) less corporation tax.

net realisable value The amount for which an asset could be disposed, less any direct selling costs (SSAP 9).

new economy The current new economy, in which IT plays a significant role, enables producers of both the tangible (computers, shoes, etc.) and intangible (services, ideas, etc.) to compete efficiently in global markets.

non-executive director A director who does not have a particular function to perform within the company's management. The usual involvement is to attend board meetings only.

non-financial performance indicators Measures of performance based on non-financial information which may originate in and be used by operating departments to monitor and control their activities without any accounting input. Non-financial performance measures may give a more timely indication of the levels of performance achieved than do financial ratios, and may be less susceptible to distortion by factors such as uncontrollable variations in the effect of market forces on operations.

non-related company A company in which a business has a long-term investment, but over which it has no control or influence. If control exists then the company is deemed to be a subsidiary.

notional cost A cost used in product evaluation, decision-making and performance measurement to represent the cost of using resources which have no conventional 'actual cost'. Notional interest, for example, may be charged for the use of internally generated funds.

off balance sheet financing The funding of operations in such a way that the relevant assets and liabilities are not disclosed in the balance sheet of the company concerned.

online Online is the condition of being connected to a network of computers or other devices and the term is usually used to describe someone who is currently connected to the Internet.

operating cycle The operating cycle, or working capital cycle, is calculated by deducting creditor days from stock days plus debtor days. It represents the period of time which elapses between the point at which cash begins to be expended on the production of a product and the collection of cash from the customer.

operating gearing The relationship of fixed costs to total costs. The greater the proportion of fixed costs, the higher the operating gearing, and the greater the advantage to the business of increasing sales volume. If sales drop, a business with high operating gearing may face a problem from its high level of fixed costs.

operating lease A lease is a contract between a lessor and a lessee for the hire of a specific asset. The lessor retains ownership of the asset but gives the right to the use of the asset to the lessee for an agreed period in return for the payment of specified rentals (SSAP 21). An operating lease is a lease other than a finance lease, where the lessor retains most of the risks and rewards of ownership.

operating profit Gross profit, or gross margin, plus/less all operating revenues and costs, regardless of the financial structure of the company and whatever exceptional events occurred during the period.

operational variance A classification of variances in which non-standard performance is defined as being that which differs from an *ex post* standard. Operational variances can relate to any element of the standard product specification.

opportunity cost The value of the benefit sacrificed when one course of action is chosen, in preference to an alternative. The opportunity cost is represented by the forgone potential benefit from the best rejected course of action.

optimised production technology (OPT) OPT is a manufacturing philosophy combined with a computerised system of shop-floor scheduling and capacity planning. It is a philosophy that focuses on factors such as manufacture to order, quality, lead times, batch sizes and set-up times, and differs from a traditional approach of balancing capacity as near 100 per cent as possible and then maintaining flow. The aim of OPT is to balance flow rather than capacity. The goal of OPT is to make money by increasing throughput and reducing stocks and operating expenses, by making better use of limited capacity by tightly controlled finite scheduling of bottleneck operations.

ordinary shares Shares which entitle the holders to the remaining divisible profits (and, in a liquidation, the assets) after prior interests, for example creditors and prior charge capital, have been satisfied.

overhead absorption rate A means of attributing overhead to a product or service, based, for example, on direct labour hours, direct labour cost or machine hours.

overhead over- and under-absorption (or overhead over- and under-recovery) The difference between overhead incurred and overhead absorbed, using an estimated rate, in a given period.

Pareto analysis Analysis of a frequency distribution with a small proportion (say 20%) of the items accounting for a large proportion (say 80%) of the total. Examples may be seen in around 80% of sales of a company being derived from about 20% of its customers, and 80% of the value of its stocks being held in 20% of its items.

password A password is a unique identifier known only to a specific individual, and used by them every time they are required to log into a computer system. Passwords do not ensure 100 per cent security, but to ensure that they provide the highest level of security possible they should not be obviously guessed words or numbers, and should be changed regularly, and protected from unauthorised users.

payback The number of years it takes the cash inflows from a capital investment project to equal the cash outflows. An organisation may have a target payback period, above which projects are rejected.

period cost A cost which relates to a time period rather than to the output of products or services.

periodicity concept The requirement to produce financial statements at set time intervals. This requirement is embodied, in the case of UK companies, in the Companies Act 1985.

planning The establishment of objectives, and the formulation, evaluation and selection of the policies, strategies, tactics and action required to achieve them. Planning comprises long-term/strategic planning, and short-term operational planning, the latter being usually for a period of up to one year.

planning variance A planning or revision variance is a classification of variances caused by *ex ante* budget allowances being changed to an *ex post* basis.

poka yoke Failsafe devices, support *jidoka* by preventing parts being mounted or fitted in the wrong way and alerting operators by flashing lights, ringing buzzers – it is a method of spotting defects, identifying, repairing and avoiding further defects.

policy deployment The process of internalising improvement policies throughout the company from translation of customer requirements, through each process of specification, design, etc. to final manufacturing and delivery.

post balance sheet events Favourable and unfavourable events, which occur between the balance sheet date and the date on which the financial statements are approved by the board of directors.

preference shares Shares carrying a fixed rate of dividend, the holders of which, subject to the conditions of issue, have a prior claim to any company profits available for distribution. Preference shares may also have a prior claim to the repayment of capital in the event of a winding up.

prepayments Prepayments include prepaid expenses for services not yet used, for example rent in advance or electricity charges in advance, and also accrued income. Accrued income relates to sales of goods or services that have occurred and have been included in the profit and loss account for the trading period but have not yet been invoiced to the customer.

present value The cash equivalent now of a sum receivable or payable at a future date.

price/earnings ratio (P/E) The market price per ordinary share divided by earnings per share shows the number of years it would take to recoup an equity investment from its share of the attributable equity profit.

price elasticity A measure of the responsiveness of the demand for a product or service to a change in the price of that product or service. Products with an inelastic demand show relatively little changes in demand to relatively large changes in price (for example, the necessities of life) – demand is therefore not significantly price sensitive. Products with an elastic demand show relatively large changes in demand to relatively small changes in price.

profit and loss account (or income statement) The profit and loss account shows the profit or loss generated by an entity during an accounting period by deducting all expenses from all revenues.

It measures whether or not the company has made a profit or loss on its operations during the period, through producing and selling its goods or services.

profit before tax (PBT) Operating profit plus or minus net interest.

profit centre A part of the business that is accountable for both costs and revenues – the manager is responsible for revenues and costs.

provision Amount charged against profit to provide for an expected liability or loss even though the amount or date of the liability or loss is uncertain (FRS 12).

prudence concept The principle that revenue and profits are not anticipated, but are included in the profit and loss account only when realised in the form either of cash or of other assets, or the ultimate cash realisation can be assessed with reasonable certainty; provision is made for all known liabilities (expenses and losses) whether the amount of these is known with certainty or is a best estimate in the light of information available.

public limited company (plc) A plc is a company limited by shares or by guarantee, with a share capital, whose memorandum states that it is public and that it has complied with the registration procedures for such a company. A public company is distinguished from a private company in the following ways: a minimum issued share capital of £50,000; public limited company, or plc, at the end of the name; public company clause in the memorandum; freedom to offer securities to the public.

pull system A system whose objective is to produce or procure products or components as they are required for use by internal and external customers, rather than for stock. This contrasts with a 'push' system, in which stocks act as buffers between processes within production, and between production, purchasing and sales.

purchase invoice A document received from a supplier by an entity showing the description, quantity, prices and values of goods or services received.

purchase invoice daybook A list of supplier invoices recording their dates, gross values, values net of VAT, the dates of receipt of the invoices, the names of suppliers, and the general ledger allocation and coding.

purchase ledger The purchase ledger contains all the personal accounts of each individual supplier or vendor, and records every transaction with each supplier since the start of their relationship with the company.

qualified accountant A member of the accountancy profession, and in the UK a member of one of the six professional accountancy bodies: CIMA; ICAEW; ICAS; ICAI; ACCA; CIPFA.

raw materials Goods purchased for incorporation into products for sale.

realisation concept The principle that increases in value should only be recognised on realisation of assets by arms-length sale to an independent purchaser.

receiver A person appointed by secured creditors or by the court to take control of company property, usually following the failure of the company to pay principal sums or interest due to debenture holders whose debt is secured by fixed or floating charges over the assets of the company. The receiver takes control of the charged assets and may operate the company's business with a view to selling it as a going concern. In practice receivership is closely followed by liquidation.

Registrar of Companies Government official agency that is responsible for initial registration of new companies and for collecting and arranging public access to the annual reports of all limited companies.

relevancy concept Management accounting must ensure that flexibility is maintained in assembling and interpreting information. This facilitates the exploration and presentation, in a clear, understandable and timely manner, of as many alternatives as are necessary for impartial and confident decisions to be taken. This process is essentially forward-looking and dynamic. Therefore, the information must satisfy the criteria of being applicable and appropriate.

relevant cost Cost appropriate to a specific management decision.

reliability concept Management accounting information must be of such quality that confidence can be placed in it. Its reliability to the user is dependent on its source, integrity and comprehensiveness.

repayable on demand This refers to the definition of cash where there is a loss of interest if cash is withdrawn within 24 hours.

reporting entity A public or private limited company required to file its annual report and accounts with the Registrar of Companies.

reserves Retained profits or surpluses. In a not-for-profit entity these are described as accumulated funds. Reserves may be distributable or non-distributable.

residual income (RI) Profit before tax less an imputed interest charge for invested capital, which may be used to assess the performance of a division or a branch of a business.

responsibility accounting A system in which a budget holder is given responsibility for all revenues and costs that can be traced to clearly defined areas of their responsibility.

responsibility centre A department or organisational function whose performance is the direct responsibility of a specific manager.

retained profits Profits that have not been paid out as dividends to shareholders, but retained for future investment by the company.

return on capital employed (ROCE) ROCE, or return on investment (ROI), is the profit before interest and tax divided by average capital employed. It indicates the profit-generating capacity of capital employed.

return on investment (ROI) See return on capital employed (ROCE).

revenue centre A centre devoted to raising revenue with no responsibility for costs, for example, a sales centre – the manager is responsible for revenues only (revenue centres are often used in not-for-profit organisations).

revenue expenditure Expenditure on the manufacture of goods, the provision of services or on the general conduct of the entity, which is charged to the profit and loss account in the accounting period of sale. This includes repairs and depreciation of fixed assets as distinct from the provision of these assets.

reverse engineering The decomposition and analysis of competitors' products in order to determine how they are made, their costs of production and the way in which future development may proceed.

rights issue The raising of new capital by giving existing shareholders the right to subscribe to new shares or debentures in proportion to their current holdings. These shares are usually issued at a discount to the market price. A shareholder not wishing to take up a rights issue may sell the rights.

risk A condition in which there exists a quantifiable dispersion in the possible outcomes from any activity. For example: credit risk – the risk that a borrower may default on his obligations; currency risk – the possibility of loss or gain due to future changes in exchange rates.

risk analysis The evaluation and quantification of all currently known uncertainty, in order to predict likely outcomes and identify strategies for reducing risk to an acceptable level and controlling residual risk.

risk management The process of understanding and managing the risks that the organisation is inevitably subject to in attempting to achieve its corporate objectives. For management purposes, risks are usually divided into categories such as: operational; financial; legal compliance; information; personnel.

Romalpa clause A contractual clause, named after a case in which its effect was litigated in 1976, by which the ownership of goods is to remain with the seller until they have been paid for. This can provide a useful protection for the seller in the event of the buyer's insolvency. Its value may be questionable if the goods are mixed with other goods in a manufacturing process or if they are resold to a third party.

sales Also called turnover or revenue, sales are amounts derived from the provision of goods or services falling within the company's ordinary activities, after deduction of sales returns, trade discounts, value added tax, and any other taxes based on the amounts so derived (Companies Act 1985/1989).

sales invoice A document prepared by an entity showing the description, quantity, prices and values of goods delivered or services rendered to a customer.

sales invoice daybook A list of customer invoices recording their dates, gross values, values net of VAT, the names of customers, and the general ledger allocation and coding.

sales ledger The sales ledger contains all the personal accounts of each individual customer, and records every transaction with each customer since the start of their relationship with the company.

scrip issue (or bonus issue) The capitalisation of the reserves of a company by the issue of additional shares to existing shareholders, in proportion to their holdings. Such shares are normally fully paid-up with no cash called for from the shareholders.

segmental reporting The inclusion in a company's report and accounts of analysis of turnover, profits and net assets by class of business and by geographical segments (Companies Act 1985/89 and SSAP 25).

semi-variable cost A cost containing both fixed and variable components and which is thus partly affected by a change in the level of activity.

sensitivity analysis A modelling and risk assessment technique in which changes are made to significant variables in order to determine the effect of these changes on the planned outcome. Particular attention is thereafter paid to variables identified as being of special significance.

separate valuation concept In determining the aggregate amount of any asset or liability, the amount of each individual asset or liability comprising the aggregate must be determined separately (Companies Act 1985).

server A server means two things: (a) a computer: or (b) a software program. (a) A server is a computer on a network that is dedicated to a particular purpose and which stores all information and performs the critical functions for that purpose. The most common example is a file server, which is a computer and a storage device dedicated to storing files. A print server is a computer, which manages one or more printers. A network server is a computer that manages network traffic. (b) A server is a program, which provides some service to other computer programs in the same computer or in other computers. An example is web server software, which transmits web pages over the Internet when it receives a web browsers' request for a page.

share A fixed identifiable unit of capital which has a fixed nominal or face value, which may be quite different from the market value of the share.

share capital Capital is the number of existing shares in the company multiplied by the nominal value of the shares.

share premium The difference in price between the original nominal value and the price new investors will have to pay for shares issued by the company.

small to medium-sized enterprise (SME) An SME is currently defined as an enterprise which has fewer that 250 occupied persons and which has either an annual turnover not exceeding 50 million euro, or an annual balance sheet total not exceeding 43 million euro.

spam Spam is unsolicited junk email sent to large numbers of people to promote products or services, and also refers to inappropriate promotional or commercial postings to discussion groups or bulletin boards.

spreadsheet A spreadsheet is a type of computer software package developed in the late 1970s and used in a variety of business operations. The spreadsheet is named after the accountant's manual spreadsheet in which text or numbers or formulae are displayed in rows and columns. Spreadsheet programs enable information to be introduced that automatically and speedily affects entries across the entire spreadsheet. Complex spreadsheet programs exist that enable the transfer of spreadsheet information through word processing techniques and there are also three-dimensional spreadsheets for multi-department, multi-division, and multi-company budgeting, planning and modelling.

standard A benchmark measurement of resource usage, set in defined conditions.

standard cost The planned unit cost of the products, components or services produced in a period. The standard cost may be determined on a number of bases. The main uses of standard costs are in performance measurement, control, stock valuation and in the establishment of selling prices.

statement of affairs Details submitted to the Official Receiver during the winding-up of a company identifying the assets and liabilities of the company. The details are prepared by the company directors, or other persons specified by the Official Receiver, and must be submitted within 14 days of the winding-up order or the appointment of a provisional liquidator.

Statement of Principles (SOP) for Financial Reporting The UK conceptual framework of accounting issued by the Accounting Standards Board in 1999.

Statements of Standard Accounting Practice (SSAPs) The accounting standards of practice published by the Accounting Standards Committee up to 1 August 1990.

statistical process control (SPC) SPC aims at achieving good quality during manufacture, through prevention rather than detection, by providing charts that plot performance (e.g. the length of steel rod compared with its specified length). If the process goes out of control, i.e. produces products outside specified upper and lower control limits, then it can be stopped before many or any defectives are produced.

stock days Stocks value divided by average daily cost of sales calculates the number of days' stocks at the current usage rate.

stocks Stocks, according to SSAP 9, are goods held for future use comprising

- goods or other assets purchased for resale
- consumable stores
- raw materials and components purchased for incorporation into products for sale
- products and services, in intermediate stages of completion (work in progress)
- long-term contracts
- finished goods.

strategic planning A process of deciding on the objectives of an organisation, the resources used to attain these objectives, and on the policies that are to govern the acquisition, use and disposition of these resources. The results of this process may be expressed in a strategic plan, which is a statement of long-term goals along with a definition of the strategies and policies which will ensure achievement of those goals.

subsidiary companies A subsidiary company, defined by the Companies Act 1985/1989, is a company for which another company – the parent company – is:

- directly a member of it and controls the composition of its board of directors; or
- holds or controls, either by itself or in agreement with other shareholders, a majority of the voting rights; or
- has the right to exercise a dominant influence over it.

substance over form concept Where a conflict exists, the structuring of reports should give precedence to the representation of financial reality over strict adherence to the requirements of the legal reporting structure.

sunk cost A cost which has already been incurred and which cannot now be recovered.

SWOT analysis Performing a SWOT analysis is a means of gaining a clear picture of the Strengths, Weaknesses, Opportunities, and Threats, which made the organisation what it is. SWOT analysis can apply across diverse management functions and activities, but is particularly appropriate to the early stages of formulating strategy.

systematic risk (or market risk) Some investments are by their very nature more risky than others. This is nothing to do with chance variations in actual compared with expected returns; it is inherent risk that cannot be diversified away.

target cost A product cost estimate derived by subtracting a desired profit margin from a competitive market price. This may be less than the planned initial product cost, but will be expected to be achieved by the time the product reaches the mature production stage.

theory of constraints (TOC) An approach to production management which aims to maximise sales revenue less materials (throughput), whilst simultaneously reducing 'inventory' and operational expense. It focuses primarily on factors which act as constraints to this maximisation.

throughput The rate of production of a defined process over a stated period of time. Rates may be expressed in terms of units of products, batches produced, turnover, or other meaningful measurements.

throughput accounting (TA) A method of performance measurement which relates production and other costs to throughput. Throughput accounting product costs relate to usage of key resources by various products.

top-down process A top-down approach usually relates to a particular type of budgeting process where a budget allowance is set or imposed without permitting the ultimate budget holder to have the opportunity to participate in the budgeting process.

total productive maintenance (TPM) Where first line maintenance, cleaning, checking for irregularities, leaks etc., and simple maintenance, become the responsibility of operators rather than of the maintenance department.

total quality control (TQC) A concept of the quality operation of a business that includes policy deployment, quality control teams, cross-function quality groups, 5S techniques of good housekeeping, the seven tools of quality, and the Deming cycle of plan-do-check-act, to involve everyone in all areas of the business to meet customer needs.

total quality management (TQM) An integrated and comprehensive system of planning and controlling all business functions so that products or services are produced which meet or exceed customer expectations. TQM is a philosophy of business behaviour, embracing principles such as employee involvement, continuous improvement at all levels and customer focus, as well as being a collection of related techniques aimed at improving quality. In addition to the features included in TQC, TQM additionally includes JIT, *heijunka*, and *jidoka*.

treasury management The corporate handling of all financial matters, the generation of external and internal funds for business, the management of currencies and cash flows, and the complex strategies, policies and procedures of corporate finance.

trial balance The list of account balances in a double-entry accounting system. If the records have been correctly maintained, the sum of the debit balances will equal the sum of the credit balances, although certain errors such as the omission of a transaction or erroneous entries will not be disclosed by a trial balance.

true and fair view The requirement for financial statements prepared in compliance with the Companies Act to 'give a true and fair view' overrides any other requirements. Although not precisely defined in the Companies Act this is generally accepted to mean that accounts show a true and fair view if they are unlikely to mislead a user of financial information in giving a false impression of the company.

turnover Also called sales or revenue, are amounts derived from the provision of goods or services falling within the company's ordinary activities, after deduction of sales returns, trade discounts, value added tax, and any other taxes based on the amounts so derived (Companies Act 1985).

uniform resource locator (url) A url is a reference or address to a resource on the Internet e.g. http://www.mcgraw-hill.co.uk/textbooks/davies.

unit cost The average cost of a product or service unit based on total costs and the number of units.

unsystematic risk Risk that can be diversified away.

value added statement An alternative presentation of the traditional profit and loss account that measures the wealth created by a company through its activities, through value added by the business rather than the profit earned by the business. It shows how value added is distributed among the relevant parties: employees; lenders; shareholders; Government; and the amount to provide maintenance and expansion of the business.

value analysis A technique for examination, by multi-disciplined teams, of design attributes and any other factors affecting the cost of the product, to identify and implement the means of achieving the specified purpose most economically at the required standard of quality and reliability. Value analysis is the broad term usually used to include both value analysis and value engineering. Value engineering applies to products under development, whilst value analysis applies to products currently in production.

value engineering The method of value analysis that applies to products under development.

variable cost Cost that varies in direct proportion to the volume of activity.

variance The difference between a planned, budgeted or standard cost and the actual cost incurred. The same comparisons may be made for revenues.

variance analysis The evaluation of performance by means of variances, whose timely reporting should maximise the opportunity for managerial action. These variances will be either favourable variances (F) or adverse variances (A).

vendor managed inventory (VMI) The management of stocks on behalf of a customer by the supplier, the supplier taking responsibility for the management of stocks within a framework that is mutually agreed by both parties. Examples are seen in separate supermarket racks maintained and stocked by merchandising groups for such items as spices, and car parts distributors topping up the shelves of dealers/garages, where the management of the stocks, racking and shelves is carried out by the merchandising group or distributor.

vertical analysis An analysis of the profit and loss account (or balance sheet) in which each item is expressed as a percentage of the total. The vertical analysis provides evidence of structural changes in the business such as increased profitability through more efficient production.

virus A computer virus is a program that usually infects the other executable programs in the computer by inserting in those files copies of itself, so that when the file is loaded into memory copies will be executed allowing them to infect still more files. Computer viruses are designed to replicate